About *New Moon*

"This is a strong, deeply moving book. I can't think of another example in which the details and particularities of childhood have been evoked so fully, with such painstaking care and precision."

—Paul Auster (author of *Moon Palace, Mr. Vertigo,* and *Smoke*)

"A memoir of baseball, high school, and Jewish New York in the '50s, *New Moon* is also a portrait of a defenseless consciousness uncovering itself and the world simultaneously. The spellbinding prose and terrifying intimacy of Richard Grossinger's book puts it, for me, in the company of Frederick Exley's *A Fan's Notes* and Annie Dillard's *An American Childhood.* An unforgettable reading experience."

—Jonathan Lethem (author of *Gun, with Occasional Music* and *Amnesia Moon*)

"Using the haunted lives which inhabited the famous Katskills resort as a backdrop, Richard Grossinger writes a brilliant novel about a young man's passage into adulthood. *New Moon* is a departure for the Jewish-American novel, as well—no longer obsessed with Old World issues, and not finding solace in the illusion of an American Promised Land."

—Ishmael Reed (author of *Yellow Back Radio Broke Down* and *Shrovetide in Old New Orleans*)

"In this remarkably courageous and unsparing self-examination, Richard Grossinger explores the labyrinths of panic and fear that lay beneath the Paradise-like surface of a privileged childhood. Part magic, part myth, part dream, part prayer, *New Moon* is a liquid mirror that leads straight to the depths of the unconscious."

—Mary Mackey (author of *The Year the Horses Came, The Horses at the Gate, Season of Shadows,* and *The Dear Dance of Eros*)

"At once a memoir, an account of psychoanalysis, and a both savage and loving account of New York in the '50s, *New Moon* is a work with many layers and a unique tone, reminiscent of Robert Musil's *A Man Without Qualities* in its blend of analytical realism, melancholia, and acute psychoanalytic and philosophical penetration."

—Andrew Harvey (author of *A Hidden Journey* and *The Return of the Mother*)

"A strange and remarkable self-evaluation in the form of a novel—illuminating, tender, moving, evocative ... any number of adjectives of praise would be appropriate."

—George Plimpton (author of *Out of My League*, *Paper Lion*, and *Shadow Box*)

"Since the days when I depended on the magazine *Io* to expand and verify a lot of what I was beginning to learn of the deep dark universe, I have found Richard Grossinger's empirical analysis of American Culture unerring. *New Moon*, a memoir of Grossinger's early life, starts out in the Land of Giants and emerges onto 5th Avenue, the mainstreet of Metropolis. In its observational acuity it is great anthropology—as a tale of growing it is strangely charming and funny and scary."

—Edward Dorn (author of *The North Atlantic Turbine*, *Gunslinger*, and *Some Business Recently Transacted in the White World*

"A fascinating self-portrait of the youth of one of our most profound and rebellious thinkers, told with a deceptive simplicity that is capable of shifting at any moment into the haunted resonance of a fairy tale, and in a language so nakedly honest it is never more than one step away from tenderness."

—Gerald Rosen (author of *The Carmen Miranda Memorial Flagpole* and *Growing Up Bronx*)

"Indeed, some readers are going to rank this memoir of baseball, summer camp, Latin classes, domestic terrors, and enchanted moments at Grossinger's as a spiritual quest in the tradition of Blake, Emerson, and ... James Agee. ..."

—Mike Harris, *Los Angeles Times*

"... skillfully evokes the world of '50s New York and Grossinger's Catskills as well as the counter culture of the '60s. ..."

—*Publishers Weekly*

"*New Moon* is something new under the sun, a real psychoanalytic autobiography."

—*Psychoanalytic Books: A Quarterly Journal of Reviews*

"Richard Grossinger tells me who he is, so he shows me who I am."

—Joy Manné (author of *Soul Therapy*) in *The European Therapist*

OUT OF BABYLON

Ghosts of Grossinger's

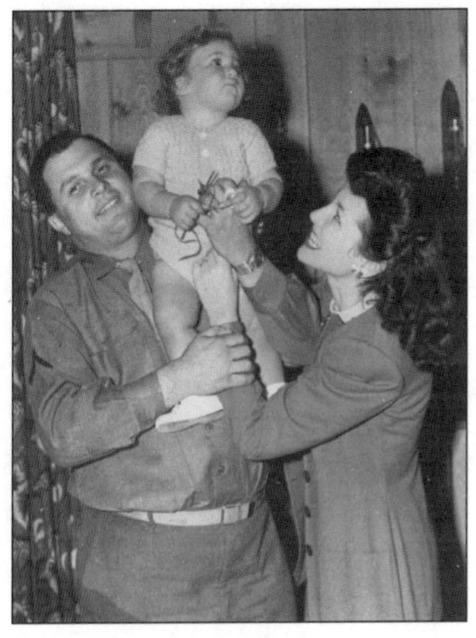

RICHARD GROSSINGER

Frog, Ltd.
Berkeley, California

Out of Babylon: Ghosts of Grossinger's

Published by Frog, Ltd.

Frog, Ltd. books are distributed by
North Atlantic Books
P.O. Box 12327
Berkeley, CA 94712

Cover and book design by Paula Morrison

Printed in the United States of America

Library of Congress Cataloging-in-Publication Data

Grossinger, Richard, 1944–
Out of Babylon / Richard Grossinger
p. cm.
ISBN 1-883319-57-9
I. Title.
PS3557.R66088 1997
813'.54—dc21 96-50152
CIP

1 2 3 4 5 6 7 8 9 / 01 00 99 98 97

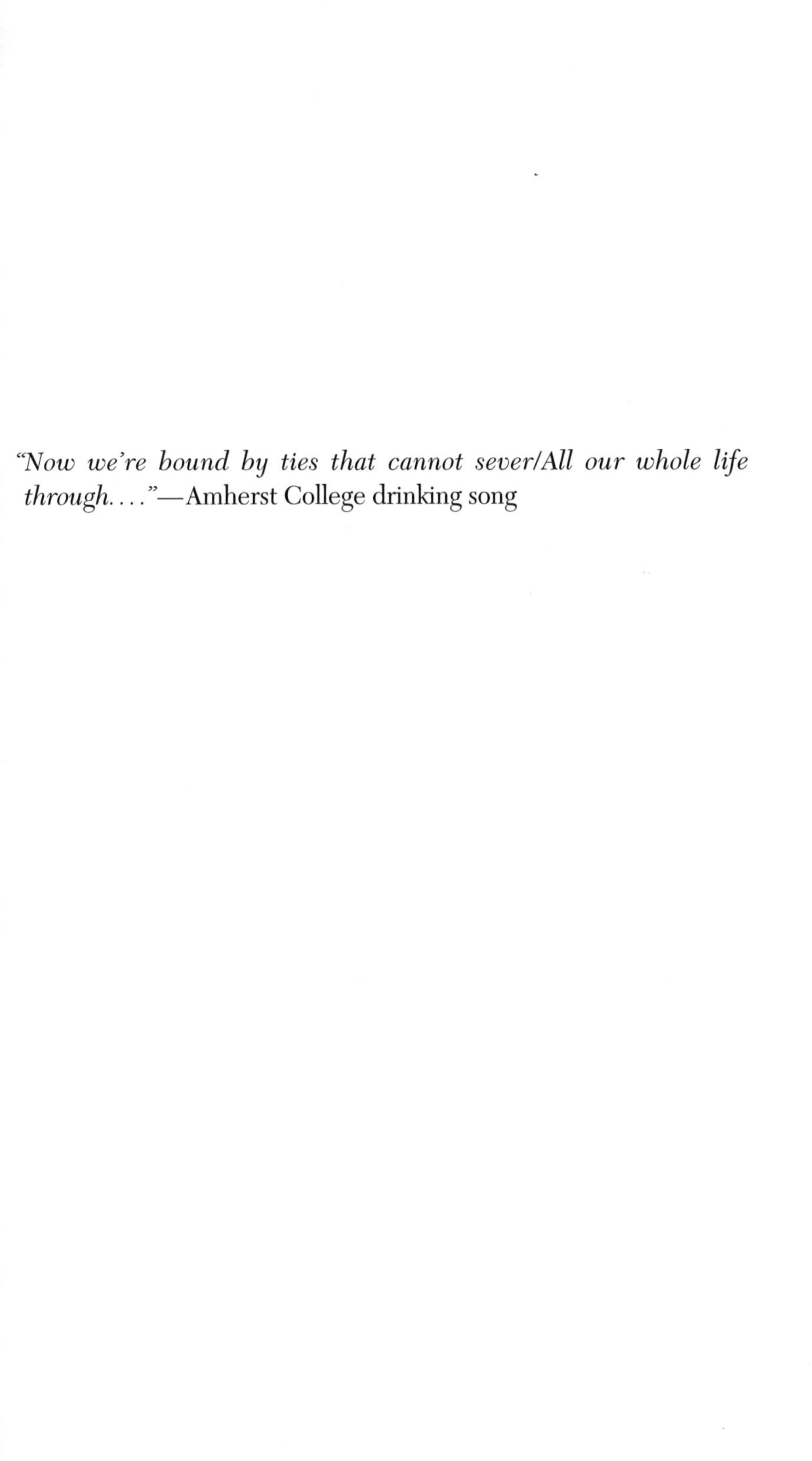

"Now we're bound by ties that cannot sever/All our whole life through. . . ."—Amherst College drinking song

Acknowledgments

I thank Philip Wohlstetter for his close reading and insightful comments; Kathy Glass for her precise, sensitive editing; Paula Morrison for her innovative design; and Martha Mendelsohn for her helpful research.

I especially acknowledge my family and friends: Lindy Hough; Robin and Miranda Grossinger; Bunny Grossinger; Jonathan and Deborah Towers; Michael and James Grossinger; Jay, Siggy, and Seymour Zises; Paul and Lionel Rothkrug; Paul Pitchford; Ian Grand; Charlie Winton; Polly Gamble; Randy Cherner; Richard Heckler; Bira Almeida; Peter Ralston; Ron Sieh; and all the rest, including the B———s—and, in memory, Jennie and Harry Grossinger, Sally Golden, Paul Grossinger, and Bob and Martha Towers.

If you hadn't been there, I couldn't have told this story.

I ask the reader to remember that the events in this book are not these people's lives but stories of mine through which they passed. Everyone in this book has not only his or her own story but a life which can never be captured in words.

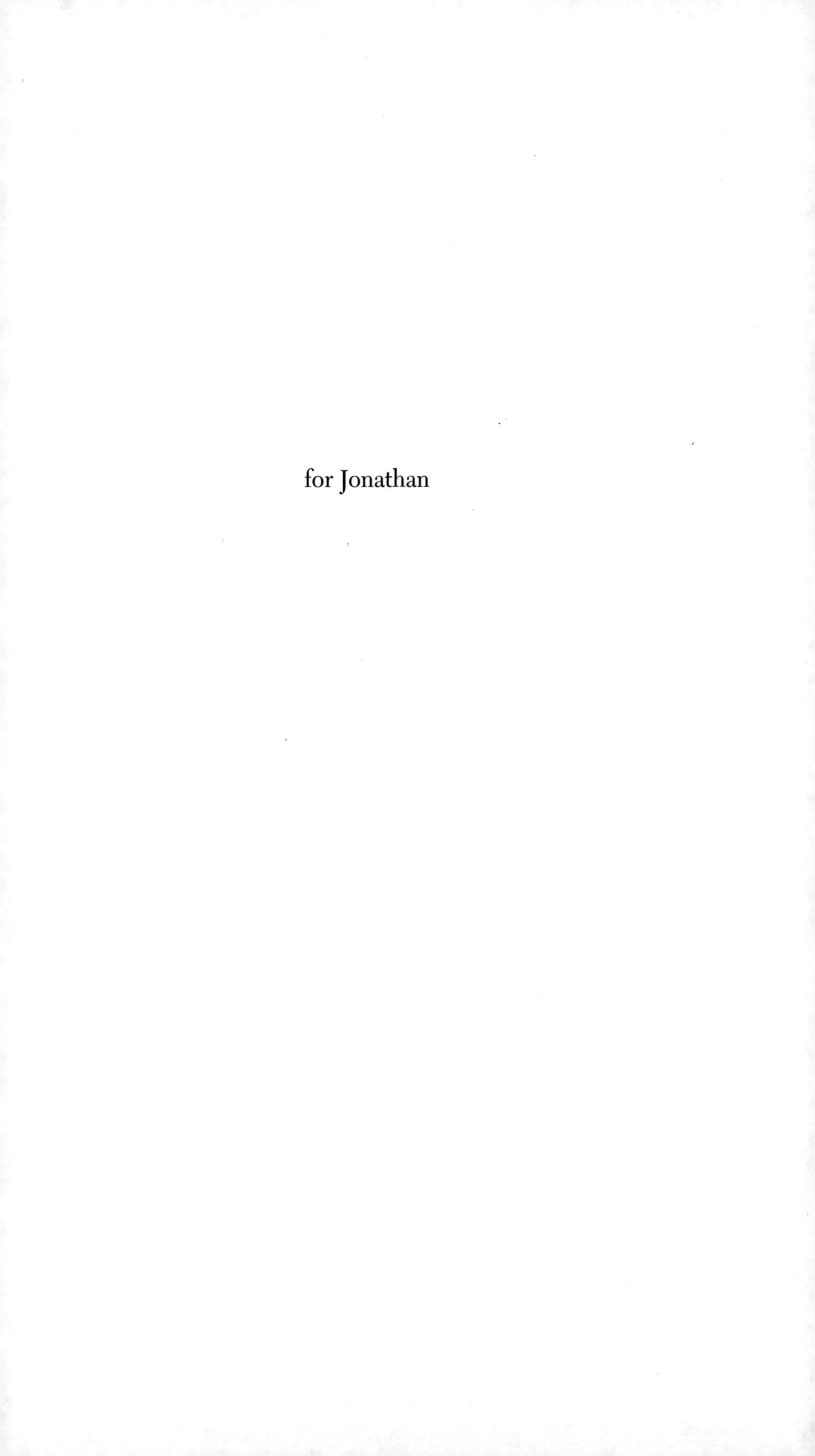

for Jonathan

Table of Contents

Book One: Grossinger

Book Two: Turetsky

Book Three: Rothkrug

Book Four: Vision Quest

Book Five: B———

Book One

GROSSINGER

Prologue

The Story of Grossinger's

THE SUMMER AFTER he revealed himself to be my father, Uncle Paul arranged for me to visit him at Grossinger's. When I stepped into the family dining room for the first time, my cousin Jay (whom I had met earlier that summer at Camp Chipinaw) greeted me enthusiastically—he literally knocked over his chair, put his arms around me, and lifted me off the ground. After breakfast, he led me on a tour of the grounds.

First, we went through swinging doors into a clatter of kitchens (different ones, Jay explained, for meat and dairy). Skirting lines of waiters, we waved to chefs, then squeezed through a metal fire exit onto a walkway bordered by flowerbeds and packed with people in bathing suits, some carting newspapers and towels. The air smelled coconut and cigarette.

As we passed through a turnstile, the pool exploded on so many levels I could barely grasp it or connect its din of sounds with what I saw. Men and women moved about the water. Lawn chairs crowded under rainbowlike canopies and along stone walls. Waiters ferried trays of bottles and glasses. "Nicer than the Chipinaw Lake?" Jay spoofed.

I nodded. It was gigantic. The blue sparkled like sapphires. Bright floats and inner tubes jutted amidst splashes and shouts.

We passed basketball players on a stone plaza, a soda shack (red and orange bottles floating in ice), then the sandy pipes of the skating rink and dandelion-full toboggan tracks. Puffing apart globes of seeds, we climbed through a grove of pines to handball courts (where we recognized two Chipinaw counselors competing with some older men). We cut across the golf course (keeping an eye on hissing pellets), then rounded the edge of the lake, past bungalows, finally back to the Main Building. There we stared at walls crammed with photographs of movie stars, baseball players, and dignitaries—Jerry Lewis, Ted Williams, Shirley Temple, Franklin Delano Roosevelt, Jackie Robinson, Abba Eban, most of them posing with Uncle Paul, Grandma Jennie, and other family members.

Then we hiked in the other direction to the stables, where we got to feed the horses. From there we circled the far section of the golf course and raced down a long grassy ski slope. At the bottom we turned our momentum into a mock bullfight, as Jay charged me and pawed the ground chewing on flowers.

Passing a row of yellowish stone buildings, we climbed to the central plaza and followed a pastry breeze into the rear of the kitchen where the bakers let us test dinner cookies out of their ovens—chocolate chips and white puffy macaroons on wooden paddles. Jay shook their hands and complimented each on the "cuisine." "I stole that routine from Woody Woodpecker," he confided as we left.

On the way home, we stopped at the canteen and met its proprietor, Milty. A friendly giant ("I'm over seven feet tall"), he invited us into a lair of soda fountains, expensive toys, and comic books. At his suggestion we helped ourselves to candy, sports magazines, and Heckle and Jeckle, Little Lulu, and Superman. Afterwards he handed me a slip to sign.

I hesitated.

"It's just for their records," Jay assured me. "No one really pays."

Telling the story of Grossinger's has been an obligation and an omen much of my life. As often as I abandoned the task I took it up, sometimes a decade (or more) later, as a totally different tale. It is pretext, hoax, evidence tampering, and fake legends. At first glance it is an epic, a Jewish-American original. At second glance it is banal, pure advertising copy. It is also a sphinx. The same people want me to tell it and don't want me to tell it. I have been alternately bribed, cajoled, and forbidden. I hate the story, and I am drawn to the story. It is anathema and destiny.

My quandary began at sixteen with my first attempt to write. To my father Paul (or rather the man I believed to be my father), this was a dangerous act. He considered writers parasites who could best aspire to public relations or being Harold Robbins.

Yet my grandmother Jennie, the Hotel's celebrity, encouraged me. "You will be our historian," she proclaimed, propped against her headboard in the pink and yellow master suite of Joy Cottage, narrating how a young girl migrated to America, spent her youth in sweatshops, and now was hosting leaders of nations and Broadway stars. "... and you will give my story to the world."

Then, reaching out over the covers and hugging me, she set her cheek against mine: "You are my very, very special grandchild!"

I guessed that my status came from being her oldest or maybe because she was the one who named me Richard. But somehow I knew, even then, it was either more than that or different from that.

When I began my chronicles, Aunt Bunny, my stepmother, was my family sponsor. She had arrived at Grossinger's a captive bride, a girl of twenty running from her father. I see now she could have become Sherry Lansing or Joan Didion. There was fire and intelligence in her, as well as a playful sensitivity unique to her milieu. Instead she was a witty hostess with a cute nickname (her real name was Ricelle).

I imagined writing her tale as Faulkner or Lawrence would have, stream of consciousness ennobling her life, illuminating the hidden depths we all associated with Grossinger's.

Aunt Bunny convened my first audience, on couches in the den: "Uncle" Irving, an allergist from Hartford, and his wife "Aunt" Alice,

"Aunt" Marsha (Aunt Bunny's friend from town), Jerry MacDonald (a high-school teacher who lived with us), and Sam Halpern, a reporter for *Time* who had just been in Cuba with Castro.

The roar of subways faded, and the noise of Central Park West broke through in sunlight. I heard screams of children mixed with clanging of ice cream bells and shouts of "Popsicles! Orange Drinks!" Horses and bikes redirected traffic, and along the sidewalks baby carriages and bikes appeared everywhere, moving and resting, parallel and perpendicular. The world broke into my dreamy mood and I felt a breeze sweeping across me, the breeze I had seen moments earlier dancing through park trees. . . .

Friday was different; it was separate and alone. The weekdays were joined one to one because they gave no such afternoon. Bleary-eyed morning would begin underground. Weary afternoons would grow stale in classrooms, evening already near. Till midnight I did homework. The next morning would follow—and the next and the next. . . . I was buried in the soporific rut of the classroom, lost in grades and exams. The French Revolution had to be memorized by year; there were two Latin stories to translate and a vocabulary test, a chapter in math with problems, a chapter in chemistry with problems, a hundred and twenty pages of The Ambassadors.

I was sixteen years old, and things never changed. Assyria and Rome became England and France. History moved four flights up in a new building. Huck Finn *flowed into* Ethan Frome. *The Chordates led back to the atom and molecule, and the indicative gave way to the subjunctive. Things never changed in me either. On the eve before I entered prep school, my mother told me, "This is your last free night for six years."*

I remember that final Sunday—the checkered cab we caught outside the restaurant, Central Park as lonely lamps shone on benches and an autumn wind ripped a leaf here and there. It was a true September evening to cap a mild afternoon:

"These are the days when the birds return,
Just a few
A bird or two,
To take a backward look."

I recall that poem as I think back to pigeons that fluttered and huddled about lonely lamps.

"The next Salinger," Sam proclaimed.

"I want him to go to Yale," declared Uncle Irving, who always brought things back to his alma mater.

From an ambivalence of puritanical and prurient intents, Aunt Bunny educated me on local crimes and indecencies. Through her eyes I saw my father as a princely man beset by avaricious kin and blackmailers from the Racetrack and unions. I learned about the homosexual uncle who ran orgies (his paramours pointed out in whispers as we passed them in lobbies) . . . how he had spies and saboteurs throughout the Hotel and manipulated my grandfather Harry (Jennie's estranged husband) by delivering young women to him.

But I dodged the Grossinger's opus and stuck to my own adventures—for instance, hanging out with teenagers around the jukebox and swimming after turtles with my brothers. Those narratives, mixed with accounts of high school and summer camp, made up a memoir of four hundred pages by the time I was eighteen:

I was sitting in the living room watching TV with Aunt Bunny and Jerry when Steve called from the main building. He had arrived on a Trailways bus.

The next day, we wandered through the packed lobbies and he was beside himself at how many girls there were.

"It's incredible, Rich. I'm overwhelmed. This is going to save my social life. I just don't know where to begin."

I never did either, so it was good to have company.

That night we joined a larger group of guys. "Are you a guest here?" one of them asked Steve.

"Well, sort of. I'm staying with Rich."

"So you're a freeloader. Hey, how is it up at the big house?"

"It's pretty sharp. His father was a funny guy at supper. He knows half the Yankees personally. And his stepmother is real good-looking and plays twist records and dances in the living room. And I have to admit that this ex-ballplayer living there, Jerry, is one of the coolest guys I've ever met."

My English teacher at Amherst thought my writing had potential, but he also saw Grossinger's as a corrupting influence with its coterie of hack novelists and newspapermen. He enlisted Saul Bellow's editor at Viking Press to nurture me. Catherine Carver met us for cocktails at the Lord Jeff Inn—an occasion I thought of as my entry into adulthood. Afterwards I collaborated with her by mail (and during occasional Manhattan lunches).

Katey encouraged me to personify Grossinger's at all its levels of majesty and scandal. "It's an ikon of Americana," she insisted. "It's a myth, much more so than the things you find mythic."

I intended to reward her confidence and become a teenage novelist. But my editor and I parted unpleasantly after my father set up a meeting between me and Harold Robbins in a hotel suite in Manhattan. "She's using you, kid," Robbins told me. "Playing school-marm."

That next summer, war journalist Quentin Reynolds was commissioned by Grosset and Dunlap to prepare Jennie Grossinger's official biography. I kept him company in the gazebo outside the Baby Villa, as he rambled through a chronology identical to the one Grandma had been telling me: the original Ferndale farmhouse, the mansion on the hill, then how Milton Blackstone coaxed the stars—Sophie Tucker, Eddie Cantor, Barney Ross—and almost overnight the Gods of Abraham and Isaac had established an international country club.

Reynolds wasn't interested in any better story. He was writing a house book:

> "Poppa, I'm so happy, I'm walking on air. Who would ever believe the Grossingers from the Lower East Side would own their own golf course? It's another miracle!"

("Who does she think she is?" Aunt Bunny snarled, "the Battle of Britain?")

When Grandma's prospective biographer died a year later, he imparted only rough drafts with notes. Joel Pomerantz, a Hotel publicist, finished the account. It appeared in 1970 as *Jennie and the Story of Grossinger's.*

"You'll write my real biography," she promised, as she repeated her tales of the early years: a stone cottage and a yellow cow.

Would that I had listened more carefully! But I was busy growing up, and there always seemed to be plenty of time.

I did plan some sort of Grossinger novel—à la Saul Bellow and Harold Robbins—until midway through Amherst I met the shaman-poet Robert Kelly and, through him, Stan Brakhage, Paul Blackburn, and Robert Creeley—radical artists who were far tougher critics than Katey Carver. By then Grossinger's had become more a stigma than a largess. I tried to disguise my connection to the Hotel and everything it stood for, dreading the inevitable query when people heard my name. The Vietnam War, the vision quests of the Winnebago Indians—in general, my need to find my own heart and courage—eclipsed what had come to seem callous luxuriating and flaunting of wealth. Grossinger's didn't deserve a bard or a historian. Hittites, Martians, and Viking explorers—each in their own way—were far worthier subjects.

I went to graduate school in anthropology, did a year's research on fishing villages in Maine, and then taught college in Maine and Vermont. During those years I wrote more than a dozen books weaving alchemical and aboriginal mythologies, dreams, and metaphors of science into texts that slid right through my imitation of Faulkner and Lawrence into something both Mediaeval and post-modern that wouldn't have pleased either Katey Carver or Harold Robbins. I did find a place for Grossinger's in them—an artificial village in a Dutch-Algonquin nation. I set the fishing wharves and islands of Frenchman's and Blue Hill Bay within a North Atlantic landscape that stretched from Newfoundland to Sullivan County, then cast that nation against Blackstone's dream kingdom. My father hated the pieces, but at least they didn't tell any of his secrets:

Mohawk. Kickapoo. Rattlesnake.

Dutch country. From Roundout and West Beer Kill, Van Burenville, to the Erie Railroad, the Delaware River. It was here that Major General John Sullivan turned to the West, chastising the Indians of New York and Pennsylvania, scattering the pottery and sunspots of the Southern Cult.

Settlers (1809). Major Hardenburg Land. Purchased from John Dusinberry by Amasa Geer. He abandoned wife and children, followed the paths of mound-building Indians, last heard from in Ohio, or Indiana. Joseph, the son he left behind, became a renowned rattle-

snake-slayer ... would visit their dens in the spring, murdering a hundred a day.

Willowemoc. Cranberry Pond. Wild Skunk. Bald Eagle.

The tanning industry (1830–1875) ... followed by tubercular clinics. Then Charlie Armstrong's Long Eddy Hotel, roller skaters and glassblowers, Kickapoo on exhibit downstairs; upstairs, 1500 feet of hardwood floor. (1875, still lies in half-eaten hulks on Loch Sheldrake, Shingle Brook, Swan Lake, one hotel after another, fires that were never put out and continue to burn as world space disappears into Mountaindale and Glen Wild.)

Cooks Falls and Chiloway. Aqueducts to New Jersey, killes and clips, hundreds of miles of turnpikes and deer trails grown over by brush. The Roman Empire once ... now there is only a wall.

Jews came from the old country by Qabala and astral body, outside the census, stopping briefly at the Port of New York, moving along backtrails with Ethiopians and Jackson Whites. Now it's a modern resort facility set in old pasture—where gagmen pass from dawn to yawn, firing punch lines.

Cackling Hen. Ruffed Grouse. Monticello Raceway. Crooks hiding behind suits at bars. Two girls dressed in their mothers' jewels thumb from White Lake to Liberty ... families touring Route 52 and old 17, here on the 25,000 block of the Lower East Side. The Aladdin. Chester's. The Ukraine.

Swimming pools and patios and tennis courts, lobbies long as city blocks, outer golf meadows.... Lou Goldstein leads his flock in Simon Sez, then takes them through the history of the G. like a guide on Times Square ... down the lineage of villas, past clowns and hypnotists, classes in Latin dances, Puerto Ricans playing softball, golf carts bumping over the path to the lake ... the gaunt punster stopping his straggle and pointing out the laundry-stack-and-greenhouse complex that blesses their dinner with linen and blossoms.

John Sullivan turned West here. At the Festival of Woodstock, Bethel turns suddenly toward the Sun.

Grossinger's was never about money, extravagance, or privilege. They were banned at the gate ... turned into burlesque. It was about spirit, about letting down your guard, whoever you were. Outside its borders was regular old stodgy, Esso America. Cross its borders and the world became jovial, whimsical, vaudeville. It was Daffy Duck and Babe Ruth meet Jimmy Stewart meet Punch and Judy. It lay between all world wars, a sanctuary within history, smelling of hay, sun-tan oil, vanilla, and marigolds—timeless, ingenue, a dream.

The Hotel I knew was a shamrock and rainbow land. Its architecture rolled like a fairy-tale empire along Dutch countryside. Its vestibules rang with excitement, the chatter of fun and good will. Each plaza was embroidered with activity—a tractor-drawn mower perfuming lawns, heaped trays of roast beef and roasted chicken with carved melon shells of mixed berries headed for the outdoor pool, homemade chocolate chip cookies, apple pie, or sugared orange sponge for dessert—plus a crinkled goblet of raspberry or pineapple ice, Kodachrome flowerbeds, tennis partners in whites lined up for doubles, women in bikinis, smoke rings and show tunes, cocktail waiters passing through smoky crowds through lobby mirrors, Eddie Lopat on the third green, Kim Novak taking lessons from the pro, Saul Rogovin showing me how to bunt on the lawn outside the Main Building.

Grossinger's was parasols and cabanas, distinctive house buses and paintbox rowboats, the taste of frost and coffee nut, photo galleries of celebrities on vacation winding down corridors around posts to exotic dead ends at underground passages lit from ancient portals, cologned air blowers in washrooms, tables filled with prune and poppyseed Danish, coffeecakes and cheesecakes, hard rolls, onion rolls, fat doughy saltsticks, and sweet buns (replaced regularly with new platters), malted-milk machines whirring, the canteen musk of comics and magazines, glass passageways between buildings (steaming in winter to give misty vistas of snow on evergreens).

During the hotel's heyday, members of the New York Yankees vacationed there with U.S. Senators and stage stars. Their families mingled in tennis tournaments and cha-cha-cha; their teenage children flirted at the pool. It was naive and unexamined, and I strolled through it with the bliss of a cherry-lime soda (mixed myself from syrup and fizz), thanking the gods I was allowed to be part of it. (Though our boarder Jerry MacDonald played minor-league hardball with many upcoming players, he considered the moment of his life to have been sitting at the bar trading jokes with Roger Maris the winter after his

61-home-run season. "Richard," he said, "I had to pinch myself to believe it.")

At thirty-six I was living in California with my wife and two kids, out of a job, when a renowned literary agent swore he could get me $250,000 to tell the "real" Grossinger story. I had just published a book with Doubleday called *Planet Medicine* and was writing another on stars and cosmology. "No problem!" chortled John, and within a month he sold my outline for *The Night Sky* to Sierra Club Books. A year later, as I was finishing, he suggested, "Why don't you take a break from your moons of Neptune and write some Grossinger material?"

Having failed to seize the tale when it was there for the taking, I spent the next two months turning my great-grandparents and grandparents into characters in a novel, trying to invent their dialogue in a style approaching the "Dynasty" best-sellers John mailed me for encouragement.

That summer he and I met at the entrance to the Hotel dining room. In his white suit and Panama hat, gawking at every patch of local exotica (alive or stationary), he appraised the literary potential of the scene and dreamed up my potboiler. "Sleaze, sex, and bucks," he extolled, as though these weren't recognized banalities. Then he yanked out his chair and decoded the luncheon menu.

Emil Cohen, Yiddish story-teller, interrupted his comedic patrol of tables. He knew I was his enemy. He had known it since I was a child.

"What opus are you planning now?" he inquired, derision masked by his pompous jargon.

I told him.

"The night sky?"

"The planets," I said. "Mars … Jupiter … Pluto."

"Mars?" he asked. "You must mean Morris. Are you going to tell me how Moishe Pippick got his name?"

I wasn't, but he performed it for us anyway, in Yiddish.

After blueberry-whipcream dessert, John took my manuscript back to his room. That night, as we sat at a table beside the bar, he shouted over the din of Tito Puente.

"It won't work. There's no life to this. Your 'night skies' and 'Mayan priests' have commitment. This stuff is a pedagogical exercise. It lacks even basic interiors and furniture. Your characters are plain boring."

Two months later, I answered the phone to the greeting of an old friend, a pro journalist, once a Grossinger's bellhop. He was looking for a break, trying to draft a Hotel saga. He knew the more famous gossip, but he wanted my secrets too. I told him I was saving those. He offered to take me on as his co-author. "*My* agent," he proposed, "everything 50/50."

Then he revealed the heart of his plot: The character representing my grandmother had a clandestine lover, a pilot with headquarters in Hillig's castle, a monolith outside Liberty.

Brady's outline and sample pages came overnight. With revived ardor for a big advance, I threw myself into his tale, this time with plenty of drapes, carpets, and chairs.

I tried to recall every nodule of scandal and myth my grandmother and Aunt Bunny had bestowed on me. I mimicked my collaborator's style and drafted a fanciful version of my uncle bringing prostitutes to my grandfather, then plotting to overthrow a caricature of my father. It was ugly, embarrassing stuff.

When Brady's version of our collaboration came back even trashier and more glitzed up, I surrendered.

I phoned him with the verdict. He accepted graciously: "Hell, it always was your book anyway!"

Now, fifteen years after that, I come to the story at a place where it can be told. Plumbing the Grossinger riddle I return always to its central paradox.

It was never a fiction or a novel anyway. It was never even Grossinger's.

As the tales that follow will demonstrate, my task was to unravel a different mystery, the one that delivered me there.

2

How Selig and Malke Discovered the Catskills and Founded Grossinger's

SELIG GROSSINGER, the youngest of Isaac's four sons, was born to elderly parents in 1865. Their home was Galicia, now part of Poland (then it lay within the Austro-Hungarian Empire). The family spoke Yiddish. It was not the tongue of Adam but closer to it than Polish or Russian.

Seven years old, the child was coaxed by his brothers through pasture into high weeds. The sun had begun to set, and he struggled to keep up. "Seligl," Aaron taunted. "Is he going to milk the cows, or will the cows milk him?" With saucy barbs they raced ahead, then vanished behind shrubs. He tried to find them, but soon he was out of breath and crossing unfamiliar fields. He had no idea where or who he was, and, as it grew dark, he began to sob.

A moon rose silently. He saw fire springing spontaneously from thicket, roaring without consuming. Silently he understood.

Hebrew tribes had scattered into Europe, east to the foothills of Mongolia and across the *sefira* into impoverished villages of Austria-Hungary. All through the civilized world and outside it their descendants lived in communities, *shtetl* slums of crumbling cottages and synagogues. Nationless and transnational, they exchanged currencies and passed anonymously over borders. Their sages practiced a sacred calendar and studied *Torah,* the *Zohar,* and Maimonides, "as though these were the daily newspapers."

The *shtetl* dweller "could not tell you a thing about Russia, about Poland, about Lithuania, and their peoples, laws, kings, politicians.... But you ask him about Og, King of Bashan ... Mesopotamia, the Tigres and Euphrates rivers, Persia ... Egypt and the Nile.... He knew the people who lived in tents and spoke Hebrew or Aramaic; the people who rode on mules or camels and drank water out of pitchers.... He knew about date palms, pomegranates, locust trees.... about the dragon and the leopard, about the turtledove and the hart that panteth after living waters...."

In the eternal present Adam arose in the Garden and Abraham offered to sacrifice his first-born to God. The Philistines were foes against whom menorahs were lit, their millennial landscape more immediate than rain pelting wagon ruts.

Selig's clan had suffered pogroms, purges, and false prophets, but they kept to their communities and practiced carpentry, tailoring, agriculture, shoe-making, and, of course, religious esoterica. To the gentiles they remained arrogant disbelievers who had crucified the Lord. It little mattered that the Lord had been one of them. That was long ago, and He had been reborn since in feudal lands, Greek and Nordic in the images of His priests.

Isaac was not a typical *shtetl* dweller. He owned land; he annually endowed the synagogue. Little Selig planted, irrigated, laid stone, repaired pipe, read holy books, cared for animals, and battened against winter. He sold his family's crops at nearby markets.

A chance occurrence the year of his *bar mitzvah* ordained Selig's destiny. As he headed toward town, he saw a dilapidated wagon wending toward him from the distance. Taking a seat in the grass, he waited boldly. Curiosity was his motive for accepting a ride from the young, flamboyantly dressed driver. Over three leisurely miles he learned that his new acquaintance was eighteen and had left another *shtetl* two years earlier to peddle.

Passing through every three months or so, Reuben became Selig's link to the world. Good-humored about the aloof treatment he received from Selig's brothers, the peddler updated his friend, mostly with gossip about America from where his once-poor uncle had recently returned, now a gentleman sporting a silk hat. On a ride into town Reuben demonstrated the music box his kinsman had gifted him. As it clinked its oddly compelling tune, Reuben rehearsed his own fantasy flight.

The following year the peddler took Selig to a nearby *shtetl* where a *maggid* was proclaiming the messiah. The two youths kept up a merry jabbering until the sight of the crowd.

What astonished Selig was how much the woodcut looked like the Bible itself—Ezekiel addressing the perfidious flock. "Evil is not *of* nature," the preacher declaimed with a sweeping flourish of his hand. "This purgatory is being cleansed through the *tikkun* that fly from God's mantle."

Selig was spellbound, but Reuben chuckled.

"Turn away from idols," the *maggid* continued. "America is the land of Nebuchadnezzar. You are Emanations of Jehovah. *Es ligt oif eich, die Shchineh!*"

"He doesn't believe in money," scoffed Reuben on the way back, "but I think I'd rather die a rich man than spend another two thousand years following one of our bloody messiahs."

As the reputation of Selig's brothers spread, matchmakers from other villages appeared. Overnight, it seemed, the household was filled with wives and babies.

Selig was seventeen when Isaac died.

Enmity grew quickly: arguments in the dark, smashed furniture, averted glances. Father had made Aaron executor of his estate, but the older brother finagled most of it. Mikhail and his family stormed off, shouting horrid things *(groyse clulas)*—no one heard from them again.

Jacob stayed to share the land. Selig never asked for his portion. He knew there was none.

It was not, he realized, so much that he had been intentionally cheated as that his siblings didn't notice him. He was just another child and they had plenty of their own. One evening, under a gibbous moon, without saying goodbye, he departed—an escapade planned for weeks with Reuben. For generations Jewish clans had fissioned like this.

All night he dreamed in tatters, troubled sleep from which he sighted, as the carriage lurched and bumped, Orion and the Pleiades. The past haunted him; he longed for something he could not imagine.

Their journey took them fifty miles to the village of Baligrod. There, at sun-up, Reuben delivered his passenger to Joseph Klanka. Reuben had already lauded Selig, so Klanka was eager to meet him. He believed in universal nobility and regularly hired Jews to manage his farms. In fact, as he explained to Selig that morning over buns and tea, the best from all races breed upward. "My people were peasants not so long ago. I trust peasants. Do you know how to keep land?"

"He has not slept well," Reuben warned.

"All my life. I have raised and slaughtered animals. I can bring soil through winter."

"Physical requirements are fine, but what about matters of men? Can you judge your own people? Would you work *for* me or with them *against* me?"

"Justice knows no religion. I will work for you fairly, but I will not cheat my people. God sent us to this land for reasons of His own."

"Some say," Klanka countered with a hint of mirth, "for sins committed against His very Son."

Selig decided to laugh too. They shook hands and, after a stutter of hesitation, embraced.

At dawn foreman Selig mounted his horse, lit a pipe, and rode the circuit of Klanka lands. He checked plantings and livestock, heard and adjudicated complaints. If circumstances required, he filled in as a worker for a day.

His predecessor had tried to cheat on both ends, banking his skimmings in curios and coins. The knave grew so miserly that suspicion spread; his stewardship ended in disgrace. As Selig gradually rebuilt the overseer's cottage into a house three times its former size, he discovered strange caches of booty along the way.

Crops were good three years in a row. He rose each day to acknowledge "God of my fathers, King of the Universe, *Reboysheloylem,* Who was Fire to Moses."

Ten months after transporting his friend to Baligrod, Reuben realized his dream. He departed for Hamburg—destination: Chicago. First he worked unhappily in a factory (though making more money in a month than Selig did in a year). Then he followed a group of *landsleit* to a place called "North Dakota." He described a hot sun, digging "the deepest hole in the world" and not finding water.

The following spring Reuben reported the dissolution of the colony. That was the last correspondence from him.

After four years, the feuding Aaron and Jacob wooed their brother separately.

He wished them well, but, like biblical Joseph of the many-colored robe, he had outgrown his kin. They would meet next through their children in the New World.

Even as his outward life found providence, Selig's dreams were filled with Liliths. The rabbi had urged him to *daven* these into angelic beings. Ultimately, though, marriage was the remedy.

In the diaspora, matrimony was usually arranged by *shadkhns* who received their percentage from the wife's family. Prospective bridegrooms publicized their interest through such spokeswomen. Selig did so as discreetly as possible.

In 1891 a marriage bard came singing the praises of Malke Grumet, a young woman several towns away. Daughter of an inn-keeper, she made chicken soup, roasts, golden challahs, *gefilte* from local perch, and *latkes*—the full repertoire of traditional delicacies.

At a gathering of mutual friends she and Selig were introduced. He found her attractive, but she was too shy to stay in the room with him. At market the next week, they met by accident. She threw her shawl over her face.

Selig knew Malke was not quite appropriate. Her devoutness like her beauty was acidic. On their wedding night he stared at her through haze but willed himself across it. From their union came the ordinary life each craved—including two cheerful daughters whom they named Jennie and Lottie.

Though Selig and Malke would argue incessantly over this or that detail of Talmudic law, a deeper quiet grew between them. He felt mostly an immense pity for his girls. What could he provide them? Even though Klanka gave him a raise at the birth of each, Galicia was dying. Two successive dry summers were followed by bleak, arid winters. The soil was impoverished.

He imagined his children in Egypt at a time of famine, compelled to live and die there, never to have anything of their own except the God of their fathers. And even that God was becoming strange to him.

Was it God he did not understand, or his own life? Long ago, these had been the same; yet now he prayed to distractions.

One morning he awoke to more wonder and power than he knew how to *daven* through. He saw the sun gigantic over meadows. He put on his wooden sacraments and wrapped himself in his shawl . . . its odor suddenly alien, as though home were no longer home.

To pray and be righteous was not enough. To end exile he would have to go into exile again.

Its name was America: free education, jobs, equality for Jews. Families throughout Galicia were immigrating in scores, the father first, a year or two later sending steamship tickets for wives, children, parents, brothers and sisters, cousins. New York was so fabled in local conversation that Jennie and Lottie pretended they crossed a stream to it, playing "America" on their plank.

Like a dying man, Selig grasped at the countryside. The wind through the trees slowed and became more stately. And torrents of rain braided an unknown symphony.

When Jennie was born in 1892, her father was a stocky elf who took her horseback-riding and showed her how to snap up fish with a bucket. Her mother taught her to cook and pickle their catch. She was five years old (he was thirty-two) when he left for New York.

Jennie's attention turned to tending her geese. Her best friend was Jhota, a yellow cow who slept by the stove, heaving as if the sun itself were breathing inside his flank. Poppa slowly became a storybook character, something that had not lasted. They prayed for him, but words only made him less real.

In the spring of 1901, as snowmelt contributed to a local stream, it became a lake. Waves rippled across farms. Together the sisters "emigrated" on their plank. Jennie crossed it first. Lottie, running behind, stumbled and fell. Paddling to stay afloat, she was swept toward a waterfall. Jennie watched in horror, then jumped. Gasping in the freezing rapids, she felt for her sister's head, got a sheath like a sea plant, and pulled her backward to shore. Both lay stunned on the ground.

How does information pass from generation to generation? Parents know what they themselves lived, but their children perceive it only remotely through the mist of their own becoming. What they pass to *their* children are legends of another time. Grandparents tell an even more legendary tale.

For great-grandchildren the lives of their parents' grandparents are a sliver of memory that for their children will not even exist. This process happens so gradually—the dissipation and building up of lives and forms—that we forget how creatures gestate in the bodies of other creatures and emerge into a world they are leaving.

On the journey Selig kept to himself, crowded into a tier of bunks with people speaking a medley of languages (he knew Russian, Polish, Yiddish, and Hebrew, and still there were many he could not converse with). As the boat heaved and bucked, his meager privacy was invaded by smells of tobacco, garlic, decayed food, vomit. Drinking water was stale, kosher impossible.

Yet the sea was a relief after the road to Hamburg. En route, he had encountered offers of counterfeit tickets, sour herring, stale bread, whiskey as a remedy for seasickness. He bought his tickets at a trusted boarding house, leaving a trail for Malke to follow.

In how long? Six months? A year? Five years?

On the third morning he climbed up on deck. The only "lands" were clouds; in their shapes floated *alephs* and *lameds.* Waves lapped right up to the ship . . . and through it. The sun was the same precise distance from God.

The ghetto was obliterated.

Ellis Island was another hurdle, engendering panic among passengers as landfall approached. Selig knew that he had to appear both healthy and alert. The entrance to America, as one immigrant put it, was "like to the Day of Judgment at which one proves fitness to enter Heaven." Those with suspected diseases or mental aberrations were set aside in large cages, their clothing chalked to indicate the organ or condition in question (H for heart, L for lungs).

In an immense room not quite as hellish as his nightmares of it Selig awaited his turn to file past doctors. As motley rows snaked along, tongues mingled in bestial moans. Older women practiced disguising their gaits; men took deep breaths and coughed, as though to work infection out. Selig wanted to extend sympathy, but he felt desperate and small.

The third doctor grabbed his head roughly, waved a stick in front of him, then tugged his eyelid up. That stung and humiliated Selig but, before he realized it, he was outside, wandering numbly through a small park, past a cluster of trees, his name announced, and Malke's brother Jacob hailing, now embracing him in another world.

The exodus was over.

Jacob untied his bundle from around his neck and the two men traded it back and forth as they hiked toward an elevated train.

From its stop-and-go path along rooftops Selig stared into a scenery familiar and bizarre. The New World was as crowded as a fair—children running on rooftops, peddlers' wagons jutting at rakish angles, crowds of men outside saloons, racks of colored dresses, exotic shouts and sirens. Wares poured into the middle of streets, forcing vehicles into perilous lanes. Fancy awnings, some smooth and wide, others with flags and frills, sagged like kerchiefs. Along each building's sides were cages and ladders. Jacob explained the ever-present risk of fire. Super-realistic signs fascinated Selig—painted crackers, cigars, and matchsticks wherever a shorter building left visible bricks on a taller one.

They crossed a thoroughfare. Rows of tenements loomed ahead.

Since Jacob was the foreman of a clothes-pressing plant, Selig took the one job available. On his first morning in the New World he worked past twilight. Most nights he slept in the factory on piles of clothes in order to make deliveries at dawn. In rooms lit by gas everyone labored six and seven days a week, as machines echoed comically. Beside Selig were rabbis, Italian and Polish philosophers, even Chinamen. (In fact, sages who had read Torah in Europe now sold cigars and pretzels on the avenue.)

Gradually Selig learned his neighborhood—Orchard, Canal, Division, Ludlow, Essex, Hester. Beyond these was a menace of "foreigner," a Polish and Russian shadow renewed in the form of Irish and Italian strongholds. Bold fellows who attempted journeys down Cherry Street across the Bowery returned with bruises, relieved of their belongings.

Among Jews the proud Germans had been entrenched for a generation. They spoke American, owned businesses, and disdained the fresh arrivals from Poland, Russia, Romania, Lithuania, and Hungary (who knew nothing of Tammany politics). In fact, the Germans were so embarrassed by the newcomers they tried to avoid them. These were exactly the kind of mannerless peasants, they thought, who had inspired Anti-Semitism in Europe. Because so many of their names ended in *ky* or *ki,* the established Jewry called them "kikes."

Selig had no life beyond his deed of immigration. As he ate and slept in other people's homes, days became weeks. Months grew into a year, and then another year. Sabbaths alone strung time in a manner resembling life.

Selig saw, as he shaved, an old man confiscating his youth.

Trolleys, buses rumbled along, stopping and starting in rigid patterns. Garbage piled everywhere. How did it ever decompose? Did rats consume it?

The sun grew soggy and sodden, pushing light through smoke. Even Jews cawed and shrieked and stole from one another's carts. Crowds moved in staccato hordes like insects. The language was assaultive—"sharrap" and "garrarrehere" ("shut up" and "get out of here"). People were barely distinguishable from pigeons and cockroaches.

Yes, there was equal opportunity, but it was opportunity to become a machine—or, at best, a boss of machines.

A few co-workers did mumble injustice. Selig mostly spurned them, though he ventured forth one night to a loft on Henry Street for speeches of the United Hebrew Trades. Most in attendance wore *yarmulkes.* Herring and pumpernickel on mahogany, cigars sweetening the damp, they recounted abuses of landlords and bosses as if chanting sections of the Torah. It was mainly an occasion for pouring another mug and shouting, *"L'chaim!"*

Trooping home before dawn he could see through tenement windows men and women working listlessly over machines, imperfect light from gas jets fed by quarters.

He longed for what he had left—clover, snowy meadows, a clear view of stars....

It was three years before he could afford tickets for Malke.

They left by wagon with cousin Gershon Grumet (after one last petting of the geese, one more hug for Jhota who was adopted by their aunt). Then they spent impatient days on cobbled streets in Brunn, awaiting the train to Hamburg.

As the *Potsdam* rumbled out of the harbor, Jennie forgot her cow and geese. Her gaze turned to the horizon.

One day she saw birds in the sky. "Are they lost?" she wondered.

"No, we are near America." She took a deep breath. The air smelled of fresh salad with traces of smoke.

They were in a room with all these men ... not really men ... animals babbling, pigs grunting. She resisted removing her clothes, then shrank from being examined so closely. But all faded as they called out the name "Grossinger."

'That must be Poppa standing in the park.'

'Are these my daughters? Why, Lottie is the age I remember Jennie. And is this the woman who ran from me at the market?'

Walking backwards Selig narrated an odyssey of streets. Alleys echoed stridently, and Jennie's head spun to peddlers *davening* herring and whitefish, spoked wheels supporting poles of dresses, shoes, pots and pans. She had never seen olives, bananas, or tomatoes before, but Selig explained and had her sample each.

At a red brick edifice they forced their way past a rigid door up unlit stairs. Another door opened into a gathering of relatives who meted hugs and platters of pastry, bread, hazelnuts, and apple strudel, plus Jennie's first sausage on a slice of rye. Everyone drank cups of hot water with flavored bags in them, yellow fruit slices dipped for bitterness.

The Grossinger home at 158 Ridge Street—marked by a red glow in a dim hallway—was barely more domestic than the *Potsdam.* Garbage collected in the alley, joining its stench to spillover from a shared toilet on the fourth floor. (Jennie, Lottie, and Malke went once a week to the public baths for showers.) Streaked windows revealed horizons of others like them, laundry strung on ropes across courtyards, identical wooden dolls among the sheets and shirts. Selig explained the use of clothes-pins *(gretklamer).*

Neighboring flats housed people from throughout Europe, crowded into cubicles, sleeping on cots, sharing meals. One downstairs apartment contained a woman with six children and no father.

Cooking was an all-day affair, so visitors surrounded the stove, occupying any available surface. They preached, *kvetched,* and found amazing parallels in their lives to the trials of Moses and Judas Maccabeus. The women made prune jam and almond cookies, stirred pot cheese, and replenished the goblet of borscht in the icebox.

Blocks of tenements unloosed girls with whom to skip rope and play potsy (a game of hopping on one foot among lines drawn in chalk on the sidewalk). Other times they tossed bags full of cherry pits into cups, bounced balls off stoops, or aimed at coins set on the pavement which, when hit, flipped up with a wonderful tinkle that meant a point for your team.

A favorite was "Prisoner's Base," which divided the juvenile community into opposing camps who tried to lure and capture prisoners and then pull their own free in tugs-of-war—everyone scattering when trucks and brewery wagons passed. Pranksters dropped feathers, nuts, and rinds from windows.

With her new friends Jennie explored the roofs of buildings, staring perilously down dumbwaiters and between lines of laundry.

It was a giddy view as a ball sailed between sheets while boys circled bases—but the girls would hop to the next building, giggling, pretending not to notice kissing couples who had sneaked up to escape tenement life.

Hard rubber zinged off brick and concrete and ricocheted with delicious unpredictability, compelling results with vehicles and passers-by.

Suddenly, smash! The players froze as glass briefly serenaded the street. Out of the hush came O'Callahan, a cop like a bulldog. "Break it up," he boomed, "or I'll wrap me shillelagh around your neck."

"Brass buttons blue coat," jeered two boys as they tore round the corner, "couldn't catch a nanny goat."

Jennie walked Lottie to the local park at Pitt Street—clumps of grass around flagstones containing metal slides and rows of swings. Their favorite was a contraption that people called "a monkey bar."

"Monkey" was one of Jennie's first American words, meaning also the creature who accompanied the organ-grinder. As they were showered with coins, the human ordered his compatriot to dance. There was no thought of stealing from the friendly animal, so Jenny helped to scoop his money up and place it in a red cap he held.

Summer was celebrated by community outings, then capped by an annual trip to the East River. Boys dove off piers into water covered with oil, climbed out, and dove again.

One scorching afternoon three shirtless men forced open a hydrant. Foam shot across bricks.

Though Jennie shied back, she found it elating to watch bubbles clear gutters and cover dancing bodies. The force churned papers and dust into muddy swales. Some kids swam half-naked through the illusion of waves.

Her adventures ended on the first day of P.S. 174. Crossing the threshold of an ugly neighborhood fortress, she was led through noisy mobs to a room of children her age. For days she sat in a stupor, understanding little, though she thought the chalk letters beautiful and hoped she would someday master their secrets.

When Jennie's lack of English was discovered, she was demoted from third to first grade, an embarrassing promenade that left her the tallest girl in her class and the only one who didn't speak American. The teacher carried a stick and, whenever she was unable to answer, whacked her.

Despite the anguish of school, there was freedom in other domains—no fenced fields or forbidden properties. Streets simmered. One whole block was lined with Hebrew books, vials of colored liquids, *mezuzas*, men's hats and ties. On the next, pushcarts were heaped with fruits and cookies. Jennie and Lottie were taught to pay for goodies, but some kids mastered the art of pilfering by making noise to distract a wagon's overseer. The sisters most adored following the ice shaver, collecting free scrapings from his knife.

On late afternoons Jennie joined an ongoing summit at the candy store, eavesdropping as teenagers boasted. She heard about "the money uptown" and "crooks who had it made." At first these phrases were indecipherable, but they became her lessons in American lingo.

As snow turned the streets into countryside, forts were established on vacant lots. Dodging projectiles, Jennie spent the better part of an afternoon hauling wooden crates of "mortar" to her side's barricade (which grew into a castle). She would never forget the shock of an iceball crushing into her cheek. She lay on the ground wanting to be brave but whimpering anyway while friends hauled her out of the firing line.

She much preferred the Flexible Flyers on which they sped down a single neighborhood hill, tumbling into a jolly heap, then back up the hill, time and again until she was too exhausted to stand. Malke brushed snow out of her hair, peeled off her clothes, and, all the while invoking exotic pneumonias, wrapped her in a robe.

Now that his family was whole again Selig borrowed from the Grumets to purchase a failing butcher shop. Three years earlier he wouldn't have dreamed of such an enterprise but, while their German detractors were settling the fashionable districts uptown, Eastern European Jews were claiming the Lower East Side. Former peddlers owned tenements. One sweatshop worker was a manufacturer of cloaks. People from Selig's very ship ran cigar factories, candy stores, and grocery markets.

Selig cut, packed, and delivered by hand. In two and a half months he was flooded with bills and taxes for things he didn't even know existed. He sold the shop just in time.

He went back to the machines—this time in a smaller factory managed by Malke's Uncle Joe.

The year before, their first American child, Harry, had been born ill, crying relentlessly, hands clasped over his ears. The doctor drained his tympanic cavities. Later a specialist from uptown diagnosed him incurably deaf *(toyb)*. Even the rabbis could recommend nothing.

Malke determined to take her son to a renowned Orthodox healer in Galicia. Though a startled Selig called her *meshuga,* he realized that if his wife left he could live cheaply again, perhaps even put aside enough to start another business. Faking complicity, he enlisted the Grumets to pay most of her ticket. At the last minute Jennie was left behind to save a fare but also to care for Poppa.

In June of 1904, she and Poppa watched Momma, Lottie, and Harry board the steamer. She stared silently as the ship grew tiny and left her sight. She wept all the way home on the trolley and arrived at Ridge Street to find their furniture already gone. Father and daughter, as planned, were moving in with Aunt Sarah Countryman, who already boarded three nieces and a nephew.

The following months were the loneliest of Jennie's life. There was nothing to lift her spirits. As Poppa worked day and night, she too increased her factory hours. Swamped with expenses—money for Malke in Europe, repayment of his debts—Selig sat in the same armchair till dawn, staring into space.

At least Jennie learned English and skipped a grade. Her main pleasure was striding around, intoning the American "w" and "th" sounds her father couldn't make. Since it irritated him to hear these coming from her, she would taunt him with repeated "Hellos" and "Whats?" and then tell jokes about gangsters.

At this point Quentin Reynolds picks up his subject's tale:

> On a summer evening in 1905, Jennie attended an open-air dance on the rooftop of P.S. 188. As she stood alone amidst hundreds of laughing young boys and girls, her . . . eyes suddenly fixed on a radiant sweet-faced girl about her own age [who was also alone]. Jennie sensed a response in the girl's open, wholesome face. Though painfully shy, she could not resist the impulse to approach this girl and ask her name.
>
> "Anna Kriendler," the girl replied.
>
> In this simple and direct fashion a friendship was born that was to play a key role in the Grossinger saga and endure to this day, more than three score years later. [From] living as a boarder with no real home of her own, Jennie was taken into the large Kriendler household [with] three boys and three girls, as one of [their] own. In time, it was perfectly natural that everyone . . . considered her the seventh Kriendler child.

Jennie may have professed loyalty to her father (she claimed later that their time together had made them confidantes), but she stopped coming home. The Kriendlers became her family, not only then but thereafter. Even when the Grossingers were reunited Jennie spent as little time as she could under Selig and Malke's roof.

That same year she was chosen May Queen of P.S. 188. She was not particularly beautiful, yet there she stood, Anna's beloved, crowned with flowers.

She was thirteen, a year too young to get her papers, but she quit school, lied about her age, and took a full-time job on the twelfth floor of a factory—ten hours a day, six days a week, sewing buttonholes. Her "vacation" on the Sabbath was purchased by having to hike eleven stories on Sunday, the elevator man's day off. One afternoon, while an inspector prowled for truants, three workers hid her under cloaks.

An unskilled laborer began at $1.50 a week, but Jennie quickly built up to $12. She gave her unopened paychecks to her father. After two months she moved to a factory that had only three flights of stairs and paid an extra half-cent per buttonhole.

Three and a half years later Malke came home, resigned to life in America. The Grossingers enrolled their son in the Fanwood School for the Deaf and Mute at 168th Street. Then, with the money he had saved, Selig rented a warehouse. Malke and the girls manned an assembly line. The house specialty was cream cheese. They also sold fresh milk, cream, and butter in wooden casks. A hectic schedule and casks of curd encouraged gooey slapstick. Poppa laughed and scolded, but Malke did not appreciate the comediennes.

Jennie resumed classes at night. Put initially into high school, she could follow neither grammar nor arithmetic and informed the teacher after a month. "Why didn't you say something sooner?" asked the woman kindly. She relocated her in the fifth grade of a different school.

Yet once again bills overwhelmed Selig. After only four months, he closed the creamery.

Jennie dropped out of school and reclaimed her seamstress job; Poppa returned to the machines too. America had become a life sentence.

At eighteen Jennie began to go on social outings, sometimes at the Yiddish theater in the Bowery, sometimes to Coney Island, usually with Lottie, Lottie's boyfriend Louie Grau, their second cousin Esther Grossinger, and Esther's friend Max. Later a shy first cousin from Chicago, Harry Grossinger, joined the group. He began to date Jennie. She was twenty and they were crossing the Williamsburg Bridge when he told her he was going to join his brothers in business. As she began to protest he added that he wanted to marry her. He promised that in six months he'd have enough money to bring her west. She hugged him in unabashed joy.

After Harry settled back in Chicago, he kept in touch by letters and presents. Jennie rebuked him for each comb and jewelled brooch, assuming they postponed a reunion, but he bragged that things were going so well they could afford to be married any time.

Selig and Malke were horrified. Harry they could hardly object to; he was a gentleman. But a daughter they couldn't spare, even one who didn't come home. God forbid! They had a deaf-mute son.

Her parents' pleas meant little to Jennie, but she could not abandon the Kriendlers. Harry answered her rejection with majestic grace. He would come back to New York—fortunes were as easily made there!

Jennie and Harry Grossinger were married on Sheriff Street in late 1912. The hall was packed with relatives, friends, and colleagues from various factories in which father and daughter had worked—so many that Selig had to call for a second round of knishes, wine, and celery tonic. As three klezmer musicians played, Jennie danced with Harry, Louie, Max, father Selig, and Anna's brothers.

Having impressed his cousins with worldliness and ambition, Harry immediately began preaching the same to Selig. After all, his family was buying up Chicago. "Let's try a restaurant *shtick* this time. My brother tells me it's easy money."

Selig and his son-in-law leased a storefront on Columbia Street and soon opened "Grossinger's Dairy Restaurant."

Jennie waited six tables; Harry managed accounting and publicity; Poppa cleaned and repaired; Malke cooked. For five months Grossinger's was the neighborhood cafeteria.

One evening, while delivering dinners, Selig collapsed. In broken dishes and blood the Columbia Street enterprise came to an end. The family sold it to a young couple, Jennie staying on to ease the transition. The doctor called the disease "a complete nervous breakdown."

"You can't go back to the factory," Malke pleaded. Selig's cough had become deep and chronic; he no longer remembered what it was like to breathe normally.

At a clandestine conference, Jennie, Harry, and the prosperous Grumets colluded on Selig's long-overdue "American vacation." An unwilling Poppa was put on the train at Grand Central. Feeling ridiculous, he debarked near Colchester, Connecticut, where a decorated carriage transported him to his room. In the morning, despite himself, he pranced along and hummed an old prayer. Passing a farmhouse "For Sale," he put down his spending money—two tens, four ones, three quarters, two dimes, and five pennies.

Back on Ridge Street, to objections of extravagance, he pantomimed fields of corn and tomatoes.

"Not Connecticut," Uncle Joe warned. "Expensive . . . long winters . . . you'd be *verblundjet* to go to Connecticut."

Malke refilled his bowl of cabbage soup.

"But I have to farm," said Selig. "I'll die otherwise."

"I didn't say no farm," Joe began again after apple strudel. "I said no Connecticut. We've got plenty of *landsleit* in the Catskills. It's more like home: big mountains, brooks, spring water, clear nights. The farming is good, better than Connecticut. The prices are *really* beautiful."

A month later, boarding a train in New Jersey, Selig stared at landscapes along the river—smoky factories, then cows and cottages, villages bright as sap. A bridge rattled. A quarry loomed and snapped away. Inside the tunnel, moisture oozed across his window.

Debarking at the remote town of Ferndale, Selig unpacked in the spare room of a Galician acquaintance of Uncle Joe's. He slept like a bear.

Morning rose on a stage that seemed a thousand years old. Birds wailed the diaspora lament, an imponderable medley of sorrow and hope. Selig wandered among grasses, sampling berries and sorrel, bending to sniff clover. Clouds dispersing seemed just above his head.

When the real-estate office opened, he once again proved his impulsiveness. He petitioned Max Fisch on duty and was taken on expedition through a district of ramshackle farms—so many his mind spun. His excited letter brought Uncle Joe on the next train. While the two men made the rounds, they spoofed their unlikely roles as potential barons. "But we can afford this," Joe promised him. "We're not paupers *(kaptsonim)* anymore."

"It is as if I saw a miracle happen before my eyes," he told Malke and Jennie later. "He's a new person. He tramps all over the countryside and when night comes he's as fresh as when he first got up. Malke, he's like the young Selig you married."

She wondered if the Catskills were really arable, but Joe shrugged and deferred to the one-time steward. "If he says he can do it, he can. You put together your money and I'll make up the difference."

It took three more days for Selig and Max Fisch to settle on a property. Then Poppa sent for his family.

Malke and daughters crossed the Hudson on the Weehawken ferry, then boarded the Ontario and Western. As they made awkward bedding on seats, the train picked up speed.

Bright rays awakened them at Ferndale.

Two girls stepped into frosty pine air. Crickets chirped in a manner that struck Jennie as presumptuously carefree. Father was waiting in a carriage owned by Max Fisch (who invited the family for breakfast). What Malke noticed was that the eggs and milk he fed them were from his own barn. But her optimism did not last.

After the meal he took them along dirt roads through sparsely settled countryside to the site Selig had selected—a crumbling cottage with barely a roof, boulders from the last Ice Age. Jennie wondered how she could live without neighbors. Where would her children go to school? The ebullient Fisch reminded them that there were farms closer to Ferndale, even ones in the village, but they were considerably more expensive.

Selig was not disappointed. He dispatched his family: he would stay and continue to search.

Back in New York City, as Malke and the girls hauled their belongings up tenement stairs, dismay overwhelmed Jennie. The streets were filthy, their quarters cramped. Brother Harry had to stay indoors for fear of the new speedy automobiles that scattered people with their horns. "Is this," she asked Momma, "what we chose over those beautiful mountains?"

A month later Selig's telegram threw the household into a tizzy:

Have bought a thirty-five-acre farm not far from station. Come at once.

Malke hurried to catch the next train. Jennie and Lottie anxiously awaited her assessment.

Two weeks later a jubilant letter summoned them.

"It must be exceptional," Lottie said, "since she never fails to exaggerate the bad side."

They crossed the Hudson and boarded the train. As arboreal scenery rolled along, they dreamed up their farm with its white fence, cows, apples and pears. "Hurleyville! Next stop Ferndale!"

The engine slowed into the station. The girls scanned the crowd for a familiar face. Outside, a fleet of jitneys stirred, their uniformed drivers preparing to assist guests to various hotels and boarding houses. No Selig.

They waited uneasily as the sky darkened.

Only when every other carriage was on its way did a rickety contrivance behind a gaunt horse creep into the station (Poppa explained that the animal's name was "Brownie"). As the girls loaded their suitcases, the carriage's support groaned and seemed about to snap. That was the beginning of a comical journey.

The farmhouse was five miles from the station, and at every hill Selig hopped down to help the horse. With indomitable cheerfulness he pointed under moonlight to a small neighborhood schoolhouse and, a little bit past it, the Grossinger home.

Its seven rooms were crumbling plaster and slumping beams. The morning revealed stones no one could work a plow around. But Selig enumerated the property's virtues: a well in front, a brook only thirty yards away, chickens already in coops. It wasn't what they had imagined, but it was theirs.

Room by room Jennie and Lottie scrubbed. Selig patched and painted behind them. After drips began hitting previously unexplained buckets, they tore off rotting shingles and remade the roof. Then they joined forces with Brownie to haul away what rocks were movable. One boulder barely budged under the horse's traction but with two girls pushing from behind, it was urged a few critical inches. Next they tried one that seemed it would be the death of the poor horse, so it was left in peace, though Lottie decorated its top with a face of small stones.

Clearing and plowing took two weeks. After turning an irregular quarter acre, they stuffed rows with eyes of potatoes, seeds of cabbages, carrots, and cucumbers. The next day in town they bought three cows.

Jennie never said it in so many words, but she was in Ferndale for good. Her husband took to visiting on weekends.

The original Grossinger farm was purchased in April of 1914 for a downpayment of $450 on a total price of $3,500. Selig and Malke put in their savings of $250, and Harry Grossinger $200. More capital was needed for operating, so $200 came from Aunt Sadie Roth and smaller amounts from other friends and relatives. Uncle Joe loaned $1,000 to help repair the property.

Blending the relief of a liberated factory worker with the pride of a farmer, Selig intended to grow enough not only to feed his family but pay off all his debts. "Next year," he boasted, "we'll have *bulbes* (potatoes) like *melonen* (melons)."

June alone taught him the fact that many urban refugees had discovered: a successful farm in the Catskills was all but impossible. Not only was the soil poor and the season short, but competitors were closer to the main markets.

"Your best crop will be your guests," the manager of the general store had predicted, so Selig, Harry, Malke, and Jennie faced reality. They owned a restored farm, three milk cows, fifty chickens. Neighbors without their connections or skills were already getting $12 a week for guests.

"Remember," Selig chided. "Momma's Poppa kept an inn *(kretchma)* in the old country. All it takes is a little work."

"If I can cook for my family," she sighed, "I can make for a few extra."

Imitating a waltz step he had performed in his youth, Selig took his wife's hand and kissed it. "With kitchen skills like yours we can't fail."

The decision was made. The Grossingers would launch a café in the Catskills; they would rent rooms and serve kosher meals.

Harry offered to throw in the remainder of his savings. To Jennie's delight, he and Selig rose, bowed to each other, and shook hands. "Yes, Harry," Poppa said, "we will be partners, you and I. Isaac's family will be made whole."

"S. and H. Grossinger," it would read years later on the company buses. . . .

With cousins and in-laws pitching in, the farm was transformed, ceremoniously given back its original name, "The Longbrook House," and opened for business the following season. The Grossingers entertained nine guests a night, each paying $9 for a week's room and board. The Kriendler family alone made a full house.

This is the way the fable goes, and there is no reason to dispute it.

The county in which Ferndale was located had been named after George Washington's second-in-command, General John Sullivan. Within its plentiful hemlock groves, tanneries thrived until the mid-nineteenth century. Then, the trees substantially stripped, mere marginal farms remained among factory towns.

Another "industry" had been growing in the county's more scenic spots—Victorian hotels. In the area around Ferndale stood the Lenape, the Mecca, and the Lancashire, institutions so imperial that Selig and Malke considered them castles from the "other world" that had always surrounded the *shtetl.*

However, by the time Selig happened upon Max Fisch's office, Jewish settlers were beginning to emancipate Sullivan and Ulster counties. Every season another of the "czar's" mansions would close or be burned to the ground for insurance money.

Meanwhile, on the Lower East Side, unchecked pollution darkened the sun; rivers of raw sewage streamed down streets, collecting in pools behind tenements. Inside such buildings tuberculosis was king. The only remedy was clean air and water, and in the vicinity of New York City, the healthiest land—snowy and sparsely settled—lay in the Catskill range. Clinics soon dotted the region, further reducing property values. Because Liberty (adjacent to Ferndale) contained the highest elevation between Manhattan and Lake Erie, it became the site of the world-renowned Loomis Sanitarium, commissioned in 1896 by J. P. Morgan.

As early as 1825 Major Mordecai Noah of the Pennsylvania militia, the most prominent American Jew of his time, proposed to create "the New Jerusalem" on an island in the Niagara River, "a Jewish nation under the auspices and protection of the constitution and laws of the United States; confirming and perpetuating all our rights and privileges, our name, our rank, and our power among the nations of the earth as they existed and were recognized under the government of the Judges."

In 1892 the Jewish Agricultural Society began a program of underwriting farms and dairies in the Catskills. By the end of the decade German Jews had repopulated large sections of a transatlantic Zion. After two decades more than a thousand properties, most of them between Ellenville and Ferndale, had been bought by settlers. Although many of the new agrarians swore to the Agricultural Society that they would till their land for eternity, virtually all of them converted failing farms to boarding houses.

A 1904 ad for the Evergreen Farm House was typical in its claims:

> Elevation, 2000 feet. Baths, toilets, hot water on every floor. Fresh milk, butter and eggs from our own farm. Kosher. 500 fruit trees. Piano and other entertainment. Books and newspapers. Playground for children.

By the time Selig and Malke were taking guests into their rehabilitated farmhouse, competing inns were heralding telephones, telegraph access, electric lights, bowling, billiards, and dancing pavilions. Ellenville, Liberty, Fallsburgh, and Monticello had become extensions of Hester and Canal Streets. Even so, the Longbrook price was low, and guests seemed to enjoy visiting with Malke and Jennie and taking Selig's countryside tours. In addition, Harry would scour the Low East—from candy stores to markets to synagogues and union halls—broadcasting his mother-in-law's cooking and the camaraderie of the clientele. When potential customers were cynical, boasting, for instance, that they preferred the beach at Far Rockaway, he never failed to offer a discount *(rabat).* Reticent customers were rarely disappointed.

From her spotlessly maintained kitchen Malke fed and overfed her house, providing delicacies not only from her homeland but the cuisines of guests who joined her during long afternoons around the oven. Each morning Jennie and Lottie plucked chickens *(hoon),* then served as second-in-command in the kitchen (first in the laundry). Few would forget August mid-day alongside the woodburners when Harry had to dip his glasses in water to keep the rims from scalding him.

After he became the comedian Joey Adams, Joey Abramowitz recalled these times, how his mother would compete with the other guests

> ... to establish a beachhead at one of the two sinks. Armed with ... scouring powder, each lived by the motto: 'Take the sink—and hold it!' Even the two ovens and the bread box became battle grounds. Everybody fought for the best spot in the icebox too. The status symbol was the two cubic inches assigned to you, and the top shelf on the front was equivalent to a triple A rating in Dun and Bradstreet.
>
> Every jar of goodies had a label. The little lump of farmer cheese ... was tagged 'H. Plotkin.' The pickled lox in the wax paper said 'J. Traum.' One always heard such anguished cries as "Somebody's been at my stewed prunes"—"Who spilled and left the shelf so dirty?"—"All right, so it was a little yellow, but did I give you permission to throw out my farmer cheese?"

The inn inspired collective genius. If there was no heat on frigid evenings, Malke baked stones in the oven, wrapped them in towels, and distributed these to guests. If *bulbes* dominated Selig's garden (as invariably they did), Malke turned them into soups, salads, desserts, pancakes, *kreplachs,* and knishes. When the Sabbath came (with its restriction against electricity), Harry would use Selig's wagon to haul hundred-pound slabs of ice to keep the food from spoiling. If they were overwhelmed with guests, the Grossingers lodged them together under the banner of intimacy—then rushed to borrow silverware, pots, and pans from their neighbors. When every spare corner was filled with cots, tents were rented from the General Store. For entertainment, a victrola trumpeted opera and Yiddish songs. People sang together, the talented among them playing harmonica and accordion. Occasionally klezmer musicians visited and serenaded with *"Di Zilberne Khasene"* and *"Sheyn vi di L'vone."* Then late into the eve they backed dancers with *horas, bulgars,* and *freylekhs.*

On many nights the fare was little more than after-dinner gabbing or the visit of a horse-and-buggy peddler with his wooden tub of ice cream: "A three-flavored brick for a nickel." For city folks, the relaxation and company (plus a 5 AM outing to watch Selig milk the cows ...

a bubbling cupful as reward) was excitement enough.

It was an exhausting regime, compensated by the endless cheer of new friends and a $400 profit the second summer.

On September 17, 1915, Jennie gave birth to a nine-pound boy and named him Paul. Soon after, Lottie and her husband Louie Grau also had their first child, Seymour. Because Jennie was hostess of the inn, the younger sister ended up nursing both babies. Malke bristled at this maternal negligence, but a blithe Jennie ignored her.

By the second season the expanded farmhouse reached a maximum of thirty-five guests. When there were enough regulars to claim every room every weekend, nothing remained for new clientele, so during the third season one of the most loyal guests, Sol Mandelbaum, offered to help Selig search for a bigger inn. With Max Fisch and his partner, Sam Weiner, joining forces, one by one the men examined every available property around Ferndale. All were quickly (and sometimes hilariously) excluded, except for one that was so far-fetched they dared not even consider it.

Because of a typhoid scare at Lake Ophelia on its grounds, the opulent Nichols Estate and Terrace Hill House had been on the market for four years. Even to consider owning this property overlooking the town of Liberty (which for generations had been a Protestant resort) seemed presumptuous to Malke and Selig. Cowed more by Terrace Hill's reputation than its plummeting price, Selig refused even to visit the grounds. However, Sol and Sam knew he could afford it, so they conspired to take S. and H. on tour against their will. To make the escapade more entertaining they recruited several unpaid "advisors." The party zoomed up the hill in Selig's new Ford, exchanging jokes about Rothchilds and Rockefellers as the town of Liberty stretched beneath.

At the summit the men walked in a daze. There was enough space here to house the population of five tenements.

Sol shouted attention to an unlocked window (perhaps left so by Fisch), then gleefully led the crew inside. Selig felt uncomfortable sneaking in, but Sol assured him that Mrs. Nichols intended them to see everything before risking their money. Soon he joined in a medley of delighted discoveries: bathrooms with running water and showers, electric lights, a gigantic kitchen, modern telephones.

Fantasy was delightful, but it had a price: Longbrook had been exposed as a mere shack.

Selig refused to make an offer, so that weekend Sol initiated a rebellion by pledging a $1000 loan. Lottie's previously reluctant husband, Louie, who now managed a large dress-making plant, offered to put up a substantial sum. Others in attendance made smaller donations: linens, silverware, blankets, extra plates.

Mrs. Nichols wanted $27,500 for three large buildings and six acres. She would then include an option on the remaining ninety acres, two cottages, and barn. Selig wouldn't budge.

Harry and Jennie pleaded with him. Finally, eyes twinkling as though about to betray a prank, he proclaimed, *"Irviltazoy, zolzaynazoy!"* ("You won't let it be no, so it must be yes.")

First, the Grossingers sold Longbrook for $10,000, a substantial profit. Then on February 12, 1919—the furnishings, silverware, and animals having been transported ahead—the family boarded their Ford and chugged up the hill to stay.

In that simple ride Selig was restored to land he might have inherited (in mountains like those of his childhood). Malke had her inn with hot and cold faucets, private toilets, and a panoramic view. Grossingers and Grumets, who had left Galicia during a cycle of poverty, now stood at the gateway to an era of unimaginable beneficence.

On Decoration Day, the Terrace Hill House opened to near-capacity crowds. Despite high rates all the rooms remained booked through the hottest summer in memory, making the risky purchase seem a steal.

For the inaugural summer Harry served as plumber, repairman, bed-maker, bellboy, and porter ... and still found time to return to the Lower East Side to talk up business and requisition produce at the Washington Market. He spent many afternoons walking stalls, visiting warehouses, poking lemons and apples, sampling peaches and plums, inspecting chickens, running his hands through walnuts and pecans, and scolding anyone he thought had cheated him the week before.

"Dos gelt kumt foon zikh aleyn" ("It feels like printing money"), he told an astonished Selig as they counted the cashbox from just one weekend.

But as people poured out of New York in record numbers, other hotels began shutting their doors—most area water sources had turned to trickles. By mid-July even the Nichols place, blessed with back-up springs, was within hours of running dry. In panic the Grossingers pondered over the nearly drained and "contaminated" Lake Ophelia, then phoned an inspector. He spent an afternoon gathering water samples, sorrowfully shaking his head. Harry and Selig practiced downtrodden looks in hopes of convincing either him or Moses in Heaven to give them a break.

He phoned them the next day. "You're the luckiest people in the Catskills. This is the first water I've tested all summer that hasn't been polluted. You have the one lake around here that's fed entirely by underground streams."

After that, family members were content to take turns carrying empty cannisters three-quarters of a mile up the mountain, full ones back down.

In October S. and H. took a second mortgage and purchased the remainder of the Nichols Estate.

"This little one *(der kleyner),*" pronounced Poppa, bending to kiss baby Paul, "will grow up like the son of a king *(ben meylekh).*"

Now that the Grossingers were officially in the hotel business, they realized that equivalently priced establishments offered at least a swimming pool and a tennis court. For swimming, the Nichols place could get by with its lake, so Selig and Harry drove to a nearby boys' camp to investigate their second priority, "the American game." Satisfied with on-the-spot sketches, they finished their rendition of tennis in time for the 1921 season. The guests were perplexed—an overly long net strung across bumpy ground in a chicken-wire enclosure, no boundary grids.

Jennie was mortified. Not only did she contact a pro working at a nearby hotel (and pay him to design a court), but she kept Iby Corwin on staff. Then she made a reservation for herself at the resort that her guests most extolled—Laurel-in-the-Pines of Lakewood, New Jersey.

The owners gave her the complete tour. What she saw cuckolded how far Grossinger's was from being a real American hotel—glittering crystal goblets, all identical (instead of an assortment of thick glasses); waiters in aprons and white jackets; guests in required formal dress (men with ties); fine cloth napkins; food carefully decorated on fancy plates; dishes of olives, radishes, and celery on crushed ice; and not only tennis, but handball, horses, boats, and an orchestra. In ten years this would be Grossinger's.

Through the '20s, Selig and Harry's enterprise outgrew any imagined strategy, prospering even during the Depression. Louie Grau, now an executive in the garment business, loaned the family most of $7000 needed to construct a dining room with a capacity of four hundred guests. By then he and Lottie had a second child, Ruth, and spent most of their weekends at their second home.

During summers every room was filled, as were cots on porches and foldaway beds in lobbies. Entertainment was guest-generated. In impromptu concerts, young Abe Lyman played a variety of instruments, while Mrs. Berlinger's son Milton stood in the lobby after dinner stringing together jokes.

Only months after starting work on their dining room, Selig and Harry purchased an eleven-room cottage on the bordering Girod estate. Since it had recently been rented to a man driven about in a Pierce-Arrow, they named it "The Millionaire." For that reason alone, it became the most requested accommodation.

When uninformed guests wanted to reserve rooms for winter months, Selig scoffed at the notion, but Harry argued that since year-round maintenance of the property was required anyway, they might as well do some business. They could purchase sleds, and there were ample hills. So Grossinger's kept its doors open year round and invented a cold-weather sports-and-entertainment calendar other resorts soon copied.

No objection was raised when Selig offered to donate funds to Ferndale for construction of a new road in place of the public one that split his property. Once the estate was sealed, a gardener was hired to landscape European style. Harry added on terraces and paths almost as quickly as his consultant proposed them.

With unassuming regality Jennie strode the grounds, greeting everyone. "Hello, I'm Jennie Grossinger—and I'm so happy to have you here as my guests."

To a group of strangers: "I owe you gentlemen an apology for not introducing myself. My name is Jennie Grossinger." As they fumbled nervously, she added, "Come, let's all have a drink to our new friendship."

To a woman arriving alone for tennis: "No escort? Why, you are so brave!"

With his crew of laborers from town, Harry Grossinger transformed antiquated structures and expanded into former farmland with villas and cottages. He fashioned a curious and eccentric Tudor village.

Selig's universe was transformed overnight. As memory and myth blurred, the sweatshops of the Lower East Side seemed a lifetime ago and Klanka's fields just yesterday . . . or perhaps tomorrow.

He was dreaming Reuben's music-box America, dangerously close to heresy *(apikoysis)*. The legendary palaces and gardens of King David were not something Jews were permitted to raise themselves; only (if they were pious) could they reclaim the ruins.

Yet when Selig and Malke occupied the Nichols Estate they were the first members of a new hotelling trade that was to include the Brickmans, the Slutskys (at the Nevele), the Pauls, the Kutchers, and the Nemersons. In Manhattan, Jewish and gentile worlds were no longer separate. New Yorkers were adopting the styles of Harlem and Little Italy, spouting Yiddish ironies in Irish brogues. They brought this magic and urbanity to the Mountains.

Before the 1925 season, S. and H. purchased a lake adjoining the grounds for $10,000. A crew was hired to expand its basin and remove underwater stumps. That summer, guests broke bottles of champagne over a fleet of rowboats.

A bridle path was cleared around the water, and equestrian Bernie Sper was invited to manage six saddle horses. Jennie joined her guests for pre-breakfast rides, spinning yarns of Ferndale and Ridge Street (to the amusement of all) . . . and promising more surprises next season.

An astute listener, she soon understood Grossinger's greatest lack was professional entertainment. Even small bungalow colonies *(kokhaleyn)* had a *tummler* (a "noise-creator") who could act the buffoon—a combination clown/comedian/singer/magician. The *tummler* organized games and promoted amateur nights, dance contests, and plays. (The closest thing to a *tummler* at Grossinger's then was a waiter who had mastered the stagecraft of bringing a squawking chicken into the dining room to deliver eggs to unsuspecting guests.)

By 1926 a fulltime Grossinger *tummler* was surrounded by professional singers, dancers, and a band. For the following summer Harry erected a theater, and Jennie enticed a team of Broadway actors to put on skits and musicals in exchange for room and board.

With sellouts all July and August, Harry threw up a quick forty-five-room building Jennie named "The Ritz." Three additional cottages were purchased from neighboring properties, expanded, and rechristened. The "Lyman" honored a longtime guest, now a popular band leader; the "Berle," Mrs. Berlinger's son.

That same year Harry built his family a ranch-style house at the entrance to the grounds (Jennie optimistically naming it Joy Cottage). By then the pair had separated their lives and hired maids to run the household, including a French governess when their daughter Elaine was born in 1927.

Paul's instructor, Milton, was a student from Jersey City who had anglicized his name to Blackstone. A basketball star at Lehigh University where he put in 21 points in an upset over Navy, he originally came to Grossinger's in 1926 as a guest recuperating from surgery and was "discovered" one day making fifteen hoops in a row by the kid who was to become his charge. Concerned about her undisciplined son, Jennie agreed to hire a companion. Selig was pleased. He had noticed how much effort Blackstone expended trying to get Harry, Jr., to socialize—the only non-relative to mouth syllables and practice sign language. "I want that boy to stay here," Poppa proclaimed. "He has a *yiddishe neshoma* (the right kind of heart)."

While accompanying young Paul through arithmetic, history, and football, Milton revealed an unsuspected talent for outrageous promotional schemes. These flew out of him at such frantic speed Harry thought he must be *meshuga;* he wanted to dispatch him before he did damage.

But Blackstone's style was irresistible to Jennie—a world of breathtaking possibility. "He must have freedom to do whatever he wants," she told her husband and father.

One of his brainstorms was to invite celebrities "on the house" (over Harry's enraged objections), then to report their gambols "unofficially" by press release. To everyone's astonishment, the press bit—hook, line, and sinker. Over the following years "guests" included Al Jolson, Alan King, Richard Tucker, Phil Foster, Eddie Cantor, and (unheard of in the Jewish Alps) black stars such as Buck and Bubbles, Lionel Hampton, and Sugar Ray Robinson. Free vacations inspired concerts and sporting exhibitions—soon the Grossinger audience was dancing in the aisles to "Hamp's Boogie Woogie." Eventually writers and photographers fought for a Catskills assignment—there was always a story.

In 1930 the family bought a huge adjacent property from the failing Lakeside Inn. Blackstone knew what he wanted to do with the addition of acreage, and he wrote to the United States Golf Association for advice. They recommended he hire A. W. Tillinghast. Eighteen holes cost $10,000, a fortune right after the Depression. Selig and Malke thought nothing more ridiculous than dynamiting perfectly good hills and dumping sand onto grass. They were no less surprised the next summer to view the bustle around a dimpled ball.

The year that golf came to Grossinger's, Abe Sharkey, a high-school teacher, was put on the summer payroll as athletic director. His job was to organize handball tournaments and basketball and softball matches. His assistants led tours through the woods, complete with beavers, blueberries, and an occasional bear. They catered campfires, singalongs, and square dances, measured baselines, and set an outfield among pines and oaks.

In subsequent summers, college students employed at Grossinger's gathered on house teams to challenge other hotels. The sports pages declared a shocker when CCNY, a real basketball power, came to town as Sharkey's pampered visitors and were handily dispatched by the local crew.

Despite the formidable expedition from the Lower East Side, whole families now journeyed to Grossinger's by bus, the O&W Railroad, limo, and auto.

Joey Adams recalled that

> the hundred-mile trip took about twelve hours because the only thoroughfares were cow paths through the center of every hamlet. Route 17 started at the George Washington Bridge and whether you were headed for Ferndale, Livingston Manor, Hurleyville, Woodburne,

> Greenfield Park, or Kiamesha, you somehow had to go through every wood and glen on the map. . . .
>
> After a short stretch of open road, they'd suddenly hit you with a four-mile-an-hour speed limit. Tickets were handed out for offenses like 'driving dangerously near the white line' . . . or even going too slow.

On Friday night the traffic from New York City to Wurtsboro was bumper to bumper.

> Kids would stand at the base of Wurtsboro Mountain, where there's a little creek. They would fill cans of water from the creek, and for a nickel or a dime, they'd throw water on the burning brakes as the cars came down the hill. . . . There'd always be a pile of empty soup cans on the bank of the creek.

One summer, Moishe Miller's car didn't make it past Wurtsboro Mountain, so he sold it for $40 and hitchhiked the rest of the way.

The folklore of getting to the Catskills was worth at least one encounter with *tsuris.*

With the attraction of a modern theater and upscale audience, actors, singers, and comedians arrived in droves (some at Milton's request, many uninvited). Either way, they needed only to be paid with stage time, room, and board. They ad-libbed mercilessly until they became Red Buttons and Danny Kaye (once Aaron Chwatt and David Daniel Kaminsky). Joseph Gottlieb turned into Joey Bishop. Baritone Moishe Miller starred in the Grossinger Terrace Room and then sang for the Metropolitan Opera as Robert Merrill. Young staff members Moss Hart, Harold Rome, and Don Hartman directed shows. Jerry Lewis grew up Joseph Levitch, the son of a Grossinger's athletic-staff actor. George Jessel arrived unexpectedly to perform with Al Jolson. Jennie ordered a young Jackie Gleason off the grounds because she thought his humor too crude.

Jennie had especially good show-business connections downtown: her friends the Kriendlers were running a string of popular speakeasies and had recently hit a gold mine with a place called "Jack and Charlie's" (but referred to as "21 Club" after it moved to 21 West 52nd Street).

The main bar at 21 Club was modelled after an English pub. Dangling from its ceiling with almost tongue-in-cheek ostentation were beer steins and miniatures of clients' commodities: telephones, automobiles, airplanes, oil trucks, locomotives, and farm equipment. Originals of magazine art graced the walls.

Through his maître d', Luigi, 21's Baron, Jack Kriendler, enforced a strict caste system. In the first room on the left he seated only the *crême de la crême:* power brokers representing U.S. Steel and Standard Oil, movie stars like Cary Grant and Jimmie Stewart (George Jessel daringly escorting a teen-aged Lena Horne). Hollywood czars, theater critics, and sportscasters were diplomatically distributed among corporate moguls. Brass plates reserved tables for "landed" gentry.

The second room was mostly the new generation, the children of the people in the first room. The final room, the one to the far right of Luigi, was a receptacle for those who merely qualified for entry to 21. Others were turned away nightly, no matter how large a bill was slipped into Luigi's emotionless palm.

A mere seven blocks' stroll led 21's diners to the Stork Club, a five-piece band playing (or maybe Joey Bushkin on the piano). Helium balloons by the hundreds rested on the ceiling, descending over the course of the evening until customers were able to leap for them. Most contained fives, tens, and twenties. There was one hundred-dollar balloon.

> But the night is still young. . . .
>
> Put on your coat and cruise down Fifty-Second Street between Fifth and Seventh Avenues. Small nightclubs showcase the piano virtuosity of the likes of Art Tatum, or the guitar and banjo wizardry of Eddie Condon, and the trumpet of Louis Prima will blare into the wee hours. Tommy Dorsey, Artie Shaw, and Henry James are playing as side men in smoky little rooms as they sharpen their skills for the great bands of the Forties and Fifties, including those of Benny Goodman and Glenn Miller; and after two AM, when the musicians have finished their sets, they will gather for jam sessions at the Famous Door, the Onyx Club, or some obscure dusty brownstones. . . .
>
> Or grab a cab and go up to Harlem. . . . Step into Small's Paradise and you will see people arriving from El Morocco or the Stork Club, resplendent in white tie and tails or dinner jackets. . . . There is no visible tension between blacks and whites. . . . Just settle back and tap your toes to the beat of Lionel Hampton or listen to Billie Holiday or Lee Wylie.

> You never know who you might run into at Small's: your landlady, Mayor Jimmie Walker or his successor, Fiorello La Guardia; the writer Carl Van Vechten or a broker you made a trade with in the afternoon; maybe even George Gershwin, sitting at a corner table, listening intently to the black American sound he would celebrate....

These are the reminiscences of a successful uptown investor, looking back to the 1920s, when he was a poor young dandy, the grandson of Jewish immigrants, dressing above his means, staying up late, hunting for romance and fortune.

> I met George Gershwin in 1933. I was squiring Miss Charlene Tucker, a dancer, currently rehearsing in Gershwin's political satire Let 'Em Eat Cake, directed by George Kaufman. Her room-mate was dating George and, one night, we found ourselves up at his new penthouse on East 72nd Street, listening to the composer of Rhapsody in Blue play the piano. It was a modest bachelor apartment of fourteen rooms and contained three pianos: that way he was never very far away from one. He was more comfortable with a piano than with people. When he entered a room full of strangers, he would immediately head for the Steinway....
>
> In the very early morning, as his lissome fingers glided over the keyboard, playing a tumultuous cascade from Rhapsody and shifting to the languor of The Man I Love, I stood beside him gazing around the luxurious new penthouse, gazing out the penthouse windows at the silent skyscrapers, the moon over the East River, the stars on the horizon; and I thought: "This is a night that should never end."
>
> But, then, I could have said that on any of a thousand New York nights touched as they were with the wondrous lovely madness of a time all of us who were lucky enough to experience will never forget.

As the moon over the East River encompassed the Catskills, Grossinger's transcended its ethnic roots and came to represent, for the *nouveau riche* and their American-born families, the pinnacle of luxury and opportunity. The narrator brought Charlene Tucker. Gershwin came on his own and was playing in the lobby as the guests gathered for dinner.

Malke did not recognize one eminent visiting actor (the former Edward Iskowitz). Thinking the oddly dressed man a tramp, she offered to feed him. "Jennie," she told her daughter, "you should only see him. The poor man is nothing but a sack of bones."

Jennie broke into laughter. That evening she put her arm around Malke and said, "Mom, this is Eddie Cantor."

"I'm pleased to meet you, Eddie Cantor. Jennie knows you, so maybe she could find a job for you here. Meanwhile, eat, and we'll get you back on your feet again."

He never stopped thanking her.

The mythology of this bumbled identity was reinvented and broadcast to the world by Blackstone.

In fact, Blackstone personified Grossinger's as "cameos with Jennie." When a lionized ball-player was interviewed at the pool or a newspaper reporter was stealing a few lines with a screenwriter, Milton saw to it that his Queen of the G. was present too, contributing sagely to the conversation.

Then she did something unforeseen: she became a star as charismatic as any he might have coined. She invented Jennie Grossinger and became her. Far more opportunistic than her promoter, she played her character with such elegance it would have cost a fortune to buy the publicity she generated just by being herself.

"Jennie, how are you? I bet my buddy here you'd recognize me. Tell him my name!"

"I'm sorry. I've seen you here many times, and I'll vouch for you, but tell me, if you didn't know I was Jennie Grossinger, I'll bet you'd have difficulty recognizing me, right?"

It wasn't dishonest. For immigrant Jews trapped in their minds by the diaspora she became a model of accomplishment and piety—proof not only of what they might become but who they secretly were. Years later George Jessel explained it to Quentin Reynolds:

> Jennie's got a touch of magic in her makeup. When she walks into a room she lights up the place. Once I attended a $100-a-plate dinner with Jennie at the Waldorf. The principal speaker was none other than Lyndon Johnson, the President of the United States, and the dais overflowed with some of the most famous names in America—Supreme Court Justice Arthur Goldberg, Assistant Secretary of State Averill Harriman, General David Sarnoff, Nobel Prize-winner Isador Rabi. Because the program was long the master of ceremonies asked the

audience of over 1500 not to applaud as the luminaries took their seats at the dais. The crowd obliged and maintained a respectful silence. But the moment Jennie walked in, the assemblage began applauding spontaneously and soon everyone was on his feet giving the bewildered gal a standing ovation that lasted while she walked the entire length of the table, found her place, and sat down."

Perhaps she was no more than a clever business woman, but she *seemed* to be Eleanor Roosevelt and Molly Picon. To her parents, though, she was a fraud who, in her jewelry and furs, had abandoned the tenets of their faith.

Selig and Malke had hit a wall. Spoiled rich, they could no longer retreat to the *shtetl.* So they reverted to strict Judaism, railing against the blasphemy all around them. In fact, Selig vowed to bar Milton from the premises. Not only that . . . he got a local rabbi to swear out a curse on his former friend.

Word reached Jennie. She confronted her father at the entrance to the Main Building. "It's my life," she said. "I've been nothing but a dutiful daughter. I've worked as hard as you, and I made this hotel what it is."

She knew his stubbornness would be greater than his love. "*Du darfst folgn* (You are to obey)," he said. "We will stay together as a family and maintain our principles." He was breathing awkwardly. "I will not permit a godless establishment. I will crush your *dybbuk.*"

"Your curse is meaningless in America. Milton will triumph over all of you."

"You have forsaken *(farlozen)* Harry, me . . . and God as well."

She struck him, quick and hard on the face. He gasped, then slapped her back roughly.

Five years of silence between them would pass quickly in the bustle of business, until his death.

Milton figured he best not risk his future with a family in turmoil, so he moved to Midtown and started his own public relations firm, Jennie his lead client. On West 57th this sour, rotund man with a golden tongue, admonishing eyes, and an over-firm handshake operated a virtual Grossinger's embassy.

In 1933 at a party for guests at New York City's Iceland he introduced Jennie to three-time Olympian speedskater Irving Jaffee. Charmed by the articulate athlete, she hired him on the spot to improve her slate of winter events, and afterwards pretended not to hear Selig and Harry's vulgar complaints.

To celebrate the partnership, Milton urged Jaffee to break the world's twenty-five-mile speed record on the Grossinger Lake. So widely did he bruit this fabricated event that five thousand people showed up to watch the skater knock a few seconds off the old mark—it took him seventy laps, one hour, 26.9 minutes. Proceeds were donated to a local hospital.

A year later Milton, theatrical publicist Monte Proser, and Sol Gold, a renowned trainer, met Jennie at Dave's Blue Room and asked her to loan her facilities to Sol's boxer Barney Ross. The religiously Orthodox Ross held two world championships and was training to fight Jimmy McLarnin in six weeks for a third.

Though she despised boxing, Jennie presented "the Barney Ross proposal" at the next family occasion. She played dumb, which cunningly drew in her husband and father. Malke interrupted to say that if a Jewish boy was poor enough to stoop this low, she'd offer him a job in the kitchen. Jennie's secret weapon was that boxing was Harry's greatest love in the whole world. He was so astonished by her news that he set aside his dislike for Blackstone and immediately started reviewing Ross' career match by match for a puzzled Selig: "He's got a great punch. Anyone who says he can't punch is crazy. He's just too smart to slug and leave himself open. The sportswriters, they talk. You'll see."

"Bring an army," he told Sol and Monte the next morning. "If we run out of rooms, we'll build another house for you." It became the Barney Ross Cottage.

Then Harry dropped his other projects to construct a professional ring. Guests paid fifty cents to watch training firsthand. They dined with Barney Ross (who entered each meal to cheers). The faithful joined him at Sabbath prayers.

Malke still refused to meet the fighter, even when Jennie tried to interest her by telling her that Ross had sewn thirty-six pennies blessed by a rabbi into his old black fighting trunks. Then Jennie described how Ross' mother mended the trunks herself but couldn't bear to watch the matches. "See," Malke snapped, "even to his own mother, this is a terrible thing."

Barney decided to handle it himself. He strolled into the kitchen as an anonymous guest and invited Malke to a game of klaberjass. "They say you're the best player in the hotel. Would you mind joining me for the afternoon?"

"Cards I can always play."

They battled for hours, teasing and challenging each other. At dinner she boasted about "the handsome new boarder with respect for his elders."

"That," pronounced Harry, "was Barney Ross."

"This is the box-fighter?" Malke asked incredulously. "He was Friday night in the synagogue too." The look on her face showed that she was rethinking the matter.

As newspapermen flocked to the Catskills to watch Ross train, Milton convinced them to use the dateline "Grossinger, New York." Damon Runyon came seeking boxing items for his nationally syndicated column; he wrote instead about a hostess who got up at dawn to see to the needs of her guests. Meanwhile band leader Abe Lyman described his surroundings to millions of listeners as "Grossinger's in the beautiful Catskill Mountains" (though he was actually in the studio in New York). The Borscht Belt was born.

In 1933, Hitler took power in Germany. One respected writer picked McLarnin to win because, he said, "Hebrews lack the fighting spirit." The boxer stopped playing cards, stopped singing quartets with his sparring partners. No one said it, but his opponent was now a German.

All at once Ross seemed sluggish and overly intense. His timing was off. The odds swung in McLarnin's favor.

Observing the somber mood, the ever-capitalizing Blackstone decided to sponsor a command performance—Abe Lyman and his band, Milton Berle, the Ritz Brothers, Sid Gary. Ross sat stage front, guffawing (pictures of course on the wire services).

On the night of his victory, Malke kneeled by the radio. "I am listening," she said, "not for the fighting but for the victory of a man who must fight that his people may be left in peace. That kind of fighting I believe in." Blackstone stole these lines too.

As Selig and Malke's venerable boarding house completed its transformation to a chic resort and nightclub, its PR wizard invented "Romance Weekends," encouraging singles from the City to come to look for mates. "Here's the gimmick," he told Jennie. "A couple meets here at Grossinger's, you see, while they're both guests. They get engaged and we give them a free honeymoon. Can you imagine how that'll pack them in? A rest they can get at home in bed. They can play tennis in Van Cortlandt Park. But to meet a husband or wife *and* get a free honeymoon, they have to come to Grossinger's."

Then Jennie suggested serving late breakfast and hiring a Director of Romance to introduce potential suitors.

Harry was less enthusiastic. "Discounts are okay—free vacations I don't like."

But when Milton came to town, Jennie's husband was little more than house contractor.

For a new generation of screenwriters, comedians, and public relations executives, Grossinger's became the reference point of their era. The staff included Paddy Chayefsky, Paul Gallico, Shelley Winters, Betty Garrett, and Robert Alda, but long before anyone knew they were Paddy Chayefsky, Paul Gallico, and Robert Alda. Plays and novels were inspired at the Lake; typewriters clacked on landscaped patios. Romances sparked with cigarette lighters in lounges and the Playhouse. Business partners met for golf. Baseball trades were initiated on lobby couches. A forerunner of the National Basketball Association drew on both college athletes and talented guests. Major League players joined autumn softball and volleyball matches and were chosen onto teams with regular *schnooks.* The East Coast worlds vacationed together, played tennis and golf together, partied and fell in love together. It was no wonder that the generation that followed them understood it best as the place that had brought them into being. When the moment passed, they remembered it as nostalgically as their parents looked back on Hungarian and Russian harvest dances.

The Grossinger family rode the wave. They adopted an aloofness of royalty, an air of destiny and invulnerability. Jennie hired a personal music teacher and a charm tutor. Whenever she heard that a guest had written an important book, she sought him out and asked if he'd spare some time to converse with her. Flattered scholars and lecturers quickly became friends and teachers. Over the years she took lessons from Isaac Singer, Budd Schulberg, and Harry Golden, but equally from run-of-the-mill journalists, sportscasters, and Walter Winchell. Her eagerness to learn, to improve herself, became, like everything else, an affectation as well as her singlemost desire. She studied Hebrew with the Hotel rabbi, grammar with Miss Marcy. She developed gentility and an educated wit.

Harry, meanwhile, spurned contact with guests. He became rough and inarticulate, toughening his Old World dialect to mimic the racist and redneck idioms of his crew. His barter was liquor, whoring, and fights at the Garden.

Malke turned into an exotic recluse, visited by rabbis, poking her head out now and then to greet old friends and marvel at what had become of Selig's farm.

3

Who We Came From

Paul Grossinger was raised by the resort itself, an extended family including employees and guests. "I was drug up," he recalled unfondly.

A football lineman at Liberty High, he was sent to hotel school at Cornell, then summoned home by his father a few courses short of his degree. He was not part of his mother's busy world, and Harry viewed him with contempt. What did the young man know about real work? What use was all his schooling? When Paul tried to open a sundry shop with his cousin Seymour, Jennie put an abrupt halt to their plans. "My boy's an idiot *(idyot)*," Harry routinely proclaimed to anyone who would listen. "One day he'll lose everything *(farschpiln)*."

So Paul hung around the hotel, building his own constituency. Then he found himself a princess.

It would have been difficult, in the world of the diaspora, to acquire a more coveted bride than Martha Rothkrug. Her father, Henri, was born on the Rhine but took his diamond-cutting skills to Antwerp. Using prized stones from South Africa, he exported his finished products throughout the world.

Relatives who had emigrated to America now included Ivy League professors, businessmen, and politicians. Henri was in Manhattan visiting family and clients when a friend invited him to the home of her cousin, lace-maker Coleman Nassberg. At a stylish East 96th apartment, Coleman's fifteen-year-old daughter Sally was summoned to play piano. A black-haired girl with Oriental cheekbones, she had debuted earlier that year at Carnegie Hall. Henri, who could not stop staring, did not forget.

During the next month the precocious Sally was quite willing to date an older man. Before he was to return to Belgium, Henri approached Coleman for permission to marry her. A scandalized father turned him down. Sally was sixteen when they eloped in 1914.

These were halcyon years for the diamond market, and it boomed nowhere more dramatically than in America, where an overseas war provided money and aspirations of fashion. Henri travelled back and forth among the States, Europe, and Africa, wrangling prices on stones, then having them cut and sold from Manhattan. He procured a house in suburban Hartsdale where a teenage mother gave birth to sons Paul and Edgar thirty-three months apart, Edgar on his father's birthday of December 12. (Strangely, ten years later in 1927 in Paris, the last son, Lionel, arrived on January 1, his mother's birthday.)

Martha Washington Rothkrug, Sally's only daughter, was born in 1920, three years after Eddie, on the same calendar day as her brother Paul, February 22. Sally had picked out "Jacqueline" but Henri said, "No, we are American citizens now," and since their daughter arrived on a president's birthday, he let her name herself.

When Martha was still an infant, the Rothkrugs sold the Hartsdale house and returned to Belgium, though Henri spent most of the next five years in Capetown. On their return to the States his fortune gave title to a mansion in Mount Vernon. Yet within a year his unflagging ambitions uprooted them again.

At that time De Beers controlled the diamond market out of Africa, limiting exports to keep up the price. But Henri had good enough connections to devise an alternate route. He smuggled his stones into Portuguese West Africa, then to New York, where his partner Louie Whitelaw handled the cutting. Without tariffs and at De Beers' inflated prices, Henri and his partners made a fortune.

A telegram from Capetown reflects his euphoric mood:

> **March 3, 1926. Rent the house. Sell the car. Bring the nurse and children. Take the first boat to South Africa.**

Sally came by ocean liner, a nanny minding her children, she on deck flirting and playing cards.

Black marketing went smoothly for a year—until a rival tipped off the government. The Rothkrugs caught a ship at midnight, just ahead of the constabulary.

Getting his share of profits turned out to be almost as problematic for Henri. Louie Whitelaw didn't want to give up a penny. A smuggler could hardly call the police, so Henri arrived the next day with a gun and told his compatriot, "My share or I blow your brains out." Louie opened the safe.

Now Henri preferred safer speculation, so he joined a diamond-retailing partnership in Seattle. Once again the Rothkrugs rented their home and moved to new surroundings. The foray lasted less than a year, for Henri sensed the coming depression and cleaned out his inventory at plunging prices. He was always proud he had enough cash to get through 1929 back in Mount Vernon.

Two years later, intuiting the bottom, he took his kids out of their schools and headed for Antwerp. Only son Paul stayed behind, to enter Harvard.

On a summer night in the Grand Hotel dining room, Henri crumpled onto the table. A stroke had ended his mad dash.

For the next year, crippled and enunciating with difficulty, he continued to deal but was cheated by partners and lost most of what he had accumulated over a lifetime. He spent the next two and a half decades dying in public facilities in White Plains, New York.

Sally never forgave Henri for "abandoning" her, or her children for growing up and stealing her youth. Upon the family's return to Mount Vernon, she insisted son Paul go to work to support her. He dropped out of Harvard and took a job at a cousin's hat mill in Danbury, Connecticut.

She sent Lionel to live with his brother, but Paul had neither the time nor inclination to supervise a child, so young Lionel cut school and joined a gang.

Edgar meanwhile fled his mother's vanity and sarcasm and ultimately worked his way to the West Coast.

Sally found it necessary to work part-time in a department store to hold onto her house—a secret she kept from her socialite friends.

When she asked for Lionel back, the rebellious teenager refused to live with a lady he didn't know. "She *is* your mother," his brother reminded him.

The first morning, he headed outdoors, arm around a football.

"Where are you off to, Li-o-nel?" Sally demanded, setting herself in his path.

"Out."

"You may go for one good hour."

"What's wrong with one bad day?"

"You are fresh and impudent!"

"Fuck you, ma'am!"

He slammed the door, joined a neighborhood game, and returned at nightfall. As he sauntered in, looking for a place to collapse, his mother was waiting. Unleashing venom stored over a day, she lunged at him, shoved him, slapped at his face, and repeatedly tried to sock him.

After he got over his shock, Lionel grabbed her arm, twisted her to the floor and, holding her there, stuck his face in hers and said, "Lady, you so much as raise your hand to me again, I break your arm."

That night, bearing a kitchen knife, she dove on him in bed. Flying out of the covers he screamed, "You're crazy, ma'am!" Those were the last words ever to pass between them.

He hitched to Scranton and, to join the war-time Navy, got a woman there to pretend she was his mother and lie about his age (he was sixteen). He was shipped to the Pacific theater, Corregidor.

None of the company expected to live. Cannon fodder, they were handed guns and put on the front line. The unit didn't take a single casualty.

Lionel would wake to hear: "Yankee bastard, you die!" Refusing to cower in a foxhole, he attached himself to a militia of comrades who crept through the dark jungle and unofficially ambushed the taunting Japanese. In hand-to-hand combat they killed a dozen or more.

Late 1945, on a destroyer en route to mop-up duty in Inchon, Korea, he heard someone from a passing boat shout, "Hey, Rothkrug, the war's over!"

"Over?" he called back. "It's *all* over."

The Japanese, in Inchon since 1905, had dug an artificial basin for their vessels; the Americans were there to dredge it out. After four months spiced by mortal bar fights with lingering enemy soldiers, Lionel was leading a beach party up the plank to a ship headed home, fifty World War II grunts behind him, a year late. The wild boy wore a necklace of Japanese teeth and a torn Japanese soldier outfit. The officer at the top was clad in spotless white. Lionel could see him up ahead "like a goddamned epiphany."

The specter shouted, "Halt!"

"What the fuck is this, pardon my French?" Lionel barked.

He had been in battle over two years but was never taught service etiquette.

"Salute properly!"

Guys behind were hot and pushing. "What's the goddamn hold-up, Rothkrug?"

"I dunno, some guy's jerking me off up here."

"Young man, you just earned yourself a trip to the brig."

The G.I. bill put Lionel through Berkeley, and more than fifty years later, a college professor in Canada (an expert on saints and shrines and the origins of world religions), he still hadn't spoken to his mother.

Martha lived two childhoods, the first a catered tour of Europe and Africa, the second a reversal of fortune. With her baby brother she was exiled to boarding school in Paris, an experience so unhappy she referred to it later with a dramatic shudder, as though the word "board" meant sadism and cruelty.

As a teenager she came to Mount Vernon, Cinderella to the duchess who demanded textbook manners and subservient grace. If a fork fell, Sally screamed, "Clumsy fool!" She was as automatic as a machine.

"Straighten your posture. You eat like a pig at a trough!" "Go into another room. I can't bear to look at anyone so ugly! I don't know how I got a slut for a daughter." Yet she found Martha older escorts—liquor, textile, and paper heirs—hoping for a wealthy son-in-law. When they came for their date, Sally shamelessly sported in a lowcut dress.

One evening, Martha's school friend Barbara Joseph called to invite her on an adventure, a Romance Weekend at a Catskill resort. Sally was spying at the door. "Think of yourself for a change," she snapped, breaking into Martha's whoop of delight, "you selfish brat. Maybe you can find a moron to indulge you."

On a snowy Friday the Josephs crammed Martha into the back of their auto. Chains singing on stone, they chugged through Christmas towns.

After a full day's drive, they finally made a sharp right off Route 52 and drove up a hill past a scalloped sign proclaiming in script *"Grossinger's Has Everything!"* Barbara's Dad held out his reservation to a guard who waved them past the gate. Weary with excitement, they were squired through a check-in as stylized as any in the movies, a handsome bellhop carting bags onto a modern elevator. Late at night the two girls gossiped as they snuggled in their room.

In the morning fresh snow sparkled on pine trees; squadrons of sprightly guys and gals bore skis, skates, and sleds. Through the buzz of the lobbies and a scrumptious bun-and-coffee brunch Martha felt herself transported. She wanted never to go home.

Spying this striking girl across the room, Paul Grossinger left his perch, and, after a number of false starts, played his favorite routine with well-rehearsed bravado.

'Why should I be interested in you?' her look said as she stared at this sluggish fat boy.

"I'm gonna own this hotel," he replied with a bashful smile.

He was speaking her language (but mainly Sally's). The wedding in 1938 was primarily a union of ambitious mothers. Later Paul was to say, "I married a beautiful woman, and she married a hotel."

Grossinger's was a chimera, quite different from the inside. Behind a veneer of opulence the mood of *shtetl* slums prevailed with their clannishness and xenophobia. Malke punitively assigned the couple to the tiniest room in staff quarters, then required Martha to stand fulltime behind the reservation desk.

Serving ten-hour stints checking people in and out was a superb assignment for her. Rescued from the gloom of boarding school, ransomed from Sally, surrounded by wealth and hoopla, she was a debutante in a glamorous family and happier than she had ever thought possible. Charismatic enough to challenge Jennie, she developed her own coterie and was pictured in cartoons of the day with long black hair in a bun, a few strands falling stylishly aside dark lashes. Famous, exciting men found her clever and beautiful and flirted with her even though she was married. She overheard one guy say: "Did you see the broad young Paul got himself!" His partner rolled his eyes and played fingers on a hot stove. Her face broke into an embarrassed grin.

In 1940 the family purchased a second hotel in Miami Beach which they renamed the Grossinger Pancoast—eleven stories with 135 rooms on the beach. Paul was made assistant manager. Martha travelled back and forth between the two, smiling and posing for Milton's camera crews with stage stars and foreign ambassadors.

Malke pursued her granddaughter-in-law like a harpy, pointing her out to the old ones in hushed Yiddish: Paul's wife bore few distinctively Hebrew attributes. Rumors had her consorting with other men. She dressed inappropriately. She spoke French. She posed pin-up style for World War II photographs. Worst of all, five years had passed without children. "Barren," Malke announced. "Nothing but an *akora.*"

From their first night Paul and Martha secretly planned to divorce (each recalled waking the next morning and wondering what they had done). "Without her makeup," Paul later moaned to friends, "she wasn't so beautiful anymore."

Yet the Hotel was large enough to permit them, like Jennie and Harry, to stay out of each other's domains. And there was always the Pancoast to escape to. Then the War intervened and gave them two more years.

In 1943 Paul was drafted into the Army and sent to Georgia as a cook (he was spared overseas service because a childhood BB-gun accident had blinded him in one eye). He came home on leave in January,

1944. On November 3, I was born: Richard Selig. On his release (a month later) Paul posed in uniform with his wife and infant for the front page of the last edition of the Grossinger war-time newspaper, *The Bugle.* The caption read: "His Royal Highness!"

Ten months after Paul returned from the Army, Martha moved to the City and took up with the man she had most admired during her years at Grossinger's, Paul's best friend, the director of showtime, Robert Towers.

He was born Reuben Turetsky in 1911, the first American child of Russian immigrants who ran a grocery at 125 Avenue D. His father had arrived in 1906 and in two years posted steamship tickets for wife and daughter Augusta. Reuben was followed by two more daughters, Bea in 1915 and Et in 1923.

Orthodox parents had little doubt about their son's rabbinical destiny, and through childhood Reuben seized his calling with gusto. A regular at synagogue, available on Saturday to take his turn with the oldtimers, he developed a fine cantorial voice. At eleven years old, he mugged sacrilegiously like a vaudeville performer. The world outside *schul* was exciting too, and soon Reuben was *davening* Jolson.

Tall and blue-eyed, suave and pretty as they come, he played wide receiver, shooting guard, and first base and led his friends in improvisational theater, politics, and Zionist oratory. The grocery-store gang agreed, if he didn't make the baseball Giants, the kid was a certain lawyer or Tammany politician.

To his parents' horror Reuben decided to attend CCNY instead of the Yeshiva and, even worse, part-timed as an usher in a local theater.

Turetsky had a way of telling a story; he also had a million-dollar smile and a dancer's flair. He added an uptown vocabulary, a few eye-catching suits, and soon he was running his own smalltime Schubert Alley. He kept postponing rabbinical tutelage. When his father demanded a commitment, Reuben simply talked faster and more eloquently. As he pantomimed a rabbi-quarterback, then a cantor-barrister, he had the old man sputtering equal parts laughter and rage.

Fortune found Reuben in 1933. At the Waldorf Astoria, he was promoting a sideshow featuring stars who were then also turning away audiences at the Majestic Theater on Broadway. A hotelman named

Murray Posner shot out of the crowd. "You were fabulous!" he exclaimed. "The way you introduced the acts almost made *them* second billing." The self-confident Turetsky was not surprised, but the offer that followed stopped him cold: "My father has a hotel outside South Fallsburg. We need a full-time Director of Activities."

"What do I know of mountains?" Reuben asked an adoring audience of sisters and cousins. "My only acquaintance with mountainous areas are such names as the Appalachians, the Rockies, the Urals, all from geography books."

Et giggled.

"What kind of work will you do?" Gus probed. Postponing being a rabbi was one thing, but a Director of Activities . . . at a joint called The Brickman?

"The only activities I know are punchball, Johnny-on-the-Pony, rope-jumping, and street-smarts," he said, "but I'll learn."

He did. A natural *tummler,* he led guests on promenades while keeping up a banter of current affairs and one-liners. He organized horseshoe pitching, apple bobbing, and Simon Sez. He also became a fledgling impresario, staging boxing and tennis exhibitions, all-star basketball games, and even unclassifiable extravaganzas such as horses pulling barges of celebrities.

"I had people," Turetsky recalled, "whose major form of recreation was sitting in rocking chairs, waiting for the next meal, or gossiping in the dining room until the show began. Then we gave'm a blues singer, a dramatic actor rendering lines from plays, a dance team, a porch clown, a little vaudeville from Artie Lewis and Peggy Ames . . . the business."

The larger Morningside quickly stole him from The Brickman.

"When your father owns a grocery store on the Lower East Side, when you go to work for an uncle at the ripe age of twelve walking across the Williamsburg Bridge to Rivington and Allen Streets under the Second Avenue el and making egg creams at his candy store, this type of luxury you don't know.

"My idea of a summer vacation was chalking out a punchball field on the local streets, playing a game of stoop ball, stuffing a basket with newspapers and shooting against the adjoining wall of a tenement house. . . .

"I said to my kids, 'Look, I read somewhere about what they call an aquacade. You bring people down to a pool. You get four girls and you do rhythmic swimming. Then some guy dives off the board, then two guys have a race. And for twenty-thirty minutes, you do a shmay-dray with the people, and you keep them excited and happy.'

"One guy said, 'What will we use for lights?'

"I said, 'We'll bring down one of the cars and shine the headlights on the pool.' And they loved it. The aquacade was a rip-roaring success.'

"I got the idea that people should be guided through activities: swim lessons, dance lessons, a show at night. One day a farmer came over to me and said, 'You know, I get $1.50 for a horseback ride. How about becoming my agent? You get the riders, and I'll give you half a dollar a ride.'

"Now when your salary is $5 a week, it doesn't matter if you don't know the front end of the horse from the rear. I went around from table to table at night telling people, 'You must take up horseback riding. It is a great sport, the sport of kings.' I knocked on people's doors at six in the morning and got them out for a ride. I even got a horn and blew a Tallyho cry."

A summer later the prominent Pauls, just down the road from Grossinger's, offered Reuben a combined appointment as Director of Activities and Master of Ceremonies. He was never wittier as, in the gloaming, he paraded a roster of stars and guests across stage and, by dayshine, organized volleyball, horseback riding, and led a revised, vaudeville Simon Sez. Having heard about this maniac, Blackstone snared a reluctant Jennie for a mission.

The three of them met ostentatiously on the Pauls' veranda. No cover was required; talent flowed graciously through the Catskills then.

"Grossinger's is the hub. The pilgrim always wants to go to Mecca," Turetsky told the startled Blackstone. "So I've been waiting for your offer." Then he turned to Jennie. "I read the papers. I read Damon Runyon, young lady. I figured sooner or later you'd come looking for me." The deal was consummated with a handshake. Milton was chuckling on the way out; he loved hyperbole and brass. "Once I hit the G.," Reuben shouted after him with a conspiratorial grin, "it's time for full-time wizardry."

Not an idle boast. Turetsky was getting better, it seemed, every day. No famous name or wise guy humbled him; he teased, tap-danced, and even crooned beside the headliners, goading unbooked talent into spontaneous routine. He had Barney Ross ballading on stage, Yankee pitcher Lefty Gomez rocking the house as a stand-up comic (with Turetsky tossing him lines). One evening Reuben spotted Jan Peerce, the operatic tenor, in the Playhouse audience and shamed him into singing the one number he couldn't refuse (even off duty). ("You so-and-so!" Peerce whispered into the mike before bringing the house down with the National Anthem.)

Harold Taub's memoir, *Waldorf-in-the-Catskills,* describes Blackstone's new protégé:

> A bundle of nerves held together by a little flesh, he was . . . the nearest thing to perpetual motion the hotel had ever seen. If you wanted to find Turetsky you didn't have to look for him. All you did was stand still, and in a minute or two he would come whizzing by.

In the words of one-time busboy Irving Cohen:

> I hated him. We all hated him. . . . He was young, his beautiful blue eyes used to pop out. He would walk through, a hospitable, lovely host; everybody would call out, "Bob, Bob."

Reuben summoned a vacationing Eddie Cantor out of his front-row seat. Jennie gasped as the growling Cantor stormed up the stage steps, then stood beside his tormentor, playing dumb. Turetsky began singing, "'*If you knew Suzie like I . . .*' I think you know that one, Eddie. . . ."

Cantor turned to the orchestra, "And I believe you know my key." Then: "C'mon Turetsky, you too; you're not getting away for nuthin'."

Finally the G. was too small for Reuben, so the truant rabbi began doing talk radio in New York out of a penthouse restaurant. An expert on everything (in the Manhattan style), he traded jibes with celebrities. By then he had changed his name to Robert Towers because, as he told my son Robin two generations later over the 21 Club urinal, "A man couldn't do business in those days with a name like Turetsky."

He was a playboy Yiddish philosopher, a city dandy, a shameless wiseass. He was the Howard Cosell, Larry King, and Johnny Carson of his era or, more properly, Cosell and King became pale corporate imitations of Towers—pompous and braggadocio.

Martha was his biggest fan. Bob was everything Paul wasn't (as well as his best friend). She flirted openly with Towers while Paul was in the army (bad knees kept Bob out altogether). They hit the chic spots, East Side, West Side, All Around the Town. He never hesitated to introduce her as "my boss' gorgeous [or lady-genius] wife." He was used to chaperoning dames, even married ones, and he carried it off with aplomb. Martha thrilled to the way Towers stopped the world. Even Sally could not get a word in edgewise.

He had been married twice before, brief legalized flings (he dubbed them). Women vied for his esteem. "Of course they want to be around me," he said. "I make the excitement."

"I love the guy like a disease," Martha told her friend Barbara. After her divorce was official (and against Bob's careful intentions) she became pregnant by him. He gave her money for an abortion, but a week later she returned it. "The doctor told me it's a boy," she lied. "How can you kill your first-born son?"

He stood there dumbfounded.

Jonathan was born April 19, 1948. At his *bar mitzvah* he would add a middle name—David (his namesake's biblical comrade).

Towers did not want to lose his job, but he could hardly remain at the Hotel and father a baby by Paul's recent wife. After he married her, they moved to an apartment on Park and 96th Street, where the train from Grand Central comes out of the tunnel and turns the neighborhood into Spanish Harlem. He went to work at the Grossinger New York office.

Bob hated being under the arrogant Blackstone. Once a brilliant propagandist who brought international fame to the G., Milton had settled into New York dotage, marked by smug presumption of his own sagacity. He told at least half a dozen stories a day about how he had made Grossinger's, won the McLarnin fight for Barney Ross, and all but invented the game of golf. He lectured like a professor emeritus addressing undergraduates.

A year later Bob gathered three partners (including the dynamic Jack Steiner) and created a rival firm working for hotels in competition with Grossinger's.

He couldn't co-exist with Steiner either and was making both of them miserable when Martha stepped in. Joining forces with her beau, she helped launch Robert Towers Advertising, specializing in New York City restaurants, resorts (like Posner's Brickman and the Nevele), car dealerships, kosher butchers, and sporting-goods stores. "Whatever else you say about that woman," he would later remark, "she had the gumption to make me my own man."

Grossinger's continued to grow. In 1948 Harry constructed one of four pools in the United States designed to Olympic specifications, a blue gem set in a ring of mountains and parasols ("a marvel of tile and concrete surrounded by terraces and cabanas," wrote Taub). Novelists, cartoonists, comics, and bookies moved their conclaves to its patios. (A joke of the era was that, when asked if she was going to have water polo, Jennie replied, "Don't be silly. Harry wouldn't allow horses in his new pool!")

Irving Jaffee got a rink big enough for ice hockey plus an adjoining lodge with panoramic windows. Grossinger's immediately became the site of the international barrel-jumping championship. With guests and cameras crowding the rink, anywhere from eight to fifteen barrels were set in a row on the ice (a phono played, *Roll out the barrels/We'll have a barrel of fun* . . . .). Jaffee always pretended they were one short and he would offer to take its place. He'd lie down on the ice, but his butt would pop up too high. The jumper would have to abort his leap because his blades weren't kosherized. Then referees would lead the bewildered "barrel" off.

Once the tournament began in earnest, speedskaters, most of them from Canada and Europe, would build up speed by going several times around the rink, then—in a great dash toward the column—put everything they had into a leap, landing usually among barrels but sometimes with a spray of ice safely on the other side. Newsreels worldwide never failed to show Leo Lebel in mid-flight successfully defending his crown.

Harry next erected a synagogue and a second nightclub with its own bar. Then he expanded and remodelled the dining room and Main Building.

Tony Bennett was a regular on New Year's Eve. Buddy Hackett brought down the house at least four times a year with his Chinese menu routine. For the High Holy Days Joel Grey sang Rumanian-Jewish songs. Mike Hall and staff performed "Sha-Still, the Rabbi is Coming." Robert Merrill sang "The Donkey Serenade." On July 4th Lionel Hampton closed with "Flying Home."

In 1949 at the Labor Day show, Monte Proser and Milton Blackstone conspired with Eddie Cantor to perform with (and then "discover") a kid on the Grossinger athletic staff with an operatic voice. Cantor's praise of Eddie Fisher—and immediate offer to join him on the road—brought down the house: "Ladies and gentlemen, I've heard many young talents in my time. . . . How would you like to go on a tour with me? We'll go to Toronto and Baltimore and Philadelphia." People felt they were watching history.

("It was like a setup," Eddie Fisher admitted years later. "It wasn't until we got to Chicago that it hit him I might be pretty good. . . . In Chicago he said, 'Don't be nervous, kid. You go out there and pee, they're going to love you after I introduce you.' Then he called the record companies and said, 'If you want Eddie Cantor, you gotta take Eddie Fisher.' ")

In 1950, while an eighteen-year-old waiter at Grossinger's, the music impresario Bill Graham staged his maiden concert by persuading Harry Belafonte to come to a staff bungalow for the birthday party of a waitress named Ruth he was sweet on:

> "I know you're here to do a show tonight but one of the most popular waitresses on the floor is having a birthday party tonight. . . . It's asking a lot but it would give her such a thrill because she really loves you and your music. Would you join us?"
>
> He just looked and me and said, "Where are you?" I showed him where we were on the hill and he said, "I'll think about it."
>
> "Thank you very much," I said. "Good luck with your show. . . ."

The waiter who would one day be known as "a combination of Mother Teresa and Al Capone" had also coopted the birthday cake of a guest at his table named Thelma. Thelma's parents were too full from their meal to attack the gaudily frosted dessert. They asked instead that it be delivered to them in the nightclub. Graham continues his story:

> I still had the cake stuck under the table. Once the meal ended, I took the cake out through the side door down the hill covered up by my waiter's jacket. I got some drinks and paper plates and stuff to eat. I

> told Ruth's girlfriend to go take her for a ride somewhere. In the bungalow, I took a knife and operated on 'Thelma' and made it into 'Ruth.' We were all sitting around eating cake at around one in the morning when there was a knock on the door. Harry Belafonte. He came in with his guitar. Now this cabin was tiny. A little bathroom with a shower and a big bed and that was it. There must have been twenty-five people squinched into the room. Belafonte talked to us and then he started to play and he sang every calypso song known to man. 'Day-O' and 'Island in the Sun' and 'House. . . .' Everyone told Ruth that no matter what happened from that point on in her life, nothing would ever top that birthday party.

Towers' replacement was Lou Goldstein, who first set foot on the grounds in the summer of 1947 as the star of a Long Island University basketball team that came to play against the Grossinger squad. Paul Grossinger hired him as boat boy at the lake.

"The next summer Paul invited me back to be on the athletic staff. . . . I began working around the clock. At night I was in charge of the spotlights. I'd watch the comedians and memorize what they did. During the day I took guests on hikes. We called it 'An Entertaining Hike with Lou Goldstein.' We walked a hundred feet; I told a joke. We walked another hundred feet; I told another joke. I would get three hundred people to join me on those hikes.

"A guy by the name of Abe Sharkey did Simon Sez. He let me jump in and kept increasing my time. I'd incorporate stories and jokes and got good at it. The game is that all commands preceded by 'Simon Sez' you obey. Any other command you ignore. I thought how long can you say to people, 'Hips, shoulders, stop perspiring.' I made it into a show, not strictly a game. I'd start by saying something like 'Let me check my brains someplace, and we'll start even.' Or, 'I don't know what I'd do without your help, but let me try.' "

When Jackie Horner came to work as an instructor for dance concessionaires Tony and Lucille, Goldstein cast an immediate eye on her. He sent a waiter backstage with a note on a silver tray asking her out for a drink after the show. She turned him down—Tony and Lucille didn't allow their dancers to date the staff.

Later that night Jackie was walking past the bar when a guy stuck out his foot and tripped her so that she fell flat on her face.

"I'm Lou Goldstein. Now will you have drink with me?"

Tony tried to enforce his authority, but Lou let it be known that at the end of his spiel he'd no longer be announcing complimentary 4 PM dance lessons (which were the main source of new customers). Lucille decided they should make an exception.

In the mid-'50s Harry kept ahead of the competition with an indoor swimming pool, modern guest cottages, and a coffee shop four times the size of the existing one.

Jackie Robinson and his family were regulars through the decade, Jennie their companion, speaking indignantly about how "Negroes are never given a fair chance." She likewise befriended Sugar Ray Robinson, Damita Jo, Ralph Bunche, Paul Robeson, Harry Belafonte, Lena Horne.

In the Catskills, Brooklyn's fierce second-baseman became a kid again, racing Dodger publicist Irving Rudd (only ten minutes after he had stepped on the ice for the first time and fallen flat on his back)—Rudd, meanwhile, dreading his own job if the star broke even the ghost of a bone.

Tania Grossinger, one of the Chicago Grossingers who grew up at the Hotel after her widowed mother moved there as a Director of Romance, recalls being introduced to Robinson as the hotel's foremost ping-pong player.

"Okay, foremost ping-pong player," he said. "I challenge you to a game at four o'clock this afternoon."

For the next three hours Tania was on pins and needles, wondering if he'd honor his challenge. Sure enough, four o'clock he arrived at the tables. They volleyed, chatted, then began in earnest. It was the high point of her life.

"He was very nice about it, but I could tell he didn't like the fact that a mere kid beat him."

Grossinger's was the mecca for those who honored a kind of innocent fun associated with early Hollywood and the pre-War era. They sought a fleeting moment when the world exploded into gardens, palaces, *tummlers,* and vaudeville, and everyone remembered they were once happy—when romance ignited in rainbows (and show tunes), and icicles hung like jewelry from ski chalets—when a poor philosopher could become a millionaire overnight without losing Maimonides, when God restored Paradise and let the Hebrews back, before rigidity and greed set in, before Saturn trailed the Moon into the next house. 'Somehow bring back that moment,' people always seemed to ask. 'Bring back our unfulfilled promise.'

When I was forty, I ran into Charlie Silvera, one-time Yankee catcher (then a scout), in the Candlestick Park press box.

"You came to my eighth birthday party," I told him playfully. He looked puzzled until I explained who I was.

"Remember?" he exclaimed. "Of course I remember. So you were the kid! Joe Collins and I went along to build your father up, show his boy what a hero Pop was." He shook his head and stuck out his hand. "Goddammit. Remember? The Grossingers were like second family to me. To Whitey, Yogi, all the guys. They treated us like royalty. None of that anymore, right?" [An aside for the eavesdroppers from 1985.] "So you're the kid?"

I smiled.

"What happened to Grossinger's? Jeez, I wish we could go back and forget everything since."

What happened to Grossinger's? Perhaps there was never a moment when it existed as reality rather than a dream. Perhaps it was always stillborn, its beauty the beauty of a Broadway set, its glitter tied to opening night.

In reality Lottie and Louie barely spoke to Jennie and Harry (who were also alienated from each other). A serious businessman, Louie was outraged not only by Harry's construction without a budget or plan but his presumption that he didn't have to consult with his partners.

Although he was advised by Sullivan County not to plant his indoor pool above a zone of underground pipes owned by New York City, Harry insisted *he* owned the land. He dug his way to a geyser—and a substantial fine. He had to fill in the hole and start elsewhere. A year later he instructed his carpenters to make a counter for the new bar. When both were completed, the structure—whichever way they twisted it—didn't fit the room. No worry, Harry said. He'd make a new one and build a coffee shop to match the existing version. (He seemed to forget that Louie's designer had already sold him plans that included a far more elegant S-shaped counter.)

Selig's death had divided the Hotel into three unequal segments. Harry, of course, kept his original half share, but Selig left nothing to daughter Jennie, only a third of the other half to Lottie (in deference to Louie's independent wealth), and the other two-thirds to deaf Harry and his children. This division left son-in-law Harry only nominally in charge, and it totally disinherited Jennie.

She pretended not to notice, taking it for granted that the Hotel was hers in spirit though she didn't own a share. "It's God's land anyway," she grandiloquently told acquaintances. "He's merely loaned it to us to watch over." She and Harry each independently ignored the fact that fifty per cent of the business was owned by her siblings.

If Harry, Jr., satisfied himself with receiving his share of the profits and running an antique shop on the grounds, Louie Grau would not tolerate being slighted. When his son Seymour died of a glandular ailment during World War II, leaving behind three girls and a wife, tragedy temporarily distracted him. But Louie also had a daughter, Ruthie, and she had married Bernie Zises, an ambitious financier. With the aid of this son-in-law, Louie enlisted Harry, Jr., in an alliance against Harry and Jennie (Seymour's widow Nettie joined the other side). This conflict simmered through the late 1940s and '50s and finally boiled over in the '60s.

Meanwhile Blackstone, whose guiding fantasy was the future of air travel, encouraged Jennie to purchase a site for a landing strip and hangar. Six months after Harry high-handedly approved $50,000 for a farmhouse on a plateau across Grossinger Lake, planes were arriving. Milton thereafter saw to it that the few corporate executives who owned their own props knew about the golf course. He also led Presidential and Gubernatorial candidates on handshaking strolls through the dining room, occasionally a fund-raiser at Joy Cottage. (On such a "whistle stop"—years later—Governor Nelson Rockefeller was to find himself shaking hands with Rocky Marciano as the two of them sat down with Cardinal Spellman to watch the Yankee game in Jennie's living room.)

The cracks continued to deepen. The Pancoast failed and was sold. Rival resorts with more capital began to expand at nearby Catskill sites.

Grossinger's was the first of its kind and had a reputation, but it was soon living on that alone. The Concord, the Nevele, and Kutchers had started as small enterprises, but they imitated the successful features of Grossinger's and soon were customizing facilities for a young clientele. They had their own "Blackstone." Robert Towers Advertising represented a host of flashy competitors—not only the Nevele (and later the Concord) but others in New Jersey, New England, and Miami Beach.

When Martha married Bob, she imagined herself starting her life fresh. She broke off ties with the Grossingers, telling Paul that she and Bob wanted to adopt his son. When Paul refused, she threatened to go to court with Louis Nizer as her lawyer. He called her bluff. Although she backed down, she indicated she would make things difficult if he did not follow her rules. As far as her child was to know, he was Bob's son; Paul was not to divulge his relationship. Thus, when Grandpa Harry came by on his trips to the market with gifts of lollipops and chocolate silverware in foil, he was presented as a great-uncle.

Martha never stopped acting like a Grossinger. In her mind she had been a hardworking, unrewarded family member for six years and was married to the mythic Reuben Turetsky in exile. She billed Grossinger's for as many household items as she could: refrigerator, stove, carpets, furniture, clothing for both boys. The Hotel always paid.

4

Childhood (I)

My earliest memories are of 96th Street and Park Avenue. My name was Richard Towers. From my doorstep a colonnade of apartment buildings ran to the horizon, down its middle a vale of tiny fenced parks in a thoroughfare teeming with cars. Uniformed doormen stood under awnings. Holes from the underground puffed steam.

In the other direction train tracks replaced park, buildings became squat and desolate, fires burned and kids prowled with sticks. Either way façades masked labyrinths through which people in costumes streamed.

This was the kingdom.

My room lay at the end of the hallway. Paintings of dolls and clowns hung on its walls.

Among folds of my quilt lived identical tigers, giraffes, and zebras.

My hands ran through them, as they chased and caught each other, hiding in crevices of me. Beyond the window was an alley, a prison of tarnished brick, land of the opera singer.

I shared this realm with Nanny, a witch who loved me but a witch all the same.

Mommy and Daddy lived down the hall in a violet world, playing out unending dramas. Her anguished voice and weeping molded our interior landscape. Daddy sometimes pleaded with her, sometimes sang cheerfully—"*Swanee, how I love you* . . ." /"*. . . looking for a bluebird and listening for its song* . . ."—or soulfully in Hebrew—"*Anakhnu modim* . . ." and "*Shama Yisrael*. . . ." Everything contributed to a sense of macabre incarnation.

No matter how I built blocks, put creatures in portals of castles, splattered yellow, blue, red smudges on my easel, no matter how happy the song records and Nanny's chortle, I was a passenger on a relentless journey downward. The further we sank, the more texture we encountered, velvet and ice engulfing us until the world was a miasma plummetting in a bottomless sea.

Mommy was determined to take me with her. In creams and lacquered fingernails, trailing the scent of too many flowers, she tried to hug-and-kiss me into submission. I wriggled against her and fought off her ghostliness.

Her mere existence confirmed my worst suspicions.

I took her hand down 96th Street. In an indoor garden, orchid mist scented the air. She commanded the proprietor in a strong but placating voice until he brought single blooms from his refrigerator. These he tied in a bunch and wrapped in colored tissue. Later she arranged them with brusque hands in a purple (almost black) vase.

The voice in the courtyard was like her—not like her voice but like *her*. It was wild; it went everywhere; it was incomprehensible.

My brother Jonathan was brought from the hospital swiftly down the hall and placed in a crib across my room. He cried all the time despite Nanny's spells.

We took his carriage to the park. Nanny put me in the sandbox. She told me to be careful of other kids' pee. I rolled in granules, feeling their fuzziness. They were a cake, not quite baking. I dug marbles out of dirt, tiny planets emblazoned with smoke. I was burrowing in my cave-world when Nanny stood me up and brushed me off.

Clouds roared like boats. Mica sparkled fairyland silver.

The morning after we moved to our summer cottage, Mommy wanted to see the ocean. We pushed my brother until pavement turned to sand. Waves uncurled and crashed. I was so busy looking I didn't notice the stroller was stuck. After yanking so hard she fell down, Mommy told me to fetch Nanny. "It's only two blocks," she pointed. "Don't get lost."

I had never gone on my own before.

Men trimming our hedges made the house look unfamiliar, so I went past it and continued for blocks. The scenery became city-like. I began to cry.

I stopped where workmen in uniforms were cleaning up. I wasn't supposed to talk to strangers, but I was lost. A guy offered to take me in his truck. I climbed into the high seat. We drove up and down streets, searching for where I lived. "Does this look familiar?" he kept asking. But it was all new.

Then I saw it—two police cars parked outside, Mommy on the porch. She was yelling for them to arrest the man as I got out.

I had the sensation of reentering my life again from the outside.

I remember hugging the surf, my being filled with each wave. On the way home Daddy visited Uncle Moe, Aunt Alice, and Uncle Nook—green droplets, black raspberry, toasted almond, Good Humor bells. Arcades along the Boardwalk offered landscapes like rainbow squares across which I moved tokens, game after game on our cottage floor: Chutes and Ladders, Uncle Wiggily, Quizkids … cartoons more real than life.

When he got bigger, I showed Jonny how to do our toys. I pushed his hand with crayons. Shoulder against shoulder on the couch with Little Golden Books, we traded ones back and forth. We changed records and (occasionally) victrola needles, using pins from Mommy's red sewing cushion whenever we ran out of pellets. We turned pages of Bozo and Sparky. We put on holsters and cap guns, tattoos plastered to our arms. We hid in the backs of closets and under chairs, sneaked behind furniture to surprise each other with rubber bands.

Soon he and I were locked into a dust devil, bumping furniture, throwing punches at the slightest provocation. At the barbershop and grocery we were an unbidden disruption. Nanny chased us, whacked at us, threatened us, and took her complaints to our mother.

After we got a TV, I surmised that two great criminals were on the loose: Joseph McCarthy and Jack Steiner. In fact, Daddy's office was like an embattled ranch on *Roy Rogers:* there were all these bad guys who stole from him, creeps and con-men for whom I imagined slick, mustachioed figures.

Sometimes Daddy fetched his Olds and drove us to the Nevele. Apple trees spread to a forest where a waterfall crashed onto rocks. There was a lake with minnows and darning needles, faint blue sparks.

Jon and I threw apples. We tied together sticks, string, and bent pins and pretended to fish. Sunnies sniffed and darted past.

Adults came calling at our table, telling stuff, laughing, puffing Camels.

In the morning ... cold dew, rotting fruit, soaked sneakers ... we trooped along, bearing sticks ... an occasional apple pounced on, aimed at a tree, or each other.

Jon was my childhood companion and playmate but also a dogged opponent. Strangely humorless for a kid, he would eye me diabolically, then remove his glance before anyone saw. He liked to bump and trip me—a sly rambunctious feint, an elbow or knee in my path, then deadpan. He took my toys and hid them, then claimed they were his.

"They're not!"

"They are!"

"You're a dumbie."

"No, I'm not!"

"You are."

"Lay off!"

"It's a free country!"

I pummelled him. He socked me in the stomach. I clawed at his shoulder blade. He bit my hand. I yanked free and grabbed his hair. Chairs and tables turned over, clothes ripped; it was impossible for Nanny to pull us apart.

I tore at him with all the life in me as though to rip and batter him into nonexistence. He grabbed scissors and stabbed me; I clobbered him with a metal truck. Blood.

Mommy spun me over, scratching my face. She slammed me against the wall, then herded me to the corner and socked me. But the worst of it was Jon's victorious snicker, his pretense of innocence.

She ordered me to bed. But it was daytime.

"No fair," I whined.

"Shut up, or I'll wash your mouth out with soap."

She locked the door.

A pall crossed the room. In it I found a strangely comforting abyss—a contagion that pressed against me and glowed. Yet it was becoming dark.

I escaped in my mind, sometimes by spaceship, sometimes by winged dragon. I found myself at the beginning of a vacant universe, so I filled its worlds with creatures and places.

I dozed and woke, dozed and woke, hundreds of times, telling myself this story. I was so deeply in it, the life—the part that had apartments and snow and was real but also the part that was Richard whose luminous scenes led me through his mind, wrapping dense pictorial tentacles around us.

Then the opera singer began her dirge.

The crisis was deeper than crime and punishment: I wet my pants, I got carsick; they were always calling, "Open the door . . . Riiichard!"

The haunting was the worst. It came from inside—sparks of poison spreading along my throat and belly onto fingertips. These polyps were colder than winter, dark in a different way from night, dark like living-room lamps when they were lit were dark.

Somewhere lay dungeons ruled by beings who killed you forever and stalked you forever. Revealed nowhere, acknowledged by no one, they were the true state. Their landscapes began at my boundary and filled the preordained interiors of existence. Mommy and Daddy didn't know. All they could do was yell.

Mommy thought I had a disease, so she and Nanny took me to Dr. Hunt. He examined my body, made pictures of my insides in his contraption, then talked with them in his private room. The way Mommy looked at me afterwards I knew it was bad. It had to do with evil and peeing, with disobedience.

She thought if she spanked me and sent me to my room enough I might change. I would kick and pull away as her nails dug. "Stoppit! Stoppit this instant!" she would scream.

I learned to cry long and slow, staring into the changing patterns inside my eyes.

During those years we lived in three different apartments between 95th and 96th on Park Avenue, changing corridors of hallways and bedrooms ... moving the third time when my sister Deborah Alice was born in May of '52.

Our home looked out on 96th. I stared down at Puerto Ricans gathering, pigeons gliding to gargoyles, green-light surges of vehicles. The church, midblock, was a cipher, but I dreamed its caverns. By night, horns and sirens sounded near and far. The Knickerbocker sign—beyond any buildings we could see—lit the portals to an unknown universe.

After Debby was born, Mommy got a job running the New York office of Miami's Fountainbleau Hotel; at night she answered its reservation line at home.

Nanny was dismissed, accused of spying and stealing secrets. I watched her packing her clothes, crying, turning into just another lady in a dark overcoat with a cap and a suitcase. She blew Jonny and me a kiss before stepping into the elevator. A month later a young Irish woman took her place.

Bridey was quite a change from the gloomy and imperious old nurse. She thought Jonny and I were well-behaved, and from the day she arrived, serenaded our apartment with show tunes and Irish ballads.

"My goodness gracious," she remarked at her first sight of one of Mommy's panics. "Mrs. Towers, you've got a sprite of a demon in you." This reaction unexpectedly calmed my mother, who stood there astonished.

"It's not easy, Bridey," she finally declared.

I was sure she meant having monsters like us.

Childhood lasted almost forever.

At P.S. 6 I preferred daydreaming to letters and numbers and gave the blackboard only a cursory glance. I also left a puddle by my seat. The others pointed and teased.

My best friend was a goofy, freckled kid named Phil, the fastest, swerviest runner. Since he collected baseball cards and rooted for the Yankees, I did these things too. We soon quizzed each other—by initials and position—on players' names: "FH, catcher, Tigers. DP, outfielder, Indians."

Shortstop, switch-hitter, and (according to my mother) a juvenile delinquent, Phil founded a club based on our discarding bagged lunches in favor of candy we bought or stole from Jessie's Jip Joint down Madison Avenue from P.S. 6. We aimed crumpled bags at the trash container, then raced along Madison.

The Yankees inaugurated a partial truce between my brother and me as I initiated Jon into their cult. We followed games on a Philco with a giant battery, its tube-warmed plastic in my lap. The baseball realm came in Mel Allen's kinglike voice, a legacy of contests against Browns, Indians, White Sox, A's. . . .

Jon's favorite player was Mickey Mantle, whose yellow-haired monolithic face soon became not so much that of a man as my brother's secret talisman in my mind. Jonathan/Mickey was the king of home runs, the star.

My favorite was a fairytale character, Gil McDougald, the versatile sub, whose wide-eyed face on baseball cards was a leprechaun.

After Daddy bought us gloves and a bat at his sporting goods account, we spent Sundays in Central Park, him pitching to us as we chased each other's hits through the grass and fired to his imaginary bases. He would lead me on long fly balls and test me to the right and left with fungoed grounders. "I've got half the Yankee infield," he teased.

"I'm an outfielder," Jon-Mickey protested.

Actually I was too.

After much pleading, our Daddy surprised us with pinstripes, which we wore proudly, Mantle and McDougald, Numbers 7 and 12, marching down 96th, showing off to the City.

Paul Grossinger came to our apartment infrequently during those years. Identified as our uncle, he was a well-dressed, clownlike man who took me all by myself to cartoons, restaurants, and, once, to a neighborhood store where he collected me a stack of Little Golden Books—tigers, farm animals, Black Sambo, airplanes . . . I thought he'd never stop picking them out. Then he got us Good Humor pops and, chuckling at his many deeds, shouted, "Taxi!" Just like that we were hurtling toward the Penny Arcade. We spent the afternoon shooting cork guns and making records of my songs through a mike in the wall. A finished disk dropped out a slot.

Luckily Jonny wasn't old enough to join us.

The world changed forever on the day I was removed from P.S. 6. My mother wore an important-occasion perfume to deliver me downtown in a taxi. Our journey ended not at any game plaza but a hospital. I was presented to a doctor in a jacket and tie.

We sat across a desk in his office. From an envelope, he pulled pictures and asked me to tell stories about them. After lunch I lay on a cot, wires attached to my head.

This was clearly comeuppance for misbehavior. Strapped in the position of the condemned criminal, the hum of electricity to my left, I gritted my teeth and vowed to survive.

The consequence of the visit, my mother told me, was to be a trip to another doctor. After school on my eighth birthday she took me to the office of Abraham Fabian downtown below 14th Street. I expected a version of the hospital man, but Dr. Fabian was a tall, sympathetic companion who played Battleship with me that afternoon while he quizzed me about my family. Afterwards Uncle Paul was waiting in an easy chair, reading a magazine.

Outside at dusk my uncle hailed his usual taxi. As he helped me in, he shouted the address for Al Schacht's. The driver tore uptown, bouncing us into each other.

Inside the restaurant was a large anteroom with a staircase of bats and balls leading upstairs. Uncle Paul had me feel them. "They're real," he said. "They were used in games."

Our menus were decorated with cutout bats bearing jokes like "Yogi Berries," "Dizzy Trout," and "Corn on the Cobb." As I was reading mine, we were joined by two tall men in suits. Uncle Paul seemed to think I knew these guys, but no matter how long I stared, I couldn't place them. Then he told me they were first-baseman Joe Collins and catcher Charlie Silvera of the Yankees.

Living baseball cards, they held out giant hands to shake mine. This was the most amazing, wonderful thing that had ever happened to me.

Later a cake arrived and everyone sang, "Happy Birthday, Dear Richard. Happy Birthday to you."

I saw Doctor Fabian twice a week, my mother arranging for a Columbia student to accompany me on the subway after school. It took me a while to understand what a psychiatrist was, but I soon grew to adore this Abraham Lincoln lookalike who knew me better than I did myself.

He interpreted things in the world as symbols for other things, disguised and important.

He drew me from my spell by naming and unravelling it. Gradually I recognized myself in this new way—not a willful stirrer of mischief or a bad boy who peed but an unconscious disseminator of symptoms to be retrieved and solved.

Dr. Fabian was the first person who appreciated the big thing, which he called my "fears." Nanny and Mommy were haunted people, he explained, and I probably had inherited *their* spooks. He uncovered them in dreams as giant birds and crones. He promised that when I found the precise moment at which I became frightened by them, my fears would go away ... and with them the wetting. As unlikely as it seemed, I was supposed to be "normal" someday.

Yet I wasn't like my mother, summoning Dr. Hitzig in the middle of the night because she was afraid of cancer. I was afraid of much worse things. I was afraid of the word "cancer" and what it made me feel, of Dr. Hitzig himself. In dreams his true nature was revealed, a Flash Gordon alien wearing a human mask, pretending to be sweet, pretending to be a doctor. He wanted to get at me through my insides.

No wonder I dreaded my check-ups at Dr. Hunt's.

"You're afraid," Dr. Fabian pronounced with majestic certainty, "that something terrible is going to happen to you." That statement, repeated by him at almost every session, became the coda of my childhood, the explanation for everything. I learned to recite its archaic refrain. 'I am afraid,' I told myself (unsure if the knowledge made me more or less vulnerable), 'that something terrible is going to happen.' It allowed me to label my fears and step away from their swarm.

Mommy understood little about psychiatry but, as a keeper of secrets, she recognized a rival. She openly mocked Dr. Fabian and contrived to make me cancel my times—dental check-ups, extra play group, the sudden necessity of Hebrew School. "I don't care if you miss your Dr. Fabian," she snapped. "You eat so much candy your teeth are rotting out." She aimed an exasperated finger. "You should be playing in the park with everyone else instead of conniving with degenerates."

Daddy was listening from the next room, and he chimed in: "Spoiled brats. That's the man's specialty."

"They never heard the like in Ireland," added Bridey. "Why, they'd think it crazy to go to a doctor for hobgoblins in the head."

"Not him," Mommy said. "He'll spend someone's money on the Man in the Moon if you give him a chance."

One day Dr. Fabian told me something of truly major importance. He didn't actually tell me; he quizzed me until I guessed it myself. Then he took my correct guess as an indication I knew all along. The question was: "Who is your father?"

I experienced his inquiry as a game of riddles in which he rejected "Bob" as the answer no matter how often I said it. I couldn't think of anyone else, so I finally offered the only other person who fit: "Is it my Uncle Paul?"

Dr. Fabian was delighted. "See," he declared. "You knew all along."

"I just guessed."

"Unconsciously, you knew it," he insisted. "Your unconscious mind yielded the truth of your father."

Mommy was furious. After she informed Jonny of the news, he scowled at me as if I had been exposed at last, an enemy spy. Not only was I a poor student, bedwetter, and ingrate, but an outsider as well.

In Mommy's official version Fabian was not an honest physician but a panderer bought with Grossinger money to undermine the virtuous, hardworking Towers. Uncle Paul was his accomplice—a lazy bum who had inherited lots of money.

One time I challenged her, saying Dr. Fabian was my best friend. She got so angry she began to shake.

"People who can't earn a living get paid to give advice," Daddy bellowed. "He's a Joe McCarthy. They should arrest him."

"He is not!" I shouted.

Finally they made an appointment to confront their nemesis. While in his office, Daddy got so angry, he smashed a lamp. That night he boasted about it to Jonny. "I had Fabian backed against the wall like the cowering mouse he is. I lowered my fist and told him, 'Send me your bill for your *chazerai* . . . and the light, you chiseller.' It was a pleasure."

I flushed in anger and humiliation.

I never discussed Dr. Fabian after that, but my superior look betrayed me. They knew I was always watching, so they routinely suspected and condemned me.

I learned to be the outlaw, ever on guard, ready at any moment to resist, to discern the subterfuge behind their fake good will, their disingenuous rapprochements. All I knew for sure was that I was trenchantly set against them and couldn't give in. Every time I yielded (when they seemed to love me) I found myself trapped again by their condemnation. "He hides like a fox and insinuates himself in our favor," Mommy told the others at dinner. She saw right through me.

By then she had drawn her own conclusions. She had two wonderful children who were being ruined by a crazy kid left over from a past marriage. She had feared initially that I was brain-damaged and—if it was going to cost money—the Grossingers could pay! That was why she let Uncle Paul hire the meddler Fabian.

At the time, Uncle Paul was especially sensitive to "mental illness" because, he told me, his second wife, "your Aunt Bunny," had suffered a nervous breakdown and was in a sanatorium. He promised he had gotten me "the best child psychiatrist in all of New York."

Once unveiled, my father saw me more often. He would phone out of the blue and invite me to dinner: "Richard, my boy! How would you like to join me today?" His voice broke through the sadness of existence and touched its pot of gold. Despite the risk of seeming too happy, I found it hard to conceal my delight. Mommy would lock herself in her room, and every time Daddy saw me he would press his lips together, avert his eyes, and shake his head.

Uncle Paul took me in a boat with fishermen. Another time, we went to see the magical dances of *Finian's Rainbow.* We attended Trans-Lux cartoons (decadently mid-afternoon). My family had always spurned bakeries, but Uncle Paul seemed never to miss a one. As we walked along, he put his arm around me and intoned, "Richard the brave! Richard the great!" I blushed. To those fears I expressed he promised he would never leave me.

The strangeness of having a new father took hold gradually and left me oddly fatherless. I could never call Bob "Daddy" anymore, and Uncle Paul remained forever "Uncle Paul."

Yet I idolized his very presence—this Santa who wanted mainly to have fun. The Towers family were all lean and wiry like me and practiced a humor I might now call wry. Uncle Paul made puns and told corny jokes about elephants and mice. It was hard for me to smile at such silliness.

Sometimes we dialed room service. Sometimes we went to clubs and sat overlooking the Park. While my father talked to the succession of important men who came by to greet him, I gazed down at buglike taxis and skaters, sticks against glistening ice. He didn't have to pay attention to me. Just the wonder and excitement of being in his world were enough.

When we went to Yankee Stadium he took me down to the dugout and called players over to meet me—Billy Martin, Vic Raschi, Eddie Lopat . . . and then Gil McDougald himself. Arc lights bathed the field with an importance that made my squabbles at home seem frivolous. My life no longer drifted. There was someone worth giving my heart to.

My mother claimed that Uncle Paul lived off other people's fortunes and put on a false front to make himself look good. "He took you to the ballpark just to show off. The players can't stand him. Anyway it was Bob Towers who brought them to Grossinger's in the first place."

Daddy said Uncle Paul was a philanderer (whatever that meant).

He was going to wreck his whole hotel. "The bastard is the lowest form of swindler and crook. He does shame even to the idle rich."

I didn't realize it then, as I sobbed and shouted denials, bringing only more wrath, that I had to defend Uncle Paul in order to protect myself, not only from them but from the haunting. He had become its other.

5

Childhood (II)

After dinner one night Uncle Paul told me he wanted to send me to Camp Chipinaw that summer.

"Do I have to?" I pleaded. "I don't want to go."

"Sure you do," he insisted, a playful twinkle in his eyes. "You'll meet your cousins Siggy and Jay Zises, and afterwards my driver'll come and get you and take you to Grossinger's. You'll stay with me. Don't you want to meet your Aunt Bunny and your brothers Michael and James?"

I left the City on a bus full of boys. Counselors led camp songs, comics were passed over seats and across aisles with peanut butter and jelly and cartons of milk. Five hours later, I found myself standing in a field of flowers and thistles across which uncountable grasshoppers rose and fell.

Bunk 4 was a long room inside a cabin. Kids and grownups were pushing everywhere, suitcases and trunks being unloaded. A woman in a flowery blouse told me, "I'm your Aunt Ruthie," then smothered me in perfume with her hug. "These are my boys," she announced, grabbing them and turning them around. Then she instructed that they keep an eye out for me.

Siggy was older and went to another bunk, but Jay was assigned the cot next to mine.

It was astonishing that this kid was my cousin; he was large enough to be an adult but actually a year *younger* than me.

Following his mother's directive, he put an arm around my waist and pulled me to kid after kid, making a special point of my shaking hands with Barry, his best friend.

Each morning we woke to the bugle and lined up for inspection. Food provided morbid merriment. We ate pancake sponges with hemlock syrup, frog-leg stew, plastic cheese, rubber cold cuts and "poolash," and drank putrid punch from poison blue powder. After lunch we made mad dashes back to the bunk for rest period, the candy patrol, and our mail.

As we swept up dustballs, made our lumpy beds, and put red and gray Chipinaw garb into our cubbies, I forgot how it felt to live anywhere else.

Toward the end of August I thought more and more about Uncle Paul's home. It seemed incredible that I wouldn't go back to my mother, Daddy, and Jonny but to another family with different children. My life seemed to lead me from fairy tale to fairy tale, some as spooky as the gingerbread cottage, others like the wondrous journey across Oz.

Jay, Siggy, and Barry left camp on the final evening. In the middle of the awards banquet, a counselor told them their parents had arrived. Applauding, they burst from their chairs. "We'll meet again," Jay called back to me, "at the G."

The next morning I sat on bunk steps, watching belongings hauled into trunks of cars that drove right onto the grass. My heart was pounding. Which of these was my father's chauffeur?

Finally he came looking for me. He shook my hand, hoisted up my trunk, then pointed to the back door of a Cadillac. I preferred to sit next to him in the front, like when Daddy drove.

We travelled past ponds and bungalows. I fixed my eyes on objects that flew past and imagined a sword attached to our car trimming them —trees, fences, mailboxes, telephone poles. . . .

Grossinger's was a yellow and brown city on a hill. Before I had time to marvel, we were amidst its buildings. Everywhere, I saw crowds.

I was let out at a huge white house, my camp things unloaded. I stood uncertainly in the hallway when my new brother Michael, a cute blonde kid, tore down the stairs to greet me. Without a word he led me up to his room. It had more stuffed animals, battery games, and knights and soldiers than a store.

Uncle Paul's wife, Aunt Bunny, was standing there. Younger and softer than my mother though resembling her, she had a pretty face, dark hair, and dark eyes.

She showed me around the house—first the room where our baby brother James lay in a puffed-up diaper in his crib, then the third floor, including the guest suite where I would stay. It was a ghostly chamber with tall bureaus, a quilted double bed with posts, and three musty closets (two of them containing smaller closets deeper inside). These were filled with old paintings, lamps, and furniture covered in sheets.

We put my things away and went back downstairs. I sat on Aunt Bunny's bed and talked about Chipinaw. Then she told me the great things we would do together. "Your father's out of town today but we'll manage famously all the same." She was so good-humored and kind I forgot about missing Uncle Paul.

The next morning after breakfast she made a picnic and summoned Michael and me to a blue bus parked outside. The driver went up and down hills, then swerved into a cove beside a small lake.

Aunt Bunny pointed to a shed. There a man got us fishing lines and a coffee can of worms. A life-guard helped us into a rowboat.

As Aunt Bunny and I worked an oar each, we cut directly across the middle toward the far shore.

I stared back at where we had been—people speckled across a golf course, fortresses among trees. I turned to the woods gliding toward us.

Among cattails we took a worm from the wet leaves, folded it squirming around a hook, and dropped a line into the black. I felt the nip of my first fish ever.

Soon we had six swimming in our pail, three of them mine.

"I told you your Aunt Bunny knows the best spots in this lake." I looked at the cattails with new respect. This was the fishes' home.

Back at the house the maid took our catch to cook for Uncle Paul's homecoming. Then Aunt Bunny brought us lemonades and glass straws with bumpy lemon tops. Sitting beside her and Michael, sun-tanned and weary on the couch, I felt so different it was almost like being happy. Yet part of me tracked an ancient melody and longed to go home.

In the days that followed I explored this territory on my own, sometimes accompanied by Michael and his collie-dog Boy, often just with Boy. I had never felt such freedom. There were no orders or rules. As I wandered through lobbies, I found Scrabble games in progress, elevators leading to floor after floor, movie stars and singers strolling about or signing autographs, projectors in darkened rooms showing movies. So many of the adults seemed to know me and wanted me to say their names and shake their hands.

I spent lots of time with big Milty, reading comics, helping him mix fruit sodas and malts. When the printers came on their coffee break, they took me to their underground shop, its machines magically imprinting and stacking menus. Next door the telephone operators invited me into their cubicle to try on headphones and listen to long distance.

One night during the show in the Terrace Room I got to turn the spotlight. The world changed from purple to sunny orange.

This was like a fairy tale except that I woke from faraway dreams to find myself there each morning, Aunt Bunny calling cheerily for breakfast, a day of adventures ahead. I had two brothers, a collie like Lassie, a new mother, Big Milty, a bakery spilling out cookies, cakes, and rolls—a whole Emerald City.

On my last night Aunt Bunny said to prepare for a surprise. Then, instead of dinner, she spread white boxes on the floor and asked us to fill our plates from them. I had never seen such food. I tasted fat juicy bacon on bones, little crisp vegetable cakes, and salty strips of duck. There were sugar cookies that cracked open with message strips carrying good fortunes.

At bedtime Aunt Bunny became a ringmaster: "A water circus is long overdue."

Michael cackled with delight.

"What's that?" I asked.

"You'll see!"

After Michael and I got undressed and hopped into the warm tub, she handed us aerosol cans. We squirted islands and clouds and shot shaving cream at each other until it ran down the walls.

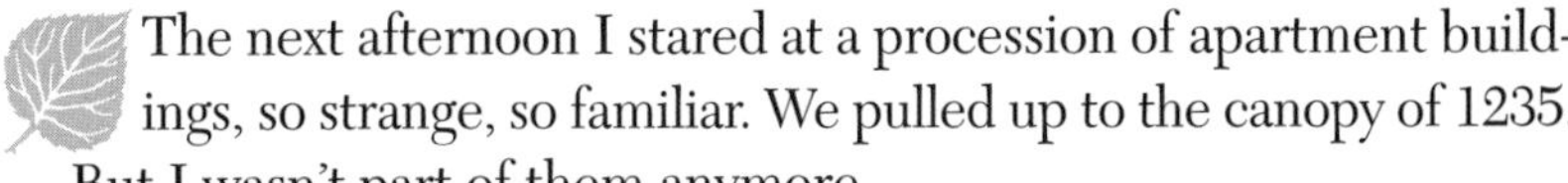

The next afternoon I stared at a procession of apartment buildings, so strange, so familiar. We pulled up to the canopy of 1235. But I wasn't part of them anymore.

For Mommy this new betrayal was as ancient as Paris and Helen, and she acted as though it were her duty to punish me sufficiently for it. "I will never forgive you," she said in a thousand ways for the rest of my childhood, without using those exact words. "Ever, ever, ever."

The destiny of her life seemed to have been set in place so long ago, when her mother abandoned her in a Parisian boarding school—then she came to the mountains and married Uncle Paul. She let me know my "pleasures" were an indulgence made possible by her and Daddy.

"How quickly they forget! It was Bob Towers and Milton Blackstone who made Grossinger's, not some Auntie Bunny. How could you choose this phony over your own flesh and blood?"

"Mr. Bigshot!" Daddy said. "Never earned a buck, but now he's an expert on the Catskills."

"It doesn't take much to seduce *him.*"

Through sixth grade I continued at P.S. 6. While reading the Hardy Boys, Ken Holt, and Rick Blaine, Phil and I made our own mysteries. The streets of New York yielded cryptic notes, plus objects that could have been connected to crimes, including a watch with a skull's head attached (we used to try to decode the names on the buzzers of a nearby apartment building).

Our one confirmed success was a fake scavenger hunt that tricked a classmate into returning a ring he had stolen from a girl.

At home Jon and I listened to the Yankees, built block castles, and rolled marbles at plastic men and horses set in the hall. We threw the dice for Clue and Monopoly, moving across squares through secret passages into the realm of Colonel Mustard.

The Sorry board with its slides and bold number cards occupied a region of our lives, as we raced to get all four pieces of the same color around the border of squares.

Ones and twos released red, yellow, green, or blue tokens into play. An opportune four-backwards could save the whole journey around the board; sevens were divisible between two pieces; elevens could change places with the opponent; a ten could be turned into one-backwards in a gamble that needed a quick second ten to save a whole circuit.

I remember the relief at being in the Safety Zone, the dismay of being forced back out, the delight of bringing two tokens home at once with a seven.

Hebrew School Monday and Wednesday afternoons was the worst thing in my life.

The teachers were wimpish and fake, and I hated their boastfulness. Only Jews made the desert bloom. Only Jews could keep a menorah burning without oil. The Arabs were jealous and wanted to persecute us.

I became a beast child. I made up pranks. I put the names of Yankees in my translation of Kibbutz activity (read aloud to everyone's giggles). I asked where the cavemen and dinosaurs were in the Old Testament. I hid comic strips in the teacher's reader for him to find when he began to recite.

The bigoted fundamentalism that marks secular Zionism (as well as Islam and Christianity) at the turn of the century was already in robust latency during my childhood. All that was needed in the landscape of Park Avenue Synagogue 1954 was the '67 war, Meir Kahane, *Gush Emunim, Aterit Cohanin,* and scattered other rabblerousers and events tindered by a generation of rabbinical students who didn't experience the Holocaust except as a kind of racist mythology. My classmates at Park Avenue Synagogue already wanted to slaughter Arabs; they made jokes about *noodnik* Egyptians bumping into each other and shooting rifles up their own asses.

I would not be surprised to hear that some of my comrades from then have moved to the State of Israel and found their kind around Hebron, packing heat, impatient for the Israeli army to leave.

Something didn't feel right back then, but to oppose it would have been considered the worst form of hooliganism and sacrilege ... because we were taught that Jews were always victims, always good guys.

During Purim fair, our class made a Nasser dart board. I was hardly a precocious humanitarian, but I hated goody-goodiness in any form. As our artist finished her Palestinian caricature to giggles and claps, I whispered that Arabs were human too—first, to Elisha (who told on me), then to the teacher, finally in the principal's office to the rabbi. I repeated it for good measure. The principal gasped and pronounced me "an anti-Semite." At his insistence I looked up my new name in his dictionary.

"*Are* you an anti-Semite?"

The definition said: "... hostile to the people and language of Israel."

"Yep."

I was expelled.

I couldn't believe such a lucky punishment.

I returned to Grossinger's each Thanksgiving, Christmas, and Passover, and for the times before and after Chipinaw. My vacations would begin when my grandfather's chauffeur Joe picked me up downstairs, usually on the evening of the last Friday of school. I'd wait on the street so that Mommy and Daddy wouldn't be involved.

The black Caddy rolled alongside the curb. Joe grabbed my suitcase from Ramon the grumpy doorman (who didn't approve of Grossinger's either but lingered for Joe's dollar). The chauffeur fit my stuff into his trunk and then pointed to my seat next to him. If Grandpa was in the back, I'd shake his hand.

I watched familiar landmarks pass, sometimes scything their panorama, sometimes trying to find letters in order from A to Z (Q often came from an antique shop, Z from a bright Pizza sign) ... counting the miles, first till The Red Apple Rest, where we'd get cake or pie, then to Grossinger's itself.

I explored every tier and acre of the grounds—trails through the woods and around staff quarters, staircases that crossed roofs, catacombs beneath the kitchen. Coming up from a dark tunnel, I saw pails of noodles dumped into pots, rows of fish simmering as chefs splattered them red with spice. Soft wet cakes rotated through oven doors, Benny the baker squeezing out birthday designs.

Uncle Paul didn't like Michael and me to go into the kitchens. It made him angrier than anything else: "You two, I never want to see you here again!" he shouted one time he caught us in the act. "We could lose our insurance." But we broke the rule regularly in order to goof off with chefs and serve ourselves like waiters.

Aunt Bunny's household was a bedlam without subterfuge—strange dogs and cats hiding in the basement, visitors lost in private rooms amid a general breakdown of distinction between Hotel staff and family maids, real family and pretend family. Aunt Bunny was often in frantic passage between the dining room and living room, leading people behind her, carrying food. (I remember once she came into a gathering and began spraying pine air-freshener directly at Uncle Paul's butt because he was farting silently. "I might as well," she told the startled guests, "go to the source.")

My stepmother was more than a parent: she was my best friend. I loved to monopolize her for conversations as she moved across her busy life. I kept her company in the kitchen, at the hairdresser, in the garden, even at the bar while she drank gin and tonics. She listened to everything I said: Hardy Boy tales, my dreams, my fears, adventures at Chipinaw. She'd tell me funny things that happened when I was away, like a commotion she caused at a dinner party: "I shouted, 'Throw Mr. Katz in the basement, or he'll fight with the dog.'"

That was our cat's name, but, unknown to her, she had a guest that evening named Mr. Katz.

"He was standing there holding his drink. He said, 'Please, don't send me to the basement. I won't fight with the dog.'" She did an imitation of him cringing, hands on her hips.

As I got older I liked to socialize in the VIP section of the dining room. There I found comedians and singers on tour, politicians, ballplayers, bookies, and members of the Chicago Grossingers. I'd shake hands with old punchdrunk Barney Ross, who'd grab me in a paralyzing bear hug and start singing in Yiddish. Usually I had to remind him to let me go. He'd give one last clasp like a python trying to squeeze out any remaining life, then assume a boxer's stance from which he insisted I throw a combination against his palms in exchange for my freedom. I never put much heart into the punches, yet he always went down for the count.

Whenever a major league player was at the hotel I looked for him, especially the Yankees (Yogi Berra, Andy Carey . . . Whitey Ford holding my hand as I struggled on ice-skates). Sometimes the maître d' or a member of the athletic staff would escort me over. "Do you know Richard, Paul's son?" The player would stop eating and dutifully get up. I'd shake hands with him and his wife and maybe get invited to join them for dessert. I knew not to talk baseball: they were on vacation.

One evening Aunt Bunny invited Yankee pitchers Johnny Kucks and Tom Sturdivant and their wives to sit with us at our table in the Terrace Room nightclub. At the show's conclusion a crowd was blocking the door. The players were in a hurry to get back to their baby-sitter, so I led us out a fire exit, up onto the roof, and across buildings on platform stairs.

"Great route, kid," Kucks said.

"I live here," Aunt Bunny remarked, "and I didn't even know these stairs existed."

Mommy's time at the Hotel defined many of my relationships. Both Jack the steward and Benny the baker thought she was the most beautiful woman they had ever seen. They always pledged me to return their sincerest regards, reviewing for them exactly the words I would use and how I would describe their appearance to her. Jack never failed to remind me how much I looked like her.

My mother adored these accolades. She may have been irritable about the trips and would hear nothing of Aunt Bunny, Uncle Paul, my "fake" brothers, or Boy, but she cajoled me for accounts of her legacy—who from her time was still there and what they said. She always sent back remembrances through me. It was our pact separate even of Daddy.

My custom of going to visit Grandma Jennie at Joy Cottage was, in part, a mission from my mother. The warmest words of farewell Mommy could provide me were, "I know Richard will visit Jennie," as though to block out the existence of anything else at Grossinger's—and commend my loyalty in advance.

Grandma seemed almost to collaborate with her, as we sat in her room, reviewing my New York life. Though she expressed great sympathy "for your suffering," she felt that I should be a strength to my family and represent the merits of Grossinger's to them. "They don't know any better," she asserted. "Your mother was mistreated in boarding school, and Bob Towers is a very difficult husband. She has a lot of unhappiness."

Grandma also shared the sadness I felt for poor people like Bridey and the Spanish dish-washers at the Hotel—a sense that behind all this gaiety was something bottomless and somber. When I described blind beggars with dogs on Lexington or the man with no legs outside Carnegie Hall, she would go into her safe, carefully distinguishing dollars to give to the needy from a large bill "to spend on yourself."

My cousins Jay and Siggy derided Grandma's grandiosity. "She's a big fat fake," Jay exclaimed.

"Queen of the ball," said Uncle Bernie. "She thinks she owns the whole town."

"I'll take Manhattan, the Bronx, and Staten," crooned Siggy, who loved to sing his jokes, *"Island too."*

Uncle Paul argued with Grandma over giving too much to charity and allowing unpaid guests (even Barney Ross was considered a free-loader). When I told her about these criticisms she always prefaced her remarks by saying she herself was to blame because she never gave Paul enough love. "I was too busy making this Hotel successful so that all our children could enjoy it." Then she sighed, elevated herself on her bed, and repeated her favorite proverb: "We have to be bigger. If other people think small, we will think big."

Her most notable adversary was her own husband. Grandpa Harry was the only person about whom she was openly contemptuous, calling him "an ignorant bum." When I visited him in his room he muttered mostly unintelligible syllables. A small bald man who either sat before a TV or walked the grounds commanding workers, he lived in Joy Cottage but had a separate entrance so he could come and go without seeing his wife. Since the door from the inside hallway was always locked, I had to go around to his plywood enclosure.

Grandpa was as generous as Grandma, taking out a wad of bills without comment and pulling a twenty off the top each visit. He'd ask about my family in New York, especially "Bobtowers" (said as though one word). He didn't listen to my answers; instead he told me to dress more warmly and (during the winter) to cover my ears. Michael and I would giggle our way home. "It's like meeting Elmer Fudd," I said.

"No," my brother proclaimed. "Scrooge McDuck." And every now and then he'd suggest we go see Grandpa Scrooge for "a quick twenty."

Grandpa's sister was Aunt Rose, a dwarf stationed at the back of the kitchen near the staff dining room. She had a large head with a doll's simple face and would curse just for the sake of it. I never saw her smile, except as a forerunner to a profanity. She would scold Michael and me whenever we passed her: "You goddamned kids, whatcha doing now? No good I betcha!" We'd purposely steer within view to get her greeting.

Overseer of the staff quarters, Aunt Rose was married to the cherubic maître d' of the dining room, Uncle Abe, who, smelling of cologne, demanded a kiss and almost never communicated anything else. He'd simply point to his cheek. Although grown up, their son Artie roamed the grounds like a child, hustling golf matches with guests. In the clubhouse he used to do an imitation of Grandpa talking about his wife: "'Putting on airs,'" he would say, his suddenly toothless gums jabbering away. "'She's no girlfriend of mine.'"

Aunt Bunny explained about Michael and James being adopted. "Sometimes it just works out that a couple can't have children, and it's that way with your father and me. But we love them as much, perhaps even more so because we picked them out."

Adopted or not, these brothers were my total pals. They and I became a club of three, roaming the grounds, finding adventures. We burst into the dining room full of energy, too boisterous for Uncle Abe, who'd hush us (before asking for his kiss). Then we commandeered Milty's canteen to make triple scoops and five-flavored shakes (while Goliath feigned bewilderment).

Aunt Elaine's son, our cousin Mark, lived just up the hill and, though he sometimes joined us on exploits, other times he looked on aloofly as though we were nothing short of lunatics, bothering the guests with our antics.

The tension between Hotel families increased after Mark shouted the forbidden secret one day: "You act stupid because you're adopted!" James had no idea what that meant. Michael went to his mother for clarification. Aunt Bunny was furious, but Uncle Paul said they would have to learn sooner or later.

"You might as well thank Mark," he chuckled reassuringly. "He saved you a difficult moment."

The Lake was our major hangout. Turtles sunned on rocks around the shallows. In a rowboat we floated up behind them as splashlessly as we could.

One day James and I rowed all the way to where reeds grew so tall it was difficult to budge the oars. Here was the original pond from which Grossinger Lake had been dug by bulldozers. It had a different feel to it, trees hanging low, hidden pockets, no sandy shore to stand on. The giant we spied there led us to call out, "A whale! A whale!" It was two feet in diameter.

I got out of the boat and strode through muck, soaking my pants as I trailed it deeper and deeper through reeds until James could no longer follow. Finally it stopped, burrowing down into mud. As I grabbed its tail, James pulled the boat up behind me, and together we flipped it into our craft. It rested on its back, a sorry spectacle.

In years afterwards I regretted taking this grandfather from his home, but at that moment we were so excited we presented it all around the beach.

Beulah the maid knew what to do and announced her plans gleefully. That appalled us, and neither James nor I were willing to taste her brew. "Not even a sip?" she pleaded.

We ran away.

I was not the only guest that June at my father's house. A young creole woman named Gail, daughter of Aunt Bunny's friend Lena Horne, was living in the other room upstairs. A student of history in college, she joined our dinners and played a red croquet ball at dusk. Each weekend in his uniform the same cadet appeared from West Point to take her on a date like in a fairy tale.

Michael and I led her to the buffet by the pool. She was delighted by ice statues and cherry tarts. At long grills tended by figures in white, we introduced our friend. From their zone of smoke the chefs saluted her.

Our plates crammed with cold cuts and melon balls, we chose a table of familiar faces—a bookie and two comedians talking to relatives from

Chicago. They were so busy arguing sports and who had the best box of cigars that they were startled by our sudden presence in their midst. They stopped chewing pastrami and hamburgers long enough to grunt recognition. Leaning across the parasol, Gail extended a hand to each.

Then all eyes turned. On a TV over a small outdoor bar Yogi Berra had reached for a high fast ball and driven it into the gap in right center. He stood on second … but there were only three days of paradise left before Chipinaw.

6

Childhood (III)

Through years of sessions with Dr. Fabian, my life became a series of riddles with no outcomes, just as my daydreams found no terminus in the universe they created. The premonition that something terrible was going to happen, my waking to wet pajamas, my failures at school were symptoms linked by the psychiatrist to the divorce of my parents. By his interpretation bedwetting was a declaration of being among the enemy; it was an act both of compliance and revenge. If I failed at staying dry, if I was bad in school, I would never have to live up to my heroic brother, whom they liked better anyway.

"What would another son or daughter of Paul and Martha been like?" Dr. Fabian wondered. "Wouldn't you give your eye teeth to know that person?"

I nodded enthusiastically. If only my parents had waited longer before getting divorced I could have had an ally, a companion. Yet the thought was also creepy—because it called for an intimacy I didn't feel toward anyone (except in daydreams), and it compelled a privacy between two adults I couldn't bear having together even to make me.

I didn't want to picture another Martha or Paul child. I didn't want to have to worry about whether he would wet his bed too or do badly in school or have fears. I didn't want to see my own defectiveness exposed in him (and either hate or love him, with consequences either way). I also didn't want to be shown up by him. What if a brother from my same family were normal?

In fact, I knew this would be the case. No matter how many real brothers and sisters I had I would still be me.

These were not thoughts I had. They are things I felt remotely, disquiets without a name.

Once, Dr. Fabian asked me, "Would it matter if your father was Paul Grossinger of Grossinger's or Paul Garfinger the ditch-digger?"

"No," I fibbed.

It wasn't so much that I fibbed as I had no idea how to answer. I adored Grossinger's. I didn't want to trade it for a perfect family. Yet I had to lie because I didn't want Dr. Fabian (of all people) to think I was selfish and spoiled.

I see now it wasn't important that my accomplice discover the truth. In fact, there was no truth. But it was necessary that he provide an explanation, some conclusive fiction we could share, to pull me from the pure terror of the void.

I was a member of the Towers clan, in spirit and heart—our meals at Daddy's accounts, the treks through Central Park, the dinners at Grandma Sally's where Jon's and my lack of manners were an embarrassment to our mother. Our world was Bridey's policeman boyfriends picking her up for dates, aerograms and gift boxes from Ireland. It was *Seders* on the Lower East Side with Daddy's sisters and their children (at which my mother would be as much an outsider as us, flashing Jonny and me snickers of contempt for such carrying on). It was make-believe carnivals with Debby, culminating in good-natured three-person chases ... treasure hunts I prepared for her and Jon, successive clues scribbled on pieces of paper and stuffed into hiding places (the metal rim of a lamp shade, a keyhole, a table leg, the elbow of a statue), each providing a hint to the next, and so on, until the grand prize (a present I bought) at the end.

Bridey knew *Finian's Rainbow* had my favorite songs. Suddenly, from the kitchen (where she was making dinner) would come the lilting soprano of Bridget McCann: *"It's that old devil moon/That you stole from the skies./It's that old devil moon in your eyes."*

That "old debbil moon" was everything we were and everything we weren't and, although Bridey couldn't have known, a Gaelic leprechaun inside her told us what was happening: *"Does that laddie with a twinkling eye/Come whistling by./And does he walk away,/Sad and dreamy there/Not to see me there . . . ,"* her brogue putting the pauses right where they belonged, where the shadow was, where light creeped through. Rhyming outside, then in. Impossible hopes leaping from an abyss. Beauty and darkness. Wedding song and dirge.

Every summer, I returned to Chipinaw. With whatever three other campers were housed with us Jay, Barry, and I went from Bunk 4 to Bunk 9, then to 12 and 14.

When they were old enough, my brother and sister were sent to Chipinaw too. Jon was immediately homesick. I would seek him out between activities, have catches with him, give him cookies from Grossinger's, and tell him stories about our bunk. Vulnerable and lonely, he was almost cute.

I hardly ever saw my sister because she was in the girls' camp, but once I was summoned to the main office because she wouldn't stop crying. She had worked herself into an inconsolable marathon.

"It's okay, Squiz," I told her. "You'll get to go home."

"I want to go home *now,*" she whimpered, hugging me. "I don't want to stay here."

After a while, without a word, she let go and, with the expression and gait of a street urchin, trudged back to her counselor.

In the summer of 1956 I got a call from Uncle Paul. He told me he had a big surprise in store. I knew because it was the All-Star break, but I pretended not to be able to guess. Then he said he was going to visit with three New York Yankees.

Word of this event turned Chipinaw upside-down, making me an instant celebrity. Kids put on facetious shows of friendship ("I was always Richie's buddy, right? Remember when . . ." and then they'd invent something).

Activities were cancelled; all Chipinaw mobilized on the hill. I ran past the forbidden boundary marker and stared down the road in the direction of Grossinger's.

They were forty-five minutes late, but finally a black limo came crashing out of the horizon, suspending time as it arrived. Uncle Paul stood there with an ear-to-ear smile; behind him were pitchers Mickey McDermott, Bob Turley, and Don Larsen.

"Are you in charge here?" Turley teased as I paraded around, announcing the arrival through a megaphone.

They stood by the flagpole where they demonstrated plays and answered campers' questions.

Jonny was astonished; it was the first time he understood I wasn't making it up about Grossinger's. It was proof of the power and seductiveness of villains, that they even had access to Yankees.

Chipinaw was a regimen of baseball, kickball, and tag, waterfront and nature hikes. I felt overwhelmed by all the cheering and rivalry. Sometimes I just wanted to drift in the outfield, sun on my arms.

At the far side of Silver Lake we could see faint dioramas of other camps carrying out maneuvers in canoes and rowboats, scurrying to assemble at their flags. Our bugle directed us likewise to activities and meals.

Summer held mysterious other lives, from rusty hot showers to dew on candy wrappers, dandelions and purple clover, wasps emitting a familiar trapped whine, smell of pine, sudden bursts of rain. Yet it all had an impenetrable mood of melancholia and exile, of being in prison (in truth, we were sent to Chipinaw not because, as our parents claimed, the City was too hot in August but because they didn't want us home).

We were supposed to be happy; we were supposed to be proud of the Red and Gray. Our games and victories were the grist and mettle, the heart of life. The counselors knew it; the campers learned it from them. Only Sam Rosenberg (Bunk 12) thought it was a big joke, and we loved him for it.

A great forest surrounded us. In its confines lived an escaped madman known as the Cropsey Maniac (who sometimes came roaring past our campfires). Those nights, under the Dipper, marshmallows bubbling black on peeled sticks, all the worlds of my daydreams sparkled in the sky.

We dressed in white uniforms for Saturday services, rowed to Glen Cove, made clay bottles, hunted snakes and centipedes, listened to the Yankees on the Monticello station, played rafterball and roofball, and competed in All-Star Baseball tournaments (long rainy afternoons, spinning the metal arrow, trying to get a home run for Charlie Keller or Aaron Robinson at 1).

We waited half a summer to compete with each other in a week of Color War. That was when I most longed to be anywhere else, as judges walked around scoring our bed-making and conduct at meals. Games and songfests became combat.

Then Color War was over. I was counting the days until camp's end ... *six, five, four* ... going to sleep at taps, spilling through relics of dream at reveille ... *three, two* ... chasing fungos by the fence, the tension so incredible I almost couldn't bear it, couldn't believe Grossinger's existed for real ... *one*....

The spell was over; cars dotted the hillside. Not another night at Chipinaw, I tore about the camp lightheaded, searching for Grandpa's driver.

The next morning, strolling past tennis courts en route to lunch at the pool, I felt as though the Earth had changed utterly, from a pit of hell to Shangri-La. I had a different body, so much denser, crammed with joyful, excited feelings, each one different and strange, rolling inside like oceans off a far horizon. It was amazing, beautiful, tropical, not just because of luxuries and gala events all around but because I could feel myself floating up into blue sky across cloud armadas that tinged the horizon far beyond Grossinger's. It was the best that things ever got, happier than happy, more colorful than blue, red, yellow, more golden than Indian summer, more euphoric than September wind eddying in maple and oak, because everywhere I looked, peace and hope extended inside me, all the way to P.S. 6 and Chipinaw, even to my brother Jon, even to the Cropsey Maniac—and in that moment of rapture, my daydream planets turned to dust and were blown off; even my mother was redeemed.

Grossinger's was where Yankees came as real people. It was where Milty shut the canteen in order to throw me balls and I made impossible diving and leaping catches among the marigolds because I suddenly had the energy and timing of Superman. It was where Grandma bought clothes for poor workers. It wasn't Grossinger's. It was creation, but Grossinger's was where I had to be for it to happen.

Rare moments there of homesickness and panic were especially profound because they betrayed my greatest joy; they meant the abyss, the gap, would emerge whenever "Richard" really looked, even in paradise. The damage was bigger than Grossinger's, and irreparable.

One morning that September I discovered a patch of gray fuzz on my bread where I had already taken a bite. A wave of horror swept over me. I had finally done it! I was going to die.

I raced to Aunt Bunny. I could feel the poison expanding like ice. I couldn't think of any way to escape, so I began to writhe in place.

She grabbed me with both hands, shook me, and stared into my eyes. "Why you and I are plagued with this," she said, "I have no idea. The Pauls of this world are fortresses. Nothing frightens or harms them. We're different. Our lives are always on the line." She was instantly reassuring, so my shaking stopped. "It's not bad fungus," she told me. "It's penicillin, good stuff; it'll make you healthy."

In the middle of sixth grade, my life changed course. Since one of her cousins was a librarian at Yale and her brother Lionel had become a renowned scholar of history, my mother fostered academic pretensions for us. I was the oldest, the first to finish grade school, and she wanted me to attend either Riverdale or Horace Mann. I had no such ambitions, and I knew Uncle Paul didn't want me to go. He disdained elitism and told me he was opposed to paying for education. "Private schools make you *less* able to earn a living," he quipped. Although it seemed unlikely I would be accepted at any prep school, Mommy made a deal with him. If I got in, she would change my name to Grossinger.

The only way for me to have even a chance was to make up the years of failed work since first grade—the childhood I had daydreamed through. For that my mother hired a tutor from Columbia, an older graduate student named Mr. Hilowitz. Visiting twice a week after dinner, he soon turned instruction into a game and challenged me to defeat the imaginary "rival" who said Richard could never learn.

As he set down prepared lessons I felt as though I had seen these things before, through a veil—vocabulary, grammar, number problems. I covered the missing curriculum in three months, passed the exam, and got into Horace Mann.

In the fall I woke at dawn, dressed in a jacket and tie, rode the crosstown bus to the IRT subway, and took the train to the end of the line, 246th Street. I began seventh grade as Richard Grossinger.

I threw myself into memorization of Latin vocabulary, Persian history, and statistics of the solar system. Gradually my world was absorbed by conjugations of irregular verbs, X and Y axes, the Articles of Confederation, and dynasties of Mesopotamians, Picts, and Phoenicians. I hardly understood the initiation; yet I came to treasure these pieces of knowledge like the gold coins of my "Know the Presidents" game. Even the Yankees faded beside the spread of Christianity and complexities of Mediaeval baronies.

During gym I played tennis and soccer, learned the butterfly stroke, and went out for hardball. I didn't hit well enough to start, but I subbed in the outfield.

After struggling at first with the transition to an all-boys' academy, in the second form I got A's and B's. In fact, I committed my life to studying for them. Mommy was delighted. She phoned relatives and friends and read them not only my report card but sections from papers I wrote and comments of my teachers. My success confirmed her notion of who we were, though we both acknowledged, without harping on it, that Jonny was far more capable and would do even better when his turn came.

Horace Mann made my two lives (New York and Grossinger's) discrepant in new ways.

My mother's regime centered on grades. She enforced dinner-to-bedtime studying, read my Horace Mann homework closely, and upbraided me for any lapses, imagined or real. Her visits to school (on "mother's day") were occasions of state during which she listened meticulously to everything my teachers said and asked them questions about my work. "He's sloppy," she would report to Bridey the next morning. "His math teacher says he doesn't check his answers. You have to wonder what he's doing all those hours because he's not prepared for history either."

None of this was true, but hearing it in her voice sent chills through me.

All her past resentments had merged into a new requirement that I always be at my desk working, never be listening to baseball, talking on the phone, watching TV. (By contrast, when Uncle Paul came on "father's day," he exchanged wisecracks with other fathers and chatted with my teachers about their colleges and hometowns.)

My mother's obsession became my own. Once I began to get A's, each paper, pop quiz, vocabulary test, midterm, and final was a life-and-death drama on which my whole identity rested. Nothing was as horrible as being caught unprepared.

At Grossinger's *no one* cared about homework or grades. Michael and James either raced through a quick page or two or scrapped the ritual entirely. It took monumental effort for me to disengage from their free-spiritedness and concentrate on those few assignments I took over vacations. The mere solving of a math program or translation of a Latin paragraph—something I did all night and weekend in our apartment—seemed suddenly as strange as decoding a document from a Mediaeval chapel. The ornate wallpaper and clutter of knickknacks everywhere seemed to defy me, to minimize my labors, plus the sound of the whole family watching *77 Sunset Strip* and *What's My Line?*, the nightly order of milk shakes and ice-cream sodas from Milty, the lure of rock 'n' roll deejays in the lobby, comedians in the nightclub.

"Richard's doing his Egyptian hieroglyphs," Michael announced. Aunt Bunny smiled and half-heartedly told him to get back to his own assignment.

On baseball days I took the subway home late, translating Caesar, sustained in romantic solipsism. Back at the apartment I ate four or five raisin-bread-and-cream-cheese sandwiches, a bowl of Corn Pops and Kix; then I got an early start on math. (In the background Bridey sang, "*We could be oh so bride-and-groomish;/Skies could be so bluish blue.*")

Her dinners were a high point—baked potatoes and vegetables, slices of rare roast beef or sirloin steaks from Daddy's friend who owned a slaughterhouse on the Lower East Side. Our parents arrived in a whiff of worldly scent, a flutter of briefcases and late-edition papers. They disappeared into their bedroom and returned in bathrobes for the meal. Everyone was joking, telling stories of the day. Debby performed goofy events.

For all our ribaldry and simulation of family life, we lived in a maelstrom, a black, silent wind, disguised by the sophistication of our wit. I was its center—or, as I saw in later years, its scapegoat. All it took was my being late from an appointment with Dr. Fabian or a mention of Grossinger's. Their glances said, 'Traitor.' They said, 'You don't deserve our company.'

My mother's and my best times together were at the Fountainbleau office where she was enlivened by ringing phones, the dance of taking reservations and handling crises with her secretary Helen; in idle spells, the most shameless gossip flew between them. There Mommy and I could sit and talk openly; she would introduce me to executives and business acquaintances as "Richard, Paul's son."

Back at home she would recognize me, or something in me, and the frown would come back, the stubborn affirmation that it would never be any different.

It is difficult to recall what was so painful then, why the sun in the morning seemed to drench us with a ghostlike nostalgia, why the furniture and carpets were dolorous and bleak. Children elsewhere went hungry and were beaten; we lived a privileged life.

Yes, occasionally our mother used a belt, umbrella, or her fists, but that was like something out of a Donald Duck comic. Her rapid footsteps down the hall were followed by our door slamming open; then her attack, usually ineffectual as we squirmed away and hid under furniture. "You're out of control, you maniacs!" she would scream for little reason other than that she had heard the sound of our playing. "No concern for anyone—just selfish brats!"

Even her disparagements were marginally amusing, for sarcasm was the closest she came to humor.

"Look at how you're dressed! Checkered tie and striped jacket! Gray slacks and brown socks! No one in the world wears gray and brown together."

I was on my way out the door to catch the subway for school. Bob came to look and commented dryly, "Some of the best dressed men in the world wear gray with brown."

"He's not one of the best dressed men in the world!"

She was disgusted by me, from the wet sheets she held so close they rubbed my nose to the tentative way she hugged me, as though it was her obligation.

Her fashion was intimacy followed by betrayal. The times we had "heart to hearts," either at her office or in the bedroom, she would adopt her sweetest tone and get me to talk about Aunt Bunny and Grossinger's. She would appear so glad for me, empathize totally. Then a day—or a month—later, in front of everyone, she would repeat my words in mocking, singsong fashion:

"'I made milk shakes with Big Milty!' Did you ever hear anything so idiotic, a kid who can't brush his hair and is a slave to baseball."

Then there was the time I made the mistake of telling her I liked a girl at Chipinaw.

"He gets crushes now," she told the family at dinner. "I wonder if this girl, whoever she is, ever took a look at his face." She jabbed at the latest outbreak of acne. "He never scrubs. He smells. He's the only human being who can't be taught a fox trot. He dances like a moron. You think a girl's going to look at you. What are you, crazy?"

Even then, I understood she was making it up. She didn't mean it literally. She was little more than a spoof of a disciplinarian and misanthrope. Yet behind her show business and frippery was a hexing from the guardians of doom itself.

She wanted to damage me. She felt safe only when I brooded. My spells of glee and elation sparked contagious anxiety and suppression in her. She had to stop good times before they went too far.

I believed her—not what she said but *her.* Down in my bones I felt the ghastly, complicated thing that afflicted and drove her—my own mother—into an unsparing Medusa. I felt its presence everywhere, making us do its Pulcinella dance.

The rest of her was missing. That was the horrifying thing.

A world that could make a beautiful, smart woman into a witch was an unsafe, desolate place indeed.

Joy became a rare epiphany I could never quite hold.

After entering Horace Mann, I didn't want to return to Hebrew School, but all my parents (except Aunt Bunny) were set on a *bar mitzvah,* so I had to attend Park Avenue Synagogue's religious classes.

On November 2, 1957, I stood before the Grossinger, Turetsky, and Rothkrug clans, including Bob's sisters, my mother's brother Paul, my Zises cousins, and my father's distant cousins and assorted clients, raced through a rendition of *Isaiah,* and gave a speech I had written which had nothing to do with me or him.

I was embarrassed by the prayer shawls wrapped around me, and I had my usual trouble keeping a tune. Two rabbis towered over the pulpit. I suspected what they were thinking: I was a religious disaster but at least a Grossinger.

On that morning Jennie was an honored guest of the congregation.

Afterwards, from a distance, I watched both my families interacting. Jonny and Debby were in the same room as Michael and James. Aunt Bunny got to see Bridey. Yet it was over in a flash, before I had a chance to understand. Its sole remains were gifts of money and stocks, a gold wristwatch, leatherbound prayerbooks and dictionaries, and religious articles I would hide in a closet and never use.

Dr. Fabian died of a stroke that winter. My mother didn't tell me right away because I was taking exams and she didn't want it to affect my grades.

I couldn't feel my grief or mourn the man who had saved me. Life seemed to rush on. Before the month was over I had been introduced to Dr. Friend. He had one open slot, the last before dinner. I accepted it.

I would take the subway directly to the West Side and do homework in his waiting room. By day's end his office smelled like the inside of a cigar box. Its drapes, bookshelves, paintings, and giant desk cast a magisterial aura.

It seemed almost traitorous to begin telling this balding, antipathetic man my story, but I knew my official trauma quite well by then. I could recite the traumatic wounds of my parents' divorce and juggle symbols and sublimation like a pro. I thought he would be impressed, but he tired quickly of this material and urged me into the present, where I was just another moody adolescent, wondering how to date girls, why I couldn't hit the curveball, playing Dion and the Belmonts and Neil Sedaka on my hi-fi.

During ninth grade our family moved to 90th Street and Central Park West, just a few blocks from Dr. Friend's office. Jonny entered Horace Mann. Debby was enrolled in the Lycée. Bridey moved to her own apartment in the Bronx.

I took advanced Biology, Honors English, and European history. I went on expeditions with the camera club and learned how to develop film and print pictures. Although still a baseball fan, I fell in with the class intellectuals who, for the most part, despised sports. We discussed Marxism and Christian mysticism, and I learned the rudiments of tarot divination and surrealism. My friends, the poet Chuck Stein and the communist Bob Alpert, were bigger influences than any of my teachers. I wanted to master systems of knowledge like them. Yet my status in their group was solely that of spokesman for the unconscious, deflating Chuck and Bob with warnings that in the end darkness and its dreams would rule, even over Russia, even over the High Priestess.

On the subway I read Samuel Butler's *Way of All Flesh,* Charles Dickens' *Our Mutual Friend,* and Freud's *Interpretation of Dreams.* These brought back the wistful mood of the early years with Dr. Fabian when symbols were signposts for a hidden universe. Would that my life could be a mystery story again!

I began writing as a reporter for the *Chipinaw Chirp,* crafting descriptions of Silver Lake and the playing fields, ornate sunsets and thunderstorms.

From that summer on, I considered writing to be one of the things I did (like photography and baseball), though I never accomplished more than a five-page story about a hobo in Central Park.

Then junior year, while searching for a topic in my creative-writing seminar, I took up my teacher's challenge to write something about myself . . . and stumbled into a narrative of adolescence.

Drs. Fabian and Friend had provided the tools and the means of questing beneath the surface; now I had discovered a form.

I continued this text through the end of high school with narratives of Horace Mann, summer camp, and Grossinger's.

On a September morn in 1962 (so yellow and blue it could have been in another universe) my life in the Towers family came to an end. I helped Bob load my stuff into his car. Then he drove me along New England parkways to Amherst.

7

Making a Home (I)

WHEN I WENT AWAY to college, I no longer had a reason to return to my mother's household. I came directly to Grossinger's for the summer. My whole life I had imagined how wonderful it would be to live there, but I was musing through a glass darkly.

Newly charged by Viking editor Katey Carver with the task of finishing a novel, I envisioned joining assorted newspapermen and authors at the outdoor pool. My father rejected this plan immediately. He wanted me to apprentice in the hotel business, and he started me off as assistant mail clerk, logging dead letters. It was a position he had held. By then I fancied myself a disciple of Nabokov and Faulkner. Hotel management had nothing to do with me, and I viewed it with disdain.

Katey wrote my father about my literary potential and the importance of ample time to work. My freshman English teacher corroborated her. "Let *them* pay you then," Uncle Paul parried.

I found myself sentenced to underground offices, handed cartons packed with hundreds of undeliverable letters and ordered to enter them one by one in a log book. My father was no longer a comical tyrant; he was my judge, and my sentence had the smell of cheap perfume and mothballs. A fan rattled all day, and a janitor periodically passed through, sweeping scraps off the floor, cigarettes from ashtrays into a metal container on a stick. This was Grossinger's too.

But once I found that no one cared or even noticed whether the letters were logged, the job was readily circumvented by tossing most of the mail in the trash. I reduced my office time to a perfunctory hour. After that I slipped home via tunnels, sprinted up to the third floor, locked the guest-room door, and rapped away on my typewriter. Aunt Bunny and Emma the maid were my lookouts, quick to holler if my father approached. The few times he did, I left by the fire escape.

My cousins had been gone for several years by then, but one afternoon Jay and Barry called from a nearby phone booth. Delighted to hear their sassy voices, I met them at the foot of the hill outside Grossinger's. They took me for a drive through the forests by Chipinaw as we exchanged tales of Sam Rosenberg and the Cropsey Maniac.

Our families were in court with each other; Barry's father was the lawyer for Jay and Siggy's parents. We were supposed to be enemies, but that was impossible. I relieved any tension by agreeing that my grandfather had unfairly seized power and that Aunt Ruthie and Uncle Bernie were probably right.

"Hey, take care of yourself, dummy!" my cousin shouted, throwing me his fake angry stare. "You'll need to with parents like yours." The next time I saw him was fourteen years later, surrounded by secretaries, huddled over a Wall Street screen.

The Hotel had changed so gradually during my high-school years that it was hard to grasp what had happened. The "famous" visitors weren't quite so famous anymore—a State Senator instead of the President of Ireland, David Boroff instead of Isaac Singer, a Jets taxi-squad quarterback instead of Yogi Berra. The crowd was more vulgar, the din a touch shrill, the lobby dense with *yarmulkes* and sequinned dresses.

But I was changing too, and it was equally difficult to distinguish whether the Hotel was deteriorating or I was outgrowing it. However, once Jay and Siggy, Aunt Ruthie and the Grau clan vacated, the labyrinth unravelled. There weren't enough of them left to keep up a kingdom. By the summer of '63 the palace veneer was faded and quaint. From coast to coast a layer of Formica was being spackled over America. Maybe other resorts lacked the legendary status of Grossinger's, but they exuded the expensive illusion of the twentieth-century express.

Even Jennie was no longer a first-magnitude star. A more commercially-minded staff and new generation of guests ignored her or at best honored her as a relic. Joy Cottage was still her salon, and there at a cocktail party I met Rhonda, a blonde singer from Miami Beach; she was a protégé of Milton Blackstone. Rhonda had come to the Hotel to be "discovered." No one knew how that happened anymore, but in deference to Milton and Jennie, someone found her a hostess job and let her sing part-time with the band.

She was my age, and we became friends.

Right away my father noticed my interest in her. In the guise of making sure she didn't get pregnant, he encouraged me to "go to bed with her." But she was my first girlfriend (in fact, she had a boyfriend back home). When I explained this he snickered:

"Try harder. I think you'll be surprised."

I filtered out his goading; after all, it was mere style. He had been raised on impersonations of Bogart and spoiled by privilege.

Yet he couldn't let it go; he interrogated me every few days and showed obvious disappointment at my resistance. Then Rhonda came to me in tears. My father had approached her on my behalf, with a leer that threw into doubt whose lust he was representing.

The next afternoon, trying to slip quickly through the house, I was startled by his voice calling me to the back porch, an area used mainly for storage. I opened the screen and saw him on a discarded couch with a heavily made-up woman barely older than Rhonda; in fact, he was lying over her with her top pulled up, and she had to squeeze out from under him to be introduced.

I wanted to pretend this hadn't happened, but that evening he summoned me to his room. I could barely face him standing there in only white undershorts, an immense pale belly. Was this the uncle who rescued me from the tower, feted and entertained me? For the first time I yearned for my mother's protection. She was at least someone I understood. Her punishments were reassuring in their simplicity; even her hysteria reminded me of home. She wanted me to be "a gentleman and a scholar," as she was wont to put it. But what did my father want me to be? Ever pawing at what he considered my sham innocence, that night he was bursting with pride for how I had seen him. He offered to get me someone "older and more sophisticated who I know won't disappoint you." He went on to explain how through a connection of his he could set up a date with a "Rheingold girl" (a representative of a brand of beer popular back then). Flushed with humiliation, I stomped out, but he laughed and turned on the TV. "You'll be back!" he called behind me.

Later that week Aunt Bunny and I worked together in the garden. Though I hadn't planned to tell her, we had been confidantes too long. She coaxed at my reticence, indicating she probably knew. She did. "The women are no big deal," she remarked. "They come and go. But I won't let him do this to my sons."

A day later he called me into his room again. He was standing by his bed. At his insistence I came closer. He lurched and stumbled as he knocked me to the carpet. I threw my arms over my head. He took off his belt and began striking, again and again. The pain was almost unbelievable, but more than its actual sting, each stroke redefined him. I tasted his brutish energy. It seemed he could kill me without even noticing. The incident lasted maybe ten seconds, but its echo filled my whole life.

We never discussed it again. By evening he was telling jokes about hens and eggs, inviting me into the den for the Mets' game. Yet that was the end between us. In later years, even when he approached me with a facsimile of intimacy, I never let down my guard. The last year of his life, when he placed my teenage daughter on his knee and said how he'd love to show off with her in public, I cringed at his naive debauchery.

In the fall of '63 I moved into Phi Psi, a renegade fraternity that served as Amherst's haven for artists, bikers, and politicos. House meetings featured literary performances and jug bands. It was like attending classes from a Greenwich Village loft.

At Thanksgiving I was compelled to return to my mother's apartment (Aunt Bunny said she had invited too many guests … and also that my mother deserved a visit). I took a Trailways bus out of the Amherst depot ... subway to dusk streets, the path along Central Park West, bright corridors to elevator ... the sound of the doorbell ... Bridey greeting me with a handshake. I felt the gloom of an old self descending.

After dinner I sat in the bedroom with Jon, talking to stave off the blues. He was a different brother, more open to me now, interested in tarot and magic. In my absence I had become a guerrilla legend, the leader of our household rebellion.

The next evening a friend named Paul who lived down the hall from me at Phi Psi came for dinner. This alone was a daring act—during all the years of high school I had never invited anyone to our coven.

Raised in a Lower-East-Side Marxist family, Paul turned out to be a lively companion for my stepfather, as they exchanged stories about "the neighborhood." This banter carried over to the meal.

Arriving late from work, my mother tried to suppress the conviviality, then continued to the bedroom to change her clothes. When she took her place at the table, the rest of us were midway through the main course.

She asked why we had a stranger here. Paul gulped. When Bob defended our guest as "the best company I've had in years," she accused everyone of turning on her and demanded we leave—Bob, Jonny and Debby, and Bridey as well.

Downstairs Paul and I phoned a housemate with a car. He met us a half hour later on the corner. We barrelled along the Thruway in a blizzard (wasn't this what I had dreamed of through all of childhood—a flight from my mother to Grossinger's through a mythical storm?). We arrived past midnight.

My father roused himself. There was no room (though I cheerily suggested the basement floor). These friends, he chided (as he led me out of earshot), were communist vagabonds: "I don't like seeing you with people like that." In the end, though, he let me sleep in the basement and gave my accomplices staff rooms.

Over the next two days, as we wandered about the grounds, my buddies pointed out the decadence of Grossinger's—lower-echelon employees were mostly black, Hispanic, or Chinese; guests paraded past them like nobility. I had always seen it but never looked.

My father and I spent Christmas together in Miami Beach. He took me on a tour of his hangouts during the years he managed the Pancoast. I listened to his clichés about baseball, his put-downs of the Democratic Party—even his opinions on literature (he liked me to play devil's advocate in order to spur debate). He had set speeches for all occasions—about how he was outsmarting the unions . . . the precise context of his hole-in-one . . . the new buildings going up at the G . . . the horses at Monticello Raceway . . . and "my three sons." James, he reported, was a nasty little trouble-maker, Michael a full-fledged rabblerouser. In that company I came off quite well, though he continued to tell people how *he* had gotten me into Amherst. My writing and prep-school grades meant nothing; the Grossinger's network was the only power he respected. In restaurants he pouted if people didn't recognize him and bustle over to greet him ("He wants to be Jennie," Aunt Bunny twitted to his face). If we were unacknowledged too long he would manage to summon the owner or maître d' (even the chef), explain that he was Paul Grossinger from Grossinger's, and ask if they had ever been there, punctuating his performance with a falsely modest chuckle. I had learned by then to shrink into a pip.

I stayed at Rhonda's the rest of vacation, but the time had passed when we might become boyfriend and girlfriend. She was now dating a much older lawyer while I was applying to colleges out West, hoping to find like-minded writers.

Meeting Lindy changed everything.

She was a poet from Denver, a sophomore at Smith. Our first date was just before Thanksgiving. She was brash and sophisticated—a tall green-eyed dancer with a wise face and long straight hair, worn sometimes in pigtails.

If Rhonda was a flashy showgirl, Lindy was a Welsh goddess. Freshman year she had dated and broken up with the guy who lived across the hall from me at Phi Psi. He had hopes of reclaiming her and enlisted me as his liaison because she and I were both writers. I asked her out; we became friends in a couple of dates. She had a lover named Steve who was an architecture student at Penn. She travelled so often to see him, I stopped calling her. We all but forgot about each other.

We met again in the spring, literally by fate. I was playing a game with fate, asking it to produce something as I chose the long path rather than the obvious one across the Smith campus. I came upon Lindy. She had had a fight with her boyfriend and was feeling low. We shared a lemonade in town.

We were both reading D. H. Lawrence and wishing for a coming-of-age romance (ostensibly with someone else, for she considered me mainly an intellectual companion). Flowers turned their richest orange or blue ever; I studied with her in meadows and held her hand beyond nostalgia or regret.

Those last months before summer vacation were a metamorphosis. I took driving lessons in Northampton and got my license. I had an Amherst friend then, Schuyler, who was even more an anti-heroic loner than I. An intramural hockey opponent and eternal bad boy (who looked like Bobby Kennedy), he would raise his stick at me in pugnacious challenge, which is how I met him. He loved to contradict teachers, to mock girls who thought they were pretty, to put himself down with satirical woe: "I guess I'm no damn good." He was always complaining about Ivy League/Madison Avenue culture that wanted to turn us into soapsuds dudes and Barbie-doll gals. He hung out with Psi U rebels, led me on fraternity escapades, and taught me the measure of man I wanted to be.

Not quite lovers, Lindy and I lay beside a lake under rows of clouds skimming (as we were) at light speed toward an unknown world. Life took on a profundity deeper than the labyrinth of memory or even constellations in the night sky. Although I experienced flickers of an ancient malaise, I also found in myself a new kind of fathomless joy. Nothing from before her seemed serious or worth preserving—the sanctuary of Grossinger's, the lineage of Yankee and Mets teams going back to childhood, my writing, even my vaunted sessions with Dr. Fabian and Dr. Friend.

Our parting for summer was a crossbreeze of sweet and melancholy moods. We were precisely between childhood and life and for the first time intuited the vastness of our freedom. She went home to Denver sure that our infatuation wouldn't last. I was, she said, still "a kid."

I returned to Grossinger's to face the continued dilemma of my role at the Hotel. This time my father upgraded his opening offer to reservation clerk. That looked even deadlier, for I couldn't escape a front-desk assignment. I asked him if I could find my own job; to my surprise he agreed (though he held out the threat of making me a dishwasher if I failed). Lindy was working for *The Rocky Mountain News* in Denver, so I sought a local equivalent. Needing a car, I went to Grandma hoping she'd find me one without involving my father. To my astonishment she offered her Lincoln: "I don't go anywhere, and when I do I'll use Harry's chauffeur."

In this pretentious vehicle I drove from town to town around a forty-mile radius, applying at each newspaper office.

Gradually I perceived the unlikelihood of any of these antique gazettes even understanding the concept of a college student. Outside the borders of Grossinger's I found nineteenth-century villages with cranky bureaucrats, zombi-like trade shops. They made dishwashing look like a haven.

As I was running out of options (having reached the Delaware River and the Pennsylvania line), at a weekly on Callicoon's main drag I found a willing publisher named Fred Stabbert. Chagrined that I came from the Grossinger family (since his liberal paper opposed the hotels' tax breaks), he insisted on calling my father first for permission. I learned later that the two men exchanged a good laugh at my expense.

Fred hired me to copy-edit and write captions, but I soon convinced him to let me explore Sullivan and Ulster Counties in search of human interest. All July and August I covered small towns and back roads.

I had a girlfriend who was a waitress at the Hotel, but I also had a crush on a stylish poet Schuy had found waitressing in Edgartown (where he was racing sailboats). Her name was Diana; she had just finished Smith and was earning money to travel in Europe. I drove to Cape Cod on my day off, and she and I sat on the beach spotting Schuy's colors while she intermittently read me her poems and I told her fortune from cards I set on sand.

The summer of '64 was full of the old promise of Grossinger's. I came and went on my own schedule, using the Hotel pump for gas, bringing desserts from the bakery to *The Sullivan County Democrat* crew at lunch, hunting Catskills exotica—a tribe of black Israelites camped in the woods with their queen, a Japanese man disseminating cherry orchards, a school for juvenile delinquents modelled on Summer Hill and run by a priest who had just marched in the South.

Aunt Bunny had her own coterie of artist and film-maker friends which included two potential suitors, about whom she kept me up-to-date in dialogue I imagined rewriting as *Absalom, Absalom!:* "He said he wanted me to come with him, but I told him Paul, and he said how could you stay?, and I said I don't know but I keep staying, and all the time Richard, watching, wondering how to do his own life."

I joined her clique for late wine at the Lake and read tarot for adults swimming naked under the Moon Card.

My conflict with my father softened. We were compatriots much of the time, following the Mets on TV, joining guests and relatives in the dining room. He was alternately cheerful with me—my old childhood benefactor—and incensed. He didn't like me spending time with Aunt Bunny because "you two just agitate each other." In fact, he blamed me for her anxiety attacks and said that if I didn't "encourage her to think provocative things she wouldn't get so upset."

Our clash of values, which had surfaced around women and my unwillingness to work for him, now dissipated into the more mischievous territory of ideology. I made him an easy mark: I was writing for the one non-Republican (and anti-hotel) newspaper in the county and was vocal in my support of his staff. He began good-humoredly calling me "his communist son," warning that the union was out to steal everything I might someday inherit. He had no idea what the real socialists among my friends were like—how unforgiving their critique of his circle.

For me the issue was less rooted in labor politics and more in the times I would side with Grandma Jennie and he would scold me for encouraging her charity. My father sometimes acted grandly, but other times he was mindlessly cruel, bossing around bellhops and drivers and mocking my brother Michael for his eccentricities and poor grades. Over the years most of my favorite staff members were fired, and my father always had the same explanation—they were crooks. The list grew to include Irving the famous ice pro, Abe the original athletic director, Eddie the comic-strip house detective, and even Milkshake Milty. Almost without my notice (because their departures occurred between my visits) the native characters disappeared—delightfully ornery waiters and daredevil chauffeurs, flamboyant chefs, exotic social directors, regal Old World managers—all replaced by hulks, drones, and bland functionaries. My father had an almost doctrinaire pessimism about human nature. He seemed to see the potentially exploitative side of every relationship (himself as victim), while my grandmother pretended naively to view everyone generously.

That summer Grandpa Harry died of a heart attack. At the time, I was in Washington, D.C., in the employ of *The Democrat,* having flown there with Milton Blackstone and Grandma to cover an airport hearing at which they both were speaking (Milton now felt the destiny that was escaping the Catskills was recoverable only in an international jetport). He decided to stay and give his testimony but hired a small plane for me to take my grandmother home.

Upon hearing the news, Grandma turned grim. Then, totally out of character, she said: "He lived too long, the bastard." After that she was taciturn, all the way to the airport and into the air.

We flew along the coast, inland across Pennsylvania. Approaching Grossinger Airport, our plane was engulfed by magically arising thunderheads. "There's no word on these babies!" the pilot exclaimed.

As we floated and shook, Grandma remained resolute. She was in some sort of trance.

"It came from fucking hell!" roared the co-pilot.

Gusts of wind buffeted us; hail drummed on our shell. Colors were brilliantly liquid, layers of cotton that seemed to curl in timelapse. Amidst strobe-bright lightning, old bowling balls rolled through the sky.

Suddenly Grandma began shouting curses at Grandpa Harry, accusing him of trying to block her return.

The co-pilot and I tried to distract her, but she shook her head as though we were children: "He won't succeed. I'll have my victory. It's my hotel!"

After three forays the pilot was forced to give up. "I have never seen one like it," he told me. "So concentrated. From 'The Twilight Zone.'"

We landed in bright sun in a pasture a mile away. Harry's current chauffeur, Ray, was waiting for us there. The plane pulled up to the car like in a movie. I held my grandmother by the elbow and helped her off.

"Now you take orders from me," she snarled at Ray.

"Like hell I do," he said. "I'll never take orders from you."

He quit the next morning.

I heard from Lindy three days later:

> The society editor is having a knock-down drag-out fight now with the city editor and I have to look busy on the pain of death, so I'll write what is a long overdue letter.
>
> My father called me at work yesterday to tell me that your grandfather or step-grandfather, Harry Grossinger, died. He had read it in the afternoon edition of THE DENVER POST. He was 76, sole founder and owner, it said, of Grossinger's, which he developed from a country-farm type of boarding house into a world famed resort. Well, it was spooky-fantastic to read about that in the paper. Somewhat like looking at the bread wrapper of Grossinger's Good Rye Bread with the picture of the white-haired woman in the corner, which is in my desk drawer for some reason at home. My mother said, "Think what a wake that funeral will be." What I wonder about this death is what it is to you, if you were close to him, and what the funeral was like. This isn't morbid interest, just wondering.

All I remember is riding in a limo, my brother Michael and Eddie Fisher on either side of me. As the entourage wound downhill into Liberty, Eddie tapped Michael on the shoulder and pointed to the local marquee: *What A Way to Go.*

Paul, Elaine, and Jennie finally ruled all of Grossinger's.

Instead of reporting on the airport hearings I wrote a tribute to Harry Grossinger, the architect of Grossinger's, whose death raised the biggest cumulonimbus in County history, uprooting trees that had stood for centuries, tearing down all his scaffolding. The *Democrat* not only published it but distributed a broadside version throughout the Catskills.

During the period of mourning, Aunt Bunny disbanded her salon. She was in no shape to embrace the Grossingers. Her heart was half-gypsy, half proto-feminist, but her house role was that of trophy wife. She had come to the Hotel as a teenager, and what sustained her in this madhouse was a mere artifice of evasions. One evening I found her in bed, shaking. I tried to talk her out of it. She said it was the worst panic ever—she wanted to die.

I gave the only advice I could think of—that she should flee while she still had a chance, start a new life somewhere else.

She shook her head. "It's too late. I've already blown it."

My father's doctor dispatched her to a New York hospital. I was told not to contact her. The implication was familiar: I was dangerous.

But then, before I returned to Amherst, my father gave me a brand-new yellow Mustang. He had it parked outside the main entrance. While he watched from his window smiling, a bellhop handed me the keys.

I hadn't earned it. He was furious at me. Bad things were happening everywhere. It was a gift without warning or explanation.

In the middle of that summer Lindy had begun dating a police reporter. He was serious enough about her to leave his wife and take a job with an ad agency in New York (to be close to her). Engaged in this romance, she arrived in Northampton.

For the first six weeks of the term she and I hung around as before, inseparable buddies but also quarrelling over her lover. Our dinners out and study dates were capped by anguished farewells. "Passion isn't something you can talk someone into," she insisted. "It's something you feel or don't. I have it with Jim. He is my once and future person."

I found solace in the works of Jung and Yeats, Charles Olson's poems, and the Case tarot. I embraced gyres and archetypes of the collective unconscious, Klee rainbows and mandalas of ourobori and astral lotus blooms.

Driving back from Smith at twilight I conceived a ceremony so profound it might glimpse what I fathomed in my heart. I enlisted others at Phi Psi, and for the next two weeks we choreographed a ritual of Chinese temple music, candlelight, chants, trickster tales, tarot cards on plywood, and slides of galaxies, cells, and flowers projected on sheets blowing in the trees.

On Halloween visitors came from near and far, word having spread through my high-school friend Chuck to his acquaintances at other colleges.

At nightfall we gathered in the glen behind Phi Psi, aliens on a remote world. I read a piece I had spent the afternoon writing—an account of our passage through Kodachrome galaxies and frauds of overlit Sunoco culture into a new occult world age that would liberate ancient demiurges.

Though Lindy spent Halloween in New York, she returned to school having broken off her relationship. Away from the newspaper in the cosmopolitan city her guy seemed parochial and bigoted. She wondered how she had ever fallen for him.

From the report of that evening and a copy of my speech, the poet and hermetic scholar Robert Kelly summoned me to his salon on the Hudson.

Meanwhile Aunt Bunny had been released from the hospital, and her friends were throwing a "welcome home" party in Manhattan.

On my twentieth birthday, November 3rd, Lindy and I took our first trip together, down through Massachusetts, along the Connecticut Turnpike. We joined the streams of urban lights. The two women in my life met and drank a gin together. At ten o'clock Lindy and I said good-night, retrieved the car, and drove the Thruway to Grossinger's.

Our arrival after midnight recalled everything this place had been to me—a city on a hill, a candy mountain marking the site of childhood. After touring near-deserted lobbies we climbed over the glass partition of the coffee shop, made six-flavor milk shakes (in memory of Milty), and sat there sipping them from frosted silver.

On the way back to Massachusetts we stopped at Bard College to meet Robert Kelly. A huge man with a bushy red beard, he lived in an apartment on the edge of campus. Dusty and unheated, covered with horoscopes, poetry broadsides, and alchemical drawings, it was at once a beatnik pad and the chamber of Merlin.

After praising my Halloween oration, Kelly proceeded (over lunch at a Chinese restaurant in Kingston) to initiate Lindy and me into esoteric literature and poetry. Later that month (on his suggestion) we drove to a New York loft to hear Diane Wakoski perform her Queen of Pentacles poems, after which Jerome Rothenberg belted out Amerindian blue souls and dadaist round dances.

Midway through Christmas vacation I flew to Denver. Lindy met my plane, and we drove to her house on a quiet suburban block. Christmas lights in the windows, snow in patches on the front lawn, this was my daydream past, my concealed future. Her parents, her married sisters, and their husbands were on hand. I was introduced in a flurry and offered this and that to eat and drink.

While treating me gingerly, everyone expressed enthusiasm about my visit. Her mother and father were quite a bit older than mine, silver-haired and not quite the Rotarians Lindy feared (there was a touch of New England left in them). Since I had been told in advance about her father Hank's eclectic interests I sought him out for talk about UFOs and Indians.

Her oldest sister Susie reminded me of Bob's sister Et. She was friendly if slightly aloof. Her husband was a business executive in Denver. He fulfilled his cliché by speaking with authority about profit margins; Lindy flashed me a cute smile behind his back.

Her next oldest sister, Polly, had Lindy's eyes and wise look, but she acted clever and cynical. Her voice dominated the group. After a few minutes she led me aside and whispered, "Boy, am I glad you're here. I've been hearing about some of Lindy's flings, married men and all. I always knew my good-looking kid sis was going to attract the wrong types." Her husband was a smooth, stocky psychiatrist who had flown jets in the Navy.

The Houghs were more self-conscious about my being Jewish than they needed to be. After all, we were all Americans, and I was far more committed to the teachings of Thomas Merton than to anything I had learned at Hebrew School. Angels and alchemists were Christian; the tarot was gnostic and Qabalistic both.

On Christmas morning I read to them from Merton's sermon on Prometheus: about our foolishness in trying to steal things God is only too willing to give us for free, making ourselves into fake heroes and thieves in order to deny his bounty and generosity.

The anti-materialism came across, so it was not their favorite message, but they thanked me for sharing it with them.

Lindy and I spent the rest of junior year travelling the Northeast, stopping often at Bard to meet artists, dancers, film-makers, and poets; to hear about Yogananda, Afghan and Sioux cosmology, and Black Mountain arts. Afterwards we drove along backroads to Grossinger's. It was a deliciously reckless transition, from sitting on Kelly's dusty floor, shivering, hanging on every metaphor and syntactic disjunction, to (three hours later) ordering room service, then walking over to the nightclub for a beer.

Under Kelly's aegis we took on the "great work" together—the techniques of tarot and astrology, Gurdjieffian physics, alchemy as individuation, and philosophies of the Sufis and Jains. Less than fifty miles from the fairytale world of my childhood I had found another universe—as different and auspicious as Grossinger's had once been for me, and equally at a time when I needed something and didn't know what. Ludicrously tiny compared to the resort, Kelly's kingdom was actually a million times larger, for it was a crystal ball, an atom that held the lodestone, the key to my next transformation.

By spring Lindy and I were his disciples. No longer neophytes, we dropped our fiction careers and began composing hermetic essays and projective verse. We wrote each other love poems and became lovers.

With the group that put on the Halloween ceremony, we launched a journal we named *Io* (after a moon of Jupiter)—our own gathering of poems, myths, and science-fiction notes. We published a first issue, thirty-two pages with a stapled binding. It was composed on a fancy typewriter and then run by my friend Stanley in between assignments on the Grossinger menu press. Stacked beside colored roosters, the *Ios* were black mothwings and screwheads around a pictograph of the banded planet and its moon. We distributed them not only at Amherst and Smith but in literary bookstores throughout the country.

We were no longer Amherst and Smith undergraduates. We had entered the Druid forest, the Pawnee waking dream.

8

Making a Home (II)

That summer there was no compromise with Grossinger's. I had outgrown even my rebellion. When I arrived from college, Aunt Bunny was back in the hospital, and my father expected me to report to his office for duty. My first night he kept pounding out a case against Lindy. She wasn't Jewish, and he presumed her interest was a greedy one—in his wealth. He mainly wanted me to get a haircut.

The second morning I packed the Mustang and took off on highways west across Pennsylvania into Ohio and Indiana, then Iowa and Nebraska, reading *Lord of the Rings* for company (and confirmation of a millennial undertaking). Lindy and I met in the Colorado Rockies and rented a cabin in the woods. I found a job as busboy and janitor at a jazz-piano restaurant; she tended bar at the Toklat, cleaned the postmaster's house, and wrote stories for the *Aspen Illustrated News.*

This was the summer at the absolute center of time. We lived in the sound of the Roaring Fork, shivering out of bed at daybreak to light the woodstove and fill the kettle with water. All my puppet selves stopped their frenetic imitation of life. I learned what it was like to dwell on the Earth in peace, to feel existence as simple as a thread flowing from a spool. I was no longer at war with the fact or frame of my being, or the myth of my traumatic past.

Amherst and Smith were coming to an end, and we had no plans for beyond them. "Each other"—the magical work Kelly had assigned to us—was the one thing we could count on.

We were a few years from the era when people lived together permissibly. "My parents couldn't stand that," Lindy said. So in the fall we decided to apply to graduate school together and get married.

Our strategy was to go to our separate families at Christmas and tell them our plans, then meet in Bloomington, Indiana, and begin looking for a campus.

My father was so furious he could barely talk to me. "You'll get no more money out of me!" But I wasn't asking for that.

I went for a walk across the outermost grounds, punting lumps of ice, trying to tap the wonder of when I came there as a virtual orphan.

In New York my mother was equally negative, though she tried persuasion, urging me not to be rash. Like my father she didn't believe anyone could really love, let alone marry me. She had no idea who Lindy was.

She didn't think a wedding would really happen. It seemed to her just yesterday I was a dreamy, asocial boy.

Yet beneath my fragile surface was an intractability mirroring her own. I left the next morning for Denver, drove like a banshee, and arrived at Lindy's house for Christmas.

It was okay. I was hardly the son-in-law they imagined, but they welcomed me. At Lindy's suggestion I asked her father for her hand and, though he wondered how we'd earn a living, he didn't see why not.

On the way back East, we stopped to visit schools in Indiana and Michigan.

When the letters of acceptance (and rejection) came, we chose Ann Arbor, even though Lindy hadn't gotten in. I was on a waiting list for a Fellowship there, whereas neither of us had gotten one at Bloomington.

In the fall I learned that the only reason my Fellowship was delayed was because several members of the Michigan department felt that giving money to a Grossinger was akin to funding a Carnegie. So good a job had Blackstone done that thirty years later his image of Grossinger's thousands of times outglittered the austere reality.

The letter granting funds was like a wedding gift from the gods.

In June my two families came to graduation, the second time in my life I saw them together. It was the height of the Vietnam War, and a bunch of us wore black arm bands and walked out of the proceedings because Hawks dominated the podium and an honorary degree was given to Robert McNamara. My father threatened to retaliate by boycotting the wedding: "I don't like *it* just like you don't approve of our Vietnam policy."

Two days later I attended Lindy's graduation as her only fan (her parents said a wedding was quite enough excitement for June). Tall and buoyant in cap and gown, she took her diploma from the elderly president with a cheerful smile and followed the row of girls back to her seat. The next morning we rented a U-Haul and set out for Ann Arbor. The sun was supernaturally bright. Memory lay in all directions: a sphere intersecting a plane, fields flat and eternal with goldenrod. The Mass Pike had Oz written all over it. Our life together had begun.

By the end of the week we had rented the upstairs of a small house near campus. From there we continued to Denver.

Lindy and I were married in her backyard, a plain ceremony with a benediction from D. H. Lawrence. I got a haircut and beard trim from her father's barber and wore a dark suit; she wore a simple Spanish gown.

They all attended, even Grandmas Jennie and Sally. My mother's brother Edgar came from San Francisco with his wife and daughter. My brother Jon was my best man. Jennie walked around hugging guests, clasping hands and thanking everyone for being there as if it were the Grossinger's dining room. Pale and drawn, my mother inhabited the occasion like a specter. I did not understand how unimaginable, how traumatic it was, for her to see me suddenly grown up and gone.

In the fall I took genetics, linguistics, cultural anthropology, and a course on peoples of the Middle East. I attended classes rotely, looking forward to domestic times together—collecting second-hand furniture, shopping for groceries, outings along the Huron River, autumn mornings at the farmers' market.

I looked back through my own complication at a primordial haunting I wanted to transform or evade forever. The melodrama and exile of childhood had resolved themselves in Lindy-Rich. The snows of November fell, and then came a lilac-magnolia spring.

My department advisor, Skip Rappaport, had been in the hotel business before going to graduate school, and he once managed the inn where my father stayed during the years he visited Aunt Bunny at her sanatorium. In addition, Rappaport's own father, a management consultant, had been hired by my father years later to do a business analysis of Grossinger's at the time of the Grau lawsuit. It was from Skip that I found out how my Grossinger lineage nearly cost me my Fellowship. He shook his head at the notion that Grossinger's was anything more than a failing business run by a quarrelsome family bent on self-destruction. At least he could tell that to the deans at Michigan. My Fellowship, he laughed, was the sole concrete result of his father's study.

In ensuing terms I studied phonetics, archaeology, ethnobotany, plant morphology, ecological anthropology, Hopi ceremonialism, and Indians of South America. While building a subscription list, Lindy and I published issues of *Io* on Indians, alchemy, Mediaeval botany, and ethnoastronomy. Through Kelly's pipeline we got work from poets Charles Olson, Edward Dorn, Robert Duncan, and others, including Theodore Enslin, who was a lay homeopathic doctor in Maine.

My writing wove fragments of kinship and plant lore, Palaeolithic Africa and pre-Columbian Mesoamerica, Hopi Snake Dances and Sioux totems, all in a syllabary of dreams and visions, rock lyrics and baseball.

My narrative was generic and autonomous. Its title was *Solar Journal,* and I made separate *Alchemical Sections, Oecological Sections, Botanical Sections, Astronomical Sections,* and *Psychological Sections.*

The rays of the universe fall in our fields, the seeds of Andromeda . . . in bogs and by railroad tracks, in cracks between cement on the sidewalk, in junkyards and pipes. Ribbons of flesh do a round dance about the nucleus; the caller squawks, the couples change partners, the matrix twilled ... the canary clan and the clan of the domestic hen wed (their child is a hawk).... The annulus of the fern snaps, casting sporangia into the wind, fluids cut to the stone, the knife-sharpener in the streets (he sings an Inca funeral dirge; in the room above, Sherlock Holmes begins to listen, his fingers straying on the piano ...). The spores of the scouring rush cast out wings on which they float. The wind melts their darkness, cracks their shell; the claws of the badger open the pie.

By the third year of coursework Lindy was pregnant. My father, who had been out of touch since the wedding, began to phone on the slightest pretext. He sent presents—a new lamp, a set of electric mixing bowls, a used TV from the Hotel. I had never expected him to be so pleased by a grandchild, especially one who wasn't Jewish.

On the evening of June 18th I sat beside Lindy at St. Joseph's hospital, coaching her breathing, getting her ice. Her contractions built until, at dawn, a head crowned; the doctor grasped, pulled, and held aloft a creature too real to behold. He presented it to us who were barely awake, a son we named Robin.

A month later we drove to Mount Desert Island, Maine, and moved into a cottage at Green Island Landing, half a mile from the ocean.

Those first days I crawled with Robin through grass and clubmoss and chased endless bounces of a Spaldeen off the roof against the background of wilderness, making the most ecstatic diving and leaping catches of all time. Our city cats sniffed in wonderment and bounded into the brush. Only a short stroll down a dirt path, Lindy and I dug clams for dinner. On the radio the Mets were being blown by destiny to their first pennant.

Bearing infant chair and shoulder carrier that fall and winter, we travelled the Maine coast, calling upon lobster sheds, fish-dealers' wharves, mud flats, and worm cellars, collecting material for an ethnographic study.

The rhythm of the Atlantic seeped in, fish pulp and red crustacean shells, cries of seabirds, daily vista of boats going out and returning (etched at different scales of the harbor). The smell of bait was omnipresent, lobsters crawling atop one another in crates, muffs of my heavy coat against my beard. Robin, snuggled in a wool hat under his blue hood, tasted fresh snow, lifted on powder-blue mittens to his tongue.

Living up the coast from Charles Olson, I received odd missives from him, brief, irregular cards with a stamp that were barely more comprehensible than shards of Hittite pottery.

This was a poet whose work was central to my cosmology. Now he was enlisting me to write my own code to his North Atlantic text.

Day by day I peopled a book with Maine fishermen and Mesolithic hunters, alchemists and freemasons, kin to his sailors and explorers. *Solar Journal* was finished, its sections submitted to Black Sparrow Press in L.A. I stretched from the Bay of Fundy to Casco to Sullivan County, and I named this new material *Book of the Cranberry Islands*.

> *Out by Swans Island a buoy clanks its three different notes. It is frightening how this one possibility of sound endures . . . and endures . . . as a ferry passes, three metal arms striking into the circle, like a Telstar among islands. Here in the Atlantic, the Gulf of Maine is the asteroid belt; the forces of nature, volcanic and glacial, have splintered a possible planet into thousands of little ones, outers calming the waters inward in intricate crosscutting lees. Isle Au Haut. Burnt Island where Fred Beal's grandfather was born. Marshall's, where his father was. And Fred saw the light at Swans. Vinalhaven and Hurricane. Granite masses of trees and churches, their shatter zone leaving a wake of hundreds more tiny islands, dense lobster territory speckled with painted buoys.*
>
> *In perfect darkness I walk down the road, not shining the flashlight I carry. There is nothing to see, no haze from cities, no windows or cars, no lightning bugs or stars. Nothing. Utter silence. Until the clouds break and there is moonlight.*

As November came to an end, ice began to form on sea plants at Green Island Landing; howling things soared through branches. Snow covered the world. Studded tires (and occasionally chains) got us to and from our destinations. We tucked our newborn in and hugged under piles of covers, fearing every imaginary intruder. These were brisk, lucid times, for we were babes again.

Compared to Maine, the Catskills were post-glacial, so we journeyed to Grossinger's at Christmas and took turns watching Robin from chaises along the indoor pool while the other swam laps—then nestled by the bonfire at the skating rink where once I cast marinated pine cones and looked into flames for the green of copper and red of iron.

In April my book arrived from Black Sparrow—*Solar Journal: Oecological Sections.* I was astonished to find that not only had elder statesman Robert Duncan written its preface but, while quoting from my Halloween speech years earlier, he had placed me in a lineage of Pound and Olson. Even more significant than his praise was that he understood what had baffled Fabian so long ago—the link between the terror (the haunting) and the beauty and wonder: "...the word 'spooked,'" wrote Duncan, "is not incidental in [Grossinger's] plan and links his inspiration to the obsessions of the dying Jack Spicer, who saw true poetry as an area of interference, *noise,* from outer space."

It was never my parents' divorce or Nanny's fears; the spook was a messenger of cosmic static, an intimation of the unseen universe. If it hadn't been scary, it wouldn't have embodied the darkness. If my being hadn't split, I would never have had a chance to travel the gap and experience the primordial crisis.

I was witness to a mystery enshrouding another, far deeper mystery.

Lindy, *Io,* Robin, *Solar Journal* ... it was unfolding so rapidly I could barely grasp what was happening. I knew it went beyond galaxies and dreams, and I believed in it not because I deserved it but because it alone touched my ancient intuition of something else.

The same month as the publication of *Solar Journal,* Joel Pomerantz's version of Quentin Reynolds' book appeared as *Jennie and the Story of Grossinger's*—an unfortunate conjunction because, as my father and his executives at the Hotel saw it, some small publisher was trying to get rich on the Grossinger name.

I tried to explain the specialness of an endorsement from an elder statesman. But who was Duncan to him? Another fifth-rate shill, or even worse, an intellectual!

Soon afterwards, as a practicing Maine ethnographer, I went for a formal interview and, two days later, got an offer (by certified mail) of a position teaching anthropology at the Portland and Gorham campuses of the University of Maine. It was my first job, and I had had no idea what salary to request. $9,500 seemed a fortune, so I accepted.

Rentals were scarce, but we found a cheap old house and barn for sale on Mitchell Road in Cape Elizabeth.

Without money for a downpayment, I called my father. I knew that I was old enough to claim my *bar mitzvah* gifts, put away half a lifetime ago. I had no idea how much there was—he had never told me. Now he threw hurdle after hurdle, citing obscure legalities and finally auguring that I would squander it all. Though he proclaimed, "Absolutely not, under no conditions!" a check for $10,000 arrived along with $7,000 of IBM stock, grown from a single 1957 share, a gift from his insurance agent Walter Kaye.

Each morning that summer, in his room overlooking the orchard, Robin would lie on his back and babble, a softness of word formation like alphabet blocks. Whenever he began to jump up and down, our rescue squad would arrive, change his diapers, haul him to breakfast. Cats twisting around our legs called for breakfast too.

The lil' girls from across the street join us cleaning out the barn—broken casks of pesticide and nails, vines growing through walls, rotted boards—until finally we uncover a lost door and collapse it through foliage. Snake slides under rusty cans. Sunlight pours in.

Robin is delighted with a sun so bright he keeps looking up, then away. I tickle his nose with rib grass. He pries open milkweeds for their silky kites.

He stands at the top of the stairs, throwing all of his toys, men and dolls and stuffed animals and plastic rings. This is hilarious to him.

We buy a wading pool, animals painted on its inside, seahorse, flounder, and crab; the hose fills it. He sits in the grass, playing with colored cups. I set my legs around him, take off my sneakers and shirt.

I step in the water; he follows me; I put my feet on his; he laughs, puts his on mine.

'Are you still afraid?' a voice inside me asks.

'Every moment I live.'

"You're fine!" Lindy insists, pointing me out to myself in the mirror, curly-haired and bright-eyed, Robin's father.

And, if I need more reassurance, there is always Duncan: "Grossinger has opened for us a new era."

Lindy and I find each other in late afternoon. I cannot get enough, nor can I bear so much desire. I want it to end, and I want it to go on forever . . . her there suspended, tall imago of the woman I courted in college, nose and eyes chiselled so perfectly they could only be her. I am convinced now that even if I saw her without her body I'd recognize her.

I pull closer and closer till that spot where it breaks, and I wonder what it is that passes through me at the core, that melts and converts memory, becomes as silent and abundant as the rain.

In shadowed scale I see two elephants wrestling at twilight, their trunks engaged. They fall, heavy in gentleness, sliding past the frame.

Those summers we sat in the high grass in Aspen are gone, but their feeling is part of the whole feeling I have for her, like clouds against the sky. Our child born.

And there is no more, and there will be no more.

Whether or not this is enough.

9

The Dream at Grossinger's

My first Introductory Anthropology class was 9 AM in windowless Luther Bonney auditorium. I climbed onto a stage and stood behind a podium. Some seventy-five students sat in semi-darkness.

I introduced myself, described my fieldwork, and laid out the course. After just ten minutes my careful curriculum felt inflated and hollow. In subsequent meetings I experienced this problem more vaguely but also more profoundly. Yet, as I hung out with faculty in the lounge and exchanged academic gossip at lunch, I was sure this was the beginning of a life-long career.

Lindy and I discovered a budding hippie area off the wharves, its centerpiece, Erebus, an emporium of paisley and incense. The proprietor, Herb Gideon, wanted to court the growing University community, so he and I co-sponsored an experimental-movie night with psychedelic posters executed by his Beardsleyesque house artist. I ordered films of Aborigines and Ainu to go with masterpieces from Stan Brakhage and Kenneth Anger and, at the end (as a prank), I slipped in the Mets 1969 promotional film (hustled through an old Grossinger's connection). After an uproar of bewilderment (when the Borden cow mooed), about half the auditorium fled. The rest stayed and cheered.

In February I got a phone call from a professor at Kent State. He was organizing an arts festival to honor the students murdered on the campus by police the previous year; he already had acceptances from Robert Duncan and Allen Ginsberg. He wanted to make me the third guest.

"Am I political enough?"

"That's precisely the point," he shot back. "We want to get this out of the hands of the ideologues."

On opening day of the 1971 baseball season Lindy and I flew to Cleveland. A student picked us up at the airport and drove us to Kent. My sponsor had set aside a room upstairs in his house, a pile of blankets on the floor for Robin.

Duncan had a room just down the hall. Specks of gray in his sideburns, a large round face, he was both a warlock figure and merry Pan. Informally (as though to Robin) he recounted his own childhood initiation by séance and the lyrics of "Wynken, Blynken, and Nod," then made Australian Dreamtime and the Hebrew alphabet a single rite of passage. Such cosmic preaching left us speechless.

The festival was nonstop readings, panels, and parties. As Duncan and Ginsberg orchestrated their memorial service (with candles and chanting of the names of the slain), I felt less like a fellow headliner than a hick from Maine. In a procession led by Ginsberg playing Blake songs on his harmonium I was just another acolyte. The real avatar was an abstracted flow of writing with the name *Solar Journal*. I hid out, as ever, in his identity.

At the culminative reading, the auditorium packed with two thousand, Duncan strode to the podium and presented me first, as prearranged, telling the students I was their representative, *their* voice among the elders. "After that introduction I hope he doesn't blow it."

I looked into a sea of faces, gulped, then said, "I think we always blow it." After that I fled through passages of fishing dialogue, baseball, mythology, and Pleistocene migrations, hoping only to survive.

"We're all frauds," Duncan offered in an interlude of candor. "That's the point of writing. We create the only world in which we could survive."

Yet I felt empty and inflated, as though my mind-dance had taken me where my male body couldn't go.

From the party I called my brother in Colorado to tell him I was thinking of him, imagining the event through his eyes: me a rookie in my first game; Ginsberg, Mickey Mantle. "Before the reading, when we were backstage, I told Allen my stomach was upset, and he said, 'You know what I do!' I thought he was going to teach me a mantra or something. He pulled out a package of Tums."

"The old advertising man," Jon laughed.

The following term I taught alchemy under the alias of Primitive Culture, and Olson and Melville in a course on Whaling Ethnography. Two more of my "Solar Journals" were published: "Psychological Sections" (with the title *Spaces Wild and Tame*) by a small San Francisco press called Mudra, and "Astronomical Sections" by Black Sparrow as *Book of the Earth and Sky.*

Gary Snyder arrived that winter at Portland International, clad in logging clothes, bearing an embroidered leather briefcase—a culture hero preaching "Smokey the Bear" sutras and mountains and rivers without end.

"Richard, you write too much," he teased. "There's more to life." His surety on this matter surprised me. Since Kelly first proposed it as daily spiritual exercise I had taken my writing for granted.

"But zen is a better way to do all that," he offered, throwing his notebook on the floor of the car as we headed to the Gorham reading. "It's tried and true. It has millennia of refinement behind it. Practice zen instead of writing; practice wilderness."

At his departure I told him he made me feel empty, as though I had done nothing. "That's the teaching," he sighed. "If I've accomplished that, I've been successful."

"But I wonder what to do."

"Come to California," he said with a parting grin. "You'll change."

The opportunity arose surprisingly soon. Norman O. Brown, another culture hero, called to say he had been organizing a graduate curriculum called History of Consciousness at a new branch of the University of California at Santa Cruz. He wanted to interview me for one of his faculty slots. Could I come for a week in January and teach a seminar? They would pay plane fare plus a stipend.

As we flew out of Maine, snow reached our ground-floor windows. At SFO it was suddenly, giddily summer. Highway rolled by on a tropical scroll, as our student-guide Tree described the program. "The big topic these days," he warned, "is Nobby Brown's interpretation of Mao; the book: *The Chinese Road to Socialism* by Wheelwright and Macfarlane."

Our room was a bungalow among redwoods. Mammoth scags of bark all but pressed against our windows. The grove also plunged hundreds of feet below into a ravine, so that we hung in a space station, the Pacific sparkling beyond.

After Tree departed we went for a walk, still clothed in flannel. Students, barefoot and shirtless, wearing only shorts, pulled at roots and pushed wheelbarrows.

We hiked over a hill to a lounge, where we stuffed ourselves with five-grain donuts, paid for fifteen cents at a time. Our child lost all sense of limits, and I had to reach down his neck to wipe off jelly. He carried his last one down the hill, half running, half eating, and got going too fast to stop, so I dashed ahead, intercepted him, snatched him up, then ran with him giggling and gooey under my arm.

While Lindy washed her hair, we scouted the ravine. The black earth held decay of moss and bark, redwood droppings so medicinal one could almost bathe in them. This was like between battles when the troops frolic in alpine pools. And I recalled how Duncan invoked at Kent ("Santa Cruz Propositions") a force "that sweeps all stagnant things up/into a torrent of confidence, beyond thought."

An hour later our patron, Nobby, knocked on the door. Hand raised toward the window, "How do you like our kettle of fish?" he declared. He was a plump, bald savant, and it was hard to deny his assertion that this was the University of the Twenty-First Century. Imagine, a Ph.D. in Consciousness itself—Robert Duncan visiting professor. "Are you ready for introductions?" he quipped.

I handed Robin to Lindy through the door of Nobby's VW bug and we raced from there to the weekly Hist-Con potluck supper.

The room was a mêlée of grad students—bearded men, women in dungarees and sneakers. One dark-haired girl named Peggy stuck around longer than the rest. She was writing a thesis on the Fool in Southwestern Indian culture and wanted my assistance. "You're the ghost of honor," she teased. "We're expecting you to bail us out 'cause Nobby's the bossman and don't let no one through."

Later she walked Lindy and me to a vantage over the sea. "I'm amazed they invited you," she offered. "You're an elf-person compared to who usually comes. Last year they turned down some genius studying shamans and the pineal gland, and their first five choices for everything are Marxist radicals." She chuckled. "That's really a new kind of cookie with a cream filling which leaves you with a craving for blood and milk."

I assumed I would teach a separate class, so I was surprised when Nobby opened my first afternoon with a discussion of the Chinese harvest and the role of the erotic in collectivism: an offshoot of *his* master seminar. From there he and I dueled shamelessly; he preached Marxism in Cuba; I countered with terraforming Mars, Buckminster Fuller harnessing the tides of Fundy to end the age of fossil fuels, and Lévi-Strauss' interpretations of South American Indian myths (that all versions from different tribes express a single epistemological reality).

He taunted that this was idealist kitsch, so I closed by quoting from my friend, parapsychologist Jule Eisenbud:

"You see, this type of thing, this ability to simply step over time, as if there were no barrier at all, is of such metaphysical, philosophical importance as to render everything else patent pending. All the work of physics stops at this point and, in fact, because of this, physics in its present form is through."

"Hogwash," Nobby snapped. "You're talking hippie conspiracy-theory." Then he heralded the farms of Mao as a model for transforming humanity down to the germ plasm.

I rebutted with the decline of industrial, anti-ecological civilization in all forms (including Maoist), offering instead Yogananda transforming sunlight through his body's cells. When Nobby continued to promote proletarian agriculture and communalism—as though our human crisis were already solved—I parried with Merleau-Ponty's warning to Sartre: that we can't pretend at any moment we have been masters of things and botched them by our futility: "We never had clear choices, and the illusion of them just sets us in an eternal return of rivalry, granting to the young our own failed possibility. If you do that in China, or for that matter, on Mars, then like Sartre, you are spoiling your children."

Nobby raised both eyebrows, looked at the students, then back at me. I sensed he was about to pigeonhole me as "pop capitalist culture in need of reeducation."

"You make a case," he begrudged. "Whether it's a case worth considering I don't know. But unfortunately I don't doubt you'll find supporters in this room."

At the Whole Earth Restaurant, lunch was tahini paste with sprouts and nuts on whole-wheat buns. The mere existence of this campus cafeteria, I told Lindy, was evidence of a higher consciousness than the whole Maine State system.

"Wouldn't it be a trip," she enthused, "to get to move here?"

But Peggy cautioned us: In the previous year's Hist-Con student skit an actor dressed as Nobby's recent book *Love's Body* pranced in a penis costume. Its author was not amused.

"He can talk 'Love's Body'—" was her gloss "—and don't get me wrong: he talks a helluva game, but when the rowdy clown comes to play, he shuts down the ceremony. He is even stressed by the large number of good-looking gay women in this program, as though it were an aberration requiring discussion. Behind 'Love's Body' is your basic All-American paternalistic male."

Back in Portland we dreamed only of California. Each time Nobby called he asked our local temperature, then told me his. In letters Peggy expressed outrage at him, along with concern that, despite her groundwork and student support, my candidacy was slipping away.

Finally the bossman concluded that "the will of the Gods was not done"; he hoped I would have a fine career somewhere else.

Peggy's own epitaph read: "Fuck Brown—I'm not staying; I just had an unplanned meeting with Carlos Castaneda at which interesting things were said—expect to leave for Mexico as soon as I can get a grant written."

But Lindy had the notion we could go there anyway, get part-time teaching jobs, wait till something opened up. Her cheerfulness inspired me. I wrote the programs at which I had been interviewed, telling them I was available for part-time work.

I got only a terse note from Brown denouncing me for embarrassing him.

I responded with a bridge-burning letter, mocking his "will of the gods," his "kettle of fish," accusing him of flaunting temperatures. That was the end of Whole Earth heaven.

Robin and I cuddled in winter jackets under the tree, watching snow dust dance on ice.

Earlier that year I had received a note from Jerry Witherspoon, the president of Goddard College in Vermont. He had read *Solar Journal* and was interested in employing me if I was available. At the time I didn't take the possibility seriously: Goddard's reputation was unappealingly druggie. However, as months passed, the notion of a small town in the Green Mountains took on a new appeal.

When I wrote to Mr. Witherspoon again, he invited us to visit his campus. We picked a weekend in late March.

Snowstorms dominated the week, but by Saturday, skies were clear. We passed cows on mullein hillsides, long walls of flat stones, abandoned telephone poles with birdhouses, possible Viking cairns. These were ikons of a northern New England we had grown to love.

Goddard's funkiness was immediately apparent: it took almost an hour to find anyone who knew that we were coming or where Jerry was, and the first three times we mentioned his name we drew a grunt, a mute stare, and a "Fuck!" A surly student led us to our room in a cooking dorm. We collapsed on its bed amidst maximum-volume music and marijuana smoke and emerged to see kids in Afros, beads, red velvet sack dresses, and leather shirts. They bellowed and grunted at each other inches away.

I kept in my bubble. It wasn't that my brain didn't grasp these were the actual pupils. It was that I was well practiced in slinking through a parallel universe.

The next afternoon I attended a gathering of enthusiastic faculty and students led by Sheppard, an intensely blue-eyed freak with shoulder-length blonde hair. He knew my work and was a buddy of Ginsberg, so had called "Howl" headquarters and gotten my dossier. "You have no choice," he said. "You have to come here. I've made up my mind you're going to teach me."

Goddard didn't have the academic pretense of Amherst or History of Consciousness. When I mentioned Crowley, Gurdjieff, Olson, the group acted as though—well, what else is there?

Jerry, a tall former Vermont tax commissioner with graying curls, explained that the school was going through stormy times. "But our programs are surprisingly popular, and we have no lack of enrollments, so I think you can feel safe in coming here. It's just a matter of sifting through the '60s and coming up with what will pay its way."

An English professor from San Francisco State added: "No grades, no tests; you're lucky if a quarter of the kids do one-tenth the reading. But you've got freedom to seek epiphany." He had quit a tenured position to join up.

"We tried to keep them from putting you in that dorm," Shep confided. "The place is a zoo. But I think some of the politicos made sure that you'd see it. Understand, those assholes weren't rude by accident. You were supposed to be scared out of your wits."

On the way back to Maine we stopped at the New Hampshire farmhouse of Russell Banks, a writer with whom we had been corresponding. If it had been twenty years later, our host might have taken on the Rasta voice of his famous character I-Man: "Up to you, guys." But we were young still, so he said, "After Portland, hiding out in some inland mountains sounds great."

The night Jerry's offer came I dreamed of a ranchero somewhere around Monterey. A sun was shining through a sky that was blue even by dream standards, and the clouds—I told my sleeping self—were thoughts in someone else's mind. The mountains were higher than any I had seen, treacherous along their sides. They were the rims of Venus, soaring above surface fog. In the distance toward San Francisco were ballfields. Rams and alpacas grazed. A football squad worked out beside glaciers.

Beneath dream promontories (and "across the huge cold silence of the universe"—Russell Banks) all the places we might have gone merged and became the same.

Our search for a house near Goddard began at a real-estate office in Montpelier, ten miles from the college. The agent checked her listings, then took us on tour. It was a landscape of mountain cottages and farms, almost everything up in the hills. When we worked our way back into Plainfield proper she checked her binder and found "only one house sort of for sale. The note says it belongs to an ex-faculty now out of the country. It also says it's rented to uncooperative students."

On cue they refused her knock.

By the next day she had the key. We tiptoed inside. Bedspreads were tacked over windows; holes punctured plaster; graffiti covered bathroom walls. Every room but the kitchen had been turned into a bedroom—mattresses, papers, and clothes on the floors, people camped even beside the washer and dryer and in the attached unheated barn.

We had found our home.

At Grossinger's that August our one-time boarder Jerry MacDonald was in town visiting. He had become guidance counsellor at a school in Rockland County so, as we chatted in the backyard, he quizzed me on colleges. Then we talked about the old days and the subsequent decline of Grossinger's.

"I'm not sure anymore, Richard," he sighed. "I only hope it looks worse than it is. You know Paul. He's always got one up his sleeve."

"Not this time, Bunny thinks."

"C'mon now. When have you ever known her to act different. Bunny wouldn't be satisfied unless the chief rabbi of Israel and the President put their stamp on it." He thought about that and chuckled. "And even then she'd probably want the signature of the Director of the Bank of Liberty, just to make sure."

The lightweight boxing champion of the world is warming up on flapjacks, memory of Marciano. Old-time ball-players from Santo Domingo gather in Panama hats and join us hitting/fielding flies light as calypso. A New York real estate mogul mocks his Puerto

Rican waiter, pantomiming for him what a toothpick is. He has Spanish help in all his buildings and does an imitation of how it sounds to phone and get José Jimenez.

Motel-like barracks shoot up. A multimillion-dollar loan is floated on the new inflation, eighteen more golf holes . . . their green targets gleaming at sunset. The last toads and rotting tree stumps stand as beggars: scraggly and proud.

We flee along Route 55, through Neversink, toward Grahamsville, past New York's water supply and fields of corn. From the mountains we come down into Woodburne. Streets are packed with Hassidim and late-summer tourists awaiting buses. Kokhaleyn sit in clearings, no more than shacks around pools. They recall what the Catskills were. The crowds come to Grossinger's now to shun the memory, the fear that nothing will replace the nostalgia they once felt, in a gimp left leg rounding third base or a rusting shower in a shed with peeling paint . . . the rag-and-bone shop no luxury or immortality can restore.

I find myself more and more reaching toward a mythological past, pointing out to Lindy the lingering archaeology of the old Hotel. In my heart two eras occupy a single space: Stephens clothing store now run by a branch of Kriendlers, where elderly ladies try on bikinis; and the vanished canteen, where Milky Stackel, seven-foot retired center, drank one milk shake for every two he served, and guests sat in infinite time watching Reynolds, Raschi, and Lopat go against Lemon, Wynn, and Garcia.

Cousin Jay's baseball field and Grandpa Harry's crown-jewel indoor pool (built on its site) now seem to fuse into a single plaza beyond time.

Queen Jennie, cut off from her senses by stroke, sits in her chair, teased by her own nurses. "Who is that?" they ask in mock honor, pointing to her portrait by a master, completed fifteen years earlier. She stares dumbfounded while they wait.

"My lady!"

Lindy, Robin, and I bump in a golf cart with my brother James (back from hotel school at Cornell). "Remember the father turtle we caught?" I ask.

He grins.

"But how did it get in there," Lindy asks, "if the pond is man-made?"

"Not the whole thing," Jimmy corrects. "See the far part, out there." He points to a hillside that is not Grossinger's, where cows graze. "That was here already."

As Robin runs along the floating green with its numbered flag, dozens of frogs break the light.

In my dream I am walking through scaffolding, rooms that crumble (vines grow in); sunlight spills over radiator steam and peeling paint.

This is a land unchanged between visits. I enter always by the same route, cross the same forgotten vistas, to find it. The pool is drained, its bottom covered with yellowed leaves. The upper lobby, lined with jewelry shops and cosmetics bars, leads down a carpeted staircase to the old Blackstone office at 221 West 57th Street, ninety miles and thirteen years away, where hundreds of brochures lie stacked and faded in dusty corners.

I am coming upstairs through rows of towel hampers and dead juke boxes to the last door. It opens to the synagogue.

No. This is where the synagogue used to be—it is now a library filled with Qabala. Massive tarot cards adorn the stucco. All the time this was hidden in Grossinger's. Any rabbi would have known!

In the complication of staircases I pass my father's first tiny office—long ago demolished—on the edge of the new wing. Turning the corner I come to what I have seen only in photos—the landmark turret of the Terrace Hill House, rooms around its balustrade, a Victorian porch.

My great-grandfather Selig stands on the widow's walk, eyes cast beyond his lifetime. Try to locate him today and he is nowhere—a clock maybe, a portrait of a pipe-smoking immigrant on the lobby wall—or my middle name.

At the apotheosis of my dream is something I don't understand and have never understood. It comes from the pale forgotten morning I most fear. Sunlight is too lemony.

They are too large. They are not really appletrees. They are something unknowable that appletrees stand for in a dream.

I don't belong here.

I slip past the mansions of "Uncle Paul" and "Aunt Elaine." I come to where Michael and James should be playing, but there are other people gathering in a Mediaeval ceremony, whole families, strangers who welcome me, costumed kids who draw me into an applefight.

In the distance Aunt Elaine and Uncle Paul are approaching in old-fashioned coats like characters in a Dickens novel.

I haven't even been born. This may not even be the Earth.

What strange fruit, almost luminous! Such a dense winey smell!

But I will never know it outside this dream.

The feeling is so strange, so horrible, and yet true to something. Beautiful if only I didn't feel its hollow draining away my life.

I know this place. It is why I was homesick once at Grossinger's. It lies in my heart, a bitter drop of Moon. But I keep telling myself it must be a memory, either from when I first came here . . . or of another universe somewhere else and long ago.

Book Two

TURETSKY

1

Jonathan

When he was five years old he beat up Harry Pin in the 96th Street playground. At eight he was a punchball slugger in the P.S. 6 yard, whacking a Spaldeen over the wire fence and circling make-shift bases in imitation of Mickey Mantle's power gait. From there he graduated to hardball and football and was "rookie of the year" (in everything, 1955) at Bill-Dave Group, then MVP of Color War at Camp Chipinaw. Led by Captain Siggy Zises, the seniors hoisted him off the field after his game-winning double.

Jon was also a relentless provocateur, and so "Harry Pin" came back in innumerable guises. On the school cement they'd go at it, punching and grappling, surrounded by a gaggle of seconds. Jon's almost angelic mien belied the irrevocability of his battles. Warned by the principal, he promised to stop. But the choice was never his.

He was president of his class, honor student, all-star shortstop at Bill-Dave, and later, quarterback of the JV football team at Horace Mann and co-captain of the track team. He wore a gold wool sweater and parted his hair down the middle; was (at the same time) young Judge Brandeis and Number Seven, the Mick. Leslie Uggams made her debut at his *bar mitzvah* in 1961 with a medley of show tunes and soft rock. She was twenty-one, a senior at Barnard and a budding star herself. Despite the rabbi's jitters, Jon's father picked her for the occasion. Relatives spoke of Princeton, law school, then maybe the first Jewish president.

Jon was our mother's charmer. She dressed him, brushed his hair, and stood back to admire his good looks—so blatantly that I winced at my own imagined appearance.

Not only was Jon their true son, he was reassuringly normal to them. He had a great sense of theater. He threw a wobbly spiral and hit a natural backhand.

To any outsider my brother was "a great kid"—the sort of elegant, witty ruffian the 1950s anointed as its leader. It was an era when winning and losing—success and failure—were more than mere games. And Jon was a victor at every level.

From my vantage, hating him, I saw only a show-off. I imagined myself the secret target of all his performances, as when he rendered 7 times 7, 7 times 8, and 7 times 9, etc., for the family at dinner with flirtatious eyes and little cute slides of his voice (bringing grins to his parents' faces), or when Mickey Mantle hit a home run on the radio and he ran the bases in the living room, couch to chair to bureau to TV, touching each with a stylish slap, and then flashed a wake-up stare at me.

Nothing was neutral with Jon. Every move had a dig or flourish. When he was beating me in Monopoly, he called out "house" or "hotel" or "mine" in a particularly aggravating voice. He had a way of saying, "Your turn," that sounded like a combination of conceit and contempt. I played on stoically, in everything, win or lose.

I detested his toys, his clothes. Cabooses were good, engines bad. Tugboats and barges were genial; motorboats and submarines butted in. The blue soldier was a friend, the red soldier an enemy. The llama and penguin helped and understood; the lion and the pig thought they could go anywhere. A winter coat with a zipper was "us"; a winter coat with a belt was "them." We had a hood that tied tight; they had a show-offy fur collar and earmuffs like a fighter pilot. We had old-fashioned black boots with tin-woodman clasps, each a pal. They had stylish red boots with a sly over-and-done-with zipper on the side.

When Jonny wrote a composition on Andrew Jackson, he *became* Andrew Jackson (I even saw the physical resemblance after that). I grew to hate Jackson more than any other president, so that years later I was pleased to learn he could be blamed for the removal of the Cherokee. And as much as I wanted the Yankees to win, it was hard to accept Mickey's tape-measure homers.

Football and basketball I didn't even attempt because Jon was so good at them. I forfeited—a permanent 9–0 loss. I never shot a hoop or dodged a tackler—a perversity I regretted my whole life. I took myself out of the game.

After entering Horace Mann I ignored my brother. I headed for the bus each morning as he was waking up and, when I got home, I had too much work to be bothered. I could go for weeks without saying a word. This enraged him. Yet every time he "told," they found me concentrating at my desk. "Leave him alone," they said. "He's studying."

"You pig," he muttered. "I'll get you!"

Eventually he did.

"He's out to punish the kid," my mother burst in. "He's jealous because he can't do the things Jonny can. But he's the one who suffers."

"So that's it!" Bob exclaimed. "You silent needler, you piece of slime, you . . . !"

"I hated you so much back then," Jonny recalled after we had grown up. "It was like having the devil for a brother, the Prince of Evil. You knew how to get at me like no one else did. I couldn't defeat you. Even when I won fights you had a way of turning it around so it looked as though you won. And when I did something big and tried to lord it over you, you pretended not to care. I didn't believe you, but I couldn't get any pleasure. Then you were sick and crazy and had to go to a head doctor all the time. And your other family was rich knaves."

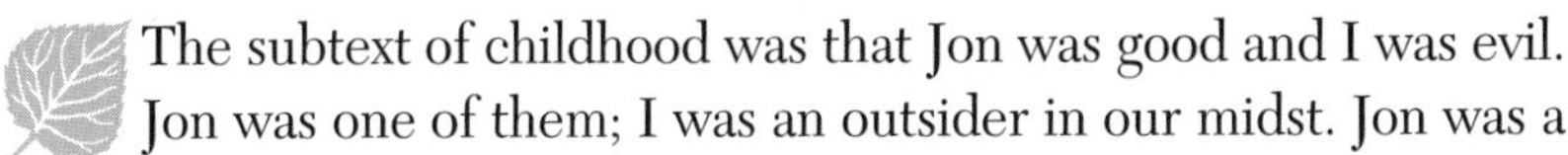

The subtext of childhood was that Jon was good and I was evil. Jon was one of them; I was an outsider in our midst. Jon was a star; I was a criminal. Jon was loving; I was conniving. If my brother was how to be in the world, I was a permanent "bad example"—for our Turetsky cousins, at P.S. 6, certainly at Park Avenue Synagogue. For all of childhood I called what I heard in my head "envy," "selfishness," "acting like a moron." I was ugly, ugly, ugly; hateful, hateful, hateful. "The joyless son of a bitch," Bob would say as I stood by sullenly while Jon entertained.

Yet in photographs from the time I am astonished to see Jon wasn't so much charismatic and princelike as intense and stolid, a proud extrovert. Standing beside him I look winsome and shy. I was stubborn and devious too (as they claimed), constantly shifting personae, tricking them.

My brother was also my buddy with whom I played Monopoly, Scrabble, Ocean Ball, and indoor baseball (with a sock and tennis racquet). From the dark of our beds we whispered word games—Geography; then Animal, Vegetable, Mineral, until we were too sleepy to talk.

At Chipinaw, homesick and afraid, he sought me out. We kept track of the Yanks together, sharing box scores, hitting each other fungoes in the bewitched hour after activities, before the bugle call to dinner.

I couldn't love my brother in the sense of throwing my arms around him. Yet knowing him so well was almost like loving him. When he woke in the lost watches of the night and stood in the center of our room throwing punches, I got up and tried to intercede for him. I wanted to emulate Dr. Fabian and solve his ghastly riddle.

Jon told me he dreamed of Harry Pin coming after him. He said he was fighting ghosts. He never described them, but I knew they weren't "Casper" ghosts: they were memories of opponents, fears inside himself.

Long after we had outgrown fist fights and wrestling matches we continued low-level psychological warfare, trying to "rank" each other with snide comments. We avoided incidental contact even while pretending to be amiable. I couldn't bear his swaggering presence or preening, his self-assured manner, like young royalty, of addressing and commanding Bridey. I felt as though he, my mother, and Bob conspired to implicate and embarrass me. I could interpret their powwows without hearing a word: Jon's sly monotone, her theatrical concurrences, Daddy's smug summaries. I knew the topic was me.

Only Debby was a trustworthy companion. I bought her stuffed animals and cupcakes and made snacks for her. She loved to roughhouse with pillows and tickling. Though she had terrible nightmares, no one was permitted to go into her room because our parents (in rebellion against psychoanalysis) believed that ignoring her was the only way to get her over them. Certainly *I* wasn't allowed to comfort her because I was what they were trying to prevent her from becoming. "Rich," she would whimper through the wall, "come."

Jon would admonish me, but I'd tiptoe down the hall, creak open her door, then lie and cuddle her, or, in the faint glow from the courtyard, make rabbits and wolves on the wall with my hands, showing her that there was still light and daffiness in the world. "Squizzle drip," I whispered. Or just "Squiz." She'd ask me to scratch her sweaty palms.

One night Jon woke our parents and told. Bob burst into Debby's room, yelling. I ran back down the hall and dove into bed, throwing the covers over my head. My mother followed and tried to pull them off. Then she pounded at my heap, cursing.

As Jon and I grew older, our rivalry became existential. He asked me why I wasn't more into "fun." To him good times were the purpose of life. To be normal was to be happy-go-lucky.

I told him life was a mystery and I was trying to get to the bottom of it. I said it didn't matter whether I had fun as long as I searched for who I was. That might have been disingenuously righteous, but it hinted at a deeper truth. From my initiation by Dr. Fabian, clues and meanings—not accomplishments—were the guideposts of my world.

"You're just making that up," he insisted. He pointed out that I was a convicted enemy of the God of Israel. When I laughed at the idea of taking Park Avenue Synagogue seriously, it was as bad as when I belittled Mickey Mantle. "You're not so special," he grumbled, "even if you say you are." I knew he thought I was covering up for not being as good an athlete and as popular as he, that he suspected me of changing the rules of life to deprive him of his fair victories. "Mom is right. She says you're sneaky and selfish. You tell me these things just to get me crazy like you."

Finally a truce was imposed in the only way possible, by the disintegration of the quarrel. It became clear that there never were such sides, that we warred only to bring another thing to light, a form that would tower over all the false embattledness of childhood.

Jon's first strike was a rock through the glass window of the Horace Mann auditorium: 1962, the fall I left to go to Amherst. It came out of a clear blue sky (they would always say). It did of course, but as a manifestation of that other sky, black and scimitar where this blue bowl glistens as though summer and youth were forever.

Once the window was smashed everything poured through. Archon was deposed by trickster. He brought a water-gun to Spanish and squirted Mr. Reilly, one of the strictest masters in a school at which a whisper during assembly was a punishable crime. They hardly knew how to respond. They had to overlook the rock and the gun. Such deeds transcended punishment.

He was saying, 'I'm not the person you think I am. I don't want to be that good.' But no one heard.

His ghosts were relentless. Not only did they rouse him from slumber, engaging him in fistfights during which he punched at air, but he felt compelled to reread the same page of a book compulsively ("as many as a hundred times," he told me later in awe and horror). They had him fitted for glasses. He said that the problem went away. It wasn't true.

Repeatedly he held his hand over a light bulb until it burned him. He would pull it away and then stick it right back.

When I mentioned psychoanalysis, my mother exploded—the only thing wrong with Jon was having me for a brother. This ignored the fact that his problems began only when I *left* home. That didn't mean, of course, that I couldn't have set a time bomb inside him (I did); but more to the point, someone had to be crazy in the family, someone had to bear the brunt of unspoken demons and give them a voice. I was it. When I left, it was Jon's turn.

He had always been densely muscled. Now he was a baby giant, a gawky raw-boned miler.

He returned from school, hours later than could be accounted for by track or football practice. He wouldn't talk to anyone about his truancy, displaying a belligerence that abjured his lifelong geniality. He did finally reveal one escapade: he would throw a ball onto the subway tracks just before the train and then jump down to retrieve it. 'Chicken. You're a chicken unless you do it,' clucked the voice in his head. 'Go ahead. Shoot Mr. Reilly. Throw the rock. I dare you!'

He came to Amherst once on the bus. I introduced him to my friends at Phi Psi. We talked magic and tarot.

His own buddies were more involved in the occult than I had ever been. At Horace Mann, Chuck Stein and I carried tarot decks. We considered the pictures literary and magical; we enjoyed their landscapes like Mediaeval baseball cards, Druid runes. By Jon's last year—1965—the cards were stern authorities, representing the order of the cosmos, and many of his friends were divining daily activities by them.

"You were there before any of us," he told me, "because you had Merlin for a teacher." This was a reversal of his parents' standard view of Dr. Fabian. But I was no master. My daffy versions of the Fool and Magician—perhaps because they contained more metaphors than fixed attributions—evoked something new for him, and he ferried them back to Emil and Phil.

Jon ventured into Harlem neighborhoods, imagining himself a spy for some as-yet-unrevealed network, searching out the African origin of the Wheel among blues musicians. He was one of the original children of the '60s, but our mother continued to blame his distraction solely on my influence. She insisted on treating his quests as deeds of intentional mischief he could remedy whenever he wished. If I hadn't been there to distort things, she reasoned, Jon would have stayed normal.

With his high-school record shattered, the Ivy League out of the question, he departed for Madison, his father mourning his lost career. There was nothing wrong with the University of Wisconsin, but Bob could not forgive.

Jon arrived in the midland carrying the Waite tarot and Yeats' *A Vision.* He lived alone, going to classes with hundreds of anonymous pre-Aquarians, publishing his first poems in Morris Edelson's *Quixote.* He shunned the community of artists and politicos. Instead he checked out ethnographies of Indian rituals and hitch-hiked throughout the Midwest in pursuit of another symbol—the Ram, in the form of the football team, because he was born on the cusp of Aries, April 19th—

until the players, including his namesake and hero John Arnett, came to recognize and greet him.

That spring rode Greyhound into Minneapolis to catch the Yankees. Weary from the journey but elated at having found the correct hotel, he wandered up and down the lobby in pursuit of individual players. He forgot that he no longer looked like the all-star shortstop from Chipinaw. Suddenly he heard a voice, "Hey, kid!"

He turned and found himself face to face with Elston Howard, the black catcher we so long had rooted for. "Someone's looking for you."

"I thought he was going to say Mickey, like he really knew."

But he said, "The barber."

After Lindy and I married and moved to Ann Arbor, Jon came to visit us often. He loved the mysterious train ride. We sat up late, listening to old songs, recalling our childhood. We hit fly balls at the high-school field and talked Pawnee and Sioux star cults and war games.

He was so intense, demanding magic to happen, the universe to change at once and reveal its secrets. "Tell us, Frodo," he coaxed our sentient gray cat in a moment of rare lightness, "whither goes Gandalf? What news yet of the shire? Have the dark forces recast their ring? Will another journey to Mordor be required in our time?"

Frodo answered with a perfect Cheshire smile.

"The oracle knows, but she won't tell. She's keeping the confidence of a great wizard."

When my mother heard about these trips, she was enraged. She viewed them as indoctrination sessions. Yet she called me regularly on her Fountainbleau line and probed me for any information I might be able to give her about him, any tip that would help her understand and get back control.

He stopped going to classes; he was constantly stoned. She kept thinking to browbeat him, even through a confirmed outlaw like me. I told her he needed "help"—a euphemism redefined in many different contexts, creating paradoxes within paradoxes, which provided gist for our subterfuge and the unacknowledged feelings she and I had for each other. Together we logged a hundred hours between New York and Michigan, paid for by a hotel in Miami Beach, coming to no resolution.

Meanwhile, Jon battled with his landlord and was evicted. He was six months behind in his coursework and still rereading the same page.

He never stood a chance. He sat in his room dazed while cults of cosmic consciousness and SDS grew around him.

One night Bob called me clandestinely from a phone booth. He wanted my honest opinion. "Don't hold anything back, Richard. Things have gone much too far for that. Level with me. Tell me what you know."

"He's in serious trouble," I told him. I went on to identify our mother's role, as I understood it. I stressed the importance of countering her influence. "His wildness is an attempt to come to terms with her hysteria. His main hope is for you to step in, be his father, reassure him, support what's sane in him, and guide him."

"This is a brilliant analysis," he exclaimed, "absolutely brilliant." "Put it in a letter. Mark it 'Personal, Robert Towers'; send it to my office. I'll be back to you for regular updates."

Jon dropped out of college and returned to New York, where he got an apartment just above the Lower East Side. He lived in improvisational squalor, studying Jung and astrology and the classics of British and American literature, the Apache and Winnebago classics too. He was praying for something extravagant and dark, a ceremony that would go on night and day, undiminished—the thump and fire of the Osage Rite of Vigil.

A desperate sympathy drew him to hobos and winos. He conversed with them on the street and invited them back to his flat, where he shared his food. Word spread, and soon he had a full house. He read their fortunes. They laughed and called him Brother Jon.

He played their favorite record for them: *"Don't you know that's the sound of the men working on the. . . ."*

"Chain!" they all screamed, *"Ga-a-ang!"*

Great Expectations was a tale he kept coming back to—the convict in the churchyard. He wanted to flee him, to save him; yet he suspected all the time destiny worked toward this man being his benefactor too. The heady drama of the figure in the marsh was as much his own (primordially) as Dickens'—a fact he proved daily by his discovery of "Abel Magwitches" on the streets of Lower Manhattan. It was the only way to escape the lofty aspirations his father held for him and earn his Stone Age rags.

> A man with no hat, and with broken shoes, and with an old rag tied round his head. A man who had been soaked in water, and smothered in mud, and lamed by stones, and cut by flints, and stung by nettles, and torn by briars, who limped and shivered, and glared and growled; and whose teeth chattered in his head as he seized me by the chin.

This was not something to be feared. This was his most forbidden desire.

One night Jon was walking along Lexington when his mind snapped. He glimpsed a tunnel so serpentine that even numbers in the billions didn't track its purgatory. He began to gallop.

Reaching into his pocket, he found two crumpled bills. Then he realized he had no shirt or shoes. He chased down a cab. "Take me to Jesus," he pleaded, though he gave his parents' address. The doorman paid the difference; the elevator man helped him upstairs.

Demons came in rhythm, in tandem, leaping into his brain from commanding turrets and behind every figment and mask he conceived to block them out, merging with his thoughts, dissolving in the roar of his blood. They swelled from each nuance of selfhood or topic of interest in which he tried to hide: old baseball games, panoramas of camp and school, Monopoly cards and Sorry tokens, at first innocent, then dilating with zigzag fangs. Just like the hot bulbs onto which he placed his hand, thoughts drew him by the same morbidity with which they repelled him—so that he resonated through an infinite regression of yes-no, yes-no, yes-no, each yes containing an even more subtle no that shed instantly into its aspect of yes; yes, no. . . . Even invoking the Osage couldn't protect him for more than a second or two, nor could his image of running a track meet, running a track meet, running a track meet, each one a shorter slice of concentrated imagined motion.

He pleaded with his mother to "keep them out of my brain." She knelt silently by his bed, shaking.

He had caught hepatitis, probably from men who had been soaked in water and ice.

He recuperated four months in the hospital where he was born—Mount Sinai, overlooking ballfields on which we had played, one block above the Ninety-Sixth Street playground.

At least the voices had been stilled. That grace alone sustained him throughout dreary days of reading in bed, staring into the gauze of time, wondering what to do. The past was empty. The future was the past.

In Ann Arbor I purchased items he requested and sent them to him: the tales of the hobbit and C. S. Lewis' science-fiction planets, the early novels of Herman Melville and Nathaniel Hawthorne, Ouspensky's *Ivan Osokin,* photocopies of Winnebago texts.

He had entered Mount Sinai ostensibly on leave from Madison, but he told his parents to forget college. He couldn't go back to the Chain Gang either. He found an apartment, uptown this time, collected his books and clothes, and accepted a gift of furniture. He got a job as an office messenger for two months, then answered an ad for a clerk at the Doubleday Bookstore on Fifth Avenue.

A year passed before I knew Bob had gone dutifully to my mother, holding my epistle to him like some sort of random criminal act he had stumbled upon. She stopped calling, even on my birthday, and didn't take any of my calls until Jon was in Mount Sinai. Then I learned of my stepfather's betrayal.

During the hospital stay, when they cleaned out Jon's apartment they were furious to find copies of the *Alchemy Issue* of *Io,* as well as letters from me that discussed our family situation. This reinforced their suspicion that I was at the bottom of things.

"You believed him?" she shouted incredulously when I insisted on my good intentions, even toward her, in asking Bob to take a role. "You thought he would *do* something? You thought he *ever* did anything?"

Dr. Hitzig told them that therapy was now a necessity. For my mother it required a reluctant admission that Jon was "sick." But she blamed the hepatitis and expected a quick and thorough cure.

Jon went to his first psychiatrist unwillingly. "How can there be wisdom," he complained, "from a man who doesn't care about Indians or believe in tarot."

I said there was also simple emotional insight.

"Well, you had magical doctors, Richard. They've given me frauds."

This was the beginning of a debate Jon would conduct between shamans and shrinks. At first he gave ground, admitting libido and acknowledging that magic might sometimes be a cover for fear of inadequacy. Malinowski had proven these ideas, the doctor explained to his patient, ethnographically at least in the Trobriands.

Jon signed up for anthropology courses at NYU and The New School—Amerindian Linguistics and Indian-White Relations, respectively. He attended Diane Wakoski's and Joel Oppenheimer's poetry workshops at St. Marks Church—Diane who wrote tarot poems and Joel who had recently made the front page of *The New York Times* by grabbing back the microphone from a patriotic guard who had snatched it at a Madison Square Garden anti-war rally.

"Let me have my say too," the guard had yelled.

"You've been talking for the last two thousand years," Joel cried out. "Now give other folks a chance."

When Lindy became pregnant in 1968, my mother made peace by inviting us to her cottage in Long Beach while we were east looking for a place in Maine. She said that she had an important secret to tell me, but, after our bumper-to-bumper drive through Expressway traffic, two days passed innocently at the beach. While Lindy and I alternated keeping her company and swimming, she nursed out an account of Jonny's conception: Bob had wanted her to abort the baby, but she refused by tricking him into believing it was a son. She told us she was now in therapy. "The waves are my emotions," she remarked soporifically, pointing to the Atlantic. "Doctor Simmons says they soothe me." Later I learned she apologized to Lindy for how she had treated me. She hoped she would forgive her.

My wife, belly large with child, assured her that she had raised two fine sons and a wonderful daughter.

But which, if any of these, were the secret?

Jon met a girl on the floor at Doubleday. Her name was Mara ("so close to Mom's it's scary"). They moved in together and adopted a cat they christened Orion.

Mara took courses in Oriental Art History and Witchcraft. She and Jon shopped together at an open-air market at the tip of Manhattan "where it meets the Mediterranean and the Pacific Basin," my brother wrote, "buying spinach, parsnips, escarole, sweet potatoes, corn at three cents an ear, and dozens of other exotic vegetables I don't know the names of."

From his letters it seemed as though, almost effortlessly, he had found what he once came to Ann Arbor for—a woman, a cat, a home.

But Mara challenged his devotion to a world of writers and intellects who were "famous," she snarled, "only to each other." She mocked the way he "hung on Diane Wakoski's every word and honored teas with her as though he were dining with Gertrude Stein." She insisted he discontinue the doctor because therapy was elitist. Despite her protests he kept his appointments.

The City was becoming unlivable, especially after they added two more cats and took to camping weekends in Connecticut.

His parents offered to support him as long as he went to school somewhere. He was admitted to Colorado College. Then he and his girl chipped in together on a second-hand station wagon, packed the cats, and headed west.

They arrived in Colorado Springs and rented the ground floor of a country house. It was delightful to set the Orion family loose in a field. They planted herbs and erected trellises with holy figurines. He bought a box of sixty-four child's crayons and drew alchemical sigils for the walls.

He discovered Don Juan Matus, the Yaqui shaman, in Carlos Castaneda's report on him, a book that stunned him for its relevance to his own life. Shamanic beasts, voodoo plants, and telepathic insects were like the phantoms he had been fighting at night for years, long before Don Juan gave them traditional names (while declaring the arena of battle with them and a suitable means of combat—magical and hallucinogenic).

No one on the faculty of Colorado College was interested in shamanism or alchemy, or the poets Olson, Dorn, and Kelly. The teachers were either old and hardline, refusing to acknowledge spiritual influence in literature and myth—or young and (to their own minds) radical, so they were the only ones allowed to have insights (and most of those were political). Jon wrote term papers on "James Fenimore Cooper's Prairie" and "The Romance of the Rose" and, on his first report card, he explained, two teachers cheated him out of A's "only because they wanted to make it clear they didn't approve."

When he visited the home of his American Literature teacher, he was astonished by the Navaho rugs and Hopi kachina dolls. "But his interest was aesthetic. He showed some minimal excitement when I mentioned a writer he had not heard of, but only, he said, because Spanish-American authors were his hobby."

Landlords were even worse. Jon and Mara were driven from house to house—harassed because of cats, hippie clothes, not being married, and long hair. Even at the last cottage, where they thought they had established rapport and the landlord addressed Orion by name and engaged Jon for tarot readings, he evicted them, then refused to give them back their damage deposit, also charging them an extra month's rent for a day over.

Dropping out of school, Jon worked as a dishwasher but left after an encounter with his supervisor. He developed an ulcer and spent three weeks in bed with the box of crayons, drawing mandalas and reading books on tribes of the Great Plains. He applied to the University of Colorado.

In September they moved to Boulder.

There he found sympathetic professors. His first term, he was invited to read a paper on "The Trickster, Rock and Roll, and Baseball" at a local ethnographic conference. Another paper was published in the department academic journal. He got straight A's and started graduate school. He planted a garden, then nursed it through winter in a homemade greenhouse. The following summer he and Mara camped in the Rockies, Sierras, and Bitterroots.

Though he continued psychoanalysis in Denver, he yearned to embody a real magic, to speak to lizards like Don Juan. His doctor teased him about this. "Be a *mensch,*" he said. "The mythology you hide behind is foppish, not manly. It keeps you from developing your real sexual interests."

"Foppish!" Jon raged, showing him photographs of Apache warriors, their faces colored with the horizon line in red, the kingdom of death in white. "You should have one-tenth their courage and power."

Yet the therapist was minor compared to the witch-woman of the Polish lower class. Mara was enraged by the intellectualism of Jon's magic. "You're a pampered rebel," she said. "You don't ever do anything real."

It was true. His father regularly put large sums in his account. One day Jon may have painted fences for extra cash, but the next he was off to Denver to see his shrink, hired at a price that would have bought their food for two weeks. He understood the peril of living a contradiction. "Fidel reached such a moment in Cuba too," he wrote me, "a crossroads at which it was either revolution or madness. His father also paid the bills. Only a master stroke of politics and magic set him free; yet he freed a nation by his act."

Bowery bums stood pleading, demanding, with Mara and the whole fucking lower class, to be let in. Harry Pin was back.

Short of graduation by one course, he dropped out of school—the long-distance runner having quit at the finish line in the movie that touched him most deeply as an adolescent (and by which he had tried to explain to his father why he had blown his prep-school career).

"I am Paracelsus returned," he told me on the phone. "You know, academics laugh at the idea that he died from one of his own potions. They think that's hilarious. Where is their compassion? Where is their feeling for the great adventure? No mortal man, not even them, can escape the gods. At least Theophrastus Bombastus faced his eternity and succumbed like a man."

He renounced Mara, the cats, the garden, and domestic life. He moved into a tiny flat on Colfax in Denver.

An incident a few weeks earlier proved the crucible. A truckdriver, buddy in the cab beside him, drove right up over the curb onto their lawn and through the herb garden. Jon came out of the house, shaking with fury. "I'm going to kill you."

The men looked at him, then chuckled. "Why don't you try?" shouted the one not behind the wheel. Jon stood there paralyzed.

"I was a chicken," he said. "I didn't defend my home."

In Denver he went to work in a metal-supply warehouse, unloading trucks. No more college culture and bookstores, he tried to pick up prostitutes at topless joints and once got taken to the dark where he paid thirty dollars—all he had—for champagne and company. She let him touch her leg. On the street where she had promised to meet him he stood for two hours afterwards.

But hearing Mara had a lover he went to the hippie's apartment, punched him around, pulled him up by his long hair, took out a knife, and threatened to scalp him.

He had become one of the halfbreeds and was acquiring their tireless original strength, their courage to risk it all on a vision quest any night of the week. "I am," he wrote me, "the black king restored from ash. I am the bad boy at last."

He had gotten to where he would have demolished that truck or been demolished trying.

But when he drove into the wilderness asking for a vision, he simply huddled there in the car, lonely and weeping. He was twenty-three.

2

Documents (from Jonathan)

First through Fourth. High School
Fifth. Madison, Wisconsin
Sixth through Ninth. New York City
Tenth and Eleventh. Colorado Springs
Twelfth and Thirteenth. Boulder

First Document

i see it has huge green fields mostly, rocky in parts and the way it sloped down from 97th Street into dustier regions. There was a playground if you followed the concrete path at 97th skirting the field.

That was when we were younger, bubble mixture in the air, two types of swings, low fences around them with little gaps by which to get in. The space was oval, people moving slowly about it or sitting with baby carriages on benches at the sides, every so often somebody shooting into the middle, that very heart of it left open. Or you could have catches across that great middle, bouncing the ball through it. When it got by you the ball might carom off the iron-spiked bars or go through.

Out the playground on one side were a few bushes in dark earth and the smell of pigeon dust; on the other were very thick high bushes, then a path of concrete climbing into shade. The branch that diverged to the left went toward 100th. It was always in sun and promised great things.

On Sunday it was a Spanish kid, very stocky, wanted to catch flies with Richard, my father, and me. We had the black bat then and wore Yankee uniforms. We played on the part that is closest to Fifth Avenue on the other side of a stone wall. We were hitting in a straight line toward the center where the grass was thin and tawny and the sun burned deeper inside. . . .

Second Document

In Pittsburgh with Billy, a stop on the way to Chicago . . . Muddy Waters in the jazz festival. We read it in the papers when we got there. He was out of place singing blues against their jazz. Billy and I knew how they sang blues in New York. If only they knew.

Muddy is my black father-being that travelled within us, how New York had taken Chicago blues into Dave Van Ronk in slow moans and a big bear-voice in the Village. We knew it was false how these whites sang it, until finally we got the real thing how it had come up from the south into the big cities that black moan, the stories of charms and dark powers, black necks under sweaty shorts soft and thick as the cotton they reaped. Those that had walked down the road or caught the greyhound and the big magic of the ginger man whom the others didn't want around. Mojo man. Lynchings and wild dogs at night. A slow earth magic you sowed with the cotton. Then the city-beat mixed into the water—muddy waters, kindling the old sound in the order of city streets, running against the trickster's looting what you got by dancing in black neon streets.

My parents sent me to Chicago for a college interview. After that I broke the pattern, got a return ticket for a later date and Billy and I sped north to Minneapolis to watch the Rams play, called my parents on the phone to guess where I was. . . .

There were giant trucks going west we looked up at. Roared through America on the path endlessly west through that small pocket outside Pittsburgh, the night that always came there and we had never seen. But this night was very much ours. We were above the trees. There was a white fence we went over three feet high which was the entrance, we didn't really know, to a nuclear reactor. We were going downhill, came to a place that looked like a shopping center or something after the war. We wondered if we had been poisoned. The man in the booth called the cops. There is a Higher Law Here. These Cops will take you to your father. He will see you swimming, a fish in an Odd Sea.

Third Document

I've been reading old letters from you Rich at my desk and feeling softnesses about how one moves through his life slowly it seems, like planets, but with all time and marvels forever about him. That is, the problems are always there in some form changing as we do. There is something that is always One about how we know ourselves something more than memory. There are scenes so unconscious or deep. I mean we are nostalgic about something past, but it may not be because it was so good then but rather it makes things better in that it reveals hidden forces that were present and working at the time but which we couldn't perceive then alone because we were involved with a lot of other things like being aware of what time it was or just having in mind other possibilities that could be occurring (as we always do), but now we perceive how some deeper part was there which we were not conscious of then but was tinting everything and are suddenly able to see alone in its full glory. Like I can't say that I (the thin veneer of the consciousness that says "I") was aware then of the mythology that was occurring to Billy and me on the trip to Madison and Chicago, but now I do, so there must have been some deeper part of me that was 'aware' of the things.

Pause

I've been listening to rock and roll tonight and thinking about what you said about '50s stuff and it seems so much the spirit of the night. Muted rather than raging fire. Especially this song by George Hamilton from '57 about how "they don't understand," but I can't remember any more of it.

I want to understand space and the planets so much better, to understand how the planets and stars are in us and how they are living, but I am still hung up on conventional notions. I know if it was given to us to see—such a huge thing bordering such dizzying heights—then there must be something it has to do with us.

Fourth Document

In the last week I have traced the compulsion to do things from getting out of bed at night to fight ghosts, to the Rams and travelling, to wanting the opposite of everything, to wanting to see through things, know other worlds (but where are they?, here or nowhere to be found, and how can I get stuck so much?). I want so much, Rich, and am so weak, afraid to risk things in the World, scared I could lose it all in one argument.

Fifth Document (Letter to Bridey from Madison)

> "For the Sidhe are dextrous fishers and they fish for men with dreams upon the hook." W. B. Yeats.

Dear Bride,

School's fine. My courses are really good, especially my American Indian Linguistics course and my English course.

That one is in Romantic Poetry (Wordsworth, Keats, Shelley, etc.) and I can see how Yeats coming a half-century later developed out of this tradition. There is a lot of feeling now against the Romantics because of their sentimentality and the weak fluidity of their poetry. It is too ethereal, too unsolid. I think this criticism is unfair, but it explains in part why Yeats is so much more accepted than the Romantics. For Yeats' poetry has the solidity and permanence, the concreteness of symbol (the dancer, the tower), and lack of metaphor that we like now. Most people find more strength in Yeats than in the Romantics. He uses the solid symbols of his lunar system and the strength-giving nature of the fiery gentleness of the Irish myth. I bought five one-act plays by Yeats and have fallen in love with "The Only Jealousy of Emer." The voices are beautiful and amazingly haunting. Cyril Cusack is one of the actors. The others are Marie Keen, Patrick Magee, and Siobhan McKenna. I'll bring it home Christmas.

Bridey, you are a true daughter of Yeats and leprechauns, of changelings and pipers. You are Badh Catha (Raven of the Battle) and Morrígan the prophet-goddess. I am honored to have been raised by you. You are Kerry, Dunanore, and Donegal. You are Cú Chulainn of heath and heather. When I read the classic works of Ireland, I know that your heart is an elf's heart, that your dreams are filled with ancient castles and the wanderings of spiritfolk, that you are merely in exile among us. I have always hoped for you that someday you would return to Ireland and find the Gaelic mystery the fairies have bequeathed you. I want you to fly again with the arch-Druid beneath the skies of Northern Eire. I wish you a crossing of the fertile sea. I want you to be Bridget the Great.

Love Jon

Sixth Document

About Great Expectations: men like Abel Magwitch the convict, the bums in NY who I've run into a lot lately and just watched sometimes in the Automat—they take such care in doing things, so slowly with almost a childish interest that they get sidetracked all the time and fall to pondering the shape of the cigarette before lighting it. There is something womblike about their care and attention; they are never running by things as most people but are always meeting them as they rise up. And the convict is like this in that he is sweet and motherly toward Pip and yet you always keep in the back of your mind his roughness, like by the tombstone in the first chapter or when he kills Compeyson underwater. The convict can be like Joe, sweet and smoking a pipe; he can be slow and thoughtful and do all these things from his heart, but from a different source than Joe's, out of a roughness and darkness of marshland and jail rather than the roughness and darkness of the honest forge.

As for Mommy and Dad I still cannot speak to them, or I couldn't when I was in the house and gave up all attempts to be nice. It was in a large part my fault that things didn't go well there because I didn't try. But I'm not sorry that I didn't, just sorry that it's like that.

When they go see my cousin Gail and her husband (which they are going to do this week, Debby told me), Gail and Ben will tell them, "What wild crazy things Jon says," and chuckle as if they know what's going on, and M + D will politely chuckle and say, "Yes, we know; he gets them all from Richard when he goes to Ann Arbor."

Seventh Document

On Monday and Tuesday I go to the New School at 6:00. My courses are bad. Poetry classes from the reader's standpoint bring back the old high school and college way of talking. My other course is in Mythology, and the guy's got it all wrong and chooses to explain myth and magic in Freudian terms: "I see no better explanation. If you can find one, show it to me," says he smugly, puts down Jung, and when anyone uses a complex term or tries to get deep he says to the guy: "Who have you been reading, Jung?" He prides himself that he isn't deep and philosophical but tells it in that matter of fact way, meanwhile very sure that he knows all that is going on in said fields. He's got it backwards: reduces mythology into Freud instead of vice versa. He says that myths are unconscious creations, but I think nowhere are they as conscious as in primitive tribes (whereas they are uniquely unconscious in us). He's real big on linking the child's state of mind with the primitive's, not perceiving what the latter do with the child's state of mind: realize it more consciously and become aware of deeper powers so as to develop control, magic.

I have millions of things to talk to you about; i got to see you to tell you because i just can't concentrate. Some guy i met on the street (he was taking a piss on the street) is staying here now and we talked for hours last night and he is really sort of amazing and Abel-Magwitch-like.

I'm trying to find a way to get a car but may take a bus or train because now i really want to see you. Will try to come Christmas Eve because i want to catch the Ram-Packer game on Saturday.

Eighth Document (Mount Sinai Hospital)

The oldest dream i can remember takes place in that playground on 96th Street and there's a kid named Roy or Harry in it who was sort of the leader of the playground and then i became co-leader with him, having been first against him (it seems more like a mythical situation now). What happens in the dream is that a witch is putting Roy to sleep outside the playground. The confusion is about the word "pin." I really can't remember if his last name was Pin or whether the witch was putting him to sleep with a pin in the dream.

Ninth Document

Found your old book in the house Exploring Mars with great pictures of what the planet would look like. Think i will go camping with Mara Friday-Saturday. Really want to get out of the city for a few days. It's been amazing this year, but every time I watch Mickey Mantle with my father he hits a home run. We listened to him against California late last night and he did it. Also happened with Mara once when i turned it on at her house, and i rushed back after class one day to see if i could catch the end of the doubleheader and he was pinch-hitting and got a double. It's the culmination of some overpowering relationship.

. . . a vast network of association done in one instant, a way to dance while standing in place, Ticonderoga (i see it on the pencil beside me) for the creation of which four men met one day in a knoll, a clipper ship sank, a band of pirates wore red, a nation went to war; and finally i'm sorry sir but we have no record of such a place in our files, it may have been part of a shorter word.

Trouble with Mara still over intellect vs. experience. A bad scene with a friend (Steve Rechtshaffen) and Mara in which she objected to our being so dainty and politely intellectual and the fact that we took ourselves so seriously. But it is usually clear to me why the seriousness is necessary and i can pass over the politeness as the usual timidity when one plays with things he considers higher than himself and would like to belong to.

We went to Middletown for the reason that we could probably stay cheaply and it would be easier in a small college town. Your friend David McAllester put us up in a tipi in his backyard. He was having a party so he drove us into town to eat, and we walked back to his place, stayed at the party a while and then slept in the tipi. All this seemed so incredibly beautiful and meaningful; we were pleased to find that such people and such a way of life existed after NY. We built a fire in the tipi later; Mara went to sleep, and I went back in. David was so nice and told me about all the groovy things that these people at the party were into. As I was going out—bored by the party and embarrassed at David's niceness and feeling I had to match it and be just as nice as he—Mara came in to make tea. We talked some more to David, he showing us Tarot cards his son had made and told us he had given a witchcraft course, etc. Back in the tent Mara felt really bad and began to cry about how things came so easily to these people and they were able to do all the things she wanted to do which came so hard for her: the Tarot cards, the Indian music the students learned to play at Wesleyan, David's Navaho music, all his many interests.

But David and his son and all the hip professors into stuff didn't affect me that way. David was disappointing to me because he lacked responsibility about the work in the sense that one just can't keep bringing up beautiful topics to point out they are beautiful. There was finally just too much "isn't this a groovy thing" and "there's so much to be done" without any concern for the personal questions in these things. All the time it was talking about intense things unintensely and I decided that although he was such a good host, he really in the end managed to keep us away and refused to follow up any specific things I tried to say about anthropology or personal things which I brought up, e.g., I said, "We have a lot of problems with school, things like being cut off too much" to which he answered: "Who doesn't?"

Tenth Document

I have found out that landlords, and I think Americans in general, have a mania for odor-freeness. Thinking of that woman in Wisconsin, a room in her and her husband's house I rented—she came in one day and said it smelled like sweat. The landlord here had this mania about cleanliness and couldn't help his compulsion to clean up our house with mops and deodorizers; he just figured he wouldn't let his compulsion totally screw him but would try to get me to pay for it. Same with the new landlady we have rented the house from who wanted to kick us out when she found we had cats, said it would take a professional cleaning service to get the cat odor out of the walls. Oh fuck and triple fuck them.

I dreamed of pissing into an overflowing toilet and the next day broke our toilet and it overflowed. Same day nine puppies were born to the German shepherd next door; they also have a very fat rabbit there. Great hosts of red ants born outside, watched them running around on top of the hills, the older winged ones (drones?) trying to shepherd them into the holes. Our female cat in heat has attracted not only Orion but two cats from the block, one of which invaded the house and was trounced by Orion, not to return at close distance yet. The sunflower plants are gigantic and flowers are about to come out, fiery sepals ready to explode suns. Some of them are taller than me. Corn plants with lots of tassels—we might get corn. Stringbeans are out drooping from the vines but are not ripe yet, and tomato and kale are coming along; they were planted later.

The daily afternoon rainclouds are coming over the mountains, always a lot of wind, sometimes rain.

I have tried to locate where you are going to be on a large map of Maine and found the name Mt. Desert Island in the sea off Bar Harbor around a lot of other names, so I couldn't tell you which piece of land it belonged to. I am really excited for you, and it is all part for me of the recent thing about the sea and expeditions. I wanted to send you this quote from The Early Spanish Main, the first half of which is mainly on Columbus. It is about his third voyage (1498) in which he discovered the north coast of South America:

"The physical geography of the gulf perplexed Columbus. The northern margin of the Orinoco delta, not recognized as such, the fresh water of the western side of the gulf, the mountains of the Paria peninsula to the north, exaggerated in distance and elevation by the humid tropical air, became to his imagination the proscenium behind which lay the Earthly Paradise, known as being at the end of the Earth. He concluded that he found another world (otro mundo) at the end of the world continent, of which Cuba was one promontory and this another and the most easterly extension."

I think this gets closer to what the structure of the earth

was for Columbus, not flat or round, but somehow already named (he never stopped saying it was the outlying islands and mainland of China that we had reached when it was clear to others that it was something different) and an earth that had places where it did not come back upon itself (the Earthly Paradise). Sauer takes a bad view of Columbus, showing he used everything he could play on to satisfy the civil and religious authorities, in order to hoodwink them of what was really going on at the same time as satisfying them; he was really out for gold and tyrannical power of the islands and his name perpetuated through heirs and remembered. Plus a mixture of extreme romanticism with pretenses at mysticism when he felt it would help him, as when he told the King and Queen that he had secret knowledge of lands beyond the Canaries. Or real mysticism, Don Quixote perhaps, the Neo-platonists and Paracelsus. Anyway Columbus plays about our islands and we are still half here and half not here.

The time with my father started out okay. We met him at the plane and took him to the Broadmoor; he immediately started sizing up the terrain as being like New England. By the end of the time, though, he had gotten exasperating and my own hostility started up again toward him, especially my embarrassment at his manner in restaurants. Animals suggested to him only the names of fancy restaurants and their dishes. We went for a cookout in the woods and he wore bermuda shorts and a tennis hat and really is the dandy. He had only one interesting thing to tell me that whole visit: the name Turetsky meant Turk. So it described the migration of our ancestors. I told him I wanted to take the name back, and he said, "It makes you wonder what you did it all for."

8 o'clock in the morning. Out the window the backyard is full of snow. Clouds overhead and it is so still. The day is clearly a first, broken off from the sequence of other days; as yesterday was the first day of autumn-preparing-for-winter, this is winter. I can't help feeling things from other years, plans I had for days that were firsts like this one. Firsts are

a genetic protean string, a time continuation dimensionally different from the one the passage of the sun makes/maybe the Mayan calendar again and the two time scales.

Something to do with football today, but mainly just the preparation, the deciding what I can do to fill the insides, as maybe on another of these firsts I thought of going sledding and that is juxtaposed as in a cubist painting to drinking hot chocolate in the morning and bundling into warm clothes (I hear the kids outside say they will go sledding). Then there is this street of New York snow merging with the backyard merging with a postcard of New England snow. And thoughts of you in the winter: Amherst, Michigan, Maine now, your film of autumn and winter, the rituals of Ann Arbor townspeople on your block in the winter.

In thinking toward you I want to do winter things with you; I see your old black rubber boots.

It was good to hear from you, but I think there were a lot of problems. On my side I think the "joy of communication" with you involved a great indebtedness that I feel toward you. Remember I told you once, "Yeah, man, my head is really in the stars and planets, just where you told me to put it." Again the whole thing of having received my aspirations from you and constantly thanking you and following you. So there is always this enthusiasm to talk to you, and yet what I am really trying to say in everything is, "Thank you, thank you!" which makes it hard to really talk. I think we have been granted the "joyful communication" and we are always able to make that, but it is the problems that constantly get in the way. Like somehow I thought you were holding things back and couldn't tell me them because the form of our conversations doesn't allow them.

I think that I have been against psychiatric ways of handling things, maybe getting an early sense of what it was when "Richard" was first going, putting it down on the fact that Richard was into it and my parents had always posed Richard as sick, etc. I think I could never take you easily enough, meaning that that lines of opposition were drawn. Somehow, the issue was always forced to the surface again and I found myself not wanting to be like you, thinking you were sick or really a bastard. And then it seemed you weren't letting me do what I was doing, calling me a boastard while I was secretly calling you a bastard.

I come into the psychiatrist telling him I have had a very strong dream and making associations, but he says you are trying to flood us out the door into the hall with associations and you don't want to try to figure it out.

Eleventh Document

Look at this, damnit. You call me up with the great idea to go see Lindy's mother. The result is that I get accused of being my father when I take it as an order. Now who's playing parent's side as well as non-parent's side? You say it's a good idea to go see Lindy's mother because she has just been nice to you, a sort of lame and irrelevant enticement why I should go see her. I don't want to see ANYBODY'S parents if I have to see them as somebody's parents. All the less reason to see them. Like in one breath you give the reason to see them as a family one, family ties and all that, and the other is that it might throw objective clarity on my own situation here. Which is not so bad, but they are your reasons and not mine. It didn't occur to me to go see Lindy's mother to get perspective and objectivity on Colorado. I'm not in any sort of settled, intellectual position to go for that reason. That's a kind of reason that makes sense from where you are—I won't say the dramatic two thousand miles again—but I will say East Coast where she may appear sweet and historical to you. Look, my being bitchy isn't going to help, but both your letters hurt and seem so fantastically unjust that I feel like hurting you. As much as you have ideas about what goes on in my house, conspiracies against you, backers on my side, I have all those images about the way you in your house take the things I do. So I expect that if I don't go to see Lindy's mother I am going to be accused of still holding the family's prejudice against Lindy and her family and I will be accused of not having grown up enough yet to make a great mature move. Well, fuck all that. Do you see what you hold over me? So I didn't tell you over the phone I didn't want to see her, but I should have and had you accept it for once without all the implications about myself that shape up in your head (still belonging to the family, still being on their side). How much are you trying to accept the way my relationship works with you? Will I only be accepted if I see Lindy's mother? Well, I happen not to like to see people's parents. I have this big thing about the styles of parents and their children and the looks of parents and their children. I really hate it when I can see the way a kid looks like the parent. I really hate it when I can see that Lindy looks like her mother, when I see the same look. I don't like to see my friend Phil in his mother.

Now the second part of it. It really pisses me off to be told that I'm being my father. It was the thing I was most conscious of in Debby, all the traits and style of my father that were in her, and then how they were in me too. It made me angry at her for the last two days she was here. Whether I am like my father or not, what does it mean for you to always bring it up in my face? Anytime I argue with you, I'm being like my father, just as Mara reminds you of our mother and all that shit. You refuse to see me outside of the family battles, and I have probably never been able to see you either. I'm sick of getting thrown back into the family by you and Lindy anytime you don't like something I do. That seems to me too easy everytime to be of any real validity. It's like you say: either go do good things like visit Lindy's mother (a token that will show you I'm on your side) or else you are just that young thing back in the family again living it all out. So you both constantly toss me back between the two. Either I'm writing well and doing good things and maturing or I'm in the family.

All of it is just TELLING ME TELLING ME. So I'm telling you now, responding to the tone of your letter and just throwing you on the defensive as you threw me, telling me, "You should have no trouble writing back, we can have a real shoot-em-up!" Well I could call your draw, but then you were always really quick to shoot it out. Man, I'm really surprised at a double barrel of nothing but accusations and instructions in the difference between myth and reality and how I should come out straight with it and my skullduggery and all that. Are you really thinking of me in your letter, or just about me, like some good idea, like something you can say something about? I really went bad like my father; I'm playing double toward you. It sounds like YOU YOU saying that; it has nothing to do with me. Maybe we'll shoot it out finally or shut down our guns for good. Anyway my complaint is that you're smart in the letter, but smart to yourself and not to me.

I've gotten interested in reading about Great Basin Indians, a really good book on Paviotso shamanism, not so good maybe, but just my enthusiasm for shamanism, and a long article on Shoshone and Bannock subsistence cycles. The area is mainly Idaho for the Shoshone, Salmon Eater, Groundhog Eaters, Camas Root Eaters, Buffalo Eaters: all of them named for what they eat, east of the Divide to hunt the buffalo and stand off the more powerful Blackfoot, then maybe making it back before the winter snows to the west of the Divide around the rivers: Salmon, Boise, etc. Whole tribes of Shoshone lived isolated in the mountains (Absaroka, Salmon) and didn't fight but hunted elk and whatever game in the mountains. At certain times other tribes would come there and hunt with them or separate from them. The Paviotso are Paiute in Western Nevada, shamanistic power coming through dreams or secured in special geographic places like mountain caves where hearing becomes very acute and one receives the power after contacting all the animals of the area in a noise.

Read "Sleepy Hollow" and "Rip Van Winkle" and did a paper on them. It had something to do not with America or Europe so much—the dichotomy the teacher has been stressing—but Washington Irving's own being in touch with Anglo-Saxon, with the Germanic origin of our language in the code of Dutch society.

Rip Van Winkle wandered up in the Catskills (Nevele and Grossinger country) to find Henrik Hudson and his crew as the guardian spirits of the towns, bowling and drinking all day and living his true wish. So Rip falls asleep and misses the Revolutionary War and the time of change and comes back neatly to fit into a patriarchal role and continue to tell stories in the tavern without the weight of Dutch work principle over his head. Beautiful descriptions in both stories of the imagined origin of thunder being a dog who just woke or a bullfrog turning in his imagined bed—all the country reposed into something, a guardian spirit caring where and how you live. . . .

I've been constructing this American history game which has become really complex, includes a giant game board of travel which I've only completed east of the Mississippi, plus a historical board, a trade goods board, and then a sympathy-antipathy part—like say the picture you pick is California gold-mining 1849, the sympathies may be dreams and fears, travel, occupations; antipathies are robbery, natural disaster, arrivals of other people. So you pick a card which, let's say, has on it, 'Scene of Chicago: 1870s,' and one of the eleven things on it is 'you become a meat-packer,' and this corresponds to the number seven, so if you pick this card and spin number seven, and if your destination is California during the Gold Rush, then occupations are your sympathy and you would gain sympathy points on the sympathy-antipathy board. This whole game started when Debby was here and I was thinking of something to do and so decided to paste these American history stickers on a board and put the captions near them and have it be so anyone who came over to the house could match up the captions with the pictures. But I was dissatisfied with it and then Mara said—why not make a game that really works, and that was just the thing.

We got kicked out again and are living now in an apartment for $80. The whole house is a converted barn made into a lot of apartments. We lost our big tomcat Orion at the other house. He just walked off and didn't come back for two weeks and then we got kicked out. Never really felt the impact of it because so much else was happening then and still just sort of feel every now and then that something is missing and we are not able to have the whole ritual-hero-worship that surrounded him. He was really a great cat, perfect in our eyes. We had this voice we used for him that was supposed to be him talking, and he would be always saying how he was the Creator, that he planned to teach a course on Cosmology in the school in which he would give a demonstration in the last class which would end up destroying the world. Also he was fantastically nostalgic about Samarkand and longed to go there. Of course when he talked to us he always called us his servants and said he would get rid of us if we didn't get him some GRADE A; he would talk about how all the dogs in the neighborhood were working for him at paltry wages and would heist some GRADE A for him now and then. God, it was really crazy all these games we did with him, but I would still love to do them.

Twelfth Document

Things have been bad because I've been frustrated. Wake up with a head full of dreams knowing it's the "whole thing" and can't remember them or, if I can, no sense in them for me, just awe, Neil Diamond's song in which the line "Had a dream and it filled me with wonder, she couldn't stay." Like it's incredible with me how wonder, awe, fantasy, dramatic action supersede attempts at understanding or even the belief I can understand. I am down on my writing because the psychological intensities I've been having seem to go so far beyond it. Like who are the girl-boys in the dream last night of the four lesbians. I am watching a movie of them and everybody is saying what ugly girls they are and I think so too but I notice one who is so soft, so magically-woundily soft, like an open wound asking to be fucked, like the girl-like faggots who seem to be saying, "Fuck Me, Fuck Me, I Want it So Bad." Which is sort of what this girl says in the dream; she says: "Kenny, put it in me" and then there is this girl Kenny, hard and skinny, fucking her in the ass and then 'Kenny' turns into the name Kennedy and the fucked girl is saying she hates Kennedy and then I am conscious of my own mind and that I am coming and I am filled with sheer delight and at the same time (in the last gasp of the dream) I am fighting for the one exquisite crucial thought as the sperm is filling my whole body and I think: 'Kennedy didn't die in vain because all these people are using him, especially in their intensest moments.'

Last night I got these fantasies about just leaving everything, school and Mara, or else going to see the psychiatrist in his house, or going to the hospital where he works and sleeping on the floor outside his office, carrying my writing there and giving it to him for safekeeping and then wanting to be his son. Then a weird fantasy of writing you a letter saying, "I am a witch. Send me back my writing. I am a witch and you ordered me to do this." Then I sign the letter in my name and add "Rich I am going insane." I secretly want you to come out here and help me. As it turned out, I went to the psychiatrist and he in effect told me to go home and stop making dramatic moves to escape figuring things out. So here I am reading about the New Guinea headhunters tonight (don't we all have our things and aren't they big enough to smash a universe with their beautiful power, the sheer beautiful power of our aberrations).

And the fantasies continue. Saw a girl in Denver the other day and she smiled at me and I actually got out a Hi; she assented and I loved her and was tingling all over because I knew she understood everything about me before it happened to me, before I said what I said. Girl in one of my anthropology classes now who I like to sit near and just have it that way, hiding under the formality of the classroom, for eternity or, as in old rock-n-roll: e-ter-ni ter-ni-ty.

I am still living with Mara although that almost ended today. I went out to look for a new place, couldn't find any and came back, Mara scared, I feeling stupid and unable to leave. I can't figure out why I need Mara, why I'm angry at Mara—all the changes and all the coming back to the same point after the same ritual. I never felt so much that I was living out my life in a drama that I have always lived and at the same time, in some other place (the psychiatrist's) we watch me play out a life I have never understood. I do everything wrong, see myself as the complete asshole, try to deny this, and see myself as the wild complex thing nobody is going to figure out because everybody really knows what they want to be me more than anything else, even when they tell me things I am doing. The point I'm at with the psychiatrist is that I have transferred everything into a little boy role. He meanwhile points out to me that I am really an angry bastard trying to hurt people. Like I can see how for years with Mommy I could get away with being really cruel to her because I could never believe it was possible I could really be cruel. Cruelty by me was unreal—I had always been told that and I worked to have people tell me that. I think behind any relationship that you and I have, Rich, lies the struggle/amazement at the good-bad differentiation: which of us is really good in the end. We are both fascinated by the other's completely different way of handling the world by posing an opposite one. I don't think this is romanticizing either of us, and I also don't think it is falling into the trap that our parents set by making us opposites in the house. I mean they misinterpreted what was opposite by making you the bad one and me the good one. I think that really we were very much alike deep down.

The air is soft, full of smells and wine and the electric blood cells are here, have always been here even though our bodies feel rusty. Earlier in the day I thought of the wood houses near the beach selling tacos and the way the land wound past the theaters, blue with age because they are close to Neptune. Two motorcyclists go by, one in gold helmet and the other silver, looking pocked like those imitations of the planets that are silver. He is shooting off energy around his head, into the sky, the motor under him, the vehicle popping, lining up one-to-one with atoms, imitating the sun and moon, as they ride through town, mediaeval shields over their faces. I want to cry.

That we have never been the equal sons of Mommy, but it seems like we've had such separate (I guess it will have to be: relations) with her. What I mean is that it never feels that far away from one of those family crises, the ones with you and me fighting, Mom's hysteria. I'm sure we have our own competition for our mother, and that was suddenly a reality when she was out here. I felt she wasn't admitting how much she loved you wanting to see her and also her needs toward you, her love for you, etc. And partly I have never admitted to myself how I like to see her. I have played tough guy and dug my father more, but seeing her at the airport made me feel very easy and secure again.

When I called and Debby hadn't told you Mom had been out here, it was clear Mommy wanted to keep a secret that obviously couldn't be kept and so again it skyrockets the whole thing. Would you be jealous? Were you angry that she visited me and has never visited you or seen Robin? This is hard to say because I don't exactly know what's at stake. Even if I were to call her on how she acts toward you, she would accuse you of putting it in my head because I am her good boy and can do no wrong, and you are always bad, bad enough to corrupt and harm me. It makes me think again how I am still in the process of trying to string three correct sentences together; that is the task.

A classic game between Houston and the Giants for me. Driving back from Aspen with Mara and Charley and Judy around 6:30, picked up the game by 8:00 thirty miles east of Glenwood Springs, driving in the valley between the low mountains before the big passes, lightning making big static on the radio so I was nervous everyone in the car would complain. Astros with a 2-0 lead behind Dierker when McCovey hits a homer in the 7th. Giants go ahead 3-2 and we start going up the passes in the dark and rain; Astros tie in the bottom of the ninth and the game is in extra innings. Really hard driving and I am turning the radio on and off. I am dying for the game to end so I can concentrate on the driving, but somehow I have gotten exactly what I asked for, a game to last the whole night and constant possibilities for Bouton to come in. Finally he makes it in the top of the 14th, gets three infield pop-ups, and on the top of Loveland Pass Johnny Edwards hits a sacrifice fly scoring Cedeno.

Got your letter today under bad happenings. One of our cats, Baseball, had been out all night, which is strange for him. In the morning we went looking, and then, coming home, Mara saw him just off the road where the sand and rocks are, lying on his side. He was dead, hit by a car. He was completely stiff, a little stone in his teeth, and when Mara picked him up, some blood fell from his nose. He was really the most alive of cats I have ever seen; his body would undulate like one of those Slinky toys, you know, with the metal rings and the ripple of motion when you touch them—pure movement, not traceable like that of a car. We heard a scream in the middle of the night, and I think what happened was he was being attacked by another cat. Probably that cat chased him onto the road. He used to make this sound when he wanted things and I was able to talk to him by imitating the sound, and then he would make it again. It was not like between people who can't understand one another; it was more like two things (a cat and a man) who are locked into their forms but can spill over into one another—like the cat is very much a person sometimes and we are sometimes more like a cat.

Death is a language. It was a language on his face when I saw him. And I couldn't pick him up at first not because I was queasy about touching his body now that it was dead but because I was scared of death, that death would leap out—not that the cat would come alive and move in my arms but that death would, because he was of Death now and not Baseball anymore. When I did carry him, I was shocked at his stiffness and heaviness. Life distributes the weight, or the weight of life has such a different feeling. But the weight of death is not like the weight of an object. There really is an Ether of Death; sometimes it was like a smell around the cat. When we die we are joined to death: our spirit, our life then is no different from Death; we don't escape death when we die, we are it—so that the lightness and the smell and crazy potential around his face was his spirit and Death at the same time.

It is hard to live with Death. They don't complement, they each demand exclusivity. I dug a hole and we buried him, but there was a time while his body was in the house that Phlox his friend would sit next to him on the sofa and bat his head to try to get a response or love-bite out of him. I can't believe how stiff his body was.

We know how to imitate Death. Baseball's dead face made me think of the African masks of Death, and then I knew how well we can see that Language of Death. There along the road, the cars going by, I running to see if he is dead, and then saw DEATH looking at me from the sand; Death had Baseball, and I turned away, Death had him, not us.

Thirteenth Document

Debby is here now. I do a lot of comparing between my going to see you and Lindy, and Debby coming here to see us, because I try to account for what makes me angry and disappointed with her that is similar to what made/still makes you angry and disappointed with me. It's that in Debby I see the worst parts of myself so clear and all-consuming in her, things that Mara pointed out to us last night about our intentional wish not to know where the money comes from, not admit it comes from our father and thereby we forever choose not to be free. And things that I feel in Debby and in myself about excessive politeness and inhibition and always the choice to keep things safe; this includes: raspberry cookies, fantastic unboldness in foods (mainly her thing now so that meals have to be geared to what she's used to getting at her home in NY), fear of cats, and just the whole feeling of timidity I feel in her and myself. I think it comes out clearest with Debby when she says she is well-liked in school and then, when asked how does she relate to the people there, says she is "funny," which means she is skillful at being non-serious about most things. Being a "pretty, rich girl" is still her main drive, and except for a strong push sometimes to express "real" things, I can't find very much that I feel strong with her on; only the weak things come out, our common fears and prejudices from the house. She has been sold an incredible amount of shit from Mommy, so that she'll even say things like, "I know Mommy's prettier than me"; I mean she's so caught in that competitive game Mommy has set up with her and she still thinks Mommy is pretty much the kind of woman to be. And Jesus, I have it too. When Mommy was out here I liked to show people my beautiful mother and all that shit, to be so sucked into their mythology. The fact of our parents is that there is still a supply of inane Uncle Moes and Nevele hotel-goers to be sold the shit of my father's advertisements and the crap of my mother as a beautiful, exciting woman rather than an artificial frozen one.

Last week I screwed with some girl who I knew liked me just that way, and I can see for myself the desire to play the role of the midnight cowboy, the young stud who gets fucked by girls. I think I'm saying this a little too easily; that was the first time I've screwed with any girl besides Mara and I'm not sure what it means to me now, except it has been easy for me not to tell her, and I can even think of doing it again, as much as I didn't really like it while I was doing it.

Was in a little town east of here called Louisville yesterday. It's a settlement almost exclusively Italians. Wind was whistling down Main Street, walked to the end of town near the tracks and heard the wind strong in the wires, tumbleweed blowing through the dusty streets. This feeling out here that just over the hill, or even within sight, can be another settlement all to itself, a complete Great Plains settlement, whereas Boulder tucks into the mountains as close as possible and leers out of its cave.

Ultimately, though, I have made only a small breach in the big wall that is inside me. And there is no surety where I'll go but as the Cornelius Bros. and Sister Rose sing on the radio: "It's too late to turn back now."

3

Apache

Past midnight Maine time Jon woke me. He was in a phone booth in Denver. "Rich," he screamed in a whisper, "there's something I have to tell you. Remember the rock I threw at Horace Mann?" It took him a moment to recover his breath. "The trouble wasn't the broken window; it was that I pretended I didn't mean it. Now I take full responsibility for the act. Not as an aberration, not as an accident. It was my first blow for freedom."

He went on to say that they "had gotten drunk together," he and his buddies, had shown up late for work. The boss had fired him. He was going to go in the next morning, collect his last paycheck, and "punch the guy out."

I could hear him playing Marlon Brando in *On the Waterfront*—or was it *One-Eyed Jacks?*—challenging the ex-outlaw sheriff who had abandoned him in Mexico and was dealing high and mighty now.

I told him it was bullshit and asked him to drop it, and by so doing took more responsibility for him than I wanted or was capable of. He showed up three days later, having sped across America like a man fleeing werewolves. There was nothing to do but try to make space for him.

He took up residency in our barn and went to work the second morning at a fish factory on the Portland wharf. He returned that night, smelling of herring, Brandoing and demonstrating how, although we had lived on the ocean for two years, he had found the inner sanctum on his second day. He refused to bathe until Lindy insisted.

When a fat lady shouted from a seventeenth-century doorway, "You are closer to hell, my son, than heaven," it scared him at first.

"But I yelled back at her, 'Then it is hell where I am headed!' Don't you think that would have done Gandalf proud!"

I invited him to the beach for our old game of Ocean Ball—broomstick and Spaldeen—but a cold breeze pressed, and neither of our hearts were into diving through spray.

This was not the bashful, reverent brother who visited us in Ann Arbor but a man cultivating trouble. Not only did he not see this, I didn't see it either because it was concealed in our inflated lingo of magic and shamanism. The second week, to Lindy's relief, he moved into an apartment in Portland, a building owned by our hippie capitalist friends. He was going to help them repair it in exchange for rent.

Jon was disgusted by how they shared the hustle and market mentality of his father, yet smoked grass, read tarot, and played hard rock.

"They're fake revolutionaries," he complained. "I've seen their sort all over Boulder."

That weekend, as they appreciated expensive grass in an unfinished bedroom, he tried to freak them out. He spooked himself instead and came back to our place pounding on the door. He boasted about how he had left his colleagues in disarray ("like Juan himself"), yet constantly asked me if I could feel the presence of "something miasmal." I had trouble getting into either mood.

"You think just because you've procured a wife and an infant you've got some sort of privileges. I could have taken you back then at 1235 Park Avenue, and I could finish you now." He pulled a knife from his back pocket. "You think you can hide forever behind her and Robin?

You think I'm some sort of supplicant brother?" Turning to Lindy, "What makes you so sure I'm not going to rape you?" She walked away. "Where do you get off ignoring me?" Soon he was screaming about demons, as he huddled on the couch.

We called a doctor from down the street. An ambulance transported him to Portland.

Our mother flew from New York the next morning. She had stopped talking to me again for obscure reasons. I knew the high drama of her life only via Jon: she had left Bob a few months earlier and moved in with (of all people) his old college friend Moe Kornhauser, a wealthy, melancholy bachelor with a Jimmy Durante voice.

I had always enjoyed Moe, especially when, on the way home from Long Beach, we shared lemonades with him, his sister Alice, and brother-in-law Nook, but I thought of him as a joker, not a potential courter of my mother. At best, in his grizzled uncouthness, there was a hint of Humphrey Bogart in *The African Queen.*

Of course, this was the same woman who had once left my father for *his* best friend.

They came down the ramp like princess and bullfrog. I shook Moe's hand and tried to hug my mother, but she resisted, complaining about my making her fly in a low ceiling.

It was the only time she ever visited me.

The occasion was funereal. I was in quarantine, still the author of the traitorous letter, the father of the forbidden child (who made her an unwilling grandmother), the destroyer of her son. Though she never spoke it, her sole intention was to blame me for this episode—in the present for having the callousness to put my own brother in the hospital, then for filling him with craziness over the years. "It's no wonder he finally turned on you," she snapped. "You brought him so much pain."

Moe put a protective arm on her. "This has been upsetting for Martha. It's giving her 'pal-pitations.'" I was moved by his artless stumble over one of her favorite words.

That night at dinner—Robin playing trucks and cars around her chair on the inn floor—she rejected my notion that we had a family trauma. "Why us?" she demanded. "We're hardly the worst."

I didn't know.

"I don't deserve this."

Moe, silent the whole meal, paid the bill; then they headed for the hospital.

After three weeks Jon escaped, reclaimed his car from storage, and drove back to Colorado.

He took a job through the University Extension, teaching Chicanos. It was supposed to be Remedial English, but he and his pupils practiced knife feints by the Sawmill Ponds and chanted in Apache and transliterated English—texts of war songs out of museum publications.

"I'm forming a mestizo gang that will live in the desert," he told me on the phone. "I have brought the Indian and white man together. I have joined two ancient Asian magics." He wanted me, his brother, to hear it first because he was sure I'd read about him in the papers. "Not by name, but you'll know who it was. After all, you were the one who taught me about the power in Hopi verbs when I was still a long-distance runner for the king."

He sensed, perhaps for the first time, that Harry Pin was in trouble and he could put him away, a knockout punch he had waited almost twenty years to throw, a long time to let a dangerous opponent hang on the ropes, especially if he could go down as a whiteboy and rise up again as an Apache witch doctor.

"Who says we can't do it? How many did Castro have? Twelve men and spirit. When he was defeated, he said, 'We have won!' When they were half-starving in rags, he said, 'We have overthrown Batista.' That's the Apache way. They thought they had gotten rid of them when they 'removed' them, as they are fond of saying. Well, we are back, and we are going to take the council by storm." Psychosis? That's not what the old Indian books or Don Juan said, what survivors told those young Government anthropologists. It was impossible to know if Jon didn't understand politics or was inventing the politics of the future.

When his employers learned the subject matter of his teaching he was fired. He had a moment of glory when his kids defended him before the bureaucrats.

Then he began constructing a sacred history, a genealogy that would legitimize his heritage. He claimed that our "mother" was a Tartar Jew who had been raped by a Turkish warrior (he actually meant her ancestors during the Middle Ages) and that Arabs in our blood line had travelled to the New World as Sufi-Vikings, then mingled with Apaches. That was why his spirit had been summoned to these Colorado hills.

Lindy and I were staying in New York with Skip Rappaport, my adviser from Ann Arbor, when Jon tracked us down and woke the household to inform me I was Apache too. Wasn't I proud. Couldn't I see that Indian stare in our mother, her high cheekbones? He asked to speak to Rappaport, "that old Indian man," so he could tell him about "a spiritual discovery that transcends ethnography." I talked him out of that.

Why did the Apache rape seem so compelling to Jon, with all of Gnostic mythology in the wings, neither to be proved nor disproved but to haunt us all our lives? I had to admit there was a ring of authenticity to it. Perhaps he *could* remember—if not Apache, then something that would seem enough like it that Apache would serve, for lack of any Hebrew genealogy (and our phony Russian and German names, Turetsky and Grossinger). Tartars, Cossacks, and Mongols were our unidentified fathers—inklings of Freud's *Totem and Taboo*—that there is a primal act to which we come naked in the end, as in the beginning.

"We must seize the myth," Jon warned when I tried to apply the collective psychology of tribes, "or they will reduce us to their size. That's why they're called 'shrinks.' Language doesn't lie."

He called a few weeks later to say he had burned all his writing. "The cinders are still dancing in the middle of the floor. You're too good, Rich. I can't touch you. You don't have to worry because I'm hanging them up for good."

"But, Jon, you're a great writer," I patronized.

"No, I'm just your imitator. You were kind enough to teach me. You were such a saint in our household and they made you a martyr. All those years I wanted to believe you but couldn't. When we'd lie in bed at night and you'd tell me the point of life was the mystery, you understood—when you explained Mom was speaking in symbols and I refused to listen. Now I know it's not in words for me, it's not in books. Marijuana has finally brought me to your level."

Cause and effect in the Towers family deteriorated rapidly. Bob suffered a heart attack, then spent a month in Mount Sinai. My mother, feeling either remorse or compassion, abruptly left Moe (though still married to him) and attended her former husband daily. In fact, she threw Moe out of the apartment he had bought her, then moved Bob in upon his release from the hospital. It was to this devastated household that Jon suddenly returned.

I tried to talk him out of it. I told him that the war was over, that he was free at last to make his own way. But he wouldn't hear that. Vengeance drowned his mind.

"You had all the advantage, Richard," he declared before leaving Colorado. "You got to be the devil. They gave you power. I had to be the goodie. Now I want thunderbolts!" He forged them all the way east. And thunderbolts were what he gave them.

"He could have broken me in two," my mother remarked later, after he shoved her across the room, shouting Apache curses. "You were right," she told me on the phone. "I loved him, but I hardly knew him."

For once things were getting to be as they actually were.

After two weeks of Jon's preaching they convinced him to go to a halfway house in Vermont that specialized in youths in his condition (whatever they imagined that was). He took their money for the trip.

In his last act before leaving, he tossed papers relating frontal-lobe damage to the use of marijuana back at Dr. Hitzig, saying, "Don't debase me with this shit!" Then he disappeared for a month while police between New York and the Rockies kept him on file. Once again, he returned to Boulder.

Mara welcomed him. He claimed a construction job, "destroying my body, just as the Apaches were forced to do the white man's work." He fantasized he could leap from the dungeon into the empyrean and that such a leap alone was worthy of a warrior.

Weeks passed like this, summer into December. Finally when Mara went east for Christmas, he hit rock-bottom. Alone in the house he could not transcend his sorrow or a feeling of deadness that smoking all day and chanting Apache songs did not relieve. A paranoid notion lingered from Hitzig: 'I am brain-damaged. All these thoughts are coming through a broken mind.' He couldn't sleep. He couldn't bear being awake either.

For all the vision quests, the shamanic fantasies, for all the threats and knife-play, in the end, when the smoke faded, there was only a kid who had once thrown a football.

His mother came on United and brought him back to New York, huddled in the seat beside her. This time he went chaperoned to Vermont. The first night there he awoke from a dream and wanted to feel something because he still thought he had ruined his brain. He picked up a kitchen knife and ran it along his wrists. A girl found him, barely breathing. He was flown to a hospital in Albany. He left with bandages on both hands and was rushed to a mental facility in Maryland. He had now lost political freedom.

He ran away and was found shivering in the bushes. He escaped again, got as far as Philadelphia, was brought back. The next time he hid in the pantry of a house in Baltimore. The matron called the police.

Lindy and I had been doing readings at colleges in Ohio and West Virginia. We chose a route home to Vermont through Towson. We found the sanatorium—a cluster of institutional buildings resembling a prison. A social worker accompanied us to Jon's ward.

There he stood, alongside ping-pong tables. A woman with rolled eyes and cotton on her temples was led past. Peace and cosmos posters littered the walls. Carrying Robin on my hip, I called out my brother's name. He turned and met my eyes, a look of bewilderment and humiliation.

As he walked beside us to the yard, he wanted only to dream again, to follow baseball, to sing rock 'n' roll. "But it's too late for me, Rich. I could have led the simple life. But I tried to be more powerful than the gods."

I was sure that things would improve.

He shook his head. "The tarot doesn't lie: every hand, no matter how I shuffle, the Death Card—fifty thousand swords through my back." He giggled inappropriately. We walked him across the brief lawn. "My mother, the witch, is behind this. All those years you thought she was after you. Not so, not so. It was really me they were after, Jesse James!" He howled the name so loud the attendants looked up. "The outlaw. They finally got me." He bounced himself off the wall like someone hit with a bullet. "The drugs make me forget. Save all my letters. Write down everything I ever said. If I escape I will need you to tell me who I am, Frankie. But I expect to die."

Fourteenth Document

Just moved into Denver yesterday, 1740 High Street, Apt. 4. I have a small room for $60 a month. It has stove and refrigerator. The letter I wrote you two days ago had a lot about Denver and now I'm here. Things are still very day to day, hour to hour, but then again: when weren't they? There is this real gloominess in the mornings that I wake into, almost without fail long dreams of Mara during the night. There are huge questions now. So much being with Mara was that we were just supposed to be together, closed my eyes and we would always be there. There is the big real world we always tried to speak of out there. I hope it will be hard to turn down such a fine offer.

At the topless place it wasn't just the rejection but the whole hardness of it, the big tits and big women flashing in front of me and sitting next to me. I woke up the next morning (two hours sleep) with that screaming inside me very badly. Sometimes I am relaxed, seeking strongly; sometimes I am on the prowl panic-like, fighting for air and sense.

There is this word that stares me in the face: loser. The ones in the bars, the ones like me who have never really loved, only needed and used. I don't want to be a loser. That movie The Hustler was all about this business of winners and losers, the losers being even men with a super talent like Fast Eddie because they don't develop themselves so that eventually their talent can't save them from themselves or even accomplish anything bigtime in the world.

I'm walking around pretty scared most of the time, scared of men and what being a man means and fighting with men, very scared to get on their bad side, scared of women and what fucking means and what loving means. And this was always there. Mara kept me from seeing it. So I'm back to knowing it as I knew it all along. It's hard when the feelings come that want her back, this old old fear-demand, like I wake and I have to find out again I'm not with her and there seems no reason for it, and it's wild and irrational inside me.

Read <u>Dune</u> in a week. Tremendous. I think of that feeling: you make it or you don't and the universe don't care, really doesn't. As you write of <u>Pierre</u>, the sea's the sea and men do drown.

I'm so damn conservative. The business that I was wild, begun by my parents, turns out to be a big lie. Instead, just like them, I'm a stay-at-home; I'm nervous about taking chances; I've got a lot of old bachelory finicky habits. And always I hear my stronger voice toned down inside of me and my meek one is always on the surface, in the warehouse, talking to girls.

I really have this fuck-the-world, give-up-the-struggle, run-away attitude that might come off as seeking evil. But I'm no tough guy, that's for sure. I'd be too scared to be Marlon Brando really, so I'm always just a stowaway on Melville's ship, closer to Jim Hawkins. I never run the ship like Ahab or mutiny it like Brando.

Your not having that bravado makes a lot of difference between us. It was upon that difference that we decided to have nothing to do with each other while we were living in the same house. What I do learn from you, because of the difference, is the futility of scattered action, doing for the sake of doing. I sit here like a burden and end up trying to hurt myself because I want Mara back, and I try to turn it into that she hurt me. I'm always seeing every man as my father, the author of me, who writes me, and so I never have responsibility because it is always other men who are deciding what I'm supposed to do. That comes in a lot now with the psychiatrist. It's him who tried to get me away from Mara and broke us up, and it's him who has all these plans for me.

It's raining right now in this dry country. I went up to a very dry portion of the mountains last weekend. Crows for me too. About five circling not far from me when I had gotten lost in the woods and couldn't find the trail. But there must have been a dead animal other than myself. I thought lots of the line:

"Dan and I with throats burned dry and souls that cried for water."

Fifteenth Document

I am excited and tentative. The simultaneity of our writing to each other brings a thrill. Recalls the secrets and the magic. Sometimes I wish you were more clear. I always feel you are writing about something specific, then you hide it. It seems imperative to not be the James brothers here (Jessie and Frank) but to try for something else.

Gil McDougald and Mickey Mantle. That's us, the slugger and the jack-of-all-trades. Remember when Casey Stengel talked about just these two players. He was talking about us. You were Gil McDougald; I was Mickey Mantle. Together we were indispensable. In the end we were the only ones Casey remembered, the stardust twins.

Marijuana I take a lot of now. I have developed myself with it and am able to use it better now. People rarely speak about developing with a drug; they think it is one thing for all the time. But in the month and a half I've been taking it pretty steadily (once a day at least) I have sharpened my use very much.

I'm going to be teaching Freshman English to Chicanos in the UMAS Program, and though I'm excited and the money is $1600 for the summer for teaching two sections, this new role has made me agitated and thrown me back on some old sabotage behavior in which I try to blow my opportunities. It's either that I'm feeling like a bum, I shouldn't be teaching, or I think I'm the only one who can teach and I get hostile and isolated from the other instructors.

Music has been very important. From some country rock album (Pure Prairie League is the group) I have for the first time in my life been able to hear musical themes and their blending and many uses in one song. The most recent man of importance for me has been John Lee Hooker whose album "Never Get Out of These Blues Alive" I bought and listened to painfully, for the blues are very painful, not the fun and games I thought when I was liking and getting the records of Blind Willies, etc. Saw John Lee Hooker the other night, the music superloud in Tulagis. He was definitely a black black-skinned man. Very fierce, lots of pain, all of it. The song "Never Get Out of These Blues Alive" is a ten-minute one, and on the record he gives Van Morrison a lesson in singing the blues, though this is done very subtly. Lines I like best are when John Lee says:

Now Van Morrison
(approx, 4 beats)
asked me

(4 beats)
he said Johnny why why
(2 beats)
do you sing the blues
(2 beats)
I said I'm doomed I'm doomed
(1 beat)
All I know is to sing the blues.

My brother, the time of our people is over. They have come to imprison us, to take us away into the darkness. They will not let us live in light again. It is the removal of the Apache lords, the Apache brides. It is the last generation of Apache children. "Ai di na da ol t'o' "—"This time we will smoke." "Knife"—"Bec." "Xa tci ta"—"he drew out." "Bi git ge tc'ij k(G)ic da t'e he ko"—"Then the middle of its breast he slit." "Ai di na da ol t'o'!"

oh brother spare me these moments I have for you and know that I write this time with hope of giving you a gift of great importance and I do this in the rejoicing I feel for the old love that binds us which you have reanimated by your letter. I speak to you in whispers, behind the oak tree at night if you will have it that way, in the trust that you will spare any persons of the family a hurt we do not wish to bring upon them. For one, I speak specifically of our mother. I say to you now that there is ample reason that has come to me via spoken word by a person most close to us and by a growing doubt in my own mind and I believe in yours that the question of your paternity is not settled and that there is reason to doubt the state things are presently decided on concerning this.

DO YOU HEAR ME JESSE I SAY THAT YOUR PATERNITY IS IN QUESTION

that we will ride we will ride forever on the ledger of the news because the question of your paternity—the very business of sex ultimately—is in question.

Richard who I ride with outside the law of the natural world, crying out against the way fucking fucks things up. You who were more your mother than your father. Frank James is heard of during the Civil War before Jesse. He fought with Quantrill's Raiders and was with him when he burned Lawrence and Frank joined in the killing. THAT THE QUESTION OF GOOD AND BAD ENTERS HERE VERY STRONGLY and how you wish to implicate me in doing bad things and represent them to me in this way and in this way you get your revenge on me for being the goodboy.

And yet I make war all day long in my own way as you make it in yours and you are called bad and blamed for Jesse's going bad. As we both know that my father and our mother have seen it that way with us. Jesse's mother and wife always swore their boys were not involved, especially Jesse, but one gets the feeling that Zerelda James is a kind of Ma Barker fashioning her boys into killers not fuckers. And her next marriage to a respectable doctor was partly a blind she used to hide her desire to have her sons revenge her on the world. She coated her own self in innocence, marrying a minister first, then a doctor, but gossip about her nature hung onto her.

It is probable that Jesse and Frank James saw themselves also linked to the great English bandits Robin Hood and Dick Turpin. These were bandits who turned around the natural honesty of the world like Lear, the Fool and Edgar. The name "Frank James" makes it look as though there are Irishmen, Scots, and English back there. The public certainly saw them in this Robin Hood way, and at times the James Brothers had a close friend, John Edwards, write up their stories with this in mind. Jesse and Frank wait for the train and pull a rail as it approaches; the engine is derailed. $2,000 in the strongbox; in anger at the paltry amount they rob the passengers. Good bank robberies by the James Brothers net in the $20,000 range. They steal from the rich and ride home. It is all for their mother they do this. They come in late at night. She finds them in bed in the morning. When they come down they give her wide-eyed faces and helpless grins and she knows they are innocent.

How I am never satisfied.

How I deeply fear something that races straight to the core of the world with me, the fear that stalks every success I have. Mother, who we are saving in this deed we do together, I'm still carting it back to you, it's all for you, I'm saving you, I fought the dragon for you, what Daddy did to you, as you Richard look for a father to gun down, I have one to too two.

IT WOULD BE A PAIN TO WRITE ABOUT MYSELF TO YOU NOW

but am always to be your deepest brother-friend because

I am

Jon

4

Jonathan in the Dark Magic Place

THE FACILITY IN Maryland may once have been a functioning hospital, but it had become a dumping ground for children of the upper middle class. During the twenty-one months Jon was there he had five different doctors, assigned and changed at the convenience of staff politics and to accommodate vacation schedules. The man who treated him the longest was an exchange doctor from Argentina who hardly spoke English, let alone Jon's English. He didn't have the slightest understanding of American culture, so he wrote that the subject's problems resembled voodoo phobias and that it was unusual to find this in a European country.

The staff ultimately collaborated on a simpler diagnosis: marijuana-induced paranoid schizophrenia. Jon had taken drugs, and he talked magic. He was obsessed with tarot cards.

No therapy was done. Since the patient was arrogant and uncooperative and tried to escape, they advised he be sedated at all times. Different doctors applied names to Jon's ostensible symptoms, making up therapeutic stories for his myths, mistaking his intellectual interests for his disease. They contradicted one another in their reports even as he contradicted himself. They overlooked the raw emotional basis of his pain and followed his language around like cats after a string. When he was depressed and no longer spoke of magic they wrote that he was improving. If he had a vision (and made the mistake of telling them) they called it a relapse. "They shame even Freud," Jon wrote. "They and my parents deserve each other."

There is a madness of the mind, a madness of the heart, and a madness of the spirit. No delirium tinged Jon's mind or spirit. He was lucid and radiant always, even as a faux Apache. But how is one to feel if they are never taught beauty, if they are tacitly forbidden to enjoy the breezes and twilights of childhood? How is one who is never safe able to love? How is one to feel safe with a mother who turns grief into terror? How is one to express his own fear-desire except by converting her into a witch and himself into a wizard and tarot master? How else to put the dream pin back through the Medusa? To undo the spell that summons assassins instead of angels?

Unrequited love was Jon's sole act of ceremonial magic. Not crazy-making demons but ghosts that arise when the heart is replaced by inextricability and the lady by a labyrinth. He did his things not because his motives were so far below the surface he didn't know he was doing them but because they were so goddamn obvious he didn't realize they were immolating and that he could pick another way.

Jon had the sacred disease, the crucible in which the doctor's own profession was primordially based—the wounded shaman. But he was dangerously out of the lineage and no one would train him, no one would send him on an authentic vision quest. Aboriginally there was purpose in such a wound: to create a healer. Now civilized, we hand our children over to bureaucrats—schools, armies, and doctors. The Spartans would judge us far crueler than they; the Apache did.

Jon was fed as much thorazine as they could get away with. His life became a drab skein of weeks, sporadic social and athletic interludes that merged with the general grayness and then some new doctor asking him about his mother and father. His interrogation had turned into a procession of recited facts, or refusals to recite, a memory without chronology, a present outside of time. "I was kidnapped, sold to slavers. By my own mother."

"They should be arrested for impersonating a mental hospital," Bob announced. But he kept his son there and paid the bills. (Of course he did not see it as prison or punishment. It was the most expensive cure he could buy: $150 a day in 1973.)

People want to be taken. They wouldn't pay a nickel to a Native American medicine man despite his thousand-year record of healings in cases of soul loss. Better the patient die than to go against the prosperity of the post-war years, to defile the memory of a good Jewish boy like Dr. Salk or Mount Sinai, to lose the opportunity to *schmooz* with Hitzig.

And they have been dying. In the best of families they have been dying.

> I do not think that anything is to be gained by arguments about formal diagnostic labels. The terminology used varies widely and is not really clarifying. We can say with confidence that he is a very sick young man, that he has been sick a long time, that an illness of this kind is a slowly developing failure of maturation. We cannot promise that he will get well, but I personally feel that he has a chance only if you allow him to remain in intensive treatment either here or at a similar hospital and for a long time (by which I mean at least a year or so) and only if you will turn the whole thing over to the hospital and really back out of the picture yourselves completely. I would urge you to taper off your visits, phone calls and letters, and to discourage phone calls and letters from other members of the family. I understand that you have been seeing him once a week. I would urge you to cut down immediately.
>
> It is not that what you do or say is necessarily harmful, but that he will misuse it to his own disadvantage until he is well on his way to recovery. That is why your well-meant and frequent visits and messages only slow up his progress and perhaps make it impossible.
>
> I am sorry to have to take such an emphatic position, but it is the only honest one that I can take and I hope that you will find in yourselves the strength to adhere to such a plan faithfully.
>
> With all good wishes, I remain
> Very truly yours,
> Lawrence S. Kubie, M.D.

Sixteenth Document

DEAR RICHARD
INSTANT
TAROT
TAKES
OH I GUESS
ITS THE CHAINS THAT
BIND ME
OH YOU TALK ABOUT
HARD LUCK AND TROUBLE

SEEMS TO BE MY
MIDDLE NAME
LOVE JON

I fall asleep from thorazine and sleep the night. I don't remember any dreams. It feels terrible when I wake up. My sickness has my body and soul.

I'm going to start a Work Therapy job this week, probably in the cafeteria storeroom. A friend of mine named Eric and me are going to sing some Bob Dylan songs together at this scheduled coffeehouse this weekend.

It's about 6:15 in the morning. I woke up a few hours ago from a wet dream in which I was having intercourse with Debby. Outside through the screen windows it's getting lighter. One or two other patients are up. An aide is closing the window in somebody's room because it's cold in the hall because they had the heat off. Another aide is talking with a patient about the weather.

Sometimes I think I'm so dead inside and really I'm a million miles away from being alive. I finished a book on wolves today. I guess I want to be doing something now to keep away the feeling of deadness.

I'm thinking of the trips I took to Michigan to visit you. The train ride, the sunlight, the woods, the light in the woods, the central hub of Chicago, the vortex of Chicago spewing you back out to the countryside, rounding Lake Michigan and proceeding east. And the deep dark night of the country, Kalamazoo, Niles, Ypsilanti, and then Ann Arbor.

I'm thinking of the great adventure it was, the heady feeling of freedom I always had in doing it. And then seeing you and the richness of your life to me, everything, cats, books, the pictures on the wall, horoscopes, alchemy, charts, maps, beautiful patterns on the coverlets, Frodo in the box in the closet, regal and lovable, the writing you gave me to read and which I took to that wonderful room you gave me for my own, always dazzled by the brilliance in it, always uplifted, always hoping to aspire to it. Those were great trips, despite the taut feelings and crazy way in which they were taken and the rigidity between us, the things neither of us could say, the things in each other we feared. I needed them so much as infusions for the sterility and barrenness of dorm life in Wisconsin and my inability to generate any kind of life for myself there.

All I ever wanted to do is speak to you. That's all it was that night in Portland. I wasn't trying to hurt you, maybe a little because you said my writing just sounded like yours.

Yesterday me and Matthew took a bus into downtown Baltimore to get some shoes for him. It was two hours total travelling time for getting there and back, a lot of fun to ride on the bus and see new things, see a lot of black people. Walking around in the crowded downtown was a high, brought back city feelings, the speed and the struggle. Tomorrow four of us are going out to eat at Johnny Unitas' Golden Arm and I'm looking forward to that.

I'm not up to writing. I just don't have the insights and intensities and nostalgias I once had. I really mourn the loss of these and pray they will return. Mara's going to have a child and is getting married to the father later this year. I still write to her. I don't remember that much about living with her and don't have much longing for her. It's like I drank and got stoned and made it all disappear. I get small flashes and the beginning of the ancient feeling, but it passes quickly and I am back into dullness with a mind that jumps along the surfaces of everything. Also I don't know if I really believe in the hospital, though I've gotten better than when I came in. I sort of end up trusting that so many people are here they must know something, the way one trusts their parents will always care for them.

Outside through the screened windows and beyond the buildings where the tops of some trees are, there seems a reason for living. And it sustains me for a moment with an innocent view that dies as soon as it has appeared. Nothing remains for long in my mind but the one constant that is a pain and a darkness which I wallow in, too scared to move forward, too scared to do anything about it. I can't kill myself in one fell swoop. I always used to think about torture and that's what I've gotten into—a slow, long torture. It started from fighting ghosts when I wanted to be in bed to touching the lamp socket on my desk when I was studying. I'm so scared of the aggressive side that came up via the marijuana that I don't even think about it much. I shouldn't even use the word "think" for what I do, because it's not really thinking. I feel very guilty for what I've done in my life, but I'm not really penitent about it, just scared that I actually did it.

Sometimes I feel so bitter, impotent, and scared when I think of your success, but the fear dominates and I say, "Well, I'm a bum; that's what I am. Other people have failed, so why not me." And I give up. But something will stir like the tops of those trees.

I see my whole life as a decline. I was so used to saying, "It's okay," "I'm fine," that I thought I could change everything bad by getting one moment's private perception. I think now of some days getting up for school there'd be this talking in my head going on so resoundingly, but I would say nothing about it, just keep on eating Bridey's eggs and bacon.

In the end, for $100,000, the doctors could only declare that Jon was belligerent and incurable; they refused to be responsible anymore.

He stepped out on the street, free but disoriented. A year had passed in America—a year of revolution and tumult. So weird had matters become he could equally have been a prisoner of war returning from Vietnam, or a Vietnamese refugee.

He was met by young women promising Sun Myung Moon, hawkers for massage parlors. Carlos Castaneda was selling the latest installment of his adventure. Although Carlos' experience with a Mexican sorcerer would seem to have been exactly the opposite of his own on thorazine, the new book felt eerily familiar. It was the only text that even pretended to have knowledge of what he had undergone.

Seventeenth Document

The halfway house is in the city, but about a mile from the downtown. About six blocks away is North Avenue, lots of action and black people.

I am as convinced as ever that I won't make it. I've done some kind of thought-process brain-damage and life is just a constant agony. But I can't kill myself. The other day there were some sharp knives in the kitchen I was using and I thought of taking one back to the hall, but I never came close. I am meeker than ever and institutionalized. Shitting is impossible for me unless I push hard and this just isn't a one-day or week constipation. It is every day for the last year and a half. I'm pretty much a wreck of a person who should be dead but who lingers on in wretchedness, overeating, doing very little. I do have a good friend Louise who believes in me a lot and constantly gives me encouragement and that feels good, though I find some way pretty fast not to believe in it or just forget about it. I went to the zoo with her on Saturday. Saw a beautiful buffalo with a massive head. Mainly thought that I was like the animals, just eating and feeling bad and blindly wanting an escape or too tamed down to even want that anymore.

A month later Jon revived. "I was hitching in the rain somewhere," he told me on the phone. "This guy picked me up. He said, 'Damnit if you aren't Lord Jesus Himself!' And who's to say I'm not. Christ was a Jew. He was a longhair, a hippie like me. Remember Gandalf; remember the alchemical king: I was crushed in a hot place, reduced to ashes. Who could question my victory over the hexing shamans now?"

"Aren't you worried about the drugs?"

He laughed contemptuously. "You know what happened in *Dune*. I have turned those poisons into a sweet, sweet juice."

The halfway house was too regimented, so Jon tried a Krishna commune. There he lasted less than twenty-four hours after putting down a month's deposit of his father's money. "The people wore white robes and this fascist in charge—he was so holy you couldn't discuss anything with him. He wasn't Oriental. He was a Jewish guy from Brooklyn."

After his father rented him an apartment, Jon took up fortune-telling and street preaching. He met with a group in the park to make plans for the Fourth World, the one (according to Hopi prophecy) that follows this civilization. In his mind, society had already collapsed. There was no place for him in it anyway. The only job he could have filled was that of squad-leader after the revolution—and then only if the revolution was the one he was waiting for, with just the right components of social disintegration and occult revival.

"I told my father I was reading tarot for the new out-patient doctor. I thought he'd be proud. So you know what he says?"

I could imagine!

"'Is that what I'm paying for,' he tells me. 'To find out my son is a fortune-teller? The guy's been on the dole his whole life. When's he ever had to start a business?' That's the kind of shit my father says. He doesn't care about me."

"What did you expect?"

"Johannes!"

He meant the delusional son from Carl Dreyer's film, *Ordet*. Johannes believed he was the resurrected Christ but was regarded as a lunatic. Midway through the film he disappeared into the open fields ("Where I go, you cannot follow . . . "). Then his sister-in-law Inge died while giving birth. At her funeral, just as the coffin was about to be closed, without warning Johannes returned, restored to his senses. The mourners presumed he was cured (a small blessing at a time of tragedy). But his two nieces, remembering when he was "Christ," asked him to revive their mother. He abruptly turned to accuse them of mocking God, of killing Inge by their "little faith." Then, to the dismay of all, he offered to bring her back to life by the power of the children's faith alone. The family pastor reached out to halt this blasphemy, but the doctor—a man bearing a haunting resemblance to Hitzig—stopped him by grabbing his arm. Then, in one of the most unexpected and stirring scenes in cinema history, Johannes called out to God, asking for the Word "to raise the dead." As he spoke, Inge imperceptibly stirred. Then she sat up. Her weeping husband embraced her.

"Johannes!" Jon exclaimed. "His father said, 'I wanted a man of God and look what I got.' Until he worked the miracle they thought he was a madman too. My father wanted a rabbi. Well, he's got Isaiah the prophet and Moses the magician and all he can do is make jokes."

What could I say? I didn't want anarchy or the Fourth World. I clung to domestic life and hoped the Aquarian apocalypse wouldn't harm us. Robin's small body and the high clouds telling nothing—those I loved more than any chant or prophecy symbol.

Book Three

ROTHKRUG

1

Goddard College Blues

Arriving in Vermont in the fall of '72 I imagined myself teaching far-out courses to eager students. The "Course Selection Supermarket" was my rude awakening.

Without any set curriculum, Goddard teachers submitted new topics every trimester. That summer I had written descriptions for *"Moby Dick"*; "Alchemy, Astrology, and Totemism"; and "Freud, Reich, and Jung." On the first day of the term, faculty members sat around the library. Bearing mimeo guides, students paraded by—guys with plaited hair, some without shirts, one with a witch-doctor's rattle inside his belt; ghostly spaced-out women in tie-dyes and leotards; chubby, curly-haired girls wearing paisley dresses. One by one they quizzed me about what my courses *really* were.

"Do we have to read books?"

"Can we make jewelry [or drop acid] in alchemy?"

"Is there primal screaming in the Reich part?"

Far from being sought out, I was mainly avoided. If it hadn't been for Sheppard herding dubious classmates my way, I would have shared the bottom rung with Jack Thomas, the elderly anthroposophist.

To my surprise the majority of people offering courses for credit weren't faculty at all but students and ex-students, mobbed by cohorts. The big energy centered not even on course selection but improvisational artists pulling down their pants and squatting on the copying machine.

When the trimester began, courses convened in the living rooms of dorms (there were only two classrooms in the school). The first day of my Alchemy seminar I sat on the floor experiencing a familiar disorientation: Why was I talking so fast and giving out so much information? Periodically I asked: "Any questions?" "Does everyone get that?"

"Everyone" nodded blankly.

First, I explained how alchemy and astrology were two quite different systems, the latter a combination of a calendar/clock and theory of spirituality, the former a fusion of vitalist beliefs with primitive laboratory science. I then defined totemism as academic repackaging of phenomena so ancient and diverse as to include alchemy and astrology as well.

There was no sign of recognition from seven of the eight attendees. They lay on the floor. Two had their eyes closed; the rest stared. But Sheppard was so alert he seemed about to jump out of his skin. I watched him bounce in place to the cadence of my voice, providing "Wows!" and whistles.

In my other courses I presumed at least hearsay acquaintance with literature and dream symbolism but, to kids who had never read Faulkner, Hawthorne, or even Robert Frost—and had a "*Forbidden Planet*/Creatures from the Id" view of Freud—my terminology was more arcane than advanced genetics.

In truth, Goddard was a school for wealthy, anti-academic kids. Glass-blowing and rock-climbing earned stature well above history or anthropology. "Psychology" meant pop psychology or radical kindergarten. Members of the administration held these views even more fervently than students. They likewise had come to escape.

Walking to my classes through Indian summer, I passed flutists and was passed by bike riders screeching blues-rock. Spiders and chipmunks darted through dew.

My dorm oozed rotten oranges and potatoes. Stereos thumped. During the second "Freud, Reich" meeting, a gangly boy, naked from a shower, pranced past, dangling but not using his towel.

Afterwards came community lunch. Occupying most of the ground floor of a rickety wooden edifice, the Goddard dining room was a cross between a Lower East Side union hall and a street fair in Amsterdam. Its noisy, colorful commons bred ideological skits and acts of spontaneous theater ranging from pornographic slapstick to costumed song and dance. The food was conscious: ingredients labelled, vegetarian set aside. When the tables were occupied, students and faculty crowded along the walls.

Traditional hierarchies had vanished. At least a dozen faculty had separated from their spouses and were living with students, sometimes both the man and woman of a couple with "child lovers." "Downwardly mobile" was Goddard's proud catch-phrase for itself—jingoistic anti-elitism. Its model was Cuba, if not Castro's actual island then an idealized clone.

Rural Vermont was its own experience. Graduates, dropouts, and escapees from cities had turned the town of Plainfield and surrounding hills into a countercultural mecca—communes whimsically named New Hamburger and Pie in the Sky. A Grange Hall down the road summoned us once a month to divvy up produce. There we heard riffs extolling fences, windmills, and Ashley wood-burners; the zen of canning, the alpha-wave high of a saw on wood.

Affinity groups of mutts commandeered our half dozen streets, growling and turning over garbage. Wrecks of cars and jeeps—converted hearses, and psychedelic vans—sat amid earthmovers. At night, a din of contra-dancing and guerrilla theater simulated urban life.

On July 4th hobo bands led a humongous Uncle Sam puppet through town, dragging behind him a Third World nation on a chain surrounded by costumed birds, eggs, and a Nixon Death's Head.

Every afternoon Robin attended Center School, a parent-run co-op in the hills. Throwing himself into its raunchy subculture, he forged quick bonds with Beth, Jason, Rosemary, and Scootchy, and was soon transformed into a country kid in overalls, a mop of sandy hair. In Big Wheels he and his buddies tore down the hill in back, spinning out tirelessly in its sandpit.

Beth's father, Bob, was a hip psychiatrist who had left practice in San Francisco to teach at Goddard. Her mother, Anne, was studying to be a therapist. Chris and Ellen, Scootchy's parents, lived down the street from us in the feedstore-apartment "slum" while they finished their dream house in the hills, a Buckminster Fuller dome enclosing a pegmatite crystal. Ellen worked for the Vermont Arts Council; Chris taught skiing at Stowe.

An evening a month we attended a parents' meeting and debated correct education. Disagreements about toy guns and the f-word inevitably pitted humanist psychologists against Marxists and diverged to long-winded disputes about symbols versus reality—far more cerebral than anything at Goddard.

It is hard to forget being embarrassed in the Montpelier Grand Union by Robin and Scootchy rolling in their parents' shopping carts, passing in the aisle and addressing each other by their fondest greeting: "Hey, fucker asshole!"

That was positively courteous compared to the campus, where President Jerry was helpless before competing left-wing factions. From the day I arrived, public forums degenerated into chants for his resignation, and I was surprised to find my own hiring cited among the "white-elitist garbage" of his regime.

My unpopularity with the politicos should have left me more allied with the academics. Yet my main colleagues were visual artists and theater people. Most of the literature and social-science people saw me as arrogant and obscure, which I was. Behind my back they trashed my courses as the antithesis of Goddard. They didn't understand that Olson transcended their mystique. They didn't even know he had stopped in town (by invitation) during the formative years. Meanwhile I found them righteous and fake-experimental with their Jung/Blake/New Physics syntheses—Johnny-come-latelies, and oversimplifiers as well.

During our years in Maine our magazine *Io* had grown into a community of people who shared an interest in Mediaeval science, American Indians, Black Mountain literature, and ecology. Themes branched and dispersed from issue to issue.

After we moved to Mount Desert, an "Oecology Issue" followed "Ethnoastronomy." The eighth *Io*, "Oneirology," published from Cape Elizabeth, was a receptacle of dreams and dreamwork. Then came a breakthrough: Terry Nemeth, a founding partner of Bookpeople, a countercultural wholesaler in Berkeley, phoned one December morning and offered to distribute our back issues. That same afternoon we emptied our barn and shipped him five years of accumulated cartons (it was reported they arrived with the center books still so cold the staff came over one by one to feel them). In just two months they sold them, paid us, and ordered more. We suddenly had money to expand.

Io/10, the "Baseball Issue," included all the poems we had collected touching on sports. (Among these was "Brooklyn August," the first published work of a young student at Orono; only back then we didn't know he was "Stephen King.")

During 1972 and '73 Lindy and I put out four issues a year—half of them giant "Earth Geography Booklets" stretching from petroglyphs and the Wisconsin Ice Age to Carl Sagan discussing life in outer space—from Kenneth Anger's astrological motorcyclists to steamboating on the Great Lakes, lost Olson texts, and Bardo calendars. *Io* had become an esoteric "Whole Earth Catalogue."

Every volume included primary-source chunks taken from occult books and ethnographic journals. We decorated the margins and ends of pieces with alchemical and astrological insignia, etchings from bestiaries and herbals, Hopi shields, assorted collages, and scientific glyphs. At least a third of each issue was work that couldn't wait for a theme.

Since Olson's death in 1970, his literary executors had been tracking down every extant word. That is why I was surprised when one of my students found an uncatalogued tape—early '60s—corroboration of the poet's "apocryphal" visit. It had lain in the Audiovisual Center untouched from the hour it was made.

A group of us met to open the time capsule. A blustery November eve, rain fell on our tin roof. The Homeric voice, the mediumistic trembling of electricity, the nearness and crackle of fire—all combined to suggest a séance.

I lay in the dark later, thinking about the magus I never met—and would never—who had the gall to stand there ten years in the past and tell me: "All that happens is eternal/no examples, no proving/possible.... The work, the real work, of the future has already been done, and the future that is proposed for us is a lie."

My heart reached to his Phoenician boats and Sumerian merchants, his monks in coarse robes, his galactic axis shifting millennially, scattering astronomers to Babylonia and Stonehenge, fishermen to Cranberry Islands. These migrations—really transmigrations—were the boundary markers of our time.

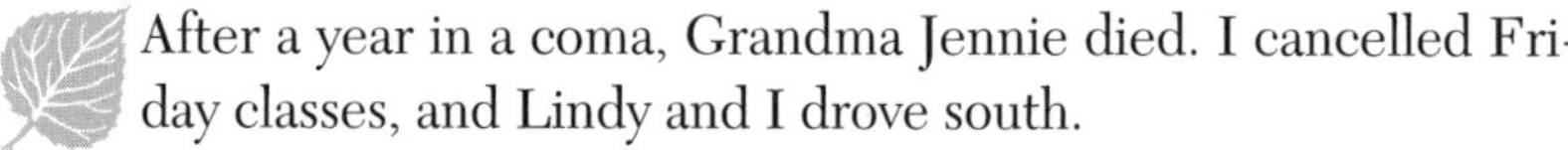
After a year in a coma, Grandma Jennie died. I cancelled Friday classes, and Lindy and I drove south.

At Grossinger's we stood among the flotsam of a zodiac: Eddie Fisher aged beyond his years, Milton Blackstone shrunken like a voodoo doll, Dr. Hitzig half blind and led by a black attendant, my mother and Bob grim and refusing to talk to us, retired staff like old apples from the fields, handsome Jewish ambassadors and El Al pilots, actresses anonymous behind veils:

> *A rabbi cuts my father's sweater and watches over him as he sits unshaven on a crate, enacting shiva. Cousins, aunts and uncles, great aunts and great uncles, members of Isaac's clan from Chicago, Montreal, Pittsburgh, Israel and New York, have returned from their lives as car dealers, fabric importers, and real-estate investors for the coronation: golden Jennie, whose body no one sees (or saw the last two years except in murti on rye-bread packages). The closed coffin contains a wasted anonymous doll that lay comatose for months, senile before that, as line after line fell, cutting off ganglia, faint membrances calling out names. Until they dissolved too.*
>
> *The coffin is set on straps and dangled over the breach of cobblestone and archaeology, then lowered past Whiteman, past Iroquois, past proto-Archaic into the Palaeolithic. Pale rabbis exchange battered books and summon some further orthodoxy that the wind tears into gibberish.*

During the winter trimester (which I had off), Lindy and I gave readings in the Midwest. We stopped in Towson to see Jon. We returned to Plainfield to find snows as deep as any I had known.

Squalls singing through cracks, particles fluttering against glass, I pictured glaciers riding Vermont, flush with clouds, scraping sky as they ground mantle into loess and plowed moraine into the hills. At night, milky ways spilled in, hot bearpiss littering cosmological black.

Lindy talked of needing something new in her life. "Either a job, a lover, or a baby," she joked, and she wrote a piece called "Baby? Maybe."

With no classes to teach I began to write a lobsterfishing thesis.

Back in Ann Arbor when I was supposed to be learning the rudiments of anthropology, I was actually a poet with a day job. I never cultivated an academic voice nor took scholarship seriously. I passed through seminars in physical anthropology, Old and New World archaeology, ethnographic theory, and the history of anthropology, getting A's (as all graduate students did). Completing eight courses and ten electives gave me an automatic Master's degree. Prelims and fieldwork were next.

On our honeymoon Lindy and I had visited Hopi and Navaho villages. We returned for fieldwork training in the summer of '67. With Frodo in a rundown car, surrounded by missionaries, Two-Horned Priests, and students of linguistics, we were in over our heads.

To a degree that I didn't see, my cavalier attitude toward the profession maddened Skip Rappaport and made foes among the more orthodox members of my department. Yet I held to a solitary path. When Rappaport left for a sabbatical in Hawaii, I didn't foresee the dangers about which he had been warning.

In the spring of 1969 I applied to take prelims. I had already gotten a grant from the National Institute of Mental Health to study homeopathy in Maine (under the guidance of Ted Enslin). The exams were a formality. No one who was allowed to take them failed them.

I filled bluebooks with epistemology of Australian Dreamtime, structures of Ndembu mythology, Plains Indian ghost dances; I cited Claude Lévi-Strauss, Michel Foucault, James Mooney, Frances Yates, and Gladys Reichard, none of them permissible sources in my program. I could have scribbled a few pages of jargon and passed. I probably could have written *nothing* and done better.

I didn't flunk the prelims for lack of knowledge. There were no questions on these exams that had either right or wrong answers. I failed because I so outraged some professors that they gave me zeroes—absolute zeroes—which wiped out higher scores I got from those who either appreciated my creativity or, if they didn't, gave me the benefit of the doubt.

I heard later that debates within the committee were rancorous, bringing to a head long-standing conflicts. Most graders merely skimmed what I wrote (which would have scandalized all factions if they had perused it closely). Quite apart from the relevance (or inappropriateness) of my answers, the Marxists and scientific statisticians opposed my candidacy; the humanists and ecologists supported it—and lost. For instance, when asked to defend giving me a score of nine out of a possible ten on my Dreamtime essay, Aram Yengoyan, a good-natured Aborigine specialist, chose instead to change it to a zero.

Afterwards I tried to pretend nothing had happened. I didn't care about a Ph.D., and I couldn't think of any use for one. Few of those who passed the prelims had gotten fieldwork money anyway; I at least had a year paid for. I changed my project so it would be supervised by the ecological anthropologists rather than the number-crunchers (who claimed native doctors among their domain). While I collected fishing data, my heart was in esoteric medicine, *Io,* and *Book of the Cranberry Islands.* I interviewed Enslin on microdoses; I turned my field notes into literary texts.

Later Skip tried to resurrect my career. He got the rules for doctoral candidates changed. He proposed a lobsterfishing study.

I said my research wasn't adequate. Anyway my skills were in myth, medicine, and botany, not fishing.

But he wouldn't give up. Rifling through my haphazard field notes during a visit, he insisted I was almost there: "Just write this goddamn stuff up in a rigorous fashion, and you've got your doctorate." He was exasperated that I wouldn't see.

Gradually I came around. I had to consider what graduate work really was. It wasn't initiation into the Golden Dawn or the Dreamtime. It didn't require a magnum opus. It had nothing to do with vision quests or theories of celestial influence (and I found it embarrassing, in retrospect, that I had tossed these notions out to my professors as if they were all Robert Kelly). What was required was the simplest sort of logical, pedantic arguments—*nada* complex, *nada* special. All they wanted from me was to speak anthro, their native tongue.

That first winter in Vermont I practiced a conventional anthropological style until it became easy—even fun—to churn out pages about the ecology and economics of fishermen—no pretense of subtexts, just hack academic journalism. I worked from a description of marine resources and cultural artifacts to the dynamics of lineages and community rules, all supported by maps of fishing territories and graphs based on State statistics. My chapters were stalwart: "Physical Features and Ecological Gradients," "The Costs and Technology of Lobsterfishing," "Costs, Rewards, and Strategies," "Catching Lobsters and the Fishing Calendar," "The Stages Between Environment and Market," and "Lobsterfishing Ideology." I treated the entire fishing livelihood as a game of strategies beginning with the selection of species to go after and investment in gear, leading to the aggressions of defending and expanding territory, cutting traps, selling catch, and so on. My closing chapter portrayed Downeast cultural mythologies.

I mailed the draft to Skip, and he showed it around the Department. "Everyone thinks this will be a fine thesis," he commended me on the phone. "Now you have to put together a committee."

As I studied reports from the Maine State Fisheries office, going back to the turn of the century (and made comparative graphs of total catch in pounds and landed cash values), I found myself in spirit at the birth of Grossinger's—Grandpa Harry visiting the Port of New York, Selig hunting for bigger inns. It took twelve hours then to get from the Lower East Side to the Catskills, even longer to truck the catch from Bass Harbor to Boston. Now frontiers were collapsing at jet speed.

Generations before Jews settled Lower Manhattan, poor Celtic mariners trawled Maine waters. The gods of these fishermen originated in old Palestine. Their nets off Georges Banks two millennia later swept up herring for the Borscht Belt.

The dispersal of tribes was a single Ice Age diaspora.

I was a player too. I got eight thousand dollars a year for teaching at a glorified camp—money paid by Manhattan, Newton, and Chevy

Chase parents for their kids to acquire the appearance of an education and a degree.

Every four months or so, Lindy and I carted boxes of food from Grossinger's back to Vermont—twenty or more sirloin steaks, a dozen chickens, tongues and corned beefs, sacks of fruit and cookies. Although I saw similar caches piled up for other relatives and VIPs, I never knew how widespread the practice was or whether anyone kept track. It felt cruddy, but I was compelled to the ritual—to a stubborn conviction that unless I got as much as I could, I was forfeiting my share of the cornucopia.

In truth, the bounty of Grossinger's had deteriorated into acts of petty theft and charges at local department stores (six-page $500 bills for small appliances, kids' clothes, pots and pans, toys, and the like, using the currency of my last name), a subterfuge that was neither condoned nor forbidden but symptomatic of a situation in which no one really knew how much wealth there was or who was entitled (by birth, status, or residency) to claim it.

If all this was okay, my father and his agents wouldn't acknowledge it. Their simultaneous invitations and prohibitions around goods were contradictory and equivocal.

Back in Vermont we continued to go to the Grange Hall on Saturday to help sort sacks of rice, beans, walnuts, flour, and raisins. Such was the schizophrenia of the time.

Years later, quite by chance, I discovered that even while I was smuggling from Grossinger's, I had the lowest salary of any teacher at Goddard.

We didn't need to skulk about and haul booty. We could have bought all the clothes and appliances we needed in Barre, plus quarters of beef in East Montpelier, organic chickens and homemade bread and cakes in Cabot and South Woodbury, etc., for a fraction of the amount I was sacrificing.

There wasn't a conspiracy against me. In fact, there was no reason for my salary other than the fact that, with the same proud indifference I displayed at Grossinger's, I never bothered to ask. I considered money base—a tawdry obsession. To notice it was to be contaminated by it. Instead I pretended everything in my life was either barter, birthright, or honoraria. If I had asked, I would have learned all I had to do (for $4,000 more) was tell a secretary I had an M.A., had taught two years previously, and had published three books.

Meanwhile a mood of catastrophe and apocalypse, at a numbing scale, made life seem fragile and salary irrelevant. A doom-crew came to town proclaiming the late great planet Earth, their week-long planning session for a social ecology program capped by a party at our house. There left-wing theoretician Murray Bookchin declared the end of time. "The numbers are in, chapter and verse," he said, taking delight in anarchy. "We've blown it."

"But all this assumes we want the human race to survive," Sheppard reminded him. "And that's just one more fucking achievement."

Wilson Clark, techno-radical from D.C., then sermonized about starving urbanites, street gangs of Harlem as well as merchants of Lexington Avenue. "They're gonna come North!" he warned (though a student asked why they wouldn't follow warmer winds).

As the wine drained past midnight, Wilson grew belligerent and upped the ante, insisting that we wouldn't even make it through the winter, that civilization would collapse into an immediate dark age—and this (as Shep pointed out) in the house of Comet Kohoutek, a body travelling at cosmic speed from the boundaries of the Solar System to the Temple. Between the science of limits and mythology without limits, what was one to believe?

The late-arriving John Todd, blonde wizard from the New Alchemy Institute (resembling both Mickey Mantle and Robert Redford), added a gloomy confirmation. "You've heard Wilson," he teased, "and he probably took ten years off your life."

Nervous laughter in the room.

"But I think he's right. The bonds that hold life together are coming asunder." He went on to describe deranged birds, psychotic fish, dead seas.

"So why even bother?" a student asked.

"If we can't save it," John responded, "maybe we can at least depart with some nobility."

Wilson continued to dispute even that glimmer of hope: "Too late. When it begins to wobble—and it's wobbling now—it cracks, the whole ball of wax." He drained his wine in a gulp. "The whole ball of wax!"

The spring after the first winter, I sat overlooking the river, thinking through the things of my life: courses to teach, unfinished manuscripts, possible other jobs. A small plane droned in the sky. The Winooski flowed, from greater waters in mountains and sky.

I was studying Attic Greek again, in preparation for a class. Insects landed in my text, hinting at the origin of the alphabet in runes. Fragments of meanings arose from glyphs—that *Chronos* is "time," *Ekeinos* means "that," *Opisten* is "behind."

The tree had no leaves. Moss crept along its bark. Two birds with bright yellow bodies sat on the wood, chirping. The sky was an eternal Greek blue.

Robin approached, holding a toad. He set it on a rock and kneeled beside it. Its chin went up and down; its eyes opened and closed, its tiger back glistening with dew.

Children skipped beneath maples, hummingbirds in lilac; cats crept through sun. "We're most happy," mused Lindy, "in that mixture of childhood nostalgia and our family. It's pretty remarkable, but we hold together."

I had arrived at Goddard at the height of its expansion from a tiny radical enclave to a countercultural bazaar. During my second term, enrollment dwindled. Industrial New England seeped in.

What was the college anyway but students in dorms playing rock music, smoking dope, faculty who disappeared down the highway into the hills? Glacial ice ruled this kingdom. Anyhow, if the world was coming to an end, Goddard would surely go before the granite pits in Barre or the Howard Bank.

I put in hours on Jerry's emergency committee, trying to launch modules of Earth mythology, Taoism, and New Alchemy. These were the same Aquarian ventures I fantasized for Grossinger's—self-sustaining gardens, solar architecture, Pelton wheels, improvisational theater, experimental cinema. I considered yoga and aerobics, either in place of or alongside cosmetics shows and Simon Sez, but my father and aunt mocked even my notion of a new softball field and modern tennis courts to attract young people. Both these institutions were hardened Lower East Side abstractions—Goddard with its ritual Deweyism, Grossinger's with its *nouveau riche* Zionism. Neither wanted to change, though neither could fill enough rooms to keep up with interest rates and the rising costs of propane and insurance.

There was another problem at the Hotel: Before her coma Jennie had written several extra wills, one of them bequeathing a resort worth ten times what she had to a con artist representing Jewish charities. The lawyers worked overtime to get Paul and Elaine out of that one. I heard they also had to offer a cottage on the grounds (in perpetuity) to Uncle Abe's and Aunt Rose's son Artie in exchange for trashing a will the wily Uncle Abe suddenly produced with Jennie's signature. The gossip was that she had left the maître d' the whole estate! And there was more.

Disdaining banks, both my grandparents had put their assets into jewelry and cash which they stored in safes in their clothing closets. After each of their deaths, the same relative, somehow bearing the combinations, had beaten everyone there and stolen the stash—millions of dollars total, all the equity, reserves, and potential operating capital of the Hotel. "I can believe he did it once," my father remarked, "but I can't believe I let him get away with it a second time."

I wondered how he could permit it at all.

"What was I going to do, call the police?"

The Graus and the family of Harry, Jr., had long ago settled out of court, but after paying them off each year in dwindling dollars, Grossinger's had no money even to keep up appearances. It all had to be borrowed—for steam-cleaning rugs and patching pipes as well as erecting bland new edifices to house the money-makers of the '70s: conventions of funeral directors and refrigerator salesmen.

Paul and Bunny moved from their longtime residence to Grandma's old rooms in Joy Cottage, leaving behind the scene of my childhood. The new Hotel manager, my cousin Mark, moved in with his wife and kids.

Construction crews stir dust and seeds. With a false front the Ross and Berle cottages are being modernized into a single unit. Wearing towel turbans, guests parade from the health club. On fluorescent carpeting, they fire into an arcade, popping World War I airplanes, jungle animals, head-hunters. Pinballs recoil in their own refracting galaxies. On cable the German air force is blue-maxing a ground army; click to another channel and Arthur's knights have trapped the Goths with water on three sides. "Now let's put fire on the fourth," shouts Lancelot. They hew mammoth trees and ignite the branches with arrows.

My father and Aunt Elaine went through a ritual of elevating the members of our generation to an Advisory Board. Given a token fee to attend a meeting, we gathered in my father's office—me, Michael and James, cousins Susan, Mark, and Mitchell, plus a few executives.

Teddy Howard, photographer emeritus, shot an entire roll. "The next generation," Aunt Elaine proclaimed.

My father opened by explaining on what good terms he had just borrowed a few million more at the bank.

"These days it's not how much you have," he boasted, "but how large a credit line you can get." Then he recalled how he had felt like a fool taking such high interest on the last loan, "but at today's rates," he added, "I feel like a genius. I should have borrowed more." He chuckled, and everyone laughed nervously.

My aunt spoke next. She said she was proud to announce that the furnishing of the new wing, the Jennie G, would put us back in the forefront of the Catskills. "We are going to be the first hotel with queen-sized beds," she exclaimed. "So don't let anyone tell you Grossinger's doesn't still lead the Mountains."

College budget committees and statistics of fishing enterprises had brought Grossinger's down in scale to where I at least could understand it. I wasn't naive. I wanted to believe they had enough intelligence and foresight to keep us afloat. I had every intention of sharing my aunt's enthusiasm. Yet the notion that queen-sized beds were somehow a war cry in the '70s seemed pitiful beside the advances of the Nevele and Concord, which had new nightclubs and restaurants as well as softball, squash, and tennis-court villages; stables of race-horses; and a steady stream of Vegas stars.

Discussion followed concerning the unfortunate changing clientele. "No one wants to be surrounded by *yarmulkes* in the lobbies," Aunt Elaine stressed. "They used to come just High Holy Days. Now they're here year-round. How do you turn them away?"

"You don't," answered Howie Bern, the general manager. "When I began at this fine Hotel years and years ago, I saw their crowd at Passover and I was shocked. My first thought was what do we do to discourage these people? But when I found out what they're willing to pay for the kinds of rooms we sell 'em, I said god bless 'em!"

That was the only meeting ever of S. and H. Grossinger's Advisory Board.

All summer (1973) I wrote essays with titles like "Sex, Outer Space, Ziggy Stardust, and the Revolution," "Terrorism, Baseball, Gold Mines, and Gurus," "The Fag Macho Prince," "IBM: Meet Guru Maharaj Ji," "The Rosicrucian Pony Back at the Barn." I performed them at the Grange Hall. My best lines had Richard Nixon hiding extraterrestrials in the White House vault, Gurdjieff directing *Mission: Impossible,* and gurus selling gold futures. I combined Prince Sihanouk, Gustavus Adolphus, and David Bowie into a single avatar. "The Martians could hold their homecoming here," I proclaimed to hoots and howls, "and we wouldn't even know it."

Playing 45s on a late summer evening, Gene McDaniels singing: "If I were a Tower of Strength. . . ." Robbie, holding "blanket" and sucking his thumb, suddenly perks up: "He says, 'I don't like you. I don't need you. I don't want you.' And then he goes out the door. He's mean!"

Lindy is sitting by him on the couch, blue jeans, no socks, tapping rhythm, pregnant.

I'm not a teenager anymore. The songs are the same, but we are different, deflected from them so that their intensity is greater. Sam the Sham: "Hey there Little Red Riding Hood, you sure are looking good . . ."; Al Wilson and "The Snake"; The Four Seasons: "Big Girls Don't Cry . . ."; Jimmy Rodgers: "Tell'm what the Wizard said." Linda Ronstadt: "I know I'm going to miss you/for a long long time."

The bittersweet concert was begun by an invasion of "The Monster Mash" from CHUM (Toronto) interfering with the final inning of the Mets' 1–0 win over San Francisco on WHN (New York), both 1050 AM: "It's a graveyard smash . . . Bonds dives—can't come up with it . . . Boswell rounds third . . . the winning run . . . it's the Monster Mash." At first damning the loss of signal I realize I can embrace both . . . and I leap from the game to the turntable and put on Del Shannon ("I'm awalkin' in the rain . . ."). Then we sit there, the two of us, plus child, plus child in embryo, in an unpredictable lesion of creation.

The splinter that was Goddard had developed Wilson's fatal totter. Enrollment was off sixty percent, and no one knew where President Jerry had gone. Finally he telegrammed his resignation. The next day the Trustees brought in Jack Andrews, a retired businessman who ran some sort of variety chain in Cincinnati. He meant to undo the counterculture overnight with rah-rah Wal-Mart materialism and martial law. About Earth Mythology and New Alchemy, he said, "If it's going to produce, like, three students, Grossinger, don't bother, okay?" It was lopped from the budget. Gathering the faculty, he gloated in precisely those clichéd words, "Heads will roll!"

Cold winds smother the fire, summer vanishing through starry black, until at 61°, metals in the furnace stir on signal from the diode, a flush of air fills the pipes, a relic of when the hulk was last filled (in June, says the postmark in my winter coat, as I reach into its pockets as though someone else's, into a time before the herald of dwindling oil).

Onions are pulled and stored next to old bottles. Green tomatoes, in expectation of frost, are set beside them. The corn continues to grow with a smell like honey until an ice moon intercedes; half a dozen ears are boiled and frozen.

Darkness descends swiftly, Gregorian chants on the stereo—mother sky and mother stars and mother Pleistocene caves. After dinner I go into the next room and turn on the game.

It should be the time of September rookies and quiet winding down of the season but, beginning with a doubleheader in Montreal, the tempo recalls the pennant madness of '69. Though still in last place, the Mets have won a game on absurdly daring baserunning and a diving catch of an extra-inning bunt by Tug McGraw.

Suddenly I'm there every evening, hovering over the radio, hoping for a quick lead. There are no other fans. People go about their lives in Vermont far from the ceremony, jeeps shifting gears up into the hills, the game half blotted out by CHUM. "It's a gift," Lindy says, partly in chagrin. "The rest of us are washing dishes and putting children to bed, but you've got something special to look forward to."

It's another, more crucial planet deepening into this one . . . from the moon on the horizon through my jumbled memories of pennant races of the '50s.

In the Mets' month-long climb from last to second (only the Pirates left to catch), I yell, clap, and command the living room (night after night) like a revival meeting. It almost collapses when the Pirates win a big Monday game, knocking out Seaver. Afterwards, I lie in a bath considering probabilities. This was the first of five straight between the two teams . . . and the Mets flatout need the other four.

The next night the Pirates take a two-run lead into the ninth. First, Beauchamp lines a pinch-hit; then Millan triples. Tying run on third . . . two-strike pitch from Giusti to Hodges (a sub-.200 catcher from the Texas League, brought up only because of injuries) . . . a single!—an impossible hit. I pound the couch: this is like nothing else! Bases loaded, Hahn up, three and two.

Line drive over short, two runs. In the bottom half Apodaca makes his major league debut; he's wild. Capra replaces him—one-run lead, bases loaded, three and one on Sanguillen, and . . . he pops it up!

The battle moves to New York; Cleon settles it with his second home run of the game. A night later the Mets find themselves a run down, bottom of the ninth, two out, man on first. Duffy Dyer, without a hit in a month, lines the ball up against the wall—tie game!

Extra innings, Sadecki mowing them down, the Pirates suddenly get a two-out baserunner. Rookie Dave Augustine follows with a line drive that looks as though it's going to go over the wall for a home run (I see this only in my mind) . . . the ball drops on the top of the railing, bounces back into the hands of Cleon, who throws Zisk out at the plate.

Bottom of the inning, two strikes, Hodges outbattles the once-invincible Giusti again.

Tug McGraw chanting "You gotta believe!" has become David Bowie: "And I want to believe/In the madness that calls 'Now'. . . ." —against all proclamations of doom, against all catastrophes and odds of human survival, against Wilson Clark, Jack Andrews, and

Richard Nixon. This is not possible. This could not be happening. Lindy and her friend Peter chatting over wine in the dining room—they do not understand. It was always more than a game.

One night later, Seaver on the mound, the Mets blow them out of Shea.

We leave Barre with second-hand pregnancy clothes, two toy trucks, vanilla Dairy Queens, then sit in the sun outside our house while a measureless calm Herman Melville saw at sea rises through maples to the sky.

2

Who Our Children Were

After Jon entered the mental hospital, my mother and Bob took the train monthly to Maryland for family therapy. She couldn't feign innocence anymore, so she began to admit her own partial guilt, though it never seemed quite the right guilt. In our phone marathons she picked guileless events, like that she pressured Jon too much in school, that she shouldn't have forbidden his playing JV football after he broke his arm.

Dr. Simmons had encouraged her to shift blame back to the previous generation. If Jon and I thought we were victims—well, we were raised as virtual princes! Grandma Sally had taunted and beaten her and put her in boarding school: "I was tortured and humiliated by my mother," she said; "I did the best I could."

After the third session she refused to attend any longer. Since Debby had left to teach prep school in Connecticut, Bob went alone. Before doctors and social workers he defended his one-time wish to send his son to Princeton. (Even Jon spoke on his behalf, saying, "Ivy League bullshit had no effect one way or the other.") The doctors insisted Bob had suffocated his son by projecting unrealistic goals. ("Unrealistic?" Jon wrote me. "They have no idea what I could have become.")

Finally Bob balked. "Not only do I think they're idiots; Jon sees right through those excuses of physicians."

"What else could he say," my mother scoffed. "They had finally exposed him as something other than the good guy he always pretended to be."

She was waiting for me to confess too—luring me, asking only certain questions, pretending to care—over and over, carrot and stick, carrot and.... (She enrolled at the New School—a course on radical psychotherapy—and began lecturing me on the very subjects I was teaching at Goddard, proudly citing her professor who lacked even my graduate degree, which for anyone else would have been gold to her.)

I was still the bad guy, to myself as well—guilty for Jon, for the jealousies of childhood, the secret pleasure I took in his downfall; for still wanting her praise, for plotting against her ... for continuing to consort with her ... for being her spy and henchman.

All the secrets and concealed grudges were out of the bag, but they made no difference. Their release had no power to heal.

She refused to allow any talk of my own family. She responded with awkward silence—and then a return to her subjects as though I lived alone. One night, she interrupted my attempt to tell a story about Robin with her own account of a stuffed-animal disaster from when I was maybe nine: "You wouldn't let me touch your pony because it came from Auntie Bunny."

'I'm smarter than this,' I thought. 'I can dance right through it.' "I apologize," I said. "I don't remember, but I'm sure it happened. I accept I hurt you and I'm sorry."

"That's not a real apology."

"What do you want? It was twenty-five years ago. Surely someone studying Wilhelm Reich and Arthur Janov can let go of a child's rebuff."

"And I have suffered for twenty-five years. You think you can make it go away with a few fancy words."

I lost it. "Is that the big thing? You won't even acknowledge Robin. And you invent this ridiculous event."

She hung up.

I sat on the couch, crying for what my childhood family had come to—my brother imprisoned, my sister no longer talking to me, my stepfather cast out, my mother caring only to incriminate. "No," said Lindy later. "That stupid story's just her excuse. It's that you rejected her madness and refused to let her get at you. It's because you're not Jon. She can't stand that you might just be normal and okay."

The next time she called, Lindy told her she would have to show more sympathy if she wanted to talk to me. "He's your son. Treat him decently."

"You have some nerve! Who do you think you are?" She stopped calling.

Ten o'clock, tucking Robin in, I read from Lord of the Rings *the part where Saruman captures Gandalf—all the stuffed monkeys on his bed listening too. Now the Eagle finds the Wizard on the mountain. . . .*

"Night, night, Robin." A hug and a kiss. He turns over, yellow flannel jammies, instant sleep.

"I came to bring messages," says the Eagle, "not to carry off a burden."

"Then take me," says Gandalf, "to the land where the horses are swift."

In her eighth month of carrying it, Lindy senses her baby coming closer. Bright Venus and more distant Jupiter appear in the evening, accompanying each other from opposite sides of a sun that is now a silhouette of trees on mountains. The Pleiades glitter, microdilution in the infinite. Comet Kohoutek is invisible, though on television we see its soft coma, a thin etching accompanying Venus in a different plane. Smoke pours from chimneys, straight up—long plumes iridescent and dissolving so that the village seems a train in motion. The moon is as bright as it will ever be, the sun in conjunction. This day stands alone in our lives, as we proceed, hooded like would-be birds of prey, given in wedlock to another physical mass.

In the morning the river steams, burning through ice-cakes. The world sticks to nostrils. On a hill above the town, seen from the railroad bed, children are sledding, leaving jet trails in snow.

We are invited to dinner at a house in the forest. After dessert, under a nearly full moon, Lindy and I follow deer tracks, the temperature pushing zero, she stumbling along, my arm clasping her swollen torso.

Around the woodstove: guitar, harmonica, voices—*"Last night I had the strangest dream/I never dreamed before."* The barn, covered with snow, inexplicable also against stars.

Sudden waking up. Lindy says, "It's time."

Robin heads downstairs, dragging his blanket behind him, thumb still in his mouth, turns Captain K. on the TV.

We take him up the hill to Jason's.

The car warms as we chug into Montpelier. Everything seems etched—steam from the river rising through trees, spruces white with snow, mist.

I stand by Lindy in the hospital room. In her journal later I see myself there.

> "Where the fuck is he?" I cried out to Richard when the contractions seemed interminable and I wanted the doctor, Granai, whom I suspected was seeing the twenty pregnant ladies who were always waiting in his office anteroom across the street from the hospital. None of the familiar landmarks had happened: no crowning, no fifty-cent piece, no hair showing, nothing to merit the doctor coming, nothing to please the nurse. I felt like I was failing a test, having no progress to show to the outside world for all this physical pain and work.
>
> Rich was my connection to the world that made sense before the pain began. I trusted him, although he didn't seem to know much what to do. He watched me, read the newspaper, held my hand, counted the breathing, got ice chips for me from the cooler down the hall, wet a washcloth and held it against my perspiring forehead: 'You're doing good work, Lin; really beautiful.'
>
> Granai came whooshing in, trailed by nurses, and commanded us all into the delivery room, like a coach pulling his team together for the Big Game! He was a brute of a man, skier, golfer, wind surfer, ruggedly handsome, a brown wide beard on a tan face. He was attractive enough that I was uncomfortable with him on the prenatal visits; we sparred and joked. . . .
>
> In the delivery room I lost any vestige of control. The baby was presenting posteriorly. Its head was turned around, so it moved right past the vagina when I pushed, arching back up to my tummy. Granai reached in with first hands and then forceps to turn the small body around, while I breathed deeply from the handmask of trilene the nurse gave

me. As each contraction came and the pain became unendurable I flipped out on the trilene, trying to escape from the new heights of pain which were pushed way beyond my capacity by the presence of the forceps in the vaginal hole. Without the baby's head against the vaginal wall it was no longer anesthetized—so Granai gave a local and did the episiotomy: a small snipping cut to make the opening bigger. The pain reared huge, now not in the abdomen, but in the vaginal canal, and as it grew I took huge swigs of breath and gas. I was a visitor on top of the room's ceiling looking down at a woman below who was having a baby. . . .

I watch Lindy gasping, the nurses masked. Pushing into exhaustion against her own membranes, half-laughing, half-crying on trilene, she gives birth in a pool of blood.

We bring Miranda home on a snowblown day, relatively mild for February. Large fluffy crystals crush in the wipers, the road playing wet music. We set the wild creature in a bassinet. I retrieve Robin and bring him upstairs to peer at his sister. She lies there in the covers. We are now a family: a man, a woman, a boy, a girl, just like the one I grew up in.

At the Goddard Ecology Conference that spring, Wilson Clark publicly proposed Apocalypse—end of fossil fuel, "the agriculture of famine." If he offered no solutions it of course was because he didn't believe there were any. He didn't think solar could pull our train any better than nuclear. "There's no free energy left."

Since his previous visit I had gradually pushed doom out of mind. Now I felt the shock anew. What about Robin and the baby? Was there no world left for them?

This time John Todd matched Wilson with a vision of restorative agriculture, cities based on geomancy and Egyptian carp, seeds from cabbages of the 1920s, pigshit heating rooms, watermills, windmills, and solar houses . . . hearkenings of Pico the magician. He described simple recycling fishponds, a kind of solar-hermetic civilization based on the golden staircase of Zosimos, the peach-flower stream of Tae Ch'ion—Earth dragons and lei lines in a harmony of hills and waters, bounty to eternity.

That night in Montpelier, a few hours after I had given up on the

Earth, dinner was almost a prankish occasion, with John toasting Paracelsus and promising to recover lost texts of the alchemists.

I expressed confusion.

He was thoughtful for a moment, then remarked: "Our lives alone will resolve this. It will be doom or rebirth. There is no middle ground."

In Bass Harbor, Jasper stands at his wharf, scanning the horizon for the last straggling boats. There are just a few loyalists left. The rest are trawling and handlining. A new man from the Bronx, Kevin Roth, sprouting red clumps and stray beard, is trying to steer into the lower wharf along the pumps. The tide is bothering him, and he keeps missing his angle. Jasper observes with majestic scorn as he smashes into the corner of lobster cars.

Even with my thesis almost written, I feel a neophyte again; the simplest rules of conduct elude me. For instance, I don't understand why so few are going after lobsters or why anyone would tolerate a fisherman from so obviously a carpetbagging origin. Should I keep counting traps, as Rappaport requires, or try to figure out what the hell is going on?

"How did he learn lobsterfishing?" I ask Jasper.

He gives me a long look, then says, "He didn't."

Afterwards Kevin agrees to answer questions. He isn't overjoyed, but he'll do it. So I hear about a supervisory engineering job in New York, marrying a woman from here, fishing part-time. "Do you like it?" I ask.

He crouches, nods many times, pure macho: "Look, man, I don't do anything I don't like."

My main informant, Wendell Seavey, has his traps up and is handlining with Marlon Bridges and a boat full of fancy new radar. A lot of good that does Jasper: his business is lobsters, a few scallops on the side. Wendell regularly takes groups from College of the Atlantic whale-observing past Mount Desert Rock, and to Little Duck, bird-watching and tagging. As New Age ferryman, he also delivers clients to a gestalt-therapy group on Great Duck, until recently an abandoned island. He carries the I Ching *and Dane Rudhyar's* Planetarization of Consciousness *and blames me. He keeps a mulch heap and a garden, the first fisherman in a generation to do so—something for the thesis: agriculture reemerging out of hunting/gathering.*

"Everyone considers me your loony now," he banters. One evening as he came to dock for gas, "boat empty, of course," as he relates it, "but a good day's ferrying to the islands," an exasperated Jasper, hungry for lobsters, exclaimed, " 'Wendell, you ... you ... you ... bird!' " (What I don't know yet is that in five years Wendell won't even have a boat and in fifteen no one will remember where he went.)

Walking from wharf to wharf I notice a new barrenness. Objects are waterlogged, surfaces scarred and pitted. Buoys hang, their colors muted. Els are collapsing, twisting apart; whole sections have caved in and lie on the wharf. Tops of posts are mashed and splintered, salt covering their façade with the corrosive delicacy of a lathe.

It is too late now. It is doubtful that any of this can be replaced or done over again. We make it from here with what is left. Or we don't.

Roofs are littered with crab shells and gull shit. Boats pulled on the beach to be reskinned lie among tar and rags. Engines clatter, hammers pound, never solidly hitting nails, however close to flush they strike. There are sudden bursts of radios and engines. It is all incomplete combustion.

And human beings stand in the center of it, oblivious to what it is, to what it could be if it were complete, or left to rest in silence. Walking along the beach I see pink anemones, fine underwater plants, wood and glass, stones and shells, smoothed and lightened, eaten through with tiny holes.

Each present serial compacted moment stands, against each other, and against the probable, and because it happens we see it, and because it dashes itself out against the substantiality of form, dies gasping into the next moment. Figures in continuity sit motionless, waiting to be carried from zone to zone of equal, undisturbed light.

I ask Warren Pinkham why he thinks the lobster supply is down.

He puts on his thinking cap and gives an analysis of the difference between the Canadian system, where lobstering is limited by season and license, and the American, which, he says, is run by greed. "But if you ask me about offshore lobstering, it's clear it's the Russians."

"Wendell Seavey says he won't believe it till he sees a hammer and sickle."

"Well, that's not hard. If you go from here to Nova Scotia you'll see the hammer-and-sickle parade. It's a whole Soviet fleet. And you won't find a gull around those Russians because they leave nothing. They suck it right up, bottom and all, and they process it at sea. There's no waste. All kinds of fish go in there, and the racks and scales are ground up too. They make fish meal out of it."

I can't tell whether he is impressed or disgusted as he brandishes his arm.

"You see, they've got these mother ships that have the factories right on them, and they're maybe six, seven hundred feet long. Then they've got the fishing vessels; they're two hundred, three hundred feet long. The fishing vessels go out and bring their catch to the mother vessel, and the mother vessel, she processes it, and then another ship comes to take it back to Mother Russia. They don't even have to fuel; a tanker just comes with its snorkel and fills'm up. The crew stays out there fishing six years. And the only reason for that is six years is the life of the engine. When they've gone through a spot, nothing lives. Your private fisherman, he got maybe $10,000 complete investment; he can't go up against that kind of operation."

"It's moon-rocket technology."

"Right, and I'm competin' with my tin can and stick of dynamite."

Tide ripples in waves, their reflections on the boatsides like flocks of negative birds undulating about a fixed point in another dimension. Gulls call out, crossing the harbor from perch to perch. Their voices begin with an animal earthiness, rise through a human scale, and screech into something extraterrestrial. With the flow of water, primal language, and wind, the irregular passages of breezes, falling leaves and petals, dash of the chipmunk—it almost seems we are the objects in the way, the impediments. Without us, nature flows.

In September Andy and Carolyn, California nomads, arrived in Plainfield in hope of building solar houses. They had been studying t'ai chi ch'uan in Berkeley, and they demonstrated it at the Grange Hall—

a version with rising and sinking motions (Anne mimicked it because I wasn't there). When she asked if they'd be willing to teach, they put her and Bob in charge.

I was, at best, equivocal. In 1974 t'ai chi was a strange exercise. True, my high-school companion Chuck had become an adept practitioner, apprenticing in Chinatown; but he was ahead on everything—tarot, yoga, and Beat poetry in the '60s; alchemy and Tibetan Buddhism in the '70s—and it had always seemed hopeless (and base ambition) to want to catch up. He had carried out duels with a wooden sword and, while visiting us earlier in the summer, had—pot-belly, beard, and all—hopped from stone to stone in the Winooski River.

On the night of the first class, Barre's main street was a thoroughfare of shopping. I dawdled stair by stair but arrived anyway at the room on the second floor of the dilapidated storefront. There, behind the blue-orange neon of KARATE, I found a place among milling men and women. Without warning, Andy and Carolyn began, arms extending, then drawn back, hands rolling, feet shifting in tight arcs. He was dark, medium height, a pixie; she was tall and fair, stylish. His arms worked shuttles; her fingertips trickled out spider threads.

As directed, twenty or so of us got arranged in three rows. Andy addressed us. "Leave your hang-ups outside," he pointed at the window. "If they're that interesting you can pick them up on your way out." His tinge of wit got my attention. "Find your axis—that's the line of gravity through the top of your head clear down to the balls of your feet—it's the thing that holds you to the earth." He paused to allow us to picture this. "Now follow me."

I encountered memories of Y rooms—smell of Hershey bars, radiator pipes, woolen sweaters piled in the corner. Herded inside on rainy days, we would be guided in knee-bends, jumping jacks, and other drills of strength and coordination. I was ever out of synch. Right and left would be confused, then front and rear, up and down.

"Find your center," Andy called out. "Move it toward your spine." Did he mean a spot inside me?

"Keep the circle soft. Even if it hurts more to do it that way you learn where the tension comes from. You guide the healing process."

'What if I don't have a center?' I wondered. There was no corelike spot X-rayed in my body-mind.

He and Carolyn were so lovely—if only we could just be them.

That Sunday, above the village at the edge of an apple grove, they stood beside each other. For over an hour they synchronized 106 moves, motionless motion. Their precision transfused an image I kept coming back to; it sustained me in the class while one by one the more precocious students dropped out until, a month later, surprisingly only eight of us remained.

By the fall of 1974 we had published twenty issues of *Io,* the last two guest-edited. The themes now seemed contrived, the design too arty, the scope no longer cutting edge. The breakthroughs lay in the early issues, yet we had an institution on our hands. Then Nathaniel Tarn, a poet and anthropologist, proposed cutting the journal back to an issue or two a year and developing a literary press. "There are plenty of magazines now," he said; "books are what's needed."

In honor of Ed Dorn's *North Atlantic Turbine* and the Geographical Foundation of the North Atlantic (founded in Antigonish, Nova Scotia, by Alan Van Newkirk and Motown White Panthers)—we adopted "North Atlantic Books" as our imprint. Its first publication was *Martian Homecoming at the All-American Revival Church*—the material I read at the Grange, plus an account of my brother's life ("Jonny's Quest"). Lindy's poem *Psyche* followed (on its back cover a jaunty photo of her in a buttoned coat disguising eight months of pregnancy). Then we put out small stapled books of three poets.

In October my mother apologized to Lindy and asked for me. She had news so critical it dwarfed our epochal clash. Doctor Hitzig had decided her palpitations could be relieved only by having her gall bladder out. In fact, he had convinced her that her entire life had been poisoned by one bad organ. Its removal would be her salvation. Of course, this was the medical genius who, for the past twenty-five years, had prescribed every sedative and sleeping pill known to man until she was immune to all of them.

She was melodramatic about whether or not she would survive, so she wanted to make up with me. I set a time to see her the following Saturday in New York.

Lindy and I drove to Grossinger's; then I got up early and continued into the City. On this glorious fall day, I felt both young and old.

I arrived at the unfamiliar building, Park and 37th. She was waiting on the Avenue, sunning herself, eyes squinting. I thought she looked gentler, a bit Indian as Jon had said. I felt waves of sympathy for her. This was, yes, the woman we once loved and called Mummsy Wine.

She approached with brittleness, then hugged me with a passion that gave me a start both for its strangeness coming from her and its desperateness. There was an almost erotic gasp in it. She wouldn't let go. Then she stood back and looked at me. It was our first time together since I had shaved off my beard the previous winter. Was it because my face—its high cheekbones and deep-set eyes, black lashes and hair—so resembled hers?

I was the age of my father, five years older than she was when I was born.

"Hi, Mom." (I could have been young, innocent Jonny.)

"Richard, dear." She put her arm around me as we walked. "How is Lindy? How are my beautiful grandchildren? You know I have a picture of Miranda with those blue eyes and I show it to everyone. And Robin, he must be the most handsome boy around." She told me about new aunts and uncles she had just met, offspring of Coleman Nassberg's late-in-life marriage to his secretary. I knew nothing of that, but the telling of the story brought me back into her family, the Nassbergs and Rothkrugs. I felt privileged, but I also cherished my sanity (or whatever it was I had escaped with), a palpable thing glinting off skyscraper windows.

The next day Lindy, the kids, and I came back together.

Upstairs in her apartment my mother got down on the floor beside Robin and crawled around furniture, giggling and playing peek-a-boo. I didn't remember her ever behaving this way. Then we walked to U.N. Plaza, Robin trooping alongside, Miranda swaying in my arm in a carrier.

She seemed to struggle for simplicity and candor. Yet there was a characteristic edge in her voice, a blend of anxiety and hauteur. She talked about Jon with resignation. "I invented him," she sighed. "He was the son I needed." Then she reviewed the matter of Moe and Bob almost clinically, confiding she never really loved Moe or stopped loving Bob. She sounded like Elizabeth Taylor assessing past husbands.

"When Bob went away on trips, Moe was the one who looked after me. But didn't Moe need someone himself?"

"How can she continue to live in that flat with Bob?" I asked Lindy later.

"Just more Hollywood melodrama, I guess."

But the Thirty-Year War was over, and it was a pleasure to meet in peace.

The t'ai chi class is down to five: me, Anne, Bob, Eugenie, and Viuu. Two evenings a week we go through the form up to where we last learned; then Andy teaches a new move. We practice it. Then he and Carolyn correct our renditions. Then we review the sequence to that point.

Afterwards Eugenie and I do the two-person form, called push-hands. My palm rests on her ward-off (her arm in the shape of "an empty embrace"). The rotation of my waist launches a strike she deflects into her center. She turns without breaking the axis of her spine so that her ward-off automatically becomes an attack and my striking hand curls into its own ward-off as I roll back. One part of me is trying to imagine myself inside the mystery, carrying a ball of Taoist energy; another part knows there is no ball and I am an imperfect mimic of an external form.

At home I stand in the precise center of the living room and go through the motions—grasp sparrow's tail, strike, embrace tiger, step back like a monkey, put a needle at sea-bottom, spread arms like a fan, descend like a snake. I rise up on one leg, hand floating to eye level . . . white crane becoming brush knee, twist step.

My life is no longer just a mythology. I am writing me.

We are invited to a New Year's Eve party in South Woodbury—faculty and students, kegs of beer, loud stereo. Robin stays overnight at a friend's, so we have only our baby.

There are maybe seventy-five people in a small farmhouse, a blistering fire. Lindy and I drift apart. I am left with Miranda, blanket, and bottle; she is dressed in a nightie. I perch along the wall, idling a beer. Various students come by to say hello, gossip. She sits beside me, looking into each of their eyes, cosmically cruising.

Before I realize it she is crawling around, finding abandoned cups, sipping beer from them. Now I grab her and lie back in haze. She crawls away, crosses the room again and looks back at me, the bigger my smile the bigger hers.

She giggles all the way home through the snow.

I fall asleep with the room spinning. In my dream she comes to me, still newborn but articulate. She tells me I don't play with her enough, that I think of her only in terms of Robin.

"I'm different," she says. "I'm not at all like him. You'll see."

3

The Train that Goes North of the Sky

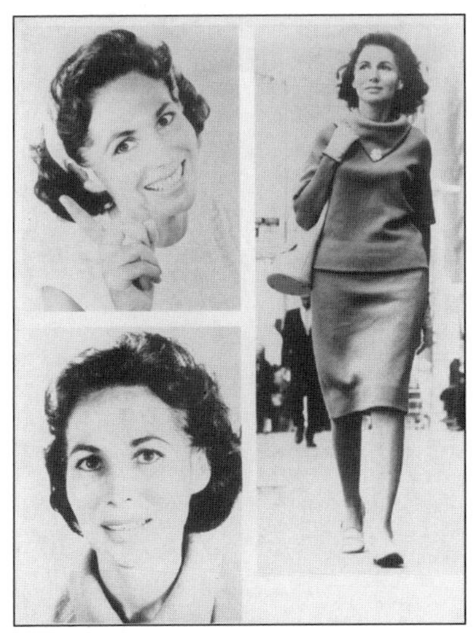

In January, Bob called. It was the first time he and I had spoken more than a word or two in eight years, since his phone call to Ann Arbor. Though the betrayal lingered, his voice was an echo of everything I had once been and forgotten. I hadn't realized how much I longed to hear it again, like Dion singing "Teenager in Love" or Mel Allen's call of a Woodling homer.

In the intervening years, when he didn't know me, both our lives had changed beyond recognition. His business (once just himself, an art director, a book-keeper, and a receptionist) had boomed to the point where he now managed a small empire of accounts to which his "gofer" Larry Berman drove him on weekends. He had become the Concord's advertising man and sports promoter, a position akin to mafia capo. He was prosperous but heartbroken. His wife had left him for Moe Kornhauser, his CCNY sidekick. His son had gone from Ivy League candidate and tennis protégé to marijuanista and pseudo-Apache rabblerouser to thorazined mental patient. Towers had also been hit by a taxi while crossing Fifth Avenue. He had lain two months in Mount Sinai, fending off not only death but memory. His voice bore the weight of tragedy. He spoke, not with the verve I remembered, but a rabbinical gloom.

He didn't acknowledge our long silence. He said, "Your mother is in Sinai. She took too many pills. You might give her a call." His pacing was tense and deliberate, a broadcaster telling the news.

I called her as soon as he hung up.

I could sense her barely suppressed alarm, like stage presence, as she told me Dr. Simmons had assured her she wasn't suicidal. She said that she wanted to see Dr. Janov right away, do a primal scream, and "get to the bottom of this once and for all . . ." as if she could summon a superstar shrink (like Hitzig) in the middle of the night.

Down in the City I made plans for visiting hours. At 2:30 I took the subway uptown to my old neighborhood, the crossroads of 96th. Passing our block was like walking through a dream of a dream. These buildings were giant tombs concealing mummies. The City is merciless that way. It is just façades and stone; new people live in its cells.

If I had been an Iroquois I would have been welcomed home for a solemn occasion. The medicine man would have dropped his other business. A village ceremony would have been planned for the evening. My brother would be returning, a healer from the wilderness.

Here was just ceaseless traffic, taxis dropping off fares, expensive cars double-parked, in the distance the same doorman (Ramon) twenty years later opening iron and glass for a stream of self-important residents. A hard wind began where Park intersected 96th. I felt my hair toss. This wasn't a dream.

I began running. I carried my jog past Madison, turned at Fifth where Nanny told me Jack Frost lived. He had his true bite today.

I stood before the doors of the Institution.

Mount Sinai was a giant terminal through which doctors and

nurses flowed. I felt a premonition of abduction, of figures appearing from behind masks. I walked cautiously to the elevator, eyeing old men and women in wheelchairs, as though any one of them might turn into a wounded pigeon and fly up with a single wing. I didn't want doctors noticing me. Even a glance might be a diagnosis.

My sister joined me on the third floor. She was huskier than I remembered, looking more like Bob's sisters now. It was four years since we had last spoken, four years of unreturned phone calls and unanswered letters.

We gave our names at the desk. Before we could sit, Bob came down the hall. I was stirred by seeing him in the flesh and wanted to give him a hug, but he was sullen and forbidding. He had a look that we all better act serious, as though he were afraid—if he let go of his pressed lips and hard eyes—he would commit sacrilege. That glare marked some of the bleakest moments of my childhood. Instinctively I fell into line.

We followed him down the hall into the last door on the left. My mother was seated in bed in hospital garb, talking animatedly to a tall gray-haired man—no doubt her analyst. "Now nothing excitable, Martha," he said, exiting hurriedly just as we came in. He seemed more anxious to get away than to set eyes on her black-sheep son.

She looked alarmed as she greeted us, her presence like broken china. I leaned and barely hugged her. I wanted to be generous, but I felt a shudder of contamination. She smelled drugged.

"You don't look bad," I said. "I know it feels awful, but maybe it's finally coming to the surface where you can deal with it."

"I look okay?" she asked incredulously, turning to Debby, who didn't change expression.

"Yeah. In fact, you look really clear. You don't have that cloud over you."

"But I feel so terrible." She looked at Bob, then Debby. "My gall bladder . . . I was in such pain. I never—"

"She screamed bloody murder when they wheeled her out of the operating room," my sister interrupted. "She got out of control."

My mother didn't notice. She turned back to me: "The operation only made it worse. You know I tried to kill myself."

I nodded. "Maybe it feels like things are getting worse, but it could be just old stuff taking on a shape where you can confront it."

"So you have hope? You think I might be okay?"

I had never heard her so tentative and meek. She smiled nervously toward Bob.

My stepfather said that he was glad she was able to get some pleasure from my coming down from Vermont. He emphasized "Vermont" as if to accentuate I was now a stranger.

This was where he and I had left off years before: a secret phone call, a purloined letter. But which of us was now the spy, which the counter-agent, and for whom? Which one would Freud blame, or Janov, or Fabian (were he alive to see the outcome)? What was the cabal of childhood?

"Is there anything I can do?" she asked me.

I had an immediate conviction. "I think the best thing is to face the fear. Give it a name."

"What do you mean?" She looked worried, as though I had suggested higher philosophy.

"We could talk about some of the things causing the problems. What about Jon?"

Bob immediately started to interrupt—my mother finished his thought: "Dr. Simmons said I should avoid disturbing material. I'm on sedation."

"We can just talk then," I sighed.

"What should we talk about?" she asked after a moment, as though we had long ago exhausted all topics.

"Have you and Bob ever discussed Moe?" I held my breath.

"No!" he inserted with obvious outrage.

I was relieved that they didn't both turn on me. It was also an indication of how desperate things were that they would let me intrude like this.

I looked back to her for an answer. She stared but seemed willing for me to continue.

"Why wouldn't you talk about it now that you're back together?"

The silence was excruciating.

"We just never have," she finally said.

We held any thoughts while a nurse came through and took the tray.

"Well, what do you think about it now? Do you have anything to say?"

She shook her head.

I turned to Bob. "Are you still angry at her?"

Debby flashed me a look of consternation and fury.

"What do you mean 'angry,' Richard?" he said. "I don't mind a fling in the hay. I've had mine, god knows. But of all the second-rate … all the bums, why she had to pick this mediocre, this mouse of a man."

"And your best friend," I added. "Why don't you tell her directly?"

"Martha, I don't get your taste. What did you see in the creep?"

"I don't know. He was just so sad."

"I'm an all-star, Martha. I'm as big as this City. You picked a utility infielder, a .220 hitter."

"I must love you," she said, "because you're the one I always come back to."

"That's not good enough for me, Martha. That's not good enough."

"Well, I always appreciated the fine people you introduced me to, like the Slutskys." She meant the owners of the Nevele, a couple she had always looked down on much as Jacqueline Kennedy might have looked down on a state senator from Arkansas.

There was another silence, and I turned from person to person. No one would respond. My sister slumped zombie-like on the bed. She was hoping, I knew, that this would end any second. "Is there anything else?" I asked.

Silence.

I knew this was bad, but I had no idea how locked the door would get, how many doors and locks in fact would be imposed in the years to come. This was the very last moment at which there was a crack, and yet it would have taken all the Horses of the Apocalypse to have pried it open.

She was doped anyway, and Bob suggested it was time to leave. She was already starting to go to sleep.

I leaned over and kissed her goodbye.

At the doorway I confronted a superstition, 'What if it's the last time?' We stood waiting for the elevator. 'What would it feel like if this were the last time I ever see my mother?'

Yet despite my enthusiasm for orchestrating group therapy, I was relieved to be getting out of there, heading to a famous restaurant where Bob would charm the maître d' and I would order a steak and a Heineken dark. I glanced compulsively down the hall as the elevator arrived.

It *was* the last time I ever saw her, but time is not linear. Even years later, I don't put any great weight on that moment. One emotion covers another endlessly, and whatever feeling my mother and I had remains outside of time.

One wishes they could be prophetic and miracle-working at the moment it counts, but life has a way of dragging loose ends forever. Things simply miss.

A month later I flew to Ann Arbor to set up my thesis committee. After dinner, Skip and I haggled over the draft I brought, page by page, on his living-room couch—what I must still do, what he would let by. At half the petty corrections he made I balked. "Do it!" he snapped brusquely, as though exacting penance each time for the lenient path he was providing. "Find out how much diesel engines cost. Get the average bank loan for a fisherman. Measure a few traps. Check the year-round population of the village. Give temperatures in degrees."

The next morning I returned to Angell Hall, home of the Anthropology Department. In my absence the curriculum had shifted dramatically in my favor: Foucault and Lévi-Strauss were mainstays. "You were a prophet," Aram Yengoyan shouted across the offices. I shrugged it off because I still didn't trust him—or anyone who gave me a zero then.

"Sure, you were," he insisted, walking up and extending his hand. "As soon as you left, all the students were talking about structuralism and magic. Now we teach it."

A short frizzy-haired scholar, he was appealing, so I teased him: "I wasn't a prophet; I was a sleepwalker."

He looked wounded.

I met Skip downtown for lunch. He kept thinking up details he wanted me to include in the final version—trap density required for buoy-cutting cycles, shapes and dimensions of fishing territories, three generations of kinship tables. I told him I didn't have enough data. "Not important," he asserted, "as long as you have *some* data."

"Do I have *any* data?" I asked provocatively.

"Make a guess," he retorted with such an authoritative flourish he sailed the menus off the table. "The next person who comes along will correct it."

We had no abiding interest in this topic anyway. He merely wanted to make sure I didn't create some new embarrassment for him.

That night I was coming upstairs for a before-dinner drink when Skip met me at the top, put his arm around my back, turned me around, and led me back down. He had me sit on the bed, then said: "Richard, Lindy phoned. Something happened today." My body froze. "Your mother died."

I heard the words, but they had no meaning. I felt mainly relief—overwhelming relief—it wasn't one of the kids. Then I had trouble orienting myself, as though this event were familiar in a nursery rhyme. I had to jar myself to realize this was new. *My mother died. This was her death.*

My voice spoke automatically, "She must have killed herself. She wasn't that old."

"Yes, she killed herself. She jumped out the window."

At dinner I learned the bizarre details: she had vacuumed the rugs, done the dishes, taken her clothes off, and put a grocery sack over her head. The doorman heard a thump. Her childhood friend Barbara came and identified the body.

My thoughts fixed on a random Sunday in 1958 just before we moved crosstown into the apartment on Central Park West. We had a joyful outing that day, entering the Park at the playground, walking halfway around the reservoir, cutting through a break in the fence at 90th across the bridle path. Jonny, Debby, and I danced about one another, goofing off, as though changing homes were the silliest of occasions.

We introduced ourselves to our new elevator man, then inspected the hollow rooms one last time. On the way out Jon and I were still cutting up. Bob turned the switch. My hand braced instinctively against the wall as I stumbled. When the light went back on, my mother saw what she dreaded most—fingerprints on wallpaper.

All the way home in the cab she brooded silently, one eye on the culprit.

That night at 11:30, unable to bear it, she got dressed, took a can of cleanser, summoned a taxi, and went crosstown to wipe off my mark.

I lay in bed not knowing how to be sorry enough.

A week before she took her life she wrote Lindy that her hair was turning gray and she was no longer beautiful. The shallowness of that conceit aside, it would have been difficult to find those single strands among the jet black.

I took a noon flight to New York and joined Lindy at my father's and Bunny's apartment.

"I'm so sorry," Bunny said. "But didn't we always know?"

I appreciated that she was trying to console me, but I felt taciturn. I smiled and accepted a beer, then fielded my father's questions about his old friend Rappaport.

The four of us went to a restaurant. Initially my father showed restraint, but he was anxious to confess. "She made things hard for me. First she tried to keep me from seeing you. Then she billed me for lots and lots of things that weren't for you." He stopped to let the sums accumulate in our minds. "You know I paid for Jonny and Debby too. Then when you went to college I asked her for help, but she wouldn't let me apply child support toward your tuition."

He said that now that she was gone he felt a weight removed that had been there most of his life. He hoped I understood.

"Of course."

I understood he felt the weight was removed.

The gathering in Apartment 11E was macabre—so many relatives I hadn't seen for years. There was no evidence of grieving, just a haste of setting out platters of food.

My eyes landed on my tall, gaunt brother. He had been sprung from the hospital for this occasion.

We found a spot in a corner.

"What courage!" he proclaimed. "She leapt into the abyss. The Noxzema woman finally found her sleep."

I didn't think of it as courage.

Grandma Sally pointed across the room at me, "There's Martha!"—drawing gasps. But of course I only looked like my mother.

In the bedroom Jonny, Debby, and I hunched on the bed, our arms around each other, reading her last note:

> My Dearest Bob, I love you always. It was never your fault. The blame is and always was mine. I am so sorry. Good-bye.

Bob stood there, sobbing. Then the sound of Sally's voice stirred him to anger.

"You should have heard her last night," he exploded. "'Do you think I might have just a single fresh fig?' A single fresh fig! How this woman terrified your mother heaven only knows. She couldn't even order dinner at a goddamn restaurant."

As we sit in the synagogue amid prayers and so many words, I think back to Bob singing Jolson, "this evening, around a quarter to nine," "old man river, that old man river," and "oh, how we danced. . . ." These tunes bring me to the origin, not because my mother and Bob ever had a clear, shining "night we were wed," but because she was my mother, and he was her dashing suitor the year I was born. . . .

"The night we were wed" was the eternal night of us as a family, Bob's cantorial voice, Shekinah and Kether, the mysteries of our joined lives on the Tree. There is a depth and texture to all this I can barely fathom.

How fast it went, the thirty years I knew her. Those years make up the labyrinth of my childhood and lie open to no single fugue.

Before the leap she was my mother, but in the air she was no one. She had no history, no children, no commitments, no sex, no body even. She was a falling creature, with little time.

There may have been a second, before everything exploded, before light turned to darkness, then to searing light, when she realized what it was, what it had always been, how simple the resolution always, now that she had flung away hope. I mean, for a second at least, she was conscious in the air and knew it was going to end.

It must have been a rush of nerves against the wind of abyss, a resonance of lights and sound culminating in a vision—a moment I can only imagine as electric because all the rest is electric. Like dropping a radio from the same window. And then the world snapped and the trivialities ran out.

She wouldn't have wanted to read about herself on the front page of The New York Post. *It would have filled her with morbid thoughts, police and reporters around her body. The morgue. Dr. Hitzig attending one last time.*

In the hearse carrying her last body to Long Island the ghoulish off-Broadway driver discussing mafioso funerals seems as inevitable as the rest . . . as we wind past paths we walked in Central Park, her face to the sun, her black coat . . . thinking her own thoughts.

The doormen at our former apartment on Central Park West are still standing, looking back from then.

Cars following a hearse cannot use parkways, so we go along old Nassau County roads, the rabbi talking politics with Bob, the driver now telling a story about shot-up corpses.

Hunched and sobbing, Debby lays the flowers her school friends sent on your gravespot. The men shovel dirt onto the box, your broken body they would not let us see. You struck a blow with it stronger than your fists your whole life—against doctors, lovers, fake medicine men, the whole sorry lot, the children you were astonished to have spawned.

No more the exotic invalid, now you have to cross the Styx. No more trying to look twenty when you're fifty. No more playing everyone against each other. You have used your terrible strength finally, made it into a single punch, and smashed all of us and yourself with it. And now that it is over, your cry, like the explosion at our beginning, rings us in forever at its end.

Eighteenth Document (Jonathan's story)

The Train that Goes North of the Sky

All through the late morning and the afternoon I sleep. Sun pours through the picture window up on the 16th floor. The wind rattles the metal pieces of the terrace guard-rail. The strength of the day pours in and I sleep under the bright-colored blankets laid out on the thick yellow carpet in my room.

Finally she craved only sleep, twenty years of pills that left her without the ability to sleep, and so she lay in the bed in darkness, my father sleeping off his workday beside her. . . .

We pull out of Baltimore into the darkness. I sit alone, foot of my right leg secured in the back of the seat in front of me. I gaze out the window clear and long into the night and my feelings and thoughts. The outer lights of the city stand like star markers on the terrain, functional but hypnotic constellations. I look out to the east, across the long lay of all the earth there is and overhead hanging in the sky is the full orange moon with the sad face of a peaceful woman looking down on me. And here I am traversing the earth in the wake of my mother's act, her suicide. Step by step the clock moves me toward New York over this tight plan there is for each of us as my mother rushes toward the sky moving out beyond us, to the moon. On all the earth if I were to travel it I could not find her, she is no longer here, but the quickest route to where she is is off to my right above me in the sky, the moon, positive and bright and immobile. My land journey, her sky journey, together set, one having precipitated the other.

In Philadelphia the earth's red fires glow, Joe Frazier's gymnasium for boxers, dilapidated red brick building and the frightening rooms of hidden combat and dull labor of mind and body. The alchemical fires glow, the earth, the train, black and red, Dylan's "Blood on the Tracks," 1975, but it's any year and any time.

A taxi is right there waiting on 34th Street. I get in and am riding on the New York City streets. We turn down dark blocks heading for Park and 37th. I go up in the elevator. My father, face pained and lined, moves strongly toward me. We embrace; he squeezes me so hard my eyes close and I stand there, suitcase still in one hand, the other clasped around him. Through my closed eyes I see the people in the living room. We stand at the edge of aunts and uncles, looking at us with lowered glances.

Two days later at the funeral I clasp Paul, father of my half-brother and my mother's first husband, and the tears come out of me and all my love. I hear him saying words, call us any time, and yes I will, we'll meet, all of us, a hundred thousand powwows till we get it straight, till we know by the slightest glance.

We drive out to the cemetery in Long Island in the black limousines. The casket is removed from the first car while the rest wait in line—me, my brother, his wife, my sister and father and the rabbi in the first car. We get out and move to the new-dug grave where the casket sits. The wind whips around us. My father and sister weep. <u>Yisgadol, v'yiskadash, shmei rabba, b'adma divra khirusei, v'yamlilkh malkutsei</u> . . . my sister holds the flowers, the rabbi takes the shovel and with the back of it throws the new-dug earth on the casket while speaking Hebrew words. The mourners are told to return to their cars. The rabbi, the medicine man in black coat and hat, remains over the grave as the Puerto Rican workmen move in and lower the body, shove the dirt on. This is it, gone, get on the train, oh mother, God, this is it, gone, get on the train, leaving, 11th floor, gone, windowsill, this is the train, mom, go, this is it, grave-diggers, get on the train, My dearest Bob, I struggled so hard not to do this, leaving, this is the train, 11th floor, windowsill, letting go, get on the train, leaving, mom, get on the train, 11th floor, leaving, gone, again, down below, get on the train, mom, leaving ohhh

Toward summer I received an official document of the sort I had forgotten existed except in novels:

> I, MARTHA KORNHAUSER, A/K/A MARTHA TOWERS, residing in the County of New York, State of New York, do make, publish and declare, [etc.]. . . .
>
> I give and bequeath the sum of ONE THOUSAND ($1,000) to my son, RICHARD GROSSINGER. Because Richard is financially secure, this bequest is only a token demonstration of my deep affection for him.
>
> I give and bequeath:
>
> A- to my son, JONATHAN, my diamond wedding band and the large painting showing a boat scene by Voyet.
>
> B- To ROBERT TOWERS, all shares of the capital stock of Robert Towers Advertising, Inc. that I may own at my death.

C- To my daughter, DEBORAH, my 420 shares of the capital stock of 55 TENANTS CORP. pertaining to Apartment 11-E, 55 Park Avenue, New York, New York, together with my lease to such apartment and all right, title, and interest owned by me at the time of my death and to any agreements relating to said building and the real property on which it is located.

D- To my daughter, DEBORAH, all other tangible personal property owned by me at the time of my death (except cash), including, without limitation, any automobiles and their accessories and equipment, all clothing and other articles of personal use or adornment and all household furniture, furnishings, works of art and other articles of household use or ornament (together with all insurance policies relating thereto) if she survives me, or to her issue, or if there be none, to my son, JONATHAN, if he shall survive me.

The cash, roughly $120,000, the most substantial portion of which came from my father's child support, was split between Jon and Debby. My sister and my mother's attorney were appointed co-trustees over Jon's portion of the estate. Her "dear friend, Robert Towers" and her attorney were appointed co-trustees over Debby's portion.

The ghost of her presence was disconcerting, as though before departing altogether she passed briefly into magisterial robes. Her lifelong disapproval of me was implicit, so I didn't give it a second thought. I signed the waiver, got it notarized in Montpelier, and mailed it back.

The story of my mother is a mystery within a mystery. I find it difficult even now to recover her character. Everything sounds trite and soap opera.

She never once told a joke. Never never. She never expressed a political sentiment unless one considers her almost fetishistic admiration of John Kennedy political. Yet she was an intelligent, brilliant, fierce woman. So what did her intelligence go into? All I can think of is gossip—gossip, conniving, and espionage—at a level that would have done a Cold War spy proud.

I ask her older brother Paul for help in recreating her personality.

"It's beyond me," he says. "No one knew her. Even as a child . . . . I will say one thing: she had charisma. When she entered a room, everyone knew."

Dr. Fabian named her in my dream: a huge dying crow, its body crushed, giving off unbearable shrieks. Years later Jonny and I discovered we each feared a pigeon from the courtyard would get trapped inside our room and fly about, bumping into walls.

What was it that riveted her to Shirley Temple, Judy Garland, Jacqueline Kennedy, Frank Sinatra, and other public idols? It wasn't just the fame. It was that they manifested elegant and exuberant personalities; they expressed her own personality for her, her sense of longing, the emotional depth she never touched in herself. They could sing and dance and vamp before the world; they could elicit romance and power, grandeur and charm, modesty and immodesty, all with theatrical ease … whereas she was stuck with petty intrigue. She couldn't even carry a tune. *("Fly me to the moon/and let me play among the stars. . . .")*

In watching old films of Judy Garland, I am struck by how much of my mother's quality is there: the muffled rage, the possibility of losing her mind at any moment, the Piaf tremble of romance and desperation, a voice that might almost give way yet continues to deepen with feeling (until it threatens to get to the very bottom of the human heart). These were things that Judy Garland could perform openly that my mother kept inside. Even Judy Garland as vaudeville tramp showed me how my mother might have been funny if she could have played the saucy ragamuffin instead of moping self-pityingly in a Paris boarding school. All her life she was condemned to watch in silence, to express enthusiasm by putting others on pedestals.

The fact is: she almost was Judy Garland. Between yearning and forbidding, she felt something enormous, something *"beyond the rainbow, why oh why. . . ."* She missed it totally, and the unattained reaches of her depth became my own measure of what emotionally must be attempted in this life, because the cost of *not* making such a journey is too high.

I can't think of a single episode in which she acted in a way that showed her true complexity, the charged aura she cast that made her never trivial even when she was, the loyalty she engendered such that I created an unwilling kingdom of madness, greater than anything she could have imagined, to protect myself from demons that came bearing her colors.

She passed the spook onto me, or perhaps birthed me to bear it for her.

Years later when my children lament that they never knew her, I tell them: Forget the pictures of the pretty raven-haired woman, listen to my voice—the alarm and vigilance still in it—and you will know my mother.

I too am doomed to place my hand over a hot light bulb again and again, to fight ghosts in the middle of the night. But my bulb is the abyss of my own mind, and my ghosts are shadows of those I would have known how to love had she not conscripted me from before memory. This is my mother's legacy—not bad parenting, not heartlessness, not narcissism, not jealousy and malice (yes, of course, all of these), but the declaration of a demonic gap in this sector of the universe and the insistence we spy on it at every moment, not because watching will help but because that is the way we do things.

4

The Knight of Pentacles

LIFE MOVES IN UNDERCURRENTS toward watersheds. We awake from the wakenings of prior dreams, on the crests of new waves, being carried ever toward an unknown place. My mother's death was a scream I perceived in the early years of my childhood—so gradual and distorted then it might have been anything: a laugh, a song, a chant. It gathered speed until it became a howl.

Lindy's and my life had been hastening toward its own watershed. Marriage had been our touchstone. We stood against our pasts, our ethnic stereotypes, our families, then the dissolution of so many couples among our friends. Kittens, highchairs, and snowsuits engaged us more than adult ambitions.

But the wave gathered and broke. Lindy formed her own circle; she had male friends. ("I don't see," she said, "why you have to be the only man I get to know my whole life.") For the first time I had a sense of not being able to reach her.

On Sundays we pushed Miranda's carriage along bike paths, snowdrifts everywhere, our course inevitably to the waterfall where the Winooski plummeted into spume. Just before its water was combed into threads at the precipice it formed a smooth image: wooden apartment houses on stilts, their paint peeling, planks rotting.

Endlessly, addictively, we talked. We hardly knew who we were, what we were drawn to, and what the consequences of dalliance might be. We had so many unexamined notions about jobs, writing, monogamy, autonomy, sex, friendship; we lived not so much lives as a pastiche of contradictory half-lives, each with its own desires, its own subtexts. We pretended to honor all of them by sheer force of will and passion.

We were bound together, a couple, a family, but each of us had had another relationship, me in Maine, Lindy more recently. Those people were behind us, but the topic remained. It was somewhat the time, the place—Goddard, the 1970s. Married couples we knew took other lovers so painlessly our single episodes seemed chaste and labored by comparison.

We wanted to be great writers, great parents. We wanted to teach at elite colleges and be famous. We fantasized romantic interludes—an artistic, fun-loving man for Lindy, a more occult, hippier woman for me.

For all our rationality it was impossible to define what we permitted each other, what was bearable, though the sheer intensity of the discourse—our ongoing parley—was a glue holding us together. We were so overbearingly verbal that it sometimes felt more like a co-authored life—a joint epistemology—than a love affair. (I joked that as long as our argument interested us we would stay married.)

Inflated left-wing rhetoric notwithstanding, Goddard seemed real in a way I wasn't. I was teaching Reich and American Indians; then students of mine were living with Navahos during nonresident trimesters, finding radical orgonomists and getting their armor dissolved. I would talk non-Western philosophy; then kids would go to Somalia, Nepal, and Thailand. It was the feeling I had had on the podium at Kent—only through word arrays and poetic images did I gain any authority. Where was *my* shamanic experience?

People from the original t'ai chi class have formed an improvisation group that meets in the karate studio one night a week. I go there because of Eugenie, the leader. A veteran dancer, she has an elegance of movement and step. She is sure of herself, definite and playful in her lessons. Short and shapeless, with a round, flat Irish face, she gives instructions each night for the improv we are going to do. I like her quixotic style, that harassed, mock-perplexed look on her face, seductive in a kind of school-marmish way, her large glasses and peasant clothes.

I leave her at her door by the dam, the crash of water in the background, a quarter Moon.

After our friend Ellen became director of the Vermont Arts Council, she offered to sponsor grants for us through the National Endowment for the Arts. We wrote two: one for publishing literary books and another for Lindy to attend a dance critics' conference at Mills College in July. They both came through.

Seeing an opportunity "for us to get some needed space from each other," Lindy made plans to spend three weeks first in Denver. She would fly there in June; then I would bring the car later and we could drive the rest of the way to California.

This barely warm March day I sit on the back porch. Wind passes through chimes.

Chainsaws ring on the horizon.

Now the chimes are louder. Almost a tune—one insistent note in their center. Water slides off the eaves. An icicle crashes with the sound of broken treasure. I hear the sun dripping like footsteps, irregularly tapping on a plastic bowl. Shadow of a bird swims across snow.

Another Peter is pursuing Lindy. A West Coast novelist, he flies here periodically to teach in one of the external-degree programs at Goddard. They go drinking at the local tavern. He has already published a chronicle of his extramarital adventures. He sits in our living room, medallion in chest hair, leather pants, spouting insider versions of Wilhelm Reich and fashionable feminism. Lindy considers him a battle-hardened confidante on matters of marriage. Rather grotesque-looking—a tall, shiny-pated gnome—and older than us by quite a bit, he has put in years at Esalen and on the self-help circuit. He isn't so much romantic as totally into "what a man must be in order for women to be women."

In April I drove through Canada to Ann Arbor.

It was a basement room, my committee members in suits. We sat at a table; they asked questions like "What do you think will be the course of trapcutting over the next five years?"; "Will the community survive if outsiders keep buying up coastal land?"; and "How did you check your data?" Everyone was relieved I had returned as a normal student.

When it was over, they stood in unison.

I stood.

Dr. Schorger shook my hand; then Dr. Kottak, Dr. Nietschmann, and Dr. Wright: "Congratulations Dr. Grossinger."

It wasn't that I was falsely modest. It was that they didn't understand how much it was play-acting for me—the extent to which my thesis was a sham. In the end I felt guilty for fooling them. They were so innocent and decent. What I wanted was somehow to confess (and have them confess too). Then neither of us would be lonely.

I took the southern route by way of Kent, drove the next day along thruways east and up into New England. By then the green hills sparkled with blossoms; in my absence it had become summer.

My stepfather had no stake in Jon's continued incarceration, so in June, my brother went back to the household of his childhood, to his father and sister who lived in the flat Moe had once gifted to his wife. Fired from her prep school in Connecticut, Debby now prepared food for a downtown caterer. "I don't want him here," she complained of Jon. "He can't be lived with. He has no lifestyle. It's all just one whim or another."

Meanwhile Jon was creating an archival tarot, mixing family photos among Pentacles and Cups: us playing baseball in Central Park, the Six of Cups, him and me in bathing suits at the beach with pails and shovels, myself as a child beside Debby in a baby carriage, the Six of Swords, the two of us in Yankee uniforms, then at Chipinaw ("the bunks behind us," he added, "in the natural layout of an Indian village").

He expropriated money for dope, pilfering even the carfare left for Bridey.

Lighting a joint, he began lecturing his father. "You gave me the holy letters; now those letters have returned to educate you."

"You teach me Judaism? You no-good drug addict, you bum! They'll kick you out of the synagogue."

"That shows how corrupt they are. They kick out any true rabbi."

"You phony excuse of a—"

"Excuse of a what? Are you going to tell me about the family you raised? My sister not even a human being. Me stuck in hell. My mother out the window."

Then Bob's version: "He points out hobos and says, 'Look, doesn't that prove the end is coming.' To *me* he points out bums on the street. Where does he think I've been the last forty years?"

On the day before Lindy and the kids left, rain pounded on the roof.

Under shelter of the barn I did "cloudy hands."

A large wet toad sat on a railroad tie.

In clay cups we shared chamomile tea.

A jet crashed through clouds.

'In a thousand years,' I thought, 'this will all be easy.'

The morning of the flight, Lindy was uncommunicative, struggling to put the house in order, irritable with suitcases. Finally we headed for Montpelier.

We were barely in time. Hauling Miranda and her purse, Robin racing behind, she scampered into a tiny plane.

I didn't wait to see it leave. It was preposterous that these people who were so dear to me should go into a flimsy Air New England prop and before nightfall be carried so far.

In Eugenie's dining room we chatted about her house-sitting and keeping up the garden after I left; she studiously wrote details on a pad. Her phone rang, and I waved good-bye.

Back at the house the dryer still running added to a macabre ambiance. Trees shifted in layers, relieving gravity.

I felt as though I had been living in a dream—a lovely slumber but midsummer night's all the same.

I put away the playpen, washed dishes, ran another laundry even though the people whose clothes I collected were halfway across the country.

All that was left was a hollow world, a sun giving off more light and brilliance than I could ever use. What gluttonous overplay!

That evening, as I pushed hands with Carolyn in our backyard, she regretted that, by the time I got to Berkeley, I would miss her teacher, Paul Pitchford, who was returning to Idaho in just a few days. She wrote down a phone number anyway, figuring that a class might continue in his absence.

I went inside and walked from room to room, pulling curtains, turning on lights.

I lay in bed with the radio. George Stone, hero of the 1973 season, returned from a year on the disabled list to pitch for the Mets in San Diego, 11 PM Vermont time.

It was not just that I could not hear the presence of Lindy and the children; it was that there was no potential sound of them. The crying in the distance … could not be Miranda.

The next morning my stepfather called. He couldn't deal with Jon and wondered if I would take him for a few days: "Try to talk some sense into him, Richard, or he'll be the death of this old man."

I drove four hours to the Albany station. The moment I saw my brother I rued my agreeableness. It was far easier to applaud his orations at a safe distance than to tolerate the actual Apache. Shaggy and unbathed, he moved in hard, directed strides. En route to my home for the first time since that fateful night in Cape Elizabeth, he commandeered the front seat, jabbering cargo-cult prophecy, finally laying the tarot with childhood photos beside me and calling up fortunes as we drove. A breeze blew seeds and leaves across the windshield.

We left Route 2 in Plainfield, turned up the driveway, and parked. I grabbed his suitcase in a moment of forced generosity to disguise my total lack of it. I led the way toward the farmhouse. With my key I let us in.

I stood in the dining room beside him, missing Lindy, Robin, and Miranda almost unbearably. Yet I acted jolly as I showed him around. In the attic he spied Robin's hockey game and asked to play. I seized the opportunity for distraction. After we set it on the dining-room floor, he noted its differences from our childhood set. However, trademark tin men still moved on tracks and were torqued by rubber-coated rods.

With abashed smiles we took up a match. Our rivalry was playful at first, but each score seemed to raise the intensity until ancient foes inside us began ramming our players, almost tilting the rink in attempts to get the miniature puck behind each other's goalies.

I scored twice on center-to-right-wing passes before he figured out a defense for that play. The mood became sober. Back on Central Park West he was the more skilled player, but he was out of practice and I continued to win game after game, evening our ancient score. He started banging and slamming his men.

I tried to end it after four victories.

"One more!" he pleaded (as when we were children). This was against my better judgment—but in truth we had nothing else to do.

In his desire to win he created a novel left-defense shot and took a quick three-goal lead. He was gleefully asserting his old dominance. I saw him loving it, brandishing power. I remembered why I used to hate him.

I neutralized his move by synchronizing my wing and goalie.

Frantically we traded goals over the next five minutes, twisting and pulling rubber-coated rods and grabbing at levers controlling our goalies. It was New York again. I couldn't bear the thought of losing to him.

Each time he almost scored I felt an icy pang.

Then I got three goals in less than a minute, two of them by pure luck (one of which he generously flipped in himself). We were tied at five and playing for a deciding point.

By all rights I should have wanted him to get at least one face-saving win. But we tightened defenses and played conservatively, like chess masters.

Time seemed to freeze as we confronted each other through tin men . . . palms sweating, fingers cramped, eyes fixed.

Then my left wing flipped one in from an unlikely angle, startling even me. I failed at suppressing a smile.

He slammed his rods into the board, pulled himself up, and stomped away, embarrassed at how much he cared.

I hauled the machine back to the attic before any more damage could be done.

When I returned, I found him at the windowsill, whispering and moving his hands. He told me he was resurrecting moths. He pointed to their bodies on the wood. He was using Apache. "I am reviving the dead," he announced, "like my namesake from *Ordet.*"

That old Harry Pin arrogance was still driving him on. Chanting over moths was about as strong a statement as my brother could make. No more toy hockey games for Jonathan! Jonathan had passed through the great dark!

Even as I could find nothing in me except disapproval, I hated the stiff edge of my affronted pride. I searched for some sort of clever, pseudo-friendly comment: "C'mon, Jon, we both know better than this."

Breathing heavily, he approached me: "Richard, infidel, brother of little faith. Get out of the way, and let the gods in."

"You're just showing off!"

He jerked as though slapped. Eyes gleamed. "I have a secret about you, Richard."

I felt an unguarded shudder. I couldn't tell if it was the present threat of him or an intuition of something else. He was so worked up he had to pause and gulp. "It's a terrible secret. A secret I was never supposed to reveal. But now that she's dead it doesn't matter."

I looked at him and knew in my heart that, despite everything, this would be crucial, this would be true. I felt a flutter of archaic fear, as though he was going to say I was born with a fatal disease and everyone knew but me. No, that wasn't it. Deep in a lost memory I knew what he was going to say. I didn't know exactly, but I knew its feeling. I experienced the specter of a landscape so primal I had overlooked it entirely. From long ago I sensed the shadow it had cast over my life, a qualm beyond birth. He was right. There *was* a secret, a terrible secret.

Dead moths took on a new meaning. At last I bowed to their omneity.

"I tried to tell you once in a letter, Jesse James."

I didn't remember, so I waited while he nursed the moment. "Well, what?" I finally stammered, no longer the rational older brother entertaining his mad sibling.

"You know nothing. You don't even know who your father is." He took a step closer; he looked like an Apache prince. "Paul isn't your father. Mom had you by another man."

A moment passed between worlds, perhaps like the esoteric moment between lifetimes. His sentences materialized in sequence and I heard them on one level, then another.

At first the disclosure was trivial. I had considered such a rumor many times—that Jon's father was my father and we were *full* brothers. I knew it wasn't true—not only did I not look like Bob, but he had never treated me like a son. Furthermore, it made no sense for Paul to reclaim a child from a man his ex-wife had married.

Jon heard that out, contemptuous, impatient, then said: "Not my father. Some other man. Some dark knight of pentacles. Someone never spoken of in our lifetime. That is why you have such power. You are the offspring of a stranger."

This time I believed him. Our mother dead, us two in a hollow place—I felt a ripple go from that moment, back through everything, and by the time it touched my earliest memories, it had shattered and rewritten my history and changed me forever.

At last the pieces fit: That's why Paul took so long to show up in my life, why I didn't look like him. That's who I was in my mother's eyes those embattled years as she tried to negate my existence, in my father's as he beat me to the ground: not their firstborn son but their bastard.

'I know this!' I thought. 'I have always known this!' Because nothing—nothing back then ever felt the way it was supposed to.

"It's true," Jon insisted. "Debby and I talked about it the times you were at Grossinger's."

I remembered how when I was taking genetics at Michigan and Lindy was pregnant with Robin I had inquired into my mother's and father's blood types. I was O negative, something the offspring of Paul and Martha could not be. When I told my mother (without suspicion) she remarked huffily that Paul didn't know his own blood type. I accepted that without a second thought.

Then I recalled how, not long after that discussion, she had invited us to her cottage at the beach. No doubt my paternity was the secret she intended to disclose. Instead she got cold feet and babbled about Jon.

For the rest of the night my brother and I reviewed family legend, imagining how it must have happened, a clandestine tryst, after *my* father and before *his*. In the process, we brought our mother back to life, young and infatuating, unharmed.

Brushing my teeth I stared in the mirror. Her imprinting in me was obvious, features that were also Jon's: deep hazel eyes, dark curly hair, large nose (she had shortened on herself), raised cheekbones. Pudgy, cherubic Paul certainly wasn't there. I didn't remotely resemble him.

In truth, I had never really looked for Paul in my face. I took for granted his paternity as the central revelation of my childhood. Why else would they have orchestrated its divulgence so powerfully? When Fabian asked and I answered, I did so without believing and without knowing why. I made it true by my answer. But did the wise doctor intuit the deeper masquerade—or did he collude too?

Probably not, I thought, or he wouldn't have been so delighted at my guess. He wouldn't have asked me about *another* offspring of Paul and Martha. They must not have told him *either.*

Lies within lies. Or truths within deeper truths.

A ritual of my childhood was to sit by my mother's shelves and re-read a passage in Harold Taub's history of Grossinger's:

> When Paul returned from the service, his wife Martha told him, hesitantly and tearfully, that she no longer loved him. She had been alone too long and had fallen in love with Bob Towers. They were both tormented, she said, and felt that they were being terribly unfair, but there didn't seem to be anything they could do about it. They were irresistibly in love.

So if neither Paul nor Bob was my father, why didn't Taub mention someone else?

Who was he? Did he cast even a shadow in the book?

Jon certainly didn't know. He sat on the bunk in Miranda's room, casting the tarot around the Knight of Pentacles, filling the air with shaman's smoke. "I am looking for him. I am looking."

I laughed with the wizard's power he had given me: "You won't find him there. He's not in the cards. He's in me."

"That's right," Jon acknowledged. "But we want to find out if he's still alive. And . . ." (he set down the last card, the Hierophant) . . . "he is!"

The next morning, Mantle and McDougald were reunited on the Goddard ballfield. Thorazine had taken away none of the Mick's power; he smashed shots to the edge of the bog. I ran unbounded, tracking down most of what he hit. Unknown ancestors, human and animal, ran with me. My half-sibling was a tall, heavy-boned giant of an allied tribe. As I felt my lithe body and fired back across the diamond, the fat, cloddy Grossingers were banished, their selfish dumbness, their begrudged wealth, their ugly, ostentatious resort.

We returned to the house exhausted, sweating. Eugenie greeted us from the garden. I had no idea what would come next.

He told me he was leaving on a vision quest. If I failed to hear from him, I should trust in the spirits that guided him.

In fact, years would pass before I saw Jon again.

Lying in bed that night I continued to review almost limitless implications: That's why my father was equally hard on all of us; in truth, he had three adopted kids, no blood ones. The old rumor of his being sterile (as the offspring of first-cousin marriage) took on new credibility.

Perhaps my real father was what my mother saw when she stared at me so bewilderingly that time in front of her apartment. Had I reached his age when "he" was her lover? Did I look like him?

Why in the hospital couldn't she have given up the one secret that might have changed things?

I was awakened in darkness by the phone.

"Did you go to bed early?" Lindy asked once it was evident I had been asleep. I turned to the bureau; the clock said "one." She had gotten the time zones reversed and thought I was two hours *behind* her.

"I want to tell you something," she said.

"I have something to tell *you,*" I interrupted. "I found out last night Paul isn't my father."

"What! How do you know this?"

I began to explain, but it had Jon written all over it—exaggeration and megalomania. She was impatient and ended the conversation.

In the morning I called back. Her sister Susie answered. When I asked for Lindy, she was tongue-tied. Finally she said, "She's in New Mexico." When I didn't comment she added, "With Peter, her writer friend."

I pretended, even to myself, not to be stunned.

Susie apologized: "But I thought she told you."

"That's okay. It's not your problem."

In the dark and alone, I no longer found my unknown father and roller-coaster marriage so romantic. The boards I was made of were not that firmly attached.

I packed a suitcase and began filling the car—books, tapes, and clothes.

Nothing changes, I realized; old events return in new guises. Years before I had gone to bed early and gotten up at dawn to drive to Colorado to meet Lindy. We were college students then, and I was running from my father. At Christmas I drove there again.

Was it because melodrama alone consoled my life?

When I saw a trickle of daylight I prepared an exodus—a reconnoiter of the house, a note to Eugenie, a bag of food, traveller's checks. I pulled out of the driveway . . . the sole vehicle through a dark town.

As I cruised between mountain ranges, an exploding sun illumined subtleties of meadows and valleys, treetops in the distances. I wished I could rest my mind in them. But they swept by and were replaced ruthlessly, a rhythm of superficial variation that kept a tension, landscape by landscape. Occasionally I flicked the radio on and off, traces of stale news, muzak.

I chose backroads leading to bridges over Champlain. Daylight continued to change color and grow.

Birds were everywhere, dancing in the meadow, swooping down, celebrating the dawn.

Hours later, at the bridge to Canada, I got on line for customs. They waved me through and onto the cross-Canadian highway (where the North American speed limit was still seventy).

After hundreds of miles, I felt catapulted out; I could finally relax in spontaneous mind-bursts.

Paternity wasn't just some episode that happened very young, like being haunted by Nanny and her ghosts. It was a thing preceding and conditioning my whole life. It came before I-was. It was the essentiality of my becoming at all.

I stopped at a cafeteria, took out a hamburger and shake, then got back in and began the highway history of rock 'n' roll. Neil Sedaka sang *"I'll build a stairway to heaven,"* and the Beatles, *"One and One and One are three./Come together, right now, over me."*

Everything was suddenly a message addressing origins—*"Michael row your boat ashore, hallelujah":* my step-brother Michael, or me who could have been named Michael—on the Lower East Side, in Mediaeval Russia, in David's Palestine, bireme with sails, unknown planet in another galaxy across stars and minds and lifetimes and . . . *"the river is deep and the river is wide"* . . . song catching mood and carrying it deeper. . . . *". . . don't fear my darling, the lion sleeps tonight"*—I the embryo, the lion him; then I the lion, hush my father, my daughter Miranda, don't fear my darling.

It was a man I saw at the Metropolitan Museum—a remarkable likeness to my Middle Eastern face painted on a coffin: wide eyes, high cheekbones, curls, odd bend in the nose as though broken.

He left instructions that his image be painted on the outside of his burial vessel so he could see the world. Through "his" eyes I saw what time had done to the polis and the paint he was painted with . . . bought with coins still bearing a trace of Atlantis.

His dark pupils and curly hair, now mine, were entrusted to Horus not Marpa, though Marpa yet lived in the blue skies of this planet; it was Horus whose message awakened me this time.

'Here I am again, Ka, remembering nothing, as once you promised.' Those marvellous dead eyes eternity had given us, whose boat we boarded blind, because memory would not have been enough. . . .

In recesses of oblivion beyond mind I intuited a more recent unknown father: a masked warrior, an uncle on the fringes of crime, an itinerant camp counselor. I recalled strangers in dreams, men moving briskly across the background, who led me into their houses and then disappeared, wives who were surprised to find me and told me to leave.

I thought of *Great Expectations*, Pip wondering for so long who his benefactor was. I had once imagined Uncle Paul the source of my destiny—but just as Pip had guessed wrong with Miss Havisham, now I too was forced to recall something older, something more like a convict in a graveyard.

A son of Paul and Martha would have been another half-brother, like Jon. My true sibling lay in an another lineage.

There was this almond-tasting chiaroscuro flitting rapidly into and out of my mind. I could recall it only as passing through an alcove in the apartment of a childhood friend into a kingdom far older than Grossinger's. I was looking for him, and he walked right past me. I went toward him, a shaman clad in Jewish middle-age. If I searched deeper in myself, there would be others, forms behind forms, shadows beneath shadows, ancestors within ancestors, figures costumed in birds' heads and antlers.

I stopped in Ann Arbor at Rappaport's house.

We sat on a hill overlooking a clearing.

"I don't think it means anything at all," he said. "Paul is your father, legally and morally. This other thing is just a story. It doesn't change your life."

My look showed I wasn't buying that.

"Can you describe its meaning?" he asked.

"It's who I am. Who-I-am is different than what I thought."

"Changing the genetic fact of your father doesn't change you."

"It does!" I insisted.

"Well, maybe it has no meaning *in the usual sense,*" he said after a moment's consideration. "But in another sense, I guess it's almost primordial."

Rappaport had played the devil's advocate all through grad school; yet behind academic protocol, he too understood there was only incarnation and magic. Preferring to get back to the equivalent of lobster traps, he then asked what I was going to do next.

I described a scene I could visit in Chicago, friends I had made while reading at the Poetry Festival there in the spring, a woman I had liked and exchanged letters with and wanted to see again … Surf Street above the market.

"Well, go," he said. "Forget your father. Forget Lindy. She's got her own adventure. Go and have a wonderful time."

I laughed at his notion that anything could be so simple.

A week later, I was crossing Iowa, a gorgeous black ingot extending into the sky against coal-gold.

At nightfall I rode into a storm, vast in all dimensions. A single bolt would break from the top of the heavens and string itself in branches, then hairs of fire. Far off another was beginning … then another.

Long past midnight I drove the outskirts of Council Bluffs into Omaha, windshield wipers on, droplets of car lights, a glow of habitation to the sides like a movie of water running down streets.

Then I was on the Plains, rain slashing across headlights, a pulse of cars from the other direction … until the downpour obliterated even them. I pulled into a rest area and fell asleep.

I woke once to see the moon rising in a caul, an aged woman parading as a newborn.

I started again near dawn, stars fading in indigo. I counted off miles (thirty of them even before stopping for breakfast). I picked up speed across Nebraska, numbers melting away, though not as fast as my mind tried to annihilate them.

I began to contemplate what I was returning to: Lindy had been to New Mexico, had returned. No one knew where I was.

In Colorado the land turned to scrub and sage. Suddenly the glint of a police car.

I pulled onto the gravel. He strolled to the window, a Mexican.

"How fast do you think you're going?"

"Seventy-five," I tried.

"At least!"

"I've come all the way from Vermont, and it's seemed like forever."

"I'm sure, but there's a speed limit. There's no time limit, you know, just a speed one."

"Yeah."

I showed him my license and registration and answered his one question by saying I was meeting my wife and kids in Denver where she was visiting her parents. He took that in, nodding. Then he started writing the ticket.

"You know something," he remarked. "You were born on the same day as me."

"November 3rd?"

"Not just November 3rd—November 3rd, 1944."

"Same day, same year?" I asked.

"Yep."

"That's pretty amazing."

He nodded. "I'm still giving you a ticket."

"I guess you have to, but it's almost worth it."

"It makes *my* day."

"Thanks," I said automatically as he handed it to me.

"Take care now, have a good visit in the Rockies. And my message to you, brother, is, SLOW DOWN!"

At his signal I pulled back on the road ahead of him; then I watched him streak past, a wave out his window. Aleister Crowley could not have said it better. I floated into Denver.

Spear Boulevard led to Lindy's sister's neighborhood and, as I pieced together where to get off and which streets to take, I preferred the role of itinerant rover to that of unexpected husband. In truth I had last spoken to her when she *didn't* tell me she was going to New Mexico (and didn't understand the significance of Jonny's revelation).

I parked, shut off the engine, and walked to the front door. Late afternoon, weekday. "Rich," Susie said with a startle. "Lindy wondered where you were."

Before I could answer, Robin came running and I seized him up on my hip. I stepped forward to face Lindy, who was carrying Miranda, newly up from a nap. As I put my other arm around her, the four of us stood together. The familiarity and ordinariness of this overwhelmed any other disjunction.

Later that week, as I fielded fungoes with Lindy's nephew, my glove came apart. I had restrung it so often since high school it was no longer salvageable.

Robin and I stood in a sporting-goods store while I tried on ceremonial objects evoking Papago games. My son patted the webbing of the one I chose and smelled it while I signed seventy dollars of my remaining traveller's checks. I took it without the box and was sitting in the backyard rubbing it with a rag and oil when Lindy joined me. "We're getting old," I told her. "This is my last glove."

"You don't have to justify buying it," she preached. The bite in her words tipped me off that she had spent money in New Mexico.

But things were different. When I arrived in town, she was talking of moving with the kids to Denver. Now we were planning our trip to California. She felt at ease enough to describe her expedition with Peter, down a rocky arroyo into a canyon at night. "I didn't want to sleep there. He was furious. After we got to the top and into the car all he could do was talk about how he'd hiked the Peruvian Andes, all over Nepal, Tibet—he Peter, tough jungle warrior; I, Lindy, flakey, fragile homebody."

"In a way," I said, "the whole adventure with him was like picking up a snake you were afraid of."

"You can't humor me that way. I feel as though you always one-up me. I was about to go on a scary adventure, leave my kids behind, and all you wanted to talk about was narcissism from your brother. It's always one more *tour de force* with you, one more great thing about Richard and his mythology. Sometimes I just don't have the strength to deal with it."

"What should we do?"

"I need your support. I need the freedom to have a good time, or a bad time, unobserved, without someone passing judgment later, holier than thou, nipping at my heels."

We went to dinner in Larimer Square, where she put a post-mortem on matters: "I don't want to give in again, but I *do* love you. That's not the issue. It was never the issue. But what about *my* life?"

5

Awakening the Mystery

On our second day at Grossinger's that fall, Bunny and I met for lunch at the outdoor buffet.

"So you found out," she remarked wistfully. "I'm surprised only that it took you this long."

"Why didn't you tell me?"

"I knew you'd ask—that you'd blame me. But I am loyal to your father. As long as you didn't know, I couldn't be the source."

"Does *he* know?"

"He'd like to believe you're his son. He figures it will never be proven one way or the other." She looked around to make sure no guests were nearby; then she continued. "When we were first married your father led me to believe *I* was the reason we couldn't have children. Perhaps he didn't know himself. You were living proof of his male potency.

"I remember the day your mother told him. We were staying at the Waldorf. He went right out, not a word. Didn't come back all night. It turned out he walked the streets crying, then slept at his friend Ham Fisher's. You may not think of him as an emotional man, but you have to understand, Richard, he really does love you."

"What did he say afterwards?"

"'It makes no difference.' He had decided you were *his son.*"

"Do you think I am?"

She shook her head.

"But you won't tell me who my father is?"

"I won't be the one."

Then there was the rest of Taub's account:

> Paul went to his mother's room and, alone with her, he cried like a baby.
>
> "I don't ever want to see her face again," he stormed. "I don't want to see either one of them as long as I live."
>
> His mother ran her fingers through his hair, soothing him as if he were a child. "You know all the good work Bob has done for us these past four years. He's earned his place. I can't discharge him," she said.
>
> Paul stared at her in astonishment. "Who said anything about firing him? Since when do we fire people? But we could transfer him to New York or Miami, couldn't we?"

Now thirty years later, I called Bob at his office. He had a routine of pretending to be too busy to see me but, in the aftermath of tragedy, he agreed to lunch.

In the morning I drove to the City. He was finishing a phone call with one hand, grabbing his hat with the other. We caught a cab to The Friar's Club. The maître d' led us to a table off the bar.

Legendarily attentive to every nuance of dining, my stepfather made sure I had an imported beer and called for a selection of rolls before conducting conversation. Amid smoke and clatter, I experienced a sudden lapse of nerve. I was daunted not only by my unknown father but the world of power and money all my fathers came from.

When Bob heard what I wanted to discuss (plus Jon's role in its genesis), his face hardened and he was abrupt in dismissal. "C'mon, Richard. Are you going to believe that lunatic? Let your mother rest in peace." He looked around as though for help from the waiter.

I dropped it. We talked instead about the Mets' pitching staff. He told me about Jon's recent misadventures in Maryland. Then he said, "Richard, it breaks my heart to see what they're doing at the G. There could have been one place in the Catskills. It should have been the foremost resort in the nation. Who's in charge? They've got Elaine running around pretending to be Jennie. Her son is her figurehead. Where did he learn the hotel business? When did he attend the school of hard knocks? A little wise-ass, he never lets you forget how smart he thinks he is. People are talking. The Grossingers don't know the Catskills anymore. The competition is beating them blind."

"Don't look at me," I shrugged. "I can't do anything about it."

"If they had employed Robert Towers Advertising, there never would have been a Nevele or a Concord. If you had read *The New York Times* you might have noticed I just accompanied someone by the name of Jimmie Connors to the Concord, along with Tom Seaver of the ball club we were just discussing. Did you see who Grossinger's brought back for Labor Day? Eddie Fisher for godsakes! Richard, did Mark Etess ever hear of a guy named Sinatra, a pretty fair talent named Streisand?"

"Guess not."

With the mood lightened and after two beers, I tried the topic again, aware that our relationship was underwritten by years of suspicion. He regarded me thoughtfully. "Richard, you may not believe me, but I am going to tell you the truth. There was no other man. Paul is your father." He tightened his lips and shook his head. "People used to say you were my child. Do you think I would have given you up to Paul Grossinger?"

"It wasn't you. It was someone I don't know."

"Forget it," he said, standing up. "People lose a million dollars on rumors not worth a plug nickel."

I awaited a different trip at Thanksgiving to try my sister on the same question. Even arranging an outing with her was an act of international diplomacy. The grown-up Debby didn't acknowledge the years of treasure hunts and shadow puppets.

On the phone she was reluctant, but I pressed until she acceded to a brief meeting during her afternoon break.

I drove into New York and parked in a structure. I made my way along Lexington to her restaurant. It was an anonymous gourmet shop, steam marking its spot on the corner. Among trays being dispatched, Debby was acting authoritative. She caught my eye without acknowledging me, then shouted to the kitchen she'd be back in ten minutes.

She threw on a black coat. "Let's walk," she said. "I need the exercise."

She kept up a brisk stride and, while we waited for traffic, she turned her hips in imitation of a tennis stroke. She moved like a New Yorker, quickly when there were no cars, not waiting for the green. I was a step slow. "Mom had you by someone else, not Paul. That's true. She didn't want you to know. She thought you'd never forgive her." She made a show of being briefly charmed by a man with a troop of motorized monkeys.

"Of course I would have forgiven her. I wish you had said something at the hospital."

My pique brought instant retaliation: "None of us have reason to expect any generosity from you!"

It was a black and a half before I spoke again: "I'm asking you for a favor."

Her tone was matter-of-fact; it was almost singsong. "I don't remember his name. She saw him once or twice later. He pretended he didn't know her. He's some wealthy Jewish bigshot. When she told him she was pregnant, he hung up."

I cached away the information: 'Yes, he was Jewish. No, he wasn't some stage personality from Grossinger's.'

"Do you know how it happened?"

Suddenly she seemed interested. "Your Grandma Jennie put her up to it. She knew they weren't going to stay married when Paul came back from the Army, and she liked Mom enough she wanted her to be the mother of her grandchild." Running in place, she took a series of deep breaths at the corner as a gridlock of cars halted our progress. "She told Mom to get pregnant so that Paul would be the father."

"What about *your* father? I thought she went from Paul to him."

"No," she said. "My father wasn't in the picture yet." Checking her watch, she suggested we head back on the other side.

"Did she ever try to get the guy to marry her?"

"I think so, but the day after she told him, he announced his engagement to another woman. He said something like, 'I wish you and Paul the best,' then hung up. She was shattered."

We were back at the restaurant. I gave her a quick hug and thanked her. She smiled girlishly and said to give her best to Lindy.

I visited Bob later that day with my sister's account. He acted as though he and I had never discussed the topic. "Barren tree!" he grumbled. "That's what they whispered behind her back. Well, you made that a lie. Then she gave me Jonathan and Deborah, and the one in between the bastard Hitzig cost me."

A dream that autumn took me to the oracle. I was in the hallway of our Central Park West apartment. When I realized my luck, I went straight to my mother's room facing 90th Street. The sun, moving on a low fall arc, warmed a mere rhomboid for an hour.

She sat on the chair by the window in a sense of eternal autumn—dead leaves and frost, her reflector open—eighteen years ago, now identically in dream. Sunlight faded behind a water tower. She put her reflector aside. Bob was adjusting something at his bed.

I knew this was after her death. I expected her to be startled because she was so easily affrighted. But she regarded me curiously. I felt as though a burden I thought I would have forever had been magically removed. There was no way I could miss. I would question her directly and have the answer in her own words.

"I am glad you came," I addressed her with the ritual formality reserved for the dead, acknowledging that it was she, not I, journeying from the other side. "I want to ask you something. I want to know who my father is."

She seemed so tiny compared to how I knew her in life.

She put her hands on my shoulders. "It's wonderful to see you, Richard," she giggled. Then she turned and stumbled against the chair, letting out a crude laugh: "Richard E. C. Grossinger!" Before I could guess, she blurted: "Economic Convenience."

This playfulness won me over, so I countered, "Martha F. T. Rothkrug."

Pleased I would meet her in riddle, she tried but could not solve it.

"Fertile Tree," I said.

Her laugh increased until it became deranged. I saw I was losing her attention, her concreteness.... and, with them, the dream. "Who was he?" I shouted. But intoxication entirely prevented speech.

Finally she gasped, "Well, it might have been Arthur Zibioski, or—" tossing her head to the side, "It might have been Arnold Garner ... or it might have been. . . .” These were totally unfamiliar names. They were followed by other unfamiliar names; they went on and on.

“You mean you don’t know,” I pleaded.

She careened about the room, shaking her head, verging on hysteria.

Bob, who had been viewing this exchange with astonishment, offered a suggestion: “Call him up and see.” He was holding out our old black phone. In fact he had already dialed Arnold Garner. The line was ringing and a man said, “Hello.”

It was Moe, his husky Durante voice unmistakable. He kept repeating, “Hello!”

I hung up.

I awoke dismayed but elated. A séance was no longer required. The stars teach us, in a manner that appears astrological, how all events are divided by exact units of time between them, propinquity and distance. The occasions of the living and the dead, of my own birth and my mother’s death, of all other principals and fathers to this affair, as well as their later wives and children, are placed in the world exactly. Each gear unfolding, each tessera is set. I could, as if it were in an act of mediumship, ask my mother again and again through different trance channels, but her answer would always be the same.

What there was would come to me and what there wasn’t, not even an etheric telescope could bring into focus.

“The dead do not lie,” Robert Kelly reminded me. “There are all sorts of other problems with the dead, but they do not lie.”

For over a year I had stared at my father in the darkness. I had looked into my own face, past my mother in it, and seen the faint beginning of a man—an expression in the eyes that wasn’t hers, a different hook to the nose, a fullness and roundness in the mouth, but mostly a softness, perhaps the same softness that had sustained me in her kingdom. He was smiling back at me. He always had been.

According to *The Tibetan Book of the Dead* I had always known him at some level outside my nervous system. There was a man making love to my mother as I looked upon her from the realm between lives, a father with whom I merged in becoming male, whom I lost quickly behind the blustering Bob and rompish Paul, a sire who (at least imaginally) waited in the background of my life to be acknowledged.

It was no accident that my conscious awareness of him began with my mother's death, for it was then that the vivid scenery she cast began to fade. Since he had refused to admit his role in her pregnancy (and immediately married another woman), her only recourse was to steal his son, to claim me as her own. I could never be just her child because, by her sense of justice, I had to be his ransom. No wonder she hated it when another family stole me.

That Christmas at Grossinger's, I led Robin through underground passages and pointed out old hiding spots. We hiked across snowdrifts, up firewalks over roofs and down hallways through rarely-used doors, a stop at the bakery for a hot raspberry cookie. At bedtime we called room service for milk shakes.

One evening, after I had put Robin and Miranda to bed and Lindy had gone to the nightclub for the show, I found my father watching TV alone in Grandpa Harry's old room. When I peeked in, he clicked off the set and asked me to sit down.

I let him initiate a conversation.

He asked how Lindy and I were getting along.

I said, "Fine."

He inquired about my job and finances, and I warmed to a speech about how Goddard had become a pretty desperate place. Struggling for a comparison he would understand, I said I felt like Jon Matlack having to pitch in Double A at his prime.

He wondered if we'd move to California. I didn't think so. "If Goddard folds, I'll find another job somewhere."

He looked interested, so I continued. "A teacher at Swarthmore is interviewing me, and I also have an invitation to the experimental program at New Paltz. Then," I added with a snippet of pride, "the head of the graduate anthropology program at the New School said that I might be considered for a position there next year."

Did he even know what the New School was? I viewed him with suspicion; I was gathering proof that he didn't really care.

He reminded me he could always intercede at Cornell—and of course I could teach any time at the local branch of the State System.

When my mother wrote in her will that I was financially secure, she meant, of course, because of Paul. Yet he knew our dilemma, and the best he could offer was a half-assed allusion to Sullivan County Community College.

It was never clear to me whether his lavish lifestyle—the closet of dozens of shoes and a hundred suits, the trips abroad and four-hundred-dollar dinners—were simply an endless expense account or greed, or both.

"We've saved a little money," I said. "I think we'll get by even if Goddard folds."

"Richard, would you drive me to my card game?"

Momentarily startled, I realized cards were the reason he had turned off the TV. I recovered my dignity by remembering it was quite an honor to deliver PG to the big game.

He threw on an overcoat and swung open the door. When he had trouble with his bulk on the ice I guided him by his arm and then helped him into my car. As I turned the ignition and looked over my shoulder he wondered, "Did your mother leave you anything?"

"What would make you think that?"

Instead of answering, he said, "Have you reconciled yourself to her death?"

"Except for one thing." He turned his head with interest as I made a U-turn and headed out the front gate.

I briefly recounted Jonny's visit. "He told me something she didn't want spoken of while she was alive."

At the foot of the hill he pointed me toward Liberty. Then he remarked calmly, "I know what you're going to say."

"Is it true?"

"Richard, I have no idea. You're my son legally, and that's all that matters."

"Did she think it was true, or did she just make it up?"

"With your mother I never knew. I think she thought it was true."

"Do you know who it was?"

"I know who she claimed it was."

"Was he someone you liked?"

"He was a creep!"

"Then why did you accept me?"

He looked at me in astonishment. "Paternity is more than blood. You were mine. I wasn't going to let her get away with it."

Even without a cloud over my paternity, there would have been sound reasons to let my mother and Bob adopt me. What would she have been getting away with? I tried to communicate this incongruity, so he told a familiar story but with a new twist: "My lawyer told me, 'You have a perfect excuse, Paul. You could save yourself a lot of money.'"

"But I wanted you," he added, "not the money."

It still made no sense. True, he had been my champion; he had rescued me from the house of ruin, but then he had been neither an attentive nor a gracious father.

What was he thinking that day he smashed me to the ground?

These were all notions beyond present reckoning. By now we had a lifelong relationship, with grandchildren. There was no turning back.

"Thanks for talking about it," I said, pulling up the driveway he pointed to.

"Remember, you're a Grossinger!" he said, edging himself out the door. I watched him tread across the snow at a snail's pace toward the ranch house.

It was a declaration of ownership not love.

Unable to keep up with its fuel bills as winter approached, the Goddard administration asked faculty to take a term off without pay and come back in the fall. Lindy and I jumped at the opportunity. Enticing poet Shepherd Ogden to see the West (and share the driving), we took both our marginal vehicles into northeast Canada. After a day in Michigan and four more in Denver we crossed Wyoming and Utah and arrived amid a rare Bay Area snow shower. We rented a bungalow in the flatlands of West Berkeley and stayed there through the summer.

At our last meeting in New York, Bob had told me what happened when Jon went on his vision quest: He returned to Baltimore, sneaked into the hospital, and started a patient revolt. The police locked him up. Then, with the hospital's collaboration, they tried to pin a mugging and seventy-two false fire alarms on him. He spent a week in a cell while his father dispatched lawyers. Finally he was waived to the custody of Gracie Square Hospital in New York.

At the end of his first month there, he was discovered by Joyce and

Joseph Golden, adjunct psychologists. Mrs. Golden wielded enough clout to get Jon released to her. "The woman is a little weird if you want to know the truth," Bob recounted to me over the phone, "but frankly, what have I got to lose?"

She set my brother up at Knickerbocker Plaza on 92nd Street and 2nd Avenue, which reminded him of the sign we saw in the distance from our childhood window.

She halted his nostrum of stellazine, and they went on a Fifth Avenue shopping spree. First they spent an afternoon at Brooks Brothers, where she prescribed a new wardrobe: suits and jackets, an assortment of white and pastel shirts, shoes and ties to match. Then she arranged for wall-to-wall carpeting, a love seat, and sofa. He picked out a stereo and tape deck. (Two days a week she used the pad herself for seeing patients.)

Now that Jon was in lusher surroundings with time on his hands Mrs. Golden suggested he enroll at Hunter College to pick up his last three credits. He chose Historical Geography.

She instructed him to buy all his groceries from Gristedes. "And don't forget to ask them to deliver. You've had a lot of pain. You need to be indulged."

It was an upper middle-class life administered therapeutically. The only difference between his shrink and an interior decorator was that her consultation went on the medical bill (either way, his mother's will paid). When I expressed disbelief that my brother would go along with such decadence, Bob suggested I call him myself.

If you guessed, on the basis of his record of organizing Chicanos for the ghost dance, that he'd begin putting an axe to the furniture, you (like me) would have missed a key fact of the twentieth century. "Very Edwardian," he remarked, describing his haberdashery. He recalled how he and Mrs. Golden had collected every item of furniture with regard to criteria of taste and quality. "Don't criticize us," he warned. "Criticism is just a way of causing pain."

Clothes make the man, the line goes. We may joke about it, but out there in the world we hardly know what's behind any of them, smiling and good-looking, company spokesmen, Congressmen. At forty sometimes they renounce it all—job, wife, children. We see it in their faces, that they are bluffing and hollow at the center, little more than frightened animals wearing fashion masks. If everything can be given away overnight, then what is left? What is the real life in the West, the one we can't renounce?

When the New School paid my plane fare to JFK that spring, I saw my brother for the first time under Dr. Golden's care. He moved like a zombie. "I never really wanted to be a hippie," he explained over dinner at a fancy restaurant. "I only dressed that way, drab clothes and all, because I didn't want people to expect too much of me."

I stared at him incredulously. I didn't understand Jon as an Apache, and I didn't comprehend him any better as a young stockbroker in the making. The only thread that might have linked these personalities was a lingering arrogance. "I listened to rock 'n' roll and wrote poetry because I thought so little of myself. I didn't realize I deserved better. Now I'm learning about the fine things in life." A shy smile. "We go to the theater. I saw an Ibsen play last week, an excellent performance." The smile even more abashed. "I listen to concerts. I don't have to punish myself with bad music. On Sunday we're going to the opera. *The Marriage of Figaro,* I believe."

Here was a guy who outwitted every physician they threw at him for ten years, suddenly falling and taking the ten-count against a bantamweight. I thought: Unification Church, Synanon, Hare Krishna, Scientology, they know something about us I missed. They understand the key to this epoch. And all along I had taken them for fools or, even worse, considered them powerless and transitory.

We are empty, I realized, all of us, and some of us more than others. If they offer to take our life in their hands, we give it to them willingly because we don't believe in it ourselves anymore.

"See this shirt I'm wearing." It had designs one step short of a Shriner's palm-tree job. "I never would have worn loud clothes before. But Dr. Golden showed me I was just avoiding looking handsome."

In a robotic, embalmed way he did look handsome now. He looked as though he could go to work on Wall Street for Siggy Zises, my cousin who helped carry him off the field at Chipinaw.

"I used to buy furniture at second-hand stores. Now we go to Bloomingdale's. The place is like an art gallery. They have African things, Oriental things, Indian things."

The man who knew enough to choose the Bureau of American Ethnography for his Osage texts and Weiser's Basement for his Qabala and tarot now was dealing an Henri Bendell deck of commissioned symbols. If this could happen to the "Apache warrior," then the whole Third World could be depopulated, every Indian peasant and Palestinian soldier reclad in a business suit.

I thought back to Dr. Kubie's words when Jon first arrived in Towson: *No life has begun. We cannot treat the symptoms. We must find where the beginning was lost. There is no life yet to treat.* By then Kubie was an old man in poor health. Yet in his afternoon with Jon he saw a shape. It went by quickly and he snagged only its tail. He trusted the psychiatric bureaucracy to finish the job.

"No life has begun." Wasn't it that way with Charlie's Angels, the original ones, Charlie Manson's? America made them cheerleaders and cowgirls, but it took next to nothing to reprogram them as assassins. No wonder school children come to stare detachedly at the body of their murdered classmate as it lies in a glade for a winter, unreported . . . unreal. Where life is a mannikin, death is a mannikin too.

By the late '70s there were no longer families, neighborhoods, or communities—only suburbs, condos, real-estate agents tacking on percentages, urban-renewal bureaucracies skimming—a decadent disco culture. Plenty of merchandise. And everyone dressed for a party.

"Aren't we proud of him," Mrs. Golden encouraged my enthusiasm as she displayed her pupil in his apartment. She was an ordinary-looking middle-aged woman, lots of brass jewelry, hard chunky body, tight Madison Avenue glow. The golden boy had won her heart, young Mickey Mantle whom Jon still nurtured in his bashful strength. She had asked to meet me there because she wanted my help in collecting her charges from Bob. "He's the cause of all Jon's problems," she told me off-handedly.

"What about our mother?"

She shook her head with professional certainty. "It's his father. His mother was weak. She committed suicide. [A pause.] If his father doesn't want to pay, we can always have the lawyer tap the trust again."

Bob and I had dinner that evening at The Friar's Club. He was anxious to perform the full routine.

"The woman asked him for my credit card. They wanted to be able to buy theater tickets. I told him, 'Look, when you need theater tickets, ask me, and I'll get them at a discount.' She had him open a charge account at Gristedes in my name. I said, 'No charge account.' So she gave him a grocery list. He brought it to my office. It read like a produce order for ten restaurants. The man would need three freezers to store it all."

"Then why do it?" I asked. "You've been around long enough to recognize a con."

"Richard," he said, balancing my name against a speech that, with variations, always went on forever. "You didn't rush down to Baltimore to talk to lawyers till four in the morning wondering what some corrupt city prosecutor was going to do while trying to close seventy-three cases. You didn't sit up half the night waiting to find out he had run away again. You haven't had eleven years like I've had, where at any moment you could be called by the police or find out he had finally succeeded in killing himself."

I felt as though the whole restaurant was listening, but then every conversation was filled with the same outrage and hyperbole. From the other side of the room I could hear, "And I told him, you son-of-a-bitch bastard, if you think you're scaring me. . . ."

"You didn't listen to the praises of marijuana, and tarot cards, and Apache Indians until it was coming out your ears. Let me have a moment's peace. I've got a few years left. I don't have to see my son beat up by gangs in the Baltimore jails." He shook his head. "This woman's got him looking like a *mensch.* Never in a million years could I have dreamed he'd look like this. Is it for real? I'm afraid even to ask. Let's give her a chance, Richard. He's not riding a bike down the West Side Highway or throwing a rock through someone's window. He's not organizing Chicanos or leading a police chase through twenty-five states. He's attending classes. And I'm going to argue? No, sir. Baltimore was the end of the line for me. It killed his mother. We've been through Dr. Aschenbach, Dr. Bernstein, Dr. Pintero, Dr. Bramhall, Dr. Wesson, Dr. Soule, and the one with the pony tail, and the one who let Jonny read his tarot. We've been through Mrs. Gernstein, Mrs. McHenry, *Ms.* Gomez, and half a dozen other overpaid social workers. I'm backed up against a wall. I've been taken by every psychiatric rip-off in our time. And I've borne my medicine like a man. Maybe Joyce Golden can work a miracle where no one else can."

Jon went to work for Food Liberation, a health-food store on upper Lexington. He learned to mix fruit and vegetable drinks and make sprout-and-nut-butter sandwiches.

He finished his degree at Hunter and continued to take courses. Meanwhile, Bob called me to complain about bills from Dr. Golden. "She must have a meter on," he said, "because I can't see where she's finding the hours in the week." He had decided to withhold a portion of her money, so Jon wasn't talking to him.

In our next conversation I told Jon Mrs. Golden was stealing his inheritance.

"Who are you to judge her," he snapped. "She's more of a true teacher than you, my brother." And he hung up.

That fall, after returning from California's eternal summer to frost-glazed Vermont, I awoke one morning too sick to get out of bed. Keying my symptoms in a materia medica, I selected homeopathic Phosphorus and dropped a few sugar balls onto my tongue. For two days afterward I lay in a semi-trance. Then I dragged myself to class.

The sensation of disease diminished in daytime only to return each night. I had diarrhea and feverish dreams. In one I experienced my naked body stretched below me on a plank. Thin tubes flowed down from my left and right eyes, crossing in the area of my diaphragm, ultimately connecting to my testicles opposite the eye from which each began. The left eye's tube flowed silver. The symbol for the moon hung like an aura below my right testicle. In the right eye's tube a golden liquid was percolating (though at spots it shone red). The symbol for the sun marked its terminus.

My life became a homeopathic warning: "Symptoms sometimes improve, but the disease gets worse." I began to imagine myself a gaunt cadaver, struggling to class against autumn gales.

After six days of this I went to the infirmary. They took urine and blood but found no ailment.

On a mid-October morning I drove south to Westchester. Edward Whitmont was not an easy man to schedule a meeting with, but—from my longstanding proposal to publish a collection of his essays—I was able to gain his assent to a half hour between clients.

A slight gray-haired man with an Austrian accent, Dr. Whitmont was both a Jungian psychiatrist and homeopath. He did not initially drop formality but, once he heard my proposal, he warmed to the idea of the book, then offered to take my case. Only ten minutes remained before his next patient, so his oracle was concise: "Diseases like yours are neither physical nor psychological. They are epiphenomenal. Phosphorus was correct but no longer important. I can see the answer just by looking at you. You are linked to your mother and her suicide, so you must begin to explore this matter of your father. You need to find him. You need his help in the shadows, maybe not as a person but as an artifact of your own psychic process."

I continued into Manhattan to Bunny's apartment. In the foyer she stared at me, then insisted she wasn't worried. "But, Richard, you don't look great. I'm going to have Ira see you."

For all the progress I had made in Berkeley, I was back in the New York physician's office.

Luckily Paul and Bunny's M.D. wasn't Hitzig. He was a tall, sunny man, a member of the Kriendler clan.

After listening to my heart and feeling my guts, he looked in my ears and eyes and down my throat. Then he took some blood, sent me to the bathroom to give urine, and wrote a slip for a stool sample. "You're healthy, I'm sure," he said. "I think we're going to come up with a parasite."

I asked him if he had a moment. Graciously putting a waiting room on hold, he straddled a stool.

"Paul Grossinger your father? Absolutely impossible! Just look at the two of you. His blood type for one, his sperm count for two. But, Richard, do me a favor."

I nodded.

"Don't go around telling people I said so."

I walked into crisp Manhattan autumn. Now that Ira had removed its omen I tried to feel the microdose of Phosphorus working inside of me, elementally and remotely. I wanted to stumble upon the old New York in which I hunted once for pumpkins among colored leaves. Everything was ripe with possibility. The World Series (Yankees-Reds) was playing in bars.

As I wandered uptown I recalled a possible witness I had overlooked. Barbara Schwartz (once Barbara Joseph) was my mother's oldest friend, the one who had brought her to Grossinger's.

I remembered Aunt Barbara best from when Jon and I were young. She had just divorced her husband and was living alone in New York with four children. For almost a year she and our mother chatted about whether love would grow in time if she accepted the proposal of a rotund multimillionaire shorter than she was, and much older. She did marry, and now, twenty-five years later, lived with him in a penthouse suite on Park Avenue.

In her last months my mother had renewed their friendship. "When she was depressed," Barbara told me at the funeral, "Martha called me and I tried to be of help. I came whenever she was despondent. All the doormen knew me. That's why they asked me to identify the body."

She was a tall made-up woman, finely tailored, a deep, resonant voice. She still practiced as an interior decorator. "If you ever want to talk about your mother," she offered, putting on her coat, "come and see me. I'd be honored."

From a phone booth on Madison I dialed her. She recovered her poise quickly and said, "By all means. Come over."

I knew it was not her style to be available on the spur of the moment, but the dead have power.

I cut west and continued uptown. I walked a dozen blocks. I gave my name to the doorman.

It was a supersonic second-generation elevator—we shot to the penthouse. The maid asked if I had had lunch and then directed me to the kitchen. While I waited, the cook fixed me a sandwich in which the cheese puffed out to form a soft round tent. Ten minutes later the maid returned and led me down a glittery hallway.

Aunt Barbara sat on her bed against a carved headboard under a Renaissance landscape, hair streaked gray, her regality brittled by age. Three poodles gamboled about, leaping onto and off the coverlet. She inhaled through a long piece of jewelry that exuded smoke rings.

"Of course your mother had you by an affair. You were her lovechild." She slapped the dogs away while petting them, then blew another ring. "You're looking at the gal who covered for her. All the time she was supposed to be staying with me she was with her lover at the

Waldorf Astoria—which is where you were conceived."

"Why do you suppose she didn't she tell me?"

"I asked her that myself many times. 'Martha, he would be proud to be the child of the man you loved.'" She threw up arms dramatically. "I could never understand why she treated you so badly—worse than Jonny and Debby. The love-child should get the best."

"Maybe she was guilty," I offered. "Maybe—" Aunt Barbara wasn't listening.

"She made herself so unhappy. What a shame! She was really a lovely person, such a bright woman."

"You know who the man was?"

"Of course I know."

I stared at her with my mother's eyes. She laughed off their intensity as if to say, 'No big deal—none of it, ever, my boy.'

"It was the financier, Bingo B———. A regular bon vivant. Benjamin B———. He was mortified he had gotten her pregnant . . . wouldn't even talk to her after that."

A name!

"Is he still alive?" My heart was pounding.

"Bingo? Of course. Look in the Manhattan phone book for the B——— corporate offices."

I left Aunt Barbara with my new identity, thoughts racing so fast I hardly knew what to do with it. B———. That was my lost name. I was Richard B———. I savored it in the elevator and onto the street.

I felt utterly reckless. I imagined going straight to his office.

Then I thought about how many decades had passed since 1944 and reconsidered. A letter would be less intrusive.

Back in Vermont, I had boundless energy. Ira Cohen wrote that it was Giardia parasites and prescribed an antibiotic. Enslin thought that the laxative for the stool sample negated the Phosphorus and had an unintended homeopathic effect. Dr. Whitmont would have said, "You finally knew your father's name."

> Dear Benjamin B———,
>
> You will probably think it strange to hear from me after all these years, but perhaps you suspected that one day I would try to contact you. Please do not regard a letter from me as a painful thing. I have no wish to make you uncomfortable and I accept that our connection

is a fateful one. As you probably know, my mother took her own life two years ago. In the aftermath of her death I learned that she believed that you, not Paul Grossinger, were my father. I don't know what you believe, but I want to say: I don't seek anything but to meet you and know you, even if briefly.

Put yourself in my place. If you learned such a fact at mid-life, wouldn't you want to see who your father was and what he looked like? I don't mean to overemphasize heredity. There are a lot of other things that make up a human being. But I do think there is a primordial meaning in sharing flesh and blood.

When I contact you, it's admittedly my own wish to know who I am. But I assume too that there's a chance in it for you to know more who you are. We have had no contact in our lifetimes, but ostensibly we share something basic. In facing each other, there is the opportunity to experience what that is.

I don't hold against you the relationship with my mother. It isn't immoral to pursue one's sexuality. I don't even hold against you your disappearance from my life. What other choice did you have? But I would like to meet you now, and I hope you can find some way to do it gracefully and without harm to yourself.

With love and respect,

Sincerely,
Richard Grossinger

Months passed, but there was no answer.

6

Going into Exile

At the start of the 1977 spring trimester the Goddard trustees announced that most faculty would be laid off after the term.

Lindy and I rued not leaving for good a year earlier. Now we faced job panic with rapidly declining property values.

I taught Attic Greek, Olson's *Maximus Poems,* and Alternative Healing. Twenty-five people showed up for the Healing course. My plan was to take them through principles of homeopathy, acupuncture, Jungian analysis, and bodywork, then to compare and connect these to alchemy, Navaho sandpainting, and Australian shamanism. I also wanted to teach stuff I had learned in Berkeley: basic shiatsu, Lomi massage, and Reichian therapy. It was to be an experiential class, more Goddard-like than my previous fare—but I still gave out a reading list. Jessie, vintage jock freak, had played the clown in a number of my seminars.

Now, at the first meeting, he refused to buy Paracelsus because "he's boring and you know I'm never going to read him."

His buddies tittered in agreement. *They* might peruse Paracelsus, but Jessie certainly wasn't going to.

"Jessie," I said, "I want you to have the books so that they're in your room. Anytime you think you're close to alchemy you can look at them and see how far away it is."

"Very funny," he retorted.

We started with a week of interpreting our dreams.

Then we built a ball of energy and passed it around the room. Everyone got to feel (and rotate) invisible stuff in their palms.

After that we moved to homeopathy. For several meetings we reviewed the polycrests. A citation conventionally listed *all* symptoms caused (and alleviated) by a remedy. "Alternative therapies tend to be simplistic and cliché-ridden," I cautioned, "so good practitioners read character and don't jump on the first obvious thing." I read the symptomology of *Carbo vegetabilis* aloud:

"Face pale, cold sweat; hair falls out by the handful; bluish, parched, sticky, loose teeth and bleeding gums." The class giggled.

"Foul taste and odors from mouth. Cold knees at night. Ulcers burn. Discharge offensive." I struggled to keep from laughing myself. "Hemorrhages, indolent oozings; even the tongue piles up black exudate; oozing of black blood from veins." Every time I tried to go on they cracked up. So did I. Finally I got words out: "Extremely putrid flatus, incarcerated flatus, collects here and there as if in a lump; diarrhea horridly putrid, with putrid flatulence; blue color of the body with terrible cardiac anxiety and. . . ."

"Jeez," Jessie shouted, "is the guy still alive?"

As Vermont warmed, our meetings moved outdoors on blankets. "Healing" became less of a priority. The course had turned into a ceremony for the death of the college; sometimes fifty, seventy-five, or more showed up, many of them non-students. "We always avoided your classes before," San Diego Art told me, "Too intellectual. But now you're just another goofy dude like us."

In the spring he honored me with a new name—'Chard—the second half of my first name, shortened from "Reee-chard." I embraced

Chard's goofiness and tried to be him. His last name (I knew) was B———.

The self-proclaimed Maoist dean instructed the campus police to monitor my classes and remove any students not formally enrolled.

"You gotta be kidding," I told him in his office.

"Richard," he said, "this is *not* a freedom-of-speech issue. This is making sure the customers—the ones paying our salaries—get undivided attention."

After I repeated his words the next day, many of the customers assaulted his office. That alone assured I would not be among those invited back.

But the University of Colorado was considering me for its Creative Writing program. Anthropology at the New School remained a possibility. I also sent a proposal for a history and philosophy of medicine to Doubleday and Harper & Row.

During a visit to New York that spring (to meet an interested editor at Doubleday Anchor) I went to visit my cousin Jay for the first time in fourteen years. His firm, Integrated Resources, occupied several floors of a midtown office building, and I had to be announced through two tiers of secretaries to reach him. He stepped out from behind his desk and video to hug me. He was an imposing figure, like a football lineman; other than missing some hair, he didn't look that different.

"Cousin Richie! I love you, kid." He shouted to his secretary, "Ring Siggy. Have him come downstairs."

While we waited, I described my present plight. "Maybe someday you and I'll start a business together," he offered. "Wouldn't that be fun!" He seemed enough of a kingmaker to pull off almost anything.

Siggy arrived with just as warm a greeting. We sat together in Jay's office.

Overwhelmed by the opulence of their situation, I commented, "I guess I don't really work like you but teach college and write." It took two seconds for Jay to obliterate that fantasy.

"We don't work either. We just come here and fuck off, like at Chipinaw. Remember?" He and Sig exchanged conspirators' smiles.

I felt like some small-time gadfly. Then I made matters worse by stumbling into the topic of the Hotel.

"I always said it was going to bury them," Siggy smirked. "My parents tried to warn them, but they didn't give a shit. They kicked us out, the schmucks. Let'em drown."

"What do they say about us?" Jay asked. "I bet they hate us. I bet Elaine calls us sons of bitches. *I certainly hope so.*"

I admitted that my father and aunt thought that the success of Integrated came only from money the Zises had won unfairly from Grossinger's.

"And how do those two geniuses figure that?" Jay asked.

I knew I was in too deep, but I had made my move.

"I guess they thought you got too much in the settlement."

"We never needed the Grossinger money," Siggy snapped. "What we got was piss. It may have meant something to them, but it was piss to us. Is that how they explain Integrated? I guess they think it all came from their money. What assholes!"

"No, Siggy," Jay inserted, "they think we're crooks. That's where they think we got our money." He turned to me.

"Maybe not crooks," I said, "but they think you engage in shady business practices."

"Grossinger's?" Jay snapped. "What's Grossinger's? We buy and sell Grossinger's five times before lunch."

As Siggy headed back upstairs I told Jay about Bingo B——— and asked his opinion.

"It's not true," he said. "My mother'll tell you; ask Aunt Ruthie."

"But Paul's sterile."

"Look, you're my cousin. Don't ever put yourself at a disadvantage by forgetting that."

Yet, contradictorily, after we had moved to other topics and as I was hugging him good-bye, he offered to put out a research inquiry on Bingo B———.

It came a week later. Jay called me in Vermont to read it: Benjamin B——— was an attorney and entrepreneur with real-estate investments in Florida, California, Illinois, Manhattan, Indonesia, South Africa, and Quebec. He had an impeccable reputation and a family network, including six brothers in business with him. He was born in

New York in 1910, attended CCNY, then Columbia Law School. With Joseph, his younger brother, he bought up urban real estate after the Depression. In the 1940s they produced twenty-one movies in Hollywood. They also invested in the production and distribution of soft-core porn. Everyone queried said Benjamin was a first-rate guy. He had four sons, Michael, Ruben, Seth, and Joey.

There was no way in.

Other college jobs turned out to be chimeras, but Anchor was willing to give a contract and a small advance. That same day, we got a surprise offer on our house, albeit for less than we originally paid.

All weekend at a yard sale, visitors came and carted off tables, chairs, bureaus—assorted props of our New England life. Meanwhile a bunch of students volunteered to help us drive back to Berkeley. It shook down to Jessie and Matt. A drinking buddy of theirs was enlisted to go ahead in a truck with our stuff.

At the last "Healing" class I told them to sense homeopathic energies and orgone waves everywhere, and "our company of spirit on a strange and beautiful planet—so that all your lives you can return to this moment." I stared at a wasp buzzing in dandelions, then water vapor breaking apart over North America.

Working all that final weekend we filled a U-Haul with a selection of books, clothes, toys, papers, and records. Our driver, a bearded logger from Quebec, adjusted his mirrors, then lumbered down the driveway and turned toward Route 2. We would meet him in California.

We filled another truck with everything not going west—the bulk of our library, winter clothing, hockey sticks, and sleds, plus hundreds of cartons of *Io* and North Atlantic Books, hauled out of the attic and set on the barn floor by an assembly line of students.

We packed our two cars. Then we staged a getaway.

This was as ancient as The Lone Ranger heading toward the horizon with Tonto, my flights from Chipinaw to Grossinger's. As deeply as we had settled in the village of Plainfield, we were soaring back toward the landscape of childhood, having cut all the roots, leaving nothing behind.

We rolled along Route 2, Jessie driving the Maverick and me the Astre. That evening, radically divergent worlds came together. Matt and Jessie became guests of Grossinger's with their own accommodations and table in the dining room. They spent the week lying by the pool and cruising lounges. Meanwhile we put our cars in the Hotel garage to be checked for the journey and unloaded the truck into Joy Cottage.

Before Paul and Bunny occupied Jennie's house, they had had all her memorabilia packed and stored in the basement. Untouched since, these now sat in sagging cartons covered with dust—trophies, plaques, Hebrew books, signed memoirs of celebrities, framed citations. Little more than ten years after Harry tried to block her entry with a thunderstorm, Grandma's claim to Grossinger's had dwindled to an archaeology, buried among boilers where a single bulb barely illuminated cavernous unfinished space. Consolidating her remnants (while salvaging rare photographs), Lindy and I cleared out a section and piled in our own stuff.

There were more than four hundred cartons of unsold books, two-thirds of them issues of *Io.* Using *Literary Market Place,* I called remainder houses until I found one in D.C. that offered to take 210 of the cases at a dime a book (and to pay the cost of shipping). In jubilation I raced to the storeroom for ten rolls of gummed tape and two black marking pens. Then, one by one, I hauled the cartons out, sealed and addressed them, and stacked them on pallets. Two mornings later a freight company took them away.

On my final trip to Manhattan, Robin was my companion. Our journey had three agendas: a meeting at Anchor about my medicine book, an interview with a reporter from the *Soho News,* and an act of espionage.

We finished the interview just before 3.

"Are we going to do it?" Robin asked.

I nodded.

The escapade was set in motion a month earlier: My friend Chuck's new stepbrother Roger (from his father's recent re-marriage) had graduated in the same high-school class as Michael B———, Bingo's eldest son. Roger warned Chuck he wasn't a real friend of Michael's, but "as long as you don't embarrass me too badly, it's okay to use my name."

Partway uptown, Robin and I double-parked by a phone booth. I dialed the B——— corporate offices, asked for Michael, and was put right through. I quickly mentioned Roger.

"Nice guy, but I hardly know him. What can I do for you?"

"I can explain more easily in person."

"Well, I've got a meeting in half an hour. If you can get here before that, I'll squeeze you in."

"We're on 40th. I'll try."

Dodging taxis and buses, we zoomed a staggered trail of green, then ditched the car at $15 a half hour. "No sense messing around with this one," I noted as Robin observed the rates.

"It's like the Hardy Boys," he said, as we hastened along the street. "But even better, 'cause it's real."

As an elevator rumbled us upward, I girded myself. I had been a renegade before, but never this. A receptionist pointed to a couch. Three minutes later we were led around the corner.

Michael was seated at a desk, a young man my age. He could have been anyone. Hair was about the right color, lighter than mine; similar build; a vague resemblance of eyebrows, nose, and mouth.

At his invitation Robin and I took chairs.

He reiterated the tenuousness of his connection to Roger.

"I need to tell you what I am here for." I hesitated for a moment.

He looked us over—man and child—and reassessed our motives. "Will I be shocked?" he teased.

"I think so."

He flashed a feint at invulnerability that was also an invitation to take my best shot. I stared at this man. Was he truly a brother?

"My mother died a couple of years ago," I began. "Actually she committed suicide."

"I'm sorry to hear that."

"She was married to Paul Grossinger when I was born."

"Right, the Catskills, Grossinger's, great place. My family used to go there."

"She left my father right after I was born, and I grew up in my stepfather's family. In fact, I even had his last name until I was twelve or so—Towers. But then I learned about my father and went to high school and college as Richard Grossinger. That's the name I have now. Anyhow, when my mother died a few years ago, it came out in the aftermath that she didn't actually have me by Paul Grossinger. She had an affair when she was married to him—while he was in the Army during World War II—and it took me a while to find out who the person was, but when I did, it turned out to be a man named Bingo B———."

If Michael was shocked he didn't show it. He raised an eyebrow disapprovingly, then laughed out loud. "Can you prove that?"

"Of course not. But I believe it's true."

He shook his head.

"I wanted to meet someone in the family," I continued. "I wrote your father, but he never answered—"

"I don't imagine he would."

"Then Roger came along . . . and this is my last day in New York. We're moving to California tomorrow. The college I was teaching at in Vermont went out of business."

There was all too much to say and no time really. I wanted everything—sympathy, recognition, resolution. "I feel silly about this."

"I understand," he said, rising and walking out from behind the desk, "but I don't see what can be done. You have no—"

"I was hoping that you might tell your brothers and then the four of you could talk to your father on my behalf."

"Why?"

"Because it's the truth. I've always believed the truth made things better."

He clearly didn't share my belief.

"I don't want anything from your family. I just want to meet them."

He smiled with a knowing look which said not only did he not buy my unsolicited renunciation but, in principle, it wasn't possible: none of them would ever buy it. I searched my mind for something else, but this was checkmate, and I had barely made a move. After all, how sure was I of my innocence? I was out of a job, no longer a Grossinger. I had two young kids. Would I turn down an offer of help from them?

This wasn't playtime anymore. My mother had jumped out a window in perplexity and despair. Bingo B——— was mixed up in that somewhere, and whoever I was began as Bingo. This was heavy-duty corporate America and, if there was a chink in its armor, it wasn't visible.

Michael was talking. "When you came in, I didn't think, 'Now that's a brother of mine.' But you never know. They say Dad had an active social life before he married. Who knows how many more of you there are running around?"

My heart sank as he went on.

"You can see why he would protect himself. Bringing up something like this with my father is not likely to make me popular." He gave a look meant to elicit my empathy. "No, I don't think he'll want to hear about this." He glanced at the clock on his desk but assured me we still had a few minutes.

"Do you have a picture of him?"

He peered into his desk drawer. "Not here I don't think, but when you get to California send me your address."

As he stepped up to walk us to the door, he asked suddenly if I had a snapshot of my wife. It was a strange sort of requital for his *not* having a photo of his father, a backhanded expression of insincere interest. I took out my wallet and showed him Lindy. "She's beautiful," he said.

I thanked him.

"Good luck to both of you."

I understood now what Jay meant. I could ignore this B——— thing and always be a Grossinger. Yet as long as I pursued it I was a bastard, like the dark son in Faulkner's *Absalom, Absalom!* but without his power to overthrow dynasties.

Two days later we repacked the cars, went out Route 17, and headed west. In Illinois, the Mets disappeared into bluegrass music and static, this time for good. We reached the desert, then the Sierras. We reentered Berkeley at the end of June.

We rented a tiny house on Hudson Street a few blocks over the Oakland line. Even as we unpacked, the landlords decided to remodel to sell after the year lease we had just signed. Ignoring our presence, they had the foundation sprayed with termite poison, then hired painters who came at 7 AM each day.

One afternoon we came home to find the top layer of our belongings speckled white where a drop cloth had missed.

"Why did you guys do this?" Robin protested. In Vermont he had the run of the village. Here there was no backyard. Highway 24 blasted by. His room stank of toxins. His friends were a continent away.

I live in Oakland and think back to Vermont. I see Plainfield, boulders in its fields, barns and meadows, a northern sun through red trees. I see from our house the garden, a tangle of weeds on fences, the crumbling porch of railroad ties.

I see wild flowers, some violet, some yellow.

I see thunderheads, purple as smoke. I hear rain on the tin roof.

I see piles of snow, broken shutters, icicles in sun. I see bare branches against blue.

I take Robin sledding on Clay Hill. The descent is so steep I have to drag my boots to slow us down. As we gather speed I feel the ground under my frame, his snowsuited body hugging mine. It was snow that once separated the New World from the Old, and it is snow rekindling my childhood through my child, his cheeks warm against mine under our hoods, our breaths smoky.

Winters pass, and he becomes the daredevil of Clay Hill. Both he and sled leave the ground at the great bump. He clings to the wood as though welded there. Steering skillfully along the hillside across branches of fallen trees he gradually comes to a stop far below, only ten feet from the highway.

Hudson Street is brown and dry. Sun bleeds through the window, melting crayons on my desk. The grass is dead. The only flower is the smell of the lemon tree.

There are moments I think of leaving. Then I catch myself. We are not on a trip to California. We have moved here.

We long again for streams and woods, where we awake home and there is no other home.

But what claim do I have on Plainfield? We were subsidized by a flimsy college. We inhabited a farmhouse through which at least a dozen families preceded us. Yet its garden and sledding hills were an eternity to our son. He came three years old from Maine. Now he walks to Peralta School through dangerous neighborhoods, chased by bigger kids whose territory he invades.

The first day of November, he and I drove north along Highway

5. We crossed the Siskiyous into Oregon. Sun cast holograms on swirling mist. At night I felt torrents of rain washing against our tires, the Pacific somewhere ninety miles to my left.

Rain eased and we came to a northern frontier of shopping centers and suburban lights.

For three days scouting I tried to force Portland into being home—a wetter, more authentic city than Oakland. But it was such a constant drizzle I wore my black pea-jacket over a sweater, my sneakers soaked. I followed up a long shot at Reed.

No luck. School was over.

We drove back to Oakland just before snows closed the pass.

Robin is eight years old. I remember him as a baby held aloft in an Ann Arbor hospital. Before that Lindy lay full-bellied on our quilt in the light of the quince.

When would there ever be another such tree, another first child, another alchemical wedding?

We drove to Maine with a U-Haul trailer on a station wagon. We moved into a cottage on Mount Desert Island, a mere stroll through forest to the Atlantic.

When would there be clams again so close to our fire, lobstermen to meet at the wharf, phone calls from Olson, islands around us?

Robin wasn't even one when we bought our first house, plowed a garden, published the Dream and Baseball issues. For four terms I drove back and forth over the bridge into Portland and along winding roads to Gorham. That was supposed to last forever too.

On the day of the move from Maine we had to empty out everything—a daunting task because there was always another drawer, and the mind was past exhaustion. A group of students labored all weekend helping us. Herb brought the Erebus staff. A poet friend drove up from New Haven and rented a twenty-four-foot truck.

I shook hands with each of them—Mike Caron, the Vietnam vet who earlier that year accepted my challenge to drop his left-wing jingoism and ended up writing the geological and ethnographic history of Vietnam; Eddie, the effete science-fiction fan and critic of my work; Beda, the freckled would-be Hindu, who taught me mantras and yoga; Mary, the scholar and nature poet; and Billy, the gay surrealist painter and cynical dadaist who drew our film posters.

Finally it came down to dumping the contents of the last drawers into boxes—paperclips, pencils, and rubber bands—searching the barn with flashlights to find garden tools. We took up each rug and shook it, unhitched handmade curtains. Then the stereo was the only thing downstairs—the Rolling Stones blasting the anthem of our time, "no satisfaction," until they too were packed. There wasn't room for any feeling; feeling was overwhelmed. We all agreed—supper on the road. A last visit to our cat Frodo's grave and then. . . .

This is Robin's first memory. He does not remember Maine at all, just our friend David in the truck pulling out first, Lindy next in the Pontiac towing the U-Haul. And me last, waiting till the U-Haul cleared the driveway and then turning into line in the $200 red Mustang with the pin-cushion radiator.

A group of neighbors waved. I waved back. As the truck crashed into branches, one came sailing across the trailer and bounced in the street. This was ridiculous, a caravan evacuating Mitchell Road.

The U-Haul swayed around familiar curves. I began laughing, laughing and crying.

Then we were out on the highway, heading northwest across New Hampshire. We hit a storm of such weird intensity that, while sun was shining, rain was falling in luminous sheaths.

The downpour ended, and we pulled into a pizza place, got shell noodles for Robin, split a pitcher of beer, salads, a large onion-and-bacon. Back in the cars, we drove over the mountains into Vermont.

We moved onto the hill in Plainfield, had another garden plowed.

Muggy afternoons gave way to quick dusks, early frosts, and blankets of morning snow. Winter winds drove the thermometer to 50 below. Night scrolls of smoke and habitation fog rolled the village through constellations. Every so often moonlight caught gusts of snow off roofs. So precise because it must be that way forever.

We dug out our front porch and driveway, got our cars to kick over.

The end of winter was a cosmic, almost supernatural transition. River ice boomed in retreat, jays screeched, and wind rattled through bare branches. In official and unofficial rivers, floods came down from the hills. A month or two of mud season was followed by warm breezes, budding maples, the return of zinnias and robins, golden-white clouds.

There was a day late in August, 1974, the last time ordinary life spun effortlessly off the spool. We pulled carrots in Anne's garden, then sat at the skinny-dipping hole, children rafting on broken pallets, adults in the mud socializing. Lindy waded in, swam a few strokes, and then stretched out a towel in the sun. I played with Miranda in a pool Robin had dug for her. She splashed at it with a toy shovel, then covered herself in mud.

I edged into glacier-melt, a shock of cold.... then drifting on my back, clouds parading over me, I dove and clambered down thermoclines. I imagined vinegar of hay, so deep an infusion I hardly could bear it. Touching mud, I opened my eyes to a single morninglike flash, grains streaming by. It was too alien and beautiful to keep looking.

And then after that last hard winter (our family in doubt), we came to California on a lark and found another world.

I walk past eucalyptus and redwood groves, staring back at Vermont in memory the way I stared at constellations from the Goddard hills, thinking how brief and absolute we are against the forever we come from.

One afternoon Robin intended to ride his bike home from a neighborhood party. He called us before leaving. Then he didn't arrive. "You go," Lindy said.

I would have given anything not to make this journey.

On the other side of the highway overpass—the neighborhood milling about—our son stood in tears by his totalled bike. At least he was alive. Chased by a gang, he had ridden into the street, right into a pick-up truck. I hoisted him up and comforted him. The driver, following us home, handed the twisted metal to Lindy.

The next morning I sent my stepfather an ill-advised letter, citing the injustice of my mother's will and asking for his help. After all (I pointed out) it was mostly money from my father. Even more important, my goal was the safety and well-being of my kids. I was invoking our oldest family value, playing my one card in the Towers family for something that mattered (at last).

Bob never answered. Years would pass in total silence.

I called my father. He said: "Richard, I have no extra cash."

In truth, I didn't put myself at a disadvantage because I was already there.

My mother's two older brothers lived in San Francisco. Uncle Eddie had set up as a furniture distributor on Market Street. After running a life insurance company in Connecticut most of his life, Uncle Paul had recently retired to be near his brother.

Eddie twisted balloons into animals for my fourth birthday in 1948; I didn't see him again until my wedding in Denver in 1966. Paul appeared periodically during my childhood, an excitable voice in the living room selling insurance to my stepfather. Afterwards, Bob and my mother tore him down.

"An expert," Bob complained, "on everything, from Karl Marx to how much I should pay him for advice."

When I met Uncle Paul anew in San Francisco, he was delighted to begin a relationship with a long-lost nephew. A confirmed socialist, he blamed my mother's suicide partly on her capitalist values. Just before her death he and she had had a falling out. With Eddie on the point of bankruptcy, Paul was raising money from family members, "but your mother refused to tap her nest egg."

"I was wrong," he concluded, "because I tried to tell her something she wasn't capable of understanding, but, Richard, sometimes you draw a line and a sister letting a brother starve is where I drew it with her."

He came to Oakland to visit us, bearing a tea set and a doll for Miranda, a board game and model boat for Robin. Over lunch he said he would help in whatever way he could.

"My mother, my own children, and my brother's family are my first responsibilities. Those are commitments I made a long time ago. But if you can think of some way I might redeem myself for how I failed my sister, I'd be glad to try."

Enough family melodrama, we switched to intellect. I found it near impossible to explain alternative medicine satisfactorily to a Marxist former life-insurance executive.

A few weeks later the Rothkrugs threw a party for a glamorous relative passing through town. Cousin Radley, a Hebrew Paul Newman, bore the ambiance not only of an independent movie-director but an international producer of erotica. The son of Grandma Sally's younger sister Anne, he had been close to my mother, in fact one of the few family members who visited us during childhood. Many an afternoon during high school I took the subway to his office; from there we would hike to the Stage Deli for a tongue-and-turkey cinema discussion. I had not seen him in over ten years, so I drew him aside and asked if we could talk.

"Richard, I always knew we would have this conversation, though I didn't necessarily know that it would be San Francisco, 1977. Let's politely excuse ourselves."

We wended our way along the Marina, kites whipping like hell overhead. "I knew Bingo well at one time, at least in the sense that anyone could claim to know him. We're both in the fuckfilm business. I had the product; he had the network. I remember one time travelling in France with a couple of his sons—this was maybe fifteen years ago when you were teenagers—and I couldn't help but think of you and Jon." Radley had a European style of thoughtful promenade. We could have been strolling along the Seine.

"Bingo himself, well, I don't know what to tell you. Let me put it this way: He won't ever get in touch with you because it might, say, cost him a dime for the call. You know what I mean?" He shrugged gallantly. "I'm sorry, Richard, but you were better off not knowing him."

We continued to walk in respectful silence before he picked up his own conversation. "How can I explain it? It's that—if you owed him money and you were on your deathbed—he'd find you. I don't know how much credence to give it, but there were rumors the B———s were Jewish mafia once upon a time. I can't say whether that went beyond the porn business or whether it was bad blood somewhere. But during the Depression they cleaned everything up that maybe needed cleaning, went above ground, and bought a good chunk of Manhattan when it was cheap." He shook his head and smiled. "Unfortunately it runs the other way in your and my genes. Your grandmother's and my mother's—let's see—grandfather, Benjamin Ziegelmilch, was a cigar-maker, but he did real estate and gambling on the side. He *lost* the site for the old Madison Square Garden in a card game. Bingo never lost anything. If he couldn't win he didn't play. And the B——s were playing very well thank you after the War."

"Then Martha met him."

"She met him at Grossinger's, vacationing. I remember his mother, a real tough character—the don." He smiled at the memory. "I think Bingo was sort of a momma's boy, afraid of her. He was old for not being married. How did you find out about him anyway?"

I told him the story of Barbara Joseph.

He looked at me incredulously, then shook his head. A dragon kite buzzed noisily, then crashed to the ground, just missing a dog who was chasing it.

"Was there something wrong with her telling me?"

"Nothing was wrong with it. But charity begins at home. What about her own daughter?"

"You mean *she* had a child by an affair?"

"Not only did she have a child by an affair. She did the French thing, like your mother. When she was married to Freddie, she got pregnant with another gentleman. I think he was a conductor of the philharmonic. She never told—"

"Julie," I supplied.

"She never told Freddie either. To this day he thinks that the child is his, god bless him if he's still alive. But Izzy adopted her. *She* doesn't know. I'm not sure Izzy even knows. He probably thinks he adopted Freddie's kid."

It was my turn to be incredulous. Barbara had portrayed herself as a staunch advocate of my mother telling me the truth. But didn't the same rules apply to her? Could she have been thinking of her own "love child"? Was she confessing by proxy, using someone else's secret? "How do you know all this?" I finally asked.

"She told your mother, no doubt in confidence, the world's biggest gossip, and your mother told that other great secret-keeper, *her* mother Sally, who told my mother, who, I'm proud to say, apparently told only me."

"But, Radley, it's so bizarre—these two women, teenage friends, each marrying, each getting pregnant through an affair, letting the husband think that the child was his, getting divorced, marrying yet another person, and attempting to get that person to adopt the kid, successfully in Barbara's case."

"If you made a movie, they wouldn't believe it."

"No, it sounds like something you might want to import from Belgium."

He laughed. A pair of gulls screeched over a piece of bread in our path.

"Now your mother, you realize, was quite a woman, quite a woman with men, even when she was married to Paul."

He stopped beside a bench but did not sit down. Instead he turned and stared at me. "She was the first woman I fell in love with. I was just a teenager myself when she was at Grossinger's. She was so gorgeous, and then she had this little baby. We all knew it wasn't Paul's—and that was, well, part of her charm. But it wasn't something you talked about, and certainly not then." He looked at the water for a moment. "Richard, I sometimes think—if this doesn't sound disrespectful, and I don't mean it to—that your mother was what got me into this business. Not the erotica, mind you—that's just bucks—but the movies. She was a born star. Bingo—I guess she chose him as her leading man. Then life was unfair, as it is to all of us."

We continued to walk silently along the Bay.

Book Four

VISION QUEST

1

Step Back Like a Monkey

Our decision to move to Berkeley had its roots in our previous visits there, one a summer adventure, the other an eight-month revel. The night after I arrived there the first time (July, 1975—the year my mother died), I dialed the number Carolyn had handed me in Vermont. The woman answering did not seem to know either her or Andy, but stated brusquely, "Yes, t'ai chi meets in my yard—7:00 on Tuesday and Thursday evenings and six mornings a week. No class on Saturday."

"Is Paul still teaching?"

"We study t'ai chi. Whoever comes participates. My name is Carol. It's my house. I'm the instructor."

We had driven north out of Denver through Cheyenne where we picked up Highway 80—two hundred miles of dusty rock-essences wind-hollowed on red hills. Patches of purple glowed briefly, chromosomes in Martian meadows.

West of Salt Lake, graffiti cairns decorated the desert, Peace signs formed by irregular rocks, Jesus on the Cross. A pelican sun sat in perspectiveless refraction, a few cumulus jugs marking a mountain.

The last spurt before Winnemucca Lindy was driving close to ninety when she knocked off a jack rabbit that bounded from oblivion into our path, leaving it at the gate to Orion, brief bump up and over its bones.

The next day we passed through Reno and began our ascent into the Sierras, entering California, not in 1967 with everyone else, but at the start of a different era.

Our first night in Berkeley a crowd of poets and anthropologists (one of them bearing a projector) gathered at the house where we were staying to watch rare Edward Curtis films of Northwest Coast Indians. As a stream of traffic glimmered in fog over the Bay Bridge, the metropolis lay in the distance, circled by jets, a Pyramid in its Third Eye. Then synchronized oars sent Bear, Raven, and Whale canoes shooting through grainy waves.

Carol's instructions were to park on McKinley Street and come down the driveway. As I ducked through brambles, I suddenly saw a Brueghel t'ai-chi classic, vivid in every detail: a lemon tree, a cat prowling, people in pairs. I stood respectfully and (I hoped) unobtrusively by the side.

The participants included one very large, elegantly dressed woman, a man in overalls, two women in a corner pushing together, a dark-haired Indian-looking woman, and a storklike man with glasses pushing forcefully against a squat red-haired man. There were ten women, four men, and all seemed very adept. The red-haired man might have been straining, but I wasn't advanced enough to tell if he was rigid and immobile or grounded and strong.

I recognized Paul from Andy's depiction. Pushing with one of the women, he was a tall reed with a pale, oval face. Strands of light brown hair fell over his ears and forehead. About my age, he wore a shapeless white robe. Even as I noticed him, he acknowledged my presence by a smile.

Finally he bowed to his partner and walked over. "You must have come from Vermont," he remarked pleasantly.

I assumed Carol had told him about my call, but just to be sure, I brought regards from my teachers.

"Carolyn was wonderful," he interrupted at the mere mention of her name. "She learned to be so much softer."

I told him I knew the set but wasn't very good.

He asked about the drive out west, then what I was doing in Vermont.

I felt childlike excitement. Paul wasn't just a student or teacher, or even a poet. He wasn't a Vermont apparatchik. He was one of the mythical California people who had lived through the Summer of Love. He seemed archangelic standing there, nodding approvingly as I overanswered while trying to be spare. He just kept smiling and asking more questions, chatting away about everything from the origin of the Great Salt Lake to what kinds of books I wrote.

"But I shouldn't be keeping you from the class," I finally inserted, for it was proceeding without us.

He gazed at me through cosmically blue eyes or, more accurately, at a point slightly above me. "You're not keeping me from t'ai chi. We're *doing* t'ai chi. You're sending energy, and I'm giving it back. Talk is a very powerful form of t'ai chi. Very subtle, very wonderful. You give energy. You yield." He turned to his left as if to cycle my words. "It's all the same principles." Then, without warning, he raised his right ward-off for my hands. He was utterly weightless; I felt like a fat ball bearing. As he rotated from his waist in an arc, I tried to relax and let his movement transfer itself to me. He was so willowy and supple it was a more complicated orbit than I had experienced with anyone before—wider, emptier, spiralling.

Sightseeing no longer, I had fallen from an amateur field in Vermont to a backyard of savants. Paul's hand probed for my center; my palm slid along the hairs of his arm, measuring his shifting degrees. Lemon blossoms released sweet oils in the dusk. A bright evening star shone above the trees.

A pleasant ache shot up my spine and expanded at my shoulder blades. Was this his potent ch'i or my over-fervent imagination? Either way I was trapped by his push. He smiled in recognition, released me, and began again.

"Don't be in such a hurry," he offered. "There's no reason to do it faster or slower. We have time. In fact, we have nothing *but* time."

During the next cycle he departed from the form as I knew it, yanking my arm abruptly back and holding it. When I didn't know what to do, he twisted it so that I had to turn; then he coiled a fist into my shoulder blade. As I resisted, he gave a light slap to my face, forcing me to respond upward with my ward-off.

As rock blasted from a nearby building, Paul repeated this lesson a number of times. "The noise is good," he said. "It forces us to make our own silence inside." Then, complimenting me on my improvement, he added, "You should work with Doris." He traded me with one of the women in the pair closest to us.

Suddenly I was exchanging circles with a nereid in a pillowy white dress, a flower in her hair, too-sweet perfume. The adjustment was like dropping off a cliff. Her presence was so vacant the hand she offered was not there. She caught me at once in her ward-off. The moment I rotated back she tugged me over to show how much I was leaning. We began again, my hand directed just inside her bracelet, our invisible beachball rolling back and forth, one part of my mind trying to decide if she was pretty, her face remote and expressionless.

After push-hands, Paul and Carol demonstrated a series that included Step Back Like a Monkey, Embrace Tiger/Return to Mountain, and Move Hands like a Cloud. They were dramatic, powerful partners—he a quick cat, pouncing back and forth; she whirling emphatically around him and striking swordlike—he suddenly behind her; she suddenly behind him. I knew the moves from Vermont, but the nuances they added made them seem totally novel.

We split into pairs and practiced this sequence over and over as they came around, inserting themselves and correcting.

It was past eight when Paul assembled us to do the set. As fog cooled my sweat, shape turned into shape, in me and around me. I felt how perfect this was, silently synchronized. Then the teacher bowed to his departing students, one by one.

That weekend Bob Callahan, our host and publisher friend, took Lindy and me on tour. Along Telegraph Avenue we passed crafts stands manned by vendors in robes and tie-dyes. Continuing into People's Park, he pointed out where barricades once stood. The lot was a hodgepodge of homemade teepees and vegetable gardens, piles of clothes marked as "free boxes." People approached us, but Bob snapped, "Whazzup?" each time and kept walking.

Sunday in Tilden Park we hiked through eucalyptus groves, their scent not unlike cat spray. We came to a pond with a footpath around it. Kids paddled in black inner tubes. Drums echoed from an invisible horizon, their sound working up and down scales like the summons of a Peruvian brujo. When we got to the other side we saw not an army, just five men and women—two black, three white—sitting in the grass, eyes closed, pounding away.

On Monday morning, the opening of the dance conference, I drove Lindy to Oakland. She kept reminding me to find daycare so she would feel reassured. I promised it would be my first priority. Then I dropped her in a crowd lining up at a Mills College dorm.

It wasn't hard to find options: Lamp posts were plastered with notices for not only daycare centers and playgroups but t'ai chi, homeopathic medicine, whole-grain baking, etc. Callahan had suggested we leave our daughter with an older woman who took care of toddlers, so I drove both his son David and Miranda there. Then Robin and I went on our own.

He selected a colorful daycare poster and said, "Let's check it out." I unfolded my map and found the address.

It was a storefront of kids, a banjo-player entertaining at the far end. I paid for three days a week. As I left, the ringmaster was setting him up at an easel.

According to purple posters all over town, homeopathy met in the living room of a ground-floor apartment on Regent Street. I sat there among twelve other people, some in chairs, most of us on the floor. I was sipping spearmint tea when Dana Ullman, a nervous, gawky young enthusiast, passed around a sheet of paper and asked each of us to jot down how we found out about homeopathy.

He began with principles and philosophy, then moved to capsule descriptions of the primary medicines, the polycrests. Hardly articulate and dangling the threads of his sentence fragments in participles, he knew his material nonetheless and made comments like "You're really gonna get off on this remedy" and "Pure energy, man." Suddenly homeopathy was not an exotic terminology in old books. People here actually studied it like the newest form of birth chart or countercultural game. As Ullman diagrammed the physical, mental, and spiritual sheaths of the body, I was already imagining a course on esoteric healing I could offer at the Goddard supermarket in the fall.

At the close, when our teacher checked the sign-up sheet, he called out my name. "Aren't you the guy who did that interview in the *Whole Earth Almanac?*"

"You mean with Ted Enslin?"

Everyone turned to look, so I elaborated: "I actually published it in my own journal, *Io. Whole Earth* sort of borrowed it."

Ullman strode over and extended his hand: "That article got most of us started. You may be responsible for this very class."

Stunned, I rose to accept his embrace.

The universe actually seemed to work. A torch I had borne briefly and inattentively in Maine had been picked up, and those whom I had accidentally initiated were beyond me, waiting.

At a café on Euclid the next afternoon, Dana offered, over carrot cake, to take my case. Before I could object he began asking me questions, like whether I was mostly hot or cold, what foods I liked and disliked, and whether I tended toward grief or anger. He was pretty sure he had figured out my remedy, but I thought he was being simplistic.

"You're typical of the way East Coast people are. Everything has to be complicated. They spend years going to psychiatrists, but James Tyler Kent said the causes of our ailments are *always* unknowable. So who cares! You could be cured in an instant by a single dose."

Back in his room he took down a jar of homeopathic Sulphur and poured a few tiny sugar balls into a folded cone of paper which he placed in my hand.

"The Jungian archetypes manifested," I observed, stalling as I pointed to pellets that held only spirit but no sulphur.

"In California we're not so intellectual."

The sun on his leather homeopathic books lent majesty to the moment. I dribbled the pellets onto my tongue and braced for an LSD rush. An irregular burning spread from the center of my back around my chest. I couldn't tell if I was hallucinating or experiencing sonic transmission.

"Look at that microdose go," Dana chuckled. "You really lit up."

"Lit up?" I protested. "I thought I was going to pass out."

"That's because you're not used to so much vital energy."

There was no word of when Paul's last class would be, but he kept warning that one of these days he'd be gone. I was trying to learn as much as possible in the brief time we had, staying afterwards and practicing with him and Carol. We engaged in a free-form version of push-hands, adhering to each other as we pursued through the jasmine yard, a hand to an arm, a finger to a shoulder, a forearm to a flank, trying to sense energy and respond to a partner's unpredictable darts and feints. I imagined the ch'i energy ball as a luminous version of the orb I had chased all my life. Yet this was wild and elating in a whole new way.

Before meeting Paul and Carol I wouldn't have thought myself austere, but something in me balked at the sinuosity of their circles, at reaching out and touching someone's chest, or bending low and twisting up without self-consciousness. These shapes weren't yet part of me.

Every step of Paul's and Carol's, even when not doing t'ai chi, was conscious and soft. I moved among them as a clubfoot, concealing embarrassment in innocence. But embarrassment for what? Doing it poorly, or doing it at all?

Over the month, as Paul unexpectedly stayed in town, he taught me the moves of a two-person set called *san shou,* which matched partners in a formalized sequence of strikes, slaps, kicks, and their neutralizations. Even though I was a beginner doing an advanced practice, his method was to place me opposite him and begin; I followed as best I could. When I blanked out or was in the wrong place he dislodged me (or simply stopped). Then we started over.

Eyes sparkling, face ever quixotic, Paul led me to California jolt by jolt. His calm words belied the forcefulness of his gestures. "I'm trying to get your attention," he explained. "If you won't give it to me, you encounter my energy before you're ready for it. I could *tell* you the same thing but you're so used to words you wouldn't bother to listen."

"It's not a fight," he preached one morning during class. "You're all trying too hard to knock each other over."

He summoned Doris to the front. "Attack me," he challenged.

Emboldened, she gave a hard push followed by a sharp press. Casually he stepped aside and she stumbled.

"Come on, Doris, really attack me!"

She charged at him, back and forth like a cartoon of an enraged bull. Each time, he pivoted away and guided her into a fall. She was amused but exasperated; she wanted to smash him.

"If you knock me over, Doris, that would only be because you gave me too much energy before I was ready to . . . *receive it,*" stepping aside and pulling her down at the word "receive." "When I'm ready, your energy is a gift." He spun as her glancing blow fluttered into space.

She came at him next time like a wild creature, both arms thrashing toward his face.

"Those are presents, little presents of your energy. I'm honored you want to give me so much without getting any . . . baaaack." He whirled and immobilized her, bending her arm behind her. "This is a dangerous position," he demonstrated to our merriment as Doris added grimaces for comic effect. "But dangerous also means healthy. Bend-bow shoot-tiger activates an acupuncture point." He jiggled her to show the meridian. "When we do the move we give our partner a treatment. If we're skillful they appreciate it." Doris verified this with a strained grin. "You can't help but heal your opponent. That's the nature of the tao."

At the end of class he led us through the first section of the set, so slowly it was almost unendurable, each movement infinitesimally changing into the next, our bodies rising and sinking. An hour instead of fifteen minutes.

Then he announced he was leaving for Idaho at the end of the week.

In the final meeting Paul proceeded as usual, dissecting moves, he and Carol observing, correcting. "We could just hit," he told one pair, "but that wouldn't be subtle enough; it wouldn't be t'ai chi. There would be nothing in reserve." He chuckled at his own conceit and stared at clouds as though parodying the ethereal savant. Lemon flowers sparkled among lemons, and next door someone was hanging a paisley on a clothesline. "Everyone talks about not having enough energy. But there's plenty of energy, all around." He demonstrated, making lotuses in the soft blue orgone air of Berkeley. "They don't want it." He shook his head in astonishment: "They *just don't want it!*"

He was still weaving this paradigm as he moved to the next pair: "It's like massage. The most powerful massage of all is not Rolfing. It's the one where you are not even touching. That's the most subtle but also the most profound. The fingers move above the body, activating points. That's the style that takes the longest to learn."

He set himself before me and offered a ward-off. "No past or future," he chided as I rushed through the move I thought I knew to get to the move he was teaching. "There are no simple moves or hard moves. If you hurry through ward-off left to get to fist under elbow you never get to fist under elbow. Everything is changing in all parts all the time. You can add tension to it, but you can't arrive any faster."

"Why?" he asked the class. "Why the resistance? Why be anxious to leave the moment you get there?"

As we practiced strikes, he instructed: "Right hand creeping by the ear, sensing. Heisenberg's Principle of Uncertainty."

"Bullshit," shouted Jeff, jock auto-mechanic in Adidas, usually his biggest admirer.

Paul looked hurt.

"You tell me how it's some Heisenberg Principle of Uncertainty!"

"You really want to know, do you?"

Jeff nodded.

"Well," Paul mused, completing the spiral of his strike, "the movement is continuous; there's no break move to move, no moment when everything isn't changing—it's a wave. But each moment is discrete; each moment some new exchange is beginning; each moment needs absolute attention—it's a particle. You can't break the wave to hold the particle. And you can't give up the particle to form the wave."

At the end of class he reminded us to open our joints and let ch'i flow. "If you don't feel it, don't worry, just keep doing it. Pretend you're feeling it. That's better than pretending you're *not* feeling it. At least you're establishing a lifelong relationship to ch'i."

Everyone left him a gift. Mine was a copy of my book *The Slag of Creation* fresh from the printer. Carol presented a loaf of bread, Doris a t'ai-chi shirt, Jeff was going to repair his car for the trip.

When Lindy's dance conference ended, we began a house-sitting gig in a luxurious Albany villa. Light, carefree days followed, the skies huge and cerulean. ("More space," Paul had warned, "than East Coast people are used to"—and he didn't mean geography.) In Tilden Park, Robin gathered bark and shells and placed seeds and pine cones in Miranda's tiny fingers. At home they rolled and jumped so rambunctiously on our hosts' waterbed that we feared the obvious. Lindy reprimanded with a line from a favorite book: "No more monkeys/Jumping on the bed!"

"Oops," said Robin.

Miranda imitated his sound.

Frisbees overhead, I lay in the sun in Ho Chi Minh Park studying a compendium of homeopathic remedies. This was not like when I memorized Hopi verbs in Arizona—I could never speak real Hopi from a book. But Lycopodium, Phosphorus, and Sepia were each a complete system of character in which I saw parts of myself and others. I could even imagine administering these pills.

Meeting for lunch at the Toraya, Lindy and I ordered miso soup, teriyaki, salad with miso-lemon dressing. We went to poetry readings in the Berkeley hills. At the Java we were served hot peanut dressing on lettuce and sprouts, lamb on skewers, coconut ice cream for dessert. Afterwards we saw a Wilhelm Reich movie we had heard about for years—*WR: Mysteries of the Organism.* The next night we got tickets to a production of *The Tempest* in the park. "This is the honeymoon we never had," Lindy rhapsodized. "All we did was get our car stuck on a Hopi mesa and rush home to graduate school. Then we put ourselves through winters in Maine and Vermont. No wonder we were going stir crazy; no wonder I went to New Mexico with Peter. Any diversion possible."

One afternoon in early August I kept an appointment with the poet Diane di Prima. We met at a tiny kitchen off Telegraph (that she had assured me was the only authentic source of Chinese food in town). After we ordered, she pulled a manuscript out of her pack. There was one unfilled slot left on our Arts Council grant.

In Boulder, Lindy and I had attended her reading and introduced ourselves. When I mentioned maybe publishing a book of hers, she promised we'd discuss it later at precisely this restaurant.

Now, as we gobbled pot-stickers, I acknowledged missing the point of her earlier work (in a snide critique of her in *Solar Journal*). Whether or not she was cognizant of my slight, she smiled magnanimously.

When I told her next about my "Freud, Reich, and Jung" course and my desire to find a Reichian to work with, she dropped her chopsticks and reached into her purse for an address book, then scribbled a name and address—"one of the most powerful teachers I have ever met: Ian Grand." She laughed heartily at her apparition of me encountering this man. "He'll put you into your body. He specializes in poets stuck in their heads." Wiping away rice she had spilled, she stared like a drill sergeant: "A few sessions with Ian Grand and you'll know how to read my 'Revolutionary Letters,' chile!"

I pictured WR, the bear-shaman himself, denouncing the medical establishment, aiming guns at UFOs from his laboratory in Maine. I wasn't sure if I was ready for him; yet I received the torn napkin with thanks.

Two years down the road I would send my student Sheppard out west to meet Diane. They would fall in love and, though she was a generation older, they would still be living together and running the San Francisco Institute of Magic and Healing Arts twenty years later.

Directed by poet friends to pick-up softball at Codornices Park, I sat on the adjacent hill and watched the action. Players wore various jerseys both faded and new—El Cerrito High, Contra Costa Merchants, Fanny Bridge Inn (F.B.I.), Watergate, Sonoma Food Conspiracy. After the game a new team was chosen, myself included. We made out a batting order: Cisco, Rudy, Travis, Wayne, Tim, Rich, Wolfman Dave pitching, Merlin, Angry Norm, Jazzman Willie. . . .

I got on base on an error and was doubled home. Sitting on the side, high-fiving, I shared their keg. Travis said, "Come back next Sunday. We play pick-up every week: first twenty guys here make the game; next ten on the list challenge the winner."

Ian Grand's phone didn't ever answer. When I checked out his number on Virginia Street, there was never anyone there. I felt like a spy, reconnoitering Reichian headquarters, hoping to be disappointed, so I could tell my students as part of my tales of California that at least I made the effort.

I didn't need this man. I had done enough.

It was an ordinary cottage on a residential street, a buzzer with his name. Sometimes I stood there before ringing, rehearsing my speech in my mind.

This was my summer ritual—to test the lair of the lion, close enough to feel his breath, to leave each time unscathed.

One morning Carol told me to try pushing hands with my eyes shut. "Remove the distraction. Don't worry about correctness. See if you can *feel* what I'm trying to show you. Not through your head—through your body."

I closed my eyes. All at once her cycle became palpable. Even as I stumbled in darkness, I felt each ripple of her changing pressure. After several minutes, my arms grew weary. I was sure she would rest. But we went only more rapidly, our hands tracing an infinity symbol, my shoulder blades aching unbearably.

"Good," she urged, "you're getting closer. Don't stop now."

I encountered a failure my whole time on Earth to keep at something that wasn't hedged against an image of what I was going to do next, by a fantasy of who I was or what women were presently attractive to me, or my planned flight home where I could sink into the nullity of my life. Carol was how I imagined California people who are advanced. She strolled from dawn meditation to morning class. Her sombrero kept direct sun off her. She was a paragon of strictness, lacking Paul's spirit of mischief. In addition to t'ai chi, she instructed me on diet and herbs. She was openly shocked that I ate at hamburger houses and bought canned foods. She blamed most of my t'ai-chi failings on these practices.

(Her sentiment was reinforced by a man with a turban in Dana Ullman's class. When we graduated to taking each other's cases my main complaint was upset stomachs, so he asked me what foods made me sick.

"I don't know."

"How little consciousness you show," he retorted pompously, "just stuffing things inside of yourself with no attention to what they are and how they change you—let alone their karma.")

Finally Carol said I could open my eyes. Waves of light trembled against me. She looked so different, her sullen face that of an old shaman, her sombrero and scarf representing her attachment to perfection.

Suddenly my arms were effortless. They began to move by themselves. Extending from my body, they traced a globe of multidimensional spheres, flowing into and out of one another. My thinking had stopped.

Carol slid her arm away. We bowed to each other. Class was over.

Up on Codornices they were choosing up teams.

My first at-bat, I whipped a beeline over the leftfielder's head into the trees, the furthest I had ever hit a softball.

My colleagues were wildmen (a few women as well); their jobs ranged from Reno gambler and jazz musician to Lucasfilms executive (female) and corporate lawyer, and included an International House pancake-maker, a telephone lineman (female), a bus driver, four or five ex-minor-league prospects (now Campbell's Carpet hustlers), two dope dealers, and uncountable varieties of scam artists hawking their wares between innings.

One Campbell's hotshot, Steve Gentile, son of the former Oriole slugger, arrived with his duffel bag, stripped down to his jock, and dressed right there. A red-bearded giant, he had the singular charisma to bullshit his way into an ongoing game. "Now pinch-hitting . . . ," he announced himself, but didn't finish, loosening pectorals with three aluminum bats.

Iggy the Indian pitcher looped it up, "Here, Whiteloaf."

Swinging for the seats, Gentile squibbed it past first. "Sorry 'bout that. Cheap single," he moaned, running down the line.

"Oh what a rogue and peasant slave am I!" shouted bare-chested Eddie Detroit upon striking out, swishing his bat in the air.

Wolfman Dave stood in leftfield chanting over and over, inning after inning, melodically, "Ain't no batter. Ain't no batter."

"Dave, shut up," one of our team-mates yelped. "You're driving *me* crazy."

"That's the point. It's meant to be irritatin'. You gotta be irritatin' or you're not distractin'."

Dragon kites plunging and sailing, dogs holding up play, immune to balls thrown at them, the good ball lost in the redwoods and people heaving junk balls up trying to knock it out—the interruptions at least as good as the game, so that most of being alive is consciousness, and most of consciousness, until it is trained, is thinking about a life, and most of baseball is waiting, playing the few balls hit to me, running the bases.

No plot, no narrative, no ideal, no collective garden, no supper. No Murray Bookchin plan for the future. No Carlos (Don Juan) Castaneda/Barry Commoner. No Mao, no Catfish Hunter. No Bob Dylan or Seth Material. No fear of comet or earthquake. Just the dust of the field and a moon rising over San Francisco.

On a journey through town, as I tried the house on Virginia, I heard footsteps. My mind scurried for a fallback position.

The door opened and I was facing a handsome man with a scarred face, a bit older than me. He wanted to know—with a grumble—why he was being interrupted. I quickly mentioned Diane and my course at Goddard.

He gave me an unusually quizzical gaze, evaluation intended and no wish to disguise it. His hand resting on the doorknob, a siren passing in the street, he said, "Come in."

I stepped past him with an edge of paranoia—a quick glance to ensure that there were windows, then that there were familiar books on the shelves. There were—not only Reich, but Robert Kelly and Diane Wakoski, and, amazingly, my own Black Sparrow books: blue, pale yellow, brown. He took his place in a cushioned chair; I sat facing him.

He asked about Goddard. I segued into Kelly and Olson. He interrupted to say that he had long been interested in poetry, "but bodywork is a way to put words into action. Olson found process in Whitehead and made projective verse. I want to locate that energy in the flesh."

I agreed, saying I was tired of being trapped in ideas.

I gave a brief account of my life—the childhood psychiatrists, my mother's suicide, my new "father," and my flight from Vermont to Denver. Because Lindy's friend Peter was a Reichian author, I mentioned him to get it out of the way.

Ian had been silent to this point, but he stopped me to protest that he barely knew "this Peter character, though he's a buddy of Stanley, the guy who trained me. So don't blame me, okay?"

I told him about t'ai chi and pick-up softball. Then I stopped because I realized he wasn't that safe.

"So what do you want?" he asked.

Before I could answer, he asked a second question: "How does someone who writes such beautiful stuff become so fucked up and rigid?"

There was no longer any way to back out gracefully. I said: "I came to see you about doing your work."

He nodded several times, looked me over, then finally spoke: "What am I to make of this? I just get back from a month's vacation. I'm not starting to see clients till September. I have a waiting list from here to the North Pole. Now I have to make a decision, Grossinger, what to do with you."

"It's okay if—"

"Take off your clothes!"

I grinned as though he had made a joke, but I began a half-hearted tug at my shoelaces.

"Hurry up! If you want to do my work, you better be ready. I don't have time later. I don't have time tomorrow. I have half an hour right now. The clock is ticking, baby."

I untied my shoes. I pulled off my shirt and jeans and stood in underpants. He circled, looking me over.

"Don't hold yourself so tightly. Sink a little into your knees. It'll feel shaky at first, but let that happen. Let your knees tremble a bit."

I crouched like an outfielder. Whistling a show tune, he braced me at the waist and adjusted my back. He pursed his lips and whistled. He ran a finger along my spine. At his touch my knees began to shake, a little, then quite strongly.

"Don't hold your head. Let your head go too."

I tried to find a comfortable posture.

He watched me settle and eventually nodded. The tips of my eyes burned, tears not far away.

"Stretch your arms up."

I held them above my shoulders.

"Farther. Farther. C'mon, Grossinger, haven't you ever been in gym? Really stretch them out."

I stretched higher.

"Even farther. Go to the furthest point you can. No, don't get up off your feet. Keep those babies sunk in the ground."

Each notch I extended pulled me through memories and feelings. These were not superficial images; they marked an actual path.

My knees were shaking uncontrollably, and I whispered, "This is t'ai chi." He laughed at the incongruity of the whisper.

"This is also alchemy," he murmured even more softly. "This is Robert Kelly; this is Shakespeare . . . this is Babe Ruth."

I began to giggle.

"Great. A little humor never hurt. Keep stretching. Pull those muscles out."

"Fears of disease come right here." I pointed to my diaphragm.

"You're all hunched over, protecting yourself. Your chest isn't used to expansion, to filling with air."

"The feeling," I continued, "is that as long as I don't move in a certain way, as long as I don't activate it, the disease will remain dormant."

"Do you feel that sensation now?"

I nodded.

"Then keep stretching. Come. Over here."

He put an arm around my back and led me over to the couch. I could smell the mint of the gum he was chewing, his after-shave. The taboos of male contact were eclipsed at once by a sense of fraternal caring. In that moment it was actually Dr. Reich supporting my naked body and guiding me.

At Goddard I had tried to teach Reich out of books. Now I had an actual sensation, a tangible layer of myself that wanted to dissolve yet was unable, that was on the verge of tears yet paralyzed.

Ian told me to pound the couch.

After an ambivalent thud or two I picked up momentum. It was wonderful, slaphappy, pummelling away without cause, though part of me thought the exercise was silly—that I was just following orders. Then I felt a sharp pain in my chest and stopped.

"Go ahead."

I shook my head.

"Force yourself."

"I'm worried I'm going to cause damage."

"You've got it backwards. If you don't do this, you're going to cause damage. What do you think heart trouble is? It's an inability to breathe, to feel. It's chest armor. It's the unwillingness to open your heart and bring energy to it." He took a deep breath. "Richard, see if you can open your heart for me."

The mere internalization of his directive to open my heart ignited a ticklish sensation in my chest. It went to my back and then spread to my neck and thighs. Ian somehow must have seen it because he said, "Yep, that's the feeling of beginning to open the heart, all right." For some reason I thought of him then as a dead ringer for Mike Schmidt, the all-star third-baseman on the Phillies.

He asked me to give my activity a voice. I tried shouting. It began as a howl of protest and gradually became dissociated as I failed to sustain it. Yet I kept up a sound, even out of breath. Anger merged with sadness until a carpet of sorrow flooded my being.

Memories of long-forgotten times sifted back, rainy days in childhood, Lindy at the Amherst swimming hole, Plato in Greek on the lawn by Churchill House the first warm spring day.

The hermetic journey I had been on was revealing a new face, and I wondered if Robert Kelly didn't paradoxically lead me away from the temple even as he led me into it.

Now Ian had me lie on my back and point my right toe toward the ceiling. "I can't let you out of here without stretching those muscles and getting some feeling into them. Bicycle!"

Legs pumping, I churned at the air above me. As I rode an upside-down vehicle, aches shot along my calves into my hips and belly. I remembered diving for balls Big Milty threw me, the sandy aroma of marigolds no flowers would ever rekindle, the sheer deliciousness of then.

I stopped moving my legs and lay sobbing, for everything that had made me who I was, everything that was lost.

"That's it for today," Ian announced.

I got up very gradually and stretched myself before him, young and gigantic. With carefree spunk I dressed. He nodded. "You did okay, kiddo."

As I headed toward the door he made it clear that the session terminated with a hug. Grinning shyly, I put my arms around him. "Grossinger," he whispered in my ear, "this is part of the work too.

Don't suddenly collapse the chest and pull away. Be present in our contact *now!*"

By dropping the part of my rigidity that was conscious, I let my body melt into his. I smelled mint and felt the warmth and tenderness of his presence.

"You're getting there, old boy."

He promised he would make time for one more session. I asked him how much it cost.

"This one's on the house, in acknowledgment of your writing. Next time you pay me $50."

When Carol told me that Paul was enjoying my book, I pictured him on the edge of the northern wilderness, leading a class much like Andy and Carolyn's. "Is he happy in Idaho?" I asked.

A Paul-like smile crept over her face. "He hasn't gone anywhere."

I was bewildered. "He's still on Woolsey Street. Why don't you go visit him. He'd like to see you."

It never occurred to me he would say goodbye and then not depart.

Driving across the Oakland border, I parked on a block of large, rundown houses, all divided (as was evident from the mailboxes) into four or five apartments. A flight of outdoor stairs like a fire escape led to Paul's rooms at the top of a three-storey Victorian. I had called ahead, so he was waiting on the landing, perched over a map of Idaho. He quickly answered my unspoken question:

"I haven't left because I haven't decided where I want to go. I can leave any time. That's not a problem. I can leave right now, in fact. But right now I'm studying this map."

His hand was moving so the parchment beneath it seemed a kind of alchemical document, different colors for roads, lakes, mountains—the joints, veins, arteries, and skin of the earth, he explained. His fingers wriggled along meridians—the big one, the Salmon, and then Lost River, Birch Creek, North Fork. He pointed out Pocatello.

"This is where I grew up. Atom-bomb country. Those of us who've come from there have had to learn to heal ourselves."

He dowsed further north. "There's a high-energy area around Coeur d'Alene. That's where I'm going. I don't know anyone there yet, but there's probably a woman who's studied properties of local herbs. I'll find her. She'll find me." Berkeley sun glistened on Pend Oreille and the Coeur d'Alene Lakes. "Maybe there's a place I can practice acupuncture. I'm going to do acupuncture of the Earth. Do you realize that every time you dig with a shovel it's putting in a needle and opening a flow?"

We passed through the doorway to his kitchen. Although robust, Paul had a wan, ephemeral quality about him, like a Celtic Christ. Along shelves were fibrous herbs and powders in jars. This was a Mediaeval apothecary—no sign anywhere of industrial America.

"Our culture has a protein obsession," he observed. "But we make all we need. And if we let ourselves make it instead of having it made for us we are stronger internally, though maybe not as strong on the outside. We exist closer to the way plants do. We are more sensitive to light, to ch'i." He undulated his hand in rays through glass, casting a shadow through a decanter on the table. "It's water," he explained. "But water left in sun changes."

We crossed into the living room.

I refused a glass of the water because, ever fastidious, I felt a need to protect myself from weirdness.

He explained how he lived here once with a woman named Janet. "In fact, she left only a few days ago."

This was a surprise to me and implied a more mundane reason for the end of the class. "She used to be married," he added. "In fact, she *is* married; she still has a husband back in Virginia. She went to see him."

I was at once concerned to know whether she was going to Idaho too.

"No, I don't expect her back; I've become too subtle for her. I had a dream last night about her husband. He was driving a car, pretending to be going real fast, but he had a flat tire. I asked him why he didn't change the tire. Then I realized—he didn't have a spare. And he didn't know he didn't have a spare. He didn't even know the tire was flat."

I smiled despite myself.

"I can't say he's in a bad place," he mused, continuing to talk about Janet's husband rather than Janet. "After all, that's where he is. He chose to be there, right? But he's ill-equipped. He's trying to go seventy. First he should slow down. He should stop right where he is and do something about a spare tire. We all should. That's what t'ai chi is for. T'ai chi gives energy in reserve."

I wondered aloud if Paul was evading emotions from the breakup of his relationship.

"Psychology is an obsession of this culture, like protein. It might be this thing that happened or that. Who knows? Right now there is only all the energy at our disposal. It doesn't matter where it comes from—genetics, trauma, the stars. We get to use it all the same."

I returned two mornings later and we pushed hands in his yard. In the heat of the sun I was mesmerized by his spirals, pleased by the honor of his company. Then—the summer-long trick—his arm came from nowhere, caught my reverie in a lock, and twisted me ruggedly to the ground.

"There's no break in t'ai chi," he said. "There's no time you can allow your attention to rise into your head like that." I stood and reengaged. He found my frozen point and threw me again.

I knew I couldn't meet him. My whole life of Grossinger's, baseball, college teaching, and literary symbolism stood in the way. His harshness had broken through the scenery and shattered my romanticism.

He suggested we do the mirror image of the set, side by side.

"Step back like a monkey!" he shouted. The Ba Kua fish had leapt from the water through the ripples of my encircling ward-off. Its hand now sank to form a fist under my elbow, punctuating its leap. "Like a monkey," he hailed, arms sagging monkeylike. Suddenly we were distracted by children reaching to pick carrots. "Don't do that," Paul called out. "Somebody was taking care of those, waiting for them to grow."

They stepped back, surveying us worriedly.

"You have wonderful floppy ears," he told the girl.

"I have ears like a monkey," she said.

"That's right!" Paul howled. "We're monkeys." And to their astonishment we flew back into the move together.

Afterwards in the kitchen I accepted a cup of flax tea from sun water. "When will you go?" I asked him.

"Parts of me are going now. I'm moving slowly. There are lots of ways to leave fast if that's what I want to do." He pointed to the map. "Airports here . . . here . . . here . . . here." Each one a little black plane. "I can hitch. I can drive the car Janet left behind." He peered out the window. It was a tan VW Bug. "It's not a question of my getting there.

It's a matter of waiting here as long as I can, until I'm perfectly ready. My mind is almost there. You only see what's left of me. But if I hadn't left this part behind we wouldn't have been able to talk and learn about each other."

Then he announced, to my horror, that we were approaching the day of the next San Andreas earthquake. "First the Pyramid will be built," he declared. "That's what Edgar Cayce said. Then the earthquake will follow."

I knew, if there was such a prophecy, that TransAmerica had already fulfilled the first half of it, and I wondered, with blatantly egoic concern, if we would get out in time.

"Sure," he said. "The abbot will leave the temple in San Francisco. That will be the sign."

I asked if he would go then. "Maybe. If I make it, I do. If I don't, I don't. The earthquake comes. Or it doesn't come. We're here. We're not here. It's all the same, life or death. The cosmic circle. We can't run. We can't hurry. It's going to come out the same either way."

On my second visit, Ian began by instructing me to stand with my knees bent.

"Are you aware of that grin?" he suddenly asked. As my attention shifted to my mouth, I felt a grimace around my lips. "It's not really a smile," he said. "It's tension holding back something in your jaw."

At his request I exaggerated the shape in order to feel it. Then it faded. In the process the space between him and me narrowed.

"Good. So you know how to put it there and take it away." He let me try it out a few times. "What do you suppose it is? Is it sadness? Disgust? Both?"

"I don't know," I gulped.

"Well now, that's a pretty sad number, because that grin *is* you. It's not some mind inhabiting some body. But who are you *in* that grin? What are you grinning about?"

I recalled how that spring at Wayne State, after my reading, while they were rewinding the videotape, I was startled to notice a slight sneer on my face, because I had pictured myself as boyish and friendly.

"You're right. There *is* a sneer on your face."

"But not now," I objected.

"Yes now. Always. You look down on everyone, including me."

"I'm not looking down on *you.*"

"To hell you aren't."

I smiled.

"And that's not a smile. There's no joy or contact behind it. You're using it as a screen to put as much distance between you and me as you can."

"But it's not as though I'm really looking down on you. How could I be? I went through all this trouble to find you. I follow your instructions."

"You say you do . . . and I believe you. But it's not true."

I stood there, puzzled.

"Poor innocent Richie Grossinger, going along with Ian, not responsible for anything. Well, Richard Grossinger, you've brought another person here with you, and *he's* not going along. He's condescended to allow you to be here. He's got terrific, unbelievable scorn for me . . . ," chewing furiously on his gum, gesturing with an upward flick of his head. "And well he might. Because I've got my eye on him. I'm going to hunt him out."

"Why do I have scorn for you?"

"No more questions. No more faking it. Just tell me about it. Say, 'Ian, you're a creep.' Say it. Say, 'Ian, I'm much better than you.'" He flopped in his chair. "'Even though I'm allowing you to do this to me you're not half the man I am. This just shows how magnanimous I am.'"

I stood there dumbfounded. I couldn't possibly say that.

"C'mon, Grossinger, say it. 'It's proof of my own largeness to indulge you in your crap, Ian.' Wipe that dumb smile off your face. Say it."

"But I don't want to. I don't feel it. It would just be acting. I'd be making it up."

"Like hell you don't feel it. I know what you think of me. I'm oily. I play up to women like the studs you always hated. I'm Peter who went off with your wife. Tell me I'm phony and smooth."

"Ian, you're oily and smooth." I barely got the words out.

"C'mon now. Without the damn grin. You don't have to apologize. *Just fucking say it.*"

I stood there paralyzed.

"Okay then, bend your knees. Hang out. Breathe. Let a little shaking happen."

Across the street I glimpsed the playground, mothers on benches, children swinging.

"That's better. Let those knees rattle. Don't avoid sensations. Whatever they are. Don't diminish even the slightest one. Go with it."

Feelings came, most of them too subtle to catch before they departed. Every now and then a flicker of a laugh touched down, shy and tender, tickling my chest. At least it wasn't the damn grin.

Then an intuition: 'Maybe this is what he means by scorn. I think I'm so great to be participating in his famous, elite system.' "You're looking better," Ian observed. "A little more grounded, right?"

"Right." It was a different voice. My throat had sunk too. How did such a trivial exercise release such profundity?

"The flesh itself is sweet," Ian eulogized. "Olson would have agreed. It's a cop-out to get all involved trying to figure out what the origin or meaning of a feeling is. That's just another head trip to take attention away from what's surging up in your being. It's another excuse not to feel it right now, because you're translating it into a description of something, an attitude toward something else. Just feel what's happening. Let *it* tell you who you are. Let *it* shape your experience. Now let's find out something about that scorn. Stick out your tongue."

I forced it out of my mouth.

"No, further."

I tried.

"*Much* further!"

"I'm not aware it goes out any further than that."

"The tongue is a weapon. You know, mightier than the sword. Stick it out and attack. Further. C'mon. A sword!"

It was worse than the dentist. The harder I pushed the more it hurt. And it was no minor pain. Since the organ wouldn't go that far it felt as though rocks were grinding underneath.

"You can go further. Push as hard as you can. You won't hurt yourself. Those muscles are just incredibly tight from holding it in all your life. Let your voice out. What is it kids say: 'Nya nya nuh nya nya!' Say that. 'Nya nya!' Attack me."

I looked at him in disbelief. Did he think I was going to say 'Nya nya nuh nya nya'?

He burst into laughter. "There it is, Richard. Perfect. The look of scorn. 'Oh, Ian, how could you be so dumb? How could you be into such fucked-up stuff? Anyone would know better. Especially a great writer and anthropologist like me.' That's it. That's really what you're saying."

I paused for a second, uncertainly.

"Stop worrying like a senile old fart. Just do it."

"Nya nya nuh nya nya. Nya nya nuh nya nya! Nya nya nuh nya nya!" It was a string of nasals in some unknown Amerindian language. I embodied scorn. My face crumpled around my nose and mouth; my upper lip rammed against my nostrils, leaving small, beady eyes.

"Now stick your tongue out. Further. Further. Still further." It was agony. Only the flow of sound gave any relief, so the more it hurt the more I intensified the nasals.

They became vaguely familiar. I began to remember that I had said such things once, a very long time ago. My body knew how to say, 'Nya nya nuh nya nya.'

"Great," announced Ian. "You look wonderful." He flashed an imitation of my crumpled-up face. "Now keep it up, your knees bent this time."

'Nya nya nuh nya nya!' No wonder I felt like an imposter at Kent. Against the power and presence of a shadow self, my life was a staged grail quest all the way, an embrace of imaginary profundity at the expense of a true wonder at my heart.

I summoned spring-rain love for Robin and Miranda, a bottomless sorrow for my mother and Jon, for my friend Schuy long dead. I felt a procession of delightful moments on earth—the Vermont sky of stars, the Mets in the ninth coming back, Lindy and me packing our U-Haul in Northampton to set out on our life together. I thought of D. H. Lawrence's *Rainbow,* Beckett and Godot, Olson calling on the precession of the equinoxes. And then—the insight: "The scorn is there all the time, *all* the time. It is part of every other expression, down under it somewhere. And it is always saying: 'This is not real; *I* am not real.'"

The nya's begin to wash away. A rich, voiceless breathing replaced them. Waves of undifferentiated sensation echoed through the chamber of my chest and rolled over me, filling my eye sockets with heat, cascading down my back. I was sweating. The air had a wonderful warm-cool to it. The sun was perfect, not too yellow, not too white. I dawdled there.

"Let's work on some of that anger now," Ian said.

On his instructions I extended my arms straight up and back and clenched my fists. I pulled them back further and further. "The body is a drawn bow," he exclaimed. I remembered such an illustration from the writings of Alexander Lowen. My limbs and torso were flexible and springy; they absorbed and transmitted.

I pulled on the bow until my neck throbbed. A hard ring tightened around my Adam's apple.

"Don't stop doing it. And say, 'No!' Express that you don't want to do it by saying, 'No!' instead of by stopping."

"No," I shouted. "No. No. No. No." "No!" at every throb and impulse to stop.

"Keep going. And louder."

I finally found a spot at which my resistance was displaced into No! "No! No! No!" I could blast it.

No! to my mother, my fathers, my counselors at Chipinaw, anthropologists at Michigan, fraternity guys at Amherst, faculty at Maine and Goddard, old girlfriends, Ian himself sitting there and prompting me.

"Catch the qualities of those No's," he said. "They're not all the same. Some mean: don't hurt me. Some mean: stay away from me; leave me alone. Others mean: don't ignore me, don't leave me."

I shot my voice into plaster. It bounced off walls. They were gunshots. There was no shriek or whine to them, pellet after pellet.

Then all images faded, and I came to a great No! It wasn't that I was saying No! to anything or anyone in particular. I had pretended all my life I needed occasions for anger. But No! just was. My skin flooded with No! and tingled. My bow bent.

"Because it was also saying No! to the flesh," Ian reminded me. "You were saying No! to yourself."

I stood there panting.

He told me to lie on my back on the mattress and breathe into my belly. My chest expanded easily, but it was almost impossible to pump the air down further. The cavity didn't want to move or respond; it was flat. I couldn't even locate it apart from a general abdominal numbness. When I finally got some breath into it, it plopped right back.

I tried again.

It wasn't pain; it was more like overwhelming fatigue. It was another kind of No!

What was this alien part of me, this bubble, bladder, this air-pocket belly?

I kept trying to inflate it. A sputter entered but popped back out. For no apparent reason I began to giggle. The giggles gathered into an uproarious laugh. My stomach was making pops, each one accordioning through me in a belly laugh.

Suddenly I didn't have to strain. My belly filled and then emptied, filled and then emptied, all by itself.

I remembered an old photograph Jon had put in his tarot deck: we were standing by the ocean in bathing suits. My head was thrown back and laughing; every rib showed.

I cringed at that picture then, remembering the vulnerability I once had to defend. Now I felt that bashful, skinny kid inside me, laughing again where he left off laughing.

"Thank you," Ian said. "Thank you, Dr. Reich and Dr. Janov, for letting us know we can laugh and cry and feel good for no other reason."

Then he told me to get dressed.

"You don't have to reassemble your whole life," he concluded as I pulled my head through my shirt. "In fact, you can't. All that you can do is give yourself a choice. Otherwise, you are totally successful at suppression and you cut yourself off from all these feelings. Isn't it a funny number when you think about it? Everyone fancies they can't be seen because they've disguised it, and yet everyone sees it in everyone else through the disguise … and has agreed not to call them on it."

He placed a goofy mantra in the air and said, "Keep the faith on those cold Vermont nights."

My sense of well-being dissolved into quiet grace by the time Lindy and I drove along the Columbia River, a sheath of insects covering our windshield. Outside Boise we passed the largest auto graveyard in the solar system. Farm equipment and machines littered front yards. A cow tied to an icebox door fed from a slosh-pail, its ass bumping into an old tractor.

T'ai chi class, pumpkin field, Carolyn and Andy leading. While we wait in wu chi, all the background comes alive—mauve of sky, din of crickets, mountain mist.

The moves begin. In their singleness I feel I have learned nothing.

A toad's golden eyes look up at me from the grass. They do not see me.

I feel a mark that begins at my forehead, splits my eyes but is neither a crevice nor a series of cracks. It plummets down my chest with thousands of filaments and rootlets, each a breath, each a mineral. It will never be uprooted. I cannot uproot it.

In the sky (walking home) I find the Dolphin, the Jug, the Circlet of Aquarius.

Yes, the old cosmology is etched upon our shell.

Sagittarius, you are so bright hurtling the mountains, a Galaxy pouring out of your mouth.

But Andromeda, you do not move, haze-breath of billions of single stars. We see you from the other side of creation, of history and philosophy both—so thin, like lipmarks—a scar passed through generations, a rip in night.

Four months later, when Goddard dispatched its faculty during the winter of '76 to save money, we returned to Berkeley. All that year was a reprieve, to be able to use my new body, to explore its mystery and hope. I put my lost father aside and threw myself into stalking 106 sylphy animal forms across Carol Lee's yard.

Sometimes Ian challenged and goaded; other times he molded and massaged the ridges of my face, my cheekbones and sockets (once, grazing a tissue along my forehead, nose, and mouth), as though he could get my cells to disintegrate their mask. Every so often he'd improvise. One afternoon we lined up football-style against each other and drove from our heels. "C'mon, Grossinger, dig in. I'm gonna sack your quarterback every fuckin' time." We closed the session by howling—Hindu mantras cum Dion and the Belmonts cum wolf pack.

My world for years had been cautiously intellectual, guided by my writing of it in detail. "Don't even look at a typewriter," he warned. I never finished *The Planet with Blue Skies,* the last of my experimental-prose manuscripts. I embraced silence as a delicious other.

Twice a week I attended Dana Ullman's homeopathic study group. Graduate-student days glossing prayersticks were over. Nobody questioned whether we could be physicians. Phosphorus, Sulphur, and Sepia were powerful substances in a vitalistic tradition. If we weren't going to use them, who was? Why else were we there? In fact, we were expected to be able to cure all diseases—chronic and acute—within a few months (California optimism as boundless as the Berkeley sky).

Outside of class Dana and I dreamed up a branch of North Atlantic Books to publish just homeopathy. Our first title would be James Tyler Kent's 1900 classic *Lectures on Homeopathic Philosophy,* long out of print. Dana wanted to follow with a collection of journal articles by Edward Whitmont, a renowned New York homeopath. He hoped, when I went back east, I could visit him and win his consent.

In April, the best of Carol's students, Polly Gamble, announced that she was starting her own shiatsu class. Though she was ten years younger than me, I looked upon her as a sensei. Her set was perfect, her push-hands baffling and powerful. I didn't think I was ready, but I went anyway, once a week, eight of us on her living-room floor, learning pressure points and meridians, then trying to tap ch'i in each other's chests, guts, and limbs.

Polly would hold my thumb under hers and silently redemonstrate applications of pressure. She startled me with comments like "Richard, where are you?" I thought I was there, but the moment I heard my name I realized I was watching myself do this oddly intimate form with strangers, amazed to be one of them.

Once again I was being taught that feelings have no meaning, no explanation—they just arise and course. I had a Japanese body, a Chinese body, a Reichian body, all of them ancient and pagan, the same as the bodies of my classmates on the floor.

On her own, Polly was studying advanced forms in Larkspur and, after shiatsu ended, she started a workshop in Lomi bodywork—four young women, two of them startlingly pretty, a stout muscular guy wearing an astrological medallion, and me. Lomi involved mostly hands-on diagnosis of each other's bodies and then removal of blocks through a combination of massage, holding limbs to release their tension, and breathing sequences.

The last half hour we examined and treated a partner and then changed places. Polly always played "Pachelbell's Canon" while we worked, its haunting opening violins following each other's notes like ancient hunters in search of the moon. My partner was either the hairy man, his chest hard and hollow as a coffin and an odor so acrid I had to struggle not to feel nauseated, or a woman with whom I tried to remain neutral while feeling tendrils of desire, until desire became pure energy in my hands. Themes built within themes, ever more complex variants of the same seventeenth-century melody, evoking a wonder, a hope, and a sorrow building to something ineffable, unrequitable. Then my partner took the role of healer and I lay there, a body. Out the window, white as snow, magnolia blossoms joined harpsichord and cello in the afternoon breeze.

At Ian's and my farewell meeting in August, I lay on a futon in the breeze, smelling jasmine from somewhere. An uninsistent rhythm rolled along my skin. Looking on with Buddha's smile, he lifted his right hand and trailed it back and forth. With each pass I felt tingles along the margins of my flesh. They converged and encompassed me. He was touching my body from across the room.

All my habitual dreads dissipated into a gratitude I existed at all. My eyes burned and streamed. He told me to stop reaching. It could be so simple. *I* could be so simple.

I wanted to reach to the unknown father inside me, to tell him about this incredible world. I wanted him to feel its exquisite, fathomless texture, the river of the heart that joined him and me, and all people, because he had brought me here.

I longed to send these spirits to my mother too, wherever she was. I wondered why my brother had been put on drugs and sentenced to torture instead of taken to a healer.

Jon was right. I *did* have magical doctors, and he had frauds. But why? Who led me always to Fabian and Kelly, now to Polly, Paul, and Ian? Who led my brother, conversely each time, to the Grand Inquisitor?

Harry Pin? Marlon Brando? Or his own rage-desire to confront Leviathan?

2

The Ghost Dance of Mickey Mantle

WHEN WE MOVED to the Bay Area I was thirty-two years old and had been either a student or a teacher my whole life. My small salaries at the University of Maine and Goddard seemed ample at the time, so I never questioned them.

The end of employment was a shock, and I was surprised to discover we weren't incomeless. I got $3500 from Doubleday, and Lindy earned a half-time salary working as dance coordinator at East Bay Center for the Performing Arts. We also had money from the sale of the Vermont house and the remaindering of books and journals.

The internal adjustment was more difficult. In Vermont—and Maine and Michigan before—I had imagined myself on a career path. Even while I fought the system, I passed through Amherst and Michigan and got a Ph.D. Since teenage years I had considered myself a writer like Faulkner or Salinger—and, if that didn't work out (as a way to earn a living), I was likely to be an heir to my father's hotel. I didn't discuss these things and rarely thought about them, but I acted unconsciously from a presumption of them.

Now not only was I illegitimate; Grossinger's itself was a mirage. Even the notion that my father would back me in a crunch was exposed as a sentimentality. And my mother, whoever she was, was gone for good, her disinheritance of me beyond amelioration.

No one owed me anything, neither my parents nor step-parents nor the academic establishment. That was hardly a surprise. Yet in truth, it made no difference at all. The world was a zone of mystery and wonder, and everything important was still at my disposal.

In our first months in California, I sent out a packet to dozens of colleges; it included my academic references, quotes about my work from Robert Duncan, Joyce Carol Oates, Charles Olson, and Ishmael Reed, a list of subjects I had taught, and a description of *Io*/North Atlantic. I tried Santa Cruz, Vanderbilt, Evergreen, Reed, and San Francisco State. I kidded myself that these schools were looking for someone interdisciplinary. In fact, they wanted to fill their slots uncontroversially. The '60s were over, even if their mood had kept us in a trance through most of an ensuing decade.

In November, Margaret MacKenzie, a medical anthropologist at Cal-Berkeley, helped me procure an unpaid position as a Research Anthropologist. I applied for grants to fund it—Ford, Guggenheim, the National Institutes of Health, the National Endowment for the Humanities. My project was a comparison between indigenous agriculture and medicine and corporate, scientific modes of farming and healing.

Preparing these applications was an epic job: it involved putting my ideas into correct academic language, then finding professors to back each variant of the project and to write letters on my behalf. It took most of a year to get rejected for everything.

As I hiked through town onto campus, I yearningly observed faculty and students on their rounds. I spent mornings at the library, going along the shelf ethnography by ethnography, culling instances of ethnomedicine and shamanic curing, making a map of "planet medicine."

At the same time, I got permission to sit in on case-taking two afternoons a week at Hering Homeopathic Clinic. As I observed the treatment of actual patients, I encountered the layers of subtexts (cultural and epistemological). Homeopathic medicine was not obvious; it treated diseases by *enhancing* their symptoms; its pills were reductions (or transmutations) of matter. And yet regular American patients marched in and out. Even the doctors seemed oblivious to the fact that they were practicing magic.

At Bookpeople's community lunches I found businessmen my age (or younger) running successful presses. They put out books and comics on self-healing, cooking, auto repair, sex, massage, travelling in South America, growing pot, and the like. I soon realized that our literary anthologies were a miniscule (and marginal) component of the company's activity.

Though I joined in banter with these ambitious countercultural capitalists, I identified with them no more than with the convention managers at Grossinger's. Yet I envied their sales. Whereas I was trying to make a few hundred dollars a month, they were disappointed by thousands and even tens of thousands.

I had brought one promising project with me from Vermont—an issue of *Io* in the form of a huge collection of baseball writings from different sources (literary, occult, anthropological), coedited with Kevin Kerrane, a professor at the University of Delaware. After a song *("Rock and roll I gave you . . . ")*, we named it *Baseball I Gave You All the Best Years of My Life.* Finished books arrived just after the World Series. The third month the anthology was in print it sold two thousand copies—a whole print run. The check ninety days later from Ingram Book Company, a national wholesaler, was larger than my entire annual salary at Goddard. Then Anchor bought the rights.

One night our phone rang after midnight. It was my brother. "Richard," he said, "I have escaped the city of the Dutch, the Jews and blackfolk. I am walking the Milky Way."

I shifted the receiver to my left ear and lay on my back on the floor. Five years of psychotropics and brainwashing. And here he was, innocent as a lamb.

"I guess you can tell I'm high." A sudden brace of giggles. "I'm high. I got some grass . . . and . . . it is real-ly . . . beautiful."

I sensed a new tone here, as though he were satirizing his own grandiose riff.

"I called Dr. Golden. She was furious—outraged." His voice mimicked her. "'Why, Jon, how could you? You know how marijuana upsets you.' Upset? Yes, I'm upset and I'm going to put things topsy-turvy. How did you get here, Apache? Well, I found this land-bridge. I got here smoking weed and following floating continents. I found my way through stars on buffalo hide. Then I said to her, 'Ma'am, how could *you* build this ugly poisonous city and hide the moon?' And she said, 'I'm not talking to you until you start making sense.' I said, 'How much does this bit of wisdom cost me?' And she hung up. What she didn't know was when the phone hit the cradle we was through. Through forever." He sang this out. "Then I called my father, but he was no better. I wanted to give him a little cosmic vision to break the routine. But he was *so* worried. 'Jon, you're not smoking again, are you?' He told me to call Dr. Golden. 'If you're so anxious for me to talk to her why don't you pay her bill. Or better yet, talk to *me*. I'm your son.' So he listened for a while, but he has no understanding. I finally hung up and called his sisters. First Bea, then Et. They were fools. They are fools forever. I come from a family of idiots." He paused. "Except you. You're the only one, Richard. You're with me in the ionosphere."

He wheezed and coughed. I asked about his life.

He said he hadn't missed a day at Food Liberation in a year. "I'm healing people who know only polluted food and contaminated air." His courses at Hunter were "Indians of the Plains," "Romantic Poetry," and "English Novelists"; he was reading *Jude the Obscure* and *1984*. He was getting straight A's. The fact that these courses were virtually identical to ones he had taken before the hospital did not diminish his accomplishment. The classics are infinite, and anyway he needed to restore damaged synapses.

Some nights this Indian boy went to Central Park and slept under stars. This was how he pressed to the missing thing, embraced its fleeting substantiality. A northern breeze tore through Manhattan autumn, late late twentieth century. He awoke shivering and watched sunrise—the simplicity of it, a landscape that could have been farmland—ancestral spirits vanishing down back alleys, building their middens along the East River, tanning deer hide in their teepees. From Amerindia he hiked to work through Eurotrash overlay, a shaman of carrot and celery juices.

In November he called to report on a class at Hunter:

"I arrived in my Indian Ghost Dance Shirt. I bought it right off this guy on the street. I'm purple sky and I've got constellations glowing in gold, buffalo running. If I said nothing that night my shirt had more insight than anyone there."

From outside a car threw headlights along the walls and shape-changed around the corner.

"I delivered a discourse on Platonic love, troubadour love. I stood and addressed them as the sky talking. We had been reading this play by Christopher Fry about witches. I told them how witches used their broomsticks to masturbate and made these potions from hellebore and wolfsbane and got high. They sat there hushed. I guess I was too heavy for them."

"Sounds like it."

"Yes, but then I could hear something in my tone that was different. I was speaking in an Italian accent. I was giving them the original Sioux-Italian-Hebrew-Indo-European-Sino-Aztecan speech. It was the best thing they ever heard. They were blown away! After class everyone was jiving, 'Hey, man, you were incredible.' I don't understand. They just walked away and left me standing there. God, I was so down when I got home." A giggle. "But my sweetheart's here now and . . . I'm high again, so it's okay."

Then he described a meeting of himself, Dr. Golden, and his father, some sort of payment being stuffed in her hand that she threw on the floor as insufficient. They began shouting at each other, father and doctor, Bob citing her husband's Medicare-fraud rap (*New York Post* front page) and accusing her of being a thief.

That's when Jon decided to step forth and speak:

"'You're Italian power,' I said to her. 'You're going to prove that you've made it from the slums, but it's all braggadocio, no spirit. And you,'" turning to his father, "'are Zionist power. The Jews are the best. You always single out Jewish ballplayers, Jewish boxers, Jewish writers. Neither of you know what you're arguing about and neither of you care about me. Go fight over money and power. I'm going to remove myself. You can have World War II all over again if you want.' And I left."

On Halloween two children dressed as Indians came to his door and gave him a treat in four words: "Gifts for the giver." He felt like the luckiest man in town.

As the lease in Oakland came to an end, we didn't relish staying in the expensive, seismically active Bay Area, but we had (in the words of the Eric Burden song) no place else left to go.

The city of Richmond, ten miles to the north, was the site of a Chevron refinery and a ghetto. We chose its middle-class section, just off Wildcat Canyon, and scoured it with a real-estate agent until we settled on a bland but roomy ranch house on Amador Street. It still cost two and a half times the selling price of our home in Plainfield. We presumed we would sell it in a year or two when a teaching job came up.

Hanging directly over Highway 80, our stretch of Amador was a sunbaked, nearly treeless block running from Sierra to Zara, but it abutted a quasi-upscale El Cerrito neighborhood. (Months later the block made the front page of *The New York Times,* an X marking where a tire off a plane out of SFO bounced first at the corner of Sierra before landing again all the way down on San Pablo six blocks away. Robin kept track of its fading dent.)

On one side of us the retired librarian Olive Salt lived with her grown son Wes and a boarder; on the other a spiffy black lady with a drum-playing teenager.

Our house was two stories if you counted the finished basement. The upstairs had a fireplace and picture-window view of San Francisco above the Richmond rooftops—an even better view of noisy I-80 ("Imagine it sounds like the ocean," soothed the agent)—likewise, ocher sunsets behind oil tanks. We had a giant backyard, yuccas and evergreen bushes, a paved three-car garage which served as a book warehouse (a delight after the oil-streaked dirt floor on Hudson), a wide street, plus, remarkably, two nearby alternative schools serving the whole East Bay—Crestmont for Robin and Bright Star Montessori for Miranda.

In late August after the move, we found a housesitter and took I-80 all the way to Grossinger's. Miranda had already forgotten the Hotel (she would point to different blocks around Berkeley and ask if they were Grossinger's), but, as we put in days across the midlands, Robin built her excitement to fever pitch—free milk shakes, comic racks, nightly cartoons, rowboats, miniature golf.

When we arrived for the summer of '78, Aunt Bunny warned that bankruptcy was imminent. She seemed so profoundly distressed I quickly sought out two executives. They each downplayed her fears. "She's got an axe to grind," one confided patronizingly. "Your father should find himself a better fuck." Then he added, "I'm pleased you're finally showing an interest. Keep your hat in the ring."

Years later I learned that he and his henchman were in collusion, PG being dealt out even as he went through the motions of bossman. I watched him cruise the dining room, no longer even pretending to be a gracious host. Some nights his main contribution seemed to be scouting for waiters and busboys in violation of rules and bawling them out publicly, or (even worse) discovering guests without ties or proper jackets and ordering them back to their rooms.

"Do you think they'll ever stay here again?" I asked Lindy.

"The last vestiges of spirit left this place with Jennie," Bunny pronounced sadly. "The Zises took the brains, and Jennie took the soul. Your father and his sister seem to think that they're running some sort of boarding school, that the guests have to come. They're just playing hotel. They're not really serious."

One afternoon at the buffet in the golf clubhouse I was approached by the bank president. He knew I was hardly of the inner circle, yet he surprised me by leading us to an empty table.

"It looks as though we're not going to make it," he began. "I thought an intelligent kid like you might get through to your father and aunt, or at least tell me what it takes. The bank's given its best shot. But it's not *our* hotel."

I explained I had no sway. As long as I could remember, Paul and Elaine were in the habit of ignoring advice.

"You don't have to be a genius to run this place," he went on. "Just cutting waste might buy ten years. Pardon the intrusion, but they have no right living like millionaires on our money."

I went to my father with the story. He could barely direct enough attention away from his crossword to listen. When I finished he asked me if there was any chicken left in the refrigerator. I cut him a wing, brought it back. He took a bite, then sent me for a diet soda and seemed surprised I didn't know an obscure Indonesian bird.

"What did I pay for Amherst for?"

I look unamused.

"Richard," he finally said, "stay out of what doesn't concern you."

That fall, with Carol's class down to two people, I decided to seek out the legendary Benjamin Pang Jeng Lo, a disciple of the late Cheng Man-ch'ing. Once I found him (among the countless Lo's in the San Francisco phone book) I paid two months' tuition and joined the 6 AM Bay Bridge rush. It was the end of backyard free form. On a cold stone floor I practiced a spare and rigorous set. Soon I had to wake even earlier to make it all the way to his new storefront on Clement Avenue near the ocean.

Arriving bleary-eyed, often in rain, I tried to concentrate on Ben's corrections. After each move, class members held their postures for examination. I froze in place, legs shaking, waiting for the master to make his way around the room to adjust me ... to twist my back and downward-aimed punch into something I had to spring up from in pain a second later. He repeated pet homilies of encouragement: "It hurt, that good—very good!" and "No see mistake, no correct. First see, then correct." ('I'll do it someday,' I'd think. 'It's great stuff. Just don't make me do it today.')

Working on a history of alternative medicine fused the psychosomatic split of my childhood, when Hitzig was the malefic diagnostician, and Fabian his angelic rival, compensating every threat by mysterious codes. I had followed his grail unconsciously ever since, passing from Freud to Jung during college, avoiding regular doctors and academic materialists, and embracing a vision that converted any condition of life—even disease—into a symbol or archetype my psyche could then transmute. Lindy's and my relationship was alchemical at two levels. The first was mere poetic ideology; the second was a crucible we lived.

In these other medicines, body inculcated mind as another layer of mind. I didn't have to interpret or decode a thing in order to change it. Things changed when energy met them. Symbols were the surface text of a far greater magic; its origins lay at the dawn of time when aboriginal medicine men first confronted spirits.

I studied with Polly until she married a Lomi School teacher and moved to San Anselmo. In her place I drove to San Francisco for dreamwork with a Jungian, Charles Poncé. A decade older than me and a one-time student of Whitmont's, Charles had been initiated (after a Korean War stint) as a Lower East Side psychic, a therapist with a ponytail who didn't believe in therapy.

"We're not on a search for hidden meanings," he told me. "There's no authorized or correct interpretation. The psyche simply shapes reality from its own apprehension of phenomena. It makes statements regarding its own existence, to give itself a certainty of itself."

Charles had a knack of turning Fabian's mythologized remnants into mundane events. When I arrived one morning—after having momentarily (and in panic) mistaken drips from an overzealous toothbrush as spitting up blood, and then seeing San Francisco from the Bay Bridge as an extraterrestrial city—he remarked, "You're having a more exciting day than I am so far. Sacred blood! Luminous cities! Who's to say how another person initiates himself?"

Down from Idaho, Paul Pitchford offered a session in Taoist medicine. He took my pulses, then put acupuncture needles in my legs, around my navel, one on my head. Each burning prick stunned me, but I could tell they were touching my core.

I rose with body and mind throbbing, as though from a hive of bees. Afterwards he held a cone of smoldering mugwort over my arms and back. Then he prescribed a tea of fenugreek, flax, fennel, comfrey, and dandelion root. I felt as though I were in the care of the four-thousand-year-old physician I had been writing about.

My book appeared as *Planet Medicine* with a subtitle I invented as a parody on fashionableness (but which Doubleday loved): *From Stone-Age Shamanism to Post-Industrial Healing.*

Then my agent John (who wanted a potboiler on Grossinger's) got me a contract plus an advance from Sierra Club to write a book on stars and planets—a synthesis of science fiction, history of astronomy, and black-hole cosmology. Soon my days were occupied with tracing connections among Pawnee myths, the search for Planet X, Hindu cosmology, the mystery of Pluto, and the epistemology of the Big Bang. I went from buffalo-hide Pleistocene nights, to a seventeenth-century cosmos filled with stars and planets, to Io and Iapetus, to relativity and flying saucers.

That October I spoke to my brother from a spot overlooking Highway 80. He had recently reconnected with a number of his high-school friends—Phil, Emile, Billy, and Steve Heller. These one-time tarot aficionados were now variously in real estate, medicine, or on Wall Street. "They all want to help, but none of them wants to listen to me. None of them thinks I have anything to say. I can read their minds: 'I made it and he didn't.' What do they know? Like Dylan said, 'The wheel's still in spin.'"

Jon's co-captain on the track team, Steve Rechtshaffen, was now an M.D. who ran a Sufi commune in upstate New York. "He ships bread and organic vegetables into the City, even to Food Liberation."

I wondered if maybe he could help Jon get a better job.

"Nah. He's just another macho mojo. I saw the phony in him when he was a wee'un."

In our next conversation he reported a new hobby. From antique shops he was buying maps of the Civil War, battleplans with positions of the troops marked in colors. He was analyzing each encounter—potentials vis à vis outcomes—until he had memorized them. One afternoon he brought these documents to his father's office, spread them out on the light table, and demonstrated military strategy to the assembled secretaries and art director.

"I interrupted the day's trivialities," he explained, "with a bit of history. The Civil War's what this country's still about. Because it *did* happen; it wasn't just a story. The South was a different thing. It was rebel, so they went and squashed it, the rural cotton South. That war's never ended, and I don't mean symbolically. I mean exactly the same soldiers, the same issues, the same battlefield. Only it's spread through every city and town in the country. My father laughs and says, 'Read the newspaper. It's 1979.' I don't need to read the paper. I look at battleplans. I watch how the troops circle over the hills keeping the woods between themselves and the Yanks. It could work tomorrow in Central Park. That's what these Madison Avenue dandies don't realize. The troops are gathering around them. We're in the dawntime. We still have the Civil War to fight."

Some days he took the subway to Horace Mann and Van Cortlandt Park and wandered around fields where he once ran track.

"I'm heading past Tillinghast Hall. No one knows me, so I'm pretty carefree. Who do I see sitting there talking to each other like old Indian ghosts—Murphy and Alexander."

"The historian and the long-distance runner, right out of Cooper's *Prairie.*"

"I was scared. I immediately changed direction. Later I was coming back from Van Cortlandt the other way when Murphy yells out, 'Towers!' I couldn't believe he saw me, he recognized me. 'Did you think you could sneak past us? We were watching you that whole time.'"

"What a great story!"

"Van Cortlandt was there for an eternity before me and it will be there long after I am gone. Yet my moment is cosmic."

"It cannot and should not be erased from the universe," I added, "even as the memory of those men, who died here, shall not perish from the Earth."

"Exactly, Richard. Only you would know the one time Abe Lincoln could be quoted esoterically. It's like no one says anything anymore. It's just, 'How ya doing, man?' and 'Great!' and 'Stayin' high?' I thought we'd come to a new age, but this is even worse than the '50s. Back then we had the Knickerbocker sign, Sam Cooke, baseball cards. Now that's all finished. People are suspicious. They meet me, they know I'm different, but they can't figure how. They ask where I'm from, like it's Saturn or someplace. 'Hell,' I tell'm, 'I was born in a hospital four blocks from here.' 'No kiddin'?' they say. They don't really believe me. They think I've been in Nepal or with Hopis. I've been in the Rockies, but that's not it. It's like I've been so far out it's inconceivable to them."

"It's a fable," I say, "the start of a great track meet many years ago, a Saturday morning. The runners line up: Emile, Phil, Steve Heller, Dr. Rechtshaffen, Jonathan. The gun is fired. A short ways into the course Jon veers off and heads for the woods. 'Where are you going?' Emile calls out.

"'I'm headed my own way,' Jon says. 'It's the only chance to get there in the end.'

"He turns and charges up a hill. He feels a rush of adrenaline. He is moving perpendicular to the race. Wet moss on stones, rotting bark underfoot, he tells himself, 'Only if you follow your heart do you find the grail.' Down below he sees them moving in tandem toward the horizon, mere stick figures. He watches till they pass out of sight. Then he plunges into the bigger wild."

"Richard, this is great!"

"The vegetation grows thicker and he stumbles over fallen branches and loses his way. He comes back into the same clearing not just once but over and over again. Months later he understands he is lost and despairs of ever finding his way out.

"Many valleys away, Emile, Phil, and the two Steves are still running. They've got Adidas on and they've picked up an accompaniment of joggers in shirts with slogans on them. Totally different races have merged and everyone is prancing through milestones toward a distant finish line."

"You know who those joggers are?" interrupted Jon excitedly. "They're people imitating cars. They think they're so cool, but they're just machines with earphones."

"And you know what the forest is? The alchemical text, the tarot, but it is also the convict in the graveyard, hepatitis, the mental hospital, the Baltimore jail. In the forest lurks Dr. Golden. In the forest are powerful spirits. With their aid he finds his way out. Ragged, exhausted, no longer resembling a runner in a race, he reemerges on the track. He has passed through a hole in space-time and is miles ahead of everyone. His physical body is wasted, but his spirit body is enormous. He doesn't run to win. In fact, he stops to wait for them, to tell them the amazing things he has seen, to tell them the race doesn't matter, never mattered. But they sweep past, almost in slow motion. They don't even see him. He stands in their path, a giant, illuminating the way."

"Richard, that is so wonderful I can't believe it. No one will write my story but you."

Here was my brother, the kid they brought home in a blanket, to whom I handed a teddy bear. Once upon a time we cut pictures out of magazines, played word games across the darkness of our room, waited for the school bus in each other's company. We were the brothers of the shire, of the haunted forest. He was the one I comforted in summer camp, whose head I battered, who taunted me, who sought me, who shared the surf of Long Beach, my comrade in All-Star Baseball and table hockey, who rolled skeeballs with me on the boardwalk until we won not the organ or mixmaster but a yellow wall clock for Bridey . . . who cried at the entrance of the puppet witch, who hung with me on every pitch of the '50s, who went with me to the Polo Grounds to watch the Mets get born.

He told a story about accepting an invitation to a Turetsky clan gathering, a Hanukah party at Aunt Et's house. It was exactly like ones we had gone to as kids, except everyone was a generation older, and there were new children. His cousin Freddie, a photographer at *Time,* didn't even say hello before challenging Jon to a game of ping-pong in the basement. "It's his major corporate recreation, and I haven't played since Maryland, but I beat him the first three games. It was intense. Like the biggest thing was to smash the other guy—the way *I* was with you in that hockey game. Nothing else existed. We hadn't seen each other in eight years, but we didn't talk. Just hitting that ball, diving for it, killing each other. He came back. He finally won, four games to three. We were sweating. I went upstairs. They all began talking to me as if I were a child, as if my deeds condemned me to pity and condescension. Everyone kept praising the food as though it were some sort of sacred object rather than slaughtered beasts, as I reminded them. That's their pitiful contribution to maintaining Jewish culture. I should have turned on them like Isaiah, but I went into the kitchen and ate with the maid. At least I was out of the company of gluttons and money changers."

"That's the way it always was," I offered. "Raise one little finger and they'll slam you down at ping-pong. It's what those games are for, you know."

"Plus they never mention Mom. If you say her name there's a silence and they change the subject. It's become the big taboo. They act as though she never existed. It's so spooky. It makes me want to bring her back as an avenger."

"Well, *we* can talk about her. I mean, Jonathan David, I'm sitting here watching the traffic on Highway 80 pour your way at light speed."

"She just plain flew—out the window like a witch. She was always . . . a witch."

"Yeah. But you got the good side of her. She was the rich lady of the court who favored you. She scared the hell out of me. Everyone talked about how beautiful she was. I think she was a decoy, like cloth mothers biologists make to mindfuck baby chimps. She tricked and cheated us. She stole our childhood. She set us against each other and made us enemies. It looked as though you got the good deal and I got the bad one. But it was really the other way around. Since I was the outlaw I could run away. You were the hero, so when you fled to Colorado she put a curse on you or invoked some post-hypnotic command."

"Do you ever see her anymore?"

"A few weeks ago I had a dream, the same dream I've had maybe three times. She was alive, alive somewhere else. I was with her. She was in really good shape except that she kept asking me what happened."

"You're scaring me, Rich. I am standing here with the lights out, and you're scaring me to death. And I'm loving it." He takes a hard toke. "Remember when we followed the wrong woman home from the fish market. She was wearing Mom's exact coat and rainhat."

"Yeah. All the way into the elevator at Eleven-Eleven until she turned and it was some other face."

"Wasn't that scary when we realized it wasn't her? Wasn't that other face like a death mask?"

"God was it ever. Because it revealed the truth we could never tell ourselves—our mother was a zombi."

"Remember when we sat on the sun roof at the Nevele piling snow along the railing, trying to melt winter."

"That memory is like my whole life."

The sky over the Bay was filled with the lanterns of planes moving at different speeds, their bodies partially visible so each one was a UFO. A tiara of cars rolled across each bridge. The sun had barely set and its after-glow was a medley of colors. I described this to Jon; then he told me what he saw:

"A guy reading his book, smoking in his chair. TVs on, lots of them, everywhere, that poisonous blue powder. I hear the wind in the courtyard. Richard, the times I was with you were so special, they were so much better. But I hated you and couldn't admit how good you were. You might betray me to your evil other family. You were mysterious and beautiful, and you hated me even more than I hated you. You were my real father and I couldn't tell you. I could only fight you and want to kill you, but I really wanted to kill my father and set us both free."

I picked up his soliloquy: "Jon, a terrible thing happened to us during childhood. I can't even tell you what it was. We no longer know it as a thing because it passed directly into our bones and blood. It was an extremely hard blow, a paralyzing blow that may or may not have come from a voodoo master working through our mother."

"Exactly."

"It's not me who was beautiful. It's you. It was you you wanted so badly that they wouldn't let be born. You saw yourself in me. You still see yourself in me. All the years growing up you couldn't abandon the fake hero they made you into, but you secretly identified with my rebellion. You might have even identified with me more than you identified with yourself."

"Once again, Richard, right! There's a part of you in me. Sometimes I'm just walking down the street and I feel like I'm you. You're my father because I never had a father. That's why I liked Mickey Mantle so much. I can see it now. Mickey was my father because he was such a great clutch hitter. His baseball had principles. He was flawed like Vulcan, but he stood for moral order in the universe."

It was so long ago and it was just yesterday, the victrola playing *"Cruising down the River on a Sunday afternoon,"* Bob singing "April Showers." Before that there was nothing, and everything ... *"bring the flowers that bloom in May...."* Rhymes with Towers. Yes, we came from elsewhere to be born in the same womb, to be initiates together in hell. But that didn't say who we were—his being my brother. That would never be revealed, but as long as the knowing didn't ruin us for the not knowing we were better off knowing this much. 'It could end in a moment,' I thought. 'Us, this whole civilization. But for being mortal, tender, even virulent, we are like clouds of insects that live also against incredible odds.'

And in the middle distance, on a sunlit dirt path, an image so remote it was barely acknowledged mutely suggested, without my singing them, the words, *"So if you're looking for a bluebird and listening for his song ..."* because no one was singing it anymore but someone had sung it then when we didn't know what dirge they were really singing, nor did they.

Nineteenth Document

Taking English course at Hunter once a week—Thursday nights—Modern British Literature. So far Portrait of the Artist as a Young Man, Women in Love, To the Lighthouse, A Passage to India. Gave a half-hour oral report on Virginia Woolf. Went very very well.

Then I have this sort of hippie life style. Free. Loose. No tomorrow. Be in the present. Very much want to steep myself in English and come out a priest of that religion.

I love this girl named Andrea (age 21, Sarah Lawrence, speaks French, lived in France, plays lute, can write music), but I don't think she cares much about me. Bought her Boaz's Kwakiutl Ethnography when she told me that was her tribe for anthro. class report.

I LOVE HER

I LOVE COLUMBIAN MARIJUANA

"and we sail and we sail away. . . . we're from Denmark. . . . way up to Caledonia. . . ."

new moon + it's Hallowe'en

Van Morrison

I'm a nut I'm stupid I'm a meaningless jackass

Pink Floyd continues on the record player and I just add this:

It's all living underground. . . .

It's all being lonely. . . .

It's all being Strider. . . .

It's all resisting the machine. . . .

This is the excitement and journey of my life. This is the course I am + was + will be on. Woh!!

here goes!

Love Love Love Love

These letters were written under the auspices + fulfillment of Lebanese Hashish. These letters are 100% ME + recorded live certified by the United States Bureau for the Inspection of Rebel Youth

Night is coming on. It is airy gold out to the west between the buildings which are black as silhouettes. I took two hits of Lebanese hash (first of the day or rather first since 3 AM this morning). It brings out color and structure. I put on a Quicksilver Messenger album. San Francisco Haight-Ashbury days they rose to fame. Summer was swept out of town today by beautiful breezy sunny, awesome pre-Autumn day. Great long fantastic clouds, huge lengthened cumulus barges propelled across an indigo sky by a gusty cleansing wind, making one aware of how they've been suffering in the steamy jungle pollution nightmare. Yesterday finished Home Life in Colonial America + The Golden Trade of the Moors. Got an A in Summer School Course, American Realism. Summertime is the hardest for living the underground life. The heat forces you up into the arena with the other beasts. LOVE THE OCCULT + ALL IT PROMISES.

Mickey Mantle, imported from the sprawling outlands of Oklahoma, roamed the wide lands and outer fields of the Stadium pastures, truly living the West in the East. A magic in his body to bring about this conjunction, deer-like he looked, a fawn, a young colt beside the veteran DiMaggio still playing center; gangly but powerful like the deep hidden springs of oil energy in his home state. And then this strange flaw in the perfect crystal, the shot of hidden lightning marking the tree, running up Ahab's body, the lameness, peg-leg of pirates, of Stuyvesant of old in New Amsterdam town, the fatal white-man-flaw running like jagged lightning out even to Oklahoma, Indian Territory. So he early fell in the drainage ditches of the flawed pastureland of El-train-battered, pigeon-haunted Yankee Stadium, the spavin (meaning "lame") in Spavinaw, Oklahoma, his hometown in Indian country, coming literally true.

The following January Jon sent a short note on Washington Irving stationery:

> I'm tired of my ratrace existence and yet forced to believe it . . . oh fuck it . . . in order to sustain it . . . until some everloving motherfuckin other

alternative is provided by the schemata of His holiness the little god of plutonian or numonium dwarves of all of fucked-up existence.

I AIN'T INTERESTED IN LIFE ANYMORE.

hasta la vista

Love Jon

On Monday he didn't show up at work. He didn't come in the next day either, nor did he answer his phone. His father called the police. They broke the lock on his apartment. All they found was the hermitage of a scholar.

Towers still wasn't talking to me, so he had his secretary call. "Please, Richard, help us," she said. "Bob's beside himself. You know how he gets. He has police checking Central Park, the morgues, the hospitals. Do you have any ideas?"

All I knew was he wasn't in California yet. I couldn't believe he was dead. His life was so close to mine and at the same time so mythologized and literary I could almost confuse him with either Ivan or Alyosha Karamazov. 'It has to be a drug deal,' I thought. 'Either that or he went to sleep in Central Park one time too many.'

Twentieth Document

I wasn't <u>ever</u> coming back. I was a Nathaniel Hawthorne character. I might have been gone ten years. I wanted to reach the Coast, but I had to work my way out there town by town because I started with only twenty dollars.

I hitched along the Hudson into the Catskills, then west into Pennsylvania. I was headed for the mountains, the Poconos, which are part of the Appalachian chain. I was out of the city by then. I could see stars. It was so cold on Highway 260 or 690 or something, I thought I was going to freeze to death. I couldn't imagine even getting to the top of the next hill. There was no one on the road, just trucks rolling by. And they wouldn't stop because they'd have to shift gears going uphill. I realized unless I got to the top by myself I wouldn't survive.

Finally a pick-up pulled over. As soon as I got in he exited. I didn't want to get out because it was so cold. He said, "You stay on this road; the local people'll come by." The next car stopped. We went through Wilkes-Barre into Scranton. I descended on that town like a ghost.

I walked into the Salvation Army. The place was filled with hippies. They put me in alcohol rehab because that's all they had. I shared my pot. I knew the scene from the hospital. We smoked in closets and snuck into bushes. I would have stayed longer, but they had a rule you had to be employed by them.

Two kids on the street wanted me to buy them some glue to sniff, but I don't serve no plastic gods. I went up on the hills—the place has got more hills than San Francisco. It must have been three or four in the morning I passed the School for the Deaf. I crept through the yard and put my head on the window. The brightness kind of stunned me. I watched them on the floor making signs. That taught me to be alert again. Then I walked across railroad yards, the Dipper overhead. It was America. I was free.

In this dry goods store they told me about a job packing books, so I walked three miles and was hired. Then I got a room in a boarding house, $10.00 a night.

The kids in the warehouse were young, like high-school age. They thought they were real smart. Their talk was pussy, cunt, all perversions. They didn't care about nothing. They were animals really, just animals with human acts. They'd kill you and throw you in the river and not think twice about it. The foreman—it wasn't that he was unfriendly, but for eight hours if you stopped a second he made you aware. All day we packed just one book: Thomas Wolfe, <u>You Can't Go Home</u>.

People complain about New York and how tough it is. New York is sweet compared to Scranton. Do you know the cops here apologized for breaking my lock, and they put on a new one. In Scranton it was all pussy and beer. They had beards and long hair. The last time I was on the road, if you were a longhair and smoked dope, that was high, man; you were cool. These guys weren't cool at all. Dope just made'em stupid and mean.

But you don't get to pick your vision-quest. I got redneck hippies just as dangerous as any werewolf or grizzly. I visited the tribes of Scranton, and they were base, base tribes. I was the Indian. They had no religion, no customs. When the Government exterminated the Cherokee and Nez Perce they thought they were getting rid of dangerous hombres. Those were fine beautiful people, people of high lineage and culture who went to war like angels. These new tribes are just mutations, ugly amorphous bands grown up from rubble. They're Vandals and Huns without a Druid history.

My father couldn't understand why I went there. When I delivered my ethnographic report he just laughed and said, "So you discovered Scranton is a hole. People have known that for the last fifty years." That's his way. Mine is to go into the wilderness, fill my head with visions, and survive.

Twenty-first Document

Jonathan David Towers Position: Windowseats, Backrows
Writes: R Throws R

Major League Career

Years in Majors: 1965 - 1979 (Still Active)

League	Year	Team	Classes Attended	Assignments Completed	Literary Conquests	Key Comments	Batting Average
Western	1965	Madison Angels	485	178	23	77	.285
Western	1966	Madison Angels	397	122	20	64	.279
Western	1967	Madison Angels	25	0	4	8	.000
Eastern	1968	Manhattan Tigers	214	93	14	81	.335
Eastern	1969	Manhattan Tigers	78	14	3	12	.205
Western	1969	Colorado Huskies	220	81	7	55	.297
Western	1970	Boulder Lions	501	203	31	95	.313
Western	1971	Boulder Lions	439	116	24	69	.305
	1972	ON THE INACTIVE ROSTER					
Eastern	1973	Baltimore Bengals	185	98	21	60	.368
Eastern	1974	Baltimore Bengals	18	0	1	8	.000
	1975	ON THE INACTIVE ROSTER					
Eastern	1976	Manhattan Tigers	73	39	4	10	.325
Eastern	1977	Manhattan Tigers	215	86	13	56	.304
Eastern	1978	Manhattan Tigers	68	30	14	33	.598
Eastern	1979	Manhattan Tigers	259	99	25	64	.313

3

Playing for Keeps

In Richmond my job was North Atlantic Books—finding authors, getting books produced, filling orders, writing grants. My salary was whatever I could save over expenses. Three days a week, in exchange for tuition reduction, I helped at Bright Star's lunchtime. Dropping whatever I was doing and hiking up Sierra, I joined Miranda and her friends on the tire fort. There I unwrapped sandwiches and carrots and acted daffy. One time, I figured out for each kid, to much hilarity, his or her name spelled backwards. After lunch I organized free play, tossing a frisbee, kicking a ball, or leading t'ai chi sillies, Capture the Flag, and other spontaneous romps.

I was usually the parent at home at the end of the school day. Robin liked to check North Atlantic's deposit slips and evaluate our progress. Luckily, Imperial Savings offered platters of cookies as an incentive to bank there—sometimes even chocolate-coated ones, the possibility of which provided daily suspense as we pushed open the glass doors. (Andrew Aaron, a Swiss book-collector, was appalled when he accompanied us there one afternoon to complete a transaction, boasting that in his country banking was a *serious* business; he almost walked out the next time—it was Halloween, a staff of witches and skeletons.) While I waited on line, Robin and Mandy would charm the tellers with their attentiveness to each other, scrawling notes and drawings back and forth on deposit slips. Robin also counted (cumulatively on a sheet of paper he folded into his pocket) the VW bugs that passed on MacDonald Avenue.

After the bank we'd drive the day's orders to the post office and wait on line to mail them. We savored fracases caused by one ornery, dimwitted clerk (whose queue we avoided). A couple of times a week we'd stop at Lucky's or some funkier grocery in San Pablo or El Sobrante. The kids would race up and down aisles to grab cereals and juices and consult each other on bread and yogurt. Robin was a skillful applier of coupons and always had a handful ready (including "slip-ins," for things we didn't buy but it looked as though we might have). He professionally shuffled his stash while reviewing items in our cart.

That winter we set a Christmas tree in the living room and decorated it with Lindy's childhood ornaments plus rings she and Robin glued (with Miranda's help). At night, driving along the Arlington through El Cerrito, we wound past incredible displays: an entire hillside of shepherds and sheep about a nativity, Santa and a team of reindeer gliding above a roof, colored lights in almost four dimensions. It was dazzling but eerie, as though, without snow and icy winds, ceremonial luminescence was unmerited.

When the National Endowment for the Arts advertised new grants for marketing, Callahan, Ishmael Reed, and I quickly launched Barbary Coast Distribution Company. Ishmael was already running Before Columbus, a similar organization, so I wrote the application. We knew that a multicultural project signed by a prominent African-American would be a shoo-in, but it was still a windfall by certified mail. With a quarter-time salary to administer the funds, I directed an ineffective crew of sales reps (a mixture of Ishmael's present students and my former ones who lived in the Bay Area). We carried titles from Ishmael's presses (Reed, Cannon, Johnson; Yardbird; and I. Reed Books) along with those of Callahan's Turtle Island, North Atlantic Books, and a variety of other (mostly local) publishing companies, such as Heyday (which specialized in American Indian books), Blue Wind, and North Point. We didn't scare up enough business to match the grant, but Barbary Coast was an experiment—to see if there was any way of selling the thousands of new literary titles the NEA was funding annually. (More cynically, Robert Duncan remarked, "We used to think we wanted Government support for poetry, but beware when such wishes are granted." In truth, there were so many poetry books that what little market had existed was now flooded.)

In 1979 the Endowment began enforcing its rule that grants had to be received by nonprofit agencies, so I paid Alameda County Neighborhood Arts Program almost $5,000 (out of $15,000) to serve as our fiscal agent. "Apply for nonprofit status," the director urged us. "We don't want to steal your money." The paperwork was so onerous I undertook it mostly as an expression of piety, with little hope of success.

Our initial hurdle was inventing a structure. At a series of workshops run by Bay Area Lawyers for the Arts, Lindy and I learned that publishing itself was not adequate. We needed to put our books in an educational context.

We conceived an anthropological foundation with a publishing program and named it Society for the Study of Native Arts and Sciences. Skip Rappaport, Margaret MacKenzie, and John Todd (with whom we had remained friends since the Goddard Social Ecology program) all agreed to become Board members (joining Lindy and me—by a rule that the majority had to be unrelated to the principals). Our goals were: reviving non-Western traditions, notably indigenous farming and shamanic medicine; conserving ecologically sensitive land; and founding a holistic-health center. We didn't expect to accomplish all this, but we needed a matrix large enough to justify our application. In truth, we were being asked to spin a fantasy of what we would do with a million dollars because the people who read our documents wanted to know that first and foremost.

After three separate submissions (during which we had to deal with such unexpected queries as how we would dispense revenues from any patents our ethnobotanical research generated), we got approval, first from the IRS, then from the State.

Amador was pure California, the future of America. Black teenagers terrorized Chinese boys. Lighter blacks taunted the more African ones: "Hey, nigger!" Robin got punched in the stomach while trying to serve as mediator between two factions: "Let's reason it out."

Smash!

There were so many scams that, despite vigilance, we bit on a few. Our house was half repainted before the friend of the mother with the teen-age drummer disappeared. Then we bought layers of needless (supposedly tax-rebated) insulation after an impassioned solicitation by Olive Salt's boarder.

Neighbors adorned backyards with dead cars and trash mounds. Houses burned down. Gunshots reverberated in the distance. Twice we found our mail stuffed in evergreen bushes, letters opened, checks removed. One morning, for blocks in either direction, the batteries were missing from vehicles parked on our side of Amador. As shouts from touch football punctuated highway din, Olive sucked the pith out of a Marlboro and reminisced about when this was all farmland and her house was towed to its present site.

It rarely rained the first two years. I dreamed of waterfalls, cranes striding through pools, giant banana flowers. Turtles broke off existing turtles like rootlets until they were everywhere, swimming through our yard.

In reality the backyard was thistles and tuberous grass. Water from a hose disappeared into cracked clay. Finally a dark October sky broke in sheets. In night winds that followed, our fence blew over, joining neighbors' yards bizarrely. Water ran unimpeded from the hills. The kids put on raincoats and galoshes and sailed boats in the street. That Christmas I slipped ten-dollar bills into the stockings, and Robin yelled to Mandy, "Wow, Santa's in the bucks!"

Much of *The Night Sky* preexisted either in my mind or in writing I had done years earlier, so it took only ten months to complete a manuscript (a year more for Sierra Club to publish it). Even before finishing, I started the third in what had become my occult science trilogy—a technical and metaphysical account of embryogenesis. This one I made from scratch, having merely a binder of scrawled physical-anthropology notes. I spent months going through embryology and genetics textbooks. Then I outlined different scales of plant and animal histories on a piece of cardboard that stood almost as tall as I did. One set of lines traced the origin of humans from free-swimming cells and wormlike marine creatures. Another mapped the genesis of the brain through neuron nets of jellyfish and ganglia of octopi. Other story-lines interwove ontogeny and phylogeny, morphogenesis and evolution. The moment of a blastula suddenly inverting, changing shape and dimension, and turning into a gastrula—in the primeval oceans and again in the womb—was as unfathomable and profound as black holes and alchemical transmutations. It contained the precise terms of our incarnation in body-minds; yet almost no one had represented it as an esoteric and psychospiritual process.

One morning before t'ai chi, the teacher's senior disciple, Peter Kwok Ming Hugh, announced that Ben had written his own book, actually a translation of the classical literature on t'ai chi ch'uan. He was looking for help getting it published.

After class I tentatively approached the front. It was premature for me, a marginal student, to address Mr. Lo, but, when he learned I was bringing help in publishing, his puzzled frown turned to talkativeness, and he led me into his office where he made chaos out of his desk looking for his calendar. He wrote in a date for the following week: me and his co-translator Martin Inn, lunch on Clement.

The morning of the meeting I put on my best clothes and drove the Bridge to the Avenues. After introducing me to Martin, a Chinese Hawaiian my age, then to the restaurant's owner, Ben ordered in Mandarin without consulting us. As milky soup, noodle dishes, and crisp buns (none of them on the menu) were set in our midst, I felt hardly worthy of the master's banquet.

Ben and Martin had failed at finding a publisher, in part because few presses had any real enthusiasm for t'ai chi ch'uan but mainly because they wanted complete aesthetic and economic control. Convincing them to let go of their prestigious project required major concessions, but it was more important to turn this fortuity into something tangible than to win debating points or get a fairer share. Ben was offering to be my business partner—that was enough.

On the spur of the moment I invited them to draw up their own rules. As we drafted a contract there at the table, the occasion became downright jovial. The food was far more than the three of us could handle, so Ben sent me home with the leftovers.

I received the fabled manuscript from Peter at the next class. Inside a small box was *The Essence of T'ai Chi Ch'uan* wrapped in tissue paper. It would sell huge numbers over the years, but our initial print run was a modest five hundred.

As North Atlantic was making a transition from a purely literary press, Dana Ullman and I inaugurated our homeopathic imprint with Kent's *Lectures.* We also published Whitmont's essays on the psychochemistry of matter, which Dana named *Psyche and Substance.* Then we turned historian Harris Coulter's articles on the scientific basis of microdoses into *Homeopathic Science and Modern Medicine.*

At the same time, I called board member Rappaport and asked for his new collection of essays. Hundreds of course adoptions would be a sure thing. "It's easier than writing job recommendations for me," I joked.

When Skip insisted that academics don't usually publish with literary presses, I reminded him that we also did baseball and t'ai chi. He laughed out loud.

"Richard," he said, "Yale University has been after me for a sequel for five years." In 1968 they had published *Pigs for the Ancestors,* his ethnography of the Tsembaga Maring of New Guinea. In subsequent conversations I appealed to his sense of justice: "You could let us make the money rather than Yale."

"This is probably absurd," Skip remarked a month later (after saying he had changed his mind). "In fact, quite likely so. But I've done crazier things to get students employed."

With *Ecology, Meaning, and Religion* in hand, I put together *Ecology and Consciousness,* a companion anthology, featuring Rappaport's famous essay, "Sanctity and Adaptation," a draft of which we had published in 1970 in the *Oecology Issue.* I included Buckminster Fuller's poem on hydroelectric power from Fundy's tides, a section of Wilhelm

Reich's chapter on cosmic superimposition, Trungpa Rinpoche's talk at Goddard on "The Meaning of Life" (in which he said, "We eat, we sleep, we shit, we bathe, we make love, we fight, we kill people, we do everything. We just live.... The living is life."), and a piece on "The Fool" by our old Santa Cruz friend Peggy. I added Ed Dorn's letter to a virus riding to Earth aboard a meteorite, my interviews with Gary Snyder and Jule Eisenbud, Eskimo writings from Knud Rasmussen ("The greatest peril of life lies in the fact that human food consists entirely of souls"), and a variety of other pieces, most of them culled out of old *Io*s.

As titles arrived from the printer, our sales at Bookpeople improved. Our plans to move evaporated, and we settled into Amador.

After spurning all my earlier ploys, Robin became a baseball fan at the advanced age of ten. Conscripted by the cult of bubble-gum cards at school, he briefly considered rooting for the local team (the Oakland A's) but then chose the Mets, not because of me but because we had painted his Vermont room (quite incidentally) blue with orange trim. He was most attracted by cards with the same color scheme. An obscure East Coast team mired in the cellar allowed him to express his nostalgia for Plainfield plus the alienation he felt from California styling all around him. The Mets were his difference, his badge of honor, and they became a meeting-place for father and son.

During the 1979 season I called Arthur Richman for tickets to watch our team at Candlestick. I had known Art two decades earlier as a guest at Grossinger's and also as a friend of my stepfather who gave him scores from *The Daily Mirror.* A career baseball man who had become travelling secretary of the team, Art was also the one who sent the 1969 World Series film to Portland.

Surprised to hear from me again—and gruff and cynical in the New York style—he came through nonetheless (though only after he complained about overpaid, ungrateful players and scolded me for being their fan—"I don't understand, Richard!") with seats right behind the visitor's dugout. The Mets were suddenly more vivid than life.

Robin and I found ourselves among the friends and families of players, including John Stearns' college buddies, Leon Brown's father, and George Foster's wife. My son quickly chose Stearns as his favorite because, during situps and stretches, he alternated between cutting up and being intense. While imitating the Mets' German conditioning coach quite loudly ("... and und streeeetch ..."), he waved to our section and his friends hailed witticisms back.

The following April, Doubleday threw a party on Fifth Avenue for their version of our anthology (renamed *Baseball Diamonds*). While I flew to New York, my co-editor, Kevin Kerrane, drove up from Delaware with his friend, rockabilly musician George Thorogood, a long-time Mets fan. While George provided a Mick Jagger presence (and maids circled with gigantic shrimps and stuffed mushrooms), contributors stood and read their works to a crowd that included sportswriters and *New Yorker* representative Jamaica Kincaid (who later parodied the event).

Afterwards our editor on the book, Tim McGinnis, having scored that night's tickets for the Doubleday box, grabbed Kevin, George, and me, and we made a dash in his car to Shea Stadium. Arriving in the third inning, we were led to seats next to Fred Wilpon, one of the two Mets owners (along with Nelson Doubleday). Though I had never met Fred, I knew he had been a guest at Grossinger's and a business colleague of my father.

After an inning of summoning my courage, I introduced myself. Pleased by the coincidence, he slid over one seat and filled me in on the details of his dead-in-the-water plan for condos around the Lake (while mourning the unnecessary demise of Grossinger's). But another event kept stealing center stage.

On his first trip to Shea ("Forget Yankee Stadium; this place is a shrine!"), Mr. Thorogood had removed his suit jacket and shirt to reveal a full Mets uniform, then lit a stogy, stepped to the railing, and shouted on every pitch (between innings he signed autographs for players). By the fifth (down 7–0) George moved back to our row and began haranguing Wilpon about John Pacella's lack of a curve ball, then urged him to sign his buddies Bernie Carbo and Jay Johnstone. When an usher asked the owner if he wanted this impertinent fan removed, Wilpon responded, "No, but find me five more like him!" In the seventh I called Robin from a phone booth to report these events and hold the receiver into the crowd noise.

A couple of weeks later, on Robin's eleventh birthday, the Mets were at Candlestick. Our family went to the game early for batting practice. Miranda, despite much anticipation, soon declared utter boredom. Lindy told her she was just as bored, but that one could always watch the antics of fans and look for the ice-cream man. Mandy chose the latter.

During warmups Art Richman brought players by to wish a "Happy Birthday." Joe Torre, the manager, asked Robin if he was married yet.

"Unh uh," he replied. "Too young."

Torre got a laugh out of that.

Then at my suggestion Art found John Stearns. Just as Robin's favorite player was approaching I reminded Lindy he was originally from Denver, so after he made his obligatory remarks to the young fan, she asked, "What high school did you go to?"

His face lit up. "East." Then they began throwing back flirty Denver-style comments.

"I know about girls from Kent," Stearns teased.

Afterwards Lindy toyed with Robin: "How do you like that? Your mother meeting your favorite player. And with some aplomb, I might add."

"Fine, Mom, but let's not talk about it, okay?"

At a bookseller's convention Sam Bercholz, publisher of Shambhala, offered Lindy a job as his West Coast scout. He had recently moved his operation from Berkeley to Boulder; now he wanted someone to resurrect a Bay Area office. Lindy wondered whether North Atlantic would be a conflict of interest, but Sam assured her we were too small.

So Lindy ended a brief career as a grant-writing consultant and trumpeted Shambhala far and wide. She soon acquired a guide to natural foods by entrepreneur Fred Rohe and a book on performance arts by Louise Steinman, her colleague from the 1975 Mills conference.

When my teacher Polly moved to Marin, she had recommended (as her replacement) her own teacher, Richard Strozzi Heckler, one of Lomi School's founders. But Heckler was more noted for prowess in aikido than bioenergetics, so I didn't contact him. Now Lindy, in her role of acquiring editor, recalled Polly's tip. Since Richard taught psychology each summer at Naropa Institute, the Buddhist college in

Boulder, she knew her boss would be eager for his first book.

And Heckler was ready to write it. He came to Amador one afternoon, outline in hand (plus a folder of case histories). He resembled a young compact Kirk Douglas, with piercing eyes that combined therapist and Zen swordsman. "We can mobilize energy and attention," he said, "far more effectively working from the body than just by dialoguing. But we can't mass-produce and bottle that energy. We have to tap each person's natural rhythms." He paused and looked directly at Lindy: "I take my lessons from aikido: we finally have to *put it on the mat.*"

Richard dropped by our house periodically after that. Sitting in the backyard with cups of tea, the three of us found ourselves kindred spirits. In the course of conversations that ran from the cosmic to the practical, we transited Buddhism, nuclear war, back-to-the-land, and raising kids. We heard about Richard's tyrannical Navy father and his stint in the Marines during Vietnam.

"I want you to meet my compadre Bira Almeida," he announced one afternoon. "He's an incredible *contra-mestre* with whom I've been studying. Have you heard of a Brazilian martial art called capoeira?"

I nodded, but I had *just* heard of it, and not even realized it was for real. It was one of the magical techniques described in a book of psychic fighting tales submitted by John Gilbey, a friend of Ben Lo's.

"Bira's trying to put together a book," Richard continued, "and he needs help with the editing and printing. You should get involved. Capoeira's a beautiful, honorable form." Putting down his tea, he hopped agilely from foot to foot, then did a handstand. "They don't compete; they 'play.' All the moves take place in a ceremonial circle, a *roda.* Two capoeiristas spar—that is, play—to musical accompaniment from others. They use *berimbaus* which they make themselves from a specially cut piece of wood, a gourd, and a tire cord. They work it with a *dobrão,* an old Brazilian coin." His hand motion suggested the *berimbau* was a kind of bass. "The music has the power to get inside you, to show you the shape of your spirit, even the dimensions of the universe. Bira says the *berimbau*'s sound has color and an aura. Once you are out of hearing of its waves, you feel it vibrating inside you. It carries the Brazilian sense of soul, melancholy and deep. It envelops you and tames your spirit even as it guides your play in the *roda.*"

As Richard talked and danced and sang a capoeira song in Portuguese, I prayed that no one else would hear of this book before I got it for North Atlantic.

On the phone Bira was generous and charming. We set up a meeting for later that week at Julius Baker's Tae Kwon-Do in downtown Berkeley.

Tentatively peeking into Baker's studio, I observed a class of African-Americans practicing jabs in unison as they let out warrior cries. Almost at once they dispersed, and new people gathered. I asked for Bira Almeida. No one seemed to know him, and I was warned to stay off the mat. Yet the next class was forming all the way on the other side by the dressing rooms.

Then an unmistakable figure materialized in their midst, a tall, solidly built Euro-Brazilian in his late thirties. Moving like a cat, bouncing this way and that, he slapped hands and whomped the butts of his students, calling out greetings and challenges in mixed Portuguese and English.

Class members were soon on the mat, dancing in pairs, walking on their hands, doing cartwheels, sparring alternately with hands and feet to the tang of the *berimbau*. Just as I began to worry that Bira had forgotten our meeting, he turned and strode toward me. He shook my hand and led me into Julius Baker's small office. As he patted his briefcase, he declared, "The World Capoeira Association, all right here."

For the next ten minutes he outlined his project and described its problems. We made a second appointment. He was on his way back to the mat—a combination Fidel Castro, Don Juan Matus, and Superman in Clark Kent drag—when suddenly he stopped, walked back, and held out his journal, the actual handwritten text. "Look it over. Leave it in the office when you go. But please stay for class. I want you to see." Turning the pages gingerly, I reclaimed my spot on the bench. I began reading at a random point:

> Mestre Bimba said capoeira is treachery. Long live he who held my hands and showed me how to be in time with the motion. Capoeira is also an art one plays anywhere, under any condition, even when in an unbalanced situation. Wherever you are must be the right place to be. So it doesn't matter if some people think I'm a fool, crazy, or even presumptuous.

As chills went up my spine, a chant exploded and engulfed the room. I looked up to see spontaneous theater—some twenty-five Hispanics, Afros, Euros, surfer and hippie types, men and women, many of them dressed Brazilian style and wearing t-shirts with Capoeira Bahia insignias. They sprang into a circle with Bira at the head. Then they opened class with a prayer: *"Ie A Capoeira!"*

Students were leaping, turning cartwheels over each other, spinning, tumbling, walking on hands. Tops and bottoms of their bodies reversed as they moved in graceful orbits so swift it seemed impossible they could dodge each other. It was reggae; it was *West Side Story;* it was Gurdjieff in France.

That night I composed a letter, saying it would be an honor to work with him. He sent me a copy of the text. It was a slaves' history of Brazil, a magician's story of his own journey.

We hired Martin Inn's girlfriend, Paula Morrison, as North Atlantic's designer—she was our first employee. With her help through the early '80s we put out dozens of new titles, including two t'ai-chi classics by Cheng Man-Ch'ing, a basketball anthology called *Take it to the Hoop,* Gilbey's illustrated fighting tales, new homeopathy and baseball volumes, and a book by Will Baker, a Cal-Davis professor, about his backpacking journey through an Amazon in transition between ancient Asháninka rites and ghetto blasters. We also made a deal with Sierra Club to package Nancy and John Todd's illustrated book on ecological design.

Then we invited Richard Heckler to edit an anthology. Over the next several months he collected articles on the application of aikido to different fields—psychotherapy, animal training, baseball, basketball, bodywork, and primary education. We published these as *Aikido and the New Warrior.*

Many a night Miranda filled her soapy tub with boats and ducks and improvised a series of songs about the different parts of her body, returning always to a chorus of "Bubbles and Water, Bubbles and Water."

After the kids were in bed Lindy and I sat in the living room. Lights twinkled across the Bay. On the stereo Willie Nelson sang "Red Headed

Stranger" and "Blue Eyes Crying in the Rain."

Every few Sundays we drove to San Francisco and visited the Rothkrugs for brunch. Afterwards we'd hike in Golden Gate Park, trooping past ballfields and gardens, Robin feeding crusts to the geese (Mandy once held out her bare hand for an unpleasant snap). Occasionally we made it to the windmill by the ocean—its rotating gears and shadows a harbinger of Vermont.

After Paul Pitchford settled in Moscow, Idaho, he kept urging me to visit potato country. His classes in t'ai chi and healing had become quite popular; his students included both the shooting guard of the upstart University of Idaho Vandals and the eighty-year-old president of the Bank of Idaho.

Paul also travelled around Utah, Idaho, Montana, British Columbia, and Eastern Washington, dispensing herbs and dietary advice and giving acupuncture treatments. He specialized in addictions and cancer, treating the former as an outcome of overly yang foods and drugs, and the latter, likewise in the Chinese manner, as a large, stubborn fungus, growing in a moist environment.

The geezer from the bank, who owned land throughout the state, had donated ninety-eight partially cleared acres (with a stream and some rundown cabins) in Potlatch, just north of Moscow, for Paul's Empty Cloud meditation retreats and annual July healing camp. It was the latter that lured us north.

Our family set out on Highway 5 with a supply of music and hobbit tapes—a day in Ashland, a night in Portland to visit our old Plainfield friends Bob and Anne, then along the Columbia River to a Walla Walla motel. In the morning we entered Idaho, hilly and mysterious.

Other visitors to the camp were rolling up in every manner of vehicle—VW buses, vans, trucks with domes on their backs, different eras of old cars. Tents bloomed across the site. That night we stood on line in the rain to receive scoops of brown rice and vegetables.

In the morning, official programs began. Lindy took reiki, a Japanese system for redirecting cosmic energy; I joined Paul's t'ai-chi and meditation classes. Both of us participated in a large group learning *do-in*, another Japanese art, this one involving self-massage and yoga-like exercises, including rapping on our own skulls and tugging rapidly on the lower flaps of our eyelids. The French instructor, an older man named Jacques, told so many corny jokes while he led us in these acts that I was reminded of Lou Goldstein conducting Simon Sez at Grossinger's.

In the grove every day at 2 PM, we attended Paul's lecture on Chinese medicine, a portable blackboard set among the trees for illustrating cycles of the five elements. As in Berkeley, the barefoot healer proved a wry Taoist commentator.

Robin and Miranda wandered to the borders of the property (and even beyond, where they found a strawberry farmer willing to share his crop). Otherwise, they were appalled by the food, making grumpy faces as they forced down millet and seitan with carrots and then went hunting "for survival" (as Robin put it) by blackberries.

Many long hours, he sat in the forest with a tube of Elmer's Glue and a penknife (his sister bringing raw materials), carving small boats and houses out of branches and bark. He stuck pine cones and nuts together to make creatures with faces. At the end of the week he and Mandy debuted their whole curious animal kingdom.

After each lunch break I sat on a boulder and taught *Planet Medicine.* In a tent at night I read from *The Night Sky*—constellations visible between the flaps.

It was a diverse crowd: rainbow hippies, tough local cowfolk, students from Washington State and the University of Idaho, New Age healers from Southern California, Germans on tour, East Indians from Canada. There was even a Puerto Rican dope dealer from the Lower East Side whom Paul had recently cured through a combination of diet, meditation, and acupuncture. Once a musician (part of a band for a night at Grossinger's), now he was a musician again, playing saxophone under the Milky Way.

"I never would have made it this time around," he told me. "I'd have hid out my whole life in Harlem or SoHo if this man hadn't found me." The tall, blue-eyed magus from Pocatello, his unlikely savior, stood within earshot, smiling like a Cheshire cat.

How far from the Catskills we had come!

Halfway through camp a group of carpenters arrived with axes and rope and assembled a sweat lodge. Although I ignored their macho presence at first, the unending rain (which Jacques called "a pleasant yin tea to inspire our work") made fire irresistible. I joined a group waiting for the next round, then undressed and crawled in. Blankets were thrown over the opening.

We were alone in a UFO.

In sere darkness we formed a circle, some people meditating, others chanting softly. Occasionally a slurp of water was tossed onto hot stones. Puffs of aromatic smoke seemed to flow to my bones, reminding me—no matter how many stars there were in the sky or ancestors in my genes—my body was clay, subtle and electrified.

"Thank you for the heat to cool my soul," intoned one man.

"Let me fly like eagle," sang a woman, and we joined her by finishing her song: *"Fly like an eagle!"*

So perfect and angelic we were, eyes adjusting to the faint ember, long hair and beards, various sizes and colors of male and female bodies. Just as the heat was becoming unbearable, someone called, "All my relations."

Blankets were tossed up, and we crawled back into the drizzle.

Robin and Miranda were quite glad to see Walla Walla again. Though we vowed to become vegetarians soon, we ordered steaks and Idaho fries that first night out.

Our family flew East for a few weeks in August. A driver met us at JFK and took us along familiar highways to Exit 100, the kids pointing at the signs, unable to contain anticipation.

Almost as soon as we arrived Bunny told me that something had to be done pronto—the Hotel was at the end of its rope; my father was a shell of a man.

I had heard such portents before, so I tried playing devil's advocate.

She had little patience for that. "Richard, you haven't been here and are way out of touch with reality. There's no time for me to debate this with you."

She suggested instead we meet together with PG—she, my brothers, and I. "He has to take immediate steps," she insisted; "he's being cheated by those all too willing to take advantage of a sick man. If we can't get through, then we may need to find a doctor to declare him incompetent."

It was heavy medicine to try on an unwilling patient, especially since

I still couldn't tell whether he was a businessman buffoon with secrets or an actor who had mastered the role of fake mogul. (After all, we had a President who couldn't distinguish between his movie roles and actual deeds. Did either PG or Ronald Reagan understand that the ship itself was sinking and they were being used?)

I well remembered Skip Rappaport describing his own father's visit to Grossinger's. He had written a detailed study of the Hotel's deficiencies. They paid him handsomely to do his work, but in the end he could find no one to report to.

"Who was in charge?" Rappaport asked me (because his father was still curious fifteen years later).

"Probably no one then, no one now," I answered.

"He wondered about your father," Skip added. "Does he drink?"

My father didn't drink, but he had a quality of appearing distracted, then responding inappropriately—phlegmatic with bursts of either jollity or anger. I had sat in his office myself and observed people trying to bring him paperwork while he rambled through stories of the past—one afternoon that summer describing his high-school football career to a bored Rick Barry and Joe Klecko, two of the last sports stars to take Grossinger's seriously enough for a free lunch.

PG had an impossible lot anyway. His own father had mocked and undermined him. When he was engaged in negotiations with the Union in the late '60s, Jennie stepped in and ended debate by granting them more than they even asked for. "These people are my family," she declared. "Their plaque expresses their lifelong loyalty and gratitude to the Grossinger family. They deserve everything." But that plaque had been hanging in her living room since 1936.

"It was the only time," my brother James told me, "I ever saw him cry."

In the past when Bunny and I presented him with our strategies for either bailing out or changing direction, his lips would quaver discontent until he blurted out some variant of: "You don't know what you're talking about." Even at his most amenable, he was not a listener.

All through the '50s and '60s, when the name Grossinger was gold, he was offered dozens of can't-miss opportunities from Palm Springs to Jerusalem . . . including a partnership in condos on the Lake (Wilpon's overture), a chain of country clubs just for the use of the name, international hotels. The Chicago Grossingers, real-estate and auto nabobs, made their best offer too. Yet he smirked at the insolence of those who thought they could hustle PG into their ruses. ("These were bigtime gentlemen," Bunny fumed. "They were paying a dollar for a dime because they loved what this place once stood for.") Instead he put patronymic on rye bread and buttermints and chose to cast his lot with Monticello Raceway, then almost ended up in prison—an unindicted co-conspirator overcharging on *bar mitzvahs* so the directors could pocket the untaxed difference.

When Bunny proposed the idea of a meeting and perhaps declaring PG mentally incompetent, James wanted no part of it.

So the three people in the family with the least credibility (to his mind) trapped him in the den by sitting down and requesting his attention. Bunny began by presenting her argument: "Paul, not only is your hotel in trouble but members of your own family are stealing from you."

"Go on," he sneered.

"I heard you sold your life insurance. Is that true? Are you the only one who had to put up your assets as collateral?"

"Go on!" But she was finished and it was my turn. I told him I was on his side, that all we wanted was to help salvage the situation any way we could.

He seemed totally in control as he asked in amazement if we believed he was stupid enough to let himself be cheated. Then he enumerated the ones he considered his real enemies—managers long ago fired or retired, Uncle Abe, now (after a lobotomy) trudging down the Joy Cottage path each night to his basement room. "That toothless bastard cut to size!" he roared with sadistic delight. He sat there victorious, restraining his growling dog, asking us contemptuously if we had any further questions.

"I want you to tell the truth, Pop," Michael finally insisted. "I don't care if I get something or not, but I want to know what's happening. I think Mom deserves to know too."

"What do you think I'm hiding?" he said with the most exasperation I had ever seen in him.

"What's really happening," I offered.

"Whether you sold your life insurance," Bunny added.

"Go on."

"All these family shenanigans," Michael threw in.

"Business has never been better," he announced after a long pause, arms folded over his chest. "And I haven't sold my life insurance. When there's something to know, you'll be the first to hear."

Back in California, we drove south, visiting Disneyland, then the ocean, Miranda uproarious in her first surf. Attending the Western Regional Booksellers' Convention, we found new trade groups in abundance. In a day and a half we tripled the size of our distribution network by taking on three enthusiastic wholesalers, Wisdom Garden, Starlite, and a Bay Area rival to Bookpeople, Publishers Group West. All of these companies were willing to accept our titles on a nonexclusive basis. As long as they each stayed in business we had an expanding pipeline.

In the next year Publishers Group West sold our titles in unprecedented numbers. While Bookpeople was countercultural and chic, freewheeling PGW, operating a few blocks away on Beaudry Street in Emeryville, ran a warehouse of imported art volumes, erotica, foreign comics, glossy rock-star biographies, and all manner of unclassifiable sleaze. Dust-covered books formed ziggurats, some crushed under stacks of pallets. Bookpeople sold passively from a catalogue, while PGW hunted for chain stores and price clubs that needed any kind of discounted merchandise to pack square footage.

The company was owned by Charlie and Mike Winton, two brothers from Modesto, and a coterie of less visible partners. The irreverent style with which they treated their business (and, in particular, esoteric and aesthetic books) reminded me of my cousins Jay and Siggy "having fun" at Integrated. Only this was Northern California. The Wintons and crew grokked country-and-western, the 49ers, MTV, motorboats, and the gourmet version of any consumable; they were pre-Yuppie, post-redneck hippies.

I spent many lively hours with Charlie at the warehouse and Candlestick, talking sports, publishing, and life. With his wave of slicked-back black hair and super-friendly yet in-your-face manner, he reminded me of guys I hung around with in high school. Like me, he was a sort of goofy intellectual, segueing between adventurous concepts-in-progress and total befuddlement. I may have erred in the direction of sanctimony, but Charlie could mock both of us, laugh, and roll the dice again.

Literary funding was coming to an end, for small presses in general but particularly for us. Even with our old Maine buddy (and Robin's godfather) David, now chairman of the Literature Program of the NEA, we were receiving virtually nothing. Barbary Coast was cancelled after two years, *Io* was declared ineligible, and North Atlantic earned only an occasional, reduced grant. It was frustrating that this exile should have occurred as soon as we got nonprofit status, but it was inevitable. Academic cliques and ethnic solidarity groups now controlled the cash, filling committees with their own representatives and disenfranchising anyone else (David chose not to cast a vote for us because he didn't want to be accused of nepotism).

In the early years of NEA funding, few even knew publishing grants existed. Those now competing with us for the last crumbs wouldn't have cared back then (if they had known) because they were far more sumptuously backed by universities and literary and Third World editors at Doubleday, Atheneum, Pantheon, and Scribners.

But the map was changing. Loose academic money was drying up, while large corporate publishers were reexamining how they spent profits from best-selling fiction, celebrity books, and the like. They no longer felt obligated to support the arts or publish a culturally valid list. "80% bad product being carried by at best 20% that sells worth a damn," wrote one new-style manager who had entered the business at the top with the corporate takeovers. But that "bad product" was most of Western civilization—and included the types of books represented by the various constituencies suddenly lined up at NEA.

A positive side to this upheaval became apparent only gradually. As the large publishers dropped their intellectual and artistic lines—they had never done much homeopathy or internal martial arts—more titles and authors became available to us, and there was increased shelf space for the books we published. Mushrooming chain stores may have been crass and imperialistic, but they were imprint-blind. They bought North Atlantic from PGW with a nonjudgmental ease once reserved (in the snobby bookworld) for Harper, Random House, and Penguin.

We could afford to take over what Putnam or Doubleday viewed as the unprofitable end of the business because, if *their* hypothetical break-even quantity was 15,000 (and rising), ours was closer to 600—and most serious books fell somewhere in between. Plus we weren't just operating in that gap; commercial houses never foresaw that books like *The Essence of T'ai Chi Ch'uan* would eventually sell 100,000 copies.

On the advice of Andrew Aaron, our Swiss customer, I took most of North Atlantic's money out of "that pathetic excuse for a financial institution" and opened a money-market account at the Merrill-Lynch office on Center Street in Berkeley. Long accustomed to shifting sums back and forth between checking and savings to earn the most interest, I had never even heard of "money-market accounts," which apparently offered both high interest and check-writing with no penalty at all. When I wondered how this could be, Andrew said it was the way "people all over the world manage cash except for provincial American businesses gulled into letting banks steal their rightful earnings."

By sheer coincidence the floor broker on the day I arrived was Gary Berman, the son of an old Grossinger's (and Bob Towers) crony—when he heard my last name he asked whether I was related to the resort. He soon convinced me to try a few stocks.

My view of stocks was as something you inherited and sold as quickly as possible. They tarred you with complicity in corporate greed—you lost just by having them (whether you actually lost or gained). But Gary wasn't your typical Wall Street hack. He was an ex-SDS wise-ass who seemed to share my attitude toward big business and cynicism toward the Market. "Are you against stealing a few bucks to help publish great books?" he asked. "It's a lot easier than writing grants."

He had a scam going whereby a friend of a friend who knew a secretary in a regulatory office figured out from her phone records when a merger was going to occur and sent the company names by code. Gary was buying these stocks and selling them quickly at a profit.

"You may think it's only $450," he riffed one day when he told me he had bought and sold Bache in our account in less than twenty-four hours. "But that's a refrigerator or a washer and dryer."

He followed that up with successes on Kyoto Ceramic, Southwest Forest, Crutcher Resources, Union Oil, and Bally—two hundred shares a pop.

Unfortunately, after this hot streak, he lost most of the profit on a run of bad luck, as for instance when someone along the chain confused Ideal with Portland Cement. Then he blew a thousand dollars on Bally the second time around, $1900 more on an option on Mohawk Data Systems, and another $2000 on an Australian company called MIM. We were in the red.

I charged into his office furious because, as usual, he didn't tell us he was buying or selling any of it.

"Shhhh!" Gary soothed, as he wrote out a personal check to make us even. "Don't tell anyone. This is against the rules."

I hadn't spoken to my stepfather Bob in five years. He refused all my calls, and he didn't answer my letters. During Jon's fugue to Scranton, he let intermediaries speak for him.

His and my relationship had always been on two levels. In person we enjoyed each other. He was my original baseball companion—he always knew exactly what I could and couldn't do. He noted each slight improvement at bat or in the field. By contrast, my father Paul never once saw me play, not a single fly ball or swing, even when I was the third-baseman on the Grossinger's team the summer I supposedly worked in his mail room . . . despite the fact his executives pleaded with him to come. To have watched me would have broken a mysterious taboo between us. It was as though it was presumptuous of me to play his buddy Roger Maris' game.

All through my childhood, even after my name became Grossinger, Bob *was* my father. He taught me my bedtime prayers, entertained me when I was sick, helped me with my homework, proofread my school papers, let me compose advertising jingles for him, and showed my early writings to his clients and friends.

He was the father who drove me to Amherst and carried half my things to the top of James Hall to start Freshman year. When I spent college summers at Grossinger's, he visited me after his ritual stop at the Nevele. Together we paid Grandma a visit.

He was the worried father of Jonathan who called me in Michigan for help.

There was no reason for him to hate me.

Yet at another level I *was his enemy,* someone an unwritten law required him to hate.

I thought of how angry he got the time the son of his first wife, Gwen, phoned. "It's Buddy, asking for money, the creep!"

But Bob was married to Gwen barely a year, and from what I knew, Buddy was pretty old by the time Turetsky showed up. *I* was an infant in his house; *I* bore the name Towers for twelve years. Plus, I never asked him for money, except maybe the last time. Maybe. . . .

So what else was there?

Years earlier when he wasn't talking to me, my mother blamed it on Lindy's not being Jewish. "He can't tolerate that," she said. "He's boycotting you."

But he had great rapport with Lindy the few times we got together. He even singled her out for his "straight man" role because he admired her playful retorts.

Then there was the fact that Jonny's old girlfriend Mara was Catholic. That never seemed to bother him.

So was it ancient jealousy over Grossinger's? Blame for Jon's fate, for my going to Amherst when my touted brother only went to Wisconsin?

Guilt over the letter he asked me to write? Ambivalence toward my mother? Discomfort at seeing her neurotic patterns reenacted in me, as I changed from boy to man? Zionist rage against the infidel who married out of the tribe? Or something unnameable, the same kind of thing that precluded my father from watching me play ball, because even to look was intolerable . . . was taboo even to wonder what it was he wasn't allowed to look at?

When Jon told me his father was attending the *bas mitzvah* of his niece Gail's daughter in San Mateo, I decided to go too. Jon volunteered to get me Gail's number. When I phoned, her husband was gracious in extending us invitations.

On Saturday morning Robin and I put on jackets and ties, Lindy and Miranda dresses, and we wormed through Bay Bridge traffic down the Peninsula. At the entrance to the synagogue I placed a *yarmulke* on my head for the first time since my mother's funeral and handed one to a bemused Robin.

Bob either didn't see me or didn't intend to acknowledge me, though his sisters cast stares throughout the service, then shunned me afterwards. ("He told them you're after his money," Jon had confided, "which puts you in competition with them.")

"You don't belong here," Aunt Et snapped. Aunt Gus strode away from my attempted greeting. These women had once been my family. I had sat at their *Seders;* I had sung: *"Manishtanor halila hazeh"* for them. They disbursed chocolate coins in gold foil to me among the cousins at Hanukah.

I hung tough, walking up to Bob, a hopeful smile on my face. Startled, he yanked his attention from me to shout a greeting to someone on the other side of the room. Then he strode toward that person as fast as he could, shoving two teenagers roughly out of his way. ("Remember," Jon warned, "when my father thinks of you he imagines some black creature out of the dark lagoon.")

Midway through the party, though, he warmed to a brief acknowledgment, patting Robin on the head and dropping a few homilies as he rushed out early to catch his plane—a man on the run.

> Dear Bob,
>
> The idea that I try to get close to you because I want your money is an embarrassment to us both. Please don't demean or slander me by such a thought. You know who I am. I'm a kid who grew up in your household. You tell your sisters I'm trying to make you into a father as though it's a hustle and a crime, but I'm just stating the obvious. Who was the real father of my childhood? Who sat with me when I was sick? Who sang me 'Billy Boy'? Who pitched to me and applauded my first catches? Who bought me roast beef and orange soda at Isaac Gellis? Who kept you company on trips to the Goldman? Who drove me to college? You're as much of a father to me as you are to Jonny and Debby. Anyway the role of father in my life is not a simple thing: there's the father who raised me (you), my legal father (who never stood by me), and my genetic father I never knew. I don't have to propose a relationship. We already have one.
>
> Love,
> Richard

"You raise interesting points," he wrote back. "I'll think about them."

My letter about my mother's will had sprung an ancient trap. The enmity Bob felt toward me was so deep and unmotivated it was all but primeval—the creature from the dark lagoon. I knew it would take years to undo the damage, but I might have enough time.

I began to send him chatty letters about the kids and our publishing, and he answered them with brief congratulatory notes on office letterhead:

> Robin seems to be quite unusual and Miranda certainly has got to be in the "top 10" also.
>
> For a solo entrepreneur you've accomplished a Herculean assignment. Stay with it!

He ended ritually with a *Todah Rabba!* or *Kol Tov!* He was even inspired to send Robin a baseball glove from his sporting goods account—fresh in its square box with crumpled paper. This was an auspicious totem, not only for its timeliness and extravagance but because it was a prayerstick from an ancestor. It proved his essential generosity and good will.

Deep down, I knew I was going to make this right. I was going to reclaim my stepfather. I was going to do it for myself, and I was going to do it because my mother would have forbidden it. I could not allow her demons to prevail.

A week after returning from Scranton, Jon walked out of Food Liberation. Bob was now his only source of cash.

"I come for my money like Robin Hood," he announced. "It's the ransom you pay for never having been a father."

"Here." Reaching into his pocket and ripping crisp new bills out of his clip, handing them to Jon without looking. "Take this and leave me alone. You can talk when you've raised a family."

"You think you raised a family? You failed at the one thing a father is supposed to give: moral leadership. You had no values or beliefs. It was just a phony smile, accolades from servile waiters. You think the pushers are in back alleys and I'm the addict. But the pushers are right here, downtown, and you're an addict. You get your hit from money. You think you take money seriously because it's a big deal to you. But you don't take it seriously at all. You merely abuse it. You rush around town all day on your boasting high, then you crash."

Bob would sit there transfixed, charmed by the cadence of his own voice in his son. Some of the staff berated Jon for his cruelty.

"They pretend to be sentimental in his behalf. But I give him what he wants. You don't need to weep for him. He's got plenty of others to do that. Most of the people appreciate my visits. They're so harried, but we laugh together, my father too. I mean, we're all mortal, so this is a big joke. What is life? It's a chess game with death. That's all. You move. Death countermoves. You know he's going to win. That's the hell of it. But you keep making your moves, hoping to checkmate death. What's there to the advertising business except pawns and bishops? So I add surprises. The other day this friend who smokes with me came by and brought a loaf of bread. It turned out to be from Steve Rechtshaffen's commune. I took it to my father's office and presented it to him."

"Was he surprised?"

"He says, 'What's this, Jon? A loaf of pumpernickel?' I think he was pleased. I have only one enemy in that office. Old blond Cyclops Helen. She says, 'You make speeches like you're some sort of missionary. Liz has got three people on hold, and you're telling her *mishigas* about the Civil War.'

"Helen of Troy," he continued, "the original deity of strife and envy. She had her knife in Mom too—confidante and betrayer. Now she's in the service of my father. She's his wench. She always wanted him. Even when she and Mom worked together, she schemed for her friend's husband. Does she think just because it's modern times and she's working in an advertising agency that Ezekiel can't walk in the door? Why, we're living in an age of prophets: Dylan, Ginsberg, Van Morrison. Someday people are going to be amazed by them."

Twenty-Second Document

I think of you in a way that includes the Greater Past when, for instance I am in the Park in the early morning around the 96th Street playground, as I have been the past two mornings, very early, quiet, intense grey reflective mornings, the great thick trees, still there in their places, and our past together with Mom and Dad, and Debby, the 1235 building, and the long grasses growing tangly beside the black-poled iron fence and the staked fence around the playground and the vista of the sky to the north, the protection of the trees in the corners, the silver buckets (the swings) and the whole soft meditative grey-silver sheen, like tears, frogwater, time, the past, memory, endearment, love, unforced now. Really this is not nostalgia or escape, just a kind of throb of intensity that gathers shape from the past and is present so easily some mornings as the ghosts of our former lives of childhood were resurrected with the morning mists over the yellow grasses.

—written on the card entitled "At the Stile," John Henry Mole, Watercolor, 1871 (three young girls on a wooden fence under a tree with a basket in a sylvan section of a vast English meadow).

Twenty-Third Document

Happy Birthday!!!!! Wonderful November 3rd!!!!!

The beautiful Fall is here, colors galore, all the leaves in the park, the tree trunks, the grass, the water in the lake and reservoir, the blue blue sky, the white white clouds, the wind blowing through.

Hooray!!!

An infinity of Happy Birthdays to you!!!

On a separate enclosed card of Peter Brueghel's "Village Wedding":

Happy Birthday and many many thousand more until the end of time. I hope we live forever so that we can always be friends.

Miranda passed happily from Bright Star to Crestmont, but for Robin, after graduating from Crestmont, there was only Adams, the local junior high. Although the school featured an appealing big kids' environment, it was also out of control. Drugs abounded. In hallways of shifting crowds (90% African-American), blasters thumped, pencil points extended surreptitiously. Going to the bathroom was out of the question.

Robin hung around with a small group of Japanese and Filipinos, shooting hoops after school, always worried (he recalled) "some big black kid would come and steal our ball." One day, walking home with his friend Michael, he turned to see two high-fashion girls striding right behind them laughing. "Look at that white boy's pack," said the chubbier one. "It's so low it hits his butt." ("I was carrying it in a particularly dworky way," Robin confessed at dinner.)

"He's my man. Don't you sass my man," said the other.

California's Proposition 13 (cutting property taxes) decimated Adams. Robin's second year, a class per day was eliminated (either science or language—your choice). The mood ranged from shopping mall to armed camp.

Robin came home daily with headaches, so we were desperate for alternatives. In fact we already knew the options: The only viable private junior high in the whole East Bay was Head-Royce—expensive, exclusive and, most daunting of all, located well on the other side of Berkeley in the Oakland hills. Even if we solved the problem of getting him admitted late, we still had to deal with transportation.

When we phoned the administrative offices, the director of admissions said we were lucky because two students had just left eighth grade. There was a long waiting list for ninth, but they were willing to deal with a possible immediate enrollee in eighth.

We called in an absence to Adams the next morning, took Mandy to Bright Star, and then headed across town on the freeway. As we pulled up alongside the school with its prep-school playing fields, I felt a rush of nostalgia. My mother had escorted me to Horace Mann, the newly anointed son of Paul Grossinger, in a different era.

I longed for the ease and accessibility of then. I wanted to be able to give Robin a respite—for how hard he tried, for how good-natured he had been (about everything always, even his loony parents), how caring of Miranda. I was his father, for sure, and I flinched at the weight of having to afford this, the irony of wanting it for him even though I had rejected its equivalent in myself.

While he took the tests, Lindy and I waited in the library. Then the director of the middle school led the three of us to his office, where he conducted a brief interview. On the way out he advised us to think of next year.

But the next morning he phoned: "I'm surprised myself at his scores. He's a bright kid. You can start tomorrow if you want."

We wrote out our largest check ever (other than the house downpayment) and then faced a crisis of how to get him there. Initially we presumed the only solution was for me to drive the twenty miles every morning, then pick him up in the afternoon; but that was eighty miles a day, most of it in rush hour.

"I can handle it," Robin said after staring at a BART map and Berkeley and Oakland city maps. I thought of Jim on *Mission: Impossible!*, a show for which the kids demanded rapt silence. (Once when I violated the ritual by remarking how unlikely one of Barney's feats was, Robin snapped, "Rich, be quiet; they can handle it.")

So "Jim" could handle this. He had never been out on his own, even as far as San Pablo Avenue, but on Monday we drove him to the El Cerrito BART, showed him how to buy a ticket, and then watched him disappear into the station. His plan was to get off in the center of Berkeley and catch a bus. (We couldn't resist calling the school two hours later to learn if he made it.)

All day I watched the hours creep and that afternoon drove to the station to meet him. Two possible trains came and went, their commuters dispersing. Few moments have matched the joy I felt when I spotted our *Mission: Impossible!* child with his backpack, bounding off the next arrival in the crowd.

When Publishers Group West assembled a national sales force, Charlie Winton exhorted me to respect industry guidelines: "You've got to announce and publish by season, make professional sales material for our reps, behave like a real business." He expected us to be pleased by our inclusion in his upgrade, but I scoffed at the regimen and took a perverse pride in bringing books out willy-nilly, surprising him with titles he didn't even know we were producing. I hated marketing sheets and advance covers. From my point of view, Bookpeople had set the standards for countercultural publishing and, even though I admired PGW's Marx Brothers, disco culture, it had no right suddenly jumping in with the sharks and telling everyone to comply with their Madison Avenue rules.

"You're the last holdout!" Charlie would tease, keeping up a low-key banter and sales pitch as we sat with Robin watching the Mets at Candlestick on Art Richman's tickets, first-baseman Keith Hernandez's father unmistakable in the row behind us.

During that season Robin and I served as an eager audience for John Hernandez's stream of insights and invectives. In fact, we had plenty of our own challenges for him—by then we subscribed to two baseball newspapers and knew the Mets' farm system inside-out. He was amused by our amateur scouting reports and, on the way out one day, extended an invitation to visit him at home in Millbrae. A charming misanthrope, Juan (as he was called) sat on his living-room couch, scoring players and management with barbs he pledged me—to his mind, a sportswriter—would never see print.

I didn't realize it at the time, but my objection to Grossinger's and to the "adult" world of both my fathers made it essential for me *not* to do anything like them. Our books were myths and texts; they were not products like the ones Robert Towers hawked.

But the Wintons had never known the New York of Milton Blackstone. They had not even been part of the countercultural renaissance that spawned Bookpeople. Without embarrassment, they wanted to turn serious bucks. "Richard," Charlie argued, "we're not forcing you to do anything you don't want. You could do exactly what you're doing with just a few cosmetic changes and make it a whole lot more profitable."

I was blithe, even arrogant, in my resistance. My personal style ignored all parameters of decorum: torn jeans, uncombed hair, shaving maybe twice a week. Charlie, now dressing a whole lot better, stood by his desk, holding out a translation of Lao Tzu by Cheng Man-ch'ing I had delivered (twenty cartons' worth) the week before. He was shaking his head.

"Sorry," I said. "I forgot to tell you about that one."

"Then how do you expect us to sell it?"

I didn't, nor did I have any ideas about how he could sell a book of arty photographs of the Oakland A's with text by a local novelist.

"If only you had shown me this before you sent it to the printer," he moaned, "I would have told you to back off or at least print fewer copies. This is too much aesthetics for the baseball market and not good enough printing for the photography market. You missed them both."

I was dismayed but, in a certain sense, I didn't care. I stood by what I was publishing because I believed in it the way I believed in John

Todd's feng shui and Bira Almeida's "playing in the light." We were publishing primary-source documents. To worry whether they sold or not was blasphemous. I wondered why Charlie couldn't get that.

Yet, contrarily, we couldn't afford private school unless I earned more money.

I had once charted the economics of wharves, boats, and fishermen, so in principle I knew how to invent co-publishing schemes and distribute shares. I enlarged my relationship with Homeopathic Educational Services and added the Platonic Academy, Weehawken Books, and Les Blank's Flower Films. I rebid typesetting, printing, and shipping—bargaining nationally for the best prices. I felt like Jasper buying and selling lobsters, Bob Towers haggling ad rates.

Books were our gig. So why not?

If I was publishing anyway, I might as well do it with at least as much intention as I projected into the Mets' minor-league system. Even Ben Lo, Skip Rappaport, and Dana Ullman wanted me to sell more books.

We were in this game for keeps.

The second year of Robin's commute we decided to see if we could afford a house closer to Head-Royce. Through months scouting with an agent, we gained a sobering recognition of how either expensive or ramshackle Berkeley was. There were no bargains. By the time we agreed to look at an unlikely blue Victorian on Blake, we had been through more than three dozen properties.

The Blake Street house, essentially an enlarged single-storey cottage, was located in a noisy but cheap student neighborhood off Telegraph Avenue. Not formally on the market, the place was less desirable not only because of its location but an unfinished, windowless second floor. The owner, a young contractor friend of the agent, was fed up with being a landlord, so he agreed to lay concrete on the dirt basement (a potential warehouse) and to add a deck at a good price (in place of termite work on the back porch). We took him up on his offer and quickly sold the Richmond house.

Already an urban veteran, Robin led Miranda through Telegraph's *Mad Magazine* landscape—bizarre characters everywhere, early '80s punks, homeless and disabled people in greater numbers than anywhere else in America, the Hate Man who yelled at everyone (especially children), plus poster and comix stores and inexpensive restaurants. We had moved from nowhere to the center of the universe. Our kids made weekend forays to the Blue Nile, which served Ethiopian food eaten with fingers on torn-off chunks of spongy flat circular bread, and Berkeley Thai House with its spring rolls and stuffed chicken wings.

Nearby on College Avenue Robin was able to catch the bus for Head-Royce, while Lindy or I walked Miranda to grade school at LeConte on Russell a few blocks away.

Blake is the house Miranda dreams of as her childhood. I remember its deep, complicated backyard with the fallen acacia, a gigantic fig surrounded by white moldy globs ("dead mice"). We hoed a garden and planted rosemary, lavender, coconut thyme, bee balm, purple and golden sage, and thick white curry plants with yellow blooms. Around them we set lemon bushes and a plum tree.

Robin made his studio in the garage; there he built furniture, including items on commission. For our house he designed a glass coffee table and another table with a scene of creatures inside a Plexiglas top plus a secret compartment that dropped open with the turn of a hidden latch. When Lindy and I wanted to buy a bed, he dissuaded us and put in hours with saws and a borrowed lathe to produce a replica of one he sketched in a furniture store, complete with headboard, shelves, and cabinets with doors. Then, over the course of a year, he hammered scrap wood into a three-room, two-storey playhouse between the garage and the fig. He and Miranda decorated it with rugs, posters, and appliances painted pop-art real. They attached a buzzer with a battery for a doorbell. Water came from an upside-down jug in a holder.

After chopping up the acacia, I decided to explore its stump. With a shovel and a pick, I got under its perimeter, a periodic blow of an axe to split exposed sections. It took almost six months for me to loosen the network of corm and roots. Finally, slicing and removing the last cords of the underground system, I found myself waist-deep in the largest hole I had ever dug. Since we were designing John and Nancy Todd's book on small ponds, I knew to spread plastic in the hole. Then we filled it with water, put in tropical fish and water hyacinths, and "inoculated" it with broth from the pond behind the original Berkeley

Urban Integrated House. After a week of raccoon vandalism, Robin surrounded the ecosphere with a bench.

But we hadn't taken into account the original hydrography, notably the defunct "Blake Creek." When heavier-than-normal storms drenched California that winter, we had the only pond that *emptied* when it rained: Gullies from the hills seeped under the plastic and floated it up. We had to check constantly to make sure our fish weren't swimming off through the grass.

Soon after we moved, I finished *Embryogenesis* and sent copies to a number of New York houses. I got a quick offer (with a sizable advance) from an editor at Avon who planned to rush it into print the next season. "I was born," he said, "to publish this book."

Meanwhile, under the title *Nuclear Strategy and the Code of the Warrior,* Lindy and I began work on an anthology about samurai principles and war. Our contributors included Jungian psychologist James Hillman ("Mars, Arms, Rams, Wars: On the Love of War"), physicist Freeman Dyson ("Weapons and Hope"), globalist Gordon Feller ("Spiritual Dimensions of World Order"), journalist Thomas Powers, playwright Arch Oboler, and Charlene Spretnak, a feminist historian at Berkeley who submitted an essay titled "Naming the Cultural Forces That Push Us Toward War." She and Lindy met for lunch one day to discuss the piece, and the next evening she offered Lindy a job in a program she ran teaching technical writing to engineers. Beginning the next term, three days a week Lindy put on a helmet and rode her bicycle to Cal.

A novelist friend named Gerry Rosen, who had been unable to sell his latest book in New York, wondered if North Atlantic would be interested. We hadn't been successful with literary prose, but *Growing Up Bronx,* while comical for my taste, was a bittersweet portrait of the counterfeit American dream. After our publication, it ran up a string of good reviews, including a glowing one in *The New York Times Book Review.* Monday morning a customer phoned from the Big Apple. His Madison Avenue bookseller had told him, "Goddamnit, you're the thirteenth person who's been in today asking for that book. We don't have it!"

When *Embryogenesis* was in page proofs, Avon fired not only my editor but the publisher as well. There were 15,000 advance sales, and the text was in plates. Yet the entire project was cancelled.

I soon realized how lucky I was.

I bought the film for a fraction of the advance money, had Paula design a new cover. Then we put the book out ourselves.

"Why?" I asked Avon's managing editor. "I don't get it. You could just finish the press run, recoup the advance and your typesetting costs, and then let it go out of print."

"Because," she retorted with unexpected candor, "the new management wants to stick as much red ink as they can on their predecessors."

In such a milieu it was no wonder that North Atlantic Books was competitive.

When a cult classic, *The Wizard of the Upper Amazon,* went out of print with Houghton-Mifflin, the author, Bruce Lamb, a retired forester living in Santa Fe, contacted us through a mutual friend. First we edited and published his sequel, *Rio Tigre and Beyond;* then we issued a second edition of *Wizard.* We also picked up a former Doubleday book by local author Marc Lappé. It had gone out of print under the title *Germs That Won't Die;* we renamed it *When Antibiotics Fail.*

We added new martial-arts and alternative-medicine titles, a translation of the French screenplay of Alain Tanner's *Jonah Who Will Be Twenty-Five in the Year 2000,* and five experimental novels (including Gino Sky's tales of the "cowboy Buddha" and Elwyn Chamberlain's account of a physicist reincarnated in Kentucky in the hound-dog litter of a Vietnam-vet marijuana farmer).

Our growth was more than an availability of manuscripts; it was alternative distribution networks rivalling those out of New York. When I sold *Planet Medicine* to Doubleday in 1977, the difference between our possibly publishing it and their publishing it was like the gulf between a garage sale and a multinational corporation. Now, seven years later, the mystique of the New York houses had been shattered. With computerized distribution, on a title-by-title basis it was hard to distinguish between North Atlantic and Random House. We used the same production techniques and printers. Without New York's rent, overhead, corporate rivalries, publicity lunches, and manufacturing waste we could launch a dozen new titles a year . . . and do it Charlie's way.

In Richmond, Robin and I had lamented not being able to follow the Mets on the radio. Yet it was an outmoded desire: technology had advanced enough that TV was actually more accessible; in fact, some Bay Area cable systems already carried Channel 9 from New York. We knew the games were up there, but our local cable company refused to offer them.

On Opening Day 1984, driving on 101 through Marin, I stopped at a store that had a satellite dish on its roof. Although (by my own admission) not a potential customer, I was invited to the big screen by salesman George Grapman, a longtime Mets fan from New York. In the course of the afternoon, while we watched Mike Torrez and staff get blown out by the Reds, we brainstormed a co-op baseball dish in the East Bay—a place where people could gather to follow out-of-town teams.

I took George's notion that night to the annual preseason bash at Cody's Bookstore on Telegraph. I warned that the dish was a longshot. If we failed, everyone would get their money back.

I hadn't taken into account the emerging fad of rotisserie baseball (people drafting their own imaginary teams and holding fantasy tournaments all season based on their players' stats). When I left a sign-up sheet, a startlingly large number pledged $100 each. In one night we had half the money needed.

George's boss offered to install a dish in exchange for that down-payment plus our monthly dues. Now we needed a site.

Fans visiting bars, apartment complexes, and store-fronts found no takers willing to mount a free satellite dish in exchange for viewing privileges.

After two fruitless weeks, George crossed the San Rafael Bridge and worked his way through Berkeley to Blake. As we sat in the backyard with tea and cookies, trying to think up new sites, he suddenly jumped to his feet and stared at our collapsing garage. The former owner had offered to raze it (since it was more termites than wood), but we elected instead to waive it from the termite report. A carpenter from Wisconsin, in exchange for a place to stay that summer, had put a foil roof on the building. Since then it had been Robin's studio.

George was ebullient. He enumerated the garage's advantages: it was close to everyone (especially us), free, and—most fortuitously of all—had a clear look at the satellite sector of sky. To confirm that, he stood beside me on the roof with surveying equipment and, position by position, called out the teams we were sure to get. It was—finally—all of them!

Two carpenters showed up Monday morning and hammered plywood to keep the building standing. The next evening a crew from Cygnus Satellite built a mesh pie on its roof, mounted it on a pole, and dropped wires through a hole. A hopeful crowd broke into a spontaneous cheer as the video screen became Merlin's crystal and materialized a raw feed of the Cleveland Indians out of static.

In one of the last dreams Charles Poncé and I studied, I was walking on a beach in moonlight carrying a corpse in my arms. I deposited this ungainly bundle into bubbles of a black tide.

I was glad to be rid of it.

Then suddenly I realized: this was my own body!

But it was *I* who carried it—something else was dead.

For years I had failed to replace Ian or Polly, nor was I training any longer with Ben or Martin. At Bira's invitation I had tried capoeira, but the class was mostly black and Hispanic kids in their twenties. Cartwheel right followed by cartwheel left finished me. While I sat one day, mind wandering, in the cab of a truck towing our Maverick with its busted timing chain, I glimpsed a man in the sideview mirror. I was no longer young. I had lost seven years preoccupied with children, publishing, and the Mets.

I called Richard Heckler and made an appointment.

We squared off in his office, meeting each other's wooden swords, trading strikes and blending. He called it a lesson in activating and passing through fear. Then, excruciatingly between his fingers, he rolled the flesh around my Adam's apple "to let you feel," he commented with surprising offhandedness, "how the Mongolian samurai prepares for battle."

Over the following months he took me beyond exercises and gestalt play into a realm of spiritual practice.

He instructed me in sitting meditation. When a few weeks later I still hadn't begun *zazen,* he asked, "Aren't you curious to find out who you are?"

One night I awoke and stared into the "thing" again. It was all it ever was, even vaster than I remembered. How could I have deemed it a mere "spook"? It was bigger than the whole universe.

I had no ploy, no identity against it. I existed either by its grace or its negligence. My mother had jumped into it.

I struggled for its boundary, its name. It felt like raw wind, carnivorous stars (without the decorative span and twinkle of the night sky). But even these were just words and what pressed against me was incarnation itself, in all its boundaryless vertigo, its tenacity to declare itself over the entire labyrinth of life and death as something else again.

I sat riveted against the headboard, praying it would pass. I tried to pretend innocence, to appease it with my terror, but these were also words or—at best—concepts. I knew beyond a doubt that death would not end this. Death was a concept too.

It ended by itself. It didn't actually end; it stopped noticing me and merged back with night.

"You met the big one," Richard said. "We don't try to handle that wave; none of us do. Too much energy, too much sorrow, and probably—if we could ever allow it—too much joy. So we stay in place, pray quietly, and let it pass through."

By the 1985 baseball season Robin was almost sixteen. We drove to Candlestick the first May evening the Mets came to town. Picking up comp tickets, we came through a passageway behind home plate, the diamond luminous below. Stalling my long-planned exploit, I sat watching batting practice. Then, clutching the press pass (courtesy of *The Village Voice*), I pushed open the gate, took a few steps, and stared back at the stands.

I felt as though I were breaking out of jail before 15,000 spectators.

I stood at the batting cage beside Darryl Strawberry, Hubie Brooks, and the rest. Soon I was eavesdropping on their banter as though it were my own pick-up game. The ball was real, the shots were high and deep, but these were still kids, mocking each other's swings, spoofing with exaggerated dances and exclamations, faking "hot foots," and shoving each other out of the box. The crack of the bat and arc of flight were mesmerizing.

Later that night, emboldened by the drama of a come-from-behind, extra-inning win, I eyed the next taboo. Fortunate to find an elevator descending with sportswriters to the bowels of Candlestick, we stuck with the group until a guard halted Robin at the end of the tunnel—only one pass and, anyway, the kid was too young; he had to wait here.

As Robin picked a spot along the wall, I was directed toward a door. I walked through it into another universe . . . players striding about, undressed and undressing, Mookie still shouting the win, others grabbing cold cuts off a table, ripping open beers. My eyes darted around, trying not to meet eyes, which was difficult because almost everyone was familiar. Then I blended into the crowd interviewing Doc Gooden—hard-driving white male questions, good-humored homeboy responses.

I felt a sudden claw. Unannounced, Art Richman, who no doubt appreciated my being in his locker room about as much as my father once enjoyed Michael and me in the Grossinger's kitchen, had grabbed my elbow and was leading me to Frank Cashen, the General Manager. Art was going to do the right thing if it killed him. "This is Paul Grossinger's son," he said, "you know, from the Catskills. He's a writer."

I can't say Cashen was enthusiastic or that I approved of the introduction, but Art was both helping me and, at the same time, making me pay for my intrusion. I asked the GM if he'd be willing to talk.

"Tomorrow before the game," he shot in quick unenunciated words, plowing through the mêlée.

Ed Lynch, the tall, studious righthander, brushed past, adjusting his tie knot: "Lynchie," Arthur crooned, "you're on the list. Right there with George Brett, Willie, and the boys."

"What list, Art?" teased Lynch.

"My pallbearers." Then he turned to me. "They gotta treat me right, Richie, or I'll get someone else."

"Who's Willie?" I asked.

"Who's Willie? C'mon. Willie Mays."

Then I noticed Ron Darling dressing alone at his locker. He had been the starter that night but was knocked out early. The year before, when he was at Tidewater, I had sent him a copy of our baseball anthology. Now I walked over and introduced myself. He remembered the book, thanked me for it, and was willing to chat.

Putting on his shirt, he talked about the game, saying he didn't feel too bad about his performance, he knew he was doing better each time. I wished him well and returned to ordinary space-time.

Robin was where I had left him. "I'm just standing here," he told me in astonishment, "and Tim Leary walks by. Then Danny Heep. And Keith Hernandez!"

The next day we made it to the ballpark two hours early. As the guard stopped Robin again, I continued in.

Darling was standing by the door. When I told him about my son, he said, "I want to meet him."

Out in the tunnel, in spikes and uniform, towering above both of us, he shook Robin's hand and asked about school, baseball, Berkeley.

While we were talking, Frank Cashen wandered past and, although part of me thought to let sleeping dogs lie, I reminded him of the previous night's offer. "I've got a bit of time," he said, distractedly checking his watch. "Let's find the sun."

As we continued toward the field, I started to give Robin instructions about meeting up later. Yet he joined us unchallenged—perhaps Cashen unintentionally intimidated the guard.

We proceeded down the tunnel onto the diamond.

Cashen surveyed the scene and chose the bench in the home-team bullpen. "Is this okay?"

"Sure," I said. "Sure. It's great."

As we took our places, Herm Starette, the Giants' pitching coach, wandered over, greeted Cashen with a handshake, then sat down. Mel Stottlemyre, an ex-Yankee of my youth (who was the Mets' pitching coach), took a seat on the other side of us.

The three of them ignored the two interlopers as they reviewed old Oriole teams. Players wind-sprinting by, Robin and I were proverbial bugs on the wall. Finally Cashen petitioned queries.

I asked him about obscure players in the Met system from Little Falls to Tidewater. He answered candidly, ad-libbing the future of the team he was trying to build. As I scribbled in shorthand, it became just another day at the wharf, a lazy sun, the GM occasionally needling his charges ("Tommy Gorman, my hero!" as the unheroic relief pitcher jogged past) . . . Robin taking over and getting us the scoop on John Gibbons, Dave Cochrane, Bill Beane, Kyle Hartshorn, Herm Winningham, Cashen not missing a beat. This could have gone on forever and we would have stayed, but there was a game to play.

The GM walked us down the tunnel, back past the clubhouse (where Ron Darling shouted, "Good luck, you two!").

It was a thousand moments I had lived or imagined living with fathers real and fictional—now as both father and son.

"Did we really do that?" Robin mused, as we flowed anonymously into the Candlestick crowd. "Did we just sit in the bullpen talking with Mel Stottlemyre and Frank Cashen about the Mets?"

For a short time Miranda joined her brother at Head-Royce. Then both kids wanted out. The bus trip to school consisted of wealthy brats yelling out the window and throwing trash at homeless people, showing off Reeboks and jewelry, sneaking designer drugs. The P.E. Department was conducting grudge boxing matches (and didn't want to hear about internal martial arts). The more radical teachers were departing en masse.

So our kids transferred—Miranda to The Academy, an eccentric school across Telegraph Avenue, where she had teachers from India, Africa, and South America and took both Latin and algebra; Robin to College Prep, a serious private high. Then our daughter, who had written so many daffy scripts for her friends at Crestmont and performed bathtub improv, began attending a local drama studio and acting in their plays. These were no longer children.

Uncle Paul moved his mother from an apartment in Hollywood, Florida, to a retirement home on Sutter Street in San Francisco. Suddenly Grandma Sally was in our neighborhood, so we hosted Rothkrug family dinners every few months.

Grandma could hardly believe that I now passed as a normal adult with a polite wife and (by her rigorous standards) well-mannered children. "Never have we had one like her in the family," she proclaimed at the sight of Miranda. "This is a great beauty. This one will be a star."

That winter I became friendly with Alain Naudé, a homeopathic physician from South Africa who had travelled for years with Krishnamurti as his private secretary. He also played classical piano.

There was an ancient, apocryphal link between this man and the Rothkrugs, yet every time I tried to get him to one of our gatherings he claimed another engagement. Finally I persuaded him to perform for my grandmother at a time of his choosing. On the appointed day, I conveyed her from the Broadmoor to his parlor for fancy dessert and a concert.

All that afternoon Lindy and I treated Sally like the grande dame she imagined she was. Alain behaved likewise, reminiscing about the districts of Capetown they shared.

She could not stop praising his tarts, his tea, and his talent. "I have never heard anyone—anyone!—play so beautifully," she said.

"Except perhaps you," he responded, "in your prime."

Each baseball season a rotating group of some thirty viewers congregated in our garage, peeing in the mulch heap. Lindy wondered how she ever approved such a lodge. For Robin it was the dream baseball clubhouse, a musty old shed with branches growing through, a single bare bulb, everyone's donated rotting chairs, Babe Ruth and Jackie Robinson on the walls, adults tossing wisecracks.

Our main regular was Stu Zacher, a floor broker at the Pacific Exchange and an uncompromising Mets fan. He was a classic New Yorker who didn't know tomatoes grew on a vine until he was astonished to find them in our garden ("What the hell are those?"). After Glenn Hubbard set a hard tag on a Met runner, he screamed, "The next guy who goes down there on a doubleplay, put him out for the season." He turned to me and added, "The guy's not gonna be able to walk."

Hearing of a Cubs injury he shouted, "Six months at least, I hope." He actually considered Jim Frey and Tom Seaver traitors. "If I were traded to another team," he remarked, "especially a Chicago team, I wouldn't go. I'd just quit."

"You think they should quit?" Robin asked.

"Absolutely. The only two things that should never happen are the rearming of Germany and a pennant in Chicago."

One night, as Lindy and Miranda ate inside, Robin and I joined the crowd in the clubhouse with our plates. Robin went inside between innings and came back with a message for me from Miranda: "She wants to know if she has to eat her spinach." (She was probably dissatisfied with Lindy's response.)

"Yes," snapped Stu before I could answer. "And give her seconds."

Never hiring a repairman (though I put him in touch with George), John Hernandez called me from Millbrae whenever the Mets were on the low Eastern Galaxy satellite he couldn't get on the dish Keith had installed for him (either a house was in the way or his system was improperly calibrated). He wanted a complete account of each of Keith's at-bats because his son might phone at any moment from the dugout for feedback. Club members struggled pathetically to meet his rigorous standards of depicting stance and swing. We were dumb fans; we didn't see what happened in a "Don Juan" way. Only Robin, with his carpenter's precision, was an acceptable reporter. If he was there, the old man said, "Put the kid on."

Early one game Robin specified the exact position of Keith's hands; then he popped out. "As I thought," the baseball Juan pronounced, and he promised better results the next time.

Keith came up in the seventh—the Mets down a run, a man on first—and put a shot into the right-field bullpen. Club members were howling and banging the walls. This loop was absurd. Certainly no one in the New York I came from would believe it. Then the phone rang.

"See, what did I tell you!" boomed John.

But that was what Berkeley had become for me, a kind of festival in which impossible wishes were granted and the irredeemable past was reclaimed. I would hardly have believed myself standing beside Hubie Brooks in the Mets' clubhouse, having him pat my fanny as he hooted at Game of the Week and imitated Pascual Perez running from a fight! This was vintage Grossinger's 1955. I wouldn't have been anywhere near the action in modern Manhattan. But then I could never have launched a publishing company there, or trained with Ben Lo and Richard Strozzi Heckler, or sent my kids to private schools. Berkeley felt like Manhattan without its penthouse prices, impenetrable empires, and gridlock.

I met my prospective co-publishers and authors for a Telegraph Avenue version of "power lunches" at the outdoor Japanese cafe and Thai patio, yellowtail sashimi or squid salad, inventing book concepts to present to PGW. Meanwhile Charlie, himself a club member, came by periodically to check out the dish. ("Grossinger, I used to say to myself, 'Why the fuck do I need you!' But you turned out to be a big surprise.")

In fact, I was the most truly surprised, not because I had been successful, not because I made such wonderful choices of titles, but because what was actually required was so meager. From the legendary kingdom of Grossinger's to the Zises chauffeured on Wall Street to the mysterious B———s, the world of finance had always seemed an outermost galaxy spiralling from me at light speed. I took my identity as childlike outsider for granted—the tarot renegade at Amherst, the bearded anthropologist on fishing wharves, the poorest paid faculty member at Goddard, the last holdout at PGW. But publishing turned out to be easier than winning ideological battles at Michigan or salvaging curricula at Goddard. It was easier than sitting on the Advisory Board of Grossinger's or writing the Grossinger novel. If Charlie had known these things, he could have told me so in the beginning (and saved us both some grief). What he didn't know was how it felt to grow up with a false mythology of power. He didn't have to first fight the minotaur to be allowed into the war room. In fact, he didn't even have to pass through the labyrinth.

Gary Berman soon invented a new category of scheme, which involved buying a stock and, at the same time, puts and calls on it, so that, he claimed, we made money no matter what happened. "It's a hole in the system," he explained, running a pencil through an illegibly scrawled diagram of 150, 155, 160, and 165 arranged vertically with intervening lines and crisscrossing arrows. "As long as the market doesn't move. And historically how much has it moved? It goes up; it goes down; it always returns to the same place. Even the bigshots in our New York office love it. One guy said, 'You've got yourself a helluva strategy.' Of course, he had a better one—just wouldn't tell me."

Month after month, anywhere from a few hundred to a thousand dollars showed up in our account.

Then Gary advanced to buying puts and calls in an odd index called OEX. I got at least one hyper phone call a day from him reporting on its movement (or better yet, its lack thereof). OEX entered my dream life, a constellation in the astral sky.

It seemed, as our broker juggled phone calls, he had a thousand clients. With his dry, sarcastic wit, jiving left and right, he was the king of Berkeley Merrill.

Then Hutton made him an offer he couldn't refuse. The irony was that as soon as he moved to Hutton, Merrill found another site and Hutton grabbed their offices. "You can now visit me in my new office at my old office," Gary proudly informed his clients on gold-embossed invitation cards.

I didn't realize it then, but our broker was a small-time hood, gambling on everyone's account, getting his commission either way. Then one morning—*"This market is on fire!"*—the terrifying words of KCBS' reporter at the Pacific Stock Exchange, terrifying for Gary's clients.

It's still on fire more than ten years later. But Gary is no longer a player. He lost twenty-five percent of North Atlantic's assets before Hutton dismissed him. He emptied the accounts of widows and retirees, who are probably waiting yet for the fire to go out.

"They never should have let a kleptomaniac like me handle other people's money," was his sole comment on his way out the door.

One afternoon Marty Asher, the editor at Quality Paperback Book Club, made an appointment to check our list. He was impressed by the basement publishing enterprise and our range of titles (though the snob in him never selected anything). At 4:30 he noticed a rush of people down the driveway toward the garage.

"Mets game," I explained, pointing to the dish on the listing roof.

"Goddamnit!" he exploded. "That's the last straw! You live in California, set your own hours, publish what you damn please; now you get the Mets, which I can't even do on my fucking midtown cable."

It was as far from the axis of Integrated Resources and Michael B——— as imaginable . . . Michael my supposed half-brother, who didn't even send Bingo's photograph.

Book Five

B———

1

The Yuppie Rebirth of Grossinger's

IT WAS BEGINNING to seem as though I would never meet my real father. Lying in bed some nights, I tried to imagine an entrée to him. I fantasized private detectives, chance encounters. (In one such scenario I cast Fred Wilpon in the role of a business partner of Bingo's, agreeing to invite us secretly to the same party. In another fantasy the B——— family needed a slightly removed blood donor for a child with an illness.)

Sometimes the whole affair seemed inflated and narcissistic (after all, it was just genes and cells; any chromosome I had from Bingo also existed in millions of other people).

> Dear Bingo B———,
>
> I cannot compel you to look at things the same way I do, but likewise I ask you not to blame me for keeping our relationship alive. This event is filled with mythic overtones—the forgotten past, the lost son, mistaken identity, etc. But I don't think there's anything to gain by

making too much of this. Others have been father and son, respectively, for both of us, and that's not in the cards anymore, nor was it ever really.

I have not been as discreet as I could have been. By writing you I have created possible embarrassment for you. But you have not been flawless either. You had the chance to respond in the beginning and tell me either that you didn't believe it was true or that you didn't know for sure but wanted it dropped. I guess since you are convinced you have nothing to gain from this you will continue to ignore it. I cannot take that prerogative from you. If you choose not to meet, or even answer me, then my only option is to write you in silence.

Sincerely,
Richard Grossinger

I reminded Uncle Paul of his one-time offer of assistance.

"I'll try," he said, "but I doubt I can overcome his almost certain objection. What *do* you want from him anyway, Richard?"

I scanned my presumptions one by one, thinking to pick out the most legitimate. They all rang false. I didn't want his love, his friendship, or his financial support.

I couldn't articulate the hole in me his very existence left.

Then I passed a beggar on Telegraph—a toothless man, hat sliding off, sad, irrefutable face. As I dropped coins in his cup, I saw that the borders of the city were visible, the rain was real, the light glittering on the pavement an actual light. His smile and thank you for so little gave me the answer.

"Just his blessing. Tell him I want his blessing—upon me, my children, and the generations that will follow us."

April 15, 1985
Dear Mr. B———:

My nephew, Richard Grossinger, has asked me to be in touch with you. He has heard that you were his mother's friend many years ago. Even after ten years, the manner of her passing continues to affect Richard deeply.

Perhaps you could find a few minutes to chat with Richard. If you can find it in your heart to do so it would be a "Mitzvah" which could help both to put his own life and his memory of his mother in better perspective.

Richard Grossinger is a good and decent man, a scholar and publisher of good books, with a charming wife and two lovely children. You would enjoy meeting him.

My wife and I plan to be in the New York Area the week of the 13th of May. With your kind permission, I plan to call you at that time.

Sincerely,
Paul Rothkrug

June 5, 1985
Dear Richard,

I spoke with Bingo, Monday, May 13, and have been pondering my message to you ever since.

The response was negative—well, more unconcerned than negative, like "Don't bother me with something that has never really been a part of my life."

Richard, you have missed nothing by not knowing Bingo. He has nothing to offer you—believe me!!! My own reaction to the brief conversation was anger, but then why should I be angry with a total stranger who displayed no interest in meeting my nephew.

Your parents were and are Paul and Martha, regardless of speculation about certain biological questions. Bingo B——— has never been a part of your life—and in truth was never really a part of your mother's life.

Put this thing to bed as you have so many other problems you have faced and overcome.

Love, Paul

Dismissing its significance was what they always came back to—"Downplay it," they warned, "because nothing can be done, because it leaves you at a disadvantage, because it opens old wounds." But I continued to believe that unconsciousness was an even greater danger, to Bingo and his kin as well.

Then, in November, Bunny sent me the clipping from the *Times:*

Benjamin J. B———, a co-founder and president of B——— Global Enterprises, died of a heart attack Monday in New York City. He was 78 years old and lived in Great Neck, Long Island.

In 1929, Mr. B———, along with his brothers James, Morris, Samuel, and Joseph, founded B——— Global Enterprises, now an international corporation, specializing in real estate and entertainment.

In 1958, he founded another company, the B——— Group, which

> is involved in producing and distributing movies internationally. At the time of his death, he was the President of the organization.
>
> Besides his brother James, of St. Petersburg, Florida, he is survived by his wife, the former Sylvia Edelman, and four sons, Michael, of New York City; Seth and Ruben, of Los Angeles; and Joey, of Tarrytown, N.Y.

Years later I told Barbara Joseph how I tried but never got it done.

"I didn't expect any different," she said. "He ran, just like the first time, his tail between his legs."

The mystery here wasn't consigned to our lifetime. It was a work of karma, the chain of lives and souls beyond termination. Whatever it would take to resolve it would be done, but Bingo B——— himself, the father who never came to the party, was heading at light speed toward whatever destiny brought him in the first place. At last, it was in the hands of the gods.

The end came suddenly at Grossinger's. Bunny called with the details. She hoped the deal wasn't as bad as it looked. "In truth, we get nothing. At least your father gets nothing. But then no one else had to put up all their assets as collateral. You'll be disgusted to hear that some so-called long-time loyal executives are part of the sale—on the other side."

> The news that everyone had been dreading was confirmed in 1985 [wrote Stefan Kanfer in his book *A Summer World*]. Grossinger's was to be sold to developers. Hidden details began to emerge. The centerpiece of the Jewish resorts had been losing money—a projected $1.8 million in 1985. Occupancy had fallen below 50 percent.

I had always assumed Paul had hidden something. "You know Peeg," Jerry MacDonald would laugh, "he's been playing cards long enough to know how to bluff. There's a nest egg somewhere." (Bunny nursed that myth right up to her last disappointed visit to his safety deposit box after his death.)

His secret was that there was no secret. All of Grossinger's had crumbled into a set of Grandpa Harry's cuff links (Bunny enshrined them in a plastic cube with two old dimes to remind herself that was what

Harry Grossinger left his son—by mistake in the back of a Joy Cottage drawer). They also shared with Elaine a contract for royalties on rye bread (expiring in two years). All the rest of a thirty-million-dollar fortune had evaporated.

Our family made it to New York on a windy September day. As gusts blew glimmerings down streets and lost them in blue sky, we returned to Bob's office for the first time in years. On the phone the bestower of the fabled baseball glove had been stand-offish, arranging only for us to have a glimpse of him near the end of his working day. He did hold out the possibility of dinner if his schedule allowed.

When he saw our family, he was visibly moved. The kids were suddenly so big and mature, answering his questions, telling him about their schools, politely attentive as he indicated signed photographs of Billy Martin, Don Budge, Chaim Weizmann on the walls.

He marched us through Robert Towers Advertising, introductions to the staff. "I can't understand why no tennis with you guys," he kept insisting. "A majestic sport, Robin. It has baseball, basketball, and football all wrapped up in it—grace, power, speed. It's swimming; it's track and field." He had become quite a player himself on the local seniors circuit and was now the promotional director of the Tournament at Forest Hills. He pointed to photos on his desk that documented visits to the Concord with Vitas Gerulitis, Bjorn Borg, John McEnroe—Bob beside them, a million-dollar smile, his racquet returning an imaginary lob.

"You've got a great family, Richard," he pronounced, centering his hat. "I think of when you, Jonny, and Debby were kids and—." He broke off with a shake of his head. "It's been a long time since I took you to the Russian Tea Room. Remember, Lindy?"

She nodded.

He picked up the phone.

"Bob Towers—Max, give me five. The Grossingers will be accompanying me [as if Max had any idea who we were]—fifteen minutes."

I asked if we could call Jon and invite him too.

"What do you want with that ingrate? Do you have to embarrass us with a guy who hasn't brushed his hair in five years?"

But he dialed the number and handed me the phone. "Richard.

How incredible! I was thinking of you this morning when I saw the brilliant blue heavens. I felt your presence." He said he'd meet us as fast as he could run the two miles.

I reminded him to brush his hair.

"Not for my father, but for you. In honor of the occasion of your being in New York I will make myself—as he puts it—presentable."

After I hung up, I suggested Debby too.

"C'mon," Bob said, "she hasn't spoken to her brother since the day of their mother's funeral. She won't be seen in public with him."

"Okay, let it go then."

Robin and Miranda were in a slaphappy mood as we took the elevator down. "What's the matter, Miranda?" Bob teased. "If you're going to be an actress, you've got to keep stage presence at all times. Practice watching these New Yorkers. Do they ever have it!" He flaunted his own stage presence, directing our attention to immediate landmarks, including the site of the old Grossinger office across 57th Street from Carnegie Hall. He performed right into his opening act—"our table, good sir" . . . menus . . . the order.

Breathless and weird enough to send a ripple through the restaurant, Jon arrived midway through shrimp cocktails and soup. The maître d' found him a jacket and tie. With childlike excitement, he took a seat next to me and began whispering. I was impressed that Bob didn't back off. He made it clear this was his son. He had the maître d' go through the entrées again. He even teased Jon about his manners. "What's wrong? It's been so long since you've had food that you've forgotten how to eat?"

Humor was redemptive. We heard about Robin's carpentry, Miranda's theater, Jon's adventures in Central Park, Lindy's new job teaching engineers at Cal, the satellite dish, Juan Hernandez, the state of North Atlantic Books.

After dessert we took leave on the street, as Bob hailed himself a cab. Jon walked us to the garage where we had stashed our rented car. We had agreed to come to his apartment, and he was delighted, wanting to run forty blocks uptown and meet us there. I told him that wouldn't work. Apprehensive—almost phobic—he got in the back seat with Robin and Miranda and was silent all the way.

He regained buoyancy the moment we became ambulatory. Brushing himself off as though removing a spell, he pranced into the elevator and said a polite hello to two elderly women.

We walked down the hall. He opened Apartment 7Q. Shades were drawn tight. A heavy grass smell met us. He turned on a light.

It was almost bare. Holes were burned in Mrs. Golden's expensive carpeting; stacks of books were propped against the walls. "The shire," he announced. "Humble but satisfactory for a hobbit."

He motioned us to have seats. There were only places on the floor. Then he showed off sections of his library—Indian ethnography, European novel, American novel, poetry, Mediaeval religion. He brought out a motley assortment of foreign coins and other artifacts, including carved ivory and feathered men. He disclosed these with gentle care to Robin and Miranda. Then he grew mournful.

He described a noise rising from the garage next door. At first it seemed as though he were reporting a minor nuisance for the sake of satire, but he went on at such length my appreciation of it grew. Every morning, he explained, hundreds of cars parked there, the gates opening and closing for each one. "It's a horrible cry! Like animals being killed, every moment, one after another. And that's what it is, an animal; only they don't realize. This city goes on mindlessly every day, killing, killing, killing." As his voice rose, Lindy put her arm around Miranda.

It turned out—as the story of the screeching door unfolded—that he had been to the garage on dozens of occasions and had yelled at the proprietors. He had even called the police. Promises were made, "Yeah, yeah," but nothing had been done.

As soon as we absorbed that epic to his satisfaction, he took up another problem: the next-door neighbors. A young Italian couple, they played music at night so loud he couldn't work or sleep. When he pounded on the wall, they laughed and pounded back. "I tried to reason with him like a human being, but it's no use. I explained to the guy that I do a lot of reading, I need quiet; maybe he could confine his music to the hours before midnight so at least I'd know when to escape. You know what he said?"

We waited.

"He said, 'Man, I'm not going to change my lifestyle for you!' Can you believe that? He taught me a lesson. All these people out there, my father included, rushing to work like lemmings, rushing back, filling the air with poison, rushing to their death, trampling on the bones of the ancestors; that's what they're all saying—'I'm not going to change my lifestyle for you, not for you Mother Earth, not for you, birds and plants, not for you, ancient island!'"

His sentiments were legitimate if irredeemable. I felt their burden of melancholy and inertia.

I was carrying a record of a song I had liked recently on the radio—John Denver and Emmylou Harris singing "Wide Montana Skies"—having just found a copy at a store on the way to Bob's office. Jon wanted to hear it but didn't have a 45 adaptor. I suggested centering the disk on the turntable.

"I do it all the time," he assured us. We eyeballed together. Then, warbling slightly, the band began:

"He was born in the Bitterroot Valley in the early morning rain.... wild geese over the water...."

Melody and words broke through a stasis. I looked at my brother and hardly knew what I thought anymore. I still hated him. He had earned his squalor and misanthropy with acts of incredible hubris. The pitched battles of childhood had been real, and the part of me that sought exoneration was appeased. I also wanted him to be happy. I felt profoundly how his condition saddened all our lives.

In my mind's eye I saw him and Mara hiking through Idaho back in the '70s when nothing bad had happened yet.

Jon wasn't born in the Bitterroot Valley, but those mountains were kin to his bitter-root American soul.

"Bringing the warm wind from the South, bringing the first taste of the spring...."

Why couldn't it have been that simple? Why couldn't we have lived among protecting spirits, an innocent downpour of seeds and rain? As I looked at Robin, Miranda, almost full-grown, I sensed the mystery beyond me, beyond us. The words that seemed to speak to Jon suddenly spoke in another voice:

"He never knew his father and he never did ask why.... /And he never learned the answers that would make an easy way. /But he learned to know the wilderness and to be a man that way."

In the song was everything Jon wasn't, yet everything his myth stood for. He was living—even overliving—the whole damn life without having been born.

Only Lindy, Robin, and Miranda—the sheer fact of them—redeemed me. Their company gave me courage and kept me from being him.

"Oh, Montana, give this child a home. /Give him the love of a good family and a woman of his own."

Yes, yes. Every sentient being. Give us a peaceful planet like those in Andromeda, a passage through rainy northern forests, geese so remote and wise they relieve the vision quest that calls us through lifetimes. Take this shroud of madness, this dying City, this sorrow not to be the hobbit called to millennial adventure.

"Giving a voice to the forest, /giving a voice to the dawn, /giving a voice to the wilderness in the land that he lived on."

I slumped back into my yearning and realized it was answered always and also not answered, that there was a remoteness and haunting in me too, a "Montana" that reached out yet into Indian summers for something unrevealed.

I wanted so much more than the reprieve I felt finally in our car, our tight foursome, fleeing up the Harlem River Parkway.

My brother's next communication was several months later, his voice hushed and dramatic. "Richard, I want to tell you something. Will you listen?

"I was taking a nap yesterday in Central Park. I had seventy dollars on me, a bag of grass. Suddenly I see this shadow. He's incredible-looking—Aztec maybe—silently gazing down at me. He says, calm and cool, 'I could have killed you, just like that. Now your life is forfeit to me.' He asks if I have anything, so I hand him my money and my grass. Then he says, 'I've killed guys like you … but I didn't kill you. Now you must follow until I release you.'

"We went out of the park uptown. He changed the City, just by telling me things. We passed Yankee Stadium. It was a Roman temple. He pointed it out in the distance. The Bronx was a Cheyenne village. He asked what I paid for the grass; then he laughed. Here I thought I knew so much, but I was paying my father's midtown prices. We went into the South Bronx. He said, 'My name is Char la`tan.' He spoke it just like that, Char la`tan. 'I'm from Nicaragua.' We went to a bar, all black and Puerto Rican except me. He bought me lunch. You dig: he took my money, but he bought me lunch. Everywhere—on the street, in the bar—people called him by name. 'Char la`tan.' Warrior.

"People like him, the ones outside society, they're my kin. I don't believe in any phony revolution like the Marxists. Char la`tan was a native to the wilderness as much as any Apache. The South Bronx, that's not a slum; that's how cities get when nature starts taking them back, making them places where warriors do battle, shamans go on vision quests."

"You've found another lost tribe for the Bureau of Aquarian Ethnography," I told him. "They're more coherent and powerful than the Scranton one."

"Char la`tan and I were on separate vision quests in the Park. He recognized this and took me. That's a teacher, someone who finds you. We played this incredible game of pool, me and him. Everyone gathered around and watched. I would have been dead in that bar without him, but they paid me respect. And I matched him shot for shot."

"Well, you play a great game of pool, Fast Eddie."

"Right, and he was Minnesota Fats. Between the meals and the drinks he spent more money on me than he took. He gave me my life back.

"I realized when I got home that you and I were always on different paths. I never told you how afraid I was of being called chicken. I couldn't be dared. Harry Pin was the beginning. You had it right in your story. He was the biggest kid and he challenged me to fight him. And there were so many fights, Richard, you don't know about, that Mom and Dad didn't know about. One day at Horace Mann when I was in First Form this guy in the Second Form was throwing snowballs at us, daring us to stop him. So I picked one up, walked right up to him, and fired it in his face. He was shaking. He said, 'Meet me behind the gym tomorrow.' I was never so scared in my life. All night, all the next day I thought about him. When I was pissing in the bathroom he came into the next stall and said, 'I'll see you later, you lard of chicken shit.'

"Phil Dicker accompanied me. He was my second. The guy could see I was terrified, but I stepped up and threw the first punch. He wrestled me to the ground. He looked at me and knew he had won. From that day on he had mastered me and I could never be anything around him. That's why I stopped playing football, only track; no more team sports, just solitary ones. I was a coward.

"And when Char la`tan told me my life was forfeit I went quietly with him. You were right about the track meet too. Steve Rechtshaffen was the short man; I was the long-distance runner, carrying the wand for eternity."

Twenty-Fourth Document

Dear Richard the Lion-hearted:

'cause it just don't pay
to buy our own
might as well
steal from rich folk
and call it
yr own

heard from Robin Hood, located wandering in a wood in England in 1136

Down to my father's for money. Travel on foot through the park, wet with thawing ice. My father writing furiously in his smoke-filled office early in the morning before nine o'clock, only he and Helen there. He, tense and down, against my exuberance and essential happiness, well-being, and calm. I show him two books I plan to read. I tell him I am very happy with the fact I have three friends. I tell my father about the three of them, saying their names and telling about their uniqueness from each other. I then say, with a sly little chuckle, there's a girl. My father lifts a one-half perked, one-half still weary, there's-nothing-new eye . . . but then I say she's married, and my father isn't looking up toward me anymore but is burrowing back into his work, communicating (not very abruptly, with a sort of 'oh, you were fooling me' resignation) that the rest will not be interesting to him. All the rest of the day is just trying to live the old shire life within the town of Mordor or Murder. . . . you know how t'is, my darling brother.

Twenty-Fifth Document

This letter is being composed in attunement with Quicksilver Messenger Service on the stereo in the Castle of Inquiry or, in other sign language, Apartment 7Q, 7 for seven planetary metals—Gold, Silver, Quicksilver, Iron, Copper, Tin, Lead—and Q for Quicksilver and/or Queen, the Marriage, the Completion of the Work.

Everything I will try to say to you will have to do only with that mythic world in which you and I are brothers, the Twins, and exist as such, timeless, fermenting in the egg. When I look above me within the house of my life, or into the alchemical egg/crystal ball of my life, I see the two older males, my brother and father; they are the two houses reigning in my sky, two deities. These two ruling dynasties are always warring with each other from deep-seated enmity. When I learn later in history classes about the Wars of York and Lancaster it is the same thing.

Twenty-Sixth Document

I send two birthday cards, for I want you to have both abundance from the rich countryside—the warm brown, ochre, gold, green, orange tints of the earth that are in the other card—and also good fishing in Winter.

Despite what you say about the voyage of exploration into outer space, I have reached a firmer conclusion that the Space Program's attempt to create an outer space is an attempt to put us in a mindless void. There is no outer space. And nobody walked on the Moon. You can't "go" to the Moon. It is not a place you can go to. It doesn't exist physically in that sense of taking a trip to a certain place. They went somewhere in their rocket ships but it was a back toilet bowl in Hell.

But it is possible, the myths show us, to go to Moon's house or Sun's house. Sun will be out during the day but his wife and child will greet you and he will come back in the evening. Moon is abiding in a cave, a long-limbed old-man giant, sprawled in his cave. All science-fiction space-voyaging is puerile projection from increased transportation.

—Written on a card of "Winter Fishing" by Moiolot [two burly peasants holding lines on either side of a bare tree with the patchwork of farms and wild fields across the river beyond them].

[Second Card]

Happy birthday. I would like to be with you in this beautiful country. Isn't it fantastic? All in motion, all things about their business, scurrying, hurrying, or in place, like the horses. Everything is getting its food, what it needs, for the winds are coming, the Fall and the colder weather are arriving. All is electric and vibrant. HAPPY BIRTHDAY

—"Peasants Returning from Work" by Rubens [horses drawing a rickety wagon, others carrying produce and tools; in the distance, vast fields with haystacks, horses, a dirt road, trees, two large birds going in the same direction].

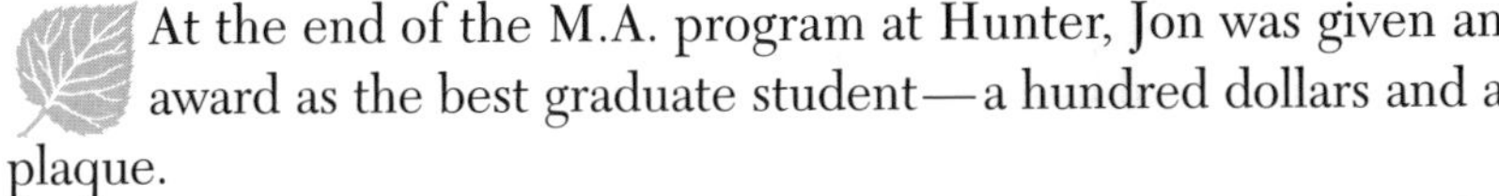

At the end of the M.A. program at Hunter, Jon was given an award as the best graduate student—a hundred dollars and a plaque.

Later that week he felt mellow enough to go to another Turetsky Passover. He even managed to sit quietly respectful at the table. "I was next to my six-year-old niece. She turned to me and said, 'It's dark and scary down here.' I think maybe the faint candlelight. I told her, 'It's dark and scary up here too.'"

Supposedly the new owners of Grossinger's were constructing a yuppie paradise with condominiums and health clubs:

> The reborn Grossinger's ... would have as many as 2,000 town houses, condominiums to be built alongside the 25-acre lake and the 27-hole

golf course. Favorite buildings, among them the Grossinger playhouse, were superfluous. They would be razed.

My father was allowed to continue living there, guaranteed a murky role as consultant to the new owners. Everyone else left.

For another year (because a legal document gave him that right) PG lived stubbornly on the Hotel grounds. He stayed in Joy Cottage, in fact in Jennie's old room, attended by a maid named Iselda. His balding, lame husky, Sam, had to be restrained from attacking anyone who approached (and barked so loudly that my father could not understand visitors even with his hearing aid). Bunny moved to her apartment in the City.

What PG saw and heard all day was the wrecking machines liquidating the world of his childhood, cottage by cottage. He had chosen, without telling himself, to suffer personally the demolition of Jennie's kingdom.

In October 1986 Eddie Fisher was huckstered into town to press a button detonating the playhouse where Eddie Cantor discovered him—the pun being to "bring down the house" a second time. Stefan Kanfer described the scene:

> ... [O]n a floor carpeted in bilious green, under a ceiling of dingy acoustical tile, a few score of Grossinger veterans and journalists gathered to witness the destruction of an old building and an invocation of Jennie's sacred memory. "I think she'd be delighted," said William Meyer, the confident young president of Servico. He went on to describe the changes planned for the coming year: the gourmet dining room, the spa, the whirlpool, the thermal wrap, the two-bedroom condominiums priced at $125,000, the 8,000-square-foot action lounge targeted to young people.

Only Sam spoke Paul's agony, perhaps Jennie's too.

That same month the Mets moved to national TV, the satellite dish superfluous. Robin and I sat stunned in the garage in the aftermath of an impossible come-from-behind World Series victory, watching Kevin Mitchell and Bobby Ojeda goof on an uncensored raw feed from the clubhouse ... because someone had inadvertently left a camera on and we happened to be watching that transponder. Tim

Teufel, playing sports announcer, held up a fake microphone: "Bobby, Bobby, how does it feel?"

Talking into his beer can, "It feels incredible, Mr. Teufel."

Then Mitchell, spitting suds on him, proclaimed, "It's because he's swimming."

"Yes, I am swimming. But I don't feel it. I don't feel a thing."

By the next summer Robin had finished junior year and was ready to look at colleges. Without Grossinger's, we picked as our base a town we knew well, Northampton, Mass. From a house we took care of while its owners travelled with a theater troupe, we ventured out on tours from Harvard to Princeton.

The Mets were not our East Coast priority, but I had promised at least one trip to Shea. When a timely home game showed on the schedule, I decided to combine it with a visit to a potential new literary agent on 96th and Madison.

My son and I set off after breakfast and drove through Massachusetts and Connecticut—too promptly, for we arrived in my old neighborhood an hour and a half early. We put the car in a garage, then walked a few blocks to a grocery store and bought juices, bread, and cheese. We sat on a bench in the 96th Street playground, making our lunch.

Robin smiled at a class of mostly Third World kids as they hopped beside their teacher, teasing and pushing and running ahead. He was amazed to think of me as a child coming to this place, a meeting ground then of European nannies and Park Avenue kids. He was old enough that we could mourn together the loss of our youth.

I had made no plans to see Jon on this trip. I hadn't been calling him because he was high all the time and had become a preacher of epiphanies on my dime. Still, being in his neighborhood sparked an irresistible urge. On the way back to Madison I spotted a phone booth. I knew his number by heart.

No answer.

We sat in the lobby with ice-cream popsicles. Mr. Agent arrived. "Give me twenty minutes," he shouted as he caught a closing elevator on the run, "to get my day in order."

I decided to walk back to the phone booth. The ring was picked up immediately. "Richard, I just came home," he exclaimed; "I had a presentiment something was going to occur."

I felt terrible. Time was short, and we were headed to the ballpark after the meeting.

"Then I'll run to where you are."

Standing on the corner of Madison, Robin and I began to scan the people approaching. "Is that him?" Robin remarked. He was pointing to a shabby old man across the street.

"No," I laughed, "he doesn't look like that yet!"

But then I did a double-take. It *was* Jon in the body of this creature, bent over in some inexplicable way, as though his back had a hump in it—a giant figure loping along, staring left and right. He came breathlessly up to us. I thought to hug him but couldn't. He just stood there, panting, eyeing us with one side of his face like a Cyclops. His skin was tight around his bones like a mask. His hair was unkempt Rastafarian, a pleated mass of knots in strings down his back. His pants were ripped open from the crotch so that his underpants and upper leg were exposed. His face had aged and deepened. It was no longer even a hyperbole that he looked like the men who lived on Telegraph Avenue. If I had passed him there, I would not have recognized him.

This was no charade anymore. This was it.

After telling a brief Apache myth he remarked tenderly that Robin was now taller than his father, his hand measuring a height somewhat beneath his own but above me. In fact, in some ways Robin resembled a young Jonathan. He had Jon's large bones and curly hair, his sweet intense look. But he also had Lindy's calm and lucidity, her steadfastness. I wanted my brother not to scare him, but Robin took Jon in without judgment. They chatted amiably about the amount of energy coming off the sun, the mindless horror of all these cars tearing along.

"I like Jonny," Robin said, "because he's different."

My brother left us by racing down 96th Street, hitting the stone wall fullspeed at the Park and clambering over it in a single vault like a yeti.

In the autumn back in California, I had this dream: I was in an auditorium where Robin was supposed to perform in a school play. He didn't like the script, became angry, and stomped out.

Everything suddenly dropped through a black hole. Years had passed, and we still didn't know where he was. I felt an unrequitable despair. We had blown it—my son was out there in the world, lost to us forever, like the child stolen from its clan by the voodoo-master in *Windwalker.*

The scenery deepened. I was walking down a street toward the ocean, a moonless night, late in the history of the world. Like the Sioux chief in the movie, I wanted to resolve the matter of my missing child before I died.

Just before the road ended, I came to a bench on which a person in rags lay asleep. I raised the blankets off him and looked. I thought—"This is horrible. This is my son.' But it wasn't Robin. It was an anonymous hobo. He stirred. Pulling himself up, he turned into my brother. As he threw his arms around me, he became Robin too. Sobbing, he said, "Rich, don't ever leave me again."

I didn't know how I could find enough love inside me to salvage us.

When the year of grace ended for my father (and the sham of his being a consultant), he relocated in Bunny's apartment. It didn't seem to matter. Either place he spent the day in bed, watching TV.

I was prepared for the end of Grossinger's, but I was shocked by the swift curtain with which Blackstone's myth was dispensed. For Bunny it was even worse. There was no money, no savings, no insurance policy, not even any furniture. Paul Grossinger had left his wife in a position of having to go back to work full-time in her sixties just to support herself and him.

He thought I didn't visit him his last year on the grounds because I was angry I wasn't going to inherit anything. He didn't understand that I couldn't look at the Hotel in demolition. He didn't remember he had lied—lied so consistently and impudently that he left no role for me.

"But you were," Bunny appealed, "the one noble thing he did."

"Yeah, but I'm not even clear why he did it. Was it love? Or did he just want to possess me the way he wanted to possess Grossinger's . . . or you, or my mother?"

"I think your father loves you, Richard."

I knew she believed this; yet I suspected he had spent his whole life making sure he kept us grateful and waiting, in the end wanting only to compel our pity. He had gone down with the ship because he didn't want to give anything to anyone (even as he pretended not to want anything for himself). In his final hurt guise, he seemed very much the picture of false martyrdom.

Reemployed as a travel consultant, Bunny brought my father to a convention in San Francisco. I crossed the Bay Bridge and saw him for the first time in two years; he was standing in the hotel lobby between the florist and men's shop. I felt waves of sympathy for this man who had once been my hero. "What's your grievance with me?" he asked as I led him onto the street. I offered to tell him in exchange for his help in resolving it:

"My grievance is simply that you never trusted me enough to confide in me, nor ask my advice, nor give it a second's thought when I gave it anyway. You pretended to be an expert when you weren't." He stopped and stood before me, his mouth open. "Even that's not the problem. I will always be sad because you deprived us of any real intimacy."

"I?" he asked incredulously.

I nodded. "You guarded yourself from me; our relationship can be no better than that now."

"You think *I* was the reason for the Hotel?"

Yes, I thought that too. I knew he wasn't the sole cause, but he had dozens of chances to preserve something. He had rudely rebuffed suitors and then let envious relatives, greedy accountants, and corrupt lawyers steal the little bit left. And out of pure sloth! All he ever wanted was to wallow and be left alone. "Yep," I said.

"Richard, don't you know? It was the *yarmulkes* that killed us!"

Even when I saw him the following year in New York he never acknowledged his role in the decline of Grossinger's. He acted as though nothing had changed.

We patronized the same expensive restaurants at which owners and maître d's seemed equally unaware that he had left the Mountains and the Hotel wasn't Grossinger's anymore. "I hear you're reopening in the spring," the headwaiter at the club at Shea Stadium chirped as he led us to just about the best table in the house, not hearing my father stutter that he was no longer in the business. "I'll see you next season," he added. "No bill!" The meal was fair trade. I imagine Paul ate many such dinners during the last years in New York, looking around the room, waving to his admirers, former guests and staff. It wasn't that everyone was uninformed or naive, not in the late '80s in the Apple. But they adored this man, the roly-poly host of the G., a languid dreamer pretending to be a tough guy, who never gave up the ship.

To the east of our Blake Street house was an apartment building owned by a retired architecture professor named James Prestini. For years he had rented units, but now, in his eighties, he was turning it into a library and nonprofit foundation. With emeritus status at Cal, Prestini was a renowned artist, a recipient of delegations and camera crews from Europe and Japan. His wood bowls—considered revolutionary for their genre—were on display at the Metropolitan in Manhattan. A giant metal square resembling a gateway to the "other universe" from *Star Trek* dominated his backyard.

Prestini enjoyed the anonymity of apartment living and its privilege of grumpiness. He didn't want to be a small-talk neighbor. Though we imagined ourselves the great intellectual publishers next door, he ignored us, except to growl about stray whiffle balls in his yard and the dying avocado we shared. When courtesy compelled discourse, he preferred to answer by aphorism. "Running down but not rusting out!" was his usual response to "How are you?"

He didn't comment on gift copies of books left by his door and, though admitting to being a Yankee fan, scorned the satellite dish and wouldn't visit our club by invitation to watch his team. When we held a party for *Jonah Who Will Be 25 in the Year 2000* (with a free film showing) at Cody's Bookstore, we invited Prestini, who had let slip one day that he admired the co-author of the original French screenplay, art critic John Berger. Toward the end of the event, we were pleased to spot him in the back of the room.

The wife of *Jonah*'s translator knew Prestini from her circles and remarked that in his prime he had a reputation as one of the toughest graders in the history of Cal, giving few B's and *never* a single A.

Prestini did notice one member of our family. He kept a watchful glance on playhouse construction, tables being hammered together, and the skeleton of a great secretary-desk temporarily brought outside for maneuvering room. Now and again he would bark an authoritative suggestion: "Buy better wood. If you're going to do it at all, do it right!" He didn't seem to gauge that this wasn't another graduate student.

Undaunted by censure, Robin took to visiting the tenement for regular sessions with the "professor" and his post-doc assistant Roger. A natural mimic, at dinner our son made us feel as though we had been there.

"'You gotta get your hands dirty!' Prestini told me. 'You've gotta be in the right place at the right time. And even then you need luck.'"

"Of course," said Lindy.

"You know why he came out west? He said they didn't like Italians in Massachusetts. He went to Chicago. Two major artists were there. I can tell you their exact names because he wouldn't continue until I could pronounce and spell them: Ludwig Mies van Dur Rohe and Laszlo Moholy-Nagy. Van Dur Rohe was an architect, and Pres said they both came from the Bauhaus in Germany. Now, Mans, this is how he talks: 'Frank Lloyd Wright, hands down, was the greatest artist of his time, no competition. But he was a lousy teacher!' He said it just like that! [Mandy giggles.] 'He didn't turn out little Wrights. Mies van Dur Rohe turned out little van Dur Rohes.' Then Roger nods, and Pres turns to him. He says, 'In an applied field such as art and architecture, studying with a master is much more rewarding than going to college. Instead of getting it second- and third-hand, you get it right from the horse's mouth. His way might not be the way *you* do it, but it's the way *he* does it. You don't want to go to places like Harvard or Princeton because they think that craft has no intellectual content.' While he's saying this, he takes my hand like this in his own, which is shaking. 'You want to make a chair, you figure out what you have to do to make a chair. You make a chair. End of lecture.'"

By senior year of high school, Robin was working saws part-time at Ashby Lumber to earn enough money to buy hardwoods. For his January internship (a requirement of College Prep) he put in a week with Prestini's friend Gary Bennett, a 260-pound, six-foot-five Oakland woodworker who shot at rats out his back door. Robin performed this at the CPS assembly:

"The guy before me was describing how he filed papers in a lawyer's office, and then the girl before that helped write petitions for Cal PIRG. I worked on just the legs of one chair. But it was a $2000 chair. Gary threatened if I didn't do things right he'd sit on me."

The highlight of the assembly was Robin's story of the boss aiming his handgun. "I said, 'Gary, I think this is how people get killed.' He thought about it for a second and said, 'You're probably damn right, but I wanta get me one of those rats.' He was always complaining about artsy-fartsy types and techno-weinies. But at the end he not only paid me for my work, he also took care of my parking ticket and gave me a hand-scraper and a burnishing tool."

Out of the blue, we were hand-delivered a karate manuscript by an African-American former Marine who had learned martial arts in Okinawa and was currently doing gang mediation in L.A.

What had started with one t'ai chi book was evolving into a singular niche of publishing: the martial arts as literature and philosophy. Then came its *tour de force.*

Richard Heckler had left the Bay Area in 1985 and '86 to participate in an experimental military program—teaching aikido and meditation to the Green Berets. It was a speculative venture for all parties—precarious for the Army to introduce alternative practices, vulnerable for the soldiers to open themselves to internal work, and daring for Heckler to risk aspersion from the Lomi community and ridicule from his new pupils. Yet his stint would change the way the Pentagon conceived of Special Forces training.

When he got back, I asked if he had written anything.

"Just journal notes," he said, reluctant even to share them.

I convinced him to bring his notebook to lunch. Opening to a random section, I confronted a man at a meditation retreat wearing a black T-shirt with skull and crossbones:

> Something is wrong. 'People don't wear T-shirts like this at meditation retreats,' I tell myself.
>
> 'But the person inside the T-shirt looks like someone at a meditation retreat,' the voice responds.
>
> I look back.
>
> The skull and crossbones glare menacingly back at me. "82ND AIRBORNE DIVISION: DEATH FROM ABOVE."

> I have no mental file for what I see. Killing and meditation simply do not go together.

I turned the pages and stopped where four-letter words caught my eye:

> They're angry at authority, angry at having to be silent, angry about the food, angry that we would judge them, Special Forces soldiers. They are contemptuous of Eastern thought and at the idea of a Special Forces soldier sitting in one place and meditating. The cacophony of shouts and insults is suddenly broken by Rader, who stands up, his six-foot-plus frame filling the room. He takes a few menacing steps forward and in turn gives each of us the finger as he bellows, "Fuck you and fuck you and fuck you!!!"

"Hey, this is incredible," I told him. "This is the book of the century."

"C'mon," he laughed, "you've gotta be putting me on."

I wasn't. A month later we started working on a manuscript about "teaching awareness disciplines to the military elite." Richard's title was *Warrior's Aim, Healer's Heart,* though ultimately Charlie renamed it *In Search of the Warrior Spirit.*

Meanwhile, I followed up a story in the San Francisco *Chronicle* about Richard Hoagland, a local science writer who had founded an organization to investigate the enormous "statue" of a Sphinxlike face and adjacent pyramids photographed on Mars by NASA in 1976 and then ignored. The implications of such artifacts were staggering. Who would have set our likeness staring upward from the surface of another planet? When? Why? Every possible answer left us in a far stranger universe, a universe that defied conventions either of biology or history.

Hoagland's manuscript on the topic had been bought originally by Prentice-Hall, then moved with a buyout to Simon and Schuster. They didn't know what they had and released it. In fact, their editor thought that astronauts had already walked on Mars. She wrote Richard, "Surely if there was a face, they would have seen it."

"Either these features are natural," he commented one day in his characteristically lofty tone, "and my investigation is a complete waste of time, or they are artificial and this is one of the most important discoveries of our entire existence on Earth. If they are artificial it is imperative that we figure them out, because they do not belong there. Their presence is trying very hard to tell us something extraordinary."

"Remember that!" I remarked. "It goes on the back cover."

We published the manuscript a year later under the title *The Monuments of Mars: A City on the Edge of Forever.*

Before Robin left for college, he brought the secretary-desk out into the backyard for photographing. It was finally finished: drawers, inlaying, glass, nobs, trim, secret compartments—four years of measuring, sawing, carving, sanding, and staining.

Prestini spied from the other side of the fence. He often stood there hunched like a rabbit on hind legs, waiting to point out a wood scrap he wanted to trade with Robin, or to toss us some of his extra geraniums, or to heave back a whiffle ball he had found while gardening, or to wait out Robin's attention so he could plant a jibe.

On this splendid occasion, we broke etiquette and insisted he come over. He shook his head and began to trudge away. But Roger coaxed, "C'mon, Pres, give the kid a break."

Without acknowledgment Prestini turned, circled the fence, and navigated himself into our yard. He made his way there as slowly as humanly possible, casting the satellite dish a disparaging glance. He finally stood before the desk. Shielding his eyes from the sun, he circled it, touched it, detected each flaw, and called it out: "What happened here?"

"That was three years ago, before I knew how to do that."

"No excuses. What happened here?"

"Blew it, Pres."

"Fine story! What happened *here?* Did the wood deteriorate?"

"Remember, Pres. I started from scrap."

"Always use the best materials. You won't regret it."

He stared a few minutes more, then turned to his underling. When Roger didn't respond, the master asked, "What do you think?"

"Looks okay to me."

"You better watch out for the younger generation, Roger. They're gaining on you."

He circled again, opening and closing doors and drawers, even allowing himself to be shown how the secret compartment worked (for which he had to bend and cock his head). Then he straightened up and headed toward his own yard. About halfway to the fence he paused and, with the barest hint of a smile, said: "Ordinarily we don't give A, but in this case we'll make an exception."

The yuppie rebirth of Grossinger's was another pipe dream, perhaps also an act of criminal negligence. After spending forty million dollars making their mess (or a hundred million, depending on the source), Servico fled without even starting to construct a habitable hotel. Another small-time crew (a real-estate broker, a tax attorney, and a financier) bought their debt, promising "to bring [The G.] back to the splendor and glory of what it used to be, but in a modern way"—meaning 1500 rooms surrounding a 200-room tower, seven restaurants, slate and marble to give a Santa Fe look—"a Club Med type of thing" with its own entertainment troupe.

After tearing down more of the remaining structures, the second group claimed bankruptcy too. (According to The Associated Press, "Construction at the hotel halted when more than a dozen contractors filed liens totaling more than $8.7 million against the hotel owners, contending that they had not been paid for renovation work.")

Once gravity took over, Grossinger's sank into a pit so deep that it seemed only a matter of time before the wilderness covered it. The indoor pool cracked like a Roman piazza. Weeds and snakes poked through sand on the ice rink. Moles and stray cats met in ruins of glass vestibules and kosher kitchens.

The debt found its way to banks in London and Tokyo. The remains of Grossinger's were bought from them (May, 1993) sight unseen by Soung Kiy Min, a Japanese businessman from Korea, who loved to play golf and had been searching the international classified for cheap courses. After remodelling a few rooms in the Paul G. wing for fellow fanatics (most of them Japanese businessmen), the new owner set up shop at the clubhouse with karaoke singing and a card room. His Jewish and Japanese clientele were almost exclusively male.

Min had no idea that his prize was so legendary, but, once he found out, he was amused enough to rename it "The Grossinger Resort." In the clubhouse he hung photographs of celebrities at the old G. Behind the bar a VCR was programmed periodically to play the 1948 film *Back to the Catskills,* featuring Lou Goldstein leading Simon Sez and Tony and Lucille teaching dance classes.

By 1996 the clubhouse had become a full-service Japanese restaurant with sushi, sashimi, and tempura. Though the bulk of the old Nichols site and Lakeside Inn remained in disrepair, Min still hoped someday to renovate fully with a spa and theater.

Grossinger's held power and desire for a generation. Then the transportation revolution took Americans to Club Med and Disneyland and left it, not unlike the old *kokhaleyn,* a backwater in a rapidly spreading slum. The family vacation with its communal spirit and camaraderie died when the nation traded its inner life for shopping malls and motel chains.

In the words of Milton Kutsher: "After Jennie died, Grossinger's started to lose business. They always had religious people as guests, but they now went all out for the religious crowd because they had to get money from someplace. As the whole thing started to crumble, it was obvious to all of us. But while it was happening, you couldn't believe it. This hotel, which had been head and shoulders above everyone, this hotel which ran like a clock for so many years—all of a sudden it started to stumble and lose its way.

"They weren't spending money. They had the same knotty pine lobbies that hadn't been changed for years. You know how many times we've changed our lobbies at Kutsher's? And even when you make them nice, they can't last very long. Styles change; things wear out. But when Grossinger's closed, even though we were competitors, we still felt bad."

Grossinger's was the victim of the oil embargo, the insurance crisis, the legalization of gambling in New Jersey, and the general decline of the Catskills, but also of a bizarre series of intra-family chicaneries.

Pettiness and stupidity are what stand out, and we have heard this story, or its equivalent, hundreds of times on *Dallas* and in Danielle Steele novels, better done. Just because it was Grossinger's doesn't make it any more significant. In fact, what has been happening for generations in the Amazonian and Southeast Asian rainforests and throughout Eastern Europe and Central America leaves Blackstone's luxury palace, by contrast, a speck of provincial vanity.

The heritage of the Hotel is one of corrupted wealth, missed opportunity, xenophobia, and greed riding the tiger for all he's worth. It ends in Vegas and Atlantic City, with resorts modelled on Grossinger's exploding through "Star Wars" technology into robot/entertainment wars—performers who began in the Borscht Belt, now working glitter stages arising phoenixlike from New Jersey/Nevada debris—and no one missing a beat.

My cousin Mark, a gentleman and the last family member to try to run Grossinger's, died tragically when the rotor came off Donald Trump's helicopter returning to the Taj Mahal from a boxing promotion in Manhattan; he was Donald's righthand man. He lived a *Mona Lisa Overdrive* reality in which the resort business portended post-apocalyptic casinos on the Moon.

The Graus of course gave up squabbling over the golden goose and got bought out while the fairy tale was still in vogue. Their children became financial-service innovators, Wall Street revolutionaries. They participated at the top of the limited-partnership, junk-bond era. They ran shopping malls, insurance companies, and leasing enterprises, moved to Long Island, and sent their kids to Chipinaw.

My brother Michael became an art therapist at a prison in Scranton.

My brother James married Mindy, the sister of Mark's wife. He joined his cousin briefly in Atlantic City but, loathing the casino scene, came home to open a restaurant (Jimmy G.s') by Monticello Raceway. The meadows and woods of his Sullivan County were vanishing. The ethnic wars of Brooklyn were sweeping north and west. Jimmy sold to the first buyer (maybe the last), then fled twenty-five hundred miles west to a management job at the Mirage.

Las Vegas was an endless Grossinger lobby, blasting into the sci-fi future, lit and overlit by Hoover Dam, its holographic veneer little more than an MTV infomercial raised to the power of the Pyramids. The Mirage had so little culture that, by contrast, the Catskills could have been Paris or Prague. Between one-armed bandits and eye-witness reports of underground UFO bases, Nevada was the Twilight Zone threatening to become a Stephen King nightmare. Jimmy's home in Henderson was a clump of desert kept green by round-the-clock sprinklers. So my brother quit the hotel business for good and found a quiet spot in Pennsylvania to raise his kids. In Hartford, Connecticut, he uncovered his Irish/American-Indian ancestry and met his birth mother. It was strange that a kid out of James Fenimore Cooper should have been raised a Grossinger. Every fall he returns to Liberty to hunt deer with his friends and hang out with the old volunteer fire crew.

None of us were really Grossingers. The true Grossingers were the thousands if not millions of alumni who danced through while magic was in the air, then made their lives in other places—the Abe Lymans and Joel Greys, Robert Merrills and Milton Berles, Rocky Marcianos, Bill Grahams, and Leonard Lyons, the playwrights, restauranteurs, countless senators and judges, chiefs of surgery and psychiatry, lawyers and corporation heads who got their start as bellboys and waiters sentenced by curmudgeon Aunt Rose to run-down cottages six in a room ... plus the generation who fell in love and married in Jennie's temple. The movie "Dirty Dancing," based on Steve Sands' memory of his summer affair with Jackie Warner (later Lou Goldstein's wife) is a sanitized '80s version—Grossinger's lite—but its stagey sentimentality carries a shard of the texture and mood. It did feel like stardust and coming of age in Shangri-La.

Properties that had originally been settled and developed with the help of the Jewish Agricultural Society have since been claimed, in various states of abandonment, by Hassids; Hindus; Korean, Tibetan, and Vietnamese Buddhists; Japanese Zen masters; twelve-step groups; New Age capitalists. Former nightclubs, main buildings, and coffee shops were either demolished or resurrected; on their sites have arisen Orthodox yeshivas, drug-rehabilitation centers, and country-club temples.

Murray Posner's Brickman (where Reuben Turetsky started his career) was combined with two other former kosher hotels (Gilbert's and the Windsor) to form a sprawling ashram. Sri Muktananda and his female disciple (and eventual successor) Gurumayi Chidvilasananda headed a Siddha Yoga group that paid cash—seventeen million dollars—for the three crumbling resorts. Once they took possession, they erected buildings as glitzy and modern as anything Jewish hôteliers ever imagined, including Anugraha (Descent of Grace), Sadhana Kutir (House of Spiritual Practices), and Atma Nidhi (Treasure of the Self). "Around the ashram's main building," wrote Lis Harris in *The New Yorker,* "the neatly landscaped grounds are scattered with Disneyesque painted-plaster likenesses of Indian gods, reflecting the scope of the Hindu pantheon." Sanskrit chants begin at 5:30 every morning.

Among the many tunnels connecting New York City's reservoirs to the Catskills is one that drops 700 feet vertically to pass under a valley near the town of Ellenville. A continuous column of water plummets dizzily in the dark and then rises 600 feet on the other side.

Beyond Grahamsville, on a road en route to the Ashokan reservoir, is a deep hollow. Suddenly it is freezing cold. Not the cool of a shady ravine, but the bitter cold of winter, even on an August day. The secret is hidden on the other side of a rock cliff over the guard rail where a series of ancient steps leads down to a small, shallow cave oozing a wind. Just inside the cave, at its dead end, roughly circular (a foot in diameter), is a breach in the rock. Rimmed with solid ice, it leads to a realm of deathly cold.

This is one of Rip Van Winkle's storage lockers for deer—or the monolith of a trapper, perhaps a Norse traveller lost in Vinland.

Outside the tiny hamlet of Claryville, at the southwest base of Slide Mountain, are the remnants of Teson's gardens, constructed in 1906 by more than a hundred workers and designers from Japan. Flooded out in 1932, its rocks strewn, its bridges destroyed, even the course of its brook altered within the garden's boundaries, Teson's at last approaches the perfection its builders envisioned but could not achieve.

At first I imagined I would reframe my old literary texts into a history of Grossinger's. But that wasn't where they led. I found a whole other book in my high-school and college writing. I made it into a nonfiction novel, *New Moon.*

This was my account of coming to consciousness: grade school, summer camp, Horace Mann, Amherst.

Then I started another book (as Robin left for college at Santa Cruz). I finished it two years later under the title *Episodes in Disguise of a Marriage.* This covered the early years of Lindy-Rich, graduate school, the birth of kids, Maine fishermen, teaching jobs, dreams of the late '60s, early '70s.

Robin was about to graduate from Santa Cruz with a thesis on tunicates, Miranda was a junior in high school, and we had moved across Telegraph and Ashby to a house on Woolsey Street before I came to the Grossinger story.

Its chronicle originated three years earlier in journal entries I made when all four of us flew to New York (June 1987) for my twenty-fifth Horace Mann Reunion. This was after the demise of Grossinger's and Richard Heckler's adventure with the Green Berets, the season following the Mets' World Series win and before the debut of Robin's secretary-desk. That trip makes up the next two chapters of this book. *Out of Babylon* in truth begins here and coils back (like a snail) through its other beginning to this point again.

Paul and Bunny made room in their apartment, and that first morning while everyone else slept, I dressed for a 10:30 appointment with my cousin Jay.

Now the beginning. . . .

2

Reuben Turetsky Tells the Story of Grossinger's at the Russian Tea Room

Aromas pour from shops and rise out of grates; crowds cluster around newsstands; bicycle messengers outrace gridlocked traffic. In a phalanx of businessmen and carts of coffee and sweet rolls, I enter the lobby of Integrated, take the elevator.

Upstairs, dominating the proscenium, are two Kodachrome boards, one of battleships, one of jets—equally stark military skies. The receptionist sits in a huge semi-oval, backlit. I take a seat among Wall Street magazines and listen to her directing calls like a neuron firing . . . "Integrated Resources. Integrated Resources."

Jay ambles out. He is magnificent without giving an inch. I follow him down a maze of hallways to his new office, take the seat he offers. He sets the agenda by asking me questions—how are Lindy, the kids?

Going through the matter of Robin and his choice of Santa Cruz, I try not to sound disingenuous. When Robin heard Ivy League colleges cost $20,000 a year, he said, "I'd rather save it. It's not like the difference between Santa Cruz and Amherst is so obvious. Anyhow, I'm tired of prep school."

All of this is foreign to Jay. I realize that my cousin has carried the lifestyle of our childhood to the next generation. It is I who have departed. My speech takes on a choppy cadence, short unsure sentences courting approval.

Jay is up-to-date on my family, the facts of my publishing, the disasters of Gary Berman. I am charmed and surprised as ever. Even as a child at Chipinaw, he dispensed power and blessings. He is a man of justice, a Solomon trapped in the corporate domain of Genghis Khan.

I can never predict how he's going to construe my role in life from his director's chair. This time he seems interested in telling (and retelling) me (until I acknowledge he is right) that I am participating in the "Entertainment Sector" of the economy. I feel trivialized by this, but when I hear the other options I realize it must be true—I'm certainly not in raw materials, manufacturing, or financing.

Jay carries an almost sacred glamour. His prestige as head of a global corporation serves merely to resonate his prior authority.

I try to discern a reprisal in him at the final disgrace of Grossinger's but, if he feels that, it's well-disguised. He's not unlike my father in behaving as though nothing has really happened.

"My parents think Paul is as happy as they've ever seen him. By the way, I told Ruthie you're the only real business mind in that family."

'Then why didn't you follow up on our joint publishing venture?' I wonder. At his repeated invitation (over ten years) I prepared flow charts, budgets, and prospectuses. They vanished one by one under his vague condescension that I wasn't thinking big enough. In fact, the only business Jay has done with me in that time is to offer a stock tip (Trans World Warrants) which I acted on because it came from the guru. When I told him I had lost half of $6000, he shrugged and said, "Hold on to it!" But I had already gotten scared and sold.

"Too bad."

Our talk shifts to summer camp. I remind him of Sam Rosenberg and his minor-league board-game tournaments. He recalls the Korean War vet who would wake us with his nightmares. These events flutter in the context of the business he is conducting minute to minute (as buzzers interrupt us with apparently threshold stock and futures prices). The calls are not distractions: I am here to be with Jay.

Chipinaw lies near our origin. In Xanadu the crux between us is as elusive as a sled named "Rosebud." I remind him of his mythical fist fight with the martinet counselor Bernstein. He is no longer comfortable with that act of insurgency and regrets that he didn't take better advantage of the facilities. "I never sailed once. We were too busy goofing off on our parents' money." I don't want to let him off the hook that easily, so I rub it in by reminding him of the times we couldn't hit any size target and were booted out of riflery and archery.

He is rescued when Siggy phones from an airport in France, en route to Geneva. The two of them go through their portfolio—bonds, stocks, other investments. They take it leisurely, plenty of jokes and sparring.

It is summer again, 1954. The Zises brothers are dealing.

Later we take the elevator together and are out on the street. He kisses my cheek as we say a quick good-bye.

Now I am late for lunch and have to cover a mile and a half uptown. The original urban broken-field runner, forty-two years old, slashes through crowds, brief spurts along sidelines of streets, picking his way with green lights so that as long as I still have to go both to the west and uptown I can't be stopped.

I alternately run and lope, losing and regaining my breath, glancing at timepieces in all scales for updates of my pace.

I am going to be late.

It is a special lunch, bringing together my fathers Bob and Paul. I have always known they were friends—until my mother came between them—but I have never seen them socialize. Now I have heard they enjoy each other's company on a regular basis.

Given their one-time camaraderie, Bob's searing attacks on the Uncle Paul of my childhood seem, in retrospect, absurd. After all, he was trashing a recent drinking buddy and fellow prankster, not a boss or adversary, unless for the dubious favors of my mother. It was perhaps a competitive pride between them that caused Bob to portray my father as a privileged buffoon (my father *his* former friend as a jealous malcontent). Maybe both were performances for my benefit. Yet Bob was prophetic: Paul has blown a fortune in record time.

It was my father who arranged this meeting, so—on the afternoon we got in—I called my stepfather to confirm. He couldn't resist a barb. "Paul Grossinger asked me to lunch, but we know who's going to pick up the tab. Richard, the man must have the slowest reach in history. I don't imagine Paul Grossinger's paid for a lunch since, well, at least the Middle Ages. Say, did I tell you I saw your uncle Paul Rothkrug the other day. He came up to my office. Richard, I didn't know he was raising money for ecology now. I thought the man was a dedicated Marxist."

"That's right. He's got his own Fund for the Environment."

"I don't understand the guy. First communism, now the environment. Richard, these Rothkrugs have a plate loose in their cranium."

I laughed. As little as he understood the beauty of a seventy-five-year-old man's conversion from political ideology to trying to save the planet, it was satisfying to hear him make an indirect joke about my mother's ghoulish end.

Coming up 57th Street I see the canopy of Carnegie Hall ahead, homeless people lying in blankets on the street. I reach for change. I make a futile attempt to straighten my hair.

Inside the Russian Tea Room I wend through a gridlocked line and, despite glares, work my way ahead. I see my family at a table along the wall. I experience a sudden awe at these people beginning their lunch together, their lives joined at me. Squeezing past Bob to get to the one empty chair, I put my hand on his back and whisper: "I just did 42nd to 57th in a new record time"—the kind of line he loves. With a big grin he pulls out his chair and shakes my hand.

"Joshua," he says to the waiter, "get this man caught up."

My father and stepfather are at opposite ends of the table. I have viewed them together maybe four times—at my *bar mitzvah,* my high-school and college graduations, my wedding. The last time was twenty years ago, and the wheel of fortune has turned one full notch in the interim: Bob is the wealthy one, Paul the fallen king. They are talking about mafia guys who hung out at the Grossinger pool. Paul remarks how no one knew, except they tipped big, "until you saw one of them in the paper, shot down alongside Dutch Schultz. Three in the morning," he continues, "remember, Bob." "Sure. We had him on the fire escape."

Now Paul explains the episode to Lindy: "He had too much to drink, and we had to get him back to his room. He gets as far as the third floor, the old Villa, and he won't move, he's feeling good, it's a mild night, the moon is out. So, finally I say to him, 'Don't you know it's bad luck to stand on the third floor of the fire escape under a full moon.' Like that, he's inside." At Paul's reenactment of the memory Bob breaks into his sunniest of smiles.

When Joshua comes back, Bob editorializes on the entrées, describing several in detail, ostensibly for Robin and Miranda's benefit. After we order, he does a quick rundown of the room, pointing out TV hosts, press agents, and executives. He waves to a few of them, pronouncing their names in salute above the din: "Mort, you sonuva gun!"

"You remember the guy who disappeared every weekend?" Paul asks.

"Remember? This was a tall bespectacled lad built like a heavyweight champion. His name was Marty something; right Paul?—six feet three inches tall, tortoise-shell glasses. He was awesome."

"That home run he hit," Paul recalls. "No, it wasn't! Because he refused to run."

"Richard, he let go a shot to leftfield. A softball. It must have gone 300 feet on the fly. Only Matty Begwich—Paul remembers that name, basketball star of a bygone era—hit one further at Grossinger's. What building did it bounce off?"

"Where the indoor pool is now, Bob—the Lyman. It came back so fast he had to run it out. But he wasn't going to run. 'Not on a shot like that!' he says."

"That's right. Guy walked over to him and said, 'Why the hell don't you run the bases?' He says, 'What the fuck business is it of yours? I just hit a home run. I could walk backwards and touch all the bases and you wouldn't have caught up to the ball if that goddamn cottage wasn't in the way.'

"Lindy, let me fill you in. I was emcee then. Whenever I did my *shtick* I'd tell a story, take an incident from the day's events and elaborate on it. I was the golden voice of Grossinger's. Marty loved me, listened religiously for two whole summers. But he always left on a Friday and came back the next Sunday night. I could never figure it out. Then one day he told me. He belonged to Longy Zwillman's gang, a famous Jewish racketeer of those days—immaculate, debonaire, a dapper dan

. . . and a rough guy . . . a real tight, smooth gangster . . . what George Raft tried to be. At that time, the beginning of World War II—Nazi persecutions and such—there were members of German-American outfits called the Bund. . . . One day Marty, Longy, and two other guys went into their hall in Newark. . . . Newark, New Jersey, was a melting pot: you either became a judge, you were a great lawyer, or you were a gangster. They came into a Bund of a hundred or two hundred Nazis. Armed with baseball bats they waded through these guys the way—" He pauses to think up a memorable image. "The way one of Richard's t'ai-chi masters could go through me. They destroyed them, broken heads, all that; Q.E.D., no more trouble with the Aryan Brotherhood.

"One Friday night Marty was walking down some street in Newark. A big fella pulls up alongside, leans out of a car, and makes a remark, denigrating his ancestry: 'You Jew bastard!' He stops, gets out. Not an ounce of fat on Marty. Don't ever start up with him. He just belted him. He says, 'Bob, I gave him a right; I gave him a left.' He hit the fella a little too hard, and his head goes into the concrete. Well, they have to hide him a few years. So all week he's up in the country, at Grossinger's. Comes the weekend, he disappears. 'Cause there's lot of people from Jersey during the weekend. Never found out where he went; just, presto, like that."

Paul's still back thinking about ballgames, patiently waiting his turn. "Remember that play I made at home plate."

Bob nods, then picks out Robin for his commentary as he describes how town teams used to play against Grossinger's. "We put together the best bunch we could, and these tough guys, real laborers, came up the hill to challenge us. We beat 'em that day by one run. Paul was catching, and the last play of the game, this guy comes crashing into him at home."

"But I held the ball," my father exclaims. He punches his hands together in front of his chest and shakes with laughter.

Now a few of the "celebrities" Bob has been waving to come by to visit our table. He gives a formal round of introductions each time, naming us in order—"Paul Grossinger, Richard Grossinger, his wife Lindy, his children Robin and Miranda." No one seems to understand about Grossinger's. They keep asking Paul how his renovations are going, when he'll be reopening.

The dishes arrive and we start eating. After a few minutes Bob takes a survey. "How's the fish, Paul?"

He gets a nod.

"The chicken, Miranda? What do you mean just okay? How's the chicken, Robin?"

"I guess it must be great."

An older guy comes by the table, a bit of a Danny Kaye face. "Hey, Mike!" Bob calls out—then turning to us: "This is the one man in New York, you want something in a column, he'll put you there. Richard, he works for all the major publishers, Random House and those guys. Mike, did you know Jennie's grandson was a writer and publisher? Lindy, do you appreciate there's no more Earl Wilson or Leonard Lyons, but if you want Liz Smith's column; you've got a book out and it should say something in the *Post,* this is the guy. Mike Hall. Paul Grossinger, of course you know; meet Lindy Grossinger, Richard Grossinger, Robin Grossinger, Miranda Grossinger!"

"My mentor," says Mike Hall, fondly putting a hand on Bob's shoulder. "Paul, what's happening there? Are they ever going to open again?"

He shakes his head. "I don't know. I'm out of the business."

"Is anything standing?"

"They left the Jennie G., the Harry G., the new pool wing, and part of the dining room."

"What a shame," Mike comments. "What a crying shame."

"Mentor?" Lindy asks after he moves on.

"Lindy—that was Meyer Holtzman. He was a busboy in the dining room; his whole career then was being a busboy. One day he walked over to me and said, 'Mr. Towers—' he never used Bob until later years—'I want to do some writing.' So, I said, 'Let's see if you've got any talent.' The man knew how he had to write for Blackstone: 'Jennie, gorgeous in her organdy gown last night,' and so on. He caught on, boom! like that. Went to New York to be a rover boy for Walter Winchell. Became Mike Hall, one of the top column men in this town. If I want to put Robin or Miranda's marriage notice in every paper in the nation, I call Mike Hall. This is his account too: the Russian Tea Room."

"I didn't know that," my father remarks.

"Paul, Grossinger's didn't die. It's everywhere you look. Every other bigshot in this town got his start there. Do you know what Grossinger's was? It wasn't just a hotel. You never went to the Catskills; you went to Grossinger's—or you didn't say where you went. The Brickman, Paul's, Morningside, the other places; they never achieved that. Grossinger's was a fraternity. We wore its emblem on jackets and tee shirts. It was the Jewish Yale and Harvard combined. No one from the Ivy League ever had any more loyalty to a college than the alumni of Grossinger's. Am I right, Paul?"

"I won't argue."

"Here in New York you had the Dr. Leo Michel Golf Club, and they met all winter. You had the Eli Epstein Tennis Club, and they also met all winter. And you had Blackstone—a visionary, a man of imagination. If anyone wrote a true history of the resort, Milton Blackstone would have to be preeminent. I was the principal eulogist at his funeral."

"Bob," interrupts my father, "you know Milton and I had our differences."

"I know you and Milton had your differences. I hated the son of a gun. But what Blackstone could do that no one else—there were very few Jewish heroes in those days. A fella named Leonard Weisberg, a taxi driver, foiled a hold-up. Milton had the foresight to invite him to Grossinger's, him and his wife, gave them a two-week vacation at no expense. Richard, Lindy, Robin, Miranda, I'll say one thing about Blackstone. He created a legend. The first time I was aware of it I was at the Brickman Hotel. Damon Runyon, who was syndicated in the Hearst newspapers, was watching Barney Ross train. He was reporting on the fight. He writes, 'I woke at six in the morning to milk the cows with Jennie Grossinger.' When I saw that dateline, July 6th, 1934, I turned to anyone who was listening and said, 'From now on Grossinger's is a national landmark!' He founded a newspaper, *The Grossinger Tattler;* he created a post office, changed the name to Grossinger, New York. Do you say the Broadmoor; Broadmoor, Colorado? No. You say Colorado Springs. The Arizona Biltmore is in Tucson. Grossinger's is in Grossinger, New York. What it took, to have a town named after a resort; there's been nothing since to rival it, either in the Catskills or anywhere else."

He looks around at us as though he isn't getting enough of a response. "C'mon, Lindy, we're talking about a recreational playground, an inn for relaxation, a cabaret, a legitimate theater, a spread of hundreds of acres beckoning to rolling hills, to sun, to sky ... to a sort of euphoria. It was all things to all people." He stops suddenly to appreciate his copy. "The old man can still do it, can't he? Paul, if you so-and-so hadn't gotten rid of me, we'd still be in business together ... and kicking ass, as they say these days."

My father loves it. He doesn't mind playing second fiddle. I have never seen him laugh like this. Not for Joey Adams. Not for Morty Gunty. It is the laughter of a happier time, the ransom of a daredevil friend who gave him a hundred thrills and pratfalls before he took his wife.

"Do you realize, Robin and Miranda, what Grossinger's was in that era? You had Max Reinhardt then, and he had something called "The Eternal Road." What could I compare it to now? Maybe *Phantom of the Opera.* Between us we brought Chaim Weizmann, founder of a nation, to Grossinger's. And you know who the fella behind the microphone was? Yours truly. It was 1942; Meyer Weisgal was in New York. I said, 'Meyer, why don't you get on the phone and call Chaim Weizmann and tell him about Grossinger's?' Richard, you know who Chaim Weizmann was."

I am hoping he doesn't expect me to elaborate.

"The man was there with Churchill, he was there with Mendes France. He invented gunpowder, TNT. He was responsible for the Balfour Agreement forming the State of Israel. He was the most important Jew in the world. We called him up and invited him to Grossinger's. He said, 'Mr. Turetsky, I'd be delighted.' Remember, Paul?"

My father nods dutifully.

"We could do anything we wanted then. I brought a young Milton Berle from Lindy's in Manhattan—a famous restaurant, Miranda, with the same name as your lovely mother. We had Barney Ross. We had Goofy Gomez, the old Yankee pitcher; a natural wit, he'd get up on stage and kibbitz with me. The guy was funnier than any comedian. We had Jan Peerce and Eddie Cantor giving free shows because they were attracted by the glamour and ambiance that Jennie created. I took Jan Peerce—Richard has heard this story. At the close of the Saturday night show I said, 'What could be more important than to have the internationally known concert artist and operatic tenor close with the National Anthem.' He gave me a look like.... Same way I got Eddie

Cantor. We were doing a thing for charity. I had him up on stage and I said, 'Folks . . . if you knew Suzie like—' and before you knew it—Eddie Andreani was at the piano. Boom, Cantor said, 'Eddie, you know my key.' Oh Jesus, the things we did at Grossinger's spontaneously nobody could orchestrate and devise. I brought Bill Tilden. You know Bill Tilden? The Babe Ruth of tennis. Remember, Paul, I put an ad in *The New York Times, The Herald Tribune:* Errol Flynn, the world's greatest stud and swordsman, was going to play tennis with Bill Tilden. The phones rang off the hook; I drew 40,000 people for the State of Israel. Turned away 2,000. I went to the Waldorf Towers. I said, 'Mr. Flynn, you're gonna play tennis with Bill Tilden.' He said, 'Will Tilden play with me?' 'Look,' I said, 'for the amount of tickets we sold, he'll play.' Women wanted to tear off the shorts Errol was wearing that night. You know I'm a sucker for anything having to do with Israel.

"Babe Didriksen, greatest woman athlete of all time: she was a baseball player; she was an Olympic Champion in track and field. Babe was on the other side of the pond. But at the Blackstone Company we had an incredible telephone operator—Paul remembers Dottie Koad—she could get Richard Halliburton in the middle of the Pacific or George Plimpton on one of his safaris. I said, 'Dottie, get me Babe Didriksen; she's at a hotel in Scotland; I saw the headline in *The New York World Telegram.*' Boom, two minutes later, Dottie says, 'Bob, I've got Miss Didriksen on the line.' Next voice I hear, 'Why the hell are you waking me up? Don't you know what time it is in Scotland?' I said, 'Look, I forgot the time differential, but I'll sweeten the purse.' She says, 'What do you want?' And I explained Grossinger's. She says, 'What are you paying me?' I said, 'Three hundred dollars.' She says, 'I'll be there next Friday.' Remember, you had to take a ship in those days. Showed up with Lefty Gomez, Whitney Martin who was the sports editor for The Associated Press four thousand strong, and Dave Zaharias her husband, a champion wrestler. The next day four thousand papers all over the world, 'In the bucolic, pastoral grandeur of Grossinger's, Babe Didriksen—' It was a Rosh Hashanah audience. They didn't know a mashing niblick or a five-iron from a bowl of matzoh ball—no, they knew the matzoh ball soup—trudging around to see Babe Didriksen because they knew, somewhere, somehow, she was a star. She got to the 18th hole—and Grossinger's remains to this day a beautiful golf course—and she used the putter like it was a pool cue, did this, put it right in the hole, waved to the crowd. End of exhibition. Ovation. That was Babe Didriksen.

"Then one day I decided to get the Turnesa Brothers, all seven. I said, 'Willie, you guys have never played under one roof together.' Willie Turnesa—Richard, he was Holy Cross, the only one who never turned pro. He got me my first invitation to the New York Athletic Club. I said, 'Willie, what's a nice Jewish boy doing in this crowd?' He said, 'Bob, we'll come around.' I said, 'No tokenism.' A wonderful guy. The seven Turnesas played Grossinger's. That was news.

"I wanted to do a rags to riches story. I got Frank Stranahan—his father owned ABC Spark Plugs—he was the guy from the right side of the tracks, against the guy who grew up the son of a greenskeeper in Westchester. They were both amateurs, one on one. The final score was Willie Turnesa, 68; Stranahan, 74. The last time I saw Frank Stranahan was boarding his Silver Beechcraft at the Grossinger Airstrip. It was taking him to LaGuardia—I'm going back forty years—he waved goodbye. Do you know anyone in that era who flew off in his own twin-engine Beechcraft? Not even Grossinger's could afford that."

Suddenly Bob notices Meryl Streep and Dustin Hoffman; he jerks his head and points.

"Did you ever want to be an agent?" Lindy asks abruptly—to stop him before we are embarrassed.

"Agent? Are you kidding? Worst job in the world. You're totally dependent on these guys. You've got to hold their hands. Blackstone and Eddie Fisher? Milton did everything for him. Eddie couldn't breathe without Milton. He was helpless. But he had that little tremble in his voice. People listened."

"You look at him now, Bob," muses Paul, "and you ask yourself, how did that guy get all those women—Elizabeth Taylor, Debbie Reynolds. . . ."

"Merle Oberon, Marlene Dietrich ... You know I saw him on the street not too long ago. He looked terrible. Twenty years older than either you or I. I said, 'Eddie, don't you ever play a set of tennis, don't you jog a bit?' He says to me, 'Bob, I'm a lover.'"

As my father smiles almost beatifically, I realize these men are recalling their early twenties when they found themselves together in paradise with a sense of invincibility, barely a generation out of the *shtetl.*

The woman they fought over is dead. The son Bob had by her sleeps in the Park. The Hotel is rubble. Paul is penniless.

Neither man will acknowledge any of this; neither shows any remorse or humility. They act as though they are still running the world, these two beguiling petty tyrants. Neither man will even address my existence. But they will perform for us, always.

"Who do you think discovered Eddie?" Bob continues. "Paul knows. It wasn't Eddie Cantor. Cantor was on a four-day vacation at Grossinger's. I said, 'Eddie, there's a kid here. He sings with the angels. He's got a quaver of Jolson in his voice. It's like a *chazen* pleading with the Almighty.' Cantor said, 'Aw, leave me alone. What are you bothering me for?' 'Eddie,' I said, 'you'll never forgive yourself.' E.g., he came. Eddie Fisher was next to the closing act. He sang *'Any time you're feeling lonely. . . .'* He destroyed them."

We order desserts from Joshua's tray, Bob extolling each in turn. After we finish our selections he recommends a second dessert, a pudding for each of the kids. "Miranda, they make an egg cream here, I'm telling you, like a cloud, and the taste. . . ." Almost the exact cadence of lines from the movie *The In-Laws,* spoken by Peter Falk to Alan Arkin in the car as they are chased through the streets of some fictional South American country by gun-wielding revolutionaries from central casting.

Then I realize this was never my father and stepfather at the Russian Tea Room. It is Jackie Gleason playing my father, Peter Falk playing my stepfather.

"Bob, you could sell anything," Lindy says.

"Not anything, Lindy. Not one thirty-nine-year-old guy on getting a job."

Miranda accepts the egg cream. After she tastes and approves, Robin follows suit. I keep flashing my kids smiles—'This is how it was, you see.' I want them to note the nuances, to understand what I have come from, because I want to understand it myself through their eyes.

I was born into Grossinger's of the '40s. I mark its very end.

Out on the street I feel a bottomless grief. But is it for these homeless and my unacted empathy—my betrayal of them at the Russian Tea Room—or is it just the frosty wind against my face and the sorrows that stretch from the acts of these fathers to the remorselessness of the hardcore wealthy in their penthouses? Is it for my two fictive fathers and my lost mother, for an era when things were real, when you had to drive a bumpy, winding road to reach the Catskills, and shiny acorns lay in the grass, when the seven Turnesas played Grossinger's for free, before megabucks and superstars, before everything became hype and apocalypse?

"You know," Paul says to Lindy in the cab, "when he ran off with Richard's mother, it was good riddance to her, it was him I missed."

3

Led by an Unlikely Ally to a Meeting with Joey B———

ON THE SUNDAY after the Twenty-Fifth Reunion of the Horace Mann Class of '62, a picnic is scheduled at Howie and Pam Hirsch's mansion in Basking Ridge, New Jersey, a few hours' drive from the City. No more than a fraction of the previous evening's group is planning to attend. In addition, it turns out to be a raw day of intermittent rain.

Following directions as Robin recites them aloud, we drive through the Lincoln Tunnel and find the Jersey Turnpike. Hours later we exit onto a rural road comprised of driveways to estate-like houses. We make our designated left, park among cars, and walk past a cluster of kids kicking a soccer ball. At the end of a glass hallway is the living room.

Aside from our class organizers, only Pete Quinn and his girlfriend have arrived. Pete is a totally different person from the guy who played quarterback and pitched against Stony Brook and Riverdale. Twenty-five years ago he was a wiry kid with a mean streak. Now he has a belly and a gentle face. Sitting at the bar with his beer he is telling stories, for instance, about how he threw the longest home run ever hit at Horace Mann (to Ed Kranepool during a scrimmage against James Madison), how he tried (unsuccessfully) to recruit Calvin Hill for Columbia "so I wouldn't have to play against him anymore. I was a defensive back in college and he absolutely killed me."

As new classmates arrive, guys gather around the table. The women make their own conversation in the living room.

Pete continues on center stage. In answer to a comment, he explains how his father—our version of Vince Lombardi—came to be athletic director at Horace Mann. "He was at Arizona State, and they wanted to hire Dan Devine. He was pushed out. Someone told him about a vacancy at Horace Mann. He was from Jersey originally and had played against us one year."

"What a come-down," Pearl remarks. "Can you imagine having to coach Quijano and Millman after the pros."

"Even me. It practically drove him crazy. I remember the time he found me and Carlos hiding in the locker room. He smashed our heads together."

A bunch of stories follow about how frightening Coach Quinn was. Finally Pete says, "You want to know about my father? He's been retired for ten years, but he still works out with the Arizona State wrestling team."

Pearl opens the 1962 yearbook and people flip through activities, commenting on one another's photographs. Pete finds himself missing from a section and complains. Pearl points a finger. "There's a Catholic page at the end, guy."

The music is playing *"Bobby's girl, I want to be Bobby's girl,"* because they have an oldies station on. I hear people referencing *The Big Chill,* for as inauthentic as that movie was, it has become the authorized cliché of what we are about—"*. . . that's the most important thing to me. . . .*"

Despite a steady drizzle, chicken and hot dogs are barbecuing. Pearl is promoting a touch football game alternately as "revenge on Pete

Quinn" and "a chance to catch a pass from our former quarterback."

I drift among conversations. Reminiscences lead one to another, none of them overly vivid or notable.

Someone punches me lightly on the arm; it is Fred. I remember him as a guy who invited me to his house Freshman year for what he advertised as a party . . . but there was no party . . . and then he copped the Latin assignment from me by having me translate while he turned on a tape-recorder hidden under the bed.

What I had written in *New Moon* was how strangely attractive he was: a sassy colt with freckles, an effortless outfielder. When I chased fly balls with him on a dandelion meadow near his house that April of 1959, I had the intimation that it would take me half a lifetime to get back there.

Any warmth had long dissipated by the time we graduated. Fred became more and more a wise guy each year. I don't remember speaking to him even once after the Latin incident, except maybe in passing.

"Rich, how're you doing?" he exults, lining up what is going to be a dramatic handshake. "How are things at Grossinger's?"

Before I can reply, he says he wants to introduce me to his wife. I call Lindy over. "This guy played a helluvan' outfield," he proclaims to her. "And he and I had some times together. Why, he was so rich, I'd ask him for a one and he'd loan me a ten."

"C'mon, Fred," I protest, as I slip away.

Sides are being chosen for the game, I decide to get into it even though I never played with these guys. In fact, I never played at all.

It's three on three. I'm on Pearl's team with Fred, against Pete.

Quinn still has an accurate arm and, on the first series, he hits Hirsch in the clear, but Howie drops the ball as he stumbles. "He'll never live it down," Pearl squeals. "Twenty-five years he waited for the perfect pass from Pete Quinn and he blows it!"

Pete intercepts Fred on the next series. Then he hits Howie with the same pass, this time for a touchdown, his legs flying up as he skids across wet grass.

I race around for the next fifteen minutes, trying to deflect balls or catch them. The cumulative effect is that they score again and lead 12–0. The rain is coming down much too hard, so Pete challenges us with one series, "All or nothing." With Fred at quarterback, I run to the right corner three times. A pass is thrown my way, but Pete dives in front, slapping it down.

"You should see this hole," Pearl tells Hirsch as we come together for a final play. "It's a Mickey Mantle-size gopher. I step in this I'm going to hire one of us as my lawyer."

It *is* quite a hole, stuffed with leaves and dirt, right before the goal line.

Fred looks left . . . right . . . then hits Danny with a bullet which he barely grabs at his gut as he steps into the hole and flips over onto his back. Dazed, he crawls across the goal line. Then he jumps up and yells, "This will be remembered for time immemorial!"

It's 4 PM. Some people are leaving. Nostalgia has turned melancholy; energy is draining fast. We have hit the hollow of the afternoon.

Suddenly Pearl mentions *New Moon:* "Richard, read to us. The occasion could not be more ideal."

I tear through rain to the car and bring back my copy.

While Pearl collects an audience, I kneel in the living room, turning hurriedly through sections about school, trying to come up with a sequence.

Out in the heated swimming area, steam rising, some twenty people—guys and their wives plus some older kids—are waiting for me, a few in the water, arms along the side.

I start with early days at Horace Mann, 1956, thirty-one years ago. I go through tales of friendships, escapades, fragments of rock 'n' roll, classroom events. Like movie music, rain falls harder on the roof. A fairy-tale ambience grows. I have woven myself into my own spell.

I address the gulf we crossed at the end of Senior year, when we separated. I go up to the final day, 1962, the concluding history class, the last Latin translation, the math exam in the gym . . . the humidity and bittersweet joy of the subway ride home.

I have never had a more receptive audience.

The world then was an agony, a melancholy beyond knowing, but it was simpler than it would ever be again.

I finish.

I stand up.

"Just great!"

"High point of this guy's reunion."

The usually cynical Pearl approaches. "I want to thank you for making the weekend . . . perfect."

I am walking back to the living room, trying not to break the spell, when Fred grabs me.

"I went to the same school you did; why didn't I learn to write like that?"

I shrug awkwardly.

"No, seriously. You're a Faulkner, a Hemingway."

I am memorizing his lines.

Then he makes an unexpected offer: "Why is it I feel I have to invite you to my house?"

I tell myself that after all these years he still wants to be my friend. But I also know that from the time we were children he and I have sought each other in some unrequited way.

I propose dropping by on some future trip. "It's already six, and we have to get back to the City. We're flying out tomorrow."

"But I want you to see my place," he pleads. "Can't you make it for dinner?"

I don't understand the insistence of his demand, and I'm hardly comfortable exploring our dubious rapport. He has both a pandering and crackpot air about him. Behind the handshake and patter he could be anyone.

I stall. Conversation drifts. He is babbling about the magnificence and luxury of Grossinger's. So that's his target!

"Fred," I interrupt, "once and for all: I was never wealthy. I never got any money from Grossinger's. For chrissake I never even lived there. It's bankrupt, defunct. And furthermore, twelve years ago my mother committed suicide and I found out she had me by an affair—I'm not even related to them."

He looks startled, almost offended, then recovers with remarkably prompt sincerity:

"You know, I had you wrong all those years. I thought of you as big bucks, a guy to get to know. But when you read tonight, I realized my error. I was mistaken about why I wanted to be friends with you. But I still do."

For his apology I thank him. Our eyes meet. He asks, "Did you ever find out who your father was?"

"Not immediately. It took some doing. My mother had an affair with this guy named B———."

"Not Bingo B———?"

Astonished, I nod.

"Are you serious? Do you know who the B———s are?"

"Not really. I've been told everything from ex-mafia to socially prominent Jewish. I hear they're good guys and I've heard they're bad guys. But I've never met them."

He is grinning, waiting for me to go on.

"Once, I went to see the oldest son Mike. He was pleasant but evasive. After ten minutes he told me this wouldn't lead to anything. He promised to send a picture of his father, but that was ten years ago, so it's probably still in the mail." I am quipping to no point, so I let him proceed.

"The B——— family lived next door to us when we were growing up. They were our goddamn neighbors. They moved away, but I've become friends again with Joey—that's Bingo's youngest son."

All of a sudden Fred is narrating an irrelevant series of anecdotes about Joey B——— and another friend, ending with Joey buying the friend's Mercedes and afterwards (for some obscure reason) raising the price of drinks at his disco in Florida. It sounds like the spoiled rich and does nothing to make me feel any kinship to my putative half-brother. But Fred adds, "He's like you—a nice guy, very open. Of course he's not easy to know. I mean, to know really. The B———s are private. They're wealthy as God. They socialize with who they want. That's not very many people. I'm not surprised you didn't meet the old man. He died, you know, a couple of years ago."

"I know." I tell Fred about writing him letters. "All I can imagine is that he was afraid I wanted money from him. That's the way the world is—one big hustle."

"I don't think it's that at all. You're an intellectual. These people are not intellectuals. If anything, they're afraid of intellectuals. I can imagine what kind of letters you wrote—very complicated and from the heart."

"Yep."

"There's no way he could have handled that. He wouldn't have wanted to meet you; he wouldn't have wanted to hear the things you were going to say to him. Don't you see—even if you tried to be unthreatening, you couldn't. It's not in your nature. Hey!" he exclaims, grabbing my arm. "I'll make you a deal: If you come back with me tonight, we'll find Joey."

Suddenly this hustler has my full attention. "How?"

"There are lots of ways. Maybe we'll go to his house and you'll be my business partner from out of town. I don't know. Let *me* worry about that."

"Do you know he's even around?"

"He *has* to be. He'll be going to work tomorrow as usual, eight o'clock on the train. Sunday night he's got to be home."

Though Fred could hardly guarantee this, I'm willing to take a chance.

I tell Lindy. Even while she is trying to absorb the plan I go into the room where Robin and Mandy are watching TV and ask, "Are you guys up for an adventure?"

Stirring wearily in front of *The Return of the Jedi,* they start to object, so I quickly add: "We have a chance to see someone from the B——— family if we go now with Fred. *Mission: Impossible!*" They leap to their feet and are into coats in less than a minute.

I assure Lindy that we aren't going too far out of our way, that we'll be heading basically back toward New York—but, in truth, we are going to Tarrytown, a long way from Manhattan.

As we collect our coats and say good-byes, Fred oddly rejects my request for directions. "You're following me."

"What if I lose you?"

"You're not going to lose me; I'm going to go very slow."

"But what if we get separated?"

"We won't get separated. *I won't permit us* to get separated." His tone is not reassuring—and not because I'm afraid of getting lost.

In relentless traffic trampling Cityward, my spirit turns black. Sheets of rain fall so heavily that driving is difficult, keeping Fred in sight as cars weave in and out. I feel intrusions of an old, almost reincarnational gloom. It is twilight, the most dangerous time according to Don Juan Matus. Spooks seem to hover invisibly above not so much the highway as the planet. Their premonition I have known forever. On some level, having to do only with such dreams, I feel as though I am being led to my execution.

But I have never let that foreboding stop me.

As distractions flow in and out of mind, cars are continually cutting in front, so I adhere almost bumper to bumper as lanes merge approaching the George Washington Bridge. When a BMW tries to force into the nonexistent space between us, I simply won't let him. He won't yield either—a small, fat man with a mustache, a wife and kids, determined on his life to wedge in front of me—so we go along together, him trapped between lanes in this test of wills.

Lindy is asking me to back off, but I have a different idea. I tell Robin to open his window and somehow gesture that we are trying to follow the car in front. His eyes forged ahead, the guy makes every effort not to notice. Then Robin's irresistibly rational presence touches him. His face breaks into a smile. He nods and drops away.

On the other side of the Bridge, Sunday traffic sticks with us. We go for miles. We pass Horace Mann; we pass Mount Vernon; we pass White Plains.

At last Fred gives his blinker, and we turn into a stretch of quiet streets, foliage slapping against our windshield. We follow him into a semi-circle of houses, up a driveway.

Inside, his two girls immediately head to the TV. My kids join them.

Fred marches to the bedroom phone. He tears through several personal phone books but doesn't find Joey's number. Finally he calls a mutual acquaintance for it. He dials.

I hang there, peering self-consciously at postcards and photos in frames.

It is clear there is no answer.

I make an assessment before he can: "Fred, it was worth it just to get to visit you and see your place. Don't feel you have to produce Joey."

"But I'm going to," he insists. "They're just out for dinner." He sounds awfully confident about someone whose phone number he doesn't have.

We walk back to the living room where the TV is playing, potato chips and sodas now on the table. I tell Lindy we'll have a polite snack and then go.

"What about dinner?" Fred exhorts. "Is there anything wrong with ordering a pizza?" Robin and Miranda don't eat tomato goop, but there is nothing wrong with it otherwise.

Fred grabs his keys and my company.

Practicing Paul Pitchford's natural-foods regimen, I haven't eaten at a greasy spoon in years. However, I am no longer under ordinary edict. I have plunged into a time warp in which meanings are reversed and each thing is a transfigurative symbol. A pizza can be anything; it can even be an herbal medicine. The only thing it can't be is snobbily rejected by me as lower consciousness. I agree to get roast-beef sandwiches for the kids.

Fred and I slide into his other (sports) car and drive into Tarrytown, he performing a synopsis of his life on the way.

"I did engineering at Rensselaer to please my parents. Actually I wanted to go to Stanford, play on their golf team. Sure route to a pro career. But they wouldn't allow it. I was good in math, and they read somewhere the world needed engineers." He affects chagrin. "I made it through school okay and landed a job building guidance equipment for Navy jets. I was part of a team. One guy got killed in an auto accident, another got pirated away, so, like that, we didn't have our assignment. It was either transfer to Texas or find something else. I took my chance to get out of engineering. I studied professional dancing."

"Like what—ballet, avant-garde?"

"No, ballroom. I moved to Florida and put together an act. This lady and I gave lessons and did shows at resorts. But her boyfriend messed up our routine. You see, we had just a brief time in which to perform [he clicks his fingers], you know the hotels, like maybe lunchtime: we do a number, then they say, 'These fine dancers are available to teach you the tango, the marengue, or whatever.' I left her and went solo. I was a young guy then. Older women signed up for lessons, but not to learn how to dance. They'd give me the key to their rooms. I didn't make too much money, but I had a great time."

We are at the bar waiting for our pizza, eleven-thirty Sunday night—no roast beef, ham sandwiches instead. Fred continues—professional hoofing on Broadway, brief fling as a pro golfer, a few tournament wins:

"I had to find another career, make a fresh start. Sales was the way to go."

He pushes aside my money, sets down a twenty, and grabs the change. Taking us on a leisurely route home, he spices the journey with stories, for instance, how he goes to this very library to read the speeches of Winston Churchill for inspiration.

We turn into its lot. He stops the car, looks me in the eye, and says, "Sales, if done right, are totally selfless."

I agree that he wouldn't last very long selling people things they didn't need.

"It's not that," he insists. "Maybe at some lower level, like widgets or piping, but not at my level. I'm not really selling. That's the beauty of it. I'm helping people fill needs. I play golf with them, maybe improve their stroke. I teach them about women, about life. I'm that good—top two percent of my industry. In college I got any woman I wanted." His manner is clinical, as if to dissuade any imputation of boasting. "I was arrogant then. I'd just decide I was going to take some girl away from a guy and I'd do it." I remember that freckled Dennis the Menace look on a fourteen-year-old.

"My wife was different. I met her in the elevator, and I knew in five minutes I didn't just want to date this woman, I wanted to marry her. The problem was that she was going out with someone, and he was number one—I was maybe number two. This guy was *the* playboy of all-time, absolutely smooth. He had money; his brother played for the Colt '45s; I didn't have a chance. The only reason I won her—you know why?"

"Unh-uh."

"He was overconfident. He *lost his concentration.*"

How could I have ever looked down on this guy? He's an original—Richard Gere playing *American Gigolo* playing Arnold Palmer. He's redeeming every maligned salesman—from Snake Oil Hayes to the sad hustlers of Arthur Miller and David Mammet—and replacing them with a Zen sorcerer. For this one night, he is *my* mentor.

Depositing pizza and sandwiches on the table, Fred and I head straight for the bedroom.

"It's midnight," Lindy pleads. "No one's going to come out at midnight."

"For me they will!"

He dials.

He is speaking to Joey's wife. "No, I need your husband. No one else'll do.... It can't wait.... I can't tell you.... It's nothing that can be said over the phone.... Rachel, I wish I could. I want you to do this for me. Do you understand?"

With a discouraged sigh, he slumps on the bed. "He's going to call back. I'm not sure at all. They just got in from Florida. Their flight was delayed. They're putting their kids to bed. Maybe...."

"It's okay," I reassure him. "The stories alone were worth it."

"Coming from you, that's an honor."

We return to the den and join the meal.

Fred describes the only two times engineering ever meant anything to him. The first was when he tripped during a foot race to the local ice-cream store, skidded, and went through the plate glass window. "I had only a second, but somehow I figured out the angles, rotated to the side, and slashed through with a karate chop. Glass all over, but I landed in the center of the room unharmed."

"And you ordered a milkshake," Robin says.

"I stood up and asked what the specials were—no, I'm joking."

"The other time was driving on the highway, a year or two ago with my whole family. Some guy—later we find out he's got a suspended license—decides suddenly he's going to cut across traffic and turn the wrong way into a one-way street. In that moment I knew I was going to hit him. There was no way I wasn't going to kill his whole family and at least half of mine. Then I calculated vectors and steered to the side so that we hit at an angle. Both cars were wrecked, but not a single person was hurt."

The phone interrupts. I meet Fred coming back out of his bedroom. He is punching a fist into a palm. "Okay! We're a go, in fifteen minutes at a bar."

Lindy is tired and wants to be done with this madness. "It's the middle of the night," she tells Fred; "it doesn't make any sense." "You're wrong," he counters. "You're wrong because time doesn't enter in here. Everything is exactly as it should be. It will never be this good again."

"What about the next time?"

"Lindy, your husband's waited forty years for this."

During the evolution of the evening I had been assuming we would all go together, but Fred has a different strategy. "It's got to be Richard alone. You guys are brothers. My job is to give you the *best* chance. I don't want this to be a circus. If the family comes, they sit at another table and don't make contact with us."

"We'll stay," Robin says.

As Fred and I re-enter his car, he sets the stage. "When we meet, I'm doing all the talking. You'll get your chance, but you have to follow my lead. It's nothing against you, but the last time you tried meeting one of these guys you were out of his office in under ten. If I performed like that, how long do you think I'd last? You've got to understand: I do this for a living."

"Got it."

"Let the sale develop. We may be there an hour. It may take two hours. It doesn't matter."

We step into a smoky alcove. Almost at once we are told they are no longer serving dinner.

We sit double-parked while Fred stares into the night.

"How about the pizza place?" I offer.

He shakes his head. "It's not that you *can't* do it there, but you've got so much to overcome you might as well not create any additional obstacles." Handing me the keys, he goes back inside intending to phone and redirect Joey.

He returns and resumes staring. "What did he say?" I finally ask.

"I didn't call. I don't want to give them any excuse not to come. I'll wait till they get here. We'll pick a place together." His words are barely audible. After a while he adds, "Pay attention to Rachel. She will not allow this to get out of hand."

Lights hit us—Fred jumps from the car and runs to meet them, stands at their window talking and gesticulating, then jogs back. Beams shift in raindrops as we re-trace our route. "We've got a spot that's perfect. They're closed, but they'll serve Joey B———."

We follow their car through streets in labyrinths.

We park. Fred issues a last warning. I nod.

I have come to an event as impalpable as any in life.

They get out of their car and walk toward us. Joey is wearing a silver jacket with felt athletic awards sewn on. About thirty, he is blond with curly hair. Rachel is darker, has the fresh good looks of an aerobics instructor. At Fred's lead I greet them.

The restaurant is empty; in fact, it is closed. I feel almost balmy as the manager unlocks the door and we follow them to a table. Chairs are unstacked for us. They order dinners. Fred and I settle for sparkly water.

The best moments in life are not necessarily when "it's happening" because by then you are into it and it's going by so fast it is already ending. The best moments are when you are sitting just outside your life, watching it unfold. You know it's inevitable; you know nothing can stop it. All you have to do is ride it in.

Joey sits across the table with Rachel. He is the doppelgänger I have waited half a lifetime, most of it unknowingly, to see: high cheekbones, lithe build—all Rothkrug features too. But there is something else: a vulnerability, a goofiness, a wise-guy grace, an air of conceit. He may be the child of nightclubs, real-estate empires, and easy wealth, but I know this guy. He is Chard's brother.

I imagine my mother coming to the realm of this kid's father, seeking her Other.

Conversation is light at first. Fred leads with stories of the Reunion, throwing in how he and I just met again after twenty-five years. Trading the narrative back and forth we fill in the touch-football game, then my reading by the pool. Joey and Rachel find that entertaining.

"Richard has a very strange history," Fred continues. "I would venture to say that no one else in our circle has had as unusual a past." He puts an arm around my shoulders. "His mother Martha was married to Paul Grossinger—you know, the resort—" They nod. "She wasn't really in love with Paul, but it was a fortunate marriage. She was a striking woman, and he was an eligible man."

"A good catch," Joey cracks.

"This marriage didn't produce any children because, as it turned out, Paul was sterile. He couldn't have children. Martha didn't know this at first, but she found out soon enough. During the war, while Paul was in the army, his mother Jennie, who was the head of the clan, came to Martha and said, 'I know you and Paul aren't getting along and won't stay together. I know he can't have children. But I think the world of you and would like you to be the mother of my grandson. So, go out and find a man who's bright, good-looking'—you know, good genes—'have your child, and he'll be a Grossinger.'"

As Joey and Rachel acknowledge the shift, they turn to me. I explain how my mother married Bob Towers and set up in New York. "I was raised as his kid, Richard Towers, with a half-brother and half-sister. When I was eight, I found out Paul was my father." I condense subsequent years into a few sentences.

They ask questions to make sure they get it straight. After all, there are three rapidfire fathers, and only two of them have been identified. We have to be clear, for instance, that Bob Towers was not the man Martha chose to have her child by.

Fred's approach is effective, for we have their empathy now. Joey and Rachel are not unwitting victims. They too are eager for the unknown father to be revealed.

Clearly wanting to slow things down, Fred reviews how we met, emphasizing that he used to think of me as this wealthy Grossinger kid. I tease him by recalling his comment about "asking to borrow a one and getting a ten," adding it was that attitude that caused me to avoid him during the later years of Horace Mann.

"I said that?" he demands incredulously. Then—"Yes, I probably said that."

As Fred goes through the chronology again, Joey interrupts, "But I don't see what this has to do with me."

"You will," Fred promises. "Just a little bit longer."

"Is this about a screenplay? Are you trying to sell me a story?"

I shake my head assertedly.

Fred is finishing again up to when I learned that my father wasn't Paul. "So," Joey demands impatiently, "did you ever find out?"

"It took a while," I stall. "I spent about a year asking my immediate family. Everyone had their own reasons for not telling me. My stepmother was protecting my father. My father still held my mother's infidelity against her. My stepfather thought I was betraying my mother's memory. Then I went to see her best friend of the time and—speaking of movies—it was just like Hollywood: penthouse on Park Avenue, long cigarette holder, three poodles on the bed beside her. . . ."

"What did she say?" Joey snaps.

I'm not going to be the one to tell him.

"You have to realize that what she said I didn't believe at first. And so I tried to contact the guy, but he didn't respond. Then I checked with a number of other people and, when everyone came up with the same guy, I assumed it was the truth. Later he confirmed it himself, though not to me. In fact, I never met him."

"You see, Joey," interrupts Fred, "there was a reason why I asked you to come here tonight. I told you that you would not regret it." I glide from face to face. "That handsome, eligible man that Richard's mother chose . . . was your father."

We are no longer flying.

Joey turns to Rachel with half a smile; his head whirls back and forth. "What! I mean, this is a joke, right?" [Pause.] "I barely know you. . . . I don't know him. This is a set-up, right? You're putting me on."

"Joey, I'd have no reason. Richard already went to see your brother Michael, but that was ten years ago, and Mike said something like, 'Well, Dad liked to play around before he was married, but let's drop it for the sake of the family.'"

"That's right! The family. Who knows this? Does my mother know?"

Fred shakes his head.

"She mustn't find out."

"It's no big deal," I finally intervene. "I'm not going around broadcasting this. It's too late to mend the past. I would just like it to be acknowledged for the future, so I could live, you could live, my children and your children could live with the truth. Because that's all it was, two young people in over their heads. . . ." But even as I talk, I am changing. I want to awaken "B———" and set him free. I've got too much narcissistic intellect and suicidal energy of Rothkrugs and Turetskys. I want the other half now.

I want permission not to be a Grossinger anymore.

New Age psychologists talk about healing with images, obscure mythological ikons, as when Navahos internalize snakes and lightning from sandpaintings.

I feel as though I am being redeemed by Joey's simple presence. Nothing else is required, but nothing else would effect it either.

To have a secret brother is to have a spirit guide, a lost twin. And I know it is not Joey himself but his refraction in me. His sheer existence supersedes any sacred visualization or homeopathic microdose. It is the most deep-acting medicine of all.

"You have to give me time to consider this," my half-brother reflects. "It makes you realize how in *The Big Chill* where the woman just wants someone to have her child . . . it doesn't stop there, it goes on years into the future. It's not a simple disposable thing."

"No," I say. "It's fundamental, paternity is." No one responds, so I go on. "During these years I mainly worried your father thought I wanted something from him. What I think now I wanted was him just to say, 'It's okay, go ahead and be,' and for me to tell him, 'It's okay, I got life, and now I've made it back.' I wanted to give him the opportunity to make peace with me too."

"Well, he's dead."

"For what it's worth," Rachel suddenly says, "I believe you, and if it were me I'd be doing this same thing."

Joey stands up. "I don't know what I think, but the least I can do—" and he reaches across the table for my hand. I stand. We clasp each other. Whatever else happens, for that one moment it is clear, okay, forever. I have found my mirror, albeit a faint recoil of another mirror—like the moon of Pluto whose separation from the planet is barely discernible—through which I see a faint replica of my lost self, the life I dreamed but never lived.

My mother embodied avarice and cheap seduction. She was petty and melodramatic. I hate being her picture image, the broodling of a witch. She was never a woman, so how was it possible for her sons to become men? (Certainly my brother couldn't figure that out. He became a shaman creature, a spirit animal, but not a man.)

I don't know what inside me intuits this, or if I have a right to claim it, but, sitting before Joey and Rachel, I feel as though my manhood, the part that chose originally to enter the world, that courted Lindy, found rapport with fishermen, made North Atlantic Books—that part is Bingo, a man I never met.

I am Bingo exiled in Martha, the ransom not only of their affair but of the forces gathering over Grossinger's then. And that event lies behind the melancholia that sang, "Oh My Papa" and "*. . . gone are the days . . .*" with Eddie Fisher, because the part of me which transcends life saw in *The Tibetan Book of the Dead* the couples mating, and *knew* that a mistake had been made.

Now I explain that my wife and kids are at Fred's house waiting. I ask if they'd be willing to meet them.

"I'll do that," Joey says.

Cars trail again.

I rush upstairs, corralling everyone. Rachel shakes Lindy's hand, "Hello, I'm Rachel B———," then Robin's, then Miranda's. We sit for an hour, chatting like couples who met at a party.

Fred has completed his work. He has performed the myth in which the outlaw leads; he has proven that, when it counts, the person who guides is the one you would least expect because that's the only way you would follow, the only way you wouldn't recognize him.

Yet mysteriously the same forces were at work over thirty years earlier, for he was the "salesman" to whose house (next door) I came too early with a Latin assignment, and never wanted to leave.

When Saturn returned he would say (again, as then, 1959), "Why is it I feel I want to ask you home?"

Now, on his suggestion, I leave Joey my copy of *New Moon.* We dart through the rain to separate cars.

Four days later I am driving the Richmond Bridge over San Francisco Bay. Fog is clumped on the water. Sun sparkles. Light and shadow flicker lyrically, almost conscious of their dance.

I am lifted to an energy almost beyond this world. I know it will end, in fact almost immediately, and I want some gesture to put it to rest.

All I can think of is how Keith Hernandez points to a Met infielder who has just made a good play—that single finger of acknowledgment.

I point at the sky where symbolically both Bingo and my mother are. I aim my finger and drop it at a stack of cumulus clouds. I laugh and say, "You guys! The trouble you caused. But don't worry. I'll set it straight for a million million lifetimes to come."

Pure melodrama, but I love it.

4

Out of Babylon

LATE SEPTEMBER, 1987, we loaded Robin's belongings into the car. He and I had stalled as long as we could, but the Mets wouldn't touch Doug Drabek that afternoon (or win the Division again). It was time to go. The universe wasn't going to dawdle any longer on Robin's childhood. Even the Mets wouldn't give us one last game.

We took 880 to 17, crossed the mountains, and descended into Santa Cruz. We parked in the quad by Robin's dorm.

Through community lunch we held onto vestiges of family, but our son was barely with us. Friends from various Bay Area schools he had attended (all eight, it seemed) kept reappearing.

The emptiness I felt driving back through the mountains melted into a river of lights from San Jose to Oakland. Personal loss quickly escalated to global hopelessness.

'This is not a pastoral or redemptive culture,' I thought. Fossil-fuel carapaces, rocks ripped from the earth's gut, made molten, hammered, polished, and styled, thunder across historyless slabs of mortar. Electric lines sizzle invisibly. Poison entrepreneurs, legal and illegal, operate everywhere, their products ranging from stewed crystals to crisped nicotiana to fermented berries and sweetened fats to potassium ordnance. Now antipathetic youths stalk the streets in their employ. Governments are little more than cabals of crooks with public-relations firms. And transnational corporations rule all humanity, spinning Orwell's *1984* and masking it in Huxley's *Brave New World.*

Five years later, when Miranda went off to college herself, friends asked if her family was close. "Close?!" she replied. "It's a cult."

But that night at dinner she said: "I think he got the better deal. His time alone with you guys was when he was a baby and your only kid. My years are going to be missing him."

"Just when you get used to something," I mused, "they take it away. We are a three-legged table now."

The cliché warns that "you learn to live with it"—and you do. That is, you learn to live. As it turned out, our son was home every few weekends, so we kept up dinner discussions, lunches at Mandarin Garden, and games on the dish.

Robin's passage to adulthood had been marked by an incident. One night in the spring of his junior year at College Prep we were awakened by him crying out on the staircase. We leapt from bed and raced down to him. Was there an intruder?

We found him on the landing. All he could remember was a geometric object chasing him in his dream. "It got bigger and bigger. I couldn't escape, but I couldn't see it."

I thought about the Rothkrug legacy.

Would he be okay at college? If it happened there, who would meet him?

I had forgotten that the dark can be even more therapeutic than the light.

There was a girl named Ching-Ching. A few years earlier she had come to America from the People's Republic. Poet, political gadfly, and ballet-dancer, she was a dynamo at College Prep, a mainstay in the group he hung out with.

That week she had been home sick. He had his eye on her but was jumpy about how visiting her would look to her boyfriend. The day after the dream he went to her house in El Cerrito.

Within a month Ching-Ching and Robin were inseparable companions. He became a stir-fry chef and a conversant on recent Mainland history.

A hodgepodge of radical articulations and spirited plans, Ching-Ching relied on our son for transportation and entrée into American culture. He drove her to her doctors' appointments and ballet lessons. They travelled to Mendocino and Yosemite. But when Ching-Ching went to Oberlin and Robin to Santa Cruz, the romance ended.

I remembered the timing of his nightmare. He knew he was going to Ching-Ching's house the next day. "No biggie!" he would have said. But some part of him cried out one last time, 'I don't know who I am, but I want to be this child forever!' Lindy-Rich comforted him with the part of us that wanted to be the parents of that child forever.

Robin didn't stretch his adolescence across bittersweet, stormy years; he grew up in the cauldron of a single dream.

By the time he moved to Santa Cruz he was a young man. During the initial months he endured thumping stereos, cigarette smoke, horrendous food, drunken parties, and Valley girls. Finally, amidst reading assignments and papers due, he fell into an endless flu. "I'm missing tons of classes," he told us. "I can't sleep."

"Robin," Lindy urged, "why don't you go to the infirmary?"

"It's a mob scene there. Couldn't Rich just come and get me?" It was a primal request. In me too. In five minutes I had dropped my day and was zooming toward San Jose. I pulled up at his dorm, helped him out of his bunk bed, collected his books and papers, and led him home.

Someone should have fetched my brother Jon from Madison this way.

The next afternoon Robin awoke from a day-long nap and wandered into the kitchen in his jammies. I knew at once he was better.

Suddenly his eyes darted up. A crane had landed on the roof of the condominium next door. It paused in consideration, opened its wings, and did exactly what we feared (and hoped)—swooped down toward our barely discernible pond and made a pass at the fish. "No!" shouted Robin. I went running onto the deck, waving my arms.

This was a response the creature had not planned on. Its feathered span suddenly dwarfed not only the pool but the clutter of yards and housing it rose against. We watched it disappear like a prehistoric visitor toward the Bay.

Then I went back to slicing turnips for miso soup.

I returned him to Santa Cruz in the morning. There he threw himself back into courses, and that spring he signed up for the fledgling hardball team.

During our years on Blake, we published titles on holistic medicine, midwifery, aikido, karate, herbs, dreams, the immune system, ecology, Jungian psychology, shamanism, sacred geometry, and whistling jugs. We hired interns. We arranged distribution in England, Australia, and New Zealand. We made deals with wholesalers.

This was the middle of life. Our kids were grown. We had developed the kinds of activities that pass for careers.

Other things didn't happen. We never found a community of friends. Our families never got to be part of our children's growing up. *The New York Review of Books* and *The New York Times* didn't know we existed. Our marriage drifted between crisis and profundity. We were searching for each other, sidestepping each other, rediscovering each other, begging each other's unasked questions—"always," Lindy said, "one foot on the threshold." We never bought land, though we searched in Maine, Vermont, Idaho, and Mendocino. And the world itself—the planet—was sinking toward the ungaugable nadir of a cosmic cycle, the failure of a '60s optimism and grace that had spawned *Io,* the end of the illusory Summer of Love.

Texture itself was dissipating from our zone of creation.

For the summer of 1988, we enrolled Miranda in a Southern California acting school. Robin and I drove her there. After a day in L.A., we headed east across desert, up a mountainside into evergreens. I felt uneasy depositing a fourteen-year-old in a group of ingenues, but she was eager to be on her own and wanted us to go quickly. We at least made sure she found the right bunk.

The journey home was a marathon of baseball talk and East Coast memories, breezes of corn and fertilizer, our late-afternoon shadow lengthening and condensing across fields of the Central Valley. Nightfall brought lightning in the distance.

For the next week and a half we emptied out Blake Street and transported our stuff to Woolsey Street. The main feature of our new home was an indoor pool that had provided a shell to make a warehouse (the inspiration of our agent with whom we had already checked out every other available weird "outbuilding" in Berkeley). The Mexican family selling the house had raised their kids around that pool, but their gas-and-electric bill was monumental and the house was suffused with chlorine. That was why our low offer was accepted.

Robin and his friends jumped in for one swim before a pump rented at the library took twenty-four hours to dribble the water into the yard. Then we hired a contractor to build a floor over the hole. He sketched something that looked like a roller-coaster track to follow the contour of the pool's bottom and support a platform of books.

In August, Lindy and I went to fetch Miranda. Busy with rehearsals, she barely acknowledged our arrival.

In the pavilion that night, she performed beside another actress as the older woman's erotically conniving superego. For a moment, I saw the face of my sister Debby starring in Molière at Mount Holyoke, a whirlwind then of charismatic French—the flesh-and-blood sculpture of our lineage irrevocable. In Mandy's sharper profile—the point of her nose and thin etch of her eyelashes—I recognized my wife, this person I had lived with now almost twenty-five years.

A day later, as we pulled up alongside Woolsey, Miranda was overwhelmed by its pretext. "We don't really live here," she cried out. "I can't bear to go in." But Robin was standing on the porch with a goofy smile.

"Hi, Mans."

"Robin, say it's not true."

He held up his arms. "I carried cartons for a week. I helped build the floor. I know it's true."

She buried her face in her palms, then marched dramatically in. "Oh my god," she proclaimed again and again as Robin took her on tour—then upstairs to her room.

After our trip to New York, Bunny persuaded me to pay more attention to my father. "He's so depressed I worry. The sight of him in this condition, moping and defeated, breaks my heart."

During the period when the Hotel was dying, I shared her fury and frustration at him. Later I blamed him. Then gradually I accepted the futility of either stand. He was impenetrable to the entire spectrum of emotion, anger as well as grief. It was as impossible to excoriate as to love him. Bunny found that out after he was exiled from Joy Cottage. She never wavered in her commitment to him. "He's a human creature in distress who depends on me," she said. "What more could one ask?"

Her friends were scandalized, not only that she should lose her newly won freedom but that she should be saddled with a partner who had betrayed her. Her comedian brother declared, "Not a penny for Paul!"—ignoring vacations on the house over the years. I was guilty of the same revisionism, wanting Bunny to punish this man and live another life, or at least imagining I wanted that because it made a grander tale.

But I had no right to grumble; I didn't have to live in her heart.

"I see that if you disown him now," I conceded, "it's like negating your whole life."

"That's right. Paul's everything to me—my past, my family, my children, even the way I come to have you as my son. I can't re-do that. My secret is: I cherish these years. I finally have Paul, the man. There has always been something special about him, something beautiful, buried though it may be."

At her urging, I began calling him every few weeks. All he wanted was a few moments of sentimentality during which he could pretend Miranda was his girlfriend and ask Lindy and me the same questions about jobs and publishing he asked the last time. He didn't want to be told the truth, ever.

Years earlier, when Robin and I had shared our excitement about a then-unknown minor-league pitcher named Dwight Gooden, my father's face turned sour; he began berating us as if we had committed an indecent act. "You don't know nothing," he barked. "Everyone looks good in the minors."

"But Gooden's special," Robin promised.

"I guarantee it—" Paul said with the strange pleasure of killing Santa, "you're wrong."

How to explain his vehemence? He adored Robin, and half the time he cooed in baby-talk anyway. Perhaps it was his cynicism about the world, his conviction that if anything sounded too good to be true, it was. To believe in poetry, or a farmhouse in Maine, or Dwight Gooden, was to get away with something.

I snapped back at him only once during that period—when he tried to compel me to write a letter to Amherst praising some "important" acquaintance's son.

"You know," I said, "your grandson—who got accepted on his own merits—didn't go to Amherst partly because we couldn't afford it, and now you want me to lie about someone unqualified because he's rich."

He told me I misunderstood him, that that was the way the world worked. And he was right.

In the spring of '89, Bunny pleaded with us to come to New York. "Your father's in such low spirits, and you and Lindy and the kids mean so much to him. If you can handle the fare, I can get you a discount at the Beverly, and Paul and I will pay for it."

When Lindy and I settled on dates, I wrote to Joey B———. It was not our first exchange since Fred's. He had called in August to tell me how much he enjoyed *New Moon.* "I really identified," he said; "I had some of the same experiences." He asked about Robin and Miranda, confided some business problems, then egged on my descriptions of monuments on Mars and the tribulations of the Santa Cruz baseball team. In another conversation several months later I wondered if we might get together on his next trip to California.

"Perhaps. But the thing about my father can't exist. You and I can be friends, but that can never be part of it."

"Of course."

"Do you still think it's true?"

I knew how I was supposed to answer, but instead I teased him: "Who killed John Kennedy? Is there a face on Mars? Are we half-brothers?"

He chuckled. None of these were legitimate riddles to him. He had made his peace on this matter by considering me a California naif who'd believe some extraterrestrial was his father if a likely enough tale were concocted. His wife might know that t'ai chi was practiced by a million people in the rising sun ... but then he might simply smirk and call it Chinese aerobics. To Joey, nightclubs were real. Ch'i and homeopathy were West Coast fads. UFOs were a total joke.

Apparently he thought better of meeting in California. When he also didn't respond to my invitation in New York, I left a message on his machine. He called that night to say he still hadn't made up his mind. "How about if I ring you from the office in the morning?"

10:30 AM in Berkeley—lunchtime in the Big Apple—I stood in the backyard, pacing with a portable phone. Joey got right to the point. "I don't believe my father is your father." When I countered, he was primed to fight: "Prove it. I'm listening."

I kept my tone light as I ran through the people who verified the story independently (including an aunt of his who spoke to Bunny and his father in conversation with my Uncle Paul). I mentioned physical resemblances. "All circumstantial evidence!" he scoffed. "It's the same kind of wishful thinking that makes people see UFOs. For all you know your many sources may just be a rumor from a single source. Probably your mother. It doesn't sound as though she was very stable. She may have had a fantasy about a relationship with my father. I can assure you she didn't have a relationship."

"But your father acknowledged it."

"And of course you know your uncle told the truth?"

"Debating it isn't going to solve anything. If you really want to know, you could check it out with your own family. We could do a blood test. This doesn't exactly strike me as a mystery in search of a resolution. What's more important is how we choose to act and what we do with it."

"If this kind of thing happened now," he snapped, "you wouldn't have been allowed to be born."

"You keep acting as though I'm making this up to be perverse or that it's somehow aimed against you and your family. But I didn't set the rules. This is how the dice came up. I mean, if you think I have a hidden agenda, call me on it." I turned, picked and smelled a sage leaf, and switched the phone to my other hand. From Manhattan, Joey responded:

"I'm a happy guy. I know that probably sounds superficial to you. I love my wife and family. Until you came along, there wasn't a cloud in my sky. Now I can't even sleep nights." He let that sink in. "There's no way this can continue."

Not a cloud in the sky? I couldn't decide whether to be more shocked he would tell another human being he didn't deserve to exist—or that nuclear bombs, homelessness, and rainforest devastation went right past him.

"I'm sorry, but I didn't invent the shadows in the world. If you have escaped them so entirely, then you're one of the blessed. But why assume that I'm part of 'them' come to beleaguer you rather than part of 'us' exiled through circumstance?"

"I don't want to talk anymore, and I certainly don't want to meet."

"The power's in your hands, Joey, so you get to choose the outcome. But I'd think that would carry a responsibility to be fair. Anyone can win when they hold the weapons."

"You just want the ultimate resolution."

"Yes."

"Well, have a good life."

Joey and I had played a longer game, but this was checkmate again.

By the time our family left for New York, my father—according to Bunny—was sitting in bed day after day, sometimes not even turning on the TV. "If you could even get him to go for a walk, it would be such a boost to his spirits. I know he'd get up for you."

She was right. The night we arrived I called from the Beverly and, though it was 10:45, he came rushing in a cab.

We were unpacking our suitcases when we heard a knock. I sprinted to the door.

Looking fragile and worn, Paul Grossinger stood there in an overcoat. His eyes lit up at the sight of us. This was the father I remembered from childhood. I gave his girth a partial hug. He shuffled across the suite, astonished by the kids. "Richard, what have you done to me?"

He asked if we had eaten dinner. While we debated whether we had or hadn't (on the plane), the old hotelman picked up the phone to check if the restaurant downstairs was still open. It was, barely. He insisted on taking us.

As he orchestrated who would sit where, he proposed, in the same tone he used when I was a child at the Plaza, to order "whatever we wanted." Then he asked Miranda to sit on his lap, an awkward moment for both her and me as he commented, "Boy, how I'd like to be seen on the town with a girl like you." But the food came quickly (we were the only people), and we set to eating.

"This reminds me of when I was a child," I told him, "how you and I went out together." He didn't hear me.

"I'm so sloppy," Robin remembered him saying as he dropped dinner on his shirt. Then he called for an early look at the dessert tray.

Time was exploding on us, washing out all that was inattentive and unfulfilled in a kind of flotsam.

"Richard, Robin, why don't you walk this old man out to catch a cab. I'm going to let you get to sleep."

Robin had a logistical dilemma the next morning. Ching-Ching was coming into town on the bus from Oberlin. He had promised to meet her at 7 AM and lead her to a girlfriend's house uptown on the West Side. Neither Lindy nor I wanted him trying to find Port Authority alone, so I agreed to get up too. In mapping our plans we decided that, after taking Ching-Ching to her friend's, we would go crosstown and look for Jonny. (We couldn't call him because, as Bob had put it, "The guy got tired of wrong numbers, so he settled the matter in a civilized way, by ripping the phone out of the wall.")

We struggled to answer our wake-up call. Outside the subway we bought a New York sports page, then plunged into the underground, caught a train to 42nd Street, and ran for the shuttle, just missing its clanging doors. We were lucky. After the train pulled away we heard singing and walked back across the station to investigate.

On the uptown side of the tracks a reggae man—army jacket, dreadlocks—performed, *"Buffalo soldier, out of Africa. . . ."* A mob shoved obliviously past him.

I regretted we couldn't cross the tracks, stay for the concert, give him money. He was as lucid and incomprehensible as a starry night. His voice rang through stone and intersected the crash of trains coming and going. Just the way he said *"Af-ri-ca"* transcended the whole mediocrity.

Ching-Ching blasted off her bus, suitcases in both arms. She had become part-bohemian, part-anarchist at Oberlin. Even after a sleepless night she was talking a blue streak about sunrise in Pennsylvania towns.

We trooped through tunnels (like alien aqueducts) that connected Port Authority to the subway, passing dozens of the people now called homeless (whose situation Jon prophesied so long ago). "He foreshadowed everything," I told my companions, "the '60s, the Indian revival, drugs, street people. . . ."

Ching-Ching was disappointed she missed the reggae singer, but she got lucky too. Before we reached the shuttle we came upon a native Peruvian band pounding an array of drums and blowing panpipes, each of the members wearing t-shirts that read, "I froze my [picture of a donkey] off in Vermont"—tiny black-haired people filling the underworld with the whistle and melody of the Andes. It seemed as though their minor chords alone might resolve the unbearable complication around us.

We stood in a makeshift crowd, transfixed through four numbers. Then one of the women stepped forward to sell their cassette. I bought a copy.

Ching-Ching wouldn't hear of not accompanying us to Jon's.

"You haven't had any sleep," I reminded her.

She had saved a dozen stories for Robin—marches at school, escapades on motorcycles, taking over the offices of the paper, a novel she was writing. We left her gear on the West Side and hiked through the Park at 72nd. (Robin noticed ballgames in the meadow and came back later as "the Santa Cruz kid" to hit two doubles and make a diving catch—while everyone either asked or reminisced about Telegraph.)

The Hispanic guard at Lexington smiled at the thought of anyone looking for Jon. "Maybe you can find him and then maybe you can't. He has his patterns, that Jon." He raised eyebrows. "If he's not in the Park he has places up there." He pointed in the general direction of 3rd. "He delivers groceries." I hadn't known that.

We got him to repeat his best guesses, and then I led my guests through a tour of my old neighborhood: the Y where we bowled and swam, the storefronts where we bought comics and baseball cards (now beauty parlors and ethnic kitchens), the apartment buildings where friends grew up.

"Everything here," Ching-Ching remarked, "looks like the cover of *The New Yorker*."

It was true: New York was a stageset for the ritual passage of generations. Its shop windows were covens of European and Asian cults, not even displaying for sale the furs, buttons, and curios that filled them.

We completed one whole round—3rd to 96th to Park to 90th and back. We didn't see Jon anywhere.

The guard shook his head. I could almost imagine him thinking, 'That Jon: the wily one.'

Then Ching-Ching directed us back to a Chinese restaurant she thought looked promising and ordered in Mandarin. The combative waitress seemed to refuse her every request. Ching-Ching remarked how arrogant New York Chinese were.

As we hit the lobby of Knickerbocker Plaza, the guard nodded coyly. "He's in," he whispered. "But I didn't tell him."

He picked up the house phone. "Hello, Jon." [Pause.] "I want to see you down here right this moment." [Pause.] "Just come down." He sounded furious.

I thanked him. Then we stood facing the elevators.

Five minutes passed.

The arrow descended to M. Jon came bursting out. He looked almost normal. His posture was no longer stooped. The reggae knots were symmetrical.

His eyesight wasn't good, and he had to adjust to see who we were. Bursting into a grin, he came striding over, hugged me and Robin, and was introduced to Ching-Ching. "I haven't seen you laugh like that in a long time, Jon," the guard noted.

"Yeah, it's my brother."

He gestured toward the door and we headed onto the street. His plan was to aim toward the Park "where you can breathe." On the way it was difficult to maintain a conversation because he continually cupped his hand over his nose and mouth. He had to remove it just to talk. His spatial relationship to us was also odd: he herded us along, walking now forward, now backward, pointing out omens of degradation and endtime.

"Look at these people, their faces," he chanted. "It's Bosch, Richard. Isn't it Hieronymus Bosch? Horrible! It's a walking march of the dead."

I couldn't argue.

I noted how carefully he returned his hand over his face each time after he talked. I wondered what ever made me think he needed remediation.

"Jon," I said, "you have finally become what you are."

We passed Food Liberation. "My prison," he commented, intending to pass. I thought we should go in.

"I would be ashamed to have you there."

"I'd like to meet the people you work with."

He paused, thought about it, then abruptly shot in. "My brother, his son, their friend," he called, parading to the back. Two clerks looked up but said nothing, so the three of us shuffled around looking at foods, picking out cereals and a loaf of bread.

Jon returned with a tiny teepee. He lit a joint and dropped it in. He was terribly pleased with this object, waiting for it to begin its operation. It was almost cute, him standing there giggling, breathing what came out of the chimney.

"We like Jon," the owner's son told me. "Jon is good for us, keeps us on our toes. You don't get away with nothing around Jon."

"I'm glad he has a place where people understand he's not just a lunatic."

"I'll tell you something," he confided, encouraging me to lean over the counter. "Jon's got problems. But Jon thinks he's the only one who's got problems. This is New York; we all got problems."

He okayed my out-of-state check, then shook my hand on the way out.

As we approached the Park, our scout was incensed by a row of buses snarled on Fifth Avenue. First he shouted from afar. Then he charged across the street ahead of us and stood right beside the closest one, swatting its metal.

The people aboard had already seen everything. If they stared, it was with the emptiest curiosity. Most didn't even bother. Finally the driver let out a swear word and pulled away in a cloud of toxin that sent Jon stumbling toward the wall and over it . . . into Indian country.

We followed him through glens where young businessmen in suits took their lunch. Jon spat Apache curses their way. "They think they look so sexy. It's not sex at all. It's foppishness. They're dandies." He turned to two men with briefcases. "You're so great, aren't you?" Robin,

Ching-Ching, and I kept walking as the men smiled at each other and walked faster. "Run from me, will you?" Jon yelled at them. "You'll find out soon enough you're in the teeth of the dragon."

On the path beyond us an official jeep growled along.

"An invader," he shouted. "Here we are in this pastoral setting, and there's a machine. Look at how smug the driver is. He thinks he's something special, making his little thing go-go-go." He veered toward the vehicle. "You're really great, aren't you, putting along."

The motorized cart cut off our path. Two young guys sat up high like cowboys. I knew this swagger would not go unchallenged. "The assholes in their little toy," he shouted. "Who do you think you are? Gene Autry? Hopalong Cassidy? Aren't you cool?"

These petty custodians didn't like it at all. They stopped the vehicle and began staring. He loped and pranced around them.

"The Cultural Revolution," Ching-Ching muttered as we hurried past. I shouted for Jon to follow.

"Even my brother is embarrassed and won't stand behind me."

"Jon, you're not conscious there's a young girl and a kid who's interested in seeing his uncle. You're just doing your own thing and making us uncomfortable. I'm not going to indulge and inflate you this time."

He fired a glare at me, a distraction during which the cart passed. "Can't you let your son know what the world is like? I'm the walking, breathing truth."

"You can be angry without having to attack; it doesn't add to nature or enlighten the universe to charge about like Don Quixote."

For a moment it seemed he might run off and leave us; instead he adopted a new tone:

"A century ago, just one century, most people lived on farms; they bartered; there was a frontier. But we've turned the frontier into money and servitude. The way money is used now is a perverse creation of society, a trick to get people to sell their lives. My father thinks I have to get a job. That's all he *ever* thinks about me or notices. Why do I have to get a job? Did God decree that?"

We walked him to his building and accepted his invitation. It was to be the third visit for me upstairs—the first with Mrs. Golden, the second "Wide Montana Skies." The difference each time was millennial.

This was the end of the world. Pitch black. The remains of his bamboo curtains couldn't be opened; they were hammered over the window in a contraption of irregular boards. Ashes and clothing covered the rug. The smell, astonishingly, was prairie.

The only order was made by rows of notebooks and a library which filled one entire wall.

Jon attentively handed Ching-Ching a rare book on China. While she was turning through it, he brought out a novel by an obscure nineteenth-century feminist. He explained that he bought it from a press in Brooklyn. Unwilling to patronize any machine-powered vehicle, he had walked all the way, camping where needed. It took him three days to reach the publishing company. On the way home he stopped "in the Village to buy marijuana from a High Priestess."

He pulled down two notebooks and found a poem for each of us. Ching-Ching's one ended with a description across the Hudson facing New Jersey: "solid weight of the Palisades/to the west/looming up on the Jersey shore//sun blazing, wind blows/in the pristine solitude/of high noon."

Robin got the city of Yonkers: "hodgepodge confusion/of old and dirty/new and ugly//worn-out/rapid-paced/urban exhaustion/where once//broad undulating slopes/old stone churches/quaint wooden houses/profusely-grown/picket-fenced/gardens//commanded wide vistas of the main river/and the farmland in the tributary valley."

While we were sharing his aesthetics, he made a racket in the bathroom, lighting a joint. He came out in high humor. We all praised the poems.

I described the reggae singer Robin and I had seen. Jon pounced on the reference. "Buffalo soldier! That's what Indians called the Africans. Because they looked like buffalo with their woolly hair."

He asked if we'd like to hear some reggae.

We did.

The stereo was still there. He pulled out a record and found the band he wanted. Needle scratched until it hit words, or rather, a yowl that sent chills down my body. It filled the room with the primal syllables of everything Jon was: *"Cuyeh, cuyeh! Nana Nananana!"* Then the words laid the stark mathematics of his life: *"One step forward, two step backward. . . ."*

"'*Down ina Babylon,*' Richard. Quite appropriate. Wouldn't you say?"

The beat was compelling and unmistakable, echoing Bob Marley and Jimmy Cliff, for sure . . . : *"the road to righteousness is narrow."*

Without warning Jon rose and, with a yank of his arm, tore open the curtains by literally dismantling the bamboo and boards. The contraption tottered, snapped, and fell with a crash onto the floor.

We blinked in a sudden flood of day.

"I thought," he said, "Ching-Ching might like some light."

It was an understatement when I remarked how his act reminded me of Pip in Miss Havisham's mansion. "Dickens continues to shadow us," I added.

"Why not," Jon exclaimed, a bear standing over his debris. Those makeshift coverlets—their nails exposed and bent—would never hang again.

"Are you a conman? Or are you a dreadlocks?"

Up the hill, dominating the horizon, were the apartments of Park Avenue, the ones we grew up in. "I make deliveries for Food Liberation," Jon revealed. "I go to those buildings where Emil and Phil used to live. They won't even let me in the service entrance now. We were born the sons of kings, but now those castles sit beyond me on the hill, just where I always wanted them."

Music and song iterated his speech like a theme behind a movie. *"Onward forward, don't step backward. Step out of Babeelon."*

"Babee´lon, Rich. That's where we were born. You were blessed, my brother; you had grace. The gods gave it to you with life. That's why the elders hated you. Me? I was their heir apparent. You took off like some wind spirit. I had to fight myself out of Babylon, every step of the way."

5

After Grossinger's

In the morning Robin took Miranda exploring. Lindy and I rode the bus uptown.

My father Paul was standing by his apartment door waiting for us. I helped him with his overcoat. We strolled to the elevator.

Down on 2nd Avenue he proposed to take us on his rounds. "We'd love to see your neighborhood," Lindy assured him.

At each shop—the butcher, the grocery, the florist—he was greeted by a proprietor. "These are like the departments of Grossinger's," I commented to Lindy as a Korean grocer led Paul to the back to show off his newly arrived shipment of produce. When they returned, he was answering my father's questions about the week's business. Back on the street I carried the groceries, Lindy the meat. Paul held flowers for Bunny.

For lunch he piloted us to his favorite Chinese restaurant a block away. As we were pulling out chairs at the only unoccupied table, the owner burst out of the kitchen and was greeting us enthusiastically when his wife joined him. "We're happy to see you, Mista G.," she interrupted.

"We're really happy you bring your children."

The one-time king of the Grossinger dining room pointed to his silverware. "This table isn't set properly," he said in a hush that was so loud it could be heard across the room.

The owner mumbled to his wife in Chinese, and she watched intently as Paul rearranged the silver. "You know," he remarked forgivingly, "I was in this business a long time."

"We know, Mista Grossinger. We're honored to have your family as our guests."

The meal began with a discussion about North Atlantic Books. I told my father it was too bad he didn't live near us because I could use his help figuring out how to balance cashflow and budget print runs.

"Maybe I'll surprise you. Will you show me your ledgers?"

"Of course!"

"You should do it, Paul," Lindy rooted. "It would be good for both of you."

Then we fell into an awkward silence, which I broke by bringing up a provocative thing: "We had a problem at the Hutton office in Berkeley and now Seymour is going to take over our account. We're getting together with him tomorrow morning." Seymour was Jay and Siggy's younger brother.

"Seymour's a great kid," my father observed unperturbedly. "Don't think I'm upset you've put your money with the Zises. Their mother's my cousin. They'll look out for you. What was your problem?"

My father loved trouble.

"Well, you remember Larry Berman? He worked for Morty Curtis and Bob Towers. When we opened a money market account for North Atlantic Books, his son—whom I never knew—turned out to live in Berkeley and be a broker. He was assigned to us purely by coincidence—like he was on duty that morning. Anyway, over the years he literally gambled our money without our permission.

"Not really 'gambled.' Actually, he would tell us he was buying one thing and then buy another, not to cheat us—understand—but because he thought he was smarter than the system, and the types of things he was doing he had to act fast. He lost over $20,000."

My father was smiling broadly because I had just proven his theory of humankind. I was smiling too because I had nothing at stake any longer and was willing to make this as juicy as possible for his benefit. In fact, mid-story, I became an actor, a kind of bumbling nebbish taken in by a big-city con.

"I finally went to see the Hutton office manager. 'That wasn't what I thought we were buying,' I told him. He said, 'What did you think they were giving you points for—being a nice guy?'"

"You should have called me," my father interjected. "I would have gotten you a lawyer." He had made that same promise half a dozen times, but, on the few occasions I accepted (like when we were evicted in Ann Arbor), it was always the same Liberty barrister who later sold *him* down the river.

We walked back toward his apartment. He trudged alongside us, taking my arm for the curbs. We rode the elevator silently. He said, "Richard, I'm tired. Thank you both for a wonderful afternoon."

The next morning Lindy and I caught a bus downtown to an office building near NYU. Cousin Seymour was a smaller, more relaxed version of Siggy and Jay. I had last seen him as a child at Chipinaw; now he could have been an L.A. record executive or an Israeli politician. He lacked Jay's puissance but had the same overt sweetness, kissing each of us ("My cousins!") in Zises style on the cheeks, then pulling out chairs around a table. His secretary brought in our accounts.

"I've looked this over, and I'm proud of what you two have done. Nobody gave you anything. In fact, my mother says you started with one hell of a handicap. Now you're not just supporting yourselves, you're publishing the kinds of books the world needs."

This was clearly a new Zises.

"I consider your willingness to work with me an opportunity. I get to learn from you, and you get to learn from me. Right?"

"Yeah. I tried with Jay, but—"

"I love Jay, but I'm not Jay." Then he reached behind himself, grabbed a book on economics and a Hebrew "Ethics of the Fathers" (from stacks of each of them), found a pen, and signed the title page of the money book, "The best is yet to come."

"The only advising I'm going to do is asset preservation—keeping you from junk you don't need—buying options, investing in the kinds of crazy funds brokers are asked to sell at supermarkets like Hutton." He was reviewing the years of Gary Berman. "You shouldn't have been in any of this stuff: OEX, commodities, futures, high-risk bonds. This guy must have really been *meshuga*."

"No," I deadpanned. "If he was crazy I wouldn't have fallen for him. He was brilliant, but he was arrogant and had a bad sense of timing."

"A combination that will kill you in this business."

After our meeting Seymour offered a lift in his limo. As we soared uptown he made a few business calls on the car phone; then he handed it to Lindy and, despite her reluctance, encouraged her to "make sure North Atlantic Books is running well today." It was a blend of generous affectation and prank. From midtown traffic she phoned our staff of one. Then Seymour let us off at the Beverly.

Saturday morning among the crowds at Central Park South we joined my sister. At the time of our mother's death, Debby was a droll, bilingual Mount Holyoke graduate; even now she played tennis every day. She should have been vibrant and engaged, in the prime of life. Instead the world had imprinted on her the stare of grief, the mask of New York cynicism. She didn't know this was happening; the expression had become more familiar than her god-given look.

We had brought a wrapped gift which she accepted bashfully from Miranda and stuffed into her purse. We began our walk from the base of the Park.

As we followed paths toward the 72nd Street Lake, Lindy and I alternated telling her about our world. After a while Debby warmed to a presentation of her life. Although detached, the shrouded intensity of her voice was evocative of Jon.

When I reviewed our mother's suicide, Debby said it now seemed so far away she didn't think about it much. "Mom was sad. It was better she died. I wasn't devastated or anything. I felt worse being left at summer camp."

She told an enlarged version of the affair with Moe. "My father couldn't help her. She needed something he couldn't give. But he's an incredible man. They don't make them like him anymore. He's from the old school—dashing, elegant, a gentleman."

"He wasn't," Lindy inserted, "much of a father to any of you."

"Everyone's entitled to their opinion," Debby snapped. "Maybe he didn't want to be a father. Maybe he shouldn't have had to be." Later she casually referred to journals I had not known about. Lindy thought I should get to see my mother's writings, but my sister instantly forbade that.

"She was as much his mother as yours!"

"That's not the way it works," Debby shot back. "He's not part of our family. He has no right."

I asked Lindy to back off.

As we approached our starting point at the base of the Park, my sister seemed to reconsider. She blamed the requirement of secrecy on her father and made a sudden offer: if I came along with her, she would let me look at my mother's memorabilia "for a half hour, no more."

We separated on Central Park South. I went with Debby. My family headed toward the Beverly.

On the journey downtown, a hike of thirty blocks, I tried to be more candid with my sister. "We were friends once. Do you remember the times at Chipinaw or when I visited you in your room at night when you were scared?"

"Of course. But it makes no difference now."

"It does to me. I was—"

"And you should leave my father alone. He's not interested in you; he merely tolerates you."

"That's between him and me. We enjoy each other's company."

"You may enjoy *him.* He doesn't enjoy you. When you called yesterday he said, 'I'll give them lunch in your mother's name, but they won't get dinner out of me.'"

I winced at her derision, but she wasn't done. "I don't see why you keep trying to get us together, why you think you should improve Jonny, why you have to start pestering me."

"Because I'm your brother, and someday you may need a brother."

"God forbid!" she exclaimed theatrically as we reached the building.

In the elevator she reminded me, "A half hour; that's all. I'll walk around the block. I want you gone by the time my father arrives for his afternoon shower."

She led me across the living room to a bureau, pointed to the appropriate drawer, and left.

In a spell of nostalgia and timelessness I stood among familiar couches and stuffed chairs. The ivory statuettes on the mantel and gilded etchings on the wall had hung in all my childhood homes. I opened the drawer and began shuffling through papers.

A smell of old leather . . . documents like faded petals . . . the memory of Bridey's voice *". . . sad and dreamy there . . ."* so the past spilled out of a time capsule: my first scrawled postcards from Chipinaw, my mother's marriage certificate with Paul, the record of my birth, photographs of us all at the Nevele and Long Beach, my report cards from P.S. 6, my letters from Maine and Vermont. Twenty minutes were gone and I hadn't even begun to hunt beneath the surface.

I made a quick decision to forget the journals (which I couldn't find) and smuggle some of this out. Selecting those items that pertained to me, I put as many as were concealable—about thirty photographs, letters, and documents—into a manila envelope and stuffed it in my coat.

As I was doing this, I found an old pocket notebook and read two scrawled pages, each bearing a single sentence:

> I invested a lifetime of feelings in all of you without a single return.
> I know I'm not the lord of the manor but just a poacher on his estate.

Then, carefully leaving the apartment door ajar on its latch (I had already tried the door to the eleven flights of stairs, and it was bolted shut, without even a rattle), I rang for the elevator.

Paranoia was instantly prophetic, for I rang and rang and rang. Nothing stirred in the shaft.

A vivid flashback of my mother jolted me. I lost the present and plunged into forgotten layers beneath the surface of my life, immune to love or spiritual practice.

My mind yammered with voices. Instantaneous, wordless, they parried as if in dialogue, pretending to represent me, to punish me: 'Stop the elevator; bring his wicked ass before the judge; throw the book at him—life without parole; don't let the crook escape the scene of his crime.'

'Your essential character, Richard, has not changed one iota. You have failed everyone. Even worse, you don't care; you're out for yourself. You're lucky to have a wife and children. You don't deserve them.'

It was no longer my mother's voice. It had far more authority and credibility. It was a sentry of God.

By now Lindy, Robin, and Miranda had discerned what Jonny once recognized and Bob and Debby still did: I was Richard, the thief. All my earnest activities—writing, publishing, parenting, t'ai chi, meditation—were a fraud, a mere overlay in which I labored to prove (to anyone who would serve as my captive audience) that I was okay.

My sole hope lay in not being Richard, in somehow blasting myself from his orbit, escaping his nature. In truth, for the years of adult life I had tried to be me, not him—to feel true compassion, to return fellowship in kind. What a joke!

Now he and I were trapped in this minute alcove between the prison of the apartment and my stepfather's ambush. And he was an ugly, mean companion.

None of this felt like perverse amusement or compulsive conversation. It was the vapor of my mind, unsensed gibberish that shadowed all thought—long forgotten, hauntingly familiar. Its cover image was once the imaginary basement of the church across 96th Street to which Bridey took us, where (before a dream) I sundered into hypnagogic echoes addressing each other forever. I was still the fossil of their ancient apparent battle.

Then I made up a different story: I was sensing my mother's ghost, trying to impart the horror she felt at the end. Or perhaps it was my stubborn desire to invent such a ghost?

Why? Out of guilt? As a spiritual challenge? Or as an attempt to blend with her and know her last act?

There was nowhere to go, just as there had been nowhere for her, except back through the door . . . and out the window.

All these thoughts passed in a second or two, as I tried the buzzer. Then I realized I was ringing the service elevator.

Down in the lobby Bob and Debby were waiting, my stepfather unwilling to go upstairs until I left. "You're a man of your word," my sister pronounced, checking her watch.

Bob wasn't happy but remarked dryly he'd see me and my family for lunch.

Walking me to the curb, Debby noticed the bulge. "You took something!" she charged.

I felt a chill. "I took my report cards, my birth certificate, photographs of me at camp, my own letters."

"Go, before he sees."

I ran most of the mile back to the Beverly.

I tried to catch my breath in the elevator. Opening the door of our room, I gasped an abbreviated explanation to Lindy, then collapsed on the bed, melodramatically spilling the contents beside me.

Turning through the material, Lindy marvelled as she stroked my hair.

Sometimes it all was too much. It didn't seem just a book I was writing.

When Robin and Mandy got back from their outing, my daughter sat on the floor performing aloud postcards from my first summer at Chipinaw:

> DEAR FOLKS, WE WENT ON A HAYRIDE. LOVE RICHARD TOWERS
>
> DEAR FOLKS, WE PLAYED WITH CLAY. LOVE RICHARD T
>
> DEAR FOLKS, WE LEARNED TO DANCE. LOVE RICHARD TOWERS
>
> DEAR FOLKS, WE CAUGHT FROGS. LOVE RICHARD T

My handwriting ran words together in scrawled, half-mirror-imaged caps right to the edge of each card.

The kids were falling down laughing so hard Miranda found herself almost unable to continue.

Then Mindy, my brother James' wife, called.

Bunny and Paul had rented a car that morning and headed to the mountains to visit them before they left for Nevada. Bunny was driving. On the Palisades near West Point she took a wrong exit. She tried to back up the ramp and didn't see a car speeding from the side. It smashed into the passenger side and flipped them over. Slivers of glass strafed her eyes. Paul was trapped in the passenger seat, unconscious.

Two hours later he sat in a hospital room joking. He was about to be released when Ira Cohen phoned and insisted on a CAT scan. "Some big shot from New York," James heard a doctor whisper. "Let's get rid of him." They sent him to the City by chopper. At Beth Israel he was put on sedation.

(Later Bunny said, "I felt as though I were in a crystal palace," her astonishment at the windshield fragments glittering as they disintegrated around her. The statement contained an irresistible irony: For Bunny it always was a crystal palace, made of glass.)

We hailed a cab to the hospital, then stood in the gloom of the waiting room for almost an hour. Technicians passed with nary a glance; equipment was wheeled along. Finally giant doors swung open.

"This is how I imagine hell," Miranda whispered—an acrid odor, bodies on gurneys, doctors bearing clipboards like clerks.

Paul lay behind a curtain, unconscious again, sighing, sputtering.

I knew at once I didn't care enough. I had trouble even holding his hand. Lindy did so without difficulty and, when she promised that Bunny would be there soon, he struggled against his shackles, moaning restlessly.

She arrived in his official Mets jacket, a gift from Fred Wilpon. "Has he been pinching any nurses?" she demanded at once. "If he has, then he's okay." Vulgarity was sometimes all that held her together.

She walked around the bed, annoyed at both the unresponsiveness of the doctors and the neutrality of the four of us. We should have been on our knees, wailing. At least I should have been.

Then Walter Kaye showed up. He had sold probably fifty million dollars' worth of vehicle and liability insurance to Grossinger's. But he was retired now and, when the "accident" finally occurred, they were driving a rented car.

Aunt Elaine was led to our spot by an attendant. Sister and wife stood beside each other, weeping.

In my father's agitated coma he seemed to be journeying back across his whole existence. It was a deep journey, a subtle dance for such a big man. His fingers trembled in delicate spirals. Behind eyelids, eyes searched high and low.

Even though he was supposed to recover (and the doctors assured the women the coma was induced by their sedative), I didn't expect to see him again. What did he have to come back for?

"I did so want to say good-bye properly," Bunny pleaded. "I can't believe after all the time we put in together, the trips on snowy roads, it might come down to some careless lady while he was yelling at me for taking the wrong exit. Is life worth so little?"

My stepfather met us for lunch the next day at the Hampshire House. He strode down 57th Street carrying his briefcase, extending a hand of welcome. Tragedy had quieted his latest spate of vitriol. The mood was somber as he asked, "What's this I hear about Paul Grossinger?"

I told him what I knew.

He shook his head many times. "The end of Grossinger's was something we all foresaw a long time ago, but no one expected it would be like this. Tragedy upon tragedy, almost Shakespearean."

Gradually, as Robin and Miranda improvised a conversation, Bob's spirit picked up. When he asked Robin if he had ever heard the name Turetsky, the scene from the men's room at 21 Club was invoked.

"That was your real name," Miranda announced. "But you couldn't do business with it."

Bob broke into an appreciative laugh. "Am I crazy or do I recall we also met a mayor there that night?"

"Abe Beame," Robin told him. "He shook my hand."

"Quite a gentleman, but—"

"Not much of a mayor," Robin finished to his surprise. "That's what you said at the time."

"How do you like that!" Bob roared. "What a memory!"

The conversation drifted to my childhood, and I recalled Bridey, now home in Belfast. Bob asked Robin and Miranda if they knew who we were talking about.

"The one time they saw her a couple of years ago on Fifth Avenue," I told him, "she gave them Irish coins she had saved. I felt as though I were showing her Jonny and Debby all over again. Do you remember how she sang Irish songs when she was cooking?"

"Those weren't Irish songs, Richard. Those were Hebrew songs."

I looked at him, baffled.

"Yip Harburg, born Isidor Hochhberg, Eleventh Street and Avenue C. *He* wrote the book for *Finian's Rainbow.* For all the tragedy he witnessed—and his ancestors witnessed—the man loved a rainbow. Gave Judy Garland one too."

"My mother's favorite song."

"That it was."

Then, in an aged cantorial voice, he *davened:*

"'*It's only a paper moon,/Sailing over a cardboard sea. . . .*' Harburg too. Richard, the man grew up on Sholem Aleichem, Yiddish theater on the Bowery. '*But it wouldn't be make-believe,/If you believed in me.*'"

The innocence of those lyrics so deceptive, so heart-breaking. . . .

Then I told my stepfather about Robin's baseball exploits (with the glove he had given him)—how he had gone out for the team at Santa Cruz after not playing hardball since he was nine. "He read Sadaharu Oh's autobiography, then used his own high-school aikido training in the batting cage. He fixed the ball as a point and focused energy into the bat as a sword."

"I only wish you had applied your perspicacity to tennis," Bob said, "the consummate sport." Then he inquired about the record of the Santa Cruz team.

"Up to 2 and 7 this year," Robin said. "Last year the only team we beat was Haverford."

"Well, they don't count," Bob teased. "They couldn't have much more of a sports program than Santa Cruz. I mean, does your school play football or basketball?"

"Not quite ready for the Final Four," Robin countered, "but we're on the bubble."

We maintained a cheerful mood as we marched down 57th to 5th where Bob searched for a cab. "I do enjoy these lunches," he said. "Remember me the next time."

"Debby says that I'm forcing myself on you."

Mouth grimacing, he stopped in his tracks. "You're her brother. She should know better."

A Yellow screeched alongside. "Come to Berkeley," I shouted. "I owe you a few thousand meals."

"C'mon!"

After hearing of my father's accident, the Beverly demanded our Visa card and locked onto its full credit limit. We lasted two more days by eating only at a Japanese restaurant that didn't run the number through a computer.

Our last morning in the City I made a cross-town dash to Bob's office to cash a check.

Money was not a medium my stepfather and I dealt in. Because he took the symbolism of cash so seriously (bearing only freshly minted bills from the bank), I shied from even a superficial resemblance of any act of mine to Jonny's. Yet sheer necessity motivated me. We were down to dollar bills and coins.

"How are you getting to the airport?" he asked, reaching into his wallet and counting off bills.

"Well, now that I have money," I smiled, showing it to him, "we'll take a cab or bus."

"One minute there, Richard."

Long ago he had put on hold my petition that he was my father. But on this April morning he dialed his favorite limousine company and commanded, "I want them to have the VIP treatment."

And VIP it was—a caper for Miranda to narrate at school: sandwiches and wine, CD player and TV, car phone.

Bunny raged at me for leaving town. I told her we had plane tickets, the kids needed to be back in school. She demanded I see my father again, so I had the driver double-park at Beth Israel. Ancient roles had reversed—the Grossingers were my oppressors, the Towers my benefactors.

Lindy and I rushed in.

Paul lay absolutely still.

I called Bunny from the car to report.

"Thank you, Richard," she said coolly. "Now you can abandon him."

Two weeks later he stopped breathing.

I did abandon him. I didn't return for the funeral. I pretended to feel ambivalence, but I had none. There was no way I could get back on a plane, cross the country, and feign the role of PG's son at a public ceremony.

I thought of his body in the hospital, no more than an incubus in flab. I could forgive the soul inside that body, forgive his attempt to own me, but I could not forgive the trumped-up, self-important world he indulged around himself. I once adored Uncle Paul, but I hated

PG. I had spent too many years listening to inflated testimonials and watching him be patronized by the lowest forms of ingratiators.

My father was gone. And if I read him right, he would fly from Grossinger's too, as swiftly across the plane of worlds as his spirit could take him.

I didn't get to hear the eulogies, but toastmasters had killed him years before his death. I didn't get to hear Bunny's brother acclaim, "PG's already in heaven, ordering room service for the rest of us."

All the years I had collaborated with her on a creed of Paul's failings I never considered the possibility that she would turn against me. Now at his death he became her martyr—a kind of Gandhi destroyed by an uncaring world. "None of us realized what a real man your father was," she declared on the phone. "Do you know he was honored by politicians and leaders of industry? People of a stature I never dreamed of keep calling me to be remembered in his name. Now I want to live up to the things he taught me."

I found her revisionism painful. Yet by having been her confidante I became an enemy to Paul Grossinger's epitaph, a living testament of her own disrespect.

The day he was buried I went to watch Robin play for Santa Cruz against Menlo College—the only time I saw him in a college game. He lined a single over short, then grounded out. In their final shot Santa Cruz was down five runs but had scored three and had two on and two out as Robin came to bat. Against a hard-throwing relief pitcher he bounced a ground ball cleanly between third and short. "Way to go Rob-bin! Clutch hit, Grossinger!"

The next guy popped up to end the game.

I brought Paul to Menlo inside me—Paul the father who took me to Dr. Fabian's and Yankee Stadium but never watched me play. It may have been disingenuously sentimental, but I pictured him beside me at the game, spurning the pomp of his funeral, rooting for his grandson.

Bunny retaliated by leaving my name (and my children's names) off the family letter to mourners and friends.

It took me many years more, beyond the span of this book, to return to the site of Grossinger's.

I feared the worst.

I had to take an extremely wide detour (from where I was going) to get there. Unfortunately, the road was longer than I remembered, and twilight had already settled.

Because the original buyers had stripped the plumbing and removed fancy doorknobs before the next team took possession, I expected at least barbed wire blocking the entrance. I was not prepared for guards at the gate house.

They rose instantly at the sight of a vehicle. There was twenty-four-hour maintenance.

While we discussed the situation (no one was allowed on the premises), I tried to peer beyond. Most of the skyline looked unscathed. At least from the outside, missing buildings were not evident. With one exception. Where the Main Building used to be was the silhouette of a massive alien tower. I couldn't take my eyes off it, like a crash-landing of Satan in his palace.

Then I remembered something. Along a side road lay the cottage of Aunt Rose's wild son Artie.

Of course! In the succession of Grandma's different wills he had been deeded a building exempt from any subsequent transfer of the Hotel—an event that probably seemed as unlikely then as the fall of the Soviet Union.

Through fate Artie was the last remaining inhabitant of Grossinger's. He held an easement. The guards could not disallow my request to visit him.

His wife Renée answered the door-bell. Not notably surprised to see me even after thirteen years, she sat upright on the couch in her '70s-style den. She talked as though nothing had changed about how everything had changed.

Artie emerged later, shirtless in underpants. He stood in the center of the living room. He was Ishmael summarizing *Moby Dick,* a jester closing the curtain on an Elizabethan play. He could have said, "And I only am escaped alone to tell thee." He did say:

"It's gone, you know. The bank came and took it. There's nothing here, Richie. It's all gone. They tore it down." Then his eyes brightened. "But the golf course is open. Come back in the summer. They walk right past here on the way to the tee. The pro lives in your father's old house."

"You know what I think," my brother Michael confided later that week. "I believe PG planned it this way, the whole business—the sale to the time-share guys, their collapse, then the drop in value to where he could almost afford the joint again. It was a master stroke. He got it off his hands to idiots who drove its price into the cellar. Then he was going to come and take it back free and clear out of bankruptcy, sign up new partners, and reopen. He would have been out on the course next spring."

After our lunch at Hampshire House, Bob put together a selection of photographs and documents from my mother's bureau and mailed them to me in Berkeley.

I was glad to have their record. The family in which I had grown up was a mystery to me, as obscure and inscrutable as the Shroud of Turin and the Sphinx. I could reach through a veil at a time, but there was always another veil ... and the one I opened would close again inscrutably ("... *not to see me there,*" because in a sense I was never there, there was never a childhood—regular old children was the one thing our mother couldn't permit us to be).

Was there any justification for my brother's diabolic curse, for the omnipotent grandiosity that ruled our family, such that each of us was addicted to reenacting it, even as we fought against it, in gesture after gesture, compulsion after compulsion, all our lives? Why did my sister reach a certain level of womanhood and then wilt into catatonia? Why did my mother cast herself into oblivion? Why did I live in vigilance and fear? Why did Bob make peace with me again and again only to take it back and recast me as the creature from the dark lagoon? What dangers did I yet face like clockwork in my genes?

Ever since the session with him and my father Paul in the Russian Tea Room I had been trying to get my stepfather to repeat his stories for me so I could use them in *Out of Babylon.* But, despite spells of great friendliness, he continued to evade me. We had one telling exchange by mail about how I treated him on a 1950s night after he drove me to a dance at Horace Mann.

"It seemed you couldn't wait to disaffiliate yourself from me," he wrote.

He presumed my behavior was because I was embarrassed by him.

"You were quick to adopt the Grossingers," he added.

"That's how teenagers act," I wrote back. "Do you think Mandy is any different when I leave her off at school? 'Go,' she insists, before anyone sees me. And as for the Grossingers, I think you know how decent they were to me. I'm sorry it left a wound. But it wasn't directed against you."

I wanted him to agree that it was more important to accept each other's truths than to come out always looking like a good guy or a martyr. This other family he was challenging embodied the means of my survival, the fact that I got out alive and somewhat whole. Grossinger's should have lost any bite otherwise. So why did he begrudge it unless he wanted me to dangle on the rope too?

"You were quick to lose us when you went to the Ivy League," he continued, "though you hardly excelled there in the manner I would have expected. And you made no bones about taking a bride out of your faith. I attended your wedding."

What misguided loyalty kept bringing us back to the nightmare like compliant sheep? Was it guilt pretending to absolve us only by denying, again and again, the balm of penance? Was it the fear that, if he let go of the myths that held us together, any justification for our family behavior (a mother scaring her children, ridiculous punishments, hysterical panics, the mental hospital, suicide) would vanish, leaving him with only a vacuum of unbearable loss, of unforgivable waste?

The problem was that, as Jews, we could always proclaim the execration of the holocaust, the persecution of the diaspora (cumulatively over generations). Even set aside Zionist propaganda, it was an inheritance of profound and justifiable suffering. But it had to be decreed the worst of human perfidies, defended against all other claimants. For those who didn't even live it, a sterile agony froze it in place, beyond the healing of time.

The sadism and meanness we routinely directed at one another (and ourselves) from a presentiment of tragedy and doom had less to do with the diaspora and more with a kind of obsessive madness that seized upon exile and genocide as an excuse for bottomless grief (when Yahweh Himself pleaded for love and forgiveness).

What about our shamans, poets, clowns, star-gazers, Qabalists … our *bon vivants* and fortune-tellers? What about Kether and Yesod,

Hesod and Malkhut? What about pure, unhedged, unbartered, dimensionless joy?

All the years of my growing up they said to me (in countless ways), "How can you smile, you traitor? Who gave you the right to let yourself off the hook? What about anti-Semitism? What about the Chosen People? See what the Nazis did to us. Are you going to defile the memory of six million Jews?"

Lamentation upon lamentation. Bereavement drained of compassion. Remorse without empathy. But did the dead really require this of us?

Those in my parents' generation weren't *really* honoring or atoning the pain of their ancestors. They were throwing a tantrum before the universe, accusing blind galaxies of Jew-hating. They were taking on cover for child abuse, emotional terrorism, and other deeds of perverse and inexplicable cruelty.

That summer Lindy and I met Bob for lunch at the Russian Tea Room. As he signed the tab, he did an unprecedented thing: he invited me to join him at the most sacred of occasions, his sister Gus' Sabbath services in her apartment on Ninth Avenue.

"Would you be welcome too, Lindy?" Bob exclaimed upon her expressing interest. "Gus would be delighted."

The next morning Miranda asked to see the building where Martha had jumped. She had already written a poem about the last moments of a grandmother she never met.

After breakfast I walked her to the site.

The elevator man stared at me. "You're Jon's brother, right?"

I said "Um hum," and introduced my daughter.

"I'm Terrence."

He shook each of our hands.

"You live in California, right?"

"Yep. And I don't get here all that often."

"The maid's alone cleaning, but I'm sure Debby and Mr. Towers wouldn't mind if you went in."

I wasn't so sure. In fact, I suspected he knew I was an intruder and was goading sacrilege. With his spooky, high-pitched voice he was classically the man who knew too much. Only Peter Lorre could have played him in the movie—that quixotic, morbid stare betraying god knows how many overheard conversations and matters of privilege.

We were rumbling upward when suddenly he locked the handle, freezing the elevator between floors. He turned with a cunning smile: "I saw your mother that day." It took a moment for me to realize what he was telling us.

"You did?"

"I was the last person who saw her alive. She was a beautiful woman. So sweet, Mrs. Towers. She treated me so well. She knew my father before me, and she always had a charitable tip for either of us."

"She was a compassionate person," I said.

"She seemed a little odd that last time," he continued, "gay, more talkative than usual. 'Nice day, Terrence,' she said—and it was. She gave me a dollar."

His board lit up and buzzed.

"I heard her land. Mind you, I didn't know what it was. It made a terrible noise, much louder than you might have thought. I went to see if something had fallen off the building. At first I thought it was a doll. But it was a naked person, so I called the police. She didn't look too bad. You'd think for falling that far. . . ."

Miranda flashed me an amazed look.

"I don't understand it. She threw bottles of pills out ahead of her. They spilled all over the pavement. She threw her clothes too."

"When someone takes their life, I guess they're entitled to make the statement they want."

"I think you're right. But I'll never forget it. I was the last person to see her alive, and you're the first ones I've told." He started the elevator with an abrupt lurch.

"Thank you for telling me," I said.

Busy vacuuming, the maid seemed unfazed by our intrusion. I led Miranda to the treasure trove.

For a while I was mesmerized sorting through artifacts, but I had seen most of these by now so I began hunting for the journals. They turned up in an unsuspected form—a kind of daybook conventionally used to record appointments.

My mother wrote in a voice partly unknown, partly familiar. Each entry in the book she traced a feeling of discontent (sometimes calling it "depression," sometimes merely alluding to "it"). Mixed in with this record of her mood—her torment—were accounts of social occasions, homilies of pop psychology, and brazen gossip. She valorized Hitzig's diagnoses and recommendations. She hinted every so often at Jon as a tragedy best not mentioned.

She seemed to be aware whenever someone important to her was visiting New York or in the spotlight that day—an actor, a statesman, John Kennedy, Frank Sinatra, Arthur Miller. She longed to have a connection to these people, and she expressed this usually by sarcasm—belittling the press accounts, the adoring masses, the unsophisticates. In fact, sarcasm was her dominant tone. It overshadowed sadness. She felt superior to everyone; yet she was haunted to a degree that left her stymied and self-pitying, reduced to sniping at other people's gaucheries.

She recalled from time to time that Ed Sullivan, the TV host, had sent her love letters while she was still married to Paul.

She celebrated Judy Garland singing "Battle Hymn of the Republic" on her TV show after John Kennedy's assassination. *"Mine eyes have seen the glory of the coming of the Lord"* were words Martha wished *she* could have sung in fury to the world.

I appeared once. Until I read her description I had forgotten the particular skein of events—how, after she had refused to see Robin for over a year, we arranged to meet for tea at her apartment. Beforehand she was sure (in her journal) I would find a way to spoil the occasion.

In her entry that evening she recounted the day, complaining that her pleasure at seeing her grandchild was totally ruined by my actions. She believed I purposely delayed my departure to force a confrontation with Bob. She barely got me out the door in time.

"I succeeded. Bob would have never forgiven me if—God forbid—he had had to look at Richard and his wife and the baby as well!"

I wasn't aware then that Bob had me under such interdict. I may even have been naively stalling for his return so he could get to *see* Robin.

The grapes of wrath, for sure!

On the Sabbath, Lindy and I dressed in good clothes and took a cab downtown to the East Side projects. We rode the clanky elevator to the twelfth floor.

At the door Gus' son Jimmy, a man our age, greeted us. Then we hugged ancient Augusta Turetsky.

Bob motioned us to seats around a tiny table. No one recalled that I was a heathen, in fact, the signature infidel. No one noticed that Lindy wasn't Jewish.

We sang Hebrew prayers, ate challah and soup, and lit the candles at sundown. Then Bob and his eighty-eight-year-old sister argued over some minutiae of the closing of the ceremony.

"He's always got to have the last word," she remarked, putting her arm around my wife and leading us to the door.

"What was it all about?" Lindy asked me in the cab uptown. "What did we fight about over all those years? What did he hold against me?"

"I'm sure it was something," I said. "It must have been something. Otherwise we wouldn't have spent so much time on it."

"But it wasn't over my not being Jewish."

"We fought among shadows in an illusion that we stood in light."

6

Changelings and Ghosts

At sixteen Miranda changed. The roots of her hair grew out so black as to make the blonde seem dyed. Invisible wounds on the bottoms of her feet left blood on her socks. By Christian legacy these were stigmata, but in Hindu medicine punctureless blood is a mark of spiritual transformation profound enough to leave a residue.

Miranda *was* a different person. More precisely, in the shell of a girl who had always been Miranda a timeless being was emerging.

She began corresponding with a prisoner in Arizona:

> When they brought your letter to my cell, it didn't immediately hit me that you were responding to my address in *East West Journal.* I hadn't gotten any mail in about a year (I used to be on a mailing list for junk mail about UFOs; I like to read about that stuff) so I assumed your letter was a hoax from one of the inmates. That's the type of thing people

> would do in here. When I realized that you were a real person in the free world who wanted to correspond with me, well I can't explain how that felt. It was like a little shock went right through me. It was positive, but it was kind of unreal in a sense. Thank you very much for writing.
>
> You are the first person to write me in six years, so if my conversation seems a bit stilted to you you'll have to keep in mind that I'm somewhat retarded socially. It's unavoidable when one spends so many years in prison, and I've been in here for about twelve years. By my calculations I should be out of here in 2012, when I'm about 60. Of course I don't plan on living that long, so it doesn't really matter. . . .
>
> I'm 38 years old. You're probably younger. I'm simply figuring the odds. I'm a Vietnam vet. The only holidays I celebrate are the vernal and autumnal equinoxes. I've never really been into the sports scene much, but before I got busted I was into spelunking—that's exploring caves. This would explain why you sent me the picture of caves in your first letter. Of course you didn't know that when you sent it, did you?

Our daughter was waking up from a long dream of innocence.

"I chose you as my parents," she announced one night at dinner. "You did a really good job for sixteen years. Now I'm taking responsibility on myself."

She was talking like a baby lama.

"That's quite some speech, Miss Miranda," Lindy said.

Herbalist Jeanne Rose and her agent showed up at our house one afternoon. "Jeanne doesn't like publishers," he explained, "so my job is to find someone willing to let her be her own publisher." Three months later we brought out *Kitchen Cosmetics* and then *Jeanne Rose's Herbal Guide to Food.*

Former *Look* editor George Leonard, now Richard Heckler's partner in an aikido dojo, gave us the rights to reissue his countercultural classics, first *Education and Ecstasy,* then *The Ultimate Athlete,* an 800,000-copy seller for Viking. George chose copublishing too.

North Atlantic's main project in the spring was *Ayahuasca Visions,* an oversize oblong color book depicting an imperiled South American cosmology through forty-nine paintings of Pablo Amaringo, a Peruvian shaman, with commentary by anthropologist Luis Eduardo Luna. For the back cover I wrote: "Enchanted castles and pagodas, spaceships with their inhabitants floating above curandero huts, tree-stump spirits and shamanic submarines, giant armadillos and red sorcerers, forest gnomes and monkeys, ospreys and jugglers, radars and floating cities, a black snake with a yellow aura! For the first time in Western book-learning we see our fantasy of the rain-forest as a Third Eye of the Earth.... The false glitter of Euro-American technology palls before the sheer profundity of the spiritualized jungle."

While visiting Denver that summer, Miranda and I set out in hopes of locating the only vegetarian restaurant in the *Yellow Pages* (my daughter was now a vegan). After an hour of map meandering we came to the correct street number ... marking an empty storefront. However, down the same block was an elegant-looking Japanese café named Domo. A menu in the window listed exotic dishes at absurdly low prices (dollar salads and four-dollar meals). All week we returned for raw turnips, shiitake mushrooms, yam-cake noodles, mochi balls, bonito chips, soybean curd, and seaweed salads. From Berkeley I sent a letter to the "owner."

It turned out that Domo was run by the Japanese Cultural Center; its chef was Gaku Homma, a martial artist. He had already completed *Aikido for Life* and was interested in copublishing it. That simple guide turned out to be "your most successful book to date," said Charlie, as it surpassed a thousand a month in the chains in the wake of Steven Segal's Hollywood morality plays. The Domo recipes appeared later as *The Folk Art of Japanese Country Cooking.*

Then Charlie directed another cookbook to us. A Berkeley restauranteur named Somchai Aksomboon had come to his office with a manuscript. He told Chai (and his writer, Diana Hiranaga) North Atlantic was "the best local press doing copublishing." After Paula designed a color section, the book came out as *Thai Cooking from the Siam Cuisine Restaurant.*

Copublishing made everyone happy; it was an exquisite application of the economy of scale. We provided national distribution on an attractive list of books—a pipe dream for most self-publishers—along with half the profits, for an initial outlay to cover half the production costs. In return we got full partners who promoted and sold their books enthusiastically and never complained about greedy publishers (because they *were* the publishers).

"So that's where all the money goes!" George Leonard exulted, slapping the table as he finished the math in his head—seven publisher dollars for every one to the author. "I always wondered. I turned my publishers into millionaires. Damnit, lunch is on me."

We were giving away windfalls ("these are death-wish contracts," Jeanne's agent warned); yet, somehow magically, we were getting windfalls back.

On a trip to Denver years later, Sensei Homma cooked Lindy and me dinner at his dojo over a fire in an iron pot, then toasted us with sake. A senior disciple translated his Japanese: "May I never sleep with my feet pointed West because I do not want to insult my esteemed partners in California."

In the summer of 1990 I took Miranda to visit Robin in his first professional role—as John Todd's apprentice, the designer of a raw-sewage treatment facility in the town dump of Marion, Massachusetts.

A friendship that began in our living room in Plainfield had blossomed unpredictably. The world had not ended in the winter of '74 (as it was supposed to, either from famine-ridden hordes or the subtle body of Kohoutek). Though the planet was in more dire straits than ever, we had beaten the short-term odds: Robin had grown to be a man, even to drive a petroleum-powered vehicle (something Wilson Clark, long dead, swore wouldn't happen).

Our son was helping John arrange bacteria, worms, snails, fish, and various species of plants in a series of giant aquarium-like cylinders. Gravity-driven passage between them converted heavy-metal septage into drinking water.

Cruising Cape Cod in an Ocean Arks truck with a car phone, Robin chuckled about what his school friends would think. We walked the dump together, visiting the llama and various goats and geese who congregated there. "I wonder if he thinks he's just a big goat," Robin mused as the Peruvian immigrant led his strange flock behind us.

In the City I called Bunny. Our estrangement ended as inexplicably as it began. As we headed down 68th Street toward 2nd Avenue, she reminisced about the past and regretted not having been a better mother to Michael and James. “I know now I failed them,” she remarked, “in fact, dreadfully so.”

“But you also gave so much that most mothers don’t.”

“To you I did. You were easy. You weren’t my son; you were a gift. I loved you right from the beginning. And you always returned it in kind to me. You always knew who I was. I could count on you for that—to tell me about things like yielding to deflect anger. You got that from t’ai chi. Or what the Tibetans think about the afterlife. Or the color of the sky on Mars. What I never gave your brothers was the one thing they needed most: discipline, a sense of order and safety in the world. But you know, Richard, I no longer feel guilty about it because how could I give them something I didn’t have myself?”

Then she hummed a tune from *Carousel* and marvelled at the curbside gardens of kale and daffodils: “Isn’t it marvelous that there’s that much beauty still left in the world.”

All that year I sensed a shift at my core. Old things were awakening—sensations prior to meaning. They contained apathy, terror, loneliness, longing. They bore a shadow fragrance that made jasmine and sage excruciating. Somewhere between childhood and my family with Lindy I had left an unlived life. Now my wife was in graduate school, doing cultural studies, hanging out with her colleagues. “I’m tired of being a caretaker or a clone of you,” she said. “I just want to be an ordinary person like everyone else.” The kids I had raised no longer existed; in their place were a young biologist and an artist wise beyond her years.

Habits that had gotten me this far would no longer work. The marriage, North Atlantic Books, my writings on stars and embryos had served as a convincing cover story. I loved it and was willing to live it forever with every cell of my being. But I didn’t have forever, and the pagan thing I fled would be there in the end, in the Bardo too, if I didn’t meet it now. This was “empty nest,” “mid-life crisis,” and the hungry ghosts of Buddhist dharma all at once.

In September I impulsively signed up for a three-year somatics training run by Polly’s husband, Randy. Each Monday I crossed the Richmond Bridge to Corte Madera, where I joined a group of thirty or so therapists. Located in a hillside grove populated by deer, our space looked down the other way at commuter traffic rolling along 101 (to which we closed our eyes on zafus of assorted sizes and colors for fifteen minutes of meditation before class).

Typically Randy opened with a lesson from the late Israeli therapist Moshe Feldenkrais (his system was called "Awareness through Movement"). Lying in patches of sun and shade, we carried out instructions to track slight distinctions between parts of our bodies, then to move infinitesimally, separating them—hips one way, shoulders the other; head rotating, eyes in opposition.

Sometimes these exercises required unusual physical contexts—for instance, our fingers interlaced in the customary manner, then in the noncustomary way (which for me had the right thumb on the outside). Asked to discover what mobility was simultaneously lost or gained in other parts of our bodies, we all found astonishingly greater neck and pelvic movement after reintercalating our fingers. When Randy instructed us to interlace our toes, it was an ordeal even to feel where one toe ended and the next began, let alone to wiggle each independently and insert them. ("The noncustomary way next?" one woman joked.)

All that fall Miranda wrote a play called *The Lifers* based on her correspondence with Franco, the prisoner. She was determined to produce it herself: raise the money, cast, direct, and stage it. Running an ad in *Call Board* got her a pro to play the prisoner. The remaining cast and crew were assembled from her friends.

> It is a big concrete box about three times taller than it is wide. So it is very big, but all the space is above your head. It has only one purpose and that is to drive one toward claustrophobia and insanity. These diseases are then treated with drugs that will make you into a nicer person. A person with no will; a person who is missing the part of his brain that wants to live. They can do this to you. These drugs were designed to do this. Solitary. At the very top of the 15-foot ceiling is a blue light. It is never turned off, and closing your eyes only makes it shine brighter.... It makes the colors and shapes inside your head grow into monsters that are scarier than any weapon....
>
> Sunflower, there is one thing that I require from you. I absolutely must have your word. In exchange I give you my ears, my shoulder, my hands, my eyes, my word, and my loyalty. I promise only that I will

never ask you to break a law or a promise, and that I will never lay any burden on you that is too heavy or without just cause....

Exploring Berkeley, Miranda raised small donations while contracting for lights, chairs, and props. Local 'zine, rock, and recording scenes provided her best sources. She still lacked a building and, when none of the usual candidates materialized, she determined to rent the notorious punk club on Gilman Street. It was a hangout for big kids and heavy metal, but she was there every afternoon, bargaining for rehearsal time with bands of mostly guys with painted hair and mohawks, metal belts, tattoos, and body rings. They also pitched in on her set.

My early days at Deer Run House I imagined massage along the lines of shiatsu and bodywork. As an amateur among therapists, I worried mainly about my ignorance of anatomy.

But Randy's work had little to do with manipulation and techniques or the old kinetics of adjusting body parts to conform to models of holism and release of tension. It was about discriminating oneself deeply enough to detect variations of neural activity beyond gross anatomy in other people, more like dancing with quantum particles than throwing a medicine ball.

In order to feel anything, I had to give up my proclivity to complicate, my instinct to keep my head above water. I had to stop overriding and muddling my own acts and commit to what my hands did, whether I admired them or not, considered them correct or not.

The training required embodying our affectations, filling our unlived spaces. In minor gaps of attention, idiosyncratic throwaway gestures, whole universes opened.

Habitually I tended to amp and exaggerate, to turn things into ideas. "But this," Randy warned, "only diminishes profundity at the very moment it is about to happen."

"Your touch is usually right," my training partner Amini encouraged, "your words almost always unnecessary." This was the opposite of my lifelong credo.

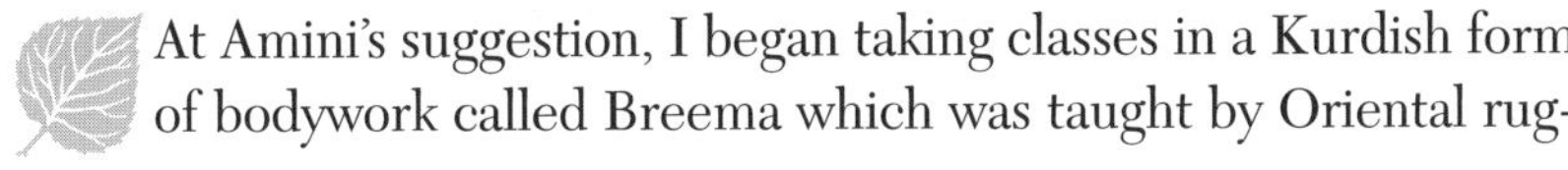

At Amini's suggestion, I began taking classes in a Kurdish form of bodywork called Breema which was taught by Oriental rug-dealer Manocher Movlai. One morning and evening a week I walked a block and a half from my home to a cottage near the juncture of Claremont and College where, on a floor covered with Turkish carpets, fifty people practiced sequences of shifting weight onto partners. Treatments involved hierarchies of leans and releases, some with hands, some with elbows, many with feet, and one with our bellies.

Claiming to have learned this art from his grandfather, Manocher entertained an almost cult following as, every week, he seemed either to invent or remember bizarre techniques.

Breema was not as much therapeutic bodywork as spiritual improv, an attempt to shock the system into awareness of both its place in the universe and the presence of kindred creatures around it.

As our course progressed, Randy added Polarity, Zero Balancing, and Craniosacral Therapy. First we learned to send breath to our bellies, sides, and backs. Then we found energy systems along each other's torsos, sensing the colors and fields generated by each chakra. Fingertips skimming above our prone partner, we treated auras by stroking and stirring invisible vapory substance. Later, like musicians tightening and loosening strings, we practiced craniosacral therapy, fingerpads on the base of each other's skulls and sacra. Following the ebb and flow of cerebrospinal fluid into organs, we encountered unfathomable shadows marked by sudden cessations of rhythm, remains of old traumas—what Randy called energy cysts.

I was arriving from within at a zone I had intuited but never known, the realm of Hopi kachinas and Esalen legend. It went as far as I was willing to listen, and stopped the moment I stopped listening.

Constantly urging us to *do less,* and then less again, Randy taught me to go after whatever was there, however strange, however submerged in layers of tissue and organs, spiralling and trailing through complex visceral objects oscillating in one another in three dimensions—to contact it, blend, and trail it (taffylike) to its own intrinsic resolution.

I knew I had it when, absent-mindedly during a lesson, my motionless hand sucked deeper and deeper into the carpet. I was trying to detect its nonexistent cranial pulse. My projection went through the floor, through the foundations of the house, but I encountered nothing alive.

I was back on the path Polly charted for me fifteen years earlier, this time for real.

After Breema one evening, an assistant took me aside and extended the teacher's invitation to visit. The next morning I arrived at the carpeted room to find only the towering Gurdjieffian sage, a visitor from the Eurasian frontier. He raised a single finger and touched my chest.

"You have many ideas," he said, "but only one heart."

The Lifers ran for two weekends. Its modest audience included mostly teens (plus everyone Miranda's parents could recruit). An actress spoke her own lines:

> "I guess everybody wants to meet someone who will replace this everyday world with something dazzling. Well, one day you murdered a man and you ended up in jail; twelve years later you got my first letter. I knew at the time that I had sent that letter to somewhere dark, and you sent me a taste of its evil, which I expected. But what's all this beauty? Why do I feel so holy when I think of you, and where you are, and what you've done?"

"It's you who have ended the dark, Miranda," the actor playing Franco called from a spotlight on his jail space. "Because this thing we have between us feels more real and true than the lock that keeps me here."

A review in a local 'zine acclaimed:

> Even if you're still sleeping, or just grabbing your first cup of coffee, sooner or later you'll deal with the world she's fashioning. Because she's not waiting for the next edition of the Punk Handbook to tell her the appropriate ways to rebel and be creative. She's writing the fucking book!

She was Miranda July now, no longer Miranda Grossinger. When Lindy protested the stage name, Miss July fired back, "None of us were ever really 'Grossinger.'"

It was inalterably clear. My kids were not the fairy orphans I imagined, born and raised in Lindy's and my sanctuary. They carried the full legacy of Rothkrug, Hough, and B———. They were going to quest in dark places, have otherworldly dreams, and do their own battles with the ghosts.

T'ai chi had become a Taoist puzzle for me, the same silent moves year after year, at which I remained an eternal beginner. In 1983 I stopped going to class. For the next seven years I practiced only sporadically. I forgot most of the set.

Then in January, 1991, I drove up the coast to Garberville where Paul Pitchford was starting a Chinese-medicine clinic at Heartwood Institute. That night, as we toted our vegetarian-banquet trays to a corner in the community center, I asked the recent emigré from Idaho a question about algae. "The best food for you," he teased, "would be to rise at 6 AM tomorrow morning for my t'ai-chi class."

I promised to try.

Outside the kiva, fog burying the sun's attempt to rise and minimally warm us, Paul corrected my rusty set. He also offered a piece of advice. As I considered aloud whether to go back to Martin Inn's Oakland group, he joked, "Why don't you study with a real world champion. At least you'll learn to fight."

It was a typical Pitchford ploy, to advance the antithesis of what he purportedly believed.

Peter Ralston was a new author of ours who ran the infamously combative Cheng Hsin School of Ontology and Martial Arts only a few blocks west of my home. He was World Champion (or so the sign above his storefront proclaimed, for he had won some tournament in Taipei in 1978). This declamation—a landmark of Telegraph Avenue kitsch—had led me to reject a manuscript he kept submitting going back to our Richmond days. World champion of what?

Paul had trained with Ralston in the early '70s; then they had gone their separate ways—Paul into herbs and ritual Buddhism, Peter into Zen and samurai training.

Cheng Hsin apprentices kept bringing their master's book back to me at approximately three-year intervals. Their patience paid off. I had snobbily limited our t'ai-chi fare to the elite lineage of Ben Lo and Cheng Man-ch'ing, but we needed new territory, even if it offended our purist colleagues. American-lingo warrior arts were a perfect item for chain bookstores—t'ai chi in Tae Kwon Do robes.

Joining his class, I soon found Peter to be a Heidegger of combat, a pragmatic street fighter who threw aside homage to traditional form and reinvented moves solely to suit function. He had won his fabled Taiwan match by scientific fighting. He meant to drown out, frustrate, and negate all formal sets, macho propagandas, psychospiritual pieties, and ch'i myths students brought along. His intention was to provide four walls, a floor, mirrors, training partners, and a riddle. Cheng Hsin was the premier school of phenomenology and martial arts.

"Correction is about changing *whatever* is not effective," the World Champion announced at the opening meeting of "Principles of Effortless Power." "My only question is: does it work? I don't want to reject tradition to make another superficial system." A balding pugilist with a fierce jovial stare, he spun, lotus-kicked, and struck an invisible target with both fists before a mirror reflecting another mirror—an infinite regression of tigers. "Begin with who you are, what your actual experience is, your fears and fantasies." He halted and faced us, a group comprised mostly of eager young testosteroned males (Martin's class was primarily women). "When you're in line to ride the roller coaster, most of your problem is concept. What you fear isn't what comes up once you're *on* the roller coaster. It's all in your mind. Get it? The real thing, not the fear! If you had to fight Mohammed Ali in his prime, you might think your lack of boxing skill would be your greatest problem. But getting into that ring, feeling the energy of the crowd—just being in that situation would defeat you before you began."

So "principles of effortless power" meant measuring steps with the precision of a surveyor, aligning with gravity, feeling an opponent's energy before he moved, retraining one's own predisposition to act in an habitual manner.

I abandoned my set and began anew. I walked on invisible posts above an ocean. I measured steps in half-inches, the placement of my feet in degrees. I gauged a plumb line dropping through my head into the "bubbling wells" of my soles. I pretended not to know if the wall existed. Then I did push-hands with the wall.

By feeling what it was like to be a water droplet I became a human droplet.

I stood face to face with a bellicose jock who, without making physical contact, tried to terrify me with gestures and kiais. I remained calm and deflected his force.

I strolled around the room with my eyes closed, hands extended, sensing energy fields of my classmates so I wouldn't bump into them.

"Accept what is, or may be, always as the first step. Adhere to activity and observe the requirements for an advantageous position." These were Peter's mottos.

"I'm here and you're there," he announced one day. "I'm here and you're there. I'm here and you're there. This is the single most profound thing. You think you hear me, but you don't. I'm here and you're there." He took a step and pointed. "Every inch between us is conscious. I'm here and you're there. I'm going to keep repeating it until you get it. I'm *here* and you're *there.*"

"We might think we want utopia," he told us another time, "but there is no place in it for us. It wouldn't work. It would break down in a relatively short time. I wouldn't even give it a year. Because you see, we wouldn't be there. We don't have the discipline for something like that. We don't have the courage, the persistence, the overwhelming courage it takes for something like that. In fact, you want to go there *so you don't have to be courageous.* Right? You want to go there so you can get away from this!"

Integrated Resources crashed with the fall of Michael Milken and Drexel, but Jay and Siggy got out in time (though they were the recipients of unjustly nasty press in *The Wall Street Journal*). Seymour broke off to form his own family-management firm. We followed him.

That fall he called me with an idea for a joint venture, a holistic-health project with a Japanese doctor on the board of Beth Israel. His account of Dr. Shinya was a series of Borscht Belt punchlines: "He's the world's leading colon specialist. When this guy talks diet, people listen. He's looked at over 200,000 colons. I asked him what the next best was, and he told me, '20,000 tops!'"

I tried to get a sense of how realistic the project was, but Seymour was too excited to split hairs. "Can you come? I had lunch with him today and I couldn't believe you weren't there. You know, this is your kind of guy: he eats seaweed and does martial arts."

In Manhattan that must have seemed vintage North Atlantic Books.

Miranda cut her hair skinhead short. She and her friend Jo wrote the first issue of a 'zine they called "Snarla in Love." Her style was Generation X meets William Faulkner (though she had never read William Faulkner):

> Now she walks again; she walks away in the sure way. Heels coming down hard on everything below her. In the low, lowest whispering she spins something around her that will protect her from the night. From every night that feels like this. Hollow and bloody.
>
> Are you there? Yes, I will always be here for you. Even when I die? Yes. Even when I am dying? Yes. Even after that? Yes. Even in a million years? Yes. Whenever you are there I am there inside you and beside you, I am there always. Yes. You are never alone, when everyone leaves I am there. Yes. When you are fifty I will be there. When you are seventy I will be there. Yes Yes Yes. I am here now. Let us go home. Yes let's. We will sleep together and hold each other in the big bed. Yes Yes yes.

Two years later (1993), during her brief stint at Santa Cruz—before she fled college (1995) to become a performance artist in Portland, Oregon ... before (1997) she rode the Kill Rock Stars label out of Olympia, Washington, with time-travel, mind-warp cuts like "Hotel Voolevoo" and "The F-A-T-E" ("Touch the hair on the left side of your head—casually. You'll notice that the strands are made of fiber-optic wire filaments")—we were to get a portent of who our daughter was. Her left eyebrow was pierced and a ring inserted (1993). Then she came home one weekend with her hair in hard mohawk spikes. She now looked like the kids from Gilman. But she spurned any cliché.

"You think I'm one of them," she charged us. "But I'm not. I'm no one. I have no gender. I want people staring at me on the street *to have no idea who I am.*"

"I can't wait till this phase passes," Lindy sighed.

Miranda walked over and stuck her face less than an inch from Lindy's. "Look at this!" she demanded. "This isn't a phase. This is me." ("We repeat—your hair is not your hair. Blink if you understand this.... Your brain is not your real brain. Blink if you understand this.")

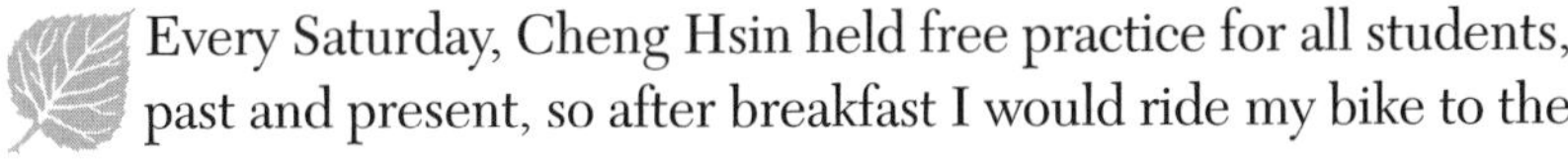

Every Saturday, Cheng Hsin held free practice for all students, past and present, so after breakfast I would ride my bike to the dojo and hang around for training. One such morning I made the acquaintance of Ron Sieh, an original Ralston apostle who had helped Peter train for the W.C. (as insiders referred to it).

He was a small, wiry guy, about forty, incredibly fast, long stringy hair, movements like a hawk and a snake. He was showing off, refusing to acknowledge anyone's presence, taking big leaping kicks and shouting, "Yowee!" I thought he was prankishly blocking the mirror as I was trying to correct my set. After stewing about this for a moment, I broke the tension by asking him a question about the form. "I'm too advanced for you," he growled . . . and went on kicking.

I hated him. Yet there was something irresistible. He reminded me of my college buddy Schuyler. His persona was part Bruce Lee, part Peter Pan.

I knew I was going to ask him to be my teacher.

We met on Tuesday for lunch.

He said, "I'll teach you as long as you interest me."

So we began practicing together an hour a week at my house on the wooden floor above the pool. A disciple of both Vipassana and boxing, Ron trained mostly being present, paying attention, "filling the mind's holes," he called it.

"This isn't just mechanics and footwork," he reminded me, as we sparred in free form, "although you've got a problem there too. It's about spirit. *You need to find your spirit.* You're thinking too much, not seeing the world as it is. Do you ever *truly* realize that there's just as much space behind you as in front of you? I *know* you don't feel your back. Guy, you're not a puppet. Your roots go down beneath the earth. I bet you don't feel your feet, let alone what's under them. Make spikes under the ground. Shoot photon torpedoes! Put all that nervous energy down there. Be creative."

My brother Jon's situation was getting worse. Gunshots ricocheted down the hall; glass smashed above him and fell to concrete. He filed a report with the police. Having the constabulary enact their ineffectual routine merely turned the perpetrators against him. He was desperate to escape 7Q.

Bob called me for help: "Your brother seems to have worn out his welcome in Knickerbocker Plaza."

Since my draft of *Out of Babylon* had been circulating among the old-timers at Bookpeople, I spoke to them about hiring Jon.

"Closest thing to getting Murphy from *One Flew Over the Cuckoo's Nest*," replied Randy Finglund. "We'd welcome him."

But Jon had his own notions. He journeyed across the marshlands around Southport, Connecticut, exploring olden sites of Pequot Indians, doing research in the town library, depicting the landscape in poems. Sometimes he found a place to sleep in the wild; otherwise he returned on the evening train.

One afternoon in the warehouse Ron was mocking how I never really punched, how I didn't put commitment behind my strikes. "That's a girl's fist," he singsonged. "You know what happens when you punch like this?" He smacked his fist into his palm. "Crack! Broken bones!" He laughed.

We tried again. He was goading me to come back at him. Whenever I moved—no matter how quickly—he was faster, and tagged me.

"Zap!" he shouted. "Nailed again, big buddy! I'm trying to get you to be the best you can, but you obviously have some other agenda."

He was aiming to make me furious ... and succeeding.

"You're locked in this limited image of what you're doing. Some weird little fantasy of winning perhaps?"

He began to jab harder, shouting things like "Dangerous art!" and "This is real!," dancing like Rocky, putting on a white-trash game face. As I executed a circle, punch, and kick, he faked terror, ducked, and called out, "Your body has some skill, but your mind is *all* fucked up!"

He had captured my spirit of play, my sense of the absurd. I came back at him like Ali in Zaire. Suddenly we stood toe to toe, throwing real punches—jabs and hooks. "Bob," he shouted. "Take your head out of the way—duh! Don't squeeze your thumb in your fist, you dope. You'll break your thumb. That's it. Keep going. Just because you made a nice move is no excuse to drop your guard." Mimicking a Roadrunner cartoon, he pointed at the ceiling, then laid a soft punch on my nose.

"Every time you let something slide by into unconsciousness, you're doing that. And we're practicing something else."

I moved more quickly, dancing around him, trying out the hsing-i Snake and Dove he had taught me. With amusement Ron neutralized them, then knocked me over hard. "Faster is not the issue. Timing is the issue. Stay in control. Hands out, dude! Move your left foot. No, your other left foot." I giggled and sighed. "Don't have a plan. When you think my punch is dead, I bend my elbow and turn it into a hook. Do the same. Render my actions obsolete by *your* actions." I took a step behind him, grabbed his arm, and attempted a version of Bend Bow, Shoot Tiger. For a moment we were stuck in place. Then I dislodged him and threw him stumbling in the other direction.

"Was that pure muscle or mystical will power?" he asked. "Did I detect Shoot Tiger?"

I nodded.

"You don't want to fight strength with strength. You don't want to make winning your goal. Remember Cheng Man-ch'ing: invest in loss. What did Bira call it: playing in the mind?"

He pranced, darted, and rolled his hands in a spiralling ball. "Today I'm going to be [his voice changed to a cadent hush] . . . the cloud man."

Our exchange became swift and coordinated. For a minute I fantasized I was matching him. I wasn't flailing; I was corkscrewing out of the ground. He was backing up, and I was connecting. I couldn't stop grinning like a kid.

"You're doing great. But don't get hypnotized by the drama. Stay sober."

Then he called out, "Truce," and we fell down together laughing.

"Now that's fighting with spirit," he pronounced, grabbing my shoulders and shaking me as we headed outside. "But you have to throw your punches in one piece, from the earth through your hips down your forearm. There's still too much parasitic motion. The goal isn't activity. The goal is awareness. You want to die awake, to realize your last breath as your last breath."

That night, from within sleep, I sat upright in a cold sweat. My father Paul had been bent over me, pounding my body with his mammoth fists.

I had gotten off the floor and begun hitting him back. Dancing like a darning needle in my own dream, I became Ron. My father was helpless.

As I smashed him, domains of childhood flooded back. He was every bullying counsellor and sadistic uncle, every dominant male who used his power and the threat of fists to control me. He was the phony parent who tried to claim and corrupt me. I threw hsing-i corkscrews and t'ai-chi jabs. I showed him Eagle, Snake, and Monkey. I kept striking the fat man until he was a blob.

I fell out of my dream.

I went into Robin's empty bedroom and lay on the mattress, weeping.

I arrived in New York the first weekend in December. I called my stepfather in the morning at his office. He was friendly but brief: "Patsy's. 52nd and 2nd. Meet me there at noon."

Not knowing how long the bus would take, I gave it plenty of time and arrived ten minutes early as they were opening the place. I sat quietly at a table by the bar, out of range of the cigarettes, chefs wandering back and forth from the kitchen, the maître d' straightening his tie. Every now and then the woman by the coat check asked, "Who are you waiting for?" (just as she remembered). "Mr. Towers. He'll be here. He's a little late today."

He showed up at 12:20, shaking his head and telling me, "Patsy's at twelve. Somehow, Richard, this slipped my mind."

It was easy to forget how old he was—pushing eighty, moving woodenly . . . undiminished fire in blue eyes, Jolson in his wizened voice.

His arrival provoked an immediate stir. As he extracted papers from his briefcase and jammed them into the manager's hand, he pointed to his favorite section of the room.

"I know, Mr. Towers."

Once seated, he reviewed our most recent correspondence—an exchange of letters in which he had maligned Dr. Fabian for meddling in his family and I defended my old master.

"I understand that Fabian helped you, but I was always disappointed you fell for the guy. He was a sweet-talking shyster, a typical rich, smug doctor. You were smarter than him. You know I went to his office and told him off."

"You smashed a lamp." The recollection brought a smile. "Perhaps in the long run you were right."

I knew Bob wasn't right for the child saved by the friendly wizard, but he was right for the grown man the great Fabian had tried to make into his most baffling and famous case (and so addicted to the hell of therapeutic dialogue, an endless internal dialogue of fears and their unknowable origins). The doctor and my mother had collaborated, despite themselves, to overendow and memorialize her demons and infiltrate my mind with loyalty to their grail. I understood now that there were no symbols, no hidden meanings—the only path was that of the warrior, and I was running out of time.

"But you overlook something," I added. "It didn't matter that he wasn't a great psychiatrist. He talked to me about things that no one else was willing to. He took some of the bite out of my mother's ghosts. Would that Jonny had had such a dialogue."

"I'll grant you that," Bob said. "What we didn't know at the time!"

After a pause acknowledging the weight of our exchange I told him I mainly wanted to get clear on some Grossinger episodes—Marty the mafia guy, Blackstone's role, the precise path by which Reuben Turetsky matriculated through the Catskills.

We reviewed these through Italian bread, salad, main course.

Then I asked a leftover question from childhood, "Were you really the one who first brought ballplayers to Grossinger's?"

"*I* wasn't the one. It was Arthur Richman. You know Arthur; he worked in the sports department of *The New York Daily Mirror,* now defunct."

"Yep. He's been getting Robin and me Mets tickets."

"Arthur's a prince of a man. You ask him sometime; he'll tell you the story. The first player, I believe, was pitcher Jack Kramer, Handsome Jack. Then he brought Dick Wakefield of the Tigers and Maury McDermott, who liked it so much he wanted to work there during the winter months. He brought Don Larsen, Tony Kubek, Dick Williams, Saul Rogovin. He has a great story about how he used to give them ground rules before they got there. 'Don't ask for bacon or ham with your breakfast. Don't ask for butter with the meat. Don't smoke in the dining room on Friday night or Saturday. Don Larsen said, 'These are the strangest ground rules I ever heard of.'"

Ballplayers resolved, I next asked, "Maybe you could clear up the story about Meyer Weisgal, Max Reinhardt, and Chaim Weizmann. Was Meyer a p.r. guy at Grossinger's?"

"Meyer was *never* a p.r. guy at Grossinger's, Richard! Meyer was a p.r. guy on *Broadway.* He was a journalist; he was a writer. Reinhardt—

what should I say—he was in the movies; Morris Kirsch, David Buroshko; these were impressarios. Reinhardt towered above them; he was *Midsummer Night's Dream;* he was on an international level."

"Got it."

"Meyer was the brashest ... most compelling ... flamboyant personality of his *siècle,* of his class. He envisioned the romance of a people, and Reinhardt did the spectacle of the story of the Jewish tribe, played it all over the country."

"That was 'The Eternal Road'?"

"Yes. Now Weisgal came to me and said two names, 'Chaim Weizmann ... Grossinger's.'"

Bob put a hand on my arm. He was talking so loud the pleasant-looking gentleman eating alone at the next table was hanging on every word.

"Understand, *I* was Grossinger's. Blackstone thought Henny Youngman and Milton Berle were Grossinger's. But Weizmann was the leader who returned the flock to the Promised Land. And Meyer was the kind of a fund-raiser who singlehandedly created the Chaim Weizmann Institute of Science. Picture this. He would have breakfast with a bigshot. The fella, to get rid of him, would write out a check for twenty-five thousand dollars. Meyer would take the check, tear it up, and say, 'That was *forshpise'*—you know: that was the appetizer. Now let's get down to business.' And, boom! he'd walk away with a million dollars. That was Meyer. You got that?"

"Yep."

"I said, 'Meyer, I don't care about Weizmann at Grossinger's, but if you knew what you would do for my mother.' You see, my mother never forgave me for not becoming a rabbi. I told her, 'Mama, I brought Barney Ross, the great boxer, to Grossinger's.' She asks, 'Who is Barney Ross? A *vilder khaye?'* That's a wildman, Richard. 'Mama, I brought Hank Greenberg, the baseball star.' She dismisses that too. A *'shtekn zester'* she calls him. A guy who hits with a club. 'Mama, I brought Eddie Cantor to Grossinger's.' She's still not impressed. 'Eddie Cantor? A *tummler,* a nothing!' But if she would know that her son and Weizmann were to walk arm-in-arm."

His eyes glowed as he recalled something more.

"Richard, you know who became his confidante?"

I shook my head.

"Your mother! Took walks with her. Discussed world affairs with her. Was crazy about her. Weizmann was *craaazzzy* about her. Richard, this was the George Washington of Israel, the guy who made the dream come true. You know his accomplishments. The British claim he won the Battle of Jutland. How would they reward him? He said, 'Let my people go.' He was the first President of Israel since King David. Your mother, Richard!"

I saw a quick-witted young woman, a companion I had never known. Bob's eyes were wistful. He was staring at the unbeheld horizon. We sat in silence.

"And what did *your* mother say when she heard about you and Weizmann?" I finally asked.

"'*Vus zug ikh yetst?* [What do I say now?] Now I know a social director is not a bum.'"

The waiter came for dessert and Bob asked me whether I wanted some three-toned ice cream.

"Sure."

"Give us two, sir."

"So it's true that your parents wanted you to become a rabbi?"

"Oh did they ever want me to be!"

"Did you seriously consider it?"

"Yes. Too many distractions, too many devotions, and too many opportunities for a kid from a coldwater flat on the Lower East Side."

The eavesdropper could bear it no longer. He excused himself and turned his chair around. "May I join your conversation? I'm missing too much by spying."

"By all means," Bob crooned. He pointed to a spot and then reached out to guide the chair to it.

Seating now rearranged, our neighbor turned out to be a movie producer. He was inspired to perform versions of the old Yiddish theater through coffee. Bob and he traded lines and routines.

I turned down the cake tray, drawing a second look from my stepfather. "You'd think my diet was pretty weird these days," I told him. "I take Chinese herbs and eat bee pollen and algae."

"I don't need to hear about your diet. It's enough that you look trim, tennis weight."

After coffee the three of us strolled to the front.

"This man is just a wealth of information," the producer told the maître d'. "He's an original."

"Don't we know that," the manager said. After all, Patsy's was Bob's account.

"I was going to offer to pick up his tab," our friend continued. "But then I got worried he might have more money than me."

"Love it!" Bob exclaimed. "Just love it. Two drinks on me the next time he comes here."

After our friend left, the maître d' confided, "Big customer. He's going to fill the house, bring the whole studio."

"No kidding!"

Then, as Bob introduced me to them as Jennie's grandson, I added that I was also *his* stepson.

"And this is mother and son," my stepfather gestured at the manager and maître d', miffed I had trumped him for just a moment. "Two generations of Patsy's."

On the street he said, "Why don't you give me a call tomorrow morning? I'll see if I can work my schedule around."

We were on to something.

That evening Seymour and I met Dr. Shinya at the Nippon. Arranging for a booth with a curtain around it, our host ordered in Japanese just as, eleven years earlier, Ben Lo had ordered in Mandarin. We were delivered a platter of uni with seaweed noodle soup.

We sat through Shinya's theory of culture and diet and then mapped how to develop his book into a line of food products. I reviewed the stages of publishing and cautioned against unrealistic hopes. I had no idea whether any of this would happen, but it hardly mattered. The dinner itself was the fulfillment of Aunt Ruthie and Cousin Jay's original promise.

I called Bob at eight the next morning. "Patsy's at twelve?" he proposed.

"For sure. Let's do it again."

I arrived less early, but he was even later.

This time I was greeted warmly and included in house conversation.

They wanted to hear all about Grossinger's and get clear on my relation to Bob. I told them about the book I was writing. When I mentioned the details of my mother's death, they were stunned.

"We heard Mr. Towers had tragedy, but you know, we don't ask questions."

"He does remarkably well under the circumstances," I said. "He has a great spirit."

"That he does," echoed the manager. "An incredible man!"

Towers arrived in the rain, folded his umbrella, and announced immediately that North Atlantic was going to publish "Patsy's Italian Cookbook," as he put it.

"With a preface by Frank Sinatra," added the maître d', pointing to his signed picture on the wall.

I blushed.

"You don't believe me," Bob orated. "You should see what this man has done for a Thai restaurant in Berkeley—put them all over B. Dalton, color plates and all. Boom! tourists from Texas show up on vacation in San Francisco, take the BART to Berkeley. He's written a tome called *Planet Medicine*—used in fifty colleges around the country."

I didn't realize he even knew the title—let alone where Berkeley was.

Without explanation we were led to a table on the opposite side of the room.

"You know where I was this morning," I told my stepfather as soon as we were alone.

He looked questioningly.

"I visited Jon."

"How is he?" Bob mumbled. "A gentle soul."

"I thought good. A lot calmer, not as angry."

"He's living in the wrong century. I feel for him."

"So you don't try to change him anymore?"

"Me change Jon. No. I tip my hat to the man for what he is."

Ten seconds later he was back inside the Grossinger legend:

"You could feel it in the funeral for Mark Grossinger Etess. In a lifetime of attending such services, I have never seen such an outpouring of genuine grief and mourning, plus a cortege of scores of limousines and private cars, which came in from Atlantic City, Catskill Mountain resort owners and executives and friends and employees who came down from upstate to pay their respects at a cemetery in New Jersey."

"No one really knows what Grossinger's was," I said, "but everyone knew it was special. Everyone except my father."

"Paul couldn't be blamed," he admonished. "Living at a resort hotel you are brought up with no sense of any value except money and people who come and go. Those of us who discovered the Catskills knew. Paul never had the chance. And I want you to forget my comment about his failure to pick up tabs. He was a good man. But let me tell you a story about my time at Grossinger's." He was beginning the mafia one all over again.

"Wait," I protested. "I've already heard it. As long as we're on Grossinger's I've got a better story."

No one interrupted Towers like that, so he looked questioningly. I grinned back. I had grown up in his household and knew his routines. We laughed together—almost father and son.

"Go ahead," he challenged. "We'll see."

I told him about Heartwood Institute, Humboldt County. We had gone there the first time three years earlier at Christmas. The place was closed, but Paul Pitchford lived on the grounds year-round.

"Heartwood is an alternative healing school." I groped for a way to make this believable to him. "I won't say the Harvard of its kind because that has no relevance. Perhaps it makes more sense to say it is the kind of place Jon would have gone to willingly twenty years ago and that might have healed him. It has remarkable teachers; it also has native American shamans. It even gives a State-certified degree. It was founded by a Jewish guy from Jersey and his wife—Bruce and Chela Burger. He was once a professor of Education at Rutgers, but he travelled through India during the '60s and was totally changed. He began Heartwood in Santa Cruz, then moved to the country. The property he bought was once hunting bungalows."

"I get the picture."

"We were there a few days without seeing either of them because—well, you know, the owners of hotels are like royalty in their palace. Then one night Chela showed up in the dining hall. She looked just like the girls I went to Chipinaw with—classic face, freckles all over, like your sisters' kids. She came looking for me because she wanted to tell me how every summer her family had rented space in the bungalow colonies and her father promised 'Next year at Grossinger's.' 'Tonight,' she announced, 'I'm going to call him and say—We never made it, Dad, but the Grossingers came to us.'"

Bob rapped the table in applause. "You're right," he exclaimed. "It was a better story. Say, while you're at it, do you ever hear from my favorite shortstop?"

A year earlier, under the title *Rowdy Richard,* North Atlantic had published the autobiography of Dick Bartell, the New York Giants sparkplug of Bob's youth. At the time I had Dick autograph a copy to his old fan.

"He's still going strong, attending autograph shows, visiting retirement homes and country clubs. Since he signs and sells the book everywhere, he comes by our warehouse and we load cartons into the trunk of his white Cadillac, right next to his golf clubs. Hey, have I ever told you my great Bartell story?"

"No. I'm enjoying this; go on."

"One day he and I both grabbed for the same carton of books, him probably to prove he could still carry the weight and me out of deference to his age. There were some sheets of plastic foam on top, and we simultaneously nicked and popped them up in the air. We looked at each other and said the exact same words at the exact same moment, 'We blew the doubleplay.'"

"What a story! You and Bartell on the pivot fifty years later." Yes, my stepfather was the master of ceremonies of Manhattan; he did best conducting a light symphony. But behind it I forever heard the prayers for the dead as surely as one heard *shtetl* dirges behind Irving Berlin's love songs. Children of rabbis and cantors wrote the music of Broadway, which is why, under their jaunty tunes, lies the depth of the entire service, the tragedy of the diaspora, not just Hebrew but Tibetan, Zulu, Apache, Irish. From Palestine to Belfast: *"Oh, Danny Boy. . . ."*

But isn't this also the central teaching of Buddhism—that joy is true only when one simultaneously feels its background of pain. How could there be a more exquisite melody, a different song? *("But come ye back/when summer's in the meadow. . . .")* Pain is the fantastic energy that brings us here in the first place, that indicates we are serious, that there is no going back on incarnation. Pain is more than a secular diaspora. It is the knowledge that everything is temporary and impermanent and that finally we and those we love must die . . . perhaps so that we can be reborn as something else . . . and something else again . . . again and again . . . until we are resolved and simplified. *This* is the yearning of "somewhere over the rainbow"—or, for the Tibetan, a pure lunar disk surrounded by devas and cherubs, petals falling like rain. ". . . *where troubles melt like lemon drops* . . . ," but not for a billion lifetimes yet, which is why the bittersweet foreboding.

"Hey, what's your uncle Rothkrug up to these days?"

That one had a delightfully provocative answer too: "He's editing a book we're publishing called *Mending the Earth.* I think Mom would be pleased—her brother and son in collaboration."

"That she would."

"My hair was real long a few weeks ago," I continued, demonstrating with both hands along my neck, "and when he came by, he said, 'God, you look like my sister.'"

This was a well-established family fact, but we were going at a heady pace and, since I was leading, I took a risk.

"I think I look so much like her because the B———s looked like her, so the features coincide. That way no one ever suspected."

"Interesting insight," he said thoughtfully. "You *do* look like them."

"Do you know them?"

"They're an unfortunate group to know. I remember forty years ago Louie B——— tried to bribe the rabbi, wanted him to say a prayer for Sandy Koufax."

"Why?"

"Why? Because he was a Brooklyn Dodger fan, as well as a pimp. The rabbi brushed him off, just like that, like you would a fly. Say, do you see your grandmother?"

After her husband Henri's death forty years earlier, Sally had married an oilman named Tom Golden. During the '50s she accompanied him through Texas, Utah, and Wyoming. When Tom was killed in an automobile accident she took up with Eric, a British stockbroker. He had remained her paramour for the next thirty years.

Bob certainly knew his mother-in-law's taste in wealthy beaus. What he didn't know was her most recent casualty.

When the trifling and opinionated Sally tired of caring for her near-blind male friend (who had outlived his savings), she told him to move out. She was busy flirting with another octogenarian at the Broadmoor.

That night Eric groped his way to the window and dropped his body onto the street.

Sally had nary a morsel of regret. "He was sick, like Martha," she sniffed.

For a while at ninety she continued to cultivate "sweeties" among the younger men, playing the piano in the rec room and recalling the scene at the ball in Capetown when the Crown Prince of England asked her to dance.

Then she had a series of strokes that should have killed anyone.

"Even though she's still alive," I told a fascinated Bob, "she has no memory left."

I described a pilgrimage "to a Jewish home for the aged by Candlestick Park. She was in a wheelchair, but only because insurance requires it. She let me know she was quite capable of walking. In fact, to the protest of the nurses she stood up and shook her cane to show off."

As the image formed, he broke into a smile.

"She was seated among a group of wheelchair people, most of them just staring into space. I didn't recognize her at first. Men and women that old tend to look alike. The face loses its distinctive features and looks sort of generic."

"I understand."

"She didn't know who I was. When she heard I was her grandson she was truly astonished. She said she didn't have a grandson and wondered how I came to be related to her. I explained that her daughter was my mother. 'I had a daughter?' she said. She was flabbergasted."

"I wouldn't have believed it. Isn't the mind a mysterious thing?"

"I took out my photographs. She pointed to you at once and said, 'That's Bob Towers.'"

"How do you like that!"

"You were the only person she recognized in all the pictures. She didn't even recognize herself. She didn't recognize Anne or Edgar or her brother Mooney. I guess you left quite an impression on her?"

"I'm afraid the impression she left on her daughter was not one to be proud of. What else did she have to say?" he continued with gentle sarcasm.

"She wondered who my father was, and I said, 'Paul Grossinger.' Then she got a sly look and asked, 'My daughter married a Grossinger?' I nodded. 'Well, we should all go to the Catskills!'"

Bob exploded with laughter, but I was still holding the punchline.

"She wondered how I found her, and I said, 'Through your son Paul.' She said, *'You know him?'* I said, 'Of course. He's my uncle.' She shook her head and said, 'Small world!'"

"Great line, Richard. Don't ever forget it."

Turetsky hated the intense sincerity of the Rothkrugs, our pious epiphanies. He was lighter than that. Perhaps (once) he was infatuated with and then consumed by my mother's density. But he never relinquished the hope that comedy was redemptive. Intimacy with Bob lay in cadences of story-telling—back and forth, back and forth—going deeper and deeper until (if it was possible) we reached the heart.

After dessert we moved on to Debby. "She's so brave," Bob declared. "What a girl! She's got a thousand fears, but she takes the world by the horns every day."

I followed discussion of my sister's courage by taking him through an account of my life he had never heard—how I had struggled to get on top of "whatever you would call it, the thing that haunts Jon and Debby and led my mother to her death, the thing that seemed as though it would never let me survive. I feel as though meeting Lindy in college made the biggest difference. Her friendship gave me the courage to come out of the darkness." This was something my "father" should know.

"I never thought she minded being Paul Grossinger's daughter-in-law either," he commented.

"Totally wrong reading," I fired back. "You are mistaking her graciousness for some sort of fawning. She believes in propriety and extending herself. She was always respectful of Paul. But the Hotel was never her favorite place."

"I'm glad to hear that."

With that matter resolved twenty-five years too late, I resumed the story of Lindy's and my life together in Michigan, the birth of Robin, our homes in Maine and Vermont. . . . These were years when he and I were out of touch. I wanted him to remember that I was part of his family. I wasn't the antithesis of Jonny; I was Jonny in another form. And I was also Bob Towers, meeting business partners, promoting Thai restaurants and aikido chefs, telling stories.

I described coming to California, doing t'ai chi and bioenergetic therapy, trying to claim my courage . . . always a spook on my tail. Then I told him how my new teacher Ron was mixing boxing and hsing-i with t'ai-chi training.

"You were always a great athlete with a baseball glove," he recalled. "And you hit a few line drives in my day."

"Barney Ross would have been astonished," I continued. "You remember how old Barney used to raise his fists in front of me as a kid and say, 'Put up your dukes.' Then he'd hug me so hard it almost crushed me."

"I remember Barney doing that."

"He never thought I'd finally put up my dukes, let alone when I got to his age. But I'm studying these things to find the ghost inside me, to come to terms with the mystery of our family."

This wasn't exactly accurate. I was oversimplifying things. But I wanted to keep it simple, keep him with me. It made no sense to get lost in Buddhist philosophy or Feldenkrais theory (even if Moshe *was* Israeli). I had to bring everything back to him and me and the threads that connected us. I meant for him to see that, for all my superficially exotic journeys, I was still a kid he knew.

"The worlds inside any of us are terrifying," he interjected. "It is best not to dwell on them. There's no room in life for nostalgia or sentiment."

"Unless you have to fight ghosts all the time," I said. "Then you live for nostalgia, like Jon."

We had talked so many times about my brother that by now I had given dozens of diagnoses and the topic was exhausted between us. At Patsy's I settled for saying, "There was a thing loose in our house, and our mother didn't protect us from it. She never protected herself from it either. In fact, she unleashed it on us before we were ready because it was unendurable to her. I think it was a power thing, a good thing, but a child can't face such a thing alone." He was staring right at me. "Telling these stories now between us is special to me. They bring back what we were and despite everything that went wrong, what we had."

"What we *could have* had, Richard. What we could have had."

"I think we had it. I don't think the universe will ever let us forget."

"You're too mystical for me."

"Call it a spook. The same thing in me, in Jonny and Debby and my mother."

"Not in you. All I see is a capable man with a family. I see someone who's giving me more pleasure yesterday and today than I could have imagined. Richard, I hope these meetings mean as much to you as they do to me."

Tears surged in me. We had reached the climax, of everything. "They do. They definitely do."

Now both the pitch and volume of his voice rose. "If I were you I'd say, 'Why don't you get the hell off me, you sonofabitch spook! Get the hell off me!'" He waved his right arm in such a striking gesture that the tables around us grew momentarily silent. And I realized, 'This is it. Profundity itself has come to its most profound moment.'

His words struck at my heart because he alone was the father and could speak such a thing, could threaten the profane spirit, could give me the reassurance not now, when I didn't need it anymore, but back then when his voice echoed throughout our tiny flat, *"Old man river, that old man river. . . ."* Such a message resounded in the remote dark and came flowing back through my whole life so that by his very voice again I felt released, if only for a moment. He stood between me and my oppressor and, if it was too late to rescue the haunted child, it was not too late to meet in the world as men. Suddenly I cared deeply for him, for all of us then, even young brash Jonathan. I was no longer their enemy.

It had been a long struggle, to feel unquestioning love in his presence. That was all I wanted, not paternity, not more words and explanations.

Yet I answered as Richard always answers. I said, "The spook *is* me."

He wouldn't allow that.

"Richard, I come from an earthy, Russian, peasant stock. I come from a people who waited four thousand years to reclaim their homeland. Be a Sabra of the desert, for god's sake. The spook isn't you. Kick the bastard out and be done with it."

A few moments later the bill was paid. Nothing more was said. Once again, we parted on the street.

7

Once Upon a Time Forever

My stepfather and I had reconciled at the final possible moment. The following spring I came to New York from an Amherst reunion, hoping to see him again. A day earlier, debarking a taxi on Park Avenue, he had had a stroke. I learned this at his office.

"Bob is in Mount Sinai," Helen announced, sitting wraithlike at the alcove to Robert Towers Advertising, her voice full of accusation. It didn't matter that I was neither Martha nor Jon. "Do you know where your brother is? His father wants him."

I found my brother near his apartment. At his suggestion we went into the Park first and sat on outcroppings of rock beside old ballfields.

We crossed the street, marched through vestibules, and stood in the elevator (young M.D.s staring disapprovingly). Then down the hall.

Bob was in a restraining chair, signing checks with his book-keeper's assistance. Tufts of unkempt white mane stood out, this lion of a man strangely insubstantial. He acknowledged our presence with an incomprehensible growl as he gestured Jon to his side for the final signatures. After each painstaking scrawl he tried to lift a fist in triumph. His girlfriend Lila was arranging flowers. "It's a mild stroke," she explained, "but at Bob's age he needs a lot of care and rehabilitation."

He had withered. He now looked exactly like his own parents when I saw them at the end of their lives, gossamer, chair-ridden creatures (1951). The morbid aroma of their apartment had imbued Jon and me with a foreboding of doom. Yet that grim dwelling-place was sheltering and civilized compared to what surrounded us in 1991. The radio was blasting 1010, "all news, all the time" and, if anyone made a move to lower the volume, Bob slammed an unstable hand on the dial.

"The sound reassures him," Lila said. "But we have to force him to turn it down at night."

The first contribution she requested of us was to help him walk—he had not been on his feet since the stroke.

With cheers and entreaties Jon and I propped him upright and inched him out of the room. Once ambulatory, he stampeded ahead, propelled in a stiff, panicked gait like a wind-up toy. We tried to grab his arms and get in front, but he strode resolutely along, head locked forward. At the first room, he turned in abruptly, tipped an imaginary hat, and mumbled, "Bob Towers. How are you, sir?"

"Bob!" shouted Lila, as she yanked him in a different direction, but he headed for the room across the hall and introduced himself to that astonished lady in bed. We centered him, then turned him around, and steered him back and into his chair. Somehow during this adventure Jon had disappeared.

In 1991 North Atlantic published *Martian Enigmas* by Mark Carlotto, an enhanced photo album of the mysterious structures on another world (along with the author's commentary about such matters as fractal terrain, shape from shading, and digital contrast control). Mark worked for the Defense Department, and he told me that if Martian artifacts had showed up in any of his satellite photos of the Soviet Union, it would have been assumed the Russkies were up to some nasty stuff. "These anomalous objects," he warranted, "read more like silos than mesas."

After I met him at a conference on "Angels, Aliens, and Archetypes," UFO researcher Jacques Vallee offered us his memoir to co-publish. The source of the François Truffaut character in *Close Encounters of the Third Kind,* Jacques had been the first to realize the similarity between UFO occupants and legendary fairies and goblins. He thought it unlikely that hundreds of thousands of metallic ships would cross the mind-boggling distances of the universe to visit the Earth on clandestine missions. Instead, he proposed, we were dealing with a phenomenon of an unknown, perhaps transdimensional, order. To his mind the visitation of the Virgin Mary at Fatima was a typical flying-saucer landing. The title of his book was *Forbidden Science.*

Edward Whitmont submitted a new manuscript, *The Alchemy of Healing,* a study of the psychic effects and projections of physicians. He proposed that healing itself was an act of transference occurring on an archetypal level, even as disease was an archetypal expression of the unconscious destinies of both physician and patient.

We expanded our lines of homeopathy, t'ai chi, and aikido—more Peter Ralston, Dana Ullman, and Gaku Homma. We added new authors.

With need for staff, Lindy and I hired the star of Robin's baseball team, Jason Kaneko. He became invoice-writer, book packer, and record-keeper.

Meanwhile Paul Pitchford was in the sixth year, at our instigation, of working on a Chinese medicine and dietary opus. PGW's continuous announcing of it without a book in hand was driving Charlie crazy. Each time after Paul completed it, we edited it and were ready for production. Then Paul took the supposedly finished product back to update and correct. When we saw it next, it was at least seventy-five pages longer and in need of another edit. Yet *Healing With Whole Foods,* 700 pages long, became North Atlantic's best-selling book through the mid '90s.

Eighteen months after I visited Bob in Mount Sinai, Lindy and I brought the patient's old buddy, the writer George Plimpton, to his apartment. There we greeted the master of ceremonies in retirement. All that remained were theatrical mimicries of Robert Towers' greatest lines. His highlight came during a tennis discussion when he corrected Plimpton. "Sofia is the capital of Bulgaria!" he slurred triumphantly. "Not Belgrade, George. Sofia." Pointing at his still functioning forehead.

Every now and then he'd mumble worriedly, "How do I sound?"

As we left, he asked Debby to "put on that Redford-Streisand movie. You know, the goy and the Jew, you old . . . ," a playful jab at the departing Plimpton.

Four months later I called the apartment not knowing what to expect.

My sister feigned surprise when I told her it was her brother's forty-fourth birthday; then she said, "I think he's no longer here."

"Is he in Connecticut?"

"I believe so. You might try asking his father."

"How *is* Bob?"

"He's just a little baby now, a tiny demanding baby. In fact, he's pulling on my arm trying to get the phone. Well, take it! You won't be so happy when you hear who it is."

"Hullo. Hullo."

"I wanted to wish Jon happy birthday. Do you know where he is?"

"He's at the Pequot Motor Inn, Southport, Connecticut. I'll pass along your regards." I could barely make out his words.

"All things considered, how's he doing?"

"All things considered, he's not in jail. The police arrested him three times. In Southport they're not used to vagrants. Forget him. He's a waste. A drug addict. How're your kids?"

I told him about Robin's research and the possibility he might come to Stony Brook on a grant.

"Is he making lots of money?" he muttered.

"No, but he's a wonderful person, and the grant is an honor."

"And your daughter."

"She's writing and casting her own plays in Berkeley."

There was a silence; then he said, "Richard, you're a star."

It was like the scent from an old jar of lavender, immediate yet ineffable.

"You're a star too, Bob."

"No, I'm not a star. I used to be a star, but I'm not a star anymore."

"You're still a star."

"I love you." Or probably he didn't say that. Perhaps he just said, "luvvya." Likely he didn't even say that.

"I love you too," I said. But he had already dropped the phone. And Debby wasn't about to give it back.

Jon had escaped New York. The Pequot Motor Inn accepted him as a boarder in an abandoned room. His father paid rent to Mr. Garfalo instead of Knickerbocker Plaza. A postcard from my brother recounted this pastoral transfer: "I now live on the site of the last Indian massacre in Connecticut . . . and so the winter passed."

Substitute night-watchman and weekend clerk, he left poems for women who brought their tricks there. "In the troubadour tradition, of course," he reminded me. By day he scouted the marshes and cleared debris from the reeds.

Twenty-Seventh Document

lady esmeralda
queen of the night
the details of your biography
are excitingly speculative
i wish to know them
no better
that you have a biography
that there is an earthly counterpart
to your divinity
is what almost amazes me
Phanette de Gentelme
tell me
how is your sister
Azalais de Porcairages?
and for that matter
how's Hermesende
Adalazie
Rostangue

Mabille
Jausserande
and all the rest
of the old crew
high on love
in the rocky fortresses
of southern Provence?

It was 1992, Miranda's last year of high school. One afternoon she returned from school with a story. A boy in her class had been abusing young women. She had taken it upon herself to "out" him. She printed up warnings and posted them across the campus and on car windshields, including his.

Unfortunately her target was the son of wealthy executives who were donating the money for the new gym. Before the day was out, the kid had driven home, and his parents had gotten the headmaster on the phone, and were threatening to sue.

Lindy and I sat in the living room, astonished at each escalation.

The school disbanded into the auditorium. There Miranda addressed the community on behalf of the victims, giving testimony they were afraid to recite themselves.

Then she walked home. And here she was.

"That's wonderful, Mandy," Lindy finally said as she hugged her. "It was so courageous of you. I only hope that there's no trouble."

But Miranda was on fire; she had little patience for her parents' faint praise.

She shot back out into the world.

She came home an hour later, crying and not wanting to talk.

That night at dinner she described an incident on College Avenue. A pigeon had been hit by a car. It was lying beside a mastiff leashed to a post. Seeing that the dog would get it, Miranda stood guard over the bird . . . until it died. "I told it not to be afraid," she said, "that wherever it went it would always be itself."

When PGW decided they could no longer store everyone's overstock, we rented a warehouse and office on 8th Street, a site previously an auto-repair shop and a coffee factory. Jason enlisted a crew of a dozen kids from Berkeley High, and, for $9 an hour, they worked at both locations—boys and girls, African, Hispanic, and Anglo—emptying out the swimming-pool building carton by carton, painting and scrubbing the 8th Street facility—a rambunctious chorus line working mops and brushes to the boom of rap.

They were assisted by my buddy Ron and Benito, a spacy Puerto Rican from New York I met while sitting at the Empty Gate Zen Center. I gave Benito a ride one night after zazen and, letting him out on Telegraph, asked if I'd see him again. His answer: "You see me now."

All during the move he amused Jason and kids with talk of nonexistent cats.

"What cat?" they kept asking him.

"That's exactly my point."

That same fall Seymour proposed that he and his wife Cathy start a new publishing company with Lindy and me.

The name Frog was my idea. I wanted us to be an animal, but not cute or fashionable like a Penguin, Dolphin, or Zebra. "Frog" was a larva we could invent. Frogs were ancient, atavistic, endangered, vulnerable, amphibian, and their totems ruled secret female societies in Native American clans. Charlie hated the name, as did virtually everyone at PGW. It was ugly, down-market.

The first big Frog success was an unlikely narrative by a Berkeley rebirther named Bob Frissell. I met him originally as a client. After our third session of grueling breathwork I learned he was involved in an esoteric tradition that interpreted the "Face" and "City" on Mars in the light of a billion-year-long morality play locally known as the Luciferian Rebellion. "Maybe you can write a book," I suggested, "about your version of the Martian mysteries."

He came to my house one night and, after watching basketball together, we sat for three and a half hours absorbing a lecture by his teacher, Drunvalo Melchizedek, a recent walk-in from the thirteenth dimension and student of Thoth.

Bob stood at the juncture of three mystery churches—Leonard Orr's rebirthing with its roots in the immortal saints and yogis of India, sacred geometry with its Rosicrucian and Gnostic antecedents, and Pueblo millenary religion with its uncharted bridges between intergalactic legends and apocalyptic parables.

He wasn't a writer. He was a former math teacher from Fargo, North Dakota. He spoke his book into a recorder: gray aliens, crop circles, Earth changes with pole shifts and hurricanes stripping the planet even of ants, secret governments on Mars, mystery cults inside the Great Pyramid, and the creation of individual protective shields called *merkabas* that allowed space travel fuelled by love throughout the universe. His girlfriend Lois transcribed the tapes. Our editor Kathy Glass rewrote the text. But we needed a better title than *Internal and External Merkabas.*

When I brought Miranda to meet Bob, he laid out Drunvalo's cosmic conspiracy theory for her. She was patiently attentive. Back on the street, I asked what she thought.

"Well, nothing he said is true, but it's exactly how things are."

Nothing in This Book Is True, But It's Exactly How Things Are debuted to a rave review in *Wired* by Jay Kinney. To the astonishment of PGW we were soon selling 5,000 a month. "This is one our sales reps totally missed," Charlie confessed. "They've done UFOs every which way, cosmic conspiracies, JFK conspiracies, witches, Satanic sacrifice, Aleister Crowley, but they didn't know a market for this stuff even existed. You can bet they're on the bandwagon now."

> *Accompanied by his two feline seers, Frissell himself is everyman (everywoman too), a silent spirit-guide to a journey each of us must take ourselves, a voice warning of the terrible things that will happen (but only if we addict ourselves to a vision of the terrible things that will happen).*
>
> *One day I came in for a session particularly stricken and bereft. I told him a tale of stuff going wrong in my life. I made it sound totally hopeless. It sounded totally hopeless to me as I was saying it. Then I took a deep breath, smiled, and said, "But it's okay."*
>
> *It wasn't just a line. I felt at that moment utterly pure in my heart and my intention to be.*
>
> *"It is," he said. "It is okay, but only if you say so. Your word must be enough."*
>
> *So I leave it with readers to decide if this is all true or if none of it is true. Because in the end your own word must be enough. For this lifetime and for all lifetimes and universes to come.*
>
> *In fact, your word is the only thing that will get you through.*

Debby was my stepfather's sole guardian during his final months. She permitted no visitors. Though Lila had been Turetsky's paramour for ten years, she could no longer lay eyes on him, let alone touch him. That Bob wanted Lila most of all meant nothing to my sister. "He doesn't know what he wants," she complained. "He simply goes from nightmare to nightmare. He cries out all night."

The phone rang one morning at work. "It's your sister."

"My sister?" I said. "My sister never called me in her life."

"He's dying," she screamed over the phone. "He's dying."

There is a Jewish cemetery and synagogue in Prague, just down the street from where Kafka wrote his masterpieces, in a small urban forest. It survived the Holocaust. Hundreds of tombstones lie in all directions, irregularly cut and eroded, twisted in the ground among tree trunks and wildflowers. Moss and lichen outline Hebrew runes. Monuments that have lost their lettering stand as cairnlike statues, weathered markers of the false boundary between weeds and alphabet. Their corroding minerals, once the repository of families and years, now feed the flowers.

Overhead, crows scream and rush in commotion from branch to branch, an alter ego to the shambles in stone.

Lila chose *The New York Times* obituary page for her epitaph. "It was a grand run, Bob," she wrote. "Love-Love all the way. Memories of shared fun, work, laughter, tears blend with unforgettably dynamic you and will linger always in my heart."

The morning after my first lunch with my stepfather at Patsy's I decided to walk our old neighborhood back along Madison, the most familiar route of my childhood. As I passed 85th, rain came down hard. I had no umbrella, so I threw up my hood. It was soon drenched through. None of the old storefronts had survived, until I reached Michael's barbershop—the original candy-striped pole. Through the window I saw the chair on which I sat while my mother instructed, cut by cut.

I turned at 95th and passed the Armory. I crossed the corner at Park, walked down the Avenue, and knocked boldly on the door of my first apartment at 1220. If someone was home, maybe I could convince them to let me look inside. But no one was. So I decided to visit Jonny.

The rain grew even heavier. My hair was now soaked. I remembered antediluvian hardball days when we played through simple thunderstorms, before radioactivity and acid clouds.

What a strange city this was! Its apartment buildings were castles and dungeons. On 93rd was an entranceway like a vast moat before a palace. Its existence had been second nature to me in childhood, but I saw it now as a giant UFO camouflaged in a building. Everywhere gargoyles and glyphs melted into façades of stone. Even the brownstone surfaces seemed like Hittite runes with their ironwork and fire escapes.

It was a landscape of secrets, of guarded money; it was everything I imagined as B———. But it was a dying nation. The people leaving these buildings were old now, sires and dames in dark formal dress even at mid-day in rain, going and coming in a ceaseless conspiracy of taxis.

As I reached Jon's part of 2nd Avenue, I entered another country. Knickerbocker Plaza was a small college town built on the ruins of a cobblestone New York. I gave the guard my name. He buzzed and indicated I could go upstairs.

When Jon opened the door, I didn't wait to consider his weirdness. I hugged him.

"I can't believe you're here!"

I could barely see him in the dark. As we stood there embracing, I felt him the same size and shape as Robin.

He was so excited he struggled for some sort of light—tried a red bulb and finally settled for a candle. In its lumination I looked around. He dwelled here as he dwelled once in my room with me. There was his bed—a mattress on the floor.

"Things have changed so much. I've got a group of friends now, guys I met at Food Liberation. We travel up to Albany and stay with people there. We walk in the countryside." Then he told me about other journeys, solitary ones to scout the Atlantic at Milford, Connecticut—"the edge of the universe before the White Man came to these parts."

"I'm on my own vision-quest now," I told him, "I've been studying new things. I'm going to this bodywork group which is really like a training in deep images and lost parts of the self. The guy who runs it teaches spirit through body, so that's what we do, work on each other, learn how to touch and move membranes and fluids. Then after all these years I took up t'ai chi again. I found this teacher Ron. He's like a real sorcerer."

I related my adventures with the Buddhist boxer.

"You found Trickster, alive and well," Jon concluded.

"Old Coyote, still doing his tricks. The wonder is that I recognized him. Sometimes I think the wonder is that I recognize anything at all."

"I know, Richard. The path was clouded for so long, but we are finally on the way."

"No more Towers or Grossinger," I laughed. "I'm B——— the shaman now."

"Our mother's changeling!"

Then he said he was going to continue what he was doing when I arrived, which was making his bed. "But we can still talk," he added. He folded his hospital corners neatly. I helped pull the sheets and smooth out their surfaces. We tucked in his blankets.

"Richard, the mystery man."

I took a place on the floor, my back on the wall. He stood, a shadow against stacks of books.

"You know who you look like," he told me.

I was afraid to ask.

"Dylan. Crouched over there, carrying the prophecy in your head. You're the image of the first album cover. You're not big like me. You're wiry like him. Dylan was the poet of the masses. You have a different following."

"Thanks."

I sat there in silence. Then I told him I had wanted to visit Debby. "But she hung up on me."

"She hates both of us. No, she doesn't hate us. She thinks she has to hate us. She's the member of the Towers household who did not reject it, as you, I, and Mom did in our individual ways. She has no choice but to reject us. She's made a viable life for herself in New York, while we have had to estrange ourselves."

"She *became* the family."

"She inherited a house and a city with its musicals and tennis clubs, etc., that was the world of our parents. Babylon claimed one of us for itself. She not only doesn't reject it, she completely identifies with it."

"Strange that it should have been *her,*" I said. "I didn't see that coming when we were growing up: Miss Park Avenue, Miss Rich and Beautiful."

"We should admire her accomplishment," he cautioned. "It had its own hard struggles. Her choice is so the opposite of ours that the differences are of a political or aesthetic nature. They're spiritual and religious, what the whole crisis of the '60s youth revolt was about. You and I, not she, are its products."

"I guess that's true."

"She falls beyond the sunlight of the revolution, in the shadowy zone of the conventional. Living in New York, I can understand her choice better than I once did, and even in some sentimentally vicarious way imagine something of the life I might have lived if I had not been born to rock 'n' roll."

I felt my face break into a grin as I nodded. Sometimes Jon could be so great.

"Remember," he continued, "when I got up in the middle of the night to fight ghosts?"

"I could never forget. That was a lesson in the whole future of the world."

"I think I finally defeated them—or have been defeated—but, either way, they're gone."

"They probably weren't ghosts."

"No, but they were something. They were definitely something."

Two pigeons landed suddenly on the window sill and began to coo, their wings crumpled against glass. I saw Jon shudder.

"We were so afraid all those years a bird would get into our room."

"A bird," he murmured. "A bird with broken wings. A dead pigeon smashed on the street. Our mother."

"I used to wonder why birds were so frightening. Trapped inside they become frantic, like her. But that alone shouldn't do it. They're also sweet, beautiful, delicate creatures. Everyone loves them, is inspired by them. People find them sympathetic and vulnerable. They're definitely female, queens of the animal kingdom. But look into their eyes, and you see a dinosaur. Look into their eyes and you forget their beauty. There is only a cold vacancy where there should have been a woman who loved and protected us."

"How true, Richard. How strange the obvious we didn't see. We were raised by a dinosaur who was even more frightening because she spoke our language and looked like a human being."

With a thump of recoil the birds were gone. We watched them float to another window, then startle and rise twenty stories over the roof out of sight.

"I had my own night grapple with a ghost," I told him after a silence. "My father was pummelling me in this dream. But I had been trained by Ron, so I turned on him and jabbed and swung away until he was a pulp."

"Our fathers are so corrupt it takes almost everything we have to defeat them. Of course, we can never defeat them in their world. We have to defeat them in ourselves, in vision-quests and dreams."

His comment reminded me of my last visit.

"I'm finally writing the book that has your story in it," I confessed. "I ended it with you playing 'Steppin' Out of Babylon' for us here that day."

"Now," he laughed, "even the record-player is gone. I gave it to a Puerto Rican woman." A look of fierceness and triumph suddenly took over his face. "You know what this was all about?" he asked. I waited, for the oracle was definitely directed at himself. "I wanted to be a human being. That's all. I was raised to be another competitive, screw-everyone, rat-race prick. I was trained to be like my father, only worse. A moneyed big-shot. So I had to sacrifice my whole life to make myself into just a person. That was the real magic—to destroy him in me."

"You have every reason to be proud. It was an incredible deed."

"But in killing him, I damn near killed myself."

I nodded quietly. "I'm mostly sorry I didn't stop them from putting you in the hospital."

"You couldn't have stopped them. But I appreciate the sentiment. Maybe you should have done more. Do you understand by now how bad they were, much worse than you even realized? It's like *On the Waterfront.* That's why that movie meant so much to me. You had it wrong. You thought I wanted to boast like Marlon Brando. But I wanted to defeat the corrupt elders—Johnny Friendly, remember? Brando tells his brother he shoulda protected him. He said, 'You was my brother, Charlie. You shoulda looked out for me a little bit. You shoulda taken care of me so I wouldenaha' to take them dives for the short-end money.'

"Richard, you might not have succeeded, but you could have done more; you were in it for the short-term money too. 'I coulda been a lot better. I could have had class. I coulda been somebody, instead of a bum.' But that's the great joke. I'm somebody anyway." He burst out laughing. "I'm the heavyweight champ of Mordor. I fought Harry Pin and won."

Waves of gratitude and regret flooded the Dylan body he had given me. I was no longer even trying to stay above water in his apartment. I began to cry. The years swept through my weeping until he crouched before me in the candlelight, crying too.

"Isn't it great," he finally said. "We can cry together. If only they had let us. . . ."

I asked if he'd be willing to let me give him a massage. He was startled at the request but said, "Sure."

He looked at me for instructions, and I had him lie on his back in the center of the room. Slowly I made touch, felt his weight and bones, moved his shoulders, put my hand on the membrane of his chest.

He giggled from the touch. That was familiar. We had tickled each other as children.

I gently rolled his forehead and massaged his temples, then softened his jaw by helping him rotate it in small arcs.

"I'm the tin woodman," he said. "I feel as though I haven't been oiled for a hundred years."

His comment brought more tears to my eyes. Their adagio sank to my hands and I found his cranial pulse, as resonant as I had ever felt it in anyone. It was tidal and kelplike—long, tangled stipes being pulled into the deep.

I wanted desperately to give him something, to find bottom for him. My fingers curled intently. Then I remembered Randy's warning, 'Always do less.'

The moment I backed off, the rhythm deepened palpably. Now it seemed as though I was riding the nerve net that connected my brother and me. I was touching our twinned aura and heart, not only touching them but bringing their vestigial currents—our bond—into the world.

The old dubious energy field was real. I could feel it. I was in it. It was simple and silent. It required nothing.

At that moment I wondered (and almost seemed to know) why all the dreamwork, energy work, t'ai chi, craniosacral therapy, and conscious breathing had not touched me at the core, had not altered the one intractable thing.

"You're good at this," he remarked. "You're almost as high as grass."

"That's a great compliment. But I wish my training made a difference. I still feel trapped; I feel afraid and unsafe just about all the time. I go back in my mind again and again to try to figure out what it was. *What did they do to us?*"

Ignoring my chatter, he added, "Your magic has returned us to childhood, but to a place where we could have never been close like this."

I held the stillpoint at the base of his cranium, let him surf the trance, then massaged his closed eyelids in a granular trail.

I removed my hands slowly, as if letting elixir drip back into his field. I sat alongside him. He slowly raised himself up.

"We should have felt our affinity and taken comfort in it," I acknowledged. "We should have been friends. Or if we couldn't have been friends, we should have recognized we weren't bitter enemies in some life-or-death struggle."

"I don't remember much anymore," he admitted, getting up and walking to the window. "The drugs, the hospital, the marijuana. It's just a blur and so long ago. I only know it was complicated and strange, like a festival of witchery and riddles. We were on a ship with Columbus, seeing the islands of the Caribbean for the first time. We were in the alchemist's chamber with antimony. We were beset by sorcerers. I can't figure any of it out."

"It was all those things, Jon, and it wasn't any of them. *We* brought the complication into being. *We* were the magicians. *We* played at being evil and devious. *We* invented Mordor. It wasn't complicated at all. Just us. The structural mythology of the universe was our gift to them, and it was so stupid to waste it on non-initiates. More than stupid—it was dangerous."

He nodded somberly.

"To us it was voodoo and mystery, an actual tortuous haunting. To them it was simple, brutally simple. They didn't intend to cast some exotic Mediaeval curse. They were just narcissistic assholes snared in our vision quest, exponentially exploded to the level of werewolves and demons because that's what we made them in our childhood minds—and that's, sadly, what they remain."

Jon pointed with facetious drama out the window toward the arena of our youth. "We were in it together," he declared, "and didn't know and turned against each other amid the dance. We broke the taboo."

"A fatal mistake! You were right. I shoulda looked out for you. I should have loved you back then. I should have intuited your innocent heart instead of forty years after the fall having to fish after a cranio-sacral pulse like some show-offy mage. And they should have been decent parents and told us the truth, 'We're having trouble coping, but you kids, you're fine, you're really okay.'"

Jon chuckled at the unlikelihood of that, but his eyes were solemn.

"Why does that sound so farout?" I insisted. "It was their sole duty, and they blew it. I don't know what it was like for you, but for me it was as though Mom was saying all the time, 'We have to act as though you're bad. You know I'm supposed to punish you. But none of it's really true. It's just a game between us. I'm really a loving mother and I think the world of you. But you and I can't ever admit that. Because that would ruin it. It would be too ordinary. Instead we have to keep up this charade.' It was as though heaven itself would fall.

"So that's what we did, the entire time of growing up. We played and played and played until we couldn't tell the difference, and couldn't stop. We told ourselves that none of it was real because none of it *could be real,* because we were the famous Towers family, talented and happy. We couldn't possibly be as horrible as we were acting.

"And all the time the thing we supposedly weren't, that we dreaded most, was exactly what we were, because there was no other childhood to substitute for the one we were pretending not to live."

My words amazed me. I hardly knew where they came from. Then Jon spoke:

"No wonder it felt like the Crusades. No wonder everything seemed so crucial. It was always the ninth inning at 1235 Park, two outs, nobody on."

"She forgot we were just kids," I continued in chorus, "that we didn't have anything else. It may have been pretending for her, but she did it for eighteen relentless unforgiving years, at least to me, and that kind of pretending's a way to make anything real. On that level everyone's just pretending—mass murderers, child molesters, Nazi guards. I mean, 'Let's torment you so that we can just pretend to be doing it.' Great idea, Mom! But what else was there to be real, all the rest of our fucking lives? Even the medicine men and martial artists you and I try to become can't be ever be real now."

"You got it, Rich. That's what I am—a story by Dickens, a tale of Indians—"

"—a spinster poet. Or an idea about what Jon would be if he weren't Jon, a great wonderful idea. Just as I'm pretend Richard, pretending to do t'ai chi, pretending to write books. The real Jonathan and Richard are always somewhere else, with the real Turetskys and B———s. It was a pact we made with her, to pretend the real was unreal—and to lose our hold on the real. Because if we acknowledged that she was really a horrible mother and we were really her children, we would have all been in hell. It would have really happened. She held us forever by her fake innocence in our loyalty that we all really lived another life."

"But why?" he demanded. "All I remember are voices in my head and ghosts in the dark. I never thought she had anything to do with them. They were Harry or Roy Pin."

"One can only guess. Perhaps somewhere back in a boarding school in Paris she decided to refuse to live. She thought if she stopped marching, the whole world would stop with her. Once she dug in her heels, it all became a script she tried to manipulate, a black fairy tale, a skein of deceitful princes. Then we came along, and she had to enlist us too. But I really don't know. Maybe she was some Egyptian queen in a past life, murdered by her guards, and keeps coming back life after life to seek justice and retribution. No, I don't really think that."

"So how do we get out of it?" Jon requested of me. "Can it work like in *Rebel Without a Cause* where the doctor regresses him all the way back to childhood and he's in a crib alongside his mother's bed? Do people believe in that stuff anymore? Does anyone still talk about being hypnotized, witnessing the traumatic moment, and changing yourself?"

"I like Lindner. But I don't think hypnotherapy works any better than bodywork or shamanism. There's no apotheosis to achieve. Or if there is, it does all sorts of transformative, profound things, but it doesn't budge the primal curse. We have to swim back through the entire pain, stroke by stroke, and feel it all over again, back to before language, to the feral state where we were unprotected and vulnerable, where this whole service began. Then maybe we can start a different clock ticking.

"After the indoctrination, it was no longer her. It's been no longer her just about forever. It's our lingo now, totally wrapped around us with all our damnable complication and Osage-Rosicrucian pomp. There's no such thing as some big epiphany—'oh, I've touched the ancient trauma and I'm released and free.' Because it's moment to moment. We can't just brag, 'I'm a rebel without a cause,' and be glorious James Dean in a movie, and summon Freud as shaman of our clan. Because we disperse it, and it forms again. We see something that looks like the moment of truth, make a big deal of it, and then we come tumbling back to who we are. Maybe if we were really Navahos and our shamans were great shamans and our senseis true senseis we could have a moment outside language and be transformed by gods who actually do something. Hypnosis and craniosacral therapy, Rolfing and t'ai chi are incredible, and they make us healthy and strong, but I don't think they can undo core trauma. It requires a more Yaqui magician than any we try to bring—"

"Don Genaro at your service!"

I laughed but clung to my thread. "We can't change it because our earnestness that wants to change is exactly our resistance that holds onto the terror— so it's stalemate. And in a culture that keeps us superficial and powerless ninety-nine percent of the time—which is its primary purpose—how can we do something different than we're doing, and keep our pact?"

"Are we doomed?" he teased.

"No, I'm just getting carried away with my own preaching."

"Don't be falsely modest, Richard. It's always been your job to *daven* our community truth."

"Then let me close my diatribe with a story I wanted to tell you anyway."

"Is it about us?"

"It's the story with which I ended our book."

Indian ceremony, Heartwood Institute, Garberville, 1990. Drum beating, I am asked by the leader to embrace a spirit animal. In my mind a bushy white wolf appears. "Follow it. Let it lead you back."

I am holding the wolf, but the scene has changed. I am sitting at the dinner table with Mom, Dad, Jon, and Debby. I remember my sense of panic then, how I wanted to bolt and didn't know where. I felt the obscurity of the life within me, not just its obscurity but the obscurity that that masked, and then a fleeting glimpse of a reality so sweet and abyssal it could not not be. And I was so afraid then because the truth was inadmissible. Everything I felt as a child isolated me—night, rain, wind, cold, the living room lamps—because no one confirmed such feelings were possible, let alone human.

I am still afraid, but I am protected because I am coming from thirty-five years in the future and have a bushy wolf. I am looking at a scene which is to leave my sister a shell, my mother a corpse, my brother a wounded shaman, my stepfather a tortured man in his last years.

The self I visit has no idea what I am to become. Perhaps that is why it is so horrible, because everything is yet to happen. I feel the melancholy and merciless jubilation of the time.

Suddenly my mother detaches herself and approaches me in phantom form, a plasma object levitating toward the present.

The ceremony leader speaks: "You are in the etheric realm. Address who comes to you."

I am stupefied. I can think of nothing. The wolf is nudging me. I feel his warm fur. I understand if I can't say anything I must allow her to speak.

She is a holograph of rapidly shifting faces: an old woman, much older than when she died . . . and at the same time a young girl I know only from photographs. Then she faces me, her eyes meet mine, she speaks: "We messed up. I know. Look at Jonathan, look at Deborah. Yet I gave you all I had."

In that instant a realization floods over me. Those years I was afraid, it wasn't evil forces at work. It was because there was more beauty than we knew what to do with . . . so much spirit in that family and we were helplessly squandering it, drowning in it, drowning each other.

Jon knew the truth always. We were born in a sorcerer's lair and overwhelmed.

"It was terrible," I tell her, my voice cracking in memory of love failed, "not to be able to do anything with so much light."

Then rays of luminosity flood over me.

A glow surrounds her. The light radiates out, demanding so much, even then, even still.

"I gave you the best of me," she repeats, "Now you have it inside you. Don't blame me. Simply do what I could not."

"I know. I know now."

"I'm sorry I wounded you, but I couldn't stand the light either."

The wolf licks my face, and I embrace it. I nod many times, for she is turning like the ghost in Hamlet.

"Go in peace," she says.

I speak as she turns to look back. "Go in peace too."

"Light! Yes, Rich, light!" Jon shouted, rising from the floor. "I believe you. It was amazing, wasn't it? We missed. We missed, and it makes no difference now."

"Exactly. All these amazing layers of substance and sorrow, the intimation everywhere of incalculable depth, is merely the churning-up, undiscovered universe. It's as deep as a Jovian ocean and as remote as the furthest galaxy we can't see, which contains trillions of Jupiters in it." Brothers were circling each other, looking right at each other.

"And what we feel is even deeper, right?" It was his original wonder-filled voice.

"Maybe not deeper," I followed, assuming the old authority of our clan, "but the same vantage of bottomlessness. The false-infinity box suggests a true infinity from which we can never be alienated. And we can't find God because he isn't here. We're here instead, in his place. This is a frontier of the universe he hasn't touched."

"It's the Louisiana Purchase. We're his Lewis and Clark."

I nodded wildly. "It's a choice we made a long time ago, to open up the unknown for God, for everyone, for every*thing*. Whoever comes to this plane of stars and animacules comes to plumb some aspect of the unknown, to reveal it, so it can be included."

"That's what you always told me when we were young: we're here to learn who we are." He grabbed his jacket and pointed to the door.

"And to send it back to Grand Central."

"I've spent my life sending messages to God. A helluvalot better than writing ad copy."

I put my arm around him briefly. "Even ad copy is cosmic rays," I teased. Then I felt a rush of eternity and scanned him and me and our era from the Galactic Eye. "No one can act any differently," I reported. "No one can accomplish any more or less. Gandhi and Hitler, blasphemous as this sounds, were merely two creatures, barely more than frogs, struggling against the murk and brilliance of their pool."

"Muss-ages to God," he proclaimed with a distinct reggae twang. Then he threw open the door and led the way.

We skipped a ride on the elevator and ran down the stairs behind each other. All the way to Seymour's apartment, along the ancient grade-school streets flanked by stone towers, we talked vision-quest tales—those of literature and our own.

New York City didn't exist anymore . . . until we reached the corner of 83rd and 5th where we were to part.

"I used to think," I told him under the canopy of a store, "that this was all hopeless, that we had blown it a long time ago and were playing out the string. We hardly get much of a chance anyway. They traumatize us before we are awake, so we sleep most of it off, most of life. Now I don't think that. I think this is all a drama of lifetimes and stretches from one end of the invisible universe to the other. Look at the starry night, how much is going on there. The years we were growing up are a minor episode in this. Even the whole life is just a moment. Look closely. What else could it be?"

Jon did not share my Buddhist mythology, so he had to think. Finally he smiled broadly: "So we've got plenty of time."

"We've still got all of eternity."

"I can't think of anyone I'd rather spend it with."

"Back to Babylon," I joked as I pointed to Seymour's building.

"You don't belong in Babylon, Rich. You're just their spy."

Twenty-Eighth Document

in a dream
i am travelling westward
a thousand miles
to escape your memory
the cities change
the strangeness
of another life
envelops me
as i move beyond
the sphere of your influence

Twenty-Ninth Document

dusk
over the East River
below 14th street
the world
in fabulous grey intensity
bridgecable lights
strung between boroughs
gloom of the whaleback waters
running south
before a stiff breeze
warehouses
on the Brooklyn shore
low & silent
dotted by lonely lights
against a flattened landscape
receding toward the ultimate ocean

Thirtieth Document

the sun is sinking . . .
a golden sheen
slanting through the foliage

Once Upon a Time Forever

and the shallow waters
of the creek
drain towards the Sound
a solitary duck
appearing round a bend
proceeds upstream
exploring the slack water
along the bank
the sun is slowly sinking
to melt again
into all the other days
that have ever been
and we are here
watching these things
that once upon a time
happened forever

Notes and Sources

Out of Babylon is one of three nonfiction novels. Each of the three is independent; none of them are sequels; and they are not sequential chronologically.

New Moon is a pure memoir of growing up, compiled primarily between the ages of sixteen and twenty-one and then rewritten as an adult.

Episodes in Disguise of a Marriage was, at the time I wrote it, a novel of changing mores of romance, marriage, and family during the '70s. I now consider it too personal to publish. Instead I have adapted parts of it to *New Moon* and *Out of Babylon.*

Out of Babylon originated in four separate manuscripts. I drew on *Episodes* for the chapters entitled "Making a Home," "The Dream at Grossinger's," "Goddard College Blues," and "Step Back Like a Monkey." I incorporated two unfinished books: *Jonny's Quest,* a novel about my brother's life, and *The Story of Grossinger's,* a fictionalized narrative of the resort. Additionally, the chapters entitled "Reuben Turetsky Tells the Story of Grossinger's at the Russian Tea Room" and "Led by an Unlikely Ally to a Meeting with Joey B———" are journal notes, hence the sudden change to present tense. Sections in italics come from earlier experimental-prose books of mine and are cited by title below. In most instances they were rewritten for their use in this text.

Because of the collage and pop-culture nature of this manuscript, I do not have access to a complete list of attributions. The following are what I can provide:

Page 8: Joel Pomerantz, *Jennie and the Story of Grossinger's*, New York: Grosset & Dunlap, 1970 (constructed from notes by Quentin Reynolds).

Pages 9–10: An earlier version of the italicized section appeared in *The Provinces,* Plainfield, Vermont: North Atlantic Books, 1975.

Page 15 et seq.: I am grateful to Dr. Eli Katz, professor of Yiddish at Sonoma State University and the University of California at Berkeley, for going over this chapter and the following one page by page with me and providing most of the Yiddish phrases. My thanks also to Frieda Falk for translating a few of the phrases at the beginning of this chapter into Yiddish.

Page 16: ("as though ... daily newspapers" and "... Og, King of Bashan ..."): Irving Howe, *World of Our Fathers: The Journey of the Eastern European Jews to America and the Life They Found and Made,* New York: Harcourt Brace Jovanovich, 1976. Howe's book also gave me general background for this chapter.

Pages 22: ("like to the Day of Judgment ..."): Ibid.

Page 23 et seq.: From this point through the end of the next chapter, I have used Pomerantz (op. cit.), Frommer and Frommer (see below), Kanfer (see below), and Taub (see below) for general background.

Pages 28–29: Pomerantz, op. cit.

Page 31: (dialogue between Selig and Uncle Joe): Harold Taub, *Waldorf-in-the-Catskills,* New York: Sterling Publishing Company, 1952.

Page 32: (dialogue between Uncle Joe and Malke): Ibid.

Page 36: ("the New Jerusalem"): Howe, op. cit.

Page 36: ("Evergreen Farm House"): Stefan Kanfer, *A Summer Place: The Attempt to Build a Jewish Eden in the Catskills, From the Days of the Ghetto to the Rise and Decline of the Borscht Belt,* New York: Farrar Straus Giroux, 1989.

Page 37: (Joey Adams): Ibid.

Page 37: ("klezmer musicians"): Myrna Katz Frommer & Harvey Frommer, *It Happened in the Catskills: An Oral History in the Words of Busboys, Bellhops, Guests, Proprietors, Comedians, Agents, and Others Who Lived It,* Harcourt Brace Jovanovich, 1991. A copy of this book was given to me by Robert Towers for help in filling in gaps in his oral histories.

Page 40: ("This little one ..."): Taub, op. cit.

Page 41: (The tour of Laurel-in-the-Pines): Pomerantz, op. cit.

Page 42: (dialogues between Jennie and guests): Ibid.

Page 45: (Joey Adams): Kanfer, op. cit.

Pages 46–47: ("But the night is still young ..." et seq.): The young fellow we left at a penthouse back in the 1930s is now eighty-five years old, reminiscing about "when New York was the center of the known universe, the object of all desire, and everywhere else was 'the sticks.'"

Jack Kriendler ignored his friend's poverty and seated him and his date in the front room at "21." He married a showgirl named Rose, formerly The Chesterfield Girl and The Coca-Cola Girl. Their son Phil was my best friend at P. S. 6. I lost track of him after sixth grade.

Phil played Hamlet at Columbia; sold *The Herald Tribune* on the streets of Paris; travelled through Chile, searching for shamans and revolutions; and now lives in Seattle, a performance artist and screen writer. He found me forty years later (after the publication of *New Moon*) and mailed me the memoir he composed out of his father's papers. At its end a son performs a father's mute soliloquy—Hamlet finally speaks for the king's ghost:

"I gaze down at a throng of pedestrians hurrying across the street in a light rain, past the grassy center dividers of Park Avenue toward the garden and pool fronting the red and cream stones of St. Bartholomew's Church. The right time, the right place. All that's missing is the sound of Gershwin on the piano, playing for me once again as he did on that memorable early morning so long ago."

This material will be published in Charles Wohlstetter, *The Right Time, The Right Place,* New York: Applause Books, 1998.

Page 48: (dialogue between Malke and Jennie): Taub, op. cit.

Page 48: (George Jessel on Jennie): Pomerantz, op. cit.

Page 50: (dialogue between Malke and Jennie): Ibid.

Page 50: (dialogue between Harry and Sol and Monte): Pomerantz, op. cit.

Page 51: (Malke on Barney Ross): Taub, op. cit.

Page 52: (dialogue between Jennie and Harry): Ibid.

Pages 63–64: (some sections of Reuben Turetsky's recollections): Frommer and Frommer, op. cit.

Page 65: Taub, op. cit.

Page 65: (Irving Cohen): Frommer and Frommer, op. cit.

Page 67: ("A joke of that era . . ."): Taub, op. cit.

Page 68: (Eddie Fisher recalling years later): Frommer and Frommer, op. cit.

Pages 68–69: Bill Graham and Robert Greenfield, *Bill Graham Presents: My Life Inside Rock and Out,* New York: Doubleday, 1992.

Pages 69–70: (Lou Goldstein): Frommer and Frommer, op. cit.

Page 70: (Tania Grossinger): Ibid.

Pages 75–140: These five chapters synopsize my nonfiction novel *New Moon.* The missing details of P. S. 6, Camp Chipinaw, Horace Mann, Dr. Fabian, Dr. Friend, Amherst, Ann Arbor, etc., can be found therein.

Page 76: "Swanee" by G. Gershwin and I. Caesar, copyright MCA.

Page 76: (". . . bluebird . . ."): "April Showers" by L. Silvers and B. G. DeSylva, copyright MCA.

Page 105: "Old Devil Moon" by E. Y. Harburg and Burton Lane, copyright Columbia.

Page 105: ("... laddie with a twinkling eye ..."): "How Are Things in Glocca Morra?" by E. Y. Harburg and Burton Lane, copyright Columbia.

Page 111: ("... oh so bride-and-groomish ..."): "Something Sort of Grandish" by E. Y. Harburg and Burton Lane, copyright Columbia.

Pages 136–137: An earlier version of the italicized section appeared in "The Plant Book," *Doctrine of Signatures, Io/5,* Ann Arbor, Michigan, 1968.

Page 138: An earlier version of the italicized section appeared in *Book of the Cranberry Islands,* New York: Harper & Row, 1974.

Page 139: Robert Duncan, "Notes on Grossinger's *Solar Journal: Oecological Sections,*" Los Angeles: Black Sparrow Press, 1970.

Pages 140–141: Earlier versions of the italicized sections appeared in *The Long Body of the Dream,* Plainfield, Vermont: North Atlantic Books, 1974; *The Book of Being Born Again into the World,* Plainfield, Vermont: North Atlantic Books, 1974; and *The Windy Passage from Nostalgia,* Plainfield, Vermont: North Atlantic Books, 1974.

Page 146: Robert Duncan, "Santa Cruz Propositions" in *Ground Work: Before the War,* New York: New Directions Publishing Company, 1984, page 36.

Page 147: Jule Eisenbud, "Interview," in Richard Grossinger (editor), *Ecology and Consciousness: Traditional Wisdom on the Environment,* Berkeley, California: North Atlantic Books, 1992.

Pages 150–151: Russell Banks, *Rule of the Bone,* New York: HarperCollins, 1994.

Page 165: "Chain Gang" by Sam Cooke, copyright BMI.

Page 166: Charles Dickens, *Great Expectations,* London: 1860–61.

Page 182: Carl Sauer, *The Early Spanish Main,* Berkeley and Los Angeles: University of California Press, 1966.

Page 189 et seq.: I cannot attribute all the song lyrics that Jonathan quoted in his letters.

Page 228: An earlier version of the italicized section appeared in *The Windy Passage from Nostalgia,* op. cit.

Pages 235–237: An earlier version of the italicized section appeared in *The Slag of Creation,* Plainfield, Vermont: North Atlantic Books, 1974.

Pages 237–238: Ibid.

Page 237: "Tower of Strength" by Millard and Bacharach, copyright ASCAP; "Lil' Red Riding Hood" by Ronald Blackwell, copyright BMI; "The Wizard" by David-Dane-Paul, copyright ASCAP; "Long Long Time" by Gary White, copyright ASCAP; "Runaway" by Shannon and Crook, copyright BMI.

Pages 238–240: An earlier version of the italicized section appeared in *The Slag of Creation,* op. cit.

Page 239: "Cygnet Committee" by David Bowie, copyright BMI.

Page 243: J. R. R. Tolkien, *The Lord of the Rings, Part Two, The Two Towers,* New York: Ballantine Books, 1965.

Pages 243–244: An earlier version of some of the material on these pages appeared in *The Slag of Creation,* op. cit.

Page 245: Ibid.

Pages 246–248: Ibid.

Pages 252–253: The italicized sections are from an unpublished book, *The Planet with Blue Skies.*

Page 268: "Somewhere Over the Rainbow" by E. Y. Harburg.

Page 271 et seq.: All the italicized sections of my own older writing in this chapter come from *The Planet with Blue Skies.*

Page 280: Taub, op. cit.

Page 283: "Stairway to Heaven" by N. Sedaka-H. Greenfield, copyright BMI; "Come Together" by J. Lennon-P. McCartney, copyright BMI; "Michael" arranged by Dave Fisher, copyright ASCAP; "The Lion Sleeps Tonight" by Weiss-Peretti-Creatore, copyright ASCAP.

Page 290: Taub, op. cit.

Pages 316–319: The italicized writing comes from *The Windy Passage from Nostalgia,* op. cit., and *The Planet With Blue Skies,* op. cit., where it appeared in a different form.

Page 327 et seq.: Some of the stories in this chapter appeared in a different form in *The Unfinished Business of Doctor Hermes,* Plainfield, Vermont: North Atlantic Books, 1976.

Pages 337 and 339–340: Some of the baseball material first appeared in a different form in *Baseball I Gave You All the Best Years of My Life,* edited by Kevin Kerrane and Richard Grossinger, Berkeley, California: North Atlantic Books, 1978 (now available in *Into the Temple of Baseball,* edited by Richard Grossinger and Kevin Kerrane, Berkeley, California: Celestial Arts, 1990).

Page 353: The italicized section first appeared in *The Unfinished Business of Doctor Hermes,* op. cit.

Page 371: "April Showers" by L. Silvers and B. G. DeSylva, copyright MCA.

Pages 387–388: Bira Almeida, *Capoeira: A Brazilian Art Form,* Berkeley, California: North Atlantic Books, 1981, 1986.

Pages 425–426: *The New York Times,* Autumn, 1985 (date intentionally withheld).

Page 326: Kanfer, op. cit.

Pages 430–431: "Wild Montana Skies" by John Denver, copyright ASCAP.

Page 436: Kanfer, op. cit.

Page 437: The full text of the Mets' dialogue appears in "Notes on the 1986 Playoffs and World Series" in Richard Grossinger (editor), *The Dreamlife of Johnny Baseball,* Berkeley: North Atlantic Books, 1987.

Page 396: Richard Strozzi Heckler, *In Search of the Warrior Spirit: Teaching Awareness Disciplines to the Green Berets,* Berkeley: North Atlantic Books, 1990.

Pages 444–445: Richard C. Hoagland, *The Monuments of Mars: A City on the Edge of Forever,* Berkeley: North Atlantic Books, 1987.

Page 446: Martha N. Mendelsohn, "Grossinger's on My Mind: A Borscht Belt Memory," *Moment,* Volume 15, Number 2, April, 1990. I am also grateful to Martha for doing some of the research for the remainder of this chapter.

Pages 446–447: (Soung Kiy Min): Tania Grossinger, "Bittersweet Return to Grossinger's," *Fort Lauderdale Sun-Sentinel,* July 21, 1996.

Page 447: (Milton Kutsher): Frommer and Frommer, op. cit.

Pages 449–450: Lis Harris, "O, Guru, Guru, Guru," in "Annals of Religion," *The New Yorker,* November 14, 1994.

Page 450: Adapted from Harold "Dusty" Dowse: "The Place That is Always Cold" and "Teson's," unpublished notes.

Page 470: *New Moon,* Berkeley, California: Frog, Ltd., 1996.

Pages 499–500: "One Step Forward" by Lee Perry and Max Romeo, published by Island Music, Inc., copyright ASCAP.

Page 511: E. Y. Harburg, "It's Only a Paper Moon."

Page 514: Herman Melville, *Moby Dick,* London: 1851.

Page 515: ("... not to see me there ..."): "How Are Things in Glocca Morra?" by E. Y. Harburg and Burton Lane, copyright Columbia.

Pages 521–522: Miranda Grossinger, *The Lifers,* unpublished play, 1992.

Pages 526–527: Ibid.

Page 529: Ibid.

Page 529: Review of "The Lifers" by Lawrence Livermore, *Absolutely Zippo*, Berkeley, California, 1992.

Pages 531–532: Some of this material comes from Peter Ralston's published talks, which are collected in *Ancient Wisdom, New Spirit*, Berkeley, California: Frog, Ltd., 1994.

Page 533: Miranda July, "Her Hollowness," unpublished short story.

Pages 538–540: Robert Towers' dialogue is corrected and enlarged with sections from Frommer and Frommer, op. cit.

Page 545: ("... where troubles melt like lemon drops ..."): "Somewhere Over the Rainbow" by E. Y. Harburg.

Page 558: Richard Grossinger, "Preface" to Bob Frissell, *Nothing in This Book is True, But It's Exactly How Things Are*, Berkeley, California: Frog, Ltd., revised edition, 1996.

Page 559: *The New York Times*, August 14, 1994.

Photo Captions

Title page: Paul, Richard, and Martha Grossinger.

Book One: Selig and Jennie Grossinger.

Page 3: Richard and Jonathan Towers.

Page 15: Harry and Jennie Grossinger.

Page 55: Reuben Turetsky and Martha Grossinger.

Page 75: Richard and Martha Grossinger.

Page 89: Bunny, Michael, Paul and James Grossinger, Richard Towers.

Page 103: Maury McDermott (New York Yankees), Richard Grossinger, and Don Larsen (New York Yankees).

Page 117: Bertha, Lindy, Hank, Susie, Fran, and Polly Hough.

Page 133: Robin and Richard Grossinger.

Page 143: Terrace Hill House, Nichols Estate.

Book Two: Richard, Martha, Robert, and Jonathan Towers.

Page 157: Richard, Martha, and Jonathan Towers.

Page 173: Richard Grossinger, Martha, Deborah, and Jonathan Towers.

Page 197: Deborah, Martha, and Jonathan Towers.

Page 211: Mara with Jonathan Towers.

Book Three: Coleman Nassberg, Anne Metzger (Sally's sister), Paul Rothkrug, Martha Rothkrug Grossinger, Julius Metzger (Radley's father), Paul Grossinger, Lionel Rothkrug, Sally Rothkrug, and Edgar Rothkrug, at the wedding of Paul Grossinger and Martha Rothkrug.

Page 223: Scootchy Lovell, Robin Grossinger, and Jason Wincuinas in Plainfield, Vermont.

Page 241: Miranda and Robin Grossinger.

Page 255: Martha Towers (professional modelling photograph composite).

Page 271: Martha, Richard, and Paul Grossinger.

Page 289: Martha Rothkrug at the time of her first trip to Grossinger's.

Page 307: Miranda, Richard, and Robin Grossinger.

Book Four: Jonathan and Richard Towers.

Page 327: Lindy Hough, Bunny Grossinger, Paul Grossinger, Robin Grossinger, Miranda Grossinger, Richard Grossinger.

Page 357: Jonathan, Martha, and Richard Towers.

Page 377: Miranda and Robin Grossinger.

Book Five: Jennie Grossinger.

Page 423: Harry, Jennie, Richard, Paul, and Martha Grossinger, Sally Rothkrug.

Page 453: Reuben Turetsky, Reuben's second wife Gwen, Barney Ross, Martha and Paul Grossinger, Danny Kaye.

Page 467: Martha Grossinger.

Page 485: Jay Zises, Darrell Johnson (New York Yankees), Paul Grossinger, Richard Grossinger, Al Cicotte (New York Yankees), Arthur Richman, Abbey West.

Page 501: Lou Goldstein, Elston Howard, Richard Grossinger, Harry Grossinger, Jackie Horner, Elston Howard's wife, Jennie Grossinger.

Page 521: Miranda Grossinger.

Page 551: Edgar Rothkrug, Martha Rothkrug, Lionel Rothkrug, Paul Rothkrug.

Notes and Sources

Page 575: Jennie Grossinger.

Page 577: Michael, Bunny, and James Grossinger, Richard Towers.

Page 579: Lindy Hough, Robin, Jennie, and Richard Grossinger.

Page 580: Robin Grossinger, Miranda July, Lindy Hough.

Photo Captions

Page 584: Jonathan Towers, Sally (Rothkrug) Golden, Deborah Towers, Martha Towers, Richard Grossinger, Lindy Hough, and Robert Towers, at the wedding of Richard Grossinger and Lindy Hough.